COMMENTARY

ON

THE BOOK OF PSALMS

VOL. I

COMMENTARY

ON

THE BOOK OF PSALMS

BY JOHN CALVIN

TRANSLATED FROM THE ORIGINAL LATIN, AND COLLATED
WITH THE AUTHOR'S FRENCH VERSION,

BY THE REV. JAMES ANDERSON

VOLUME FIRST

WIPF & STOCK · Eugene, Oregon

Wipf and Stock Publishers
199 W 8th Ave, Suite 3
Eugene, OR 97401

Commentaries on the Book of Psalms, Volume 1
By Calvin, John and Anderson, James
Softcover ISBN-13: 979-8-3852-1498-3
Hardcover ISBN-13: 979-8-3852-1499-0
eBook ISBN-13: 979-8-3852-1500-3
Publication date 1/26/2024
Previously published by Baker Book House, 2005

This edition is a scanned facsimile of the original edition published in 2005.

INTRODUCTORY NOTICE.

THE BOOK OF PSALMS, viewed merely as a poetical composition, has very high claims on our attention. Men of the most refined and cultivated taste have often been attracted to the study of it from the poetical beauties with which it abounds, and have admitted, in this respect, the superiority of its claims. The greatest of our English poets[1] thus speaks of these sacred songs: "Not in their divine argument alone, but in the very critical art of composition, they may be easily made appear over all the kinds of lyric poesy to be incomparable." Another elegant scholar,[2] speaking on the same subject, says, "In lyric flow and fire, in crushing force and majesty, that seems still to echo the awful sounds once heard beneath the thunder clouds of Sinai, the poetry of the ancient Scriptures is the most superb that ever burned within the breast of man."

But the intrinsic excellence of this Book gives it still higher claims on our attention. Written under the influence of the Spirit of inspiration, its subject-matter is worthy of its celestial origin. In general, it contains details of the national history of the Jewish people, records of particular portions of the life and experience of individuals, and predictions of future events. Each of these heads embraces a wide field, and they include illustrations of every religious truth which it

[1] Milton.   [2] Sir Daniel K. Sandford.

is necessary for us to know, exemplifications of every devout feeling which it is our duty to cherish, and examples of every spiritual conflict which it is possible for us to experience. We meet with many disclosures of the greatness, majesty, and perfections of the only true God; his government of the world; and his special care over his chosen people. We meet with the varied exercises of the regenerated soul, and behold it at one time offering up fervent supplications to the Hearer of prayer, at another celebrating his perfections and works; at one time giving utterance to the ardent breathings of love to God, and trust in him, at another struggling with unbelief and corruption; at one time mourning under the divine chastisement on account of sin, at another rejoicing in a sense of forgiving mercy, and enjoying the peace which passeth all understanding. We have presented to us many wonderful predictions concerning the Messiah, his humiliation, sufferings, death, resurrection, and ascension to his Father's right hand; his work in heaven as the intercessor of his people, and his authority as universal King; the effusion of the influences of the Holy Spirit, and the conversion of all nations to the faith of the Gospel. In short, we have unfolded to our view the final judgment, the gathering of all the righteous to God, and the eternal exclusion of the wicked from happiness and from hope.

These and similar topics which are set forth in the noblest strains of poetry, and in a diction whose magnificence and sublimity correspond to the importance and grandeur of the sentiments, constitute the materials of this Book; and while they afford an incontestable proof that it is inspired, that it does not consist of the creations of mere human genius, but is an emanation from heaven, they show that its character and tendency are altogether different from the character and tendency of the most admired poetry, which the genius of heathen nations has ever produced. It ministers to no depraved passion; it fosters no fictitious virtue; it disdains to offer its delicious incense at the shrine of degrading superstition. It teaches the most exalted piety, and the purest morality. It tends only to refine and exalt the nature of man, to elevate the soul to God, and inspire it with the admiration and love of his character, to curb the passions, purify the affections, and excite to the cultivation of whatsoever things are true, honest, just, pure, lovely, and of good report. It has guided the saint in doubt and difficulty; it has nerved him for self-denial and suffering; it has imparted support and comfort to him in the hour of death. This Book has accordingly been highly appreciated by the best of men in every age, and they have laboured to find expressions in which to set forth its excellence. Athanasius styles it, "An epitome of the whole Scriptures;" Basil, "A compendium of all theology;" Luther, "A little Bible, and the summary of the Old Testament;" Melancthon, "The most elegant work extant in the world;" and for Calvin's estimate of its value we refer to the excellent preface with which he introduces this department of his labours to the attention of the reader.

CALVIN'S COMMENTARY ON THE PSALMS, a new Translation of which is now in course of being presented to the English reader, is distinguished by many of the excellencies which have acquired for his Commentaries on other parts of Scripture so great reputation. In this, as in his other Commentaries, his first and great object is to ascertan the mind of the Holy Spirit. To ascertain this, he proceeds on the principle laid down by Melancthon, "that Scripture cannot be understood theologically, unless it be first understood grammatically." Before his time the mystical and allegorical method of explaining the Scriptures was very prevalent; according to which, the interpreter, dwelling very little or not at all upon the literal sense, sought for hidden and allegorical meanings. But rejecting this mode of interpretation, which contributed little to the right understanding of the word of God, and according to which the meaning was made to depend entirely upon the fancy of the interpreter, Calvin set himself to the investigation of the grammatical and literal sense, by a careful examination of the Hebrew text, and by a diligent attention to the drift and intention of the writer's discourse.

This principle of interpretation cannot be too highly commended. It should first engage the attention of the commentator; and when it is neglected, the fundamental principle of sacred criticism is violated. Calvin was deeply alive to its importance. His only defect lies in his acting upon it too exclusively. Many of the Psalms, in addition to the literal meaning, have a prophetical, evangelical, and spiritual sense. While referring primarily to David and the nation of Israel, they have, at the same time, a reference to Christ and the New Testament Church, founded on the fact that the former were typical of the latter. Calvin, indeed, explains some of the Psalms on this principle. But he applies the principle less frequently than he might have done, without contravening the canons of sound hermeneutics. His great aversion to the mystical method of interpretation, and to the absurd and extravagant lengths to which it was carried by the Fathers, perhaps made him err on the other extreme of confining his attention too much to the literal meaning, and directing his attention too little to the prophetical and spiritual character of the Book, and to the reference which it has to Christ and the Church. In consequence of this, his expositions have less unction, and contain less of rich evangelical sentiment, than would otherwise have distinguished them. There are, however, two principles of evangelical truth which he is at pains to inculcate, whenever a fit opportunity presents itself —the doctrine of justification by faith in Christ without the works of the Law; and the necessity of personal holiness in order to salvation.

Another excellence of this COMMENTARY is its practical character. The author does not confine himself to the dry and lifeless detail of mere grammatical praxis, as if he had been commenting on a Greek or Roman classic. He turns all his explanations to practical account, and thus his work exhibits a happy combination of critical and philological remark with practical exposition.

Here, again, we find displayed the sound and penetrating judgment for which CALVIN has been universally admired. This is manifest in the judicious selection which he makes from amongst a variety of interpretations, of that which is evidently the true one, or which appears to be the most probable. Sometimes he pronounces a certain interpretation to be meagre and unsatisfactory. At other times, he simply states his preference of one interpretation to another, when, after careful examination, it appeared to him to have the balance of arguments in its favour; without, however, expressing any decided opposition to the other, when the view which he preferred to it was supported only by a slight preponderance of evidence. At other times, he does not decide between different interpretations, showing that with respect to certain words and expressions he had not come to a fixed opinion. In all these instances,[1] he generally shows

[1] From the variety of interpretations of the same passages which we meet with in Calvin's Commentary, and of which we have still more numerous specimens in Poole's Synopsis Criticorum, it is by no means to be supposed that the meaning of the language of Scripture is vague, uncertain, and unsettled. Had the professed interpreters of Scripture always performed their task with judgment, as well as learning and talent, and been guided by the rules of sound hermeneutics, the reader would not have been bewildered with so many different and contradictory interpretations. Still, however, there are words and sentences, the exact import of which is more or less doubtful and uncertain, so that it is difficult to determine between different senses which have been put upon them. The reasons of

much penetration and judgment. He is, no doubt, sometimes mistaken in his interpretation of particular passages. But when it is considered that the Scriptures had long been a sealed book, and that his helps were few and imperfect com-

this are so well stated by Cresswell, in his preface to The Book of Psalms with Notes, (pp. 14, 15, 16,) and the passage has so direct a bearing on a number of the various interpretations, which Calvin deals with in this Commentary, that we shall quote it entire though it is long.

"The Hebrew is not only a *dead* language, but the oldest of all dead languages; it is, moreover, the language of a people that lived under institutions and in a climate very different from those of our own country, so that the idioms with which it abounds cannot but be strange to our habits of thinking, and our modes of speech; nor have we any book but the Bible itself to consult for an illustration of these phraseological peculiarities. The paucity of the words also contained in that ancient tongue is such, that the same Hebrew term very often bears a great variety of significations, the connexion of which with each other cannot always be satisfactorily ascertained: and, again, there are words, each of which is found but once in the whole volume of Scripture, so that their meanings can only be conjectured, either from their affinity to other words, or from the purport of the passage wherein they occur.

"The following are amongst the many grammatical Hebraisms which we meet with in The Book of Psalms. The *future* and *past* tenses are put almost indiscriminately, the one for the other, and the former of them is used occasionally to designate not that which *will* happen, but that which is *accustomed* to happen. The *infinitive* is put for every other mood, and also for nouns even in the accusative case. The *future* tense is sometimes expressed by a verb in the imperative mood. Two substantives are put instead of a substantive and an adjective; a substantive is frequently used adverbially; and the same substantive repeated denotes multitude. When the *negative* particle occurs in the first member of a sentence, it is sometimes to be understood, and must be supplied, in the following members. Hebrew sentences are also in other respects very often elliptical, broken, and imperfect; and in the same sentence there is in many instances a change of person in the speaker, without any express intimation of it.

"From the peculiarities above mentioned, and especially from the different ways in which an ellipse may be supplied, it is plain that the text of Scripture must needs admit of a considerable latitude of interpretation; so that although none of its important doctrines, whether they relate to faith or morals, are thereby left doubtful, yet does it contain passages the exact meanings of which are more or less uncertain. The candid and pious reader, however, will with Augustine gladly acknowledge that all which he fully comprehends in the sacred volume is most excellent; whilst he looks with feelings of veneration upon that smaller portion of it which he less perfectly understands, but which the diligence and erudition of future times may, through divine aid, be enabled to elucidate."

pared with those which we now possess, the wonder is, that he should have succeeded so well in bringing out their true meaning. This was chiefly owing to vigour and acuteness of intellect, combined with a sound and discriminating judgment. These, indeed, were the mental qualities by which he was peculiarly distinguished. We meet with no flashes of poetry, no brilliant corruscations of fancy, giving evidence of a powerful imagination. The eloquent passages which occur are the eloquence of reason, not the bursts of imagination. But his strength of thought, the vigour and perspicacity of his intellect, the extraordinary power of his judgment, command our willing admiration.

Since this COMMENTARY was first published, a great number of Translations of The Psalms, as well as numerous critical and explanatory works upon them, have made their appearance, while much new light has been thrown upon many passages from more extensive philological research, from an attention to the parallelism of Hebrew poetry,[1] and from the fuller information which we now possess, by the discoveries of modern travellers, of the natural history, customs, and manners of the East, to which frequent allusion is made in The Psalms. But such is the acuteness of judgment, and

[1] Parallelism is the distinguishing characteristic of Hebrew poetry, and an attention to it, it must be admitted, affords much assistance in elucidating obscure, and explaining difficult passages. Some modern translations of The Psalms, as French and Skinner's, have the lines so arranged as to make the parallelisms apparent to the eye; which enables the reader to discover at a glance niceties both of structure and of meaning, which, in the ordinary mode of printing, might pass unnoticed after frequent and even close perusal. For a full investigation of this subject, the reader is referred to Dr Lowth's elegant Lectures on Sacred Poetry, and his Preliminary Dissertation prefixed to his translation of the prophet Isaiah, works which created a new era in sacred literature, by the light which they cast on the character of Hebrew poetry, with respect to which the learned world were previously unsettled and perplexed, from the obscurity which rested on the subject. Bishop Jebb, in his "Sacred Literature," has also investigated the parallelism of Hebrew poetry with much ability, and successfully controverted some of Bishop Lowth's positions.

success in discovering the mind of the Spirit which distinguish these prelections, that they are not superseded by any modern Commentary on the same subject: and though it is nearly three centuries since they were written, there are few separate works on The Psalms from which the student of the present day, who wishes critically to examine them, will derive more important assistance.

Nor is CALVIN's impartiality and integrity as an interpreter less apparent in this Work than his judgment. It being his first and leading object to ascertain the mind of the Holy Spirit, he came to the Word of God not for the purpose of finding arguments to establish some preconceived opinion or theory, but in the humble character of a learner, and we never find him perverting or twisting a passage to support even those doctrines which he most deeply cherished. So far from doing this, he not unfrequently gives up a text which has been explained by other commentators as a proof of some important doctrine, and which he would have viewed in the same light had it not been for his aversion to put on Scripture a forced construction, and his determination rigidly to adhere to the principles of fair and logical interpretation. For example, these words in Psalm ii. 7, "Jehovah hath said unto me, Thou art my Son; this day have I begotten thee," have been quoted by Augustine and many other eminent divines, in proof of the eternal generation of the Son of God. But as Paul, in Acts xiii. 33, explains them as receiving their fulfilment in the resurrection of Christ, Calvin sets them aside from the class of proofs which support the doctrine of an eternal generation, although he held that doctrine,[1] and considers them

[1] That Calvin held this doctrine is evident from his Commentary on Acts xiii. 33, where, after stating that the words of the second Psalm, above quoted, refer to the unequivocal evidence by which the Father proved that Christ was his Son in raising him from the dead, he observes, "This, however, is no objection to the doctrine that Christ, the personal Word, was begotten by the eternal Father before time; but that generation is an inscrutable mystery." With respect to those who argue from

as referring merely to the manifestation afforded of Christ's Sonship by his resurrection from the dead.[1] Again, Psalm viii. 5, &c., "Thou hast made him a little lower than God, and hast crowned him with glory and honour," &c., has been often explained as prophetic of the temporary humiliation and subsequent exaltation of Christ, an opinion which is supported by reasons far from contemptible; but Calvin, judging from the scope of the passage, considers it as exclusively referring to man, and that when Paul quotes it in Heb. ii. 7, and applies it to Christ, he applies it to him only by way of accommodation.[2] Again, these words in Psalm xxxiii. 6, "By the word of Jehovah were the heavens established, and all the host of them by the spirit of his mouth," have been viewed by many judicious divines as a proof of the Trinity, "Jehovah," denoting the Father, "the word of Jehovah," the Son, and "the spirit of Jehovah's mouth," the Holy Spirit; but while Calvin admits that the "word of Jehovah" means the Eternal Word, the only begotten Son of God, yet reasoning from the sense which the phrase, "the spirit of Jehovah's mouth," ordinarily bears in Scripture, he argues that it does not there mean the third person of the adorable Trinity, but simply *sermo*, *speech*, although there were no truths which he held more firmly, and regarded as more essential to the Christian system, than the doctrines of the Trinity and of the Divinity of the Holy Spirit.[3] "It is very possible," says Tholuck, "that in following this direction of mind, he may have unnecessarily sacrificed this and the other proof text; still the principle upon which he proceeded is in all cases to be approved."

this passage in support of that doctrine, he says, "I know that Augustine, and the greatest number of commentators, are better pleased with the subtile speculation that 'to-day' denotes a continued or an eternal act. But when the Spirit of God himself is his own interpreter, and explains by the mouth of Paul what was spoken by David, we are not warranted to invent and put upon the words any other meaning."

[1] P. 18.   [2] Pp. 103-105.   [3] P. 543.

This COMMENTARY, again, bears evident marks of the learning of its author. His intimate acquaintance with the Hebrew language, the knowledge of which is of so much importance to the interpretation of the Old Testament Scriptures, is everywhere apparent. Father Simon, whom the acrimony of controversy led to indulge too much in depreciating and abusing those who differed from him, asserts, indeed, that Calvin was so ignorant of the Hebrew language, that he knew nothing more than the letters. But we have only to examine his Commentary on The Psalms, not to speak of his Commentaries on other parts of the Old Testament, to be convinced that his knowledge of the Hebrew language was accurate and minute, considering the age in which he lived. He frequently enters into a critical examination of the original text, and manifests by his philological remarks, brief though they be, an intimate acquaintance with that language; arriving, in his interpretations, at the same results to which a more profound exegesis and a more minute attention to philology have conducted modern critics. Often, when he does not professedly criticise the Hebrew text, or make his statements in the form of criticism, the Hebrew scholar will perceive that his remarks are founded upon a close attention to the strict meaning of the Hebrew words, and that he frequently states their precise import with much force, felicity, and delicacy of expression. Nor is proof wanting, from this Commentary, that Calvin had travelled over the whole field of knowledge, in so far as it had been explored in his day. From ancient and modern systems of philosophy, from civil and ecclesiastical history, as well as from the Greek and Roman classics, he draws materials, and shows how he could employ with ease and power, and yet without the least ostentation or pedantry, his varied acquisitions for the illustration of sacred truth.

In short, this Work is pervaded by earnest piety and much

Christian experience. Its whole tone evinces it to be the fruit of a soul which felt the deep workings of piety; of a soul in which the love of God was supreme, which sought its rest and happiness in him alone, which recognised his hand and providence in every event, which confided in him in all circumstances, which looked to him as a Father and a friend for every blessing, and which, in all its powers, was consecrated with entire devotedness to Christ and the Gospel. It everywhere, too, bespeaks the man of large religious experience. Whether the author comments on the plaintive songs in which grief pours forth its bitterness, or on the triumphant and joyful songs in which the perfections and providence of God, individual and national deliverances are celebrated; whether he speaks of David's religious exercises, or of the trials of his life, or of his inward conflicts, we perceive a mind which had itself experienced much of what it illustrates. This experience eminently qualified Calvin to be an interpreter of The Psalms. Placed often in circumstances similar to those of David, as he graphically describes in his Preface, he was thus enabled accurately to conceive of David's train of thinking, to see things as it were with his eyes, to trace the complexion and character of his feelings, and thus to portray them in so just and natural a manner, that we are almost ready to think, in perusing the description of them, that they are described by David himself.

This Work has been translated from the original Latin, and collated with the French version, which was written by the author himself. The French edition which has been used, and which was doubtless the last corrected under the author's eye, was printed in 1563, and is described on the title-page as "So carefully revised, and so faithfully compared with the Latin version, that it may be considered a new translation." While the Translator has made the Latin version his text book, he has throughout carefully collated it with the French version, by which he has been greatly aided in giving a clearer and fuller representation of his author's meaning. The French version having made its appearance after the Latin, and being written in Calvin's native tongue, in which he might be expected to write with greater ease than in a dead language, admired though his Latin works are for the purity of their classic diction, it contains numerous expansions of thought and expression, by which he removes the occasional obscurities of the Latin version, which is written in a style more compressed and concise. Sometimes, though not often, we meet with a complete sentence in the French version which is not to be found in the Latin; but the cases are of frequent occurrence, in which, by inserting into the French version a clause at the beginning, the middle, or the end of a sentence, which does not occur in the Latin, he explains what is obscure in the latter version, or introduces a new thought or expresses his meaning with greater clearness and with greater copiousness of language. These additional clauses the Translator has introduced into the text in their proper place, and indicated them by adding the original French in the form of notes at the foot of the page. He, however, sometimes translates from the French version where it seems fuller and more perspicuous than the Latin, without indicating this by foot-notes. In a few instances, where the expression in the two versions is different, he has given the expression of both, retaining that of the Latin version in the text, and transferring that of the French to the foot of the page.

With respect to the principle on which he has proceeded in the task of translating, it is sufficient simply to state, that he has endeavoured to express the meaning of his author in language as true to the original as possible, avoiding being too literal on the one hand, and too loose on the other; as this, in his apprehension, is the method by which a translator can best succeed in faithfully representing to the reader the sense as well as the style and manner of his author.

CALVIN's version of the Sacred Text has been given in preference to that of our English Bible, as this was necessary to the clear understanding of his illustrations. The two versions, however, nearly resemble each other: often our English version is an accurate translation of Calvin's, at other times the marginal readings which are in some of our English Bibles. He, however, not unfrequently differs from both; and in some instances, though not in all, where he does differ, his translation appears to be superior in accuracy, and places the sentiment of the original in a clearer light, and with greater effect than is done in our English version. The Scriptural quotations which he makes have been given in the words of our English Bible, except in those cases in which his argument required his own translation of the passage to be retained.

This Work was translated into English some years after its first appearance by ARTHUR GOLDING, whose translation was published at London in 1571. Arthur Golding, who was of a gentleman's family and a native of London, was one of the most distinguished translators of the Roman classics in the age of Queen Elizabeth, when the translation of these valuable works of antiquity into the English language employed every pen. He translated Justin's History, Cæsar's Commentaries, Ovid's Metamorphoses, Seneca's Benefits, and other classic authors; as well as various modern French and Latin works, among which are a number of Calvin's writings, besides The Psalms. His only original work appears to have been, "A Discourse upon the Earthquake that happened through the Realme of Englande, and other places of Christendom, the sixt of Aprill 1580," published in 16mo. "It is to be regretted," says Warton, "that he gave so much of his time to translation."[1] Golding was no doubt a good classical scholar, and well acquainted with the style of Calvin; but as his translation was executed nearly three hundred years ago, it every where abounds with words and phrases which are become antiquated and obsolete, from the great change which the English language has undergone since that period. Being on this account frequently very obscure, often unintelligible, it fails in giving a just representation to an English reader of the present day of Calvin's work, and leads him to form a less favourable estimate of its value than is due to its high merits. Besides, Golding does not appear to have seen the French version, which affords to a translator so much assistance in the faithful representation of Calvin's meaning.

With respect to the NOTES with which this Translation is accompanied, they are intended to enable the reader clearly to understand the meaning of such of Calvin's philological remarks and criticisms as are obscure, from the brevity with which they are stated; or to exhibit Calvin's merits as a commentator, by showing how frequently his interpretations are adopted and supported by the most eminent Biblical critics; or to illustrate the Sacred Text, by showing the precise meaning of the Hebrew words, or by explaining some portion of natural history, or some eastern custom or manner to which there is an allusion. The ancient versions afford important assistance in the explanation of difficult passages, and their rendering of particular texts has been occasionally given when this contributes to elucidate them, or to throw light on Calvin's observations. Of these versions the Septuagint, the Vulgate, and Jerome's, are the only ones which he appears to have consulted, and to the first he frequently refers.

As the Translations of THE CALVIN SOCIETY are in-

[1] See Biographica Dramatica; Lowndes' Biographer's Manual of English Literature; and Warton's History of English Poetry, vol. iii. pp. 409-414.

tended for the whole Christian community, it has been deemed out of place to enter upon theological questions, on which difference of opinion exists among the various denominations of the Christian community. In making these Notes, the Editor has often compared Calvin's translation of the Sacred Text with the original Hebrew, and with the Septuagint, Vulgate, and Jerome's versions. He has also consulted a considerable number of critical works on The Psalms by some of the most eminent Biblical scholars who have written on this book, either as a separate undertaking, or in common with the other books of Scripture. Of the rich stores of erudition thus supplied he has freely made use; and in the course of the work he has carefully marked his authorities, as this will give greater weight to his statements. Many of the authors who are quoted were men of distinguished learning, judgment, and piety, possessed a profound acquaintance with the Hebrew language, and had devoted years of laborious study to the investigation of the meaning of this sacred book; and it is wonderful to find how closely the results of Calvin's investigations, even on the most difficult passages, harmonise with the results to which modern critics, guided by the principles of accurate hermeneutics, have arrived. This has often forced itself upon the attention of the Editor, and the more he has compared Calvin's criticisms and interpretations with the labours of these learned men, the higher has been raised his admiration of the ingenuity, penetration, learning, and critical acumen of this great commentator. Not a few, indeed, of the most beautiful interpretations which are to be found in Commentaries and critical works, were first given forth by Calvin, although the source in which they originated has been forgotten. It may here be stated, that the examination of the philology of the Sacred Text, and of critical works on the subject, has led the Editor to observe how closely Calvin often adheres in his interpretations to the import of the original Hebrew, and enabled him in many cases in the course of the translation to represent the meaning of his author more correctly than he could otherwise have done, as well as to avoid mistakes into which Golding has sometimes fallen, evidently from his not being acquainted with the philology of the passage, or the criticism which Calvin briefly states or refers to, and which it is difficult for the reader clearly to understand, unless he find it more fully stated in some other critical work.

The Editor has to express his obligations to two of his friends who materially aided in the preparation of the latter part of this volume,—the late Rev. ALEXANDER DUNCAN, A.M., formerly of Dundee, and the Rev. JAMES M'LEAN, whose able translation of several of the Psalms left him little more to do than the labour of revision and annotation. The Editor and the Society have also been much indebted to the Rev. THOMAS M'CRIE, Professor of Divinity, Edinburgh, not only in general for the benefit of his experience, but also for the trouble he has taken in examining the sheets of this Volume while passing through the press, and for many important suggestions. The Editor has great satisfaction in thus publicly acknowledging his obligations.

A *fac-simile* of the TITLE-PAGE of the French version which we have used, and of the title-page of Arthur Golding's translation, together with his Dedication, are prefixed to this Volume.

It remains only to be added, that the last Volume will contain copious INDICES of the principal matters contained in the Commentary and Notes, of the passages of Scripture more or less illustrated, and of the Hebrew words referred to or explained. J. A.

EDINBURGH, *June* 1845.

COMMENTAIRES
de M. Iean Caluin sur le liure des Pseaumes.

CESTE TRADVCTION EST TELLEMENT reueuë & si fidelement conferee sur le Latin, qu'on la peut iuger estre nouuelle.

AVEC VNE TABLE FORT AMPLE DES PRINCI-paux points traittez és Commentaires.

Imprimé par François Estiene.
M. D. LXIII.

THE
Psalmes of
Dauid and others.

With M. Iohn
Caluins Commentaries.

ANNO. DO. M.D. LXXI.

[IT has been thought proper to preserve THE DEDICATION which is prefixed to the English Translation by ARTHUR GOLDING in the original orthography. Besides affording a vivid idea of the style and phraseology of this Translator, the slightest inspection of this singular composition will demonstrate how very unsuitable the publication of such a version would have been for general use in these times.

The only liberty which has been taken in reprinting this Dedication, is in reference to the supplying of modern punctuation, and the division of it into paragraphs; but in other respects it is given *verbatim et literatim*. There is only *one* paragraph in the whole of Golding's Dedication. It is dated 20th October 1571.

GOLDING's version of CALVIN's COMMENTARY ON THE PSALMS is throughout equally obscure and quaint; and it may justly be characterised as being wholly unfit for the perusal of all classes of readers of the present day, who do not happen to be minutely acquainted with the language and idiom of the sixteenth century in its most uncouth and repulsive form.]

THE EPISTLE DEDICATORY.

[PREFIXED TO THE ORIGINAL ENGLISH TRANSLATION, 1571.]

TO

THE RIGHT HONORABLE AND HIS VERIE GOOD LORD,

EDWARD DE VERE, ERLE OF OXINFORD,

LORD GREAT CHAMBERLAIN OF ENGLAND, VICOUNT BULBECKE, &c.[1]

ARTHUR GOLDING

VVISHETH INCREACE OF GODLY KNOWLEDGE, WITH HEALTH, HONOUR, AND PROSPERITIE.

It may, peraduenture, be thought in respect of the matter wherof this woork treateth, that it ought rather to haue bin dedicated to som of my very good Lords, the Lords Spirituall, or to some of the Clergie, as to whom such things seeme to perteine more peculiarly, by reason of theyr charge and call-

---

[1] Edward de Vere, 17th Earl of Oxford, was highly distinguished for his wit, valour, and patriotism. In two several tournaments he was honoured by receiving the prize from the hand of his mistress, Queen Elizabeth, having been led armed, by two ladies, into the Royal Presence-Chamber. Walpole notes that he was an admired poet, and reckoned the best writer of comedy in his time. He died at a very advanced age, June 24, 1604.

It is extremely probable that ARTHUR GOLDING, the old Translator, was related, perhaps not distantly, to this nobleman. It appears from

ing. VVhich opinion, as I purpose not to encounter, but rather most willingly submit my selfe and my doings to the iudgement and reformation of such reuerend Fathers and learned men, as God hath put in trust with the care of his flock, and the charge of his Church within this Realm, euen so forasmuch as the things which the Holy Ghost vttereth in the Sacred Scriptures belong indifferently vntoo all men, of what estate, degree, sex, age, or calling, so euer they be, without exception: I haue at this time set all other respects and considerations aside, and only had an eye to my dutie toward your Lordship.

And bicause my continuall troubles and sutes in the Lawe (as yit vnended after more than three yeeres trauel) haue bereft mee of the greatest part of my time, so as I could not dispatch things with such expedition as otherwise I might haue done; my care and indeuer hath bin too recompence mine ouerlong silence with goodnes of matter, that might redound to the furtherance of our Christen common weale, and also be meete for your Lordship too looke vpon. But you, perchaunce, according too the noble courage and disposition of your yeeres, doo looke I should presente vntoo you some Historie of the Conquestes and affaires of mightie Princes, some treatise of the gouernment of common weales, some description of the platte of the whole Earth, or some discourse of chiualrie and feates of Armes. These things are, in deede, meete studies for a noble manne, and in their season right necessary for the common welth; but as nowe I present vntoo your honour muche greater things, that is, to wit, true Religyon, true Godlynesse, true Vertue, wythout the whych, neyther force, policie, nor freendship, are of any value, neyther can any common weale, any Citie, any householde, or any company, bee wel gouerned, or haue any stable and long continuance. These be the things wherin your Lordship may do God, your Prince, and your Cuntrie, best seruice, and which do giue true nobilitie, or rather are the very nobilitie it self.

Dugdale, and other authorities, that John, 16th Earl of Oxford, his father, married Margaret, daughter of John Golding, and sister of *Sir Edward Golding*, for his second wife, by whom he had Earl Edward, after whom it is likely he was named, and a daughter.

The greater that you are of birth and calling, the more doo these things belong vnto you. The greater gifts of Nature, the mo graces of mind, the mo worldly benefites that God hath bestowed vppon you, the more are you bound to be thankful vnto him. But thankful you cannot bee without the true knoweledge of him, neyther can you know him rightly but by his woord. For his woord is the lanterne of your feete, and the light of your steppes. VVhosoeuer walketh without it, walketh but in darkenesse, though he were otherwise as sharpe sighted as *Linceus* or *Argus*, and had all the sciences, artes, conning, eloquence, and wisedome of the worlde. No sound and substantiall truthe is too bee founde any where els saue onely there. And, therfore, the Holy Ghost, by the mouth of Moyses, willeth you that the lawe of God (that is to say, his word and doctrine) shoulde not departe from your mouth, but that you should bynde it about your wrists, imbroyder it vpon your garments, ingraue it vpon the postes of your house, and write it in the tables of your hart. And Dauid, speaking by the same spirite, exhorteth you by his owne example to set your whole delight in it, too occupy your selfe in it day and night, too lay it vp in your hart, too set more store by it than by riches, to be mindeful of it, to make it your counsayler, to stick too it, too talke of it afore Kings and greate men, to loue it, too make your songs of it, to remember it night and day, too count it sweeter than Hony, too take it as an heritage, and too make it the ioy of your hart. Neyther is it without cause that GOD calleth so ofte vppon Magistrates and noble men by name, that they should be diligent in his worde. For looke how muche the greater burthen and charge lyeth vpon their shoulders, and the greater accounte they haue to make afore him; so muche the greater wisedome and knoweledge haue they need of, which are not to be atteyned elsewhere than in his lawe. I beseeche your Lordship consider how God hath placed you vpon a high stage in the eyes of all men, as a guide, patterne, insample, and leader vnto others. If your vertues be vncounterfayted, if your religion be sound and pure, if your doings be according to true godlines, you shalbe a stay to your cuntrie, a comforte too good men, a bridle too euil men, a ioy too your freends, a corzie too your enemies, and an increace of honor to your owne house. But if you should become eyther a counterfayt Protestant, or a peruerse Papist, or a colde and carelesse newter, (which God forbid,) the harme could not be expressed which you should do to your natiue Cuntrie. For (as *Cicero*, no lesse truely than wisely affirmeth, and as the sorrowfull dooings of our present dayes do too certeinly auouch) greate men hurt not the common weale so much by beeing euil in respect of themselues, as by drawing others vnto euil by their euil example.

I assure your Lordshippe I write not these things as though I suspected you to be digressed from that soundnes and sinceritie wherein you were continually trayned and traded vnder that vigilant *Vlisses* of our common welth, sometyme your Lordship's careful *Chyron* or *Phoenix*, and nowe your faithful *Patroclus*, or as though I mistrusted your Lordship to be degenerated from the excellent towardnes, which by foreward proof hath giuen glad foretokens, and (I trust also) luckye hansels of an honorable age too ensue; but bycause the loue that I owe to God and his religion, the care that I haue of the church and my natiue cuntrie, the dutie wherin Nature hath bound mee to your Lordship, and (which is an occasion too make all good and honest men look about them) the perilousnes of this present time, wherin all meanes possible are practized to ouerthrowe Christe's kingdome, and to abolishe all faithfulnes from among men, make mee to feare and forecast, not so much what is true, as what may bee noysome and hurtful; and, therfore, I seek rather too profite by wholesome admonition, than to delight by pleasant speeches. These be no dayes of daliance; for Sathan, the workmaster of all mischeef, being greued that his own kingdome draweth to an end, not onely goeth about like a roring Lyon too deuoure folke by open force, but also like a slie Serpent setteth snares and pitfalles innumerable, to intrap men and bring them to destruction by policie, laying wayt for all men, but specially for such as are of high estate, as who alwayes carye greatest nombers with them which waye so euer they incline. Hee turneth himselfe intoo mo shapes than euer did *Proteus:* and suche as himselfe is, suche are his ministers. First and foremost, the obstinate and stubborne-harted *Papistes*, the sworne enemies of God, the pestilent poyson of mankinde, and the very welsprings of all error, hipocrisie, and vngraciousnes, (who, while they beare sway, bee more cruel than Beares, VVolues, and Tigres; and when they bee kept vnder, more deceitfull than *Cerastes* and *Crocodyles;* and at all times more mischeuous than the Diuel himselfe,) labour with tooth and nayle too winde their owne trash into credit with all men, and to bring the heauenly doctrine of the Gospel in hatred.

Ageine, the *Atheistes,* which say in their hartes there is no God; and the *Epicures,* which depriue GOD of his prouidence in gouerning the world, as though hee eyther vnderstoode not what is doone vppon Earth, or els cared not for mennes affaires : seeke they not by all meanes possible too weede all Religion, all feare of GOD, all remorse of conscience out of mennes harts? Out of these rootes spring other impes, no lesse pernicioue than the stockes of whiche they come, men of all Religions, Shippemen that canne sayle with all wethers, Carpenters that can hewe with bothe handes, Laddes that canne holde with the Hare and hunt with the Hounde, and (as the Scripture termeth them) time-seruers and menpleasers. Of which sorte be the picthank Preests of *Hammon,* who, with the venemouse blaste of their filthie flattery, corrupt the wel instructed mindes of our *Alexanders,* (that is to say, of our noble men,) by bearing them in hand, that they bee the sonnes of *Iupiter,* and making them beleeue themselues too bee Gods, yea, sometimes before they be scarce men. These, after the maner of *Panthers* and *Mermaides,* astonne the senses with a deadly sweetnes, and work destruction by delighting. Moreouer, to the further withdrawing of men's minds from the estimation of the sound Religion, it falleth out that euen in the outward face of the Church there be many Hipocrites, many looce liuers, many Sectaries, and many wranglers, whiche pretending the countenance of Chryste's flock, but beeing in deede the Deuil's hirelings, confessing GOD with their mouth, but denying him in their works, cause his holy, pure, and reuerend doctrine to bee slaundered and ill-spoken of among the *Gentiles,* (that is, too wit, among the *Papist* and worldlings,) and so alienate men from Christ.

The ignorant sort also deeming things vntowardly by the outward shew, charge the Gospell with the faultes of men, which it reprooueth and bringeth too lyght, as who would say, that hee whiche bewrayeth a Murtherer, or rebuketh an Adulterer, were too bee counted an offender in the same caces, bicause hee discouereth their wickednesse, too the intent too haue it punished or redressed. And these are stumbling-blocks common to all sortes of men; but more peculiar to great menne are those that I spake of in the third place, and also these ensuing, namely, noblenesse of birth, renowne of Aunceters, fauor of their Prince, freendship of their peeres, awe of their inferiours, great alyances, greate retinewes depending vpon them, libertie aboue the common rate, welth, honour, riches, ease, sumptuouse fare, costly apparel, gorgeouse buildings, attendaunce of seruants, and suche other like, whiche as they bee the singuler good giftes and benefites of God bestowed vpon them for their comfort, to the end they should the more loue him and imbrace his truthe: So Sathan abusing the infirmitie and corruption of man's nature, dooth in many menne wrest them all too a contrary ende, namely, too the proude contempt and impugning, or at leastwise to the carelesse neglecting of God's true Religion and seruice.

As for the fraylnesse of youth it self, the open manaces and priuie practizes of *Antichrist*, the common hatred and disdeine of the VVorlde ageinst the sincere worshippers of GOD, the hardnesse and aduersities which they endure in this life, and infinite other by matters whiche are no small hinderances too the proceeding of the Gospel, I wil not stand too intreat of them. For doubtlesse, although *Antichrist* were abolished, although Sathan were a sleepe, although the world were at one with vs, although wicked counsel were vtterly put too silence, although no euil example were giuen vs, although no outwarde stumbling-blocke were cast in our waye; yit haue wee one thing in our selues and of our selues, (euen originall sinne, concupiscence, or lust,) which neuer ceaseth too egge vs and allure vs from God, and too staine vs with all kinde of vnclennes, according as Sainct Iames sayth: Euery man is tempted of his owne lust. This is the breth of the venemouse *Cockatrice* which hath infected the whole offspring of *Adam*. This is the sting of that olde Serpent whose wounds neither *Chyron, Aesculapius,* nor *Apollo,* can heale, no, nor any wight in Heauen or Earth, saue onely God. This is the bitter fountaine *Exampeus,* which with his brackishnesse marreth the sweete Riuer *Hipanis,* that is to say, the flowing streame of all God's graces, benefites, and gifts in vs.

Good cause haue we therfore to bee forewarned and continually admonished to beware of the mischeef that is armed with so many weapons and policies to anoy: specially considering how the operation therof is to slea both bodie and soule, and to drown them togither in to endles damnation. For this I dare be bolde to say vpon the warrant of assured truthe, that whosoeuer is but lightly blasted with the poyson of Papistrie, is the vnapter to all the duties of true vertue and godlines, like as a Cripple or lame man is the vnmeeter and vnabler for the affaires of this life. But as for him that is throughly saped in it, and hathe digested it into his bowels, and hath setled the roots of it in the bottome of his hart; depending vpon the *Antichrist* of *Rome* as vpon the mouth of God, He can neyther be the faithful seruant of God, nor a hartie Subiect too his Prince, nor a good and sound member of the common welth, vntill hee haue done as the Snake dooth when he commeth to engender with the Lamprey.

For the better manifestation of all the which things, I beseech your good Lordship to peruse this present booke, which doubtlesse, for the excellency therof, not onely deserueth more singular commendation than man's wit is able to yeeld, but also is worthy too be had continually in all mennes hands, or rather too bee printed in their hartes. For if you haue an eye too the Authors, it was written by Prophets, Preestes, and Kinges, inspired with the Holye Ghost, the fountaine of all vnderstanding, wysedom, and truth, and auouched vnto vs by Christ, the Sonne of the euerlasting God. Or if you haue an eye to the matter, it conteineth a treatise of the Doctrine of lyfe and euerlasting Saluation, the particulars wherof are as many as are the points of true Religion and holinesse to Godward, or the points of faithfull meening and honest dealing too manward. And these things are common to it with the residue of holy Scripture.

The thing that is peculiar to it, is the maner of the handling of the matters wherof it treateth. For whereas other partes of holy writ (whither they be historicall, morall, iudiciall, ceremoniall, or propheticall) do commonly set down their treatizes in open and plaine declarations; this parte consisting of them all, wrappeth vp things in types and figures, describing them vnder borowed personages, and oftentimes winding in matters by preuention, speaking of thinges too come as if they were past or present, and of things past as if they were in dooing, and euery man is made a bewrayer of the secretes of his owne hart. And forasmuche as it consisteth cheefly of prayer and thanksgiuing, or (which comprehendeth them bothe) of inuocation, whiche is a communication with God, and requireth rather an earnest and deuout lifting vp of the minde, than a loud or curious vtterance of the voice: there be many vnperfect sentences, many broken speeches, and many displaced words, according as the voice of the partie that prayed was eyther preuented with the swiftnesse of his thoughtes, or interrupted with vehemency of ioy or greef, or forced to surcease through infirmitie, that hee might recouer newe strength and cheerfulnesse, by interminding God's former promises and benefites. Notwithstanding, the obscuritie of those places is not so great but that it may be easely ouercome, by such as, when they pray, doo vtterly sequester their mindes from all earthly imaginations and fleshly conceits, and after a sort forsaking their bodies for the time, do mount vppe aboue the world by faith, and present themselues before the heauenly throne of grace, to seek the vnspeakable and inestimable comfort of their soules.

Suche are the conteints, and suche is the maner or disposition of the ground-worke of this booke, that is to say, of the Psalmes themselues. VVhervnto (for the better vnderstanding of them) heere is added an exposition or Commentarie written in Latin by that learned Clerk and faithful minister of Chryst in the church of *Geneua,* Master *Iohn Caluin,* whose worthy praise and commendation, his owne manifolde woorks moste peinfully, sincerely, and soundly set foorth too the greate furtherance and profite of the whole Christen common weale, doo better declare than my pen can vtter or my wit deuice. And among the reste of them, it is thoughte of most learned men, that next vntoo his Institutions, this presente volume beareth the Bel, bothe for varietie of matter, substantialnes of doctrine, depth of iudgement, and perfectnesse of penning. For it is not puffed vp with vaine sound of emptie woords, nor with Rhetorical inlarging of painted sentences, but it is stuffed with piththy and grounded matter, such as plainly sheweth him too haue bin a man indued with the Spirite of God, and also well practized and tryed in the affaires and troubles of this world.

VVhat is to bee thought of the translation of it, that I remitte to your Lordship's fauourable acceptation, vnder whose Antesigne it is my desire that it may fight in the defence and maintenance of the true religion ageinst Antichrist and his wicked members. Onely thus muche I may safely say of it, that in all pointes (to the vttermoste of my power, and according to the abilitie which God hath giuen me to edifie withall) I haue sincerely performed the dutie of a faithfull Interpreter, rather indeuering too lay foorth things plainlye (yea, and sometimes also homely and grossely) too the vnderstanding of many, than to indyte things curyously too the pleasing of a fewe. For in this and suche other workes, the rude and ignorant haue more interest than the learned and skilful. If any thing be amisse, (as I dare not presume too vpholde that nothing hath escaped mee in so great a woorke,) my hartie desire is, that the same may be amended by such as are of sound iudgement and knowledge in God's woorde, so as no inconuenience may ensue of it too the churche of Christ. And look what I request in the behalfe of this present booke, the same do I request for all other books whiche I haue or (by God's grace and permission) shall heerafter put foorth for the edifying of Chrystes flock: for I knowe how suche things are the woork of God and not of man.

VVhat remayneth then, but that your Lordship, framing your selfe according to the rule of God's most holy word, should hie you apace to the atteinment of the true honour and immortall glory, by subduing sinne, the world, and the Deuil, the *Hectors* that cannot bee vanquished but by a christen *Achilles*; and by your good guyding bring many vnto Christ, that in the end you may receiue the rewarde of true and perfect blissednesse, euen the euerlasting saluation of the soule, whiche is the faire *Helen* for whose safetie it behooueth all good men too endure, not tenne yeeres warre, but continuall warre all their life long. To the furtherance wherof, God hath by householde alyance lincked vnto your Lordship a long experienced *Nestor*, whose counsaile and footsteps if you folowe, no doubt but you shalbee bothe happie in your selfe, and singularly profitable to your common welth; and moreouer, God shall blisse you with plentiful and godly issue by your vertuous and deerbeloued Spouse, to continew the honour and renowne of your noble house after the happy knitting vp of bothe your yeeres, which I pray God may bee many in vnseperable loue, like the loue of *Ceix* and *Alcyonee*, to the glory of God, and the contentation of bothe your desires.
VVritten at *London*, the xx. of October 1571.

¶ Your good Lordship's moste humble to commaund, *Arthur Golding*.

THE AUTHOR'S PREFACE.

JOHN CALVIN

TO THE GODLY AND INGENIOUS READERS,

GREETING.

IF the reading of these my COMMENTARIES confer as much benefit on the Church of God as I myself have reaped advantage from the composition of them, I shall have no reason to regret that I have undertaken this work. Having expounded here, in our small school, the Book of Psalms, about three years ago, I thought that I had by this means sufficiently discharged my duty, and had resolved not to publish to the world what I had familiarly taught those of my own household. And, in fact, before I had undertaken to expound this book in my lectures, at the request of my brethren, I said what was true, that I had kept away from this subject, because that most faithful teacher of the Church of God, Martin Bucer, had laboured in this field with such singular learning, diligence, fidelity, and success, that at least there was not so great need that I should put my hand to the work. And had the Commentaries of Wolphangus Musculus at that time been published, I would not have omitted to do them justice, by mentioning them in the same way, since he too, in the judgment of good men, has earned no small praise by his diligence and industry in this walk. I had not yet come to the end of the book, when, lo! I am urged by renewed solicitations not to suffer my lectures, which certain persons had carefully, faithfully, and not without great labour, taken down, to be lost to the world. My purpose still remained unaltered; only I promised what for a long time I had been thinking of, to write something on the subject in the French language, that my countrymen might not be without the means of being enabled to understand so useful a book when perusing it. Whilst I am thinking of making this attempt, suddenly, and contrary to my first design, it occurred to me, by what impulse I know not, to compose in Latin, only as it were in the way of trial, an exposition of one Psalm. When I found that my success corresponded to my desire far beyond what I had ventured to anticipate, I was encouraged, and accordingly began to make the same attempt in a few other Psalms. On perceiving this, my intimate friends, as if in this way they held me bound, urged me with the greater confidence not to desist from my course. One reason which made me comply with their solicitations, and which also had from the commencement induced me to make this first attempt, was an apprehension that at some future period what had been taken down from my lectures, might be published to the world contrary to my wishes, or at least without my knowledge. I can truly say, that I was drawn to execute this work rather from such an apprehension, than led to it from my own free will. At the same time, as I continued to prosecute the work, I began to perceive more distinctly that this was by no means a superfluous undertaking, and I have also felt from my own individual experience, that to readers who are not so exercised, I would furnish important assistance in understanding The Psalms.

The varied and resplendid riches which are contained in this treasury it is no easy matter to express in words; so much so, that I well know that whatever I shall be able to say will be far from approaching the excellence of the subject. But as it is better to give to my readers some taste, however small, of the wonderful advantages they will derive from the study of this book, than to be entirely silent on the point, I may be permitted briefly to advert to a matter, the greatness of which does not admit of being fully unfolded. I have been accustomed to call this book, I think not inappropriately, "An Anatomy of all the Parts of the Soul;" for there is not an emotion of which any one can be conscious that is not here represented as in a mirror. Or rather, the Holy Spirit has here drawn to the life all the griefs, sorrows, fears, doubts, hopes, cares, perplexities, in short, all the distracting emotions with which the minds of men are wont to be agitated. The other parts of Scripture contain the commandments which God enjoined his servants to announce to us. But here the prophets themselves, seeing they are exhibited to us as speaking to God, and laying open all their inmost thoughts and affections, call, or rather draw, each of us to the examination of himself in particular, in order that none of the many infirmities to which we are subject, and of the many vices with which we abound, may remain concealed. It is certainly a rare and singular advantage, when all lurking places are discovered, and the heart is brought into the light, purged from that most baneful infection, hypocrisy. In short, as calling upon God is one of the principal means of securing our safety, and as a better and more unerring rule for guiding us in this exercise cannot be found elsewhere than in The Psalms, it follows, that in proportion to the proficiency which a man shall have attained in understanding them, will be his knowledge of the most important part of celestial doctrine. Genuine and earnest prayer proceeds first from a sense of our need, and next, from faith in the promises of God. It is by perusing these inspired compositions, that men will be most effectually awakened to a sense of their maladies, and, at the same time, instructed in seeking remedies for their cure. In a word, whatever may serve to encourage us when we are about to pray to God, is taught us in this book. And not only are the promises of God presented to us in it, but oftentimes there is exhibited to us one standing, as it were, amidst the invitations of God on the one hand, and the impediments of the flesh on the other, girding and preparing himself for prayer: thus teaching us, if at any time we are agitated with a variety of doubts, to resist and fight against them, until the soul, freed and disentangled from all these impediments, rise up to God; and not only so, but even when in the midst of doubts, fears, and apprehensions, let us put forth our efforts in prayer, until we experience some consolation which may calm and bring contentment to our minds.[1] Although distrust may shut the gate against our prayers, yet we must not allow ourselves to give way, whenever our hearts waver or are agitated with inquietude, but must persevere until faith finally come forth victorious from these conflicts. In many places we may perceive the exercise of the servants of God in prayer so fluctuating, that they are almost overwhelmed by the alternate hope of success and apprehension of failure, and gain the prize only by strenuous exertions. We see on the one hand, the flesh manifesting its infirmity; and on the other, faith putting forth its power; and if it is not so valiant and courageous as might be desired, it is at least prepared to fight until by degrees it acquire perfect strength. But as those things which serve to teach us the true method of praying aright will be found scattered through the whole of this Commentary, I will not now stop to treat of topics which it will be necessary afterwards to repeat, nor detain my readers from proceeding to the work itself. Only it appeared to me to be requisite to show in passing, that this book makes known to us this privilege, which is desirable above all others—that not only is there opened up to us familiar access to God, but also that we have permission and freedom granted us to lay open before him our infirmities, which we would be ashamed to confess before men. Besides, there is also here prescribed to us an infallible rule for directing us with respect to the right manner of offering to God the sacrifice of praise, which he declares to be most precious in his sight, and of the sweetest odour. There is no other book in which there is to be found more express and magnificent commendations, both of the unparalleled liberality of God towards his Church, and of all his works; there is no other book in which there is recorded so many deliverances, nor one in which the evidences and experiences of the fatherly providence and solicitude which God exercises towards us, are celebrated with such splendour of diction, and yet with the strictest adherence to truth; in short, there is no other

---

[1] " Jusqu'à ce que nous sentions quelque allegement qui nous appaise et contente."—*Fr.*

book in which we are more perfectly taught the right manner of praising God, or in which we are more powerfully stirred up to the performance of this religious exercise. Moreover, although The Psalms are replete with all the precepts which serve to frame our life to every part of holiness, piety, and righteousness, yet they will principally teach and train us to bear the cross; and the bearing of the cross is a genuine proof of our obedience, since by doing this, we renounce the guidance of our own affections, and submit ourselves entirely to God, leaving him to govern us, and to dispose of our life according to his will, so that the afflictions which are the bitterest and most severe to our nature, become sweet to us, because they proceed from him. In one word, not only will we here find general commendations of the goodness of God, which may teach men to repose themselves in him alone, and to seek all their happiness solely in him; and which are intended to teach true believers with their whole hearts confidently to look to him for help in all their necessities; but we will also find that the free remission of sins, which alone reconciles God towards us, and procures for us settled peace with him,[1] is so set forth and magnified, as that here there is nothing wanting which relates to the knowledge of eternal salvation.

Now, if my readers derive any fruit and advantage from the labour which I have bestowed in writing these Commentaries, I would have them to understand that the small measure of experience which I have had by the conflicts with which the Lord has exercised me, has in no ordinary degree assisted me, not only in applying to present use whatever instruction could be gathered from these divine compositions, but also in more easily comprehending the design of each of the writers. And as David holds the principal place among them, it has greatly aided me in understanding more fully the complaints made by him of the internal afflictions which the Church had to sustain through those who gave themselves out to be her members, that I had suffered the same

---

[1] " Et nous acquiert tranquillite de conscience devant luy."—*Fr.* "And acquires for us tranquillity of conscience before him."

or similar things from the domestic enemies of the Church. For although I follow David at a great distance, and come far short of equalling him; or rather, although in aspiring slowly and with great difficulty to attain to the many virtues in which he excelled, I still feel myself tarnished with the contrary vices; yet if I have any things in common with him, I have no hesitation in comparing myself with him. In reading the instances of his faith, patience, fervour, zeal, and integrity, it has, as it ought, drawn from me unnumbered groans and sighs, that I am so far from approaching them; but it has, notwithstanding, been of very great advantage to me to behold in him as in a mirror, both the commencement of my calling, and the continued course of my function; so that I know the more assuredly, that whatever that most illustrious king and prophet suffered, was exhibited to me by God as an example for imitation. My condition, no doubt, is much inferior to his, and it is unnecessary for me to stay to show this. But as he was taken from the sheepfold, and elevated to the rank of supreme authority; so God having taken me from my originally obscure and humble condition, has reckoned me worthy of being invested with the honourable office of a preacher and minister of the gospel. When I was as yet a very little boy, my father had destined me for the study of theology. But afterwards, when he considered that the legal profession commonly raised those who followed it to wealth, this prospect induced him suddenly to change his purpose. Thus it came to pass, that I was withdrawn from the study of philosophy, and was put to the study of law. To this pursuit I endeavoured faithfully to apply myself, in obedience to the will of my father; but God, by the secret guidance of his providence, at length gave a different direction to my course. And first, since I was too obstinately devoted to the superstitions of Popery to be easily extricated from so profound an abyss of mire, God by a sudden conversion subdued and brought my mind to a teachable frame, which was more hardened in such matters than might have been expected from one at my early period of life. Having thus received some taste and knowledge of true godliness, I was immediately inflamed with so intense a desire to make progress therein, that although I did not altogether leave off other studies, I yet pursued them with less ardour.

 I was quite surprised to find that before a year had elapsed, all who had any desire after purer doctrine were continually coming to me to learn, although I myself was as yet but a mere novice and tyro. Being of a disposition somewhat unpolished and bashful, which led me always to love the shade and retirement, I then began to seek some secluded corner where I might be withdrawn from the public view; but so far from being able to accomplish the object of my desire, all my retreats were like public schools. In short, whilst my one great object was to live in seclusion without being known, God so led me about through different turnings and changes, that he never permitted me to rest in any place, until, in spite of my natural disposition, he brought me forth to public notice. Leaving my native country, France, I in fact retired into Germany, expressly for the purpose of being able there to enjoy in some obscure corner the repose which I had always desired, and which had been so long denied me. But lo! whilst I lay hidden at Basle, and known only to a few people, many faithful and holy persons were burnt alive in France; and the report of these burnings having reached foreign nations, they excited the strongest disapprobation among a great part of the Germans, whose indignation was kindled against the authors of such tyranny. In order to allay this indignation, certain wicked and lying pamphlets were circulated, stating, that none were treated with such cruelty but Anabaptists and seditious persons, who, by their perverse ravings and false opinions, were overthrowing not only religion but also all civil order. Observing that the object which these instruments of the court aimed at by their disguises, was not only that the disgrace of shedding so much innocent blood might remain buried under the false charges and calumnies which they brought against the holy martyrs after their death, but also, that afterwards they might be able to proceed to the utmost extremity in murdering the poor saints without exciting compassion towards them in the breasts of any, it appeared to me, that unless I opposed them to the utmost of my ability, my silence could not be vindicated from the charge of cowardice and treachery. This was the consideration which induced me to publish my Institute of the Christian Religion. My objects were, first, to prove that these reports were false and calumnious, and thus to vindicate my brethren, whose death was precious in the sight of the Lord; and next, that as the same cruelties might very soon after be exercised against many unhappy individuals, foreign nations might be touched with at least some compassion towards them and solicitude about them. When it was then published, it was not that copious and laboured work which it now is, but only a small treatise containing a summary of the principal truths of the Christian religion; and it was published with no other design than that men might know what was the faith held by those whom I saw basely and wickedly defamed by those flagitious and perfidious flatterers. That my object was not to acquire fame, appeared from this, that immediately after I left Basle, and particularly from the fact that nobody there knew that I was the author.

Wherever else I have gone, I have taken care to conceal that I was the author of that performance; and I had resolved to continue in the same privacy and obscurity, until at length William Farel detained me at Geneva, not so much by counsel and exhortation, as by a dreadful imprecation, which I felt to be as if God had from heaven laid his mighty hand upon me to arrest me. As the most direct road to Strasburg, to which I then intended to retire, was shut up by the wars, I had resolved to pass quickly by Geneva, without staying longer than a single night in that city. A little before this, Popery had been driven from it by the exertions of the excellent person whom I have named, and Peter Viret; but matters were not yet brought to a settled state, and the city was divided into unholy and dangerous factions. Then an individual who now basely apostatised and returned to the Papists, discovered me and made me known to others. Upon this, Farel, who burned with an extraordinary zeal to advance the gospel, immediately strained every nerve to detain me. And after having learned that my heart was set upon devoting myself to private studies, for which I wished to keep myself free from other pursuits, and finding that he gained nothing by entreaties, he proceeded to utter an imprecation that God would curse my retirement, and the tranquillity of the studies which I sought, if I should withdraw and refuse to give assistance, when the necessity was so urgent. By this imprecation I was so stricken with terror, that I desisted from the journey which I had undertaken; but sensible of my natural bashfulness and timidity, I would not bring myself under obligation to discharge any particular office. After that, four months had scarcely elapsed, when, on the one hand, the Anabaptists began to assail us, and, on the other, a certain wicked apostate, who being secretly supported by the influence of some of the magistrates of the city, was thus enabled to give us a great deal of trouble. At the same time, a succession of dissensions fell out in the city[1] which strangely afflicted us. Being, as I acknowledge, naturally of a timid, soft, and pusillanimous disposition, I was compelled to encounter these violent tempests as part of my early training; and although I did not sink under them, yet I was not sustained by such greatness of mind, as not to rejoice more than it became me, when, in consequence of certain commotions, I was banished from Geneva.

By this means set at liberty and loosed from the tie of my vocation, I resolved to live in a private station, free from the burden and cares of any public charge, when that most excellent servant of Christ, Martin Bucer, employing a similar kind of remonstrance and protestation as that to which Farel had recourse before, drew me back to a new station. Alarmed by the example of Jonas which he set before me, I still continued in the work of teaching. And although I always continued like myself, studiously avoiding celebrity;[2] yet I was carried, I know not how, as it were by force to the Imperial assemblies, where, willing or unwilling, I was under the necessity of appearing before the eyes of many. Afterwards, when the Lord having

---

[1] "Cependant surveindrent en la ville seditions les unes sur les autres."—*Fr.*

[2] "C'est, asçavoir de ne vouloir point apparoistre ou suyvre les grandes assemblees."—*Fr.* "That is, not wishing to appear before, or wait upon, the great assemblies."

compassion on this city, had allayed the hurtful agitations and broils which prevailed in it, and by his wonderful power had defeated both the wicked counsels and the sanguinary attempts of the disturbers of the Republic, necessity was imposed upon me of returning to my former charge, contrary to my desire and inclination. The welfare of this church, it is true, lay so near my heart, that for its sake I would not have hesitated to lay down my life; but my timidity nevertheless suggested to me many reasons for excusing myself from again willingly taking upon my shoulders so heavy a burden. At length, however, a solemn and conscientious regard to my duty, prevailed with me to consent to return to the flock from which I had been torn; but with what grief, tears, great anxiety and distress I did this, the Lord is my best witness, and many godly persons who would have wished to see me delivered from this painful state, had it not been that that which I feared, and which made me give my consent, prevented them and shut their mouths.

Were I to narrate the various conflicts by which the Lord has exercised me since that time, and by what trials he has proved me, it would make a long history. But that I may not become tedious to my readers by a waste of words, I shall content myself with repeating briefly what I have touched upon a little before, that in considering the whole course of the life of David,[1] it seemed to me that by his own footsteps he showed me the way, and from this I have experienced no small consolation. As that holy king was harassed by the Philistines and other foreign enemies with continual wars, while he was much more grievously afflicted by the malice and wickedness of some perfidious men amongst his own people, so I can say as to myself, that I have been assailed on all sides, and have scarcely been able to enjoy repose for a single moment, but have always had to sustain some conflict either from enemies without or within the Church. Satan has made many attempts to overthrow the fabric of this Church; and once it came to this, that I, altogether feeble and timorous as I am, was compelled to break and put a stop to his deadly assaults by putting my life in

---

[1] "Qu'en considerant tout le discours de la vie de David."—*Fr.*

danger, and opposing my person to his blows. Afterwards, for the space of five years, when some wicked libertines were furnished with undue influence, and also some of the common people, corrupted by the allurements and perverse discourse of such persons, desired to obtain the liberty of doing whatever they pleased, without control, I was under the necessity of fighting without ceasing to defend and maintain the discipline of the Church. To these irreligious characters and despisers of the heavenly doctrine, it was a matter of entire indifference, although the Church should sink into ruin, provided they obtained what they sought,—the power of acting just as they pleased. Many, too, harassed by poverty and hunger, and others impelled by insatiable ambition or avarice and a desire of dishonest gain, were become so frantic, that they chose rather, by throwing all things into confusion, to involve themselves and us in one common ruin, than to remain quiet by living peaceably and honestly.[1] During the whole of this lengthened period, I think that there is scarcely any of the weapons which are forged in the workshop of Satan, which has not been employed by them in order to obtain their object. And at length matters had come to such a state, that an end could be put to their machinations in no other way than cutting them off by an ignominious death; which was indeed a painful and pitiable spectacle to me. They no doubt deserved the severest punishment, but I always rather desired that they might live in prosperity, and continue safe and untouched; which would have been the case had they not been altogether incorrigible, and obstinately refused to listen to wholesome admonition.

The trial of these five years was grievous and hard to bear; but I experienced not less excruciating pain from the malignity of those who ceased not to assail myself and my ministry with their envenomed calumnies. A great proportion of them, it is true, are so blinded by a passion for slander and detraction, that to their great disgrace, they betray at once their impudence, while others, however crafty and cunning, cannot so cover or disguise themselves as to escape being shamefully convicted and disgraced; yet when a man has

[1] " Que se tenir quois en vivant paisiblement et honnestement."—*Fr.*

been a hundred times found innocent of a charge brought against him, and when the charge is again repeated without any cause or occasion, it is an indignity hard to bear. Because I affirm and maintain that the world is managed and governed by the secret providence of God, a multitude of presumptuous men rise up against me, and allege that I represent God as the author of sin. This is so foolish a calumny, that it would of itself quickly come to nothing, did it not meet with persons who have tickled ears, and who take pleasure in feeding upon such discourse. But there are many whose minds are so filled with envy and spleen, or ingratitude, or malignity, that there is no falsehood, however preposterous, yea, even monstrous, which they do not receive, if it is spoken to them. Others endeavour to overthrow God's eternal purpose of predestination, by which he distinguishes between the reprobate and the elect; others take upon them to defend free will; and forthwith many throw themselves into their ranks, not so much through ignorance as by a perversity of zeal which I know not how to characterise. If they were open and avowed enemies, who brought these troubles upon me, the thing might in some way be borne. But that those who shroud themselves under the name of brethren, and not only eat Christ's sacred bread, but also administer it to others, that those, in short, who loudly boast of being preachers of the gospel, should wage such nefarious war against me, how detestable is it? In this matter I may very justly complain with David, "Yea, mine own familiar friend, in whom I trusted, who did eat of my bread, hath lifted up his heel against me," (Ps. xli. 9.) "For it was not an enemy that reproached me; but it was thou, a man mine equal, my guide, and mine acquaintance. We took sweet counsel together, and walked unto the house of God in company," (Ps. lv. 12, 13, 14.) Others circulated ridiculous reports concerning my treasures; others, of the extravagant authority and enormous influence which they say I possess; others speak of my delicacies and magnificence. But when a man is content with scanty food and common clothing, and does not require from the humblest more frugality than he shows and practises himself, shall it be said that such an one is too sumptuous, and lives in too high a style? As to the power and influence of which they envy me, I wish I could discharge this burden upon them; for they estimate my power by the multitude of affairs, and the vast weight of labours with which I am overwhelmed. And if there are some whom I cannot persuade whilst I am alive that I am not rich, my death at length will prove it. I confess, indeed, that I am not poor; for I desire nothing more than what I have. All these are invented stories, and there is no colour whatever for any one of them; but many nevertheless are very easily persuaded of their truth, and applaud them; and the reason is, because the greatest part judge that the only means of cloaking their enormities is to throw all things into disorder, and to confound black and white; and they think that the best and shortest way by which they can obtain full liberty to live with impunity just as they please, is to destroy the authority of Christ's servants.

In addition to these, there are "the hypocritical mockers in feasts," of whom David complains, (Ps. xxxv. 16;) and I mean by these not only lick-dish characters, who seek a meal to fill their belly,[1] but all those who by false reports seek to obtain the favour of the great. Having been long accustomed to swallow such wrongs as these, I have become almost hardened; yet when the insolence of such characters increases, I cannot but sometimes feel my heart wounded with bitter pangs. Nor was it enough that I should be so inhumanly treated by my neighbours. In addition to this, in a distant country towards the frozen ocean, there was raised, I know not how, by the frenzy of a few, a storm which afterwards stirred up against me a vast number of persons, who are too much at leisure, and have nothing to do but by their bickering to hinder those who are labouring for the edification of the Church.[2] I am still speaking of the

---

[1] " Et je n'enten pas seulement les frians qui cherchent quelque lippee pour farcir leur ventre."—*Fr.*

[2] " Mais encore ce n'estoit pas assez d'estre traitté ainsi inhumainement par mes voisins, si non qu'en un pays lointain vers la mer glacee le temps se troublast aussi je ne scay comment par la phrenesie d'aucuns, pour puis apres faire lever contre moy comme un nuee de gens qui sont trop de loisir et n'ont que faire s'ils ne s'escarmouschent à empescher ceux qui travaillent à edification."—*Fr.*

internal enemies of the Church—of those who, boasting mightily of the gospel of Christ, nevertheless rush against me with greater impetuosity than against the open adversaries of the Church, because I do not embrace their gross and fictitious notion concerning a carnal way of eating Christ in the sacrament; and of whom I may protest, after the example of David, "I am for peace; but when I speak, they are for war," (Ps. cxx. 7.) Moreover, the cruel ingratitude of all of them is manifest in this, that they scruple not to assail both in flank and rear a man who strenuously exerts himself to maintain a cause which they have in common with him, and whom therefore they ought to aid and succour. Certainly, if such persons were possessed of even a small portion of humanity, the fury of the Papists which is directed against me with such unbridled violence, would appease the most implacable animosity which they may bear towards me. But since the condition of David was such, that though he had deserved well of his own people, he was nevertheless bitterly hated by many without a cause, as he complains in Ps. lxix. 4, "I restored that which I took not away," it afforded me no small consolation when I was groundlessly assailed by the hatred of those who ought to have assisted and solaced me, to conform myself to the example of so great and so excellent a person. This knowledge and experience have been of much service in enabling me to understand The Psalms, so that in my meditations upon them, I did not wander, as it were, in an unknown region.

My readers, too, if I mistake not, will observe, that in unfolding the internal affections both of David and of others, I discourse upon them as matters of which I have familiar experience. Moreover, since I have laboured faithfully to open up this treasure for the use of all the people of God, although what I have done has not been equal to my wishes, yet the attempt which I have made deserves to be received with some measure of favour. Still I only ask that each may judge of my labours with justice and candour, according to the advantage and fruit which he shall derive from them. Certainly, as I have said before, in reading these Commentaries, it will be clearly seen that I have not sought to please, unless in so far as I might at the same time be profitable to others. And, therefore, I have not only observed throughout a simple style of teaching, but in order to be removed the farther from all ostentation, I have also generally abstained from refuting the opinions of others, although this presented a more favourable opportunity for plausible display, and of acquiring the applause of those who shall favour my book with a perusal. I have never touched upon opposite opinions, unless where there was reason to fear, that by being silent respecting them, I might leave my readers in doubt and perplexity. At the same time, I am sensible that it would have been much more agreeable to the taste of many, had I heaped together a great mass of materials which has great show, and acquires fame for the writer; but I have felt nothing to be of more importance than to have a regard to the edification of the Church. May God, who has implanted this desire in my heart, grant by his grace that the success may correspond thereto!

GENEVA, *July* 22, 1557.

COMMENTARY

ON

THE BOOK OF PSALMS.

COMMENTARY

UPON

THE BOOK OF PSALMS.

PSALM I.

He who collected the Psalms into one volume, whether Ezra or some other person, appears to have placed this Psalm at the beginning, by way of preface, in which he inculcates upon all the godly the duty of meditating upon the law of God. The sum and substance of the whole is, that they are blessed who apply their hearts to the pursuit of heavenly wisdom; whereas the profane despisers of God, although for a time they may reckon themselves happy, shall at length have a most miserable end.

1. *Blessed is the man who walketh not in the counsel of the ungodly, nor standeth in the way of sinners, nor sitteth in the seat of the scorner.*
2. *But his delight is in the law of Jehovah; and in his law doth he meditate day and night.*

1. *Blessed is the man.*[1] The meaning of the Psalmist, as I have stated above, is, that it shall be always well with God's devout servants, whose constant endeavour it is to make

---

[1] In the Septuagint, the reading is, $\mu\alpha\kappa\acute{\alpha}\rho\iota o\varsigma\ \acute{\alpha}\nu\eta\rho$, *blessed is the man*. Both Calvin and our English translators have adopted this rendering. But the Hebrew word אשרי, *ashre*, rendered *blessed*, is in the plural number, and האיש, *ha-ish*, *the man*, in the singular. Accordingly, the words have been considered as an exclamation, and may be literally rendered, *O, the blessednesses of the man!* a beautiful and emphatic form of expression.

progress in the study of his law. The greater part of mankind being accustomed to deride the conduct of the saints as mere simplicity, and to regard their labour as entirely thrown away, it was of importance that the righteous should be confirmed in the way of holiness, by the consideration of the miserable condition of all men without the blessing of God, and the conviction that God is favourable to none but those who zealously devote themselves to the study of divine truth. Moreover, as corruption has always prevailed in the world, to such a degree, that the general character of men's lives is nothing else but a continual departure from the law of God, the Psalmist, before asserting the blessedness of the students of the divine law, admonishes them to beware of being carried away by the ungodliness of the multitude around them. Commencing with a declaration of his abhorrence of the wicked, he teaches us how impossible it is for any one to apply his mind to meditation upon God's law, who has not first withdrawn and separated himself from the society of the ungodly. A needful admonition surely; for we see how thoughtlessly men will throw themselves into the snares of Satan; at least, how few comparatively there are who guard against the enticements of sin. That we may be fully apprised of our danger, it is necessary to remember that the world is fraught with deadly corruption, and that the first step to living well is to renounce the company of the ungodly, otherwise it is sure to infect us with its own pollution.

As the prophet, in the first place, enjoins the godly to beware of temptations to evil, we shall follow the same order. His affirmation, that they are blessed who have no fellowship with the ungodly, is what the common feeling and opinion of mankind will scarcely admit; for while all men naturally desire and seek after happiness, we see how securely they can indulge themselves in their sins, yea, that those of them who have departed farthest from righteousness, in the gratification of their lusts, are accounted happy, because they obtain the desires of their heart. The prophet, on the contrary, here teaches that no man can be duly animated to the fear and service of God, and to the study of his law, until he is firmly persuaded that all the ungodly are miserable, and that they who do not withdraw from their company shall be involved in the same destruction with them. But as it is no easy matter to shun the ungodly with whom we are mingled in the world, so as to be wholly estranged from them, the Psalmist, in order to give the greater emphasis to his exhortation, employs a multiplicity of expressions.

In the first place, he forbids us to *walk in their counsel;* in the second place, to *stand in their way;* and, lastly, to *sit in their seat.*

The sum of the whole is, that the servants of God must endeavour utterly to abhor the life of ungodly men. But as it is the policy of Satan to insinuate his deceits, in a very crafty way, the prophet, in order that none may be insensibly deceived, shows how by little and little men are ordinarily induced to turn aside from the right path. They do not, at the first step, advance so far as a proud contempt of God; but having once begun to give ear to evil counsel, Satan leads them, step by step, farther astray, till they rush headlong into open transgression. The prophet, therefore, begins with *counsel,* by which term I understand the wickedness which does not as yet show itself openly. Then he speaks of *the way,* which is to be understood of the customary mode or manner of living. And he places at the top of the climax *the seat,* by which metaphorical expression he designates the obduracy produced by the habit of a sinful life. In the same way, also, ought the three phrases, *to walk, to stand,* and *to sit,* to be understood. When a person willingly *walks* after the gratification of his corrupt lusts, the practice of sinning so infatuates him, that, forgetful of himself, he grows hardened in wickedness; and this the prophet terms *standing in the way of sinners.* Then at length follows a desperate obstinacy, which he expresses by the figure of *sitting.* Whether there is the same gradation in the Hebrew words רשעים, *reshaim,* חטאים, *chataim,* and לצים, *letsim,* that is to say, a gradual increase of evil, I leave to the judgment of others.[1] To me it does not appear that there is, unless, perhaps, in the last word. For those are called *scorners* who, having thrown off all fear of God, commit sin without

[1] C'est à dire, un accroissement de mal comme par degrez.—*Fr.*

restraint, in the hope of escaping unpunished, and without compunction or fear sport at the judgment of God, as if they would never be called to render up an account to him. The Hebrew word חטאים, *chataim*, as it signifies the openly wicked, is very properly joined with the term *way*, which signifies a professed and habitual manner of living.[1] And if, in the time of the Psalmist, it was necessary for the devout worshippers of God to withdraw themselves from the company of the ungodly, in order to frame their life aright, how much more in the present day, when the world has become so much more corrupt, ought we carefully to avoid all dangerous society, that we may be kept unstained by its impurities. The prophet, however, not only commands the faithful to keep at a distance from the ungodly, from the dread of being infected by them, but his admonition further implies, that every one should be careful not to corrupt himself, nor abandon himself to impiety.[2] A man may not have contracted defilement from evil examples, and yet come to resemble the wicked by spontaneously imitating their corrupt manners.

In the second verse, the Psalmist does not simply pronounce those happy who fear God, as in other places, but designates godliness by *the study of the law*, teaching us that God is only rightly served when his law is obeyed. It is not left to every man to frame a system of religion according to his own judgment, but the standard of godliness is to be taken from the Word of God. When David here speaks of *the law*, it ought not to be understood as if the other parts of Scripture should be excluded, but rather, since the whole of Scripture is nothing else than an exposition of the law, under it as the head is comprehended the whole body. The prophet, therefore, in commending the law, includes all the rest of the inspired writings. He must, therefore, be understood as meaning to exhort the faithful to the reading of the Psalms also. From his characterizing the godly as *delighting* in the law of the Lord, we may

---

[1] Il est bien conjoint avec le verbe signifiant une profession de vivre et un train tout accoustumé.—*Fr.*

[2] Et s'adonner de soy-mesme à impiete.—*Fr.*

learn that forced or servile obedience is not at all acceptable
to God, and that those only are worthy students of the law
who come to it with a cheerful mind, and are so delighted
with its instructions, as to account nothing more desirable
or delicious than to make progress therein. From this love
of the law proceeds constant *meditation* upon it, which
the prophet mentions in the last clause of the verse; for all
who are truly actuated by love to the law must feel pleasure
in the diligent study of it.

3. *He shall be like a tree planted by the rivers of waters, that
bringeth forth his fruit in his season; whose leaf shall not
wither; and whatsoever he doeth shall prosper.*

The Psalmist here illustrates, and, at the same time, confirms by a metaphor, the statement made in the preceding verse; for he shows in what respect those who fear God are to be accounted happy, namely, not because they enjoy an evanescent and empty gladness, but because they are in a desirable condition. There is in the words an implied contrast between the vigour of a tree planted in a situation well watered, and the decayed appearance of one which, although it may flourish beautifully for a time, yet soon withers on account of the barrenness of the soil in which it is placed. With respect to the ungodly, as we shall afterwards see, (Ps. xxxvii. 35,) they are sometimes like "the cedars of Lebanon." They have such an overflowing abundance of wealth and honours, that nothing seems wanting to their present happiness. But however high they may be raised, and however far and wide they may spread their branches, yet having no root in the ground, nor even a sufficiency of moisture from which they may derive nourishment, the whole of their beauty by and by disappears, and withers away. It is, therefore, the blessing of God alone which preserves any in a prosperous condition. Those who explain the figure of the faithful *bringing forth their fruit in season,* as meaning that they wisely discern when a thing ought to be done so as to be done well, in my opinion, show more acuteness than judgment, by putting a meaning upon the words of the prophet which he never intended. He obviously meant nothing more than that the children of God constantly flourish, and are always watered with the secret influences of divine grace, so that whatever may befall them is conducive to their salvation; while, on the other hand, the ungodly are carried away by the sudden tempest, or consumed by the scorching heat. And when he says, *he bringeth forth his fruit in season*,[1] he expresses the full maturity of the fruit produced, whereas, although the ungodly may present the appearance of precocious fruitfulness, yet they produce nothing that comes to perfection.

4. *The ungodly are not so; but are like the chaff which the wind driveth away.*

The Psalmist might, with propriety, have compared the ungodly to a tree that speedily withers, as Jeremiah likens them to the heath which grows in the wilderness, (Jer. xvii. 6.) But not reckoning this figure sufficiently strong, he debases them by employing another, which represents them in a light still more contemptible: and the reason is, that he does not keep his eye on the prosperous condition of which they boast for a short time, but his mind is seriously pondering on the destruction which awaits them, and will at length overtake them. The meaning, therefore, is, although the ungodly now live prosperously, yet by and by they shall be like chaff; for when the Lord has brought them low, he shall drive them hither and thither with the blast of his wrath. Besides, by this form of speech, the Holy Spirit teaches us to contemplate with the eye of faith, what might otherwise seem incredible; for although the ungodly man rise high, and appear to great advantage, like a stately tree, we may rest assured that he will be even as chaff or refuse, whenever God chooses to cast him down from his high estate, with the breath of his mouth.

[1] " And it bringeth forth all its produce to maturity."—*(Street's New Literal Version of the Psalms.)*

5. *Therefore the ungodly shall not stand in the judgment, nor sinners in the congregation of the righteous.*
6. *For Jehovah knoweth the way of the righteous; but the way of the ungodly shall perish.*

In the fifth verse, the prophet teaches that a happy life depends on a good conscience, and that, therefore, it is not wonderful, if the ungodly suddenly fall from the happiness of which they fancied themselves in possession. And there is implied in the words a kind of concession; the prophet tacitly acknowledges that the ungodly please and enjoy themselves, and triumph during the reign of moral disorder in the world; just as robbers revel in the woods and caves, when beyond the reach of justice. But he assures us, that things will not always remain in their present state of confusion, and that when they shall have been reduced to proper order, these ungodly persons shall be entirely deprived of their pleasures, and feel that they were infatuated when they thought themselves happy. We now see how the Psalmist pronounces the ungodly to be miserable, because happiness is the inward blessing of a good conscience. He does not deny, that before they are driven to judgment, all things succeed well with them; but he denies that they are happy, unless they have substantial and stedfast integrity of character to sustain them: for the true integrity of the righteous manifests itself when it comes at length to be tried. It is indeed true, that the Lord daily executes judgment, by making a distinction between the righteous and the wicked, but because this is done only partially in this life, we must look higher if we desire to behold *the assembly of the righteous*, of which mention is here made.

Even in this world the prosperity of the ungodly begins to pass away as often as God manifests the tokens of his judgment; (for then, being awakened out of sleep, they are constrained to acknowledge, whether they will or no, that they have no part with the assembly of the righteous;) but because this is not accomplished always, nor with respect to all men, in the present state, we must patiently wait for the day of final revelation, in which Christ will separate the sheep from the goats. At the same time, we must maintain it as a general truth, that the ungodly are devoted to misery; for their own consciences condemn them for their wickedness; and, as often as they are summoned to give an account of their life, their sleep is broken, and they perceive that they were merely dreaming when they imagined themselves to be happy, without looking inward to the true state of their hearts.

Moreover, as things appear to be here driven about at the mercy of chance, and as it is not easy for us, in the midst of the prevailing confusion, to acknowledge the truth of what the Psalmist had said, he therefore presents to our consideration the grand principle, that God is the Judge of the world. Granting this, it follows that it cannot but be well with the upright and the just, while, on the other hand, the most terrible destruction must impend over the ungodly. According to all outward appearance, the servants of God may derive no advantage from their uprightness; but as it is the peculiar office of God to defend them and take care of their safety, they must be happy under his protection. And from this we may also conclude that, as he is the certain avenger of wickedness, although, for a time, he may seem to take no notice of the ungodly, yet at length he will visit them with destruction. Instead, therefore, of allowing ourselves to be deceived with their imaginary felicity, let us, in circumstances of distress, have ever before our eyes the providence of God, to whom it belongs to settle the affairs of the world, and to bring order out of confusion.

PSALM II.

David boasts that his kingdom, though assailed by a vast multitude of powerful enemies, would, notwithstanding, be perpetual, because it was upheld by the hand and power of God. He adds, that in spite of his enemies, it would be extended even to the uttermost ends of the earth. And, therefore, he exhorts kings and other rulers to lay aside their pride, and receive, with submissive minds, the yoke laid upon them by God; as it would be vain for them to attempt to shake it off. All this was typical, and contains a prophecy concerning the future kingdom of Christ.

1. *Why do the nations rise tumultuously, and the peoples murmur in vain?*
2. *The kings of the earth have confederated, and the princes have assembled together, against Jehovah and against his Christ.*
3. *Let us break off their bonds, and cast away their yoke from us.*

WE know how many conspired against David, and endeavoured to prevent his coming to the throne, and from their hostile attempts, had he judged according to the eye of sense and reason, he might have been so full of apprehension, as forthwith to have given up all hope of ever becoming king. And, doubtless, he had often to struggle sorrowfully with very grievous temptations. But, as he had the testimony of an approving conscience, that he had attempted nothing rashly, nor acted as ambition and depraved desire impel many to seek changes in the government of kingdoms; as he was, on the contrary, thoroughly persuaded that he had been made king by divine appointment, when he coveted no such thing, nor even thought of it;[1] he encouraged himself by strong confidence in God against the whole world, just as in these words, he nobly pours contempt both on kings

---

[1] Ne mesme y pensait.—*Fr.*

and their armies. He confesses, indeed, that he had a sore battle to fight, inasmuch as it was no small party, but whole nations with their kings, who had conspired against him; but he courageously boasts that their attempts were vain, because they waged war, not against mortal man, but against God himself. It is not certain from the words, whether he speaks only of enemies in his own kingdom, or extends his complaints to foreign invaders. But, since the fact was, that enemies rose up against him in all quarters, and that as soon as he had settled the disturbances among his own people, the neighbouring states, in their turn, became hostile to him, I am disposed to think that both classes of enemies are meant, Gentiles as well as Jews. It would be a strange mode of expression to speak of many nations and people when only one nation was meant, and to speak of many kings when he had in eye Saul only. Besides, it agrees better with the completeness of the type to suppose that different kinds of enemies were joined together; for we know that Christ had not only to do with enemies in his own country, but likewise with enemies in other nations; the whole world having entered into a common conspiracy to accomplish his destruction. The Jews, indeed, first began to rage against Christ as they had formerly done against David; but afterwards the same species of madness seized upon other nations. The sum is, that although those who endeavoured to overthrow him might be strengthened by powerful armies, yet their tumults and counsels would prove vain and ineffectual.

By attributing to the people commotion and uproar, and to kings and rulers the holding of assemblies, to take counsel, he has used very appropriate language. Yet he intimates that, when kings have long and much consulted together, and the people have poured forth their utmost fury, all of them united would make nothing of it. But we ought carefully to mark the ground of such confidence, which was, that he had not thrust himself forward to be king rashly, or of his own accord, but only followed the call of God. From this he concludes, that in his person God was assailed; and God could not but show himself the defender of the kingdom of which he was the founder. By honouring himself with the title of Messias, or the Anointed, he declares that he reigned only by the authority and command of God, inasmuch as the oil brought by the hand of Samuel made him king who before was only a private person. David's enemies did not, indeed, think they were making a violent attack against God, yea, they would resolutely deny their having any such intention; yet it is not without reason that David places God in opposition to them, and speaks as if they directly levelled their attacks against him; for by seeking to undermine the kingdom which he had erected, they blindly and ferociously waged war against Him. If all those are rebels against God who resist the powers ordained by him, much more does this apply to that sacred kingdom which was established by special privilege.

But it is now high time to come to the substance of the type. That David prophesied concerning Christ, is clearly manifest from this, that he knew his own kingdom to be merely a shadow. And in order to learn to apply to Christ whatever David, in times past, sang concerning himself, we must hold this principle, which we meet with everywhere in all the prophets, that he, with his posterity, was made king, not so much for his own sake as to be a type of the Redeemer. We shall often have occasion to return to this afterwards, but at present I would briefly inform my readers, that as David's temporal kingdom was a kind of earnest to God's ancient people of the eternal kingdom, which at length was truly established in the person of Christ, those things which David declares concerning himself are not violently, or even allegorically, applied to Christ, but were truly predicted concerning him. If we attentively consider the nature of the kingdom, we will perceive that it would be absurd to overlook the end or scope, and to rest in the mere shadow. That the kingdom of Christ is here described by the spirit of prophecy, is sufficiently attested to us by the apostles, who, seeing the ungodly conspiring against Christ, arm themselves in prayer with this doctrine, (Acts iv. 24.) But to place our faith beyond the reach of all cavils, it is plainly made manifest from all the prophets, that those things which David testified concerning his own kingdom are properly applicable to Christ. Let this, therefore, be held as a settled point, that all who do not submit themselves to the authority of Christ make war against God. Since it seems good to God to rule us by the hand of his own Son, those who refuse to obey Christ himself deny the authority of God, and it is in vain for them to profess otherwise. For it is a true saying, " He that honoureth not the Son, honoureth not the Father which hath sent him," (John v. 22.) And it is of great importance to hold fast this inseparable connection, that as the majesty of God hath shone forth in his only begotten Son, so the Father will not be feared and worshipped but in his person.

A twofold consolation may be drawn from this passage :—First, as often as the world rages, in order to disturb and put an end to the prosperity of Christ's kingdom, we have only to remember that, in all this, there is just a fulfilment of what was long ago predicted, and no changes that can happen will greatly disquiet us. Yea, rather it will be highly profitable to us to compare those things which the apostles experienced with what we witness at the present time. Of itself the kingdom of Christ would be peaceable, and from it true peace issues forth to the world; but through the wickedness and malice of men, never does it rise from obscurity into open view without disturbances being excited. Nor is it at all wonderful, or unusual, if the world begin to rage as soon as a throne is erected for Christ. The other consolation which follows is, that when the ungodly have mustered their forces, and when, depending on their vast numbers, their riches, and their means of defence, they not only pour forth their proud blasphemies, but furiously assault heaven itself, we may safely laugh them to scorn, relying on this one consideration, that he whom they are assailing is the God who is in heaven. When we see Christ well nigh overwhelmed with the number and strength of his enemies, let us remember that they are making war against God over whom they shall not prevail, and therefore their attempts, whatever they may be, and however increasing, will come to nought, and be utterly ineffectual. Let us learn, farther, that this doctrine runs through the whole gospel; for the prayer of the apostles which I have just quoted, manifestly testifies that it ought not to be restricted to the person of Christ.

3. *Let us break, &c.* This is a prosopopœia,[1] in which the prophet introduces his enemies as speaking; and he employs this figure the better to express their ungodly and traitorous design. Not that they openly avowed themselves rebels against God, (for they rather covered their rebellion under every possible pretext, and presumptuously boasted of having God on their side;) but since they were fully determined, by all means, fair or foul, to drive David from the throne, whatever they professed with the mouth, the whole of their consultation amounted to this, how they might overthrow the kingdom which God himself had set up. When he describes his government under the metaphorical expressions of *bonds, and a yoke,* on the persons of his adversaries, he indirectly condemns their pride. For he represents them speaking scornfully of his government, as if to submit to it were a slavish and shameful subjection, just as we see it is with all the enemies of Christ who, when compelled to be subject to his authority, reckon it not less degrading than if the utmost disgrace were put upon them.

> 4. *He who dwelleth in heaven will laugh at them; the Lord*[2] *will have them in derision.*
> 5. *Then will he speak to them in his wrath, and vex them in his sore displeasure.*
> 6. *I have anointed my King upon my holy hill of Sion.*

After David has told us of the tumult and commotions,

---

[1] A rhetorical figure, in which persons or things are feigned or supposed to speak; a personification.

[2] The word in our Hebrew Bibles is *Elohai;* but in a considerable number of MSS. it is *Jehovah.* "The Jews in latter ages had a superstitious dread of pronouncing the word *Jehovah,* and frequently inserted *Adonai* and *Elohim* instead of it in their manuscripts of the Scriptures. But the more ancient MSS. have *Jehovah* frequently, where the more modern have *Adonai* and *Elohim.* Sixty MSS. of Dr Kennicott's collation and twenty-five of De Rossi's have *Jehovah* here."—*Street,* ii. 4.

the counsels and pride, the preparation and resources, the strength and efforts of his enemies, in opposition to all these he places the power of God alone, which he concludes would be brought to bear against them, from their attempting to frustrate his decree. And, as a little before, by terming them *kings of the earth*, he expressed their feeble and perishable condition; so now, by the lofty title of *He that dwelleth in heaven*, he extols the power of God, as if he had said, that power remains intact and unimpaired, whatever men may attempt against it. Let them exalt themselves as they may, they shall never be able to reach to heaven; yea, while they think to confound heaven and earth together, they resemble so many grasshoppers, and the Lord, meanwhile, undisturbed beholds from on high their infatuated evolutions. And David ascribes *laughter* to God on two accounts; first, to teach us that he does not stand in need of great armies to repress the rebellion of wicked men, as if this were an arduous and difficult matter, but, on the contrary, could do this as often as he pleases with the most perfect ease. In the second place, he would have us to understand that when God permits the reign of his Son to be troubled, he does not cease from interfering because he is employed elsewhere, or unable to afford assistance, or because he is neglectful of the honour of his Son; but he purposely delays the inflictions of his wrath to the proper time, namely, until he has exposed their infatuated rage to general derision. Let us, therefore, assure ourselves that if God does not immediately stretch forth his hand against the ungodly, it is now his time of laughter; and although, in the meantime, we ought to weep, yet let us assuage the bitterness of our grief, yea, and wipe away our tears, with this reflection, that God does not connive at the wickedness of his enemies, as if from indolence or feebleness, but because for the time he would confront their insolence with quiet contempt. By the adverb *then*, he points to the fit time for exercising judgment, as if he had said, after the Lord shall have for a time apparently taken no notice of the malpractices of those who oppose the rule of his Son, he will suddenly change his course, and show that he regards nothing with greater abhorrence than such presumption.

Moreover, he ascribes speech to God, not for the purpose of instructing his enemies, but only to convict them of their madness; indeed, by the term *speak*, he means nothing else than a manifestation of God's wrath, which the ungodly do not perceive until they feel it. The enemies of David thought it would be the easiest thing in the world for them to destroy one who, coming from a mean shepherd's cot, had, in their view,[1] presumptuously assumed the sovereign power. The prophecy and anointing of Samuel were, in their estimation, mere ridiculous pretences. But when God had at length overthrown them, and settled David on the throne, he, by this act, spoke not so much with his tongue as with his hand, to manifest himself the founder of David's kingdom. The Psalmist here, then, refers to speaking by actions, by which the Lord, without uttering a single word, makes manifest his purpose. In like manner, whenever he defends the kingdom of his Son against the ungodly, by the tokens and inflictions of his wrath, although he does not speak a single word, yet in effect he speaks enough to make himself understood.[2] David afterwards, speaking in the name of God, shows more clearly how his enemies were guilty of wickedly fighting against God himself in the hatred which they bore towards him whom God had made king. The sum is this: Wicked men may now conduct themselves as wickedly as they please, but they shall at length feel what it is to make war against heaven. The pronoun *I* is also emphatical, by which God signifies that he is so far exalted above the men of this world, that the whole mass of them could not possibly obscure his glory in the least degree. As often, then, as the power of man appears formidable to us, let us remember how much it is transcended by the power of God. In these words there is set before us the unchangeable and eternal purpose of God effectually to defend, even to the end, the kingdom of

---

[1] Il avoit a leur avis.—*Fr.*
[2] Encore qu'il ne dise un seul mot, si est ce qu'en effect il parle assez pour se faire entendre.—*Fr.*

his Son, of which he is the founder; and this may well support our faith amidst the troublous storms of the world. Whatever plots, therefore, men may form against it, let this one consideration be sufficient to satisfy us, that they cannot render ineffectual the anointing of God. Mention is here made of *mount Sion* in express terms, not because David was first anointed there, but because at length, in God's own time, the truth of the prophecy was manifested and actually established by the solemn rite of his consecration. And although David in these words had a regard to the promise of God, and recalled the attention of himself and others to it, yet, at the same time, he meant to signify that his own reign is holy and inseparably connected with the temple of God. But this applies more appropriately to the kingdom of Christ, which we know to be both spiritual and joined to the priesthood, and this is the principal part of the worship of God.

> 7. *I will declare the decree : The Lord hath said unto me, Thou art my Son; this day have I begotten thee.*
> 8. *Ask of me, and I will give thee the heathen for thine inheritance, and the uttermost parts of the earth for thy possession.*

7. *I will declare, &c.* David, to take away all pretence of ignorance from his enemies, assumes the office of a preacher, in order to publish the decree of God; or at least he protests that he did not come to the throne without a sure and clear proof of his calling; as if he had said, I did not, without consideration, publicly go forward to usurp the kingdom, but I brought with me the command of God, without which, I would have acted presumptuously, in advancing myself to such an honourable station. But this was more truly fulfilled in Christ, and doubtless, David, under the influence of the spirit of prophecy, had a special reference to him. For in this way all the ungodly are rendered inexcusable, because Christ proved himself to have been endued with lawful power from God, not only by his miracles, but by the preaching of the gospel. In fact, the very same testimony resounds through the whole world. The apostles first, and

after them pastors and teachers, bore testimony that Christ was made King by God the Father; but since they acted as ambassadors in Christ's stead, *He* rightly and properly claims to himself alone whatever was done by them. Accordingly, Paul (Eph. ii. 17) ascribes to Christ what the ministers of the gospel did in his name. "He came," says he, "and preached peace to them that were afar off, and to them that were nigh." Hereby, also, the authority of the gospel is better established; because, although it is published by others, it does not cease to be the gospel of Christ. As often, therefore, as we hear the gospel preached by men, we ought to consider that it is not so much they who speak, as Christ who speaks by them. And this is a singular advantage, that Christ lovingly allures us to himself by his own voice, that we may not by any means doubt of the majesty of his kingdom.

On this account, we ought the more carefully to beware of wickedly refusing the edict which he publishes, *Thou art my Son*. David, indeed, could with propriety be called the son of God on account of his royal dignity, just as we know that princes, because they are elevated above others, are called both gods and the sons of God. But here God, by the singularly high title with which he honours David, exalts him not only above all mortal men, but even above the angels. This the apostle (Heb. i. 5) wisely and diligently considers, when he tells us this language was never used with respect to any of the angels. David, individually considered, was inferior to the angels, but in so far as he represented the person of Christ, he is with very good reason preferred far above them. By the Son of God in this place we are therefore not to understand one son among many, but his only begotten Son, that he alone should have the pre-eminence both in heaven and on earth. When God says, *I have begotten thee*, it ought to be understood as referring to men's understanding or knowledge of it; for David was begotten by God when the choice of him to be king was clearly manifested. The words *this day*, therefore, denote the time of this manifestation; for as soon as it became known that he was made king by divine appointment, he came forth as one who had been lately begotten of God, since so great an honour could not belong to a private person. The same explanation is to be given of the words as applied to Christ. He is not said to be begotten in any other sense than as the Father bore testimony to him as being his own Son. This passage, I am aware, has been explained by many as referring to the eternal generation of Christ; and from the words *this day*, they have reasoned ingeniously as if they denoted an eternal act without any relation to time. But Paul, who is a more faithful and a better qualified interpreter of this prophecy, in Acts xiii. 33, calls our attention to the manifestation of the heavenly glory of Christ of which I have spoken. This expression, *to be begotten*, does not therefore imply that he then began to be the Son of God, but that his being so was then made manifest to the world. Finally, this begetting ought not to be understood of the mutual love which exists between the Father and the Son; it only signifies that *He* who had been hidden from the beginning in the sacred bosom of the Father, and who afterwards had been obscurely shadowed forth under the law, was known to be the Son of God from the time when he came forth with authentic and evident marks of Sonship, according to what is said in John i. 14, " We have seen his glory, as of the only begotten of the Father." We must, at the same time, however, bear in mind what Paul teaches, (Rom. i. 4,) that he was declared to be the Son of God with power when he rose again from the dead, and therefore what is here said has a principal allusion to the day of his resurrection. But to whatever particular time the allusion may be, the Holy Spirit here points out the solemn and proper time of his manifestation, just as he does afterwards in these words, (Psalm cxviii. 24,) " This is the day which the Lord hath made; we will rejoice and be glad in it."

8. *Ask of me.* Christ, it is true, besought his Father (John xvii. 5) to " glorify him with the glory which he had with him before the world was;" yet the more obvious meaning is, that the Father will deny nothing to his Son which relates to the extension of his kingdom to the ut-

termost ends of the earth. But, in this wonderful matter, Christ is introduced as presenting himself before the Father with prayers, in order to illustrate the free liberality of God in conferring upon men the honour of constituting his own Son governor over the whole world. As the eternal Word of God, Christ, it is true, has always had in his hands by right sovereign authority and majesty, and as such can receive no accessions thereto; but still he is exalted in human nature, in which he took upon him the form of a servant. This title, therefore, is not applied to him only as God, but is extended to the whole person of the Mediator; for after Christ had emptied himself, there was given to him a name which is above every name, that before him every knee should bow, (Philip. ii. 9.) David, as we know, after having obtained signal victories, reigned over a large extent of territory, so that many nations became tributaries to him; but what is here said was not fulfilled in him. If we compare his kingdom with other monarchies, it was confined within very narrow boundaries. Unless, therefore, we suppose this prophecy concerning the vast extent of kingdom to have been uttered in vain and falsely, we must apply it to Christ, who alone has subdued the whole world to himself, and embraced all lands and nations under his dominion. Accordingly, here, as in many other places, the calling of the Gentiles is foretold, to prevent all from imagining that the Redeemer who was to be sent of God was king of one nation only. And if we now see his kingdom divided, diminished, and broken down, this proceeds from the wickedness of men, which renders them unworthy of being under a reign so happy and so desirable. But although the ingratitude of men hinders the kingdom of Christ from prospering, it does not render this prediction of none effect, inasmuch as Christ collects the dispersed remnants of his people from all quarters, and in the midst of this wretched desolation, keeps them joined together by the sacred bond of faith, so that not one corner only, but the whole world, is subjected to his authority. Besides, however insolently the ungodly may act, and however they may reject his sovereignty, they cannot, by their rebellion, destroy his authority and power. To this subject also belongs what immediately follows:—

9. *Thou shalt break them with a rod of iron, and dash them in pieces like a potter's vessel.*

This is expressly stated, to teach us that Christ is furnished with power by which to reign even over those who are averse to his authority, and refuse to obey him. The language of David implies that all will not voluntarily receive his yoke, but that many will be stiff-necked and rebellious, whom notwithstanding he shall subdue by force, and compel to submit to him. It is true, the beauty and glory of the kingdom of which David speaks are more illustriously displayed when a willing people run to Christ in the day of his power, to show themselves his obedient subjects; but as the greater part of men rise up against him with a violence which spurns all restraint, it was necessary to add the truth, that this king would prove himself superior to all such opposition. Of this unconquerable power in war God exhibited a specimen, primarily in the person of David, who, as we know, vanquished and overthrew many enemies by force of arms. But the prediction is more fully verified in Christ, who, neither by sword nor spear, but by the breath of his mouth, smites the ungodly even to their utter destruction.

It may, however, seem wonderful that, while the prophets in other parts of Scripture celebrate the meekness, the mercy, and the gentleness of our Lord, he is here described as so rigorous, austere, and full of terror. But this severe and dreadful sovereignty is set before us for no other purpose than to strike alarm into his enemies; and it is not at all inconsistent with the kindness with which Christ tenderly and sweetly cherishes his own people. He who shows himself a loving shepherd to his gentle sheep, must treat the wild beasts with a degree of severity, either to convert them from their cruelty, or effectually to restrain it. Accordingly, in Psalm cx. 5, after a commendation is pronounced upon the obedience of the godly, Christ is immediately armed with power to destroy, in the day of his wrath, kings and their armies who are hostile to him. And certainly both these characters are with propriety ascribed to him: for he was sent by the Father to cheer the poor and the wretched with the tidings of salvation, to set the prisoners free, to heal the sick, to bring the sorrowful and afflicted out of the darkness of death into the light of life, (Isaiah lxi. 1;) and as, on the other hand, many, by their ingratitude, provoke his wrath against them, he assumes, as it were, a new character, to beat down their obduracy. It may be asked, what is that iron sceptre which the Father hath put into the hand of Christ, wherewith to break in pieces his enemies? I answer, The breath of his mouth supplies to him the place of all other weapons, as I have just now shown from Isaiah. Although, therefore, Christ move not a finger, yet by his speaking he thunders awfully enough against his enemies, and destroys them by the rod of his mouth alone. They may fret and kick, and with the rage of a madman resist him never so much, but they shall at length be compelled to feel that he whom they refuse to honour as their king is their judge. In short, they are broken in pieces by various methods, till they become his footstool. In what respect the doctrine of the gospel is an iron rod, may be gathered from Paul's Epistle to the Corinthians, (2 Ep. x. 4,) where he teaches that the ministers of Christ are furnished with spiritual weapons to cast down every high thing which exalteth itself against Christ, &c. I allow that even the faithful themselves may be offered in sacrifice to God, that he may quicken them by his grace, for it is meet we should be humbled in the dust, before Christ stretch forth his hand to save us. But Christ trains his disciples to repentance in such a way as not to appear terrible to them; on the contrary, by showing them his shepherd's rod, he quickly turns their sorrow into joy; and so far is he from using his iron rod to break them in pieces, that he rather protects them under the healing shadow of his hand, and upholds them by his power. When David speaks, therefore, of *breaking* and *bruising*, this applies only to the rebellious and unbelieving who submit to Christ, not because they have been subdued by repentance, but because they are overwhelmed with despair. Christ does not, indeed, literally speak to all men; but as he denounces in his word whatever judgments he executes upon them, he may be truly said to slay the ungodly man with the breath of his mouth, (2 Thess. ii. 8.) The Psalmist exposes to shame their foolish pride by a beautiful similitude; teaching us, that although their obstinacy is harder than the stones, they are yet more fragile than *earthen vessels.* Since, however, we do not see the enemies of the Redeemer immediately broken in pieces, but, on the contrary, the Church herself appears rather to be like the frail earthen vessel under their iron hammers, the godly need to be admonished to regard the judgments which Christ daily executes as presages of the terrible ruin which remains for all the ungodly, and to wait patiently for the last day, when he will utterly consume them by the flaming fire in which he will come. In the meantime, let us rest satisfied that he "rules in the midst of his enemies."

10. *And now, O ye kings, be wise; and ye judges of the earth be instructed.*
11. *Serve Jehovah with fear, and rejoice with trembling.*

David having, as a preacher of the judgments of God, set forth the vengeance which God would take upon his enemies, proceeds now, in the character of a prophet and teacher, to exhort the unbelieving to repentance, that they may not, when it is too late, be compelled to acknowledge, from dire experience, that the divine threatenings are neither idle nor ineffectual. And he addresses by name kings and rulers, who are not very easily brought to a submissive state of mind; and who are, besides, prevented from learning what is right by the foolish conceit of their own wisdom with which they are puffed up. And if David spare not even kings themselves, who seem unrestrained by laws, and exempted from ordinary rules, much more does his exhortation apply to the common class of men, in order that all, from the highest to the lowest, may humble themselves before God. By the adverb *now*, he signifies the necessity of their speedy repentance, since they will not always be favoured with the like opportunity. Meanwhile, he tacitly gives them to understand, that it was for their advantage that he warned them, as there was yet room for repentance, provided they made haste. When he enjoins them *to be wise*, he indirectly condemns their false confidence in their own wisdom, as if he had said, The beginning of true wisdom is when a man lays aside his pride, and submits himself to the authority of Christ. Accordingly, however good an opinion the princes of the world may have of their own shrewdness, we may be sure they are arrant fools till they become humble scholars at the feet of Christ. Moreover, he declares the manner in which they were to be wise, by commanding them to *serve the Lord with fear.* By trusting to their elevated station, they flatter themselves that they are loosed from the laws which bind the rest of mankind; and the pride of this so greatly blinds them as to make them think it beneath them to submit even to God. The Psalmist, therefore, tells them, that until they have learned to fear him, they are destitute of all right understanding. And certainly, since they are so much hardened by security as to withdraw their obedience from God, strong measures must at the first be employed to bring them to fear him, and thus to recover them from their rebelliousness. To prevent them from supposing that the service to which he calls them is grievous, he teaches them by the word *rejoice* how pleasant and desirable it is, since it furnishes matter of true gladness. But lest they should, according to their usual way, wax wanton, and, intoxicated with vain pleasures, imagine themselves happy while they are enemies to God, he exhorts them farther by the words *with fear* to an humble and dutiful submission. There is a great difference between the pleasant and cheerful state of a peaceful conscience, which the faithful enjoy in having the favour of God, whom they fear, and the unbridled insolence to which the wicked are carried, by contempt and forgetfulness of God. The language of the prophet, therefore, implies, that so long as the proud profligately rejoice in the gratification of the lusts of the flesh, they sport with their own destruction, while, on the contrary, the only true and salutary joy is that which arises from resting in the fear and reverence of God.

12. *Kiss the Son, lest he be angry, and ye perish from the way, when*[1] *his wrath is kindled in a moment. O blessed are all who put their trust in him.*

David expresses yet more distinctly what kind of fear and service God requires. Since it is the will of God to reign by the hand of his Son, and since he has engraven on his person the marks and insignia of his own glory, the proper proof of our obedience and piety towards him is reverently to embrace his Son, whom he has appointed king over us, according to the declaration, " He that honoureth not the Son, honoureth not the Father who hath sent him," (John v. 23.) The term *kiss* refers to the solemn token or sign of honour which subjects were wont to yield to their sovereigns. The sum is, that God is defrauded of his honour if he is not served in Christ. The Hebrew word בר, *Bar*, signifies both a son and an elect person; but in whatever way you take it, the meaning will remain the same. Christ was truly chosen of the Father, who has given him all power, that he alone should stand pre-eminent above both men and angels. On which account also he is said to be " sealed " by God, (John vi. 27,) because a peculiar dignity was conferred upon him, which removes him to a distance from all creatures. Some interpreters expound it, *kiss or embrace what is pure,*[2] which is a strange and rather

---

[1] *Ou, car son;* or, for his.—*Fr. marg.*

[2] The word בר, *Bar*, which here signifies *son*, is also sometimes used to denote *pure*, as in Job xi. 4, Ps. xxiv. 4, and lxxiii. 1. In the former sense it is a Chaldee word, in the latter it is a Hebrew one. This rendering, of which Calvin disapproves, is substantially that of the Septuagint, which reads δραξασθε παιδειας, literally, lay hold upon instruction. But as the Arabic version of the Psalms, which generally follows the Septuagint, has used here (and in many other places, where the Septuagint has παιδειας) a word which signifies not only instruction, but *good morals, virtue,* Street thinks that the authors of the Septuagint, by παιδειας, meant good morals, or virtue in general, and that they understood בר, *Bar,* as a general expression for the same thing. The Chaldee, Vulgate, and Æthiopic versions, also render בר, *Bar,* by a word meaning *doc-*

forced interpretation. For my part, I willingly retain the name of son, which answers well to a former sentence, where it was said, " Thou art my Son, this day have I begotten thee."

What follows immediately after is a warning to those who despise Christ, that their pride shall not go unpunished; as if he had said, As Christ is not despised without indignity being done to the Father, who hath adorned him with his own glory, so the Father himself will not allow such an invasion of his sacred rights to pass unpunished. And to teach them to beware of vainly deceiving themselves with the hope of a lengthened delay, and from their present ease indulging themselves in vain pleasures, they are plainly told that his wrath will be kindled *in a moment*. For we see, when God for a time connives at the wicked, and bears with them, how they abuse this forbearance, by growing more presumptuous, because they do not think of his judgments otherwise, than according to sight and feeling. Some interpreters, I know, explain the Hebrew word כמעט, *Camoat*, which we have rendered, *in a moment*, in a different way, namely, that as soon as God's wrath is kindled in even a small degree, it will be all over with the reprobate. But it is more suitable to apply it to time, and to view it as a warning to the proud not to harden themselves in their stupidity and indifference, nor flatter themselves from the patience of God, with the hope of escaping unpunished. Moreover, although this word appears to be put for the purpose of giving a reason of what goes before,[1] namely, why those who refuse to kiss the Son shall perish, and although the Hebrew word כי, *Ki*, signifies more frequently *for* than *when*, yet I am unwilling to depart from the commonly received translation, and have thought it proper

---

trine or *discipline*. " This is a remarkable case," says Dr Adam Clarke, " and especially that in so pure a piece of Hebrew as this poem is, a Chaldee word should have been found, בר, *Bar*, instead of בן, *Ben*, which adds nothing to the strength of the expression, or the elegance of the poetry. I know it is supposed that בר, *Bar*, is also pure Hebrew as well as Chaldee; but, as it is taken in the former language in the sense of *purifying*, the versions probably understood it so here. *Embrace that which is pure*, namely, the *doctrine* of God."

[1] Pour rendre raison du precedent ascavoir pour quoy c'est qu'ils periront.—*Fr.*

to render the original word by the adverb *when,* which denotes both the reason and time of what is predicated. Some explain the phrase, *to perish from the way,* as meaning a perverse way, or wicked manner of living. Others resolve it thus, *lest your way perish,* according to that saying of the first psalm, *the way of the ungodly shall perish.* But I am rather inclined to attach to the words a different meaning, and to view them as a denunciation against the ungodly, by which they are warned that the wrath of God will cut them off when they think themselves to be only in the middle of their race. We know how the despisers of God are accustomed to flatter themselves in prosperity, and run to great excess in riot. The prophet, therefore, with great propriety, threatens that when they shall say, Peace and safety, reckoning themselves at a great distance from their end, they shall be cut off by a sudden destruction, (1 Thess. v. 3.)

The concluding sentence of the psalm qualifies what was formerly said concerning the severity of Christ; for his iron rod and the fiery wrath of God would strike terror into all men without distinction, unless this comfort had been added. Having, therefore, discoursed concerning the terrible judgment which hangs over the unbelieving, he now encourages God's faithful and devout servants to entertain good hope, by setting forth the sweetness of his grace. Paul likewise observes the same order, (2 Cor. x. 6;) for having declared that vengeance was in readiness against the disobedient, he immediately adds, addressing himself to believers, "When your obedience is fulfilled." Now, we understand the meaning of the Psalmist. As believers might have applied to themselves the severity of which he makes mention, he opens to them a sanctuary of hope, whither they may flee, in order not to be overwhelmed by the terror of God's wrath;[1] just as Joel (chap. ii. 32) also, after having summoned the ungodly to the awful judgment-seat of God, which of itself is terrible to men,[2] immediately subjoins the comfort, "Whosoever shall call on the name of the Lord shall be saved." For it appears to me that this exclamation, *Blessed are all they that put their*

---

[1] Pour n'estre point accablez de la frayeur d'ire de Dieu.—*Fr.*
[2] Qui de soy est espouvantable aux hommes.—*Fr.*

trust in him,[1] should be read as a distinct sentence by itself. The pronoun *him* may be referred as well to God as to Christ, but, in my judgment, it agrees better with the whole scope of the psalm to understand it of Christ, whom the Psalmist before enjoined kings and judges of the earth to kiss.

PSALM III.

David, although driven from his kingdom, and pressed down with utter despair of relief from every earthly quarter, ceases not to call upon God, and supports himself from his promise against the greatest terrors, against the mockery and cruel assaults of his enemies; and, finally, against death itself, which then forced itself upon his consideration. In the end of the psalm, he congratulates himself and the whole Church on the happy issue of all.

¶ A Psalm of David, when he fled from Absalom his Son.[2]

How bitter David's sorrow was under the conspiracy of his own household against him, which arose from the treachery of his own son, it is easy for every one of us to conjecture from the feelings of nature. And when, in addition to this, he knew that this disaster was brought upon him by God for his own fault in having defiled another man's wife, and for shedding innocent blood, he might have sunk into despair, and been overwhelmed with anguish, if he had not been encouraged by the promise of God, and thus hoped for life even in death. From his making no allusion here to his sins, we are led to infer, that only one part of his prayers is comprised in this psalm; for as God punished him expressly on account of his adultery, and his wicked treachery towards Uriah, there can be no doubt that he was at first distressed with grievous and dreadful torments of mind. But after he had humbled himself before God, he took courage; and being well assured of having obtained

---

[1] The word אשרי, *ashre*, which occurs in the beginning of the psalm, is also used here; and therefore the words may be rendered, *O the blessednesses of all those who put their trust in him.*

[2] The inscription or title of the psalm refers it to the conspiracy of Absalom, and that the psalm refers to this is evident from the whole tenor of it. "But these titles are destitute of authority, as the careful reader of The Psalms will soon remark; they are to be regarded merely as marginal glosses of the Jews, but poor guides to the interpretation of Scripture."—*Fry's Translation and Exposition of the Psalms.*

forgiveness, he was fully persuaded that God was on his side, and knew that he would always preside over his kingdom, and show himself its protector.[1] But he, nevertheless, complained of his son, and of the whole faction involved in the conspiracy, because he knew that they wickedly rose up for the purpose of frustrating the decree of God. In like manner, if at any time God makes use of wicked and mischievous men, as scourges to chastise us, it becomes us first diligently to consider the cause, namely, that we suffer nothing which we have not deserved, in order that this reflection may lead us to repentance. But if our enemies, in persecuting us, rather[2] fight against God than against us, let the consideration of their doing so be immediately followed by the confident persuasion of our safety under the protection of him, whose grace, which he hath promised to us, they despise and trample under foot.

1. *O Lord, how are my oppressors multiplied! many rise up against me.*
2. *Many say to my soul, There is no help for him in God. Selah.*

SACRED history teaches that David was not only dethroned, but forsaken by almost all men; so that he had well nigh as many enemies as he had subjects. It is true there accompanied him in his flight a few faithful friends; but he escaped in safety, not so much by their aid and protection as by the hiding-places of the wilderness. It is therefore not wonderful though he was affrighted by the great numbers who were opposed to him, for nothing could have taken place more unlooked for, on his part, than so sudden a rebellion. It was a mark of uncommon faith, when smitten with so great consternation, to venture freely to make his complaint to God, and, as it were, to pour out his soul into his bosom.[3] And certainly the only remedy for allaying our fears is this, to cast upon him all the cares which trouble us; as, on the other hand, those who have the conviction that they are not the objects of his regard, must be prostrated and overwhelmed by the calamities which befall them.

---

[1] Et s'en monstreroit le protecteur.—*Fr.*
[2] En nous poursuyvant.—*Fr.*
[3] Il a osé venir familierement faire sa complainte a Dieu et comme se discharger à lui.—*Fr.*

In the third verse he expresses more distinctly, and more emphatically, the pride of his enemies in deriding him as a castaway, and as a person whose circumstances were past hope. And he means, that their boldness increased hereupon, because they were confident he had been rejected by God. Perhaps, in these words also, their ungodliness is indirectly referred to, inasmuch as they made no account of the help of God in preserving the king whom he had chosen. And this second view is the more probable, for Absalom did not flatter himself with the hope of the favour of God, but, entirely disregarding him, hoped for victory from his own power. David, therefore, expressly introduces both him and the rest as speaking after this manner, to show that it was by a monstrous and outrageous contempt of God that they were driven to such fury against him, as if they made no account whatever of the fact of his having been often wonderfully delivered from the greatest dangers. The ungodly, when they rise up to destroy us, may not openly break forth into such daring presumption as to maintain it to be impossible for us to derive any advantage from the favour of God; yet, as they either ascribe every thing to fortune, or hold the opinion that a man's success will be in proportion to his strength, and therefore fearlessly rush forward to gain their object, by all means, whether right or wrong, as if it would be equally the same, whether God is angry with or favourable towards them, it is evident that they set no value whatever upon the favour of God, and mock at the faithful as if it would avail them nothing to be under the care and protection of God.

The translation of some, *Many say* OF *my soul*, does not give the true meaning of this passage. The letter ל is indeed sometimes used as meaning *of* in Hebrew, but David here intended to express something more, namely, that his heart was in a manner pierced with the mockery of his enemies. The word *soul*, therefore, in my opinion, here signifies the seat of the affections. And it has a corresponding meaning in a passage which we shall meet with in another Psalm, (xxxv. 3,) " Say to my soul, I am thy salvation." David thus teaches us by his own example, that although the whole world, with one voice, should attempt to drive us to despair, instead of listening to it, we ought rather to give ear to God alone, and always cherish within us the hope of the salvation which he hath promised; and as the ungodly use their endeavours to destroy our souls, we ought to defend them by our prayers. With respect to the word *Selah,* interpreters are not agreed. Some maintain it is a mark of affirmation, and has the same signification as truly or amen. Others understand it as meaning *for ever*. But as סלל, *Selal,* from which it is derived, signifies *to lift up,* we incline to the opinion of those who think it denotes the lifting up of the voice in harmony in the exercise of singing. At the same time, it must be observed, that the music was adapted to the sentiment, and so the harmony was in unison with the character or subject-matter of the song; just as David here, after having complained of his enemies for shamefully laughing to scorn his hope, as if the protection of God would be of no avail to him, fixes the attention on this blasphemy, which severely wounded his heart, by the use of the word *Selah;* and as a little after, when he has added a new ground of confidence with regard to the safety of his person, he repeats the same word.

3. *And thou, Jehovah, art a shield for me, my glory, and he that exalteth my head.*
4. *I have cried to the Lord with my voice, and he heard me out of his holy hill. Selah.*

The copulative *and* should be resolved into the disjunctive particle *but,* because David employs language full of confidence, in opposition to the hardihood and profane scoffings of his enemies,[1] and testifies that whatever they may say, he would nevertheless rely upon the word of God. It besides appears that he had previously entertained an assured hope of deliverance, from the circumstance of his here making no mention of his present calamity as a chastisement inflicted upon him by the hand of God; but rather depending upon

---

[1] L'audace de ses ennemis et risee accompagnee de sacrilege.—*Fr.*

the divine aid, he courageously encounters his enemies, who were carrying on an ungodly and wicked war against him, seeing they intended to depose a true and lawful king from his throne. In short, having acknowledged his sin before, he now takes into consideration only the merits of the present cause. And thus it becomes the servants of God to act when molested by the wicked. Having mourned over their own sins, and humbly betaken themselves to the mercy of God, they ought to keep their eyes fixed on the obvious and immediate cause of their afflictions, that they may entertain no doubt of the help of God when undeservedly subjected to evil treatment. Especially when, by their being evil entreated, the truth of God is opposed, they ought to be greatly encouraged, and glory in the assurance that God without doubt will maintain the truth of his own promises against such perfidious and abandoned characters. Had it been otherwise with David, he might seem to have claimed these things to himself groundlessly, seeing he had deprived himself of the approbation and help of God by offending him.[1] But being persuaded that he was not utterly cut off from the favour of God, and that God's choice of him to be king remained unchanged, he encourages himself to hope for a favourable issue to his present trials. And, in the first place, by comparing God to *a shield*, he means that he was defended by his power. Hence also he concludes, that God *was his glory*, because he would be the maintainer and defender of the royal dignity which he had been pleased to confer upon him. And, on this account, he became so bold that he declares he would walk with unabashed brow.[2]

4. *With my voice have I cried unto the Lord.* He here informs us that he had never been so broken by adversity, or cast down by impious scornings,[3] as to be prevented from addressing his

---

[1] En l'offensant.—*Fr.*
[2] De là procede l'asseurance dont il fait mention puis apres qu'il marchera hardiment la teste levée.—*Fr.* From this proceeded the confidence of which he makes mention a little after, that he will boldly walk with unabashed brow.
[3] Par les mocqueries mal-heureuses des meschans.—*Fr.* By the pitiful scornings of the wicked.

prayers to God. And it was an infallible proof of his faith to exercise it by praying even in the midst of his distresses. Nothing is more unbecoming than sullenly to gnaw the bit with which we are bridled, and to withhold our groaning from God,[1] if, indeed, we have any faith in his promise. Nor is there a redundancy of expression in these words, *I have cried with my voice.* David distinctly mentions his voice, the better to express that how much soever the ungodly might rage against him, he was by no means struck dumb, but pronounced, in a loud and distinct voice, the name of his God; and to do this was a difficult matter under so grievous and severe a temptation. He also particularly mentions his voice, in order to show that he opposes the voice of prayer to the tumultuous outcries of those who either blame fortune or curse God, or give way to excessive complainings; those, in short, who with passionate confusion pour forth their immoderate sorrow. But David's meaning appears to me to be principally this, that amidst the blasphemies of his enemies, by which they endeavoured to overwhelm his faith, he was not put to silence, but rather lifted up his voice to God, whom the ungodly imagined to have become his enemy. He adds that he cried not in vain, to encourage all the godly to the like constancy. As to the expression, *from the hill of his holiness,* or, which signifies the same thing, *from his holy hill,* it is improperly explained of heaven, as has been done by some. Heaven, I indeed confess, is often called, in other places, God's holy palace; but here David has doubtless a reference to the ark of the covenant, which at that time stood on Mount Sion. And he expressly affirms that he was heard from thence, though he had been compelled to flee into the wilderness. The Sacred History relates, (2 Sam. xv. 24,) that when Abiathar the priest commanded the ark to be carried by the Levites, David would not suffer it. And in this the wonderful faith of the holy man appears conspicuous. He knew that the Lord had chosen Sion to be the dwelling place of the ark, but he was, notwithstanding, willing rather to be torn from that sacred symbol of the divine pre-

---

[1] D'esloigner de Dieu nos gemissemens, et les luy cacher.—*Fr.* To withhold our groanings from God, and to conceal them from him.

sence, (which was painful to him as if his own bowels had been torn from him,) than make any innovation not sanctioned by the will of heaven. Now, he boasts, that although he was deprived of the sight of the ark, and notwithstanding the distance to which he was removed from it, God was near him to listen to his prayers. By these words he intimates that he kept a due medium, inasmuch as he neither despised the visible sign, which the Lord had appointed on account of the rudeness of the times, nor by attaching a superstitious importance to a particular place, entertained carnal conceptions of the glory of God. Thus, he did not idly scatter words which would vanish into air, as unbelievers are wont to do, who pray also, but are in doubt to what place they ought to direct their speech. David turned himself directly towards the tabernacle, whence God had promised to be merciful to his servants. Hence the confidence with which he prayed; and this confidence was not without success. In our day, since there is fulfilled in Christ what was formerly shadowed forth by the figures of the law, a much easier way of approach to God is opened up for us, provided we do not knowingly and willingly wander from the way.

5. *I laid me down and slept, I awaked; for the Lord sustained me.*
6. *I will not be afraid of ten thousands of people, who have set their camps against me on all sides.*

According to the usage of the Hebrews, these words, which are in the past tense, *I laid me down and slept*, are taken sometimes for the future, *I will lie down and sleep*.[1] If we retain the reading of the verb in the past tense, David expresses a wonderful and almost incredible stedfastness of mind in that he slept so soundly in the midst of many deaths, as if he had been beyond the reach of all danger. He had doubtless been tossed amidst the merciless waves of anxiety, but it is certain their violence had been allayed by means of

[1] Selon l'usage des Hebrieux, ces mots qui sont en un temps passé, Je suis couché et endormi se prenent ancunesfois pour un temps à-venir, Je me coucheray et dormiray.—*Fr.*

faith, so that however much he was disquieted, he reposed in God. Thus the godly never fail in ultimately proving victorious over all their fears, whereas the ungodly, who do not rely upon God, are overwhelmed with despair, even when they meet with the smallest perils. Some think there is here a change of tenses; and, therefore, translate the verbs into the future tense, *I will lay me down and will sleep, and will awake,* because immediately after a verb of the future is subjoined, *The Lord shall uphold me.* But as he expresses, by these last words, a continuous act, I thought it unnecessary to change the tenses in the three first verbs. Still we ought to know, that this confidence of safety is not to be referred peculiarly to the time of his affliction, or, at least, is not to be limited to it: for, in my judgment, David rather declares how much good he had obtained by means of faith and prayer; namely, the peaceful and undisturbed state of a well regulated mind. This he expresses metaphorically, when he says, that he did the ordinary actions of life without being disturbed by fear. "I have not lain," says he, "waking and restless on my bed; but I have slept soundly, whereas such manner of sleeping does not generally happen to those who are full of thought and fear." But let us particularly notice that David came to have this confidence of safety from the protection of God, and not from stupidity of mind. Even the wicked are kept fast asleep through an intoxication of mind, while they dream of having made a covenant with death. It was otherwise with David, who found rest on no other ground but because he was upheld by the power of God, and defended by his help. In the next verse, he enlarges upon the incalculable efficacy of this confidence, of which all the godly have some understanding, from their experience of the divine protection. As the power of God is infinite, so they conclude that it shall be invincible against all the assaults, outrages, preparations, and forces of the whole world. And, indeed, unless we ascribe this honour to God, our courage shall be always failing us. Let us, therefore, learn, when in dangers, not to measure the assistance of God after the manner of man, but to despise whatever terrors may stand in our way, inasmuch as all the attempts which men may make against God, are of little or no account.

> 7. *Arise, O Lord, save me, O my God; for thou hast smitten all mine enemies upon the cheek-bone; thou hast broken the teeth of the ungodly.*
> 8. *Salvation belongeth unto the Lord; thy blessing is upon thy people. Selah.*

7. *Arise, O Lord.* As in the former verses David boasted of his quiet state, it would now appear he desires of the Lord to be preserved in safety during the whole of his life; as if he had said, Lord, since thou hast overthrown my enemies, grant that this thy goodness may follow me, and be continued even to the end of my course. But because it is no uncommon thing for David, in the Psalms, to mingle together various affections, it seems more probable, that, after having made mention of his confidence in God, he returns again to make the same prayers as at the beginning.[1] He therefore asks to be preserved, because he was in eminent peril. What follows concerning *the smiting* of his enemies, may be explained in two ways: either that in praying he calls to his remembrance his former victories, or that having experienced the assistance of God, and obtained the answer of his prayers, he now follows it up by thanksgiving: and this last meaning I am much inclined to adopt. In the first place, then, he declares that he fled to God for help in dangers, and humbly prayed for deliverance; and after salvation had been granted him, he gives thanks, by which he testifies, that he acknowledged God to be the author of the deliverance which he had obtained.[2]

8. *Salvation belongeth unto the Lord.* Because ל is some-

---

[1] A faire les mesmes prieres qu'au commencement.—*Fr.*
[2] Et puis a cause qu'il a obtenu cela, c'est à dire, qu'il est demeuré, en sauveté, il luy en rend graces; tesmoignant par cela qu'il tient de Dieu sa deliverance et la recognoist de luy.—*Fr.* And then having obtained this, that is to say, having been preserved in safety, he gives thanks to God; testifying by this, that he owed his deliverance to him, and recognised it as coming from him.

times used by the Hebrews for מִן, *Min,* some not improperly translate this clause, *Salvation is of the Lord.* I, however, consider the natural and obvious meaning to be simply this, that salvation or deliverance is only in the hands of God. By these words, David not only claims the office and praise of saving for God alone, tacitly opposing his power to all human succour; but also declares, that although a thousand deaths hang over his people, yet this cannot render God unable to save them, or prevent him from speedily sending forth without any effort, the deliverance which he is always able to impart. In the end of the psalm, David affirms that this was vouchsafed, not so much to him as an individual, as to the whole people, that the universal Church, whose welfare depended on the safety and prosperity of his kingdom, might be preserved from destruction. David, therefore, acknowledges the dispersion of this wicked conspiracy to have been owing to the care which God had about the safety of his Church. From this passage we learn, that the Church shall always be delivered from the calamities which befall her, because God who is able to save her, will never withdraw his grace and blessing from her.

PSALM IV.

After David in the beginning of the psalm has prayed to God to help him, he immediately turns his discourse to his enemies, and depending on the promise of God, triumphs over them as a conqueror. He, therefore, teaches us by his example, that as often as we are weighed down by adversity, or involved in very great distress, we ought to meditate upon the promises of God, in which the hope of salvation is held forth to us, so that defending ourselves by this shield, we may break through all the temptations which assail us.

¶ To the chief musician on Neginoth. A psalm of David.

It is uncertain at what time this psalm was composed. But from the tenor of it, it is conjectured, with probability, that David was then a fugitive and an exile. I therefore refer it to the time when he was persecuted by Saul. If, however, any person is disposed rather to understand it as referring to the time when he was compelled by the conspiracy of Absalom to secure his safety by flight, I will not greatly contend about the matter. But as, a little after, he uses an expression, namely, "How long?" (verse 3,)[1] which indicates that he had a lengthened struggle, the opinion which I have already brought forward is the more probable. For we know with what varied trials he was harassed, before he obtained complete deliverance, from the time when Saul began to be his enemy. Concerning the words which are contained in this verse, I shall only make one or two brief observations. Some translate the word למנצח, *Lamnetsah, for ever;* and they say that it was the commencement of a common song, to the tune of which this psalm was composed:[2] but this I reject as a forced translation. Others, with more truth, are of opinion, that מנצח, *Menetsah,* signifies one who excels and surpasses all others. But because expositors are not agreed as to the particular kind of excellence and dignity here spoken of, let it suffice, that by this word is denoted the chief master or president of the band.[3] I do not approve of rendering the word, *conqueror;* for although it answers to the subject-matter of the present psalm, yet it does not at all suit other places where we shall find the same Hebrew word used. With respect to the second word, *Neginoth,* I think it comes from the verb נגן, *Nagan,* which signifies to strike or sound; and, therefore, I doubt not, but it was an instrument of music. Whence it follows, that this psalm was designed to be sung, not only with the voice, but also with musical instruments, which were presided over, and regulated by the chief musician of whom we have just now spoken.

1. *Answer me when I cry, O God of my righteousness; thou hast enlarged me in distress; have pity upon me, and hear my prayer.*

IN these words there is shown the faith of David, who, although brought to the uttermost distress, and indeed almost consumed by a long series of calamities, did not sink under his sorrow; nor was he so broken in heart as to be prevented from betaking himself to God his deliverer. By his praying,

---

[1] Ascavoir, Jusques à quand, a vers. 3.—*Fr.*
[2] Et ils disent que c'estoit le commencement d'une chanson commune au chant de laquelle ce pseaume a este compose.—*Fr.*
[3] Le principal *chantre,* ou maitre de la musique qui avoit charge de mettre les pseaumes en chants et accords.—*Fr.* The chief singer or leader of the music who had the charge of setting the psalms to tunes and harmonies.

he testified, that when utterly deprived of all earthly succour, there yet remained for him hope in God. Moreover, he calls him *the God of his righteousness,* which is the same thing as if he had called him the vindicator of his right;[1] and he appeals to God, because all men everywhere condemned him, and his innocence was borne down by the slanderous reports of his enemies and the perverse judgments of the common people. And this cruel and unjust treatment which David met with, ought to be carefully marked. For while nothing is more painful to us than to be falsely condemned, and to endure, at one and the same time, wrongful violence and slander; yet to be ill spoken of for doing well, is an affliction which daily befalls the saints. And it becomes them to be so exercised under it as to turn away from all the enticements of the world, and to depend wholly upon God alone. *Righteousness,* therefore, is here to be understood of a good cause, of which David makes God the witness, while he complains of the malicious and wrongful conduct of men towards him; and, by his example, he teaches us, that if at any time our uprightness is not seen and acknowledged by the world, we ought not on that account to despond, inasmuch as we have one in heaven to vindicate our cause. Even the heathen have said there is no better stage for virtue than a man's own conscience. But it is a consolation far surpassing this, to know when men vaunt themselves over us wrongfully, that we are standing in the view of God and of the angels. Paul, we know, was endued with courage arising from this source, (1 Cor. iv. 5,) for when many evil reports were spread abroad concerning him among the Corinthians, he appeals to the judgment-seat of God. Isaiah also, fortified by the same confidence, (l. 6, and following verse,) despises all the slanders by which his enemies calumniated him. If, therefore, we cannot find justice anywhere in the world, the only support of our patience is to look to God, and to rest contented with the equity of his judgment.

It may, however, be asked, by way of objection, Since all

---

[1] Mon protecteur, celuy qui maintient mon droict.—*Fr.* My protector, he who maintains my right.

the purity of men is mere pollution in the sight of God, how can the godly dare to bring forward their own righteousness before him? With respect to David, it is easy to answer this question. He did not boast of his own righteousness except in reference to his enemies, from whose calumnies he vindicated himself. He had the testimony of a good conscience that he had attempted nothing without the call and commandment of God, and therefore he does not speak rashly when he calls God the protector and defender of his right. Hence we learn that David honoured God with this title of praise, in order the more readily to set him in contrast with the whole world. And as he asks twice to be heard, in this there is expressed to us both the vehemence of his grief and the earnestness of his prayers. In the last clause of the verse, he also shows whence he expected to obtain what he needed, namely, from the mercy of God. And certainly, as often as we ask anything from God, it becomes us to begin with this, and to beseech him, according to his free goodness, to relieve our miseries.

Thou hast enlarged me when I was in distress. Some think that David here promises himself what he had not yet experienced; and in the exercise of hope anticipates the manifestations of God's grace with which he should afterwards be favoured. But, in my opinion, he rather mentions the benefits which he formerly received from God, and by these strengthens himself against the time to come. Thus the faithful are accustomed to call to their remembrance those things which tend to strengthen their faith. We shall, hereafter, meet with many passages similar to this, where David, in order to give energy to his faith against terrors and dangers,[1] brings together the many experiences from which he had learned that God is always present with his own people and will never disappoint their desires. The mode of expression which he here employs is metaphorical, and by it he intimates that a way of escape was opened up to him even when he was besieged and enclosed on every side. The distress

---

[1] Contre les effrois et dangers qui se presentoyent.—*Fr.* Against the terrors and dangers which presented themselves.

of which he speaks, in my opinion, refers not less to the state of his mind than to circumstances of outward affliction; for David's heart was not of such an iron mould as to prevent him from being cast into deep mental anguish by adversity.

2. *O ye sons of men, how long will ye try to turn my glory into shame? how long will ye love vanity, and seeking after lying? Selah.*
3. *But know that Jehovah hath chosen for himself one who is merciful: Jehovah will hear when I call upon him.*

2. *O ye sons of men.* The happy result of the prayer of David was, that resuming courage, he was able not only to repel the fury of his enemies, but also to challenge them on his part, and fearlessly to despise all their machinations. That our confidence, therefore, may remain unshaken, we ought not, when assailed by the wicked, to enter into conflict without being furnished like David with the same armour. The sum is, that since God was determined to defend David by his own power, it was in vain for all the men in the world to endeavour to destroy him; however great the power which they otherwise might have of doing him injury. By calling those whom he addresses the sons, not of Adam, or of some common person, but *of men*, he seems by the way to reprove their pride.[1] I do not agree with certain Jewish expositors who think that nobles or men of rank are meant. It is rather an ironical concession of what they claimed to themselves, by which he ridicules their presumption, in esteeming themselves to be noble and wise, whereas it was only blind rage which impelled them to wicked enterprises. In the words *how long*, he condemns their perverse obstinacy; for what he means, is not that they were stirred up against him merely by some sudden impulse, but that the stubborn purpose of injuring him was deeply fixed in their hearts. Had not their maliciousness deprived them of their understanding, the many

---

[1] Le mot Hebrieu ne signifie pas simplement Homme, mais homme viril et robuste; en quoy il semble taxer, en passant, leur arrogance.—*Fr.* The Hebrew word signifies not simply *man*, but a strong and robust man; and by this word he seems, in passing, to rebuke their arrogance.

instances in which God had proved himself to be David's defender would have compelled them to desist from their attempts against him. But as they were fully determined to disgrace *him* whom God had exalted to the royal throne, he asks them, How long they will persevere in their endeavours *to turn his glory into shame.* And it is to be observed, that although loaded with every kind of reproach, both among the high and the low, he yet courageously keeps fast hold of the glory or the honour of royalty which God had graciously promised him, or had conferred upon him, and is fully persuaded that God will at length vindicate his right to it, however much his enemies might wickedly endeavour to blot and obscure it by treating his pretensions with derision and scorn.

How long will ye love vanity? In these words, he partly reproaches his enemies for the wicked and perverse passions with which he saw them to be impelled, although they falsely pretended to be actuated by a godly zeal; and he partly derides their folly in flattering themselves with the hope of success while fighting against God. And it is a most pointed rebuke. Even when the ungodly rush headlong into all manner of wickedness with the grossest[1] malice, they soothe themselves with deceitful flatteries in order not to be disturbed with the feelings of remorse. David, therefore, cries out, that wilfully to shut their eyes, and varnish their unrighteousness with deceitful colours, would avail them nothing. The ungodly may indeed flatter and delude themselves, but when they are brought in good earnest to the trial, it will be always manifest that the reason why they are deceived is, because from the beginning they were determined to deal deceitfully. Now, from this place, we ought to take a shield of invincible stedfastness as often as we see ourselves overmatched in prudence and subtlety by the wicked. For with whatever engines they assault us, yet if we have the testimony of a good conscience, God will remain on our side, and against him they shall not prevail. They may greatly excel in ingenuity, and possess

---

[1] D'une malice si evidente qu'on la pourroit toucher au doigt.—*Fr.* With a malice so evident that one could touch it with the finger.

much power of hurting us, and have their plans and subsidiary aid in the greatest readiness, and be very shrewd in discernment, yet whatever they may invent, it will be but lying and vanity.

3. *Know that Jehovah hath set apart, &c.* This is a confirmation of the preceding verse; for it shows that the cause of David's boldness consisted in this, that he depended upon God, the founder of his kingdom. And surely we may then safely triumph over our enemies when we are assured of having the call of God to the office which we hold, or the work in which we are engaged. Accordingly, David does not here boast of his own strength, or riches, or armies by which he obtained the kingdom. But as he was chosen by God, he intimates that the many attempts of his enemies against him would be without success, because they would find from experience, that God, whose power they could not successfully resist, was against them. In the first place, he says that he was *set apart* by God, by which he means that he was advanced to the throne, not by the will of man, or by his own ambition, but by the appointment of God. The Hebrew word פלה, *Phalah*, signifies to separate, and it here refers to separation to honour and dignity; as if he had said, you admit no one as king but he who is chosen by your own suffrages, or who pleases you; but it is the peculiar prerogative of God to make choice of whom he will. By the word *merciful* or *bountiful*, he doubtless vindicates his right to be king, from the fact that this was a quality which belonged to himself; it is as if he had produced the mark or badge of his calling. For it was truly said in the old proverb, Mercy is the virtue most suitable for kings. Now, God usually furnishes those whom he reckons worthy of having this honour conferred upon them, with the endowments requisite for the exercise of their office, that they may not be as dead idols. Some understand the word חסיד, *chasid*, in a passive sense, not as denoting a beneficent person, but one who is placed on the throne by the favour of God. As, however, I meet with no examples of this signification of the word in Scripture,

I think it safer to follow the common interpretation, which is this : God has chosen a king, who answers to the character which should be possessed by all who are called to fill such an exalted station, in as much as he is merciful and beneficent. Hence, he infers that he would be heard by God as often as he called upon him; for God principally proves his faithfulness in this, that he does not forsake the work of his own hands, but continually defends those whom he has once received into his favour. Hence, we are taught fearlessly to proceed in our path; because, whatever we may have undertaken according to his will, shall never be ineffectual. Let this truth then, obtain a fixed place in our minds, that God will never withhold his assistance from those who go on sincerely in their course. Without this comfort, the faithful must inevitably sink into despondency every moment.

> 4. *Tremble then, and sin not : commune with your own heart upon your bed, and be still. Selah.*
> 5. *Sacrifice the sacrifices of righteousness, and put your trust in the Lord.*

4. *Tremble then.* Now he exhorts his enemies to repentance, if peradventure, their madness was not wholly incorrigible. In the first place, he bids them *tremble,* or *be troubled;* a word by which he rebukes their stupidity in running headlong in their wicked course, without any fear of God, or any sense of danger. And certainly the great presumption of all the ungodly in not hesitating to engage in war against God, proceeds from their being hardened through an infatuated security; and by their thoughtlessness, they render themselves stupid, and become more obdurate by forgetting both God and themselves, and following whithersoever lust leads them. He tells them that the best remedy to cure their rage, and prevent them from *sinning* any longer, would be to awaken from their lethargy, and begin to be afraid and tremble; as if he had said, As soon as you shall have shaken off your drowsiness and insensibility, your desire of sinning will abate; for the reason why

the ungodly are troublesome to the good and the simple, and cause so much confusion, is because they are too much at peace with themselves.

He afterwards admonishes them *to commune with their own heart upon their bed,* that is, to take an account of themselves at leisure, and as it were, in some place of deep retirement;[1] an exercise which is opposed to their indulgence of their unruly passions. In the end of the verse he enjoins them *to be still.* Now, it is to be observed, that the cause of this stillness is the agitation and trembling, of which he before made mention. For if any have been hurried into sin by their infatuated recklessness, the first step of their return to a sound mind is to awaken themselves from their deep sleep to fearfulness and trembling. After this follows calm and deliberate reflection; then they consider and reconsider to what dangers they have been exposing themselves; and thus at length they, whose audacious spirits shrink at nothing, learn to be orderly and peaceable, or, at least, they restrain their frantic violence.

To commune upon one's bed, is a form of expression taken from the common practice and experience of men. We know that, during our intercourse with men in the day time, our thoughts are distracted, and we often judge rashly, being deceived by the external appearance; whereas in solitude, we can give to any subject a closer attention; and, farther, the sense of shame does not then hinder a man from thinking without disguise of his own faults. David, therefore, exhorts his enemies to withdraw from those who witnessed and judged of their actions on the public stage of life, and to be alone, that they may examine themselves more truthfully and honestly. And this exhortation has a respect to us all; for there is nothing to which men are more prone than to deceive one another with empty applause, until each man enter into himself, and commune alone with his own heart. Paul, when quoting this passage in Eph. iv. 26, or, at least, when alluding to the sentiment of David, follows

---

[1] Et estans retirez à part pour sonder leurs consciences.—*Fr.* And being retired by themselves to probe or examine their consciences.

the Septuagint, "Be ye angry and sin not." And yet he has skilfully and beautifully applied it to his purpose. He there teaches us that men, instead of wickedly pouring forth their anger against their neighbours, have rather just cause to be angry with themselves, in order that, by this means, they may abstain from sin. And, therefore, he commands them rather to fret inwardly, and be angry with themselves; and then to be angry, not so much at the persons, as at the vices of others.

5. *Sacrifice ye.* Many are of opinion that David exhorts his enemies to give some evidence of their repentance; and I certainly admit, that sacrifices were partly enjoined for the purpose of inducing men to walk in newness of life. But when I consider the character of the men who opposed David, I am satisfied that he here censures their hypocrisy, and beats down their groundless boasting. David, when he wandered as a fugitive in deserts, or in caves, or on mountains, or in the regions beyond his own country, might seem to have been separated from the Church of God; and certainly he was commonly accounted as a corrupt member cut off from the body and the communion of the saints. Meanwhile the ark of the covenant was in the hands of his enemies, they kept possession of the temple, and they were the first in offering sacrifices. They, therefore, vaunted themselves against David with the same boldness and presumption with which we know hypocrites to have been always puffed up. Nor is it to be doubted, but they proudly abused the name of God as if they only had been his true worshippers.[1] But as Jeremiah (chap. vii. 4) rebukes the ungodly, because of the false confidence which they placed in the temple of the Lord; so David also denies that God is pacified by mere outward ceremonies, since he requires pure sacrifices. There is in the words an implied contrast between the sacrifices

---

[1] Comme s'ils eussent este gens de bien, adonnez a son service et qu'il n'y eust eu zele qu'en eux.—*Fr.* As if they had been his genuine people, devoted to his service, and that there was no zeal but among them.

of righteousness, and all those vain and spurious rites[1] with which the counterfeit worshippers of God satisfy themselves. The sum, therefore, is, "You boast of having God on your side, because you have free access to his altar to offer your sacrifices there with great pomp; and because I am banished from the Holy Land, and not suffered to come to the temple, you think that I am not an object of the divine care. But you must worship God in a far different manner, if you would expect any good at his hand; for your unclean sacrifices with which you pollute his altar, so far from rendering him favourable to you, will do nothing else but provoke his wrath." Let us learn from this passage, that, in contending with the corruptors of true religion, who may have the name of God continually in their mouth, and vaunt themselves on account of their observance of his outward worship, we may safely rebuke their boasting, because they do not offer the right sacrifices. But, at the same time, we must beware lest a vain pretence of godliness foster in us a perverse and ill founded confidence, in place of true hope.

6. *Many say, Who will show us good?*[2] *Lift thou up upon us the light of thy countenance, O Jehovah.*
7. *Thou hast given more joy to my heart than they have in the time when their corn and their wine are increased.*

6. *Many say.* Some are of opinion that David here complains of the cruel malice of his enemies, because they greedily sought for his life. But David, I have no doubt, compares the sole wish with which his own heart was burning, to the many desires with which almost all mankind are

---

[1] Entre les sacrifices de justice et toutes les ceremonies, quand elles sont destituees de la verite interieure et destournees de leur droit usage et par consequent falsifiees.—*Fr.* Between the sacrifices of righteousness, and all ceremonies, when they are unaccompanied with sincerity of heart, and perverted from their proper use, and are consequently spurious.

[2] The reader will observe, that Calvin does not use the word *any*, a supplement which is to be found in our English version. The question is certainly more emphatic without this word. "The word *any*," says Dr Adam Clarke, "is not in the text, nor any thing equivalent to it; and yet not a few have quoted *it*, and preached upon the text, placing the principal emphasis upon this illegitimate word."

distracted. As it is not a principle held and acted upon by
ungodly men, that those only can be truly and perfectly happy
who are interested in the favour of God, and that they
ought to live as strangers and pilgrims in the world, in order
through hope and patience to obtain, in due time, a better
life, they remain contented with perishing good things;
and, therefore, if they enjoy outward prosperity, they are not
influenced by any great concern about God. Accordingly,
while, after the manner of the lower animals, they grasp
at various objects, some at one thing, and some at another,
thinking to find in them supreme happiness, David, with
very good reason, separates himself from them, and proposes to himself an end of an entirely opposite description.
I do not quarrel with the interpretation which supposes that
David is here complaining of his own followers, who, finding their strength insufficient for bearing the hardships
which befel them, and exhausted by weariness and grief,
indulged in complaints, and anxiously desired repose. But
I am rather inclined to extend the words farther, and to view
them as meaning that David, contented with the favour of
God alone, protests that he disregards, and sets no value on
objects which others ardently desire. This comparison of the
desire of David with the desires of the world, well illustrates
this important doctrine,[1] that the faithful, forming a low estimate of present good things, rest in God alone, and account
nothing of more value than to know from experience that
they are interested in his favour. David, therefore, intimates,
in the first place, that all those are fools, who, wishing to
enjoy prosperity, do not begin with seeking the favour of
God; for, by neglecting to do this, they are carried about by
the various false opinions which are abroad. In the second
place, he rebukes another vice, namely, that of gross and
earthly men in giving themselves wholly to the ease and
comforts of the flesh, and in settling down in, or contenting
themselves with, the enjoyment of these alone, without

---

[1] Or ceste comparaison du desir de David avec ceux des mondains amplifie bien la substance de ceste doctrine.—*Fr.*

thinking of any thing higher.[1] Whence also it comes to pass, that as long as they are supplied with other things according to their desire, they are altogether indifferent about God, just as if they had no need of him. David, on the contrary, testifies, that although he may be destitute of all other good things, the fatherly love of God is sufficient to compensate for the loss of them all. This, therefore, is the purport of the whole: "The greater number of men greedily seek after present pleasures and advantages; but I maintain that perfect felicity is only to be found in the favour of God."

David uses the expression, *The light of God's countenance,* to denote his serene and pleasant countenance—the manifestations of his favour and love; just as, on the other hand, the face of God seems to us dark and clouded when he shows the tokens of his anger. This light, by a beautiful metaphor, is said to be *lifted up,* when, shining in our hearts, it produces trust and hope. It would not be enough for us to be beloved by God, unless the sense of this love came home to our hearts; but, shining upon them by the Holy Spirit, he cheers us with true and solid joy. This passage teaches us that those are miserable who do not, with full resolution, repose themselves wholly in God, and take satisfaction therein,[2] even although they may have an overflowing abundance of all earthly things; while, on the other hand, the faithful, although they are tossed amidst many troubles, are truly happy, were there no other ground for it but this, that God's fatherly countenance shines upon them, which turns darkness into light, and, as I may say, quickens even death itself.

7. *Thou hast given more joy to my heart.* By another comparison he better expresses and illustrates the strength of his affection, showing that, having obtained the good which he had longed for, he does not in the least degree envy the wealth and enjoyments of others, but is altogether contented with his own lot. The sum is, that he had more satisfac-

[1] Se contentent d'en jouir sans panser plus haut.—*Fr.*
[2] Se repose totalement en Dieu et y prendre contentement.—*Fr.*

tion in seeing the reconciled countenance of God beaming upon him, than if he had possessed garners full of corn, and cellars full of wine.¹ Interpreters are not agreed as to the word מֵעֵת, *me-eth,* which we have translated, *in the time.* Some give this rendering, *Thou hast put gladness into my heart,* SINCE THE TIME *that their corn and wine increased;* as if David had said, I rejoice when I see mine enemies prospering in the world.² But the former translation appears to me much more suitable; according to which David declares, that he rejoices more in the favour of God alone, than earthly men rejoice when they enjoy all earthly good things, with the desire of which they are generally inflamed. He had represented them as so bent upon, and addicted to, the pursuit of worldly prosperity, as to have no great care about God; and now he adds, that their joy in the abundance and increase of their wine and corn is not so great as is his joy in a sense of the divine goodness alone. This verse contains very profitable instruction. We see how earthly men, after they have despised the grace of God, and plunged themselves over head and ears in transitory pleasures, are so far from being satisfied with them, that the very abundance of them inflames their desires the more; and thus, in the midst of their fulness, a secret uneasiness renders their minds uncomfortable. Never, therefore, shall we obtain undisturbed peace and solid joy until the favour of God shine upon us. And although the faithful also desire and seek after their worldly comforts, yet they do not pursue them with immoderate and irregular ardour; but can patiently bear to be deprived of them, provided they know themselves to be the objects of the divine care.

> 8. *I will lay me down, and will sleep together in peace; for thou, Lord, hast placed me alone³ in safety.*

He concludes by stating, that as he is protected by the

¹ The allusion is to the joy of the harvest and vintage.
² "Or combien que les expositeurs varient en ce mot que nous avons traduit, Au temps : pource qu'aucuns traduisent, Tu m'as donné liesse au cœur depuis le temps que, &c., comme s'il disoit, Je suis joyeux quand je voy prosperer mes ennemis en ce monde."—*Fr.*
³ "Seul ou à part."—*Fr.*

power of God, he enjoys as much security and quiet as if he had been defended by all the garrisons on earth. Now, we know, that to be free from all fear, and from the torment and vexation of care, is a blessing to be desired above all other things. This verse, therefore, is a confirmation of the former sentence, intimating that David justly prefers the joy produced by the light of God's fatherly love before all other objects: for inward peace of mind certainly surpasses all the blessings of which we can form any conception. Many commentators explain this place as expressing David's hope, that his enemies will be reconciled to him, so that he may sleep with them in peace, God having granted him the peculiar privilege of being able to rest without being disturbed or disquieted by any man. But in my judgment the proper meaning is this, that he will live as quietly and securely alone, as in the midst of a great host of men, because God defends him: for in the words, *I will sleep together*, I consider the particle *as* to be understood, as if the reading were *as together*, that is to say, as with a multitude. Some refer לבדד, *lebadad, alone,* to God, translating the words thus, *Thou alone, O Lord, hast set me in safety;* but this I do not at all approve, because, by taking away the contrast between these two words, *together* and *alone*, much of the beauty of the sentence is lost. In short, David boasts that the protection of God alone was sufficient, and that under it he sleeps as securely, although destitute of all human guardianship, as if he had had many to keep watch and ward continually over him, or as if he had been defended on all sides by a great company. Let us, therefore, learn from his example, to yield this honour to God—to believe, that although there may appear no help for us from men, yet under his hand alone we are kept in peace and safety, as if we were surrounded by a great host.

PSALM V.

David being grievously oppressed by the cruelty of his enemies, and apprehending still more mischief, earnestly beseeches God for help. And the more easily to obtain what he asks, after having, by the earnestness of his prayers, manifested the greatness of his grief, he first brings forward the intolerable malice of his enemies, showing how inconsistent it would be with the character of God, were they to be left unpunished. He next speaks of his own faith and patience, and even comfort; having no doubt whatever of a happy issue. Finally, he concludes, that when he shall be delivered, the benefits resulting from his deliverance would not be limited to himself, but would extend to all the godly.

¶ To the chief musician upon Nehiloth. A psalm of David.

Some translate the Hebrew word *Nehiloth, heritages,* and others, *armies.* The former assign this reason for their opinion, that David prayed for the welfare of the twelve tribes, whom he calls *heritages.*[1] The latter assert in support of their view, that being besieged by a vast multitude of men, he betook himself to God for succour; and, according to this sense, the word *upon* will signify *against.* But not approving of the conjectures of many who speak upon these inscriptions of The Psalms as if they were riddles,[2] I adopt the opinion of those who hold that it was either a musical instrument or a tune; but of what particular kind I consider it of little importance to ascertain.

1. *Give ear unto my words, O Jehovah ; attend to my speech.*
2. *Hearken to the voice of my cry, my King and my God : for unto thee will I pray.*

I presume not positively to determine whether David, in this psalm, bewails the wrongs which he suffered from his enemies at some particular time, or whether he complains generally of the various persecutions with which, for a long time, he was harassed under Saul. Some of the Jewish commentators apply the psalm even to Absalom; because,

---

[1] " Qu'il appelle Heritages."—*Fr.*
[2] " Mais pource que je n'approuve point ce que devinent plusieurs parlans comme par enigmes sur ces inscriptions des Pseaumes."—*Fr.*

by *the bloody and deceitful man,* they think Doeg and Ahithophel are pointed out. To me, however, it appears more probable, that when David, after the death of Saul, had got peaceable possession of the kingdom, he committed to writing the prayers which he had meditated in his afflictions and dangers. But to come to the words :—First, he expresses one thing in three different ways; and this repetition denotes the strength of his affection, and his long perseverance in prayer. For he was not so fond of many words as to employ different forms of expression, which had no meaning; but being deeply engaged in prayer, he represented, by these various expressions, the variety of his complaints.[1] It therefore signifies, that he prayed neither coldly nor only in few words; but that, according as the vehemence of his grief urged him, he was earnest in bewailing his calamities before God; and that since it did not immediately appear what would be their issue, he persevered in repeating the same complaints. Again, he does not expressly state what he desires to ask from God :[2] but there is a greater force in this kind of suppression, than if he had spoken distinctly. By not uttering the desires of his heart, he shows more emphatically that his inward feelings, which he brought with him before God, were such that language was insufficient to express them. Again, the word *cry,* which signifies a loud and sonorous utterance of the voice, serves to mark the earnestness of his desire. David did not cry out as it were into the ears of one who was deaf; but the vehemence of his grief, and his inward anguish, burst forth into this cry. The verb הגה, *hagah,* from which the noun הגיג, *hagig, speech,* which the prophet here uses, is derived, means both *to speak distinctly,* and *to whisper* or *to mutter.* But the second sense seems better suited to this passage.[3] After David has said in general, that God hears his words, he seems, immediately after, for

---

[1] "Il a aussi representé et exprimé ses gemissemens qui estoyent en grand nombre et de beaucoup de sortes."—*Fr.*
[2] "Ce qu'il veut requerir à Dieu."—*Fr.*
[3] Bishop Horne beautifully renders the word, "dove-like mournings," and Bishop Horsley, "sighing." "The word," says Hammond, "regularly signifies *sighing* or *cry,* not a *loud, sonorous voice,* but such as complaints are made in."

the purpose of being more specific, to divide them into two kinds, calling the one obscure or indistinct moanings, and the other loud crying.[1] By the first he means a confused muttering, such as is described in the Song of Hezekiah, when sorrow hindered him from speaking distinctly, and making his voice to be heard. " Like a crane, or a swallow, so did I chatter; I did mourn as a dove," (Isaiah xxxviii. 14.) If, then, at any time we are either backward to pray, or our devout affections begin to lose their fervour, we must here seek for arguments to quicken and urge us forward. And as by calling God *his King* and *his God*, he intended to stir up himself to entertain more lively and favourable hopes with respect to the issue of his afflictions, let us learn to apply these titles to a similar use, namely, for the purpose of making ourselves more familiar with God. At the close, he testifies that he does not sullenly gnaw the bit, as unbelievers are accustomed to do ; but directs his groaning to God : for they who, disregarding God, either fret inwardly or utter their complaints to men, are not worthy of being regarded by him. Some translate the last clause thus, *When I pray to thee;* but to me it seems rather to be the reason which David assigns for what he had said immediately before, and that his purpose is, to encourage himself to trust in God, by assuming this as a general principle— that whoever call upon God in their calamities never meet with a repulse from him.

3. *O that thou wouldst hear my voice in the morning ; O Jehovah, in the morning will I direct unto thee, and I will keep watch.*

The first sentence may also be read in the future tense of the indicative mood, *Thou shalt hear my prayer.* But, in my opinion, the verb is rather in the optative mood, as I have translated it. Having besought God to grant his

---

[1] " Il semble que puis apres, pour mieux specifier, il en met deux sortes, appelant les unes Complaintes obscures, et les autres Cri."—*Fr.*
[2] " Quand la douleur l'empesche de parler distinctement et faire entendre sa voix."—*Fr.*

requests, he now entreats him to make haste. Some think he alludes to the morning prayers which were wont to be joined with the daily sacrifices in the temple, according to the appointment of the law. Although I do not disapprove of this opinion, yet I have no doubt but that, constrained by the weariness of a somewhat lengthened delay, he wishes his deliverance to be hastened; as if he had said, " As soon as I awake, this will be the first subject of my thoughts. Therefore, O Lord, delay no longer the help of which I stand in need, but grant immediately my desires." The expression, *To direct unto God*, I take to signify the same thing as directly to approach to God. Many, as if the language were elliptical, supply the words, *my prayer*. But in my judgment, David rather intends to declare that he was not turned hither and thither, nor drawn different ways by the temptations to which he was exposed, but that to betake himself to God was the settled order of his life. There is, in the words, an implied contrast between the rambling and uncertain movements of those who look around them for worldly helps, or depend on their own counsels, and the direct leading of faith, by which all the godly are withdrawn from the vain allurements of the world, and have recourse to God alone. The Hebrew word ערך, *arac*, signifies to set in order or dispose, and sometimes to dress or make fit. This sense is very suitable to the passage, in which David plainly declares it to be his determination not to be drawn away in any degree from his orderly course into the indirect and circuitous paths of error and sin, but to come directly to God. By the word, *watch*, he conveys the idea of hope and patience as well as of anxiety. As צפה, *tsapah*, in Hebrew means, *to wait for*, as well as *to look for*, David, I have no doubt, intended to say, that after he had disburdened his cares into the bosom of God, he would, with an anxious mind, look out, as it were, like a sentinel, until it should appear, that in very deed God had heard him. No doubt, in the exercise of longing, there is always implied some degree of uneasiness; but he who is looking out for the grace of God with anxious desire, will patiently wait for it. This passage, therefore, teaches us the uselessness of those prayers to which there is not added that hope which may be said to elevate the minds of the petitioners into a watch-tower.

> 4. *For thou art not a God that hath pleasure in wickedness;*[1] *evil shall not dwell with thee.*
> 5. *The foolish shall not stand in thy sight; thou hatest all that commit iniquity.*
> 6. *Thou shalt destroy them that speak falsehood; Jehovah will abhor the blood-thirsty* [2] *and deceitful man.*

Here David makes the malice and wickedness of his enemies an argument to enforce his prayer for the divine favour towards him. The language is indeed abrupt, as the saints in prayer will often stammer; but this stammering is more acceptable to God than all the figures of rhetoric, be they ever so fine and glittering. Besides, the great object which David has in view, is to show, that since the cruelty and treachery of his enemies had reached their utmost height, it was impossible but that God would soon arrest them in their course. His reasoning is grounded upon the nature of God. Since righteousness and upright dealing are pleasing to him, David, from this, concludes that he will take vengeance on all the unjust and wicked. And how is it possible for them to escape from his hand unpunished, seeing he is the judge of the world? The passage is worthy of our most special attention. For we know how greatly we are discouraged by the unbounded insolence of the wicked. If God does not immediately restrain it, we are either stupified and dismayed, or cast down into despair. But David, from this, rather finds matter of encouragement and confidence. The greater the lawlessness with which his enemies proceeded against him, the more earnestly did he supplicate preservation from God, whose office it is to destroy all the wicked, because he hates all wickedness.

---

[1] " Ou le mauvais."—*Fr. Marg.* " Or the wicked."
[2] The words in the original are אִישׁ דָּמִים, *ish damim*, literally, *the man of bloods.* The plural number is used, probably to teach us, that the man who thirsts for human blood is rarely satisfied with one victim.

Let all the godly, therefore, learn, as often as they have to contend against violence, deceit, and injustice, to raise their thoughts to God in order to encourage themselves in the certain hope of deliverance, according as Paul also exhorts them in 2 Thess. i. 5, "Which is," says he, "a manifest token of the righteous judgment of God, that ye may be counted worthy of the kingdom of God, for which ye also suffer: seeing it is a righteous thing with God to recompense tribulation to them that trouble you; and to you who are troubled, rest with us." And assuredly he would not be the judge of the world if there were not laid up in store with him a recompense for all the ungodly. One use, then, which may be made of this doctrine is this,—when we see the wicked indulging themselves in their lusts, and when, in consequence, doubts steal into our minds as to whether God takes any care of us, we should learn to satisfy ourselves with the consideration that God, who hates and abhors all iniquity, will not permit them to pass unpunished; and although he bear with them for a time, he will at length ascend into the judgment-seat, and show himself an avenger, as he is the protector and defender of his people.[1] Again, we may infer from this passage the common doctrine, that God, although he works by Satan and by the ungodly, and makes use of their malice for executing his judgments, is not, on this account, the author of sin, nor is pleased with it because the end which he purposes is always righteous; and he justly condemns and punishes those who, by his mysterious providence, are driven whithersoever he pleases.

In the 4th verse some take רע, *ra*, in the masculine gender, for a wicked man; but I understand it rather of wickedness itself. David declares simply, that there is no agreement between God and unrighteousness. He immediately after proceeds to speak of the men themselves, saying, *the foolish shall not stand in thy sight;* and it is a very just inference from this, that iniquity is hateful to God, and that, therefore, he will execute just punishment upon all the wicked. He calls those *fools*, according to a frequent use of

---

[1] "Comme il est protecteur et defenseur des siens."—*Fr.*

the term in Scripture, who, impelled by blind passion, rush headlong into sin. Nothing is more foolish, than for the ungodly to cast away the fear of God, and suffer the desire of doing mischief to be their ruling principle; yea, there is no madness worse than the contempt of God, under the influence of which men pervert all right. David sets this truth before himself for his own comfort; but we also may draw from it doctrine very useful in training us to the fear of God; for the Holy Spirit, by declaring God to be the avenger of wickedness, puts a bridle upon us, to restrain us from committing sin, in the vain hope of escaping with impunity.

7. *And I, in the multitude* [or *abundance*] *of thy mercy, will enter into thy house; I will worship in thy holy temple in thy fear.*

Some think that the word *and*, by which this sentence is joined to the preceding, is put for *but;* as if David, comparing himself with the ungodly, declared and assured himself that God would be merciful to him, while he abhorred and would destroy the wicked. But I leave it to my readers to judge whether it does not suit the passage better to consider this verse as an inference from what goes before, which might be put in this form: "O Lord, thou canst not bear with the wicked; when, therefore, I am saved out of their hands by thy power, I will come to present myself before thee in thy temple, to give thee thanks for the deliverance which thou hast vouchsafed to me." If the former interpretation be preferred, then the prophet, by simply commending his own piety towards God, separates himself from the class of whom he spoke. The scope of the passage leads us to understand him as promising to give thanks to God. He had before spoken of his enemies as hated of God; and now, being persuaded that God will keep him in safety, he calls himself to the exercise of gratitude. *I will come into thy temple,* says he, *in the multitude of thy mercy;* as if he had said, I may now seem to be in a condition almost desperate, but by the favour of God, I shall be kept in perfect safety. This passage, therefore, teaches us, that when we are afflicted by the most distressing temptations, we ought to set the grace of God before our eyes, in order thereby to be supported with the hope of the divine interposition amidst the greatest dangers. Farther, as our carnal minds either wickedly undervalue the grace of God, or put the low estimate upon it which is commonly put by the world, let us learn to extol its wonderful greatness, which is sufficient to enable us to overcome all fears. The primary object of David was to encourage himself in the assured hope of preservation from the mercy of God; but at the same time he shows, that upon obtaining deliverance, he will be grateful to God for it, and keep it in remembrance. And as hypocrites, in giving thanks to God, do nothing else but profane his name, inasmuch as they themselves are unholy and polluted, he therefore resolves to come in *the fear of God,* in order to worship him with a sincere and upright heart. Again, we may hence draw the general truth, that it is only through the goodness of God that we have access to him; and that no man prays aright but he who, having experienced his grace, believes and is fully persuaded that he will be merciful to him. The fear of God is at the same time added, in order to distinguish genuine and godly trust from the vain confidence of the flesh.

> 8. *O Jehovah, lead me forth in thy righteousness, because of mine adversaries: make thy way straight before my face.*
> 9. *For there is no faithfulness in their mouth; their inward parts are very wickedness; their throat is an open sepulchre; with their tongues they deal deceitfully.*
> 10. *Cause them to err, O God; let them fall from their counsels; destroy them in the multitude*[1] *of their transgressions; for they have rebelled against thee.*

8. *O Jehovah, lead me forth, &c.* Some explain these words thus: Show me what is right, and make me wholly devoted to the practice of that righteousness which adorns thy character; and do this because of my adversaries; for the saints, impelled by the wicked practice and deceitful arts of the

---

[1] "Pour la multitude."—*Fr.* "For the multitude."

ungodly, are in danger of turning aside from the right way. This meaning is unquestionably a pious and a useful one. But the other interpretation is more suitable, which views the words as a prayer that God would lead his servant in safety through the midst of the snares of his enemies, and open up to him a way of escape, even when, to all appearance, he was caught and surrounded on every side. *The righteousness of God,* therefore, in this passage, as in many others, is to be understood of his faithfulness and mercy which he shows in defending and preserving his people. Consequently, *in thy righteousness,* means the same thing as *for* or *according to thy righteousness.* David, desiring to have God as the guide of his path, encourages himself in the hope of obtaining his request, because God is righteous; as if he had said, Lord, as thou art righteous, defend me with thine aid, that I may escape from the wicked plots of my enemies. Of the same import is the last clause of the verse, where he prays that *the way of God may be made straight before his face,* in other words, that he might be delivered by the power of God from the distresses with which he was so completely surrounded, that, according to the judgment of the flesh, he never expected to find a way of escape. And thus he acknowledges how impossible it was for him to avoid being entangled in the snares of his enemies,[1] unless God both gave him wisdom, and opened up for him a way where no way is. It becomes us, after his example, to do the same thing; so that distrusting ourselves when counsel fails us, and the malice and wickedness of our enemies prevail, we may betake ourselves speedily to God, in whose hands are the issues of death, as we shall see afterwards, (Ps. lxix.)

9. *For there is no faithfulness in their mouth.* He still repeats the same complaints which he made before, in order thereby to render his enemies the more odious in the sight of God, and to call forth in his own behalf the mercy of God,

---

[1] "Par ainsi il confesse n'avoir ne dexterite ne force, ne mesme aucun moyen pour eviter les embusches des ennemis."—*Fr.* "Thus he confesses that he has neither skill nor power, nor any means whatever, by which to avoid the snares of his enemies."

who has promised to succour those who are unjustly oppressed. And this is to be particularly attended to, that the more our enemies manifest their cruelty against us, or the more wickedly they vex us, we ought, with so much the greater confidence, to send up our groanings to heaven, because God will not suffer their rage to proceed to the uttermost, but will bring forth their malice and wicked devices to the light. In the first place, he accuses them of treachery, because they speak nothing uprightly, or in sincerity; and the cause which he assigns for this is, that inwardly they are full of iniquity. He next compares them to sepulchres, *their throat is an open sepulchre;* as if he had said, they are devouring gulfs;[1] meaning by this, their insatiable desire of shedding blood. In the close of the verse, he again speaks of their deceitfulness. From all this we conclude, that the wrongs with which he was tried were of no ordinary kind, but that he had to contend with enemies the most wicked, who had neither humanity nor moderation. Being so miserably oppressed, he not only perseveres in prayer, but finds ground of hope even from the confusion and apparent hopelessness of his outward condition.

When Paul, (Rom. iii. 13,) in quoting this passage, extends it to all mankind, both Jews and Gentiles, he does not give to it a meaning of greater latitude than the Holy Spirit intended to give. Since he takes it as an undeniable point, that under the person of David, there is here described to us the church, both in the person of Christ, who is the head, and in his members, it follows that all those ought to be reckoned among the number of his enemies, who have not been regenerated by the Spirit of God, whether they are without the pale of the visible church, or within it. For David, in this passage, does not summons either the Assyrians or the Egyptians to the judgment-seat of God, but the degenerate Jews, who, being circumcised in the flesh, gloried in their descent from the holy lineage of Abraham. Paul, therefore, does not wrest these words from their genuine meaning when he applies them to all mankind, but asserts,

---

[1] "Gouffres qui devorent tout."—*Fr.* "Gulfs which devour all."

with truth, that David showed in them what is the character of the whole human family by nature.

10. *Cause them to err.* As the Hebrew word אשם, *asam*, signifies *to cut up* or *to destroy*, as well as *to sin*, and is taken metaphorically for *to err*, or *be deceived*, either of these senses is suitable in this passage; but, as David immediately after subjoins, *Let them fall from their counsels*, I have no doubt but this first prayer is allied and similar to the second. I therefore join these two clauses together, as the cause and the effect. In the first, he prays that God would deprive them of their understanding, and drive them into error; and in the second, he prays that, as the effect of this, their counsels might come to nought, in other words, that their undertakings might prove unsuccessful.[1] For how is it that the ungodly take counsel in vain, and are carried hither and thither without consideration or judgment, and become so basely obstinate, if it is not because the Lord takes them unawares in their own craftiness, breaks their artful schemes, intoxicates them with the spirit of phrenzy and giddiness, so that they act foolishly even in the smallest matters? If, therefore, we are afraid of the snares and deceits of men, and if we find those who desire to do us mischief to be clear-headed and sharp-witted persons, let us remember, that it is the continual office of God to strike with stupidity and madness those who are wise to commit iniquity. Thus it will come to pass, that although we may be asleep, the Lord will dissipate with the breath of his mouth their devices, be they never so subtle, and, in the end, expose them to the mockery of the whole world. In short, David wishes God to lay his hand upon his enemies, and to put a stop to their wicked deliberations. And in fact it is necessary that God bring to nothing the schemes which the wicked cunningly devise, since it is Satan, the contriver of all deceits, who suggests to them all their methods of doing mischief. By praying, *Let them fall from their counsels*, he means that they may not obtain or accom-

---

[1] " C'est à dire, ne vienent à bout de leurs enterprises."—*Fr.*

plish what they had determined. Again, he prays to God to punish them as they deserved, because, in wrongfully and wickedly making war against an innocent person, they *rebelled against God.* The proud, indeed, never think of this, that the poor, whom they afflict and despise, are of such estimation in the sight of God, that he feels himself insulted and injured in their persons: for they do not imagine that the blows aimed at them are struck against heaven, any more than if they trampled a little dust or clay under their feet. But God bestows upon his servants the inestimable reward of taking their cause into his own hand. Whoever, therefore, has an approving conscience, and does not turn aside from his uprightness, although troubled wrongfully, has no reason to doubt of his warrant to improve God as a buckler against his enemies.

> 11. *And let all rejoice who put their trust in thee, yea, let them rejoice for ever; and cover thou them, and let those that love thy name delight in thee.*[1]
> 12. *For thou, O Jehovah, shalt bless the righteous, thou shalt encompass them with thy loving kindness as with a shield.*

11. *And let all rejoice, &c.* It makes little difference as to the sense, whether we read these words in the future tense, *All shall rejoice, &c.,* or in the optative mood, *Let all rejoice, &c.;* for in both ways the meaning of the prophet will be the same; namely, that if God deliver him, the fruit of this deliverance will be common to all the godly; as if he had said, Lord, if thou succourest me, the goodness which thou conferrest upon me will not rest on me alone, but will extend to all thy servants: for this will serve the more to confirm their faith, and make them praise thy name the more. In order, therefore, to induce God to grant him deliverance, he employs as an argument the end or effect which it would produce, inasmuch as it would stir up all the godly to exer-

[1] In the older Latin editions, and in the French edition, the verbs for *rejoice* and *delight* are rendered, on the margin, in the future tense, thus:—" And all who trust in thee shall rejoice; yea, they shall rejoice for ever; and cover thou them, and those that love thy name shall delight in thee."

cise greater trust in God, and encourage them to give praise and thanks to him. This passage teaches us, that we are ungrateful to God if we do not take encouragement and comfort from whatever blessings he confers upon our neighbours, since by these he testifies that he will always be ready to bestow his goodness upon all the godly in common. Accordingly, the reason of this joy is added, *because the Lord will cover* or *protect them.* As often as God bestows any blessings upon any of the faithful, the rest, as I have said before, ought to conclude that he will show himself beneficent towards them. Again, this passage teaches us, that true joy proceeds from no other source than from the protection of God. We may be exposed to a thousand deaths, but this one consideration ought abundantly to suffice us, that we are covered and defended by the hand of God. And this will be the case, if the vain shadows of this world do not so beguile us as to excite us to take shelter under them. We ought also particularly to notice the statement, that those who trust in the Lord *love his name.* The remembrance of God must be sweet to us, and fill our hearts with joy, or rather ravish us with love to him, after he has caused us to taste of his goodness; as, on the other hand, all unbelievers wish the name of God to be buried, and shun the remembrance of him with horror.

12. *For thou, O Jehovah, wilt bless the righteous.* The Psalmist here confirms the concluding sentence of the preceding verse, namely, that all the servants of God in common will take support to their faith from what he had experienced, for he would have us from one example to form our judgment of the immutability and perpetuity of God's grace towards all the godly. Again, by this he teaches us that there is no true and right joy but that which is derived from the sense of God's fatherly love. The word, *to bless,* in Hebrew, (when we speak of this as the act of men,) signifies to wish happiness and prosperity to any one, and to pray for him;[1]

---

[1] " Signifie, souhaitter bien et prosperite a quelqu'un et prier pour luy."—*Fr.*

but when it is spoken of as the act of God, it signifies the same thing as to prosper a man, or to enrich him abundantly with all good things; for since the favour of God is efficacious, his blessing of itself produces an abundance of every good thing. The name *righteous* is not restricted to any one man, but signifies in general all the servants of God. Those, however, who are called righteous in Scripture, are not so called on account of the merit of their works, but because they aspire after righteousness; for after God has received them into his favour, by not imputing their sins to them, he accepts their upright endeavours for perfect righteousness. What follows is of the same import as the preceding clause, *Thou wilt crown them with thy free favour*, or good will, *as with a shield*. The Psalmist's meaning is, that the faithful shall be completely defended on all sides, since he will, in no case, withhold from them his grace, which is to them an invincible fortress, and brings along with it certain safety. The word, *to crown*, which the Psalmist employs, often denotes in Hebrew, *ornament* or *glory*; but as there is added the similitude of a shield, I have no doubt but he uses it metaphorically for, *to fortify*, or *to compass about*.[1] The meaning, therefore, is, that however great and various may be the dangers which besiege the righteous, they shall, notwithstanding, escape, and be saved, because God is favourable to them.

[1] Bishop Horsley thinks כצנה, *katsinah*, *as with a shield*, should be construed with רצון, *ratson*, *favour* or *good will*, and translates the words thus: "Like a shield of good will, thou wilt stand guard around him." The reading of the Septuagint is the same: Ὡς ὅπλῳ εὐδοκίας, *as with a shield of good will*. The word צנה, *tsinah*, means that kind of shield, from the middle of which there arose a large boss, surmounted by a dagger, and which was highly useful both as a defensive and an offensive weapon in ancient warfare.

PSALM VI.

David, being afflicted by the hand of God, acknowledges that he had provoked the Divine wrath by his sins, and, therefore, in order to obtain relief, he prays for forgiveness. At the same time, he regrets, that by being taken out of the world, he would be deprived of an opportunity of praising God. Then, having obtained confidence, he celebrates the grace of God, and directs his discourse to his enemies, who triumphed over his calamities.

¶ To the chief musician on Neginoth, upon the eighth. A song of David.

The name of *Song* shows that David composed this psalm, in which he describes the passionate workings of his grief in the time of his trouble, after he had obtained deliverance from the evils which he deplores. What the kind of chastisement was of which he speaks is uncertain. Those who restrict it to bodily disease do not adduce in support of their opinion any argument of sufficient weight. They insist on the word אמל, *amal*, which occurs in verse third, where he says, " I am weak," which indeed signifies to be sick ; but it is more probable that it is here used metaphorically. They allege that Hezekiah, after his recovery from sickness, sung in the same strains as are here recorded, concerning death. But in Psalm cxvi., where no mention is made of bodily disease, the same complaint is uttered by the Psalmist in the name of the whole Church. We can, indeed, gather from these words that the life of David was in the utmost danger, but it may have been some other kind of affliction than bodily sickness under which he laboured. We may, therefore, adopt this as the more certain interpretation, that he had been stricken by some severe calamity, or that some punishment had been inflicted upon him, which presented to his view on every side only the shadow of death. It ought also to be considered, that this psalm was not composed at the very time when he presented to God the prayers recorded in it ; but that the prayers which he had meditated and uttered in the midst of his dangers and sadness were, after he had obtained respite, committed to writing. This explains why he joins the sorrow with which he certainly had struggled for a time with the joy which he afterwards experienced. With respect to the word *eighth*, as we have before said that נגינות, *Neginoth*, signifies a musical instrument, I do not know whether it would be correct to say, that it was a harp of eight strings. I am rather inclined to the opinion that it refers to the tune, and points out the particular kind of music to which the psalm was to be sung.[1] However, in a matter so obscure and of so little importance, I leave every one at liberty to form his own conjecture.

---

[1] *Sheminith,* or *the eighth,* " is thought to be the shrillest or loftiest note,

1. *Jehovah, rebuke me not in thine anger, and chastise me not in thine indignation.*

THE calamity which David now experienced had, perhaps, been inflicted by men, but he wisely considers that he has to deal with God. Those persons are very unsuitably exercised under their afflictions who do not immediately take a near and a steady view of their sins, in order thereby to produce the conviction that they have deserved the wrath of God. And yet we see how thoughtless and insensible almost all men are on this subject; for while they cry out that they are afflicted and miserable, scarcely one among a hundred looks to the hand which strikes. From whatever quarter, therefore, our afflictions come, let us learn to turn our thoughts instantly to God, and to acknowledge him as the Judge who summons us as guilty before his tribunal, since we, of our own accord, do not anticipate his judgment. But as men, when they are compelled to feel that God is angry with them, often indulge in complaints full of impiety, rather than find fault with themselves and their own sins, it is to be particularly noticed that David does not simply ascribe to God the afflictions under which he is now suffering, but acknowledges them to be the just recompense of his sins. He does not take God to task as if he had been an enemy, treating him with cruelty without any just cause; but yielding to him the right of rebuking and chastening, he desires and prays only that bounds may be set to the punishment inflicted on him. By this he declares God to be a just Judge in taking vengeance on the sins of men.[1] But as soon as he has confessed that he is justly chastised, he earnestly beseeches God not to deal with him in strict justice, or according to the utmost rigour of the law. He does not altogether refuse punishment, for that would be unreasonable; and to be without it, he judged would be more hurtful than

---

as *Alomoth* is the lowest; of which see 1 Chron. xv. 20, 21. But all this is only conjecture; and the Jews themselves have no certain knowledge of their ancient music, and of the signification of the terms belonging to it."—*Poole's Annotations.*

[1] " En faisant vengence des forfaits des hommes."—*Fr.*

beneficial to him: but what he is afraid of is the wrath of God, which threatens sinners with ruin and perdition. To anger and indignation David tacitly opposes fatherly and gentle chastisement, and this last he was willing to bear. We have a similar contrast in the words of Jeremiah, (ch. x. 24,) " O Lord," says he, "correct me, but with judgment; not in thine anger." God is, indeed, said to be angry with sinners whenever he inflicts punishment upon them, but not in the proper and strict sense, inasmuch as he not only mingles with it some of the sweetness of his grace to mitigate their sorrow, but also shows himself favourable to them, in moderating their punishment, and in mercifully drawing back his hand. But, as we must necessarily be stricken with terror whenever he shows himself the avenger of wickedness, it is not without cause that David, according to the sense of the flesh, is afraid of his anger and indignation. The meaning therefore is this: I indeed confess, O Lord, that I deserve to be destroyed and brought to nought; but as I would be unable to endure the severity of thy wrath, deal not with me according to my deserts, but rather pardon my sins, by which I have provoked thine anger against me. As often, then, as we are pressed down by adversity, let us learn, from the example of David, to have recourse to this remedy, that we may be brought into a state of peace with God; for it is not to be expected that it can be well or prosperous with us if we are not interested in his favour. Whence it follows, that we shall never be without a load of evils, until he forgive us our sins.

2. *Have mercy upon me, O Jehovah, for I am weak; heal me, O Jehovah, for my bones are afraid.*

3. *And my soul is exceedingly troubled;*[1] *and thou, O Jehovah, how long?*[2]

2. *Have mercy upon me.* As he earnestly calls upon God

---

[1] Or greatly terrified. This is a very correct rendering of the original words נבהלה מאד, *nibhalah meod;* and they are very like those uttered by the Saviour in his agony, "My soul is exceeding sorrowful, even unto death."

[2] " Mais toy, Seigneur, jusques à quand m'affligeras-tu?"—*Fr.* " But thou, O Lord, how long wilt thou afflict me?"

to be merciful to him, it is from this the more clearly manifest, that by the terms *anger* and *indignation* he did not mean cruelty or undue severity, but only such judgment as God executes upon the reprobate, whom he does not spare in mercy as he does his own children. If he had complained of being unjustly and too severely punished, he would now have only added something to this effect: Restrain thyself, that in punishing me thou mayest not exceed the measure of my offence. In betaking himself, therefore, to the mercy of God alone, he shows that he desires nothing else than not to be dealt with according to strict justice, or as he deserved. In order to induce God to exercise his forgiving mercy towards him, he declares that he is ready to fail: *Have mercy upon me, O Jehovah, for I am weak.* As I have said before, he calls himself weak, not because he was sick, but because he was cast down and broken by what had now befallen him. And as we know that the design of God in inflicting punishment upon us, is to humble us; so, whenever we are subdued under his rod, the gate is opened for his mercy to come to us. Besides, since it is his peculiar office to heal the diseased, to raise up the fallen, to support the weak, and, finally, to give life to the dead; this, of itself, is a sufficient reason why we should seek his favour, that we are sinking under our afflictions.

After David has protested that he placed his hope of salvation in the mercy of God alone, and has sorrowfully set forth how much he is abased, he subjoins the effect which this had in impairing his bodily health, and prays for the restoration of this blessing: *Heal me, O Jehovah.* And this is the order which we must observe, that we may know that all the blessings which we ask from God flow from the fountain of his free goodness, and that we are then, and then only, delivered from calamities and chastisements,[1] when he has had mercy upon us.—*For my bones are afraid.* This confirms what I have just now observed, namely, that, from the very grievousness of his afflictions, he entertained the hope of some relief; for God, the more he sees the wretched oppressed

---

[1] " Des maux et chastiemens."—*Fr.*

and almost overwhelmed, is just so much the more ready to succour them. He attributes fear to his *bones*, not because they are endued with feeling, but because the vehemence of his grief was such that it affected his whole body. He does not speak of his flesh, which is the more tender and susceptible part of the corporeal system, but he mentions his bones, thereby intimating that the strongest parts of his frame were made to tremble for fear. He next assigns the cause of this by saying, *And my soul is greatly afraid.* The connective particle *and*, in my judgment, has here the meaning of the causal particle *for*, as if he had said, So severe and violent is the inward anguish of my heart, that it affects and impairs the strength of every part of my body. I do not approve of the opinion which here takes *soul* for *life*, nor does it suit the scope of the passage.

3. *And thou, O Jehovah, how long?* This elliptical form of expression serves to express more strongly the vehemence of grief, which not only holds the minds of men bound up, but likewise their tongues, breaking and cutting short their speech in the middle of the sentence. The meaning, however, in this abrupt expression is doubtful. Some, to complete the sentence, supply the words, *Wilt thou afflict me, or continue to chasten me?* Others read, *How long wilt thou delay thy mercy?* But what is stated in the next verse shows, that this second sense is the more probable, for he there prays to the Lord to look upon him with an eye of favour and compassion. He, therefore, complains that God has now forsaken him, or has no regard to him, just as God seems to be far off from us whenever his assistance or grace does not actually manifest itself in our behalf. God, in his compassion towards us, permits us to pray to him to make haste to succour us; but when we have freely complained of his long delay, that our prayers or sorrow, on this account, may not pass beyond bounds, we must submit our case entirely to his will, and not wish him to make greater haste than shall seem good to him.

4. *Return, O Lord, deliver my soul; save me for thy mercy's sake.*
5. *For in death there is no remembrance of thee; and in the grave who shall acknowledge thee?*[1]

4. *Return, O Lord.* In the preceding verses the Psalmist bewailed the absence of God, and now he earnestly requests the tokens of his presence; for our happiness consists in this, that we are the objects of the Divine regard, but we think he is alienated from us, if he does not give us some substantial evidence of his care for us. That David was at this time in the utmost peril, we gather from these words, in which he prays both for the deliverance of his soul, as it were, from the jaws of death, and for his restoration to a state of safety. Yet no mention is made of any bodily disease; and, therefore, I give no judgment with respect to the kind of his affliction. David, again, confirms what he had touched upon in the second verse *concerning the mercy of God*, namely, that this is the only quarter from which he hopes for deliverance: *Save me for thy mercy's sake.* Men will never find a remedy for their miseries until, forgetting their own merits, by trusting to which they only deceive themselves, they have learned to betake themselves to the free mercy of God.

5. *For in death there is no remembrance of thee.* After God has bestowed all things freely upon us, he requires nothing in return but a grateful remembrance of his benefits. To this gratitude reference is made when David says, that *there will be no remembrance of God in death, nor any celebration of his praise in the grave.* His meaning is, that if, by the grace of God, he shall be delivered from death, he will be grateful for it, and keep it in remembrance. And he laments, that if he should be removed out of the world, he would be deprived of the power and opportunity of manifesting his gratitude, since in that case he would no longer mingle in the society of men, there to commend or celebrate

---

[1] "Car il n'est fait nulle mention de toy en la mort: qui est-ce qui te louëra au sepulchre?"—*Fr.* "For there is no mention made of thee in death; and who shall praise thee in the grave?"

the name of God. From this passage some conclude, that the dead have no feeling, and that it is wholly extinct in them; but this is a rash and unwarranted inference, for nothing is here treated of but the mutual celebration of the grace of God, in which men engage while they continue in the land of the living. We know that we are placed on the earth to praise God with one mind and one mouth, and that this is the end of our life. Death, it is true, puts an end to such praises; but it does not follow from this, that the souls of the faithful, when divested of their bodies, are deprived of understanding, or touched with no affection towards God. It is also to be considered, that, on the present occasion, David dreaded the judgment of God if death should befall him, and this made him dumb as to singing the praises of God. It is only the goodness of God sensibly experienced by us which opens our mouth to celebrate his praise; and whenever, therefore, joy and gladness are taken away, praises also must cease. It is not then wonderful if the wrath of God, which overwhelms us with the fear of eternal destruction, is said to extinguish in us the praises of God.

From this passage, we are furnished with the solution of another question, why David so greatly dreaded death, as if there had been nothing to hope for beyond this world. Learned men reckon up three causes why the fathers under the law were so much kept in bondage by the fear of death. The first is, because the grace of God, not being then made manifest by the coming of Christ, the promises, which were obscure, gave them only a slight acquaintance with the life to come. The second is, because the present life, in which God deals with us as a Father, is of itself desirable. And the third, because they were afraid lest, after their decease, some change to the worse might take place in religion. But to me these reasons do not appear to be sufficiently solid. David's mind was not always occupied by the fear he now felt; and when he came to die, being full of days and weary of this life, he calmly yielded up his soul into the bosom of God. The second reason is equally applicable to us at the present day, as it was to the ancient fathers, inasmuch as God's fatherly love shines forth towards us also even in this life, and with much more illustrious proofs than under the former dispensation. But, as I have just observed, I consider this complaint of David as including something different, namely, that feeling the hand of God to be against him, and knowing his hatred of sin,[1] he is overwhelmed with fear and involved in the deepest distress. The same may also be said of Hezekiah, inasmuch as he did not simply pray for deliverance from death, but from the wrath of God, which he felt to be very awful, (Isaiah xxxviii. 3.)

6. *I have become wearied in my groaning; I make my bed to swim[2] every night; I water my couch with my tears.*
7. *Mine eye hath waxed dim for vexation; it hath waxed old among my persecutors.*

These forms of expression are hyperbolical, but it must not be imagined that David, after the manner of poets, exaggerates his sorrow;[3] but he declares truly and simply how severe and bitter it had been. It should always be kept in mind, that his affliction did not proceed so much from his having been severely wounded with bodily distress; but regarding God as greatly displeased with him, he saw, as it were, hell open to receive him; and the mental distress which this produces exceeds all other sorrows. Indeed, the more sincerely a man is devoted to God, he is just so much the more severely disquieted by the sense of his wrath; and hence it is that holy persons, who were otherwise endued with uncommon fortitude, have showed in this respect the greatest softness and want of resolution. And nothing prevents us at this day from experiencing in ourselves what David describes concerning himself but the stupidity of our flesh. Those who have experienced, even in a moderate degree, what it is to contend with the fear of eternal death, will be satisfied that there is nothing extravagant in these

---

[1] "Ascavoir que sentant la main de Dieu contraire, veu qu'il l'advertissoit de sa vengence contre le peche."—*Fr.*

[2] "Je baigne ma couche."—*Fr.* "I soak my couch." "Ou, jefaynager."—*Fr. marg.* "Or, I make to swim."

[3] "Il ne faut pas penser toutesfois que David amplifie sa tristesse à la façon des Poëtes."—*Fr.*

words. Let us, therefore, know that here David is represented to us as being afflicted with the terrors of his conscience,[1] and feeling within him torment of no ordinary kind, but such as made him almost faint away, and lie as if dead. With respect to the words, he says, *Mine eye hath waxed dim;* for grief of mind easily makes its way to the eyes, and from them very distinctly shows itself. As the word עָתְקָה, *athak,* which I have translated *it hath waxed old,* sometimes signifies to depart from one's place, some expound it, that the goodness of his eyesight was lost, and his sight, as it were, had vanished. Others understand by it that his eyes were hidden by the swelling which proceeds from weeping. The first opinion, however, according to which David complains of his eyes failing him, as it were, through old age, appears to me the more simple. As to what he adds, *every night,* we learn from it that he was almost wholly wasted away with protracted sorrow, and yet all the while never ceased from praying to God.

8. *Depart from me, all ye workers of iniquity; for the Lord hath heard the voice of my weeping.*
9. *The Lord hath heard my supplication; the Lord will receive[2] my prayer.*
10. *Let all mine enemies be put to shame and greatly confounded; let them turn back, and be ashamed suddenly.[3]*

After David has disburdened his griefs and troubles into the bosom of God, he now, as it were, assumes a new character. And, without doubt, he had been afflicted with long-continued despondency of spirit before he could recover himself, and attain to such a degree of assurance as he here displays;[4] for we have already seen that he had spent many nights in continual weeping. Now, the more he had been distressed and wearied by the long delay of his deliver-

---

[1] " Des frayeurs de la morte."—*Fr.* " With the terrors of death."
[2] " A receu."—*Fr.* " Hath received." This is the rendering which is adopted in all the ancient versions, although the Hebrew verb is in the future tense.
[3] " En un moment."—*Fr.* " In a moment."
[4] " Avant que pouvoir se relever et venir à sentir telle asseurance qu'il monstre yci."—*Fr.*

ance, with so much the more alacrity does he stir up himself to sing of victory. Directing his discourse against his adversaries, he represents it as not the least part of his temptation, that ungodly men triumphed over him, and derided him as lost, and in a hopeless condition; for we know with what insolence their pride and cruelty magnify themselves against the children of God, when they see them oppressed under the cross. And to this Satan moves them, in order to drive the faithful to despair, when they see their hope made the subject of mockery. This passage teaches us, that the grace of God is the only light of life to the godly; and that, as soon as He has manifested some token of his anger, they are not only greatly afraid, but also, as it were, plunged into the darkness of death; while, on the other hand, as soon as they discover anew that God is merciful to them, they are immediately restored to life. David, it is to be noticed, repeats three times that his prayers were heard, by which he testifies that he ascribes his deliverance to God, and confirms himself in this confidence, that he had not betaken himself to God in vain. And if we would receive any fruit from our prayers, we must believe that God's ears have not been shut against them. By the word *weeping*,[1] he not only indicates vehemence and earnestness, but also intimates that he had been wholly occupied in mourning and sorrowful lamentations. The confidence and security which David takes to himself from the favour of God ought also to be noticed. From this, we are taught that there is nothing in the whole world, whatever it may be, and whatever opposition it may make to us,[2] which we may not despise, if we are fully persuaded of our being beloved by God; and by this also we understand what his fatherly love can do for us. By the adverb *suddenly*, he signifies, that when there is apparently no means of delivering the faithful from affliction, and when all seems desperate or hopeless, then they are

---

[1] "*The voice of my weeping*, my loud weeping," says Hengstenberg, and then he adds, quoting from *Roberts' Orient. Illustr. of the Sacred Scrip.*, "Silent grief is not much known in the East. Hence, when the people speak of lamentation, they say, Have I not heard the voice of his mourning?"

[2] "Qu'il n'y a rien en tout le monde qui se dresse contre nous."—*Fr.*

delivered by the power of God contrary to all expectation. When God suddenly changes men's afflicted condition into one of joy and happiness, he thereby manifests more illustriously his power, and makes it appear the more wonderful.

PSALM VII.

David, loaded with unjust calumny, calls upon God to be his advocate and defender, and commits his innocence to the Divine protection. In the first place, he protests that his conscience did not accuse him of the wickedness laid to his charge. Secondly, he shows how greatly it concerns the glory of God that he should execute judgment against the ungodly. Thirdly, to inspire his mind with confidence, he seriously reflects upon the goodness and righteousness of God, and sets before him the divine promises. Lastly, as if he had obtained the desire of his heart, he derides the folly and the vain attempts of his enemies; or rather, depending upon the aid of God, he assures himself that all their endeavours against him shall turn to their own destruction.

¶ Shiggaion of David, which he sung unto Jehovah, upon the words of Cush the Benjamite.

With respect to the word *Shiggaion*, the Jewish interpreters are not agreed. Some understand it to mean a musical instrument. To others it seems to be a tune to which a song is set. Others suppose it to have been the beginning of a common song, to the tune of which David wished this psalm to be sung. Others translate the Hebrew word, *delight*, or *rejoicing*.[1] The second opinion appears to me the most probable, namely, that it was some kind of melody or song, as if one should term it Sapphic or Phaleucian verse.[2] But I do not contend about a matter of so small importance. Again, the psalm is said to have been composed upon the *words of Cush*. I cannot subscribe to the interpretation, (although it is the commonly received one,) that *words* here mean *affairs*, or *business*. To put *word* for a *matter*, or *an affair*, is, I allow, a common form of speech among the Jews; but as David a little after de-

---

[1] "Delectation, ou Resjouissance."—*Fr.*

[2] "Ascavoir que c'a este une espece de melodie ou certain chant, comme nous scavons que selon la diversite des nations et langues, il y a diverses mesures de vers."—*Fr.* "Namely, that it was a kind of tune or song, as we know, that, according to the diversity of nations and languages, there are different measures of verse."

clares that he was falsely accused of some crime, I doubt not but he here speaks of the accusation or calumny itself, of which, as I judge, Cush, some one of Saul's kindred, was the author, or, at least, the instrument who preferred and circulated it. The opinion of some who say that Saul is here spoken of under a fictitious name, is not supported by any argument of sufficient weight. According to them, David avoided calling him by his own name, in order to spare the royal dignity. David, I admit, had great reverence for the holy anointing; but as he expressly names Saul in other places where he reprehends him not less severely, and paints him in colours no less black than he does in this psalm, why should he suppress his name here, and not in these passages? In my opinion, therefore, he here expresses by his proper name, and without figure, a wicked accuser, who had excited hatred against him by falsely charging him with some crime, and who had either been bribed by the king to do this, or, currying the royal favour, had calumniated David of his own accord; for David, we know, was very much slandered, as if he had been ungrateful and treacherous towards the king, his father-in-law. Saul, indeed, belonged to the tribe of Benjamin. We do not, however, think that he is the person here mentioned, but that it was one of Saul's relations, one who belonged to the same tribe with him, who falsely accused David.

1. *O Jehovah, my God, in thee do I trust: save me from all them that persecute me, and deliver me.*
2. *Lest* HE *seize upon my soul as a lion, and tear it in pieces, while there is none to deliver it.*

AT the commencement of the psalm, David speaks of having many enemies, and in the second verse he specifies some one in the singular number. And certainly, since the minds of all men were inflamed against him, he had very good reason for praying to be delivered from all his persecutors. But as the wicked cruelty of the king, like a firebrand, had kindled against him, though an innocent person, the hatred of the whole people, he had good reason also for turning his pen particularly against him. Thus, in the first verse, he describes the true character of his own circumstances—he was a persecuted man; and, in the second verse, the fountain or cause of the calamity he was enduring. There is great emphasis in these words which he uses in the beginning of the psalm, *O Jehovah, my God, in thee do I trust.* The verb, it is true, is in the past tense in the Hebrew; and, therefore, if literally translated, the reading would be, *In thee have I trusted;* but as the Hebrews often take one tense for another,[1] I prefer to translate it in the present, *In thee I do trust,* especially since it is abundantly evident that a continued act, as it is termed, is denoted. David does not boast of a confidence in God, from which he had now fallen, but of a confidence which he constantly entertained in his afflictions. And this is a genuine and an undoubted proof of our faith, when, being visited with adversity, we, notwithstanding, persevere in cherishing and exercising hope in God. From this passage, we also learn that the gate of mercy is shut against our prayers if the key of faith do not open it for us. Nor does he use superfluous language when he calls Jehovah *his own God;* for by setting up this as a bulwark before him, he beats back the waves of temptations, that they may not overwhelm his faith. In the second verse, by the figure of *a lion,* he represents in a stronger light the cruelty of Saul, as an argument to induce God to grant him assistance, even as he ascribes it to *Him* as his peculiar province to rescue his poor sheep from the jaws of wolves.

3. *O Jehovah, my God, if I have done this thing, if there be iniquity in my hands:*
4. *If I have rewarded evil to him that was at peace with me, and have not delivered him that persecuted me without cause:*
5. *Let the enemy pursue my soul and take it; and let him throw down my life to the ground,[2] and hold down[3] my glory in the dust. Selah.*

3. *O Jehovah, my God.* Here David, to induce God to show him favour, protests that he is molested unjustly, and without being guilty of any crime. To give his protestation the greater weight, he uses an imprecation. If he has done any wrong, he declares his readiness to bear the blame; yea, he offers to endure the severest punishment, if he is not altogether innocent of the crime of which all men thought him almost convicted. And by entreating God to succour

---

[1] "Mais pource que les Hebrieux prenent souvent un temps pour l'autre."—*Fr.*
[2] "Et foulle ma vie en terre."—*Fr.* "And let him trample my life on the ground."
[3] "Et qu'il mette."—*Fr.* "And lay."

him upon no other condition than this, that his integrity should upon trial be found to be untarnished, he teaches us, by his example, that as often as we have recourse to God, we must make it our first care to be well assured in our own consciences with respect to the righteousness of our cause; for we do him great wrong if we wish to engage him as the advocate and defender of a bad cause. The pronoun *this* shows that he speaks of a thing which was generally known; whence we may conclude, that the slander which had been raised by Cush was spread far and wide. And as David was condemned, by the false reports and unrighteous judgments which men advanced against him, and saw no remedy on earth, he betakes himself to the judgment-seat of God, and contents himself with maintaining his innocence before the heavenly Judge; an example which all the godly should imitate, in order that, in opposition to the slanderous reports which are spread against them, they may rest satisfied with the judgment of God alone. He next declares more distinctly, that he had committed no crime. And in the fourth verse, he mentions two particulars in self-vindication; first, That he had done no wrong to any one; and, secondly, That he had rather endeavoured to do good to his enemies, by whom notwithstanding he had been injured without any just cause. I, therefore, explain the fourth verse thus: If I have wronged any man that was at peace with me, and have not rather succoured the unworthy, who persecuted me without a cause, &c. Since David was hated of almost all men, as if ambition to reign had impelled him perfidiously to rise up in rebellion against Saul, and to lay snares for the monarch to whom he was bound by the oath of allegiance,[1] in the first part of the verse, he clears himself of such a foul slander. The reason, perhaps, why he calls Saul *him that was at peace with him* is, that on account of his royal dignity his person ought to be sacred, and secure from danger,[2] so that it should be unlawful to make any hostile

---

[1] "Apres luy avoir fait le serment."—*Fr.* "After having sworn the oath of allegiance to him."

[2] "Pource que le nom et titre royal luy devoit estre une sauvegarde et le tenir en seureté."—*Fr.* "Because the royal name and title ought to be to him a safeguard, and secure the safety of his person."

attempt against him. This phrase, however, may be understood generally, as if he had said, No one who has meekly restrained himself from injuring me, and has conducted himself kindly towards me, can with truth complain that I have ever injured him in a single instance. And yet it was the general persuasion, that David, in the midst of peace, had stirred up great confusion, and caused war. From this it is just so much the more manifest, that David, provided he enjoyed the approbation of God, was contented with the consolation arising from this, though he should have comfort from no other source.

In the second clause of the fourth verse, he proceeds farther, and states, that he had been a friend, not only to the good, but also to the bad, and had not only restrained himself from all revenge, but had even succoured his enemies, by whom he had been deeply and cruelly injured. It would certainly not be very illustrious virtue to love the good and peaceable, unless there were joined to this self-government and gentleness in patiently bearing with the bad. But when a man not only keeps himself from revenging the injuries which he has received, but endeavours to overcome evil by doing good, he manifests one of the graces of a renewed and sanctified nature, and in this way proves himself to be one of the children of God; for such meekness proceeds only from the Spirit of adoption. With respect to the words: as the Hebrew word חלץ, *chalats*, which I have translated *to deliver*, signifies to *divide* and *to separate*, some, to prevent the necessity of supplying any word to make out the sense,[1] thus explain the passage, *If I have withdrawn myself from my persecutors, in order not to succour them.* The other interpretation, however, according to which the verb is rendered *to deliver* or *rescue from* danger, is more generally received; because the phrase, *to separate* or *set aside*, is applied to those things which we wish to place in safety. And thus the negative word *not* must be supplied, an omission which we will find not unfrequently occurring in The Psalms.

[1] In the clause, "And have NOT delivered him that persecuted me without cause," the word *not* is a supplement, there being nothing for it in the Hebrew text.

5. *Let mine enemy pursue.* It is a striking proof of the great confidence which David had in his own integrity, when he is willing to endure any kind of punishment, however dreadful, provided he should be found guilty of any crime. If we could bring a good conscience like this before God, his hand would be more quickly stretched forth to afford us immediate assistance. But as it often happens that those who molest us have been provoked by us, or that we burn with the desire of revenge when offended, we are unworthy of receiving succour from God; yea, our own impatience shuts the gate against our prayers. In the first place, David is prepared to be given over to the will of his enemies, that they may *seize his life, and throw it down to the ground;* and then to be publicly exhibited as an object of their mockery, so that, even after he is dead, he may lie under eternal disgrace. Some think that the word כבוד, *kebod,* which we have translated *glory,* is here to be taken for *life,* and thus there will be three words, *soul, life, glory,* signifying the same thing. But it appears to me, that the meaning of the passage will be fuller if we refer the word *glory* to his memory, or his good name, as if he had said, Let my enemy not only destroy me, but, after having put me to death, let him speak of me in the most reproachful terms, so that my name may be buried in mire or filth.

6. *Arise, O Jehovah, in thine anger, lift up thyself against the rage of mine enemies: and awake thou for me to the judgment which thou hast ordained.*[1]
7. *And then the assembly of peoples* [or *nations*] *shall compass thee about: and on account of this, return thou on high.*
8. *Jehovah shall judge the peoples,* [or *nations:*] *judge me, O Jehovah, according to my righteousness, and according to the integrity that is in me.*

6. *Arise, O Jehovah.* David here sets the anger of God in opposition to the rage of his enemies; and when we are

---

[1] *Street's* rendering is, "And exert in my favour the judgment thou hast ordained."

in similar circumstances we should act in the same manner. When the ungodly are inflamed against us, and cast forth their rage and fury to destroy us, we ought humbly to beseech God to be inflamed also on his side; in other words, to show in truth that he has no less zeal and power to preserve us, than they have inclination to destroy us. The word, *Arise,* is taken in a figurative sense, for *to ascend into a judgment-seat,* or rather *to prepare one's self to make resistance;* and it is here applied to God, because, while he delays to succour us, we are very apt to think him asleep. Accordingly, David also, a little after, beseeches him *to awake;* for it seemed on the part of God something like the forgetfulness of sleep to give no assistance to an individual who was so much afflicted and oppressed on all hands.

In the end of the verse he shows that he asks nothing but what is according to the appointment of God. And this is the rule which ought to be observed by us in our prayers; we should in every thing conform our requests to the divine will, as John also instructs us, (1 John v. 14.) And, indeed, we can never pray in faith unless we attend, in the first place, to what God commands, that our minds may not rashly and at random start aside in desiring more than we are permitted to desire and pray for. David, therefore, in order to pray aright, reposes himself on the word and promise of God; and the import of his exercise is this: Lord, I am not led by ambition, or foolish headstrong passion, or depraved desire, inconsiderately to ask from thee whatever is pleasing to my flesh; but it is the clear light of thy word which directs me, and upon it I securely depend. Since God, of his own good pleasure, had called him to be one day king, it belonged to him to defend and maintain the rights of the man whom he had chosen for his servant. David's language, therefore, is the same as if he had said, "When I was well contented with my humble condition in private life, it was thy pleasure to set me apart to the honourable station of being a king; now, therefore, it belongs to thee to maintain this cause against Saul and his associates, who are using their efforts to defeat thy decree in making war upon me." The Hebrew word עוּרָה, *urah*, which we have rendered, *awake thou*,[1] might also be taken transitively for *to build up*, or *to establish* the right of David. The sum of the whole, however, comes to this, that David, trusting to the call of God, beseeches him to stretch forth his hand for his relief. The faithful must, therefore, take care not to exceed these bounds, if they desire to have God present with them to maintain and preserve them.

7. *And a congregation of peoples.* Some limit this sentence exclusively to the people of Israel, as if David promised that, as soon as he should ascend the throne, he would endeavour to reunite together, in the pure worship of God, the people who before had been as it were in a state of dispersion. Under the reign of Saul, religion had been neglected, or such an unrestrained license in wickedness had prevailed, that few paid any regard to God. The meaning, therefore, according to these expositors, is this: Lord, when thou shalt have constituted me king, the whole people, who have so basely gone astray from thee,[2] shall return from their wanderings and disorderly courses to thee and to thy service, so that all shall know that thou rulest in the midst of them, and shall worship thee as their only King. But I am rather inclined to view this as language which has a respect in common to many nations. David here speaks in high terms of the effects resulting from his deliverance, the report of which would be spread far and wide, and his words are, as if he had said, "Lord, when thou shalt have put me in peaceable possession of the kingdom, this will not only be a benefit conferred on me personally, but it will be a common lesson to many nations, teaching them to acknowledge thy just judgment, so that they shall turn their eyes to thy judgment-seat."[3] David here alludes to the practice of a people who surround their king, as in a circle, when he holds a solemn assembly. In the same sense, he adds immediately after, that God, who, for a

---

[1] "Lequel nous avons traduit Veille."—*Fr.*
[2] "Tout le peuple qui s'estoit ainsi vilenement destourné de toy."—*Fr.*
[3] "Mais ce sera un enseignement commun a plusieurs peuples, pour recognoistre ton juste jugement, tellement qu'ils dresseront les yeux vers ton siege judicial."—*Fr.*

time, lay still and kept silence, would raise himself on high that not only one or two, but whole nations, might behold his glory: *And on account of this return thou on high.*[1] There is, in these words, a tacit comparison, that although it might not be necessary to have a regard to one man alone, it is requisite that God should keep the world in the fear and reverence of his judgment.

8. *Jehovah shall judge the nations.* This sentence is closely connected with the preceding verse. David had prayed God to show himself as judge to the nations; and now he takes it for a certain and admitted truth, that it is the peculiar office of God to judge the nations: for the word put in the future tense, and rendered *shall judge,* denotes here a continued act; and this is the signification of the future tense in general sentences. Besides, he does not here speak of one nation only, but comprehends all nations. As he acknowledges God to be the judge of the whole world, he concludes a little after from this, that he will maintain his cause and right. And as often as we seem to be forsaken and oppressed, we should recall this truth to our remembrance, that as God is the governor of the world, it is as utterly impossible for him to abdicate his office as to deny himself. From this source there will flow a continual stream of comfort, although a long succession of calamities may press upon us: for from this truth we may assuredly conclude, that he will take care to defend our innocence. It would be contrary to every principle of just reasoning to suppose, that he who governs many nations neglects even one man. What happens with respect to the judges of this world can never take place with respect to him; he cannot, as may be the case with them, be so occupied about great and public affairs as to neglect, because unable to attend to them, the concerns of individuals.

He again brings into view *his integrity,* that he may not

---

[1] Fry reads, "And over it resume thy high tribunal." He supposes that the word עליה, *aleha,* which Calvin has rendered *on account of this,* may be understood, "concerning this affair," and gives the following paraphrase: "Resume thy judgment-seat, in order to investigate the cause in which I have been prejudged by the adversary."

seem, after the example of hypocrites, to make the name of God a mere pretext for the better furthering of his own purposes. Since God is no respecter of persons, we cannot expect him to be on our side, and to favour us, if our cause is not good. But it is asked, how can David here boast of his own integrity before God, when in other places he deprecates God entering into judgment with him? The answer is easy, and it is this: The subject here treated of is not how he could answer if God should demand from him an account of his whole life; but, comparing himself with his enemies, he maintains, and not without cause, that, in respect of them, he was righteous. But when each saint passes under the review of God's judgment, and his own character is tried upon its own merits, the matter is very different, for then the only sanctuary to which he can betake himself for safety, is the mercy of God.

> 9. *Let the malice of the wicked come to an end, I beseech thee; and direct thou the righteous: for God, who is righteous, proves* [or *searches*] *the hearts and the reins.*
> 10. *My defence* [or *shield*] *is in God, who saves the upright in heart.*
> 11. *God judgeth the righteous, and him who despiseth God, daily.*

9. *Let the malice of the wicked come to an end, I beseech thee.* David, in the first place, prays that God would restrain the malice of his enemies, and bring it to an end; from which it follows, that his affliction had been of long duration. Others suppose that this is rather a dreadful imprecation, and they explain the Hebrew word גמר, *gamar*, somewhat differently. Instead of rendering it *to cease,* and *to come to an end,* as I have done, they understand it *to make to cease,* which is equivalent *to destroy* or *to consume.*[1] Thus, according to them, David wishes that God would cause the mischief which the wicked devise to fall upon their own heads: *Let the wickedness of the wicked consume them.* But, in my opinion, the former inter-

---

[1] "Les autres estiment plustost que ce soit une vehemente imprecation, et exposent ce mot Hebrieu un peu autrement. Car en lieu que nous le traduisons Cesser et Prendre fin, ils le prenent pour Faire cesser, qui est Destruire et Consumer."—*Fr.*

pretation is the more simple, namely, that David beseeches God to bring his troubles to a termination. Accordingly, there follows immediately after the corresponding prayer, *Direct thou the righteous,* or *establish him;* for it is of little importance which of these two readings we adopt. The meaning is, that God would re-establish and uphold the righteous, who are wrongfully oppressed, and thus make it evident that they are continued in their estate by the power of God, notwithstanding the persecution to which they are subjected.—*For God searcheth the hearts.* The Hebrew copulative is here very properly translated by the causal particle *for,* since David, without doubt, adds this clause as an argument to enforce his prayer. He now declares, for the third time, that, trusting to the testimony of a good conscience, he comes before God with confidence; but here he expresses something more than he had done before, namely, that he not only showed his innocence, by his external conduct, but had also cultivated purity in the secret affection of his heart. He seems to set this confidence in opposition to the insolence and boasting of his enemies, by whom, it is probable, such calumnies had been circulated among the people concerning him, as constrained him in his deep affliction to present his heart and reins to be tried by God. Perhaps, also, he speaks in this manner, in order to divest them of all those plausible but false and deceitful pretences, which they made use of for the purpose of deceiving men, and if they succeeded in doing this they were satisfied.[1] He shows that, although they might triumph before the world, and receive the applause of the multitude, they, nevertheless, gained nothing, inasmuch as they would, by and by, have to make their appearance before the judgment-seat of God, where the question would not be, What were their titles? or, What was the splendour of their actions? but how it stood as to the purity of their hearts.

10. *My shield.* It is not wonderful that David often

---

[1] "Il se peut faire aussi qu'il parle ainsi pour oster toutes ces belles apparances bien fardees dont ils se servoyent pour abuser les hommes et ce leur estoit assez."—*Fr.*

mingles meditations with his prayers, thereby to inspire himself with true confidence. We may go to God in prayer with great alacrity; but our fervour, if it does not gather new strength, either immediately fails or begins to languish. David, therefore, in order to continue in prayer with the same ardour of devotion and affection with which he commenced, brings to his recollection some of the most common truths of religion, and by this means fosters and invigorates his faith. He declares, that as God *saves the upright in heart,* he is perfectly safe under his protection. Whence it follows, that he had the testimony of an approving conscience. And, as he does not simply say *the righteous,* but *the upright in heart,* he appears to have an eye to that inward searching of *the heart and reins* mentioned in the preceding verse.

11. *God judgeth the righteous, &c.* Others read, *God is a righteous Judge, and God is angry every day.* The words will certainly admit of this sense; but as the doctrine is fuller according to the first reading, I have preferred following it, as I see it is more approved of by the most learned divines, and, besides, it is more suitable to the subject which David is now considering. As Saul and his accomplices had, by their calumnious reports, so far succeeded in their wicked design as to have produced a general prejudice against David, so that he was condemned by almost the whole people, the holy man supports himself from this one consideration, that whatever may be the confusion of things in the world, God, notwithstanding, can easily discern between the righteous and the wicked. He, therefore, appeals from the false judgments of men to Him who can never be deceived. It may, however, be asked, How does the Psalmist represent God *as judging every day,* when we see him delaying punishment frequently for a long time? The sacred writings certainly most justly celebrate his long-suffering; but, although he exercises patience long, and does not immediately execute his judgments, yet, as no time passes, yea, not even a day, in which he does not furnish the clearest evidence that he discerns between the righteous and the wicked, notwithstanding the confusion of things in the world, it is certain that he never ceases to

execute the office of a judge. All who will be at the trouble to open their eyes to behold the government of the world, will distinctly see that the patience of God is very different from approbation or connivance. Surely, then, his own people will confidently betake themselves to him every day.

12. *If he turn not, he will whet his sword ; he hath bent his bow and made it ready.*[1]

13. *And he hath prepared for it*[2] *the instruments of death ; he shall make fit his arrows for them that persecute.*[3]

14. *Behold, he shall travail to bring forth iniquity ; he hath conceived wickedness, and he shall bring forth falsehood.*[4]

12. *If he turn not.* These verses are usually explained in two ways. The meaning is, that if David's enemies should persevere in their malicious designs against him, there is denounced against them the vengeance which their obstinate wickedness deserves. Accordingly, in the second clause, they supply the name of *God,—If he turn not,* GOD *will whet his sword ;*[5] as if it had been said, If my enemy do not repent,[6] he shall, at length, feel that God is completely armed for the purpose of maintaining and defending the righteous. If it is understood in this sense, the third verse

---

[1] " Il a *ja* tendu son arc, et l'a dressé *ascavoir pour tirer.*"—*Fr.* " He hath *already* bent his bow and made it ready, *namely, to shoot.*" The words in italics are supplementary, there being nothing for them in the Hebrew text. Calvin, in his French version, has uniformly distinguished supplementary words by printing them in smaller characters.

[2] According to Calvin, the pronoun refers to bow. Fry renders it differently. "It is," says he, " literally *for himself—for his use.* We must keep in view the metaphor of the warrior preparing for action."

[3] " Pour les bailler aux persecuteurs."—*Fr.* " To give them to the persecutors."

[4] " Car il a conceu meschancete, *ou moleste,* mais il enfantera mensonge."—*Fr.* " For he hath conceived wickedness, *or mischief,* but he shall bring forth falsehoods."

[5] This is the view adopted by Hengstenberg in his excellent Commentary on The Psalms. " The apparently coarse manner of expression in our text," says he, " representing God as a warrior equipped with sword and bow, has besides for its foundation the coarseness of sinners, and the weakness of faith on the part of believers, which does not direct itself against the visible danger with pure thoughts of God's controllable agency, but seeks to clothe those thoughts with flesh and blood, and regards the judge as standing over against the sinner, man against man, sword against sword."

[6] " Ne cesse de me poursuyvre."—*Fr.* "Do not cease from pursuing me."

is to be considered as a statement of the cause why God will thus equip himself with armour, namely, because the ungodly, in conceiving all kinds of mischief, in travailing to bring forth wickedness, and in at length bringing forth deceit and falsehood, directly assail God, and openly make war upon him. But, in my judgment, those who read these two verses in one continued sentence, give a more accurate interpretation. I am not, however, satisfied that even they fully bring out the meaning of the Psalmist. David, I have no doubt, by relating the dreadful attempts of his enemies against him, intended thereby to illustrate more highly the grace of God; for when these malicious men, strengthened by powerful military forces, and abundantly provided with armour, furiously rushed upon him in the full expectation of destroying him, who would not have said that it was all over with him? Moreover, there is implied in the words a kind of irony, when he pretends to be afraid of their putting him to death. They mean the same thing as if he had said, "If my enemy do not alter his purpose, or turn his fury and his strength in another direction, who can preserve me from perishing by his hands? He has an abundant supply of arms, and he is endeavouring, by all methods, to accomplish my death."

But Saul is the person of whom he particularly speaks, and therefore he says, *he hath made fit his arrows for the persecutors.* This implies, that Saul had many agents in readiness who would willingly put forth their utmost efforts in seeking to destroy David. The design of the prophet, therefore, was to magnify the greatness of the grace of God, by showing the greatness of the danger from which he had been delivered by him.[1] Moreover, when it is here said, *if he do not return, returning* does not signify repentance and amendment in David's enemy, but only a change of will and purpose, as if he had said, "It is in the power of my enemy to do whatever his fancy may suggest."[2] Whence it appears the more clearly, how

---

[1] "Duquel il avoit este delivré par luy."—*Fr.*

[2] "Au reste, quand il est yci parlé *de se retourner,* ce n'est pas pour signifier ce que nous appelons repentance et amendement en son ennemi,

wonderful the change was which suddenly followed contrary all expectation. When he says that Saul had *prepared the instruments of death for his bow*, he intimates that he was driving after no ordinary thing, but was fully determined to wound to death the man whom he shot at. Some, referring the Hebrew word דולקים, *doulekim*, which we have rendered *persecutors*, to *arrows*, have rendered it *burning*,[1] because it has also this signification;[2] but the translation which I have given is the more appropriate. David complains that he had reason to be afraid, not only of one man, but of a great multitude, inasmuch as Saul had armed a powerful body of men to pursue and persecute a poor fugitive.

14. *Behold, he shall travail.* David has hitherto shown how great and formidable the danger was which was near him. In this verse, laughing to scorn the presumptuous and foolish attempts of Saul, and his magnificent preparations, he declares that they had failed of accomplishing their object.[3] By the demonstrative adverb *Behold*, he enhances the wonder, inasmuch as such a result fell out, on his part altogether unlooked for. *Behold*, says he, *after he has travailed to bring forth wickedness, like as he had conceived mischief*, at length

---

mais tant seulement une volonte et deliberation diverse; comme s'il dit qu'il estoit en la puissance de l'ennemi de parfaire tout ce qui luy venoit en la fantasie."—*Fr.*

[1] Those who adopt this rendering, support it from the reading of the Septuagint, Vulgate, and Syriac versions, although the Chaldee version reads *persecuting*; and they generally view the 12th and 13th verses as a representation of God under the image of a warrior ready to shoot his flaming, burning, fiery arrows, against the object to which he is opposed. "I read, דולקים, *urentes, inflammatos*; the arrows of the Almighty, (Deut. xxxii. 24.) Languishments of famine, the burnings of the carbuncle, and the bitter pestilence. Schultens, (Prov. xxvi. 23.) Lightnings are also called God's arrows, (Psal. xviii. 15,) and represented as the artillery of heaven."—*Dr Kennicott's note on this place in his Select Passages of the Old Testament.* Hengstenberg takes the same view. His rendering is, *He* [*that is, God*] *makes his arrows burning.* "דלק, *to burn.* In sieges it is customary to wrap round the arrows burning matter, and to shoot them after being kindled."

[2] "Là ou nous avons mis *Persecuteurs* aucuns le rapportans aux *fleches*, traduissent Ardentes; pource que le mot Hebrieu emporte aussi ceste signification."—*Fr.*

[3] "Disant que tout cela est allé en fumee."—*Fr.* "Saying that the whole ended in smoke."

there comes forth only empty wind and vanity, because God frustrated his expectations, and destroyed all these wicked attempts.[1] Iniquity and mischief are here put for every kind of violence and outrage[2] which Saul intended to inflict upon David. Some interpreters think that the order of the words is inverted, because *travailing to bring forth* is put before *conceiving;* but I think that the words have their proper place if you explain them thus: Behold, he shall travail to bring forth wickedness, for he hath conceived mischief; that is to say, as he long ago devised with himself my destruction, so he will do his utmost to put his design into execution. David afterwards adds, *he hath brought forth falsehood.* This implies that Saul had been disappointed in his expectation; as Isaiah, (ch. xxvi. 18,) in like manner, speaks of unbelievers " bringing forth wind," when their success does not correspond to their wicked and presumptuous attempts. As often, therefore, as we see the ungodly secretly plotting our ruin, let us remember that they speak falsehood to themselves; in other words, deceive themselves, and shall fail in accomplishing what they devise in their hearts.[3] If, however, we do not perceive that they are disappointed in their designs until they are about to be brought forth, let us not be cast down, but bear it with a spirit of patient submission to the will and providence of God.

15. *He hath digged a pit, and hollowed it out;*[4] *and he hath fallen into the ditch which he hath made.*
16. *His wickedness shall return upon his own head, and his violence shall descend upon his own crown.*

Here David says not only that their wicked devices were without success, but that, by the wonderful providence of

---

[1] " Pource que Dieu l'a frustré de son attente et renverse toutes ces meschantes entreprises."—*Fr.*

[2] " Pour toutes violences et outrages."—*Fr.*

[3] " C'est a dire, se deçoyvent et ne viendront à bout de ce qu'ils couvent en leurs cœurs."—*Fr.*

[4] Fry, from a comparison of the Hebrew word which Calvin renders *hollowed it out,* with the cognate Arabic word, supposes that it means " dug it over, so as to cover and hide it." The imagery is taken from the common method of catching lions and other wild beasts in the east, by

God, the result was the very opposite of what had been contemplated. He sets this forth in the first place metaphorically, by employing the figure of *a pit and a ditch;* and then he expresses the same thing in simple terms without figure, declaring, that the *mischief intended for others returned upon the head of him who had devised it.* There is no doubt that it was a common proverb among the Jews, He who hath digged a pit falleth into it; which they quoted when they meant to say, that wicked and crafty men are caught in the snares and traps which they have set for others, or that the contrivers of the ruin of others perish by their own devices.[1] There is a twofold use of this doctrine: In the first place, however skilled in craft our enemies may be, and whatever means of doing mischief they may have, we must nevertheless look for the issue which God here promises, that they shall fall by their own sword. And this is not a thing which happens by chance; but God, by the secret direction of his own hand, causes the evil which they intend to bring upon the innocent to return upon their own heads. In the second place, If at any time we are instigated by passion to inflict any injury upon our neighbours, or to commit any wickedness, let us remember this principle of retributive justice, which is often acted upon by the divine government, that those who prepare a pit for others are cast into it themselves; and the effect will be, that every one, in proportion as he would consult his own happiness and welfare, will be careful to restrain himself from doing any injury, even the smallest, to another.

---

digging pits on the spots which they were observed to frequent, and covering them slightly over with reeds or small branches of trees. Luther's translation of this clause is precisely the same with that of Calvin; and, in his Commentary on the place, he well explains the force of the expressions of the Psalmist. "See," says he, "how admirably he expresses the hot burning fury of the ungodly, not simply declaring, *he has dug a pit,* but adding to this, *and hollowed it out.* So active and diligent are they to have the pit dug and the hole prepared. They try every thing, they explore every thing, and not satisfied that they have dug a pit, they clear it out and make it deep, as deep as they possibly can, that they may destroy and subvert the innocent."

[1] "Tomboyent au mal qu'ils avoyent brassé."—*Fr.* "Fall into the destruction which they had contrived."

17. *I will praise Jehovah according to his righteousness ; and I will sing to the name of Jehovah, Most High.*

As the design of God in the deliverances which he vouchsafes to his servants is, that they may render to him in return the sacrifices of praise, David here promises that he will gratefully acknowledge the deliverance which he had received, and at the same time affirms that his preservation from death was the undoubted and manifest work of God. He could not, with truth, and from the heart, have ascribed to God the praise of his deliverance, if he had not been fully persuaded that he had been preserved otherwise than by the power of man. He, therefore, not only promises to exercise the gratitude which was due to his deliverer, but he confirms in one word what he has rehearsed throughout the psalm, that he is indebted for his life to the grace of God, who had not suffered Saul to take it from him. *The righteousness of God* is here to be understood of his faithfulness, which he makes good to his servants in defending and preserving their lives. God does not shut up or conceal his righteousness from our view in the secret recesses of his own mind, but manifests it for our advantage when he defends us against all wrongful violence, delivers us from oppression, and preserves us in safety, although wicked men make war upon us and persecute us.

PSALM VIII.

David, reflecting upon God's fatherly beneficence towards mankind, is not content with simply giving thanks for it, but is enraptured by the contemplation of it.

¶ To the chief musician upon Hagittith. A song of David.

1. *O Jehovah[1] our Lord, how wonderful is thy name in all the earth, to set[2] thy glory above the heavens!*

WHETHER גִּתִּית, *Gittith*, signifies a musical instrument or some particular tune, or the beginning of some famous and well-known song, I do not take upon me to determine. Those who think that the psalm is so called because it was composed in the city of Gath, give a strained and far-fetched explanation of the matter. Of the other three opinions, of which I have spoken, it is not of much importance which is adopted. The principal thing to be attended to is what the psalm itself contains, and what is the design of it. David, it is true, sets before his eyes the wonderful power and glory of God in the creation and government of the material universe; but he only slightly glances at this subject, as it were, in passing, and insists principally on the theme of God's infinite goodness towards us. There is presented to us in the whole order of nature, the most abundant matter for showing forth the glory of God, but, as we are unquestionably more powerfully affected with what we ourselves experience, David here, with great propriety, expressly celebrates the special favour which God manifests towards mankind; for this, of all the subjects which come under our contemplation, is the brightest mirror in which we can be-

---

[1] This first word is the incommunicable name of God; the next word, אֲדֹנֵנוּ, *Adonenu, our Lord*, is derived from the root דן, *dan*, which signifies *to rule, to judge, to support.*

[2] " Pourceque tu as mis."—*Fr.* " Because thou hast set." " Ou, qui as mis, ou que de mettre."—*Fr. Marg.* " Or, who hast set, or even to set."

hold his glory. It is, however, strange why he begins the psalm with an exclamation, when the usual way is first to give an account of a thing, and then to magnify its greatness and excellence. But if we remember what is said in other passages of Scripture, respecting the impossibility of expressing in words the works of God, we will not be surprised that David, by this exclamation, acknowledges himself unequal to the task of recounting them. David, therefore, when reflecting on the incomprehensible goodness which God has been graciously pleased to bestow on the human race, and feeling all his thoughts and senses swallowed up, and overwhelmed in the contemplation, exclaims that it is a subject worthy of admiration, because it cannot be set forth in words.[1] Besides, the Holy Spirit, who directed David's tongue, doubtless intended, by his instrumentality, to awaken men from the torpor and indifference which is common to them, so that they may not content themselves with celebrating the infinite love of God and the innumerable benefits which they receive at his hand, in their sparing and frigid manner, but may rather apply their whole hearts to this holy exercise, and put forth in it their highest efforts. This exclamation of David implies, that when all the faculties of the human mind are exerted to the utmost in meditation on this subject,[2] they yet come far short of it.

The *name* of God, as I explain it, is here to be understood of the knowledge of the character and perfections of God, in so far as he makes himself known to us. I do not approve of the subtle speculations of those who think the name of God means nothing else but God himself. It ought rather to be referred to the works and properties by which he is known, than to his essence. David, therefore, says that the earth is full of the wonderful glory of God, so that the fame or renown thereof not only reaches to the heavens, but ascends far above them. The verb תנה, *tenah*, has been rendered by some in the preterite tense, *hast set*, but in my judgment, those give a more accurate translation who render

---

[1] "Puis que langue ne bouche ne la scauroit exprimer."—*Fr.* "Because neither tongue nor mouth can express it."

[2] "A louer les graces de Dieu."—*Fr.* "In praising the grace of God."

it in the infinitive mood, *to place* or *to set;* because the second clause is just an amplification of the subject of the first; as if he had said, the earth is too small to contain the glory or the wonderful manifestations of the character and perfections of God. According to this view, אשר, *asher*, will not be a relative, but will have the meaning of the expletive or exegetic particle *even,* which we use to explain what has preceded.[1]

2. *Out of the mouth of babes and sucklings thou hast founded thy strength because of the adversaries, that thou mightest put to flight the enemy and avenger.*

He now enters upon the proof of the subject which he had undertaken to discourse upon,[2] declaring, that the providence of God, in order to make itself known to mankind, does not wait till men arrive at the age of maturity, but even from the very dawn of infancy shines forth so brightly as is sufficient to confute all the ungodly, who, through their profane contempt of God, would wish to extinguish his very name.[3]

The opinion of some, who think that מפי, *mephi, out of the mouth,* signifies כפי, *kephi, in the mouth,* cannot be admitted, because it improperly weakens the emphasis which David meant to give to his language and discourse. The meaning, therefore, is, that God, in order to commend his providence, has no need of the powerful eloquence of rhetoricians,[4] nor even of distinct and formed language, because the

---

[1] " Mais vaudra autant comme Que, dont on use pour declarer ce qui a precedé."—*Fr.*

[2] The doctrine proposed to be illustrated in this psalm is the excellence of God's name, or his power, goodness, and other perfections, as manifested in his providence and government of the world; and this the Psalmist states in the first verse. He then proceeds to establish and illustrate this doctrine: 1. From the case of infants; 2. From the starry heavens; and, 3. From God's being mindful of man, and visiting him, notwithstanding his unworthiness, sinfulness, and misery.

[3] " Qui voudroyent que son nom fust totalement aboli de la memoire des hommes."—*Fr.* " Who would wish that his name were totally extinguished from the memory of men."

[4] " Que Dieu pour magnifier et exalter sa providence n'ha pas besoin de la rhetorique et eloquence de grans orateurs."—*Fr.* " That God, in order to magnify and exalt his providence, has no need of the rhetoric and eloquence of great orators."

tongues of infants, although they do not as yet speak, are ready and eloquent enough to celebrate it. But it may be asked, In what sense does he speak of children as the proclaimers of the glory of God? In my judgment, those reason very foolishly who think that this is done when children begin to articulate, because then also the intellectual faculty of the soul shows itself. Granting that they are called babes, or infants, even until they arrive at their seventh year, how can such persons imagine that those who now speak distinctly are still hanging on the breast? Nor is there any more propriety in the opinion of those who say, that the words *for babes and sucklings* are here put allegorically for the faithful, who, being born again by the Spirit of God, no longer retain the old age of the flesh. What need, then, is there to wrest the words of David, when their true meaning is so clear and suitable? He says that babes and sucklings are advocates sufficiently powerful to vindicate the providence of God. Why does he not entrust this business to men, but to show that the tongues of infants, even before they are able to pronounce a single word, speak loudly and distinctly in commendation of God's liberality towards the human race? Whence is it that nourishment is ready for them as soon as they are born, but because God wonderfully changes blood into milk? Whence, also, have they the skill to suck, but because the same God has, by a mysterious instinct, fitted their tongues for doing this? David, therefore, has the best reason for declaring, that although the tongues of all, who have arrived at the age of manhood, should become silent, the speechless mouth of infants is sufficiently able to celebrate the praise of God. And when he not only introduces babes as witnesses and preachers of God's glory, but also attributes *mature strength* to their mouth, the expression is very emphatic. It means the same thing as if he had said, These are invincible champions of God who, when it comes to the conflict, can easily scatter and discomfit the whole host of the wicked despisers of God, and those who have abandoned themselves to impiety.[1]

[1] "Et desconfire toute l'armee des meschans contempteurs de Dieu, et gens adonnez à impiete."—*Fr.*

We should observe against whom he imposes upon infants the office of defending the glory of God, namely, against the hardened despisers of God, who dare to rise up against heaven to make war upon God, as the poets have said, in olden time, of the giants.[1]

Since, therefore, these monsters,[2] with furious violence, pluck up by the roots, and overthrow whatever godliness and the fear of God[3] there is in the world, and through their hardihood endeavour to do violence to heaven itself, David in mockery of them brings into the field of battle against them the mouths of infants, which he says are furnished with armour of sufficient strength, and endued with sufficient fortitude, to lay their intolerable pride[4] in the dust. He, therefore, immediately subjoins, *On account of the adversaries.* God is not under the necessity of making war with great power to overcome the faithful, who willingly hearken to his voice, and manifest a ready obedience, as soon as he gives the smallest intimation of his will. The providence of God, I confess, shines forth principally for the sake of the faithful, because they only have eyes to behold it. But as they show themselves willing to receive instruction, God teaches them with gentleness; while, on the other hand, he arms himself against his enemies, who never submit themselves to him but by constraint. Some take the word *founded* as meaning, that, in the very birth or generation of man, God lays foundations for manifesting his own glory. But this sense is too restricted. I have no doubt that the word is put for *to establish,* as if the prophet had said, God needs not strong military forces to destroy the ungodly; instead of these, the mouths of children are sufficient for his purpose.[5]

To put to flight. Interpreters differ with respect to the

---

[1] " Comme les poëtes ont dit anciennement des geans."—*Fr.*
[2] " Cyclopes."—*Latin version.* " Ces monstres."—*French version.*
[3] " Et crainte de Dieu."—*Fr.*
[4] " Leur orgueil intolerable."—*Fr.*
[5] " Comme si le prophete eust dit que Dieu se sert des bouches des petis enfans, comme d'une puissante armee et bien duite à la guerre et qu'elles luy suffisent pour destruire et exterminer les meschans."—*Fr.* " As if the prophet had said, God makes use of the mouths of little children as of a powerful and well-fitted army, and these suffice him to destroy and exterminate the wicked."

word הִשְׁבִּית, *hashebith*. It properly signifies, *to cause to cease;* for it is in the conjugation *Hiphil* of the neuter verb שָׁבַת, *shabath*, which signifies *to cease.* But it is often taken metaphorically for *to destroy*, or *to reduce to nothing*, because destruction or death brings to an end. Others translate it, *that thou mayest restrain*, as if David meant that they were put to silence, so that they desisted from cursing or reviling God. As, however, there is here a beautiful allusion to a hostile combat, as I have a little before explained, I have preferred the military phrase, *to put to flight.* But it is asked, How does God put to flight his enemies, who, by their impious slanders and detractions, do not cease to strike at, and violently to rush forward to oppose all the proofs of a Divine Providence which daily manifest themselves?[1] I answer, They are not routed or overthrown in respect of their being compelled to become more humble and unassuming; but because, with all their blasphemies and canine barkings, they continue in the state of abasement and confusion to which they have been brought. To express the whole in a few words: so early as the generation or birth of man the splendour of Divine Providence is so apparent, that even infants, who hang upon their mothers' breasts, can bring down to the ground the fury of the enemies of God. Although his enemies may do their utmost, and may even burst with rage a hundred times, it is in vain for them to endeavour to overthrow the strength which manifests itself in the weakness of infancy. A desire of revenge reigns in all unbelievers, while, on the other hand, God governs his own children by the spirit of meekness and benignity:[2] but, according to the scope of the present passage, the prophet applies this epithet, *the avenger*, to the despisers of God, who are not only cruel towards man, but who also burn with frantic rage to make war even against God himself.

I have now discharged the duty of a faithful interpreter in opening up the mind of the prophet. There is only one

---

[1] "Lesquels par leurs mesdisances et detractions plenes de sacrilege ne cessent de heurter et choquer impetueusement encontre tout ce en quoy la providence de Dieu se manifeste journellement."—*Fr.*

[2] "De douceur et benignite."—*Fr.*

difficulty remaining, which is this, that Christ (Matth. xxi. 16) seems to put upon this passage a different meaning, when he applies it to children ten years old. But this difficulty is easily removed. Christ reasons from the greater to the less in this manner: If God has appointed children even in infancy the vindicators of his glory, there is no absurdity in his making them the instruments of showing forth his praise by their tongues after they have arrived at the age of seven years and upwards.

> 3. *When I see thy heavens, the works of thy fingers; the moon and the stars which thou hast arranged:*
> 4. *What is man,*[1] *that thou art mindful of him? and the son of man, that thou visitest him?*[2]

As the Hebrew particle כִּי, *ki*, has often the same meaning as *because* or *for*, and simply affirms a thing, both the Greek and the Latin fathers have generally read the fourth verse as if it were a complete sentence by itself. But it is, doubtless, closely connected with the following verse; and, therefore, the two verses ought to be joined together. The Hebrew word כִּי, *ki*, might be very properly translated into the disjunctive particle, *although*, making the meaning to be this: Although the infinite majesty of God shines forth in the heavenly bodies, and justly keeps the eyes of men fixed on the contemplation of it, yet his glory is beheld in a special manner, in the great favour which he bears to men, and in the goodness which he manifests towards them. This interpretation would not be at variance with the scope of the passage; but I choose rather to follow the generally received opinion. My readers, however, must be careful to mark the design of the Psalmist, which is to enhance, by this comparison, the infinite goodness of God; for it is, indeed, a wonderful thing that the Creator of heaven, whose glory is so surpassingly great as to ravish us with the highest admiration, condescends so far as graciously to take upon him the

---

[1] "*Alors je pense*, Qu'est-ce de l'homme?"—*Fr.* "Then I think, what is man?"
[2] "Ou, as souvenance de luy?"—*Fr. marg.* "Or, art mindful of him?"

care of the human race. That the Psalmist makes this contrast may be inferred from the Hebrew word, אֱנוֹשׁ, *enosh*, which we have rendered *man*, and which expresses the frailty of man rather than any strength or power which he possesses.[1] We see that miserable men, in moving upon the earth, are mingled with the vilest creatures; and, therefore, God, with very good reason, might despise them and reckon them of no account if he were to stand upon the consideration of his own greatness or dignity. The prophet, therefore, speaking interrogatively, abases their condition, intimating that God's wonderful goodness is displayed the more brightly in that so glorious a Creator, whose majesty shines resplendently in the heavens, graciously condescends to adorn a creature so miserable and vile as man is with the greatest glory, and to enrich him with numberless blessings. If he had a mind to exercise his liberality towards any, he was under no necessity of choosing men who are but dust and clay, in order to prefer them above all other creatures, seeing he had a sufficient number in heaven towards whom to show himself liberal.[2] Whoever, therefore, is not astonished and

---

[1] The other phrase by which man is described, בן אדם, *ben Adam*, is literally *the son of Adam*,—man, the son of Adam, and who, like him, is formed of the dust of the ground, as the name *Adam* implies, man, the son of apostate and fallen Adam, and who is depraved and guilty like him. " As before, men are called *Enosh* for their doleful estate by sin, so are they called *Adam* and *sons of Adam*, that is, *earthly*, to put them in mind of their original and end, who were made of *Adamah*, the earth, even of the dust, and to dust shall return again, Gen. ii. 7; iii. 19."—*Ainsworth*. Some are of opinion that this expression, *ben Adam*, means man in his most exalted state, and that it is contrasted with the former, אנוש, *enosh*, which represents man in a frail, weak, and miserable condition. Dr Pye Smith renders the words thus :—
"What is man, that thou art mindful of him?
Even the [noblest] son of man, that thou visitest *him?*"
And adds, in a foot note, " Our language has no single terms to mark the distinction so beautifully expressed by אנוש, *frail, miserable man*, βροτὸς, and אדם, *man at his best estate*, ἀνθρωπος. I have endeavoured to approach the idea by the insertion of an epithet."—*Scripture Testimony to the Messiah*, vol. i. p. 217. Bishop Patrick observes, that " *Ben Adam* and *bene ish*, *the son of man* and *the sons of men*, are phrases which belong in the Scripture language to princes, and sometimes the greatest of princes;" and he explains the phrase, *the son of man*, as here meaning " the greatest of men;" " the greatest prince in the world."—*Preface to his Paraphrase on the Book of Psalms.*

[2] " Veu qu'il avoit assez au ciel envers qui se monstrer liberal."—*Fr.*

deeply affected at this miracle, is more than ungrateful and stupid.

When the Psalmist calls the heavens *God's heavens,* and *the works of his fingers,* he has a reference to the same subject, and intends to illustrate it. How is it that God comes forth from so noble and glorious a part of his works, and stoops down to us, poor worms of the earth, if it is not to magnify and to give a more illustrious manifestation of his goodness? From this, also, we learn, that those are chargeable with a very presumptuous abuse of the goodness of God, who take occasion from it to be proud of the excellence which they possess, as if they had either obtained it by their own skill, or as if they possessed it on account of their own merit; whereas their origin should rather remind them that it has been gratuitously conferred upon those who are otherwise vile and contemptible creatures, and utterly unworthy of receiving any good from God. Whatever estimable quality, therefore, we see in ourselves, let it stir us up to celebrate the free and undeserved goodness of God in bestowing it upon us.

The verb, at the close of the third verse, which others translate *to prepare,* or *to found,* or *to establish,* I have thought proper to render *to arrange;* for the Psalmist seems to have a reference to the very beautiful order by which God has so appropriately distinguished the position of the stars, and daily regulates their course. When it is said, *God is mindful of man,* it signifies the same thing as that he bears towards him a fatherly love, defends and cherishes him, and extends his providence towards him. Almost all interpreters render פקד, *pakad,* the last word of this verse, *to visit;* and I am unwilling to differ from them, since this sense suits the passage very well. But as it sometimes signifies *to remember,* and as we will often find in the Psalms the repetition of the same thought in different words, it may here be very properly translated *to remember;* as if David had said, This is a marvellous thing, that God thinks upon men, and remembers them continually.

5. For[1] thou hast made him little lower than God,[2] and hast crowned him with glory and honour.
6. Thou hast set him over the works of thy hands : Thou hast put all things under his feet.

5. *Thou hast made him little lower.* The Hebrew copulative כִּי, *ki,* I have no doubt, ought to be translated into the causal particle *for,* seeing the Psalmist confirms what he has just now said concerning the infinite goodness of God towards men, in showing himself near to them, and mindful of them. In the first place, he represents them as adorned with so many honours as to render their condition not far inferior to divine and celestial glory. In the second place, he mentions the external dominion and power which they possess over all creatures, from which it appears how high the degree of dignity is to which God hath exalted them. I have, indeed, no doubt but he intends, by the first,[3] the distinguished endowments which clearly manifest that men were formed after the image of God, and created to the hope of a blessed and immortal life. The reason with which they are endued, and by which they can distinguish between good and evil; the principle of religion which is planted in them; their intercourse with each other, which is preserved from being broken up by certain sacred bonds; the regard to what is becoming, and the sense of shame which guilt awakens in them, as well as their continuing to be governed by laws; all these things are clear indications of pre-eminent and celestial wisdom. David, therefore, not without good reason, exclaims that mankind are adorned with glory and honour. *To be crowned,* is here taken metaphorically, as if David had said, he is clothed and adorned with marks of honour, which are not far removed from the splendour of the divine majesty. The Septuagint render אֱלֹהִים, *Elohim,* by *angels,* of which I do not disapprove, since this name, as is well known, is often given to angels, and I explain the words of David as meaning the same thing as if he had said, that the condition

---

[1] " Ou, Et tu l'as."—*Fr. marg.* " Or, And thou hast."
[2] " Ou, les anges."—*Fr. marg.* " Or, the angels."
[3] " Qu'il n'entende par la premier."—*Fr.*

of men is nothing less than a divine and celestial state. But as the other translation seems more natural, and as it is almost universally adopted by the Jewish interpreters, I have preferred following it. Nor is it any sufficient objection to this view, that the apostle, in his Epistle to the Hebrews, (chap. ii. 7,) quoting this passage, says, *little less than the angels,* and not *than God;*[1] for we know what freedoms the apostles took in quoting texts of Scripture; not, indeed, to wrest them to a meaning different from the true one, but because they reckoned it sufficient to show, by a reference to Scripture, that what they taught was sanctioned by the word of God, although they did not quote the precise words. Accordingly, they never had any hesitation in changing the words, provided the substance of the text remained unchanged.

There is another question which it is more difficult to solve. While the Psalmist here discourses concerning the excellency of men, and describes them, in respect of this, as coming near to God, the apostle applies the passage to the humiliation of Christ. In the first place, we must consider the propriety of applying to the person of Christ what is here spoken concerning all mankind; and, secondly, how we may explain it as referring to Christ's being humbled in his death, when he lay without form or beauty, and as it were disfigured under the reproach and curse of the cross. What some say, that what is true of the members may be properly and suitably transferred to the head, might be a sufficient answer to the

---

[1] Certainly the fact that Paul uses the word *angels* instead of *God*, does not prove the inaccuracy of Calvin's rendering. As the Septuagint version was in general use among the Jews in the time of Paul, he very naturally quotes from it just as we do from our English version. And this was sufficient for his purpose. His object was, to answer an objection which the Jews brought against the Christian dispensation, as being inferior to the Mosaic, inasmuch as angels were mediators of the latter, while the mediator or head of the former was in their estimation but a man. This objection he answers from their own Scriptures, and quotes this psalm to show, that Christ, in his human nature, was little inferior to the angels, and that he is exalted far above them in respect of the glory and dominion with which he is crowned. If the apostle had quoted from the Hebrew Scriptures, and used אלהים, *Elohim,* God, meaning the Most High, his argument in support of the dignity of Christ in human nature would have been still stronger.—See *Stuart's Commentary on the Hebrews,* vol. ii. pp. 68-71.

first question; but I go a step farther, for Christ is not only the first begotten of every creature, but also the restorer of mankind. What David here relates belongs properly to the beginning of the creation, when man's nature was perfect.[1] But we know that, by the fall of Adam, all mankind fell from their primeval state of integrity, for by this the image of God was almost entirely effaced from us, and we were also divested of those distinguishing gifts by which we would have been, as it were, elevated to the condition of demigods; in short, from a state of the highest excellence, we were reduced to a condition of wretched and shameful destitution. In consequence of this corruption, the liberality of God, of which David here speaks, ceased, so far, at least, as that it does not at all appear in the brilliancy and splendour in which it was manifested when man was in his unfallen state. True, it is not altogether extinguished; but, alas! how small a portion of it remains amidst the miserable overthrow and ruins of the fall. But as the heavenly Father hath bestowed upon his Son an immeasurable fulness of all blessings, that all of us may draw from this fountain, it follows that whatever God bestows upon us by him belongs of right to him in the highest degree; yea, he himself is the living image of God, according to which we must be renewed, upon which depends our participation of the invaluable blessings which are here spoken of. If any person object that David first put the question, What is man? because God has so abundantly poured forth his favour upon a creature so miserable, contemptible, and worthless; but that there is no cause for such admiration of God's favour for Christ, who is not an ordinary man, but the only begotten Son of God. The answer is easy, and it is this: What was bestowed upon Christ's human nature was a free gift; nay, more, the fact that a mortal man, and the son of Adam, is the only Son of God, and the Lord of glory, and the head of angels, affords a bright illustration of the mercy of God. At the same time, it is to be observed, that whatever gifts he has received

---

[1] "Lorsque la nature de l'humain n'estoit point encore corrompue."— *Fr.* "When the nature of man was not yet corrupted."

ought to be considered as proceeding from the free grace of God, so much the more for this reason, that they are intended principally to be conferred upon us. His excellence and heavenly dignity, therefore, are extended to us also, seeing it is for our sake he is enriched with them.

What the apostle therefore says in that passage concerning the abasement of Christ for a short time, is not intended by him as an explanation of this text; but for the purpose of enriching and illustrating the subject on which he is discoursing, he introduces and accommodates to it what had been spoken in a different sense. The same apostle did not hesitate, in Rom. x. 6, in the same manner to enrich and to employ, in a sense different from their original one, the words of Moses in Deut. xxx. 12 : " Who shall go up for us to heaven and bring it to us, that we may hear it and do it?" &c. The apostle, therefore, in quoting this psalm, had not so much an eye to what David meant; but making an allusion to these words, *Thou hast made him a little lower;* and again, *Thou hast crowned him with honour,* he applies this diminution to the death of Christ, and the glory and honour to his resurrection.[1] A similar account may be given of Paul's declaration in Eph. iv. 8, in which he does not so much explain the meaning of the text, (Ps. lxviii. 18,) as he devoutly applies it, by way of accommodation, to the person of Christ.

6. *Thou hast set him over.* David now comes to the second point, which I have just now spoken of, namely, that from the dominion over all things which God has conferred upon men, it is evident how great is the love which he has borne towards them, and how much account he has made of them. As he does not stand in need of any thing himself, he has destined all the riches, both of heaven and earth, for their use. It is certainly a singular honour, and one which cannot be sufficiently estimated, that mortal man, as the representative of God, has dominion over the world, as if it pertained

---

[1] " Tu l'as fait un peu moindre ; puis Tu l'as couronné d'honneur, il approprie ceste diminution à la mort de Christ, et la gloire et honneur a la resurrection."—*Fr.*

to him by right, and that to whatever quarter he turns his eyes, he sees nothing wanting which may contribute to the convenience and happiness of his life. As this passage is quoted by Paul in his First Epistle to the Corinthians, (ch. xv. 27,) where he discourses concerning the spiritual kingdom of Christ, some may object and say, that the meaning he puts upon it is very different from the sense which I have given. But it is easy to answer this objection, and the answer which I give to it is this, That generally the whole order of this world is arranged and established for the purpose of conducing to the comfort and happiness of men. In what way the passage may properly apply to Christ alone, I have already declared a little before. The only thing which now remains to be considered is, how far this declaration extends —that all things are subjected to men. Now, there is no doubt, that if there is any thing in heaven or on earth which is opposed to men, the beautiful order which God had established in the world at the beginning is now thrown into confusion. The consequence of this is, that mankind, after they were ruined by the fall of Adam, were not only deprived of so distinguished and honourable an estate, and dispossessed of their former dominion, but are also held captive under a degrading and ignominious bondage. Christ, it is true, is the lawful heir of heaven and earth, by whom the faithful recover what they had lost in Adam; but he has not as yet actually entered upon the full possession of his empire and dominion. Whence the apostle concludes, that what is here said by David[1] will not be perfectly accomplished until death be abolished. Accordingly, the apostle reasons in this manner: " If all things are subdued to Christ, nothing ought to stand in opposition to his people. But we see death still exercising his tyranny against them. It follows then, that there remains the hope of a better state than the present." Now, this flows from the principle of which I have spoken, that the world was originally created for this end, that every part of it should tend to the happiness of man as its great object. In another part of his writ-

---

[1] " Que ce qui est yci dit par David."—*Fr.*

ings, the apostle argues on the same principle, when, in order to prove that we must all stand at the last day before the judgment-seat of Christ, he brings forward the following passage, "Unto me every knee shall bow," (Rom. xiv. 10.) In this syllogism, what Logicians call the minor proposition must be supplied,[1] namely, that there are still too many who proudly and obstinately cast off his yoke, and are averse to bow the knee in token of their submission to him.

7. *All sheep and oxen, and also the beasts of the fields;*
8. *The birds of the air, and the fish of the sea, and whatsoever passeth through the paths of the seas.*
9. *O Jehovah, our Lord, how wonderful is thy name in all the earth!*

The preceding question, with respect to the extent of man's dominion over the works of God, seems not yet to be fully answered. If the prophet here declares, by way of exposition, to what extent God has put all things in subjection to us, this subjection, it seems, must be restricted to what contributes to the temporal comfort and convenience of man while he continues in this world. To this difficulty I answer, That the Psalmist does not intend in these verses to give a complete enumeration of all the things which are subjected to man's dominion, and of which he had spoken generally in the preceding verse, but he brings forward an example of this subjection only in one part or particular; yea, he has especially chosen that part which affords a clear and manifest evidence of the truth he intended to establish, even to those whose minds are uncultivated and slow of apprehension. There is no man of a mind so dull and stupid but may see, if he will be at the trouble to open his eyes, that it is by the wonderful providence of God that horses and oxen yield their service to men,—that sheep produce wool to clothe them,—and that all sorts of animals supply them with food for their nourishment and support, even from their own flesh. And the more that this dominion is apparent, the more ought we to

---

[1] "Car il faut suppleer en ceste argument la proposition que les Dialecticiens appellent."—*Fr.*

be affected with a sense of the goodness and grace of our God as often as we either eat food, or enjoy any of the other comforts of life. We are, therefore, not to understand David as meaning that it is a proof that man is invested with dominion over *all* the works of God, because he clothes himself with the wool and the skins of beasts, because he lives upon their flesh, and because he employs their labour for his own advantage; for this would be inconclusive reasoning. He only brings forward this as an example, and as a mirror in which we may behold and contemplate the dominion over the works of his hands, with which God has honoured man. The sum is this: God, in creating man, gave a demonstration of his infinite grace and more than fatherly love towards him, which ought justly to strike us with amazement; and although, by the fall of man, that happy condition has been almost entirely ruined, yet there is still in him some remains of the liberality which God then displayed towards him, which should suffice to fill us with admiration. In this mournful and wretched overthrow, it is true, the legitimate order which God originally established no longer shines forth, but the faithful whom God gathers to himself, under Christ their head, enjoy so much of the fragments of the good things which they lost in Adam, as may furnish them with abundant matter of wonder at the singularly gracious manner in which God deals with them. David here confines his attention to God's temporal benefits, but it is our duty to rise higher, and to contemplate the invaluable treasures of the kingdom of heaven which he has unfolded in Christ, and all the gifts which belong to the spiritual life, that by reflecting upon these our hearts may be inflamed with love to God, that we may be stirred up to the practice of godliness, and that we may not suffer ourselves to become slothful and remiss in celebrating his praises.

PSALM IX.

David, after having recounted the former victories which he had gained, and exalted in lofty strains the grace and power of God in their happy issue, now again, when he sees new enemies and dangers rising up, implores the protection of the same God by whom he had before been delivered, and beseeches him to overthrow the pride of his enemies.

¶ To the chief musician Almuth Laben. A Psalm of David.

This inscription is variously explained. Some translate it, *Upon the death of Laben*, and are of opinion that he was one of the chief captains of David's enemies. Others are inclined to think it was rather a fictitious name, and that Goliath is the person spoken of in this psalm. According to others, it was a musical instrument. But to me it seems a more correct, or, at least, (as I am accustomed to speak when the matter is obscure,[1]) a more probable opinion, that it was the beginning of some well-known song, to the tune of which the psalm was composed. The disputes of interpreters as to what victory David here celebrates, in my judgment, are unnecessary, and serve no good purpose. In the first place, their opinion that it is a song of victory, in which David simply gives thanks to God, is confuted, and shown to be erroneous from the scope of the psalm. The greater part is indeed occupied in singing the praises of God, but the whole ought to be considered as a prayer; in which, for the purpose of elevating his mind to confidence in God, he calls to his remembrance, according to his usual manner, by what wonderful displays of the power of God he had formerly been delivered from the violence and power of his enemies. It is therefore a mistake to limit to one victory this thanksgiving, in which he intended to comprehend many deliverances.

1. *I will praise Jehovah with my whole heart ; I will tell of thy marvellous works.*
2. *I will rejoice and exult[2] in thee ; yea, I will celebrate in songs thy name, O thou Most High.*

---

[1] "Comme on a accoustumè de parler quand la chose est obscure."—*Fr.*
[2] Or, leap for joy. This is the precise meaning of the Hebrew word אֶעֶלְצָה, *E-elisah.* The Septuagint render it ἀγαλλιάσομαι, which means the same thing.

3. *When my enemies are turned back, they fall down, and are put to flight*[1] *at thy presence.*

1. *I will praise the Lord.* David begins the psalm in this way, to induce God to succour him in the calamities with which he was now afflicted. As God continues his favour towards his own people without intermission, all the good he has hitherto done to us should serve to inspire us with confidence and hope, that he will be gracious and merciful to us in the time to come.[2] There is, indeed, in these words a profession of gratitude for the favours which he has received from God;[3] but, in remembering his past mercies, he encourages himself to expect succour and aid in future emergencies; and by this means he opens the gate of prayer. *The whole heart* is taken for an upright or sincere heart, which is opposed to a double heart. Thus he distinguishes himself not only from gross hypocrites, who praise God only with their lips outwardly, without having their hearts in any way affected, but also acknowledges that whatever he had hitherto done which was commendable, proceeded entirely from the pure grace of God. Even irreligious men, I admit, when they have obtained some memorable victory, are ashamed to defraud God of the praise which is due to him; but we see that as soon as they have uttered a single expression in acknowledgment of the assistance God has afforded them, they immediately begin to boast loudly, and to sing triumphs in honour of their own valour, as if they were under no obligations whatever to God. In short, it is a piece of pure mockery when they profess that their exploits have been done by the help of God; for, after having made oblation to Him, they sacrifice to their own counsels, skill, courage, and resources. Observe how the prophet Habakkuk, under the person of one presumptuous king, wisely reproves the ambition which is common to all, (Hab. i. 16.) Yea,

---

[1] " Et sont ruinez devant ta face."—*Fr.* " And are overthrown before thy face."
[2] " Doit servir pour nous asseurer et faire esperer qu'il nous sera propice et debonnaire à l'advenir."—*Fr.*
[3] " De la faveur qu'il a receuë de Dieu."—*Fr.*

we see that the famous generals of antiquity, who, upon returning victorious from some battle, desired public and solemn thanksgivings[1] to be decreed in their name to the gods, thought of nothing less than of doing honour to their false deities; but only abused their names under a false pretence, in order thereby to obtain an opportunity of indulging in vain boasting, that their own superior prowess might be acknowledged.[2] David, therefore, with good reason, affirms that he is unlike the children of this world, whose hypocrisy or fraud is discovered by the wicked and dishonest distribution which they make between God and themselves,[3] arrogating to themselves the greater part of the praise which they pretended to ascribe to God. He praised God with his whole heart, which they did not; for certainly it is not praising God with the whole heart when a mortal man dares to appropriate the smallest portion of the glory which God claims for himself. God cannot bear with seeing his glory appropriated by the creature in even the smallest degree, so intolerable to him is the sacrilegious arrogance of those who, by praising themselves, obscure his glory as far as they can.

I will tell of all thy marvellous works. Here David confirms what I have already said, that he does not treat in this psalm of one victory or one deliverance only; for he proposes to himself in general all the miracles which God had wrought in his behalf, as subjects of meditation. He applies the term *marvellous* not to all the benefits which he had received from God, but to those more signal and memorable deliverances in which was exhibited a bright and striking manifestation of the divine power. God would have us to acknowledge him as the author of all our blessings; but on some of his gifts he has engraven more evident marks in order the more effectually to awaken our senses, which are otherwise as if asleep or dead. David's language, therefore, is an acknowledgment that he was preserved of God, not by ordinary means, but by the special power of God, which was conspicuously displayed in this matter; inasmuch as he had

---

[1] " Processions."—*Fr.*
[2] " Afin que leurs belles prouesses veissent en cognoissance."—*Fr.*
[3] " Qu'ils font entre Dieu et eux."—*Fr.*

stretched forth his hand in a miraculous manner, and above the common and usual way.

2. *I will rejoice and exult in thee.* Observe how the faithful praise God sincerely and without hypocrisy, when they do not rest on themselves for happiness, and are not intoxicated with foolish and carnal presumption, but rejoice in God alone; which is nothing else than to seek the matter of their joy from the favour of God, and from no other source, since in it perfect happiness consists. *I will rejoice in thee.* We ought to consider how great is the difference and opposition between the character of the joy which men endeavour to find in themselves, and the character of the joy which they seek in God. David, the more forcibly to express how he renounces every thing which may keep hold of or occupy him with vain delight, adds the word *exult,* by which he means that he finds in God a full and an overflowing abundance of joy, so that he is not under the necessity of seeking even the smallest drop in any other quarter. Moreover, it is of importance to remember what I have previously observed, that David sets before himself the testimonies of the divine goodness which he had formerly experienced, in order to encourage himself with the more alacrity to lay open his heart[1] to God, and to present his prayers before him. He who begins his prayer by affirming that God is the great source and object of his joy, fortifies himself before-hand with the strongest confidence, in presenting his supplications to the hearer of prayer.

3. *While my enemies are turned back.* In these words he assigns the reason why he undertakes to sing the praises of God, namely, because he acknowledges that his frequent victories had been achieved, not by his own power, nor by the power of his soldiers, but by the free favour of God. In the first part of the verse he narrates historically how his enemies were discomfited or put to flight; and then he adds, what faith alone could enable him to say, that this did not

---

[1] " Afin de descouvrir son cœur a Dieu plus alaigrement."—*Fr.*

take place by the power of man or by chance, but because God fought for him,[1] and stood against them in the battle. He says, *they fall,*[2] *and are put to flight* AT THY PRESENCE. David therefore acted wisely, when, upon seeing his enemies turn their backs, he lifted up the eyes of his mind to God, in order to perceive that victory flowed to him from no other source than from the secret and incomprehensible aid of God. And, doubtless, it is He only who guides the simple by the spirit of wisdom, while he inflicts madness on the crafty, and strikes them with amazement,—who inspires with courage the faint and timid, while he causes the boldest to tremble with fear,—who restores to the feeble their strength, while he reduces the strong to weakness,—who upholds the faint-hearted by his power, while he makes the sword to fall from the hands of the valiant;—and, finally, who brings the battle to a prosperous or disastrous issue, just as he pleases. When, therefore, we see our enemies overthrown, we must beware of limiting our view to what is visible to the eye of sense, like ungodly men, who, while they see with their bodily eyes, are yet blind; but let us instantly call to our remembrance this truth, that when our enemies turn back, they are put to flight by the presence of the Lord.[3] The verbs, *fall* and *put to flight*, in the Hebrew, are in the future tense, but I have translated them in the present, because David anew presents to his own view the goodness of God which had formerly been manifested towards him.

---

[1] " Mais pource que Dieu a battaillé pour luy."—*Fr.*
[2] The idea implied in the verb כשל, *cashal*, is that of stumbling, and it is here employed in a military sense. In Psalm xxvii. 2, where it is said of David's enemies, " they stumbled and fell;" this is the verb used for *stumbled*. The idea there is not properly that of falling, but of being wounded and weakened by the stumbling-blocks in the way, previous to falling. The word כשל, *cashal*, has been viewed as having the same meaning in the passage before us. "It refers," says Hammond, " to those that either faint in a march or are wounded in a battle, or especially that in flight meet with galling traps in their way, and so are galled and lamed, rendered unable to go forward, and so fall, and become liable to all the ill chances of pursuits, and as here are overtaken and perish in the fall."
[3] " C'est la face de Dieu qui les poursuit."—*Fr.* " It is the face of God which pursues them."

4. *For thou hast maintained my right and my cause; thou sattest upon the throne a righteous judge.*[1]

5. *Thou hast rebuked the nations; thou hast destroyed the wicked; thou hast blotted out their name for ever and ever.*

The Psalmist proceeds a step farther in the 4th verse, declaring that God stretched forth his hand to give him succour, because he was unrighteously afflicted by his enemies. And surely if we desire to be favoured with the assistance of God, we ought to see to it that we fight under his standard. David, therefore, calls him *a judge of righteousness*, or, which is the same thing, *a righteous judge;* as if he had said, God has acted towards me according to his ordinary manner and constant principle of acting, for it is his usual way to undertake the defence of good causes. I am more inclined to render the words, *Thou sittest a just judge*, than to render them, *O just judge, thou sittest*,[2] because the form of expression, according to the first reading, is more emphatic. The import of it is this: God at length has assumed the character of judge, and is gone up into his judgment-seat to execute the office of judge. On this account he glories in having law and right on his side, and declares that God was the maintainer of his right and cause. What follows in the next verse, *Thou hast destroyed* [or *discomfited*] *the wicked*, belongs also to the same subject. When he beholds his enemies overthrown, he does not rejoice in their destruction, considered simply in itself; but in condemning them on account of their unrighteousness, he says that they have received the punishment which they deserved. Under the name of *nations* he means, that it was not a small number of ungodly persons who were destroyed, but great armies, yea, even all who had risen up against him from different quarters. And the goodness of God shines forth the brighter in this, that, on account of the favour which he bare to one of his servants, he spared not even whole nations. When he says, *Thou hast blotted out their name for ever*, it may be understood as meaning, that they were destroyed without any hope of ever

---

[1] "Ou pour juger justement."—*Fr. marg.* " Or to judge righteously."
[2] " J'ay mieux aimé traduire, Tu t'es assis juste juge ; que, O juste juge tu t'es assis."—*Fr.*

being able to rise again, and devoted to everlasting shame. We could not otherwise discern how God buries the name of the ungodly with themselves, did we not hear him declare that the memory of the righteous shall be for ever blessed, (Prov. x. 7.)

> 6. *O thou enemy, desolations are come to an end for ever; and thou hast destroyed* [or *demolished* [1]] *cities; their memory has perished with them.*
> 7. *And Jehovah sitteth for ever, he hath prepared his throne for judgment.*
> 8. *And he shall judge the world in righteousness, he shall judge the nations in uprightness.*

6. *O thou enemy, desolations are come to an end for ever.* This sixth verse is explained in different ways. Some read it interrogatively, viewing the letter ה as a mark of interrogation, as if David, addressing his discourse to his enemies, asked whether they had completed their work of devastation, even as they had resolved to destroy every thing; for the verb תמם, *tamam,* signifies sometimes *to complete,* and sometimes *to put an end to any thing.* And if we here take it in this sense, David, in the language of sarcasm or irony, rebukes the foolish confidence of his enemies. Others, reading the verse without any interrogation, make the irony still more evident, and think that David describes, in these three verses, a twofold state of matters; that, in the first place, (verse 6,) he introduces his enemies persecuting him with savage violence, and persevering with determined obstinacy in their cruelty, so that it seemed to be their fixed purpose never to desist until the kingdom of David should be utterly destroyed; and that, in the second place, (verses 7, 8,) he represents God as seated on his judgment-seat, directly over against them, to repress their outrageous attempts. If this sense is admitted, the copulative, in the beginning of the seventh verse, which we have translated *and,* must be rendered by the adversative particle *but,* in this way: Thou, O enemy, didst seek after nothing except slaughter and the

---

[1] "*Demolished.* The Hebrew word expresses the tearing up of the foundations of the buildings."—*Horsley.*

destruction of cities; but, at length, God has shown that he sits in heaven on his throne as judge, to put into proper order the things which are in confusion on the earth. According to others, David gives thanks to God, because, when the ungodly were fully determined to spread universal ruin around them, he put an end to their devastations. Others understand the words in a more restricted sense, as meaning that the desolations of the ungodly were completed, because God, in his just judgment, had made to fall upon their own heads the calamities and ruin which they had devised against David. According to others, David, in the 6th verse, complains that God had, for a long time, silently suffered the miserable devastation of his people, so that the ungodly, being left unchecked, wasted and destroyed all things according to their pleasure; and in the seventh verse, they think he subjoins for his consolation that God, notwithstanding, presides over human affairs. I have no objection to the view, that there is first described ironically how dreadful the power of the enemy was, when they put forth their highest efforts; and next, that there is set in opposition to it the judgment of God, which suddenly brought their proceedings to an abrupt termination, contrary to their expectation. They anticipated no such issue; for we know that the ungodly, although they may not presume openly to deprive God of his authority and dominion, yet run headlong to every excess of wickedness, not less boldly than if he were bound with fetters.[1] We have taken notice of an almost similar manner of speaking in a preceding psalm, (vii. 13.)

This contrast between the power of the enemies of God and his people, and the work of God in breaking up their proceedings, very well illustrates the wonderful character of the succour which he granted to his people. The ungodly had set to themselves no limit in the work of doing mischief, save in the utter destruction of all things, and at the commencement complete destruction seemed to be at hand; but when things were in this state of confusion, God seasonably made

[1] "Que s'il avoit les pieds et mains liees."—*Fr.* "Than if he were bound hand and foot."

his appearance for the help of his people.[1] As often, therefore, as nothing but destruction presents itself to our view, to whatever side we may turn,[2] let us remember to lift up our eyes to the heavenly throne, whence God beholds all that is done here below. In the world our affairs may have been brought to such an extremity, that there is no longer hope in regard to them; but the shield with which we ought to repel all the temptations by which we are assailed is this, that God, nevertheless, sits Judge in heaven. Yea, when he seems to take no notice of us, and does not immediately remedy the evils which we suffer, it becomes us to realise by faith his secret providence. The Psalmist says, in the first place, *God sitteth for ever*, by which he means, that however high the violence of men may be carried, and although their fury may burst forth without measure, they can never drag God from his seat. He farther means by this expression, that it is impossible for God to abdicate the office and authority of judge; a truth which he expresses more clearly in the second clause of the verse, *He hath prepared his throne for judgment*, in which he declares that God reigns not only for the purpose of making his majesty and glory surpassingly great, but also for the purpose of governing the world in righteousness.

8. *And he shall judge the world in righteousness.* As David has just now testified, that the power of God is not inactive, so that he dwells in heaven only indulging himself in pleasures; but that it is a constantly operating power which he exercises in preserving his authority, and governing the world in righteousness and equity; so in this verse he adds the use of this doctrine, which is this, that the power of God is not shut up in heaven, but manifests itself in succouring men. The true doctrine on this subject is not, like Epicurus, to imagine that God is a being wholly devoted to ease and pleasures, and who, satisfied with himself alone, has no care whatever about mankind, but to place him on the throne of power and equity, so that we may be fully persuaded, that

---

[1] "Dieu s'est monstré bien à propos pour secourir les siens."—*Fr.*
[2] "De quelque costé que nous-nous scachions tourner."—*Fr.*

although he does not immediately succour those who are unrighteously oppressed, yet there is not a moment in which he ceases to take a deep interest in them. And when he seems for a time to take no notice of things, the conclusion to which we should come most assuredly is, not that he deserts his office, but that he wishes hereby to exercise the patience of his people, and that, therefore, we should wait the issue in patience, and with tranquillity of mind. The demonstrative pronoun *He*, in my opinion, is of great weight. The import of it is, as if David had said, No one can deprive God of his office as Judge of the world, nor prevent him from extending his judgments to all nations. Whence it follows, that he will much more be the judge of his own people. David declares these judgments to be *righteous*, in order to induce us, when we are unrighteously and cruelly molested, to ask assistance from God, in the confident expectation of obtaining it; for since he judges the nations in righteousness, he will not suffer injustice and oppression always to reign with impunity in the world, nor deny his aid to the innocent.

9. *And Jehovah will be a refuge to the poor, and a protection in seasonable times in trouble.*
10. *And they that know thy name will put their trust in thee: for thou forsakest not them that seek thee, O Jehovah.*
11. *Sing unto Jehovah, who dwelleth in Sion, and proclaim his doings among the nations.*
12. *For in requiring blood, he hath remembered it: he hath not forgotten the cry of the afflicted.*

9. *And Jehovah will be a refuge for the poor.* David here furnishes a remedy for the temptation which greatly afflicts the weak, when they see themselves, and those who are like them, abandoned to the will of the ungodly, while God keeps silence.[1] He puts us in mind that God delays his aid, and to outward appearance forsakes his faithful ones, in

---

[1] "Exposez a l'appetit et cruaute des meschans, sans que Dieu face semblant d'en rien veoir ne scavoir."—*Fr.* "Exposed to the desire and cruelty of the wicked, while God seems neither to see nor to know any thing about it."

order at length to succour them at a more convenient season, according to the greatness of their necessity and affliction. From this it follows, that he by no means ceases from the exercise of his office, although he suffer the good and the innocent to be reduced to extreme poverty, and although he exercise them with weeping and lamentations; for by doing this he lights up a lamp to enable them to see his judgments the more clearly. Accordingly, David expressly declares, that God interposes his protection *seasonably* in the afflictions of his people. *The Lord will be a protection to the poor in seasonable times in trouble.* From this we are taught the duty of giving his providence time to make itself at length manifest in the season of need. And if protection by the power of God, and the experience of his fatherly favour, is the greatest blessing which we can receive, let us not feel so uneasy at being accounted poor and miserable before the world, but let this consolatory consideration assuage our grief, that God is not far from us, seeing our afflictions call upon him to come to our aid. Let us also observe, that God is said to be at hand in *seasonable times* when he succours the faithful during their affliction.[1] The Hebrew word בצרה, *batsarah*, which occurs in the end of the 9th verse, is understood by some as if it were the simple word which signifies *defence;* but here they render it metaphorically *distress,* denoting those trying circumstances in which a person is so closely shut up, and reduced to such extremity, that he can find no escape. I, however, think there is more probability in the opinion of those who take ב, the first letter of בצרה, *batsarah,* as a servile letter meaning *in,* which is its ordinary signification.[2] What is here said, then, is, that God assists his own people in the time of need, namely, in affliction, or when they are weighed down with it, for then assistance is most necessary and most useful.

In the tenth verse, the Psalmist teaches us, that when the

---

[1] "Notons aussi que Dieu est dit estre prest en temps opportun quand il subvient aux fideles lors qu'ils sont affligez."—*Fr.*

[2] "*In critical times,* לעתות, *leitoth; in* [*the season of*] *distress,* בצרה, *batsarah.* בצרה *is the substantive* צרה, *under its own preposition* ב, *and is not so well rendered as a genitive following* עתות."—*Horsley.*

Lord delivers the righteous, the fruit which results from it is, that they themselves, and all the rest of the righteous, acquire increasing confidence in his grace; for, unless we are fully persuaded that God exercises a care about men and human affairs, we must necessarily be troubled with constant disquietude. But as most men shut their eyes that they may not see the judgments of God, David restricts this advantage to the faithful alone, and, certainly, where there is no godliness, there is no sense of the works of God. It is also to be observed, that he attributes to the faithful *the knowledge of God;* because from this religion proceeds, whereas it is extinguished through the ignorance and stupidity of men. Many take the *name of God* simply for God himself; but, as I have observed in my remarks on a preceding psalm, I think something more is expressed by this term. As God's essence is hidden and incomprehensible, his name just means his character, so far as he has been pleased to make it known to us. David next explains the ground of this trust in God to be, that he *does not forsake those who seek him.* God is sought in two ways, either by invocation and prayers, or by studying to live a holy and an upright life; and, indeed, the one is always inseparably joined with the other. But as the Psalmist is here treating of the protection of God, on which the safety of the godly depends, *to seek God*, as I understand it, is to betake ourselves to him for help and relief in danger and distress.

11. *Sing unto Jehovah.* David, not contented with giving thanks individually, and on his own account, exhorts the faithful to unite with him in praising God, and to do this not only because it is their duty to stir up one another to this religious exercise, but because the deliverances of which he treats were worthy of being publicly and solemnly celebrated; and this is expressed more clearly in the second clause, where he commands them to be published among the nations. The meaning is, that they are not published or celebrated as they deserve, unless the whole world is filled with the renown of them. To proclaim God's doings among the nations was indeed, as it were, to sing to the deaf; but

by this manner of speaking, David intended to show that the territory of Judea was too narrow to contain the infinite greatness of Jehovah's praises. He gives God this title, *He who dwelleth in Sion,* to distinguish him from all the false gods of the Gentiles. There is in the phrase a tacit comparison between the God who made his covenant with Abraham and Israel, and all the gods who, in every other part of the world except Judea, were worshipped according to the blinded and depraved fancies of men. It is not enough for persons to honour and reverence some deity indiscriminately or at random; they must distinctly yield to the only living and true God the worship which belongs to him, and which he commands. Moreover, as God had particularly chosen Sion as the place where his name might be called upon, David very properly assigns it to him as his peculiar dwelling-place, not that it is lawful to attempt to shut up, in any particular place, Him whom "the heaven of heavens cannot contain," (1 Kings viii.;) but because, as we shall afterwards see, (Ps. cxxxii. 12,) he had promised to make it his rest for ever. David did not, according to his own fancy, assign God a dwelling-place there; but he understood, by a revelation from heaven, that such was the pleasure of God himself, as Moses had often predicted, (Deut. xii.) This goes far to prove what I have said before, that this psalm was not composed upon the occasion of David's victory over Goliath; for it was only towards the close of David's reign that the ark of the covenant was removed to Sion according to the commandment of God. The conjecture of some that David spake by the Spirit of prophecy of the residence of the ark on Sion, as a future event, appears to me to be unnatural and forced. Farther, we see that the holy fathers, when they resorted to Sion to offer sacrifices to God, did not act merely according to the suggestion of their own minds; but what they did proceeded from faith in the word of God, and was done in obedience to his command; and they were, therefore, approved of by him for their religious service. Whence it follows, that there is no ground whatever to make use of their example as an argument or excuse for the religious observances which superstitious men have, by their own fancy, invented for themselves. Besides, it was not enough for the faithful, in those days, to depend upon the word of God, and to engage in those ceremonial services which he required, unless, aided by external symbols, they elevated their minds above these, and yielded to God spiritual worship. God, indeed, gave real tokens of his presence in that visible sanctuary, but not for the purpose of binding the senses and thoughts of his people to earthly elements; he wished rather that these external symbols should serve as ladders, by which the faithful might ascend even to heaven. The design of God from the commencement in the appointment of the sacraments, and all the outward exercises of religion, was to consult the infirmity and weak capacity of his people. Accordingly, even at the present day, the true and proper use of them is, to assist us in seeking God spiritually in his heavenly glory, and not to occupy our minds with the things of this world, or keep them fixed in the vanities of the flesh, a subject which we shall afterwards have a more suitable opportunity of discussing more fully. And as the Lord, in ancient times, when he called himself, *He who dwelleth in Sion*, intended to give his people full and solid ground of trust, tranquillity, and joy; so even now, after the law has come out of Sion, and the covenant of grace has flowed to us from that fountain, let us know and be fully persuaded, that wherever the faithful, who worship him purely and in due form, according to the appointment of his word, are assembled together to engage in the solemn acts of religious worship, he is graciously present, and presides in the midst of them.

12. *For in requiring blood.* In the original, it is *bloods*, in the plural number, and, therefore, the relative which follows immediately after, *And remembereth* THEM, may very properly be referred to that word in this way, He requireth bloods, and remembereth them. But as it is sufficiently common in Hebrew to invert the order of the antecedent and the relative, and to put *them* before the word to which it refers,[1] some explain it of *the poor*, thus: In requiring blood, he hath

---

[1] "Et de mettre Eux, devant le mot auquel il se rapporte."—*Fr.*

remembered them, namely, the poor, of whom he speaks a little after. As to the sum and substance of the matter, it is of small importance in which of these ways we explain the relative; but the former is, in my view, the more natural explanation. There is here a repetition of what the Psalmist had said a little before, that we ought especially to consider God's power, as it is manifested in the mercy which he exercises towards his servants, who are unrighteously persecuted by wicked men. From the numerous works of God, he selects one which he commends as especially worthy of being remembered, namely, his work in delivering the poor from death. God sometimes leaves them in his holy providence to be persecuted by men; but at length he takes vengeance for the wrongs inflicted upon them. The words which David uses denote a continued act; but I have no doubt that he intends from those examples, which he has related in the preceding part of the psalm, to lead men to acknowledge that God requireth innocent blood, and remembers the cry of his people.

He again insists on what I adverted to before, that God does not always put a stop to injuries so speedily as we would wish, nor break the attempts of the wicked at the first, but rather withholds and delays his assistance, so that it may seem that we cry to him in vain, a truth which it is of importance for us to understand; for if we measure the help of God according to our senses, our courage will ever and anon fail us, and in the end our hope will be entirely extinguished, and will give place to despondency and despair. We would fondly wish him, as I have said, to stretch forth his hand to a distance, and drive back the troubles which he sees to be prepared for us; yet he seems to take no notice, and does not prevent the blood of the innocent from being shed. Let this consolatory consideration, however, sustain us, that he will at length actually show how precious our blood was in his sight. If it is objected, that God's assistance comes too late, after we have endured all calamities, I answer, God delays to interfere no longer than he knows it to be of advantage for us to be humbled under the cross, and if he chooses rather to take vengeance after we have suffered outrage, than to aid us previous to the infliction of evil, it is not because he is not always willing and ready to succour us; but because he knows it is not always a proper time for manifesting his grace. By the way, it is a striking evidence, not only of his fatherly love towards us, but of the blessed immortality which is the portion of all the children of God, that he has a care about them even after they are dead. Were he always by his grace to prevent affliction from befalling us, who is there amongst us who would not be wholly attached to the present life? When, however, he avenges our death, from this it appears that, though dead, we still remain alive in his presence. For he does not, after the manner of men, hold in estimation the memory of those whom he could not preserve alive,[1] but he actually shows that he cherishes in his bosom, and gives protection to those who seem to be no more, viewing them according to the flesh. And this is the reason why David says that he remembereth blood when he requireth it; for, although he may not presently deliver his servants from the swords of the wicked, yet he suffers not their murder to pass unpunished. To the same purpose is the last clause, *He forgetteth not the cry of the afflicted.* God may not show, by granting instant deliverance or relief, that he lends an immediate ear to the complaints of his servants; but at length he proves unanswerably that he has regarded them. Express mention is made of *crying*, to encourage all who desire to experience God as their deliverer and protector, to direct their wishes, groanings, and prayers to him.

13. *Have mercy upon me, O Jehovah, see my affliction which I suffer from those who persecute me, thou that liftest me up from the gates of death.*
14. *That I may recount all thy praises in the gates of the daughter of Sion; and that I may rejoice in thy salvation.*

13. *Have mercy upon me, O Jehovah.* I think that this is

---

[1] "Car ce n'est pas qu'il face comme les hommes qui auront en estime et reverence apres la mort la memoire de leurs amis quand ils ne leur ont peu sauver la vie. —*Fr.* "For he does not act like men, who hold in estimation and reverence after death the memory of their friends, when they can no longer preserve their life."

the second part of the psalm. Others, however, are of a different opinion, and consider that David, according to his frequent practice, while giving thanks to God for the deliverance wrought for him, mingles with his thanksgiving an account of what had been the matter of his prayer in the extremity of his distress; and examples of the same kind, I confess, are every where to be met with in the Psalms. But when I consider all the circumstances more attentively, I am constrained to incline to the other opinion, namely, that in the commencement he celebrated the favours conferred upon him in order to make way for prayer; and the psalm is at last concluded with a prayer. He does not, therefore, in passing here insert the prayers which he had formerly made in the midst of his dangers and anxieties; but he purposely implores help from God at the present time,[1] and asks that *He*, whom he had often experienced as his deliverer, would continue the exercise of the same grace towards him. His enemies, perhaps, whom he had already vanquished on various occasions, having gathered new courage, and raised new forces, made a desperate effort, as we often see those who are driven to despair rush upon their enemies just with the greater impetuosity and rage. It is indeed certain, that David, when he offered this prayer, was seized with the greatest fear; for he would not, on account of a small matter, have called upon God to witness his affliction in the way he here does. It ought to be observed, that while he humbly betakes himself to the mercy of God, he bears, with a patient

---

[1] " In the 12th verse," says Horsley, " the Psalmist having mentioned it as a part of the divine character, that God forgetteth not the cry of the helpless, naturally thinks upon his own helpless state, and in the 13th and 14th verses cries for deliverance. The promise of the overthrow of the faction, which were the principal instruments of his affliction, recurring to his thoughts, he breaks out again in the 15th verse in strains of exultation." The transition from the language of triumph, in the preceding part of the psalm, to the language of prayer and complaint in the 13th verse, and the mixture of triumph and complaint in the sequel of the psalm, are very remarkable. This was the natural effect of the Psalmist's present distressed condition. The pressure of his affliction excited him, on the one hand, to utter the language of dejection; while his confident expectation of deliverance prompted him, on the other hand, to utter the language of triumph.

and submissive mind, the cross which was laid upon him.[1] But we ought chiefly to mark the title which he gives to God, calling him *his lifter up from the gates of death;* for we could not find a more appropriate expression than *to lift up* for the Hebrew word מרומם, *meromem.* By this the Psalmist, in the first place, strengthens his faith from his past experience, inasmuch as he had often been delivered from the greatest dangers. And, in the second place, he assures himself of deliverance, even in the very jaws of death; because God is accustomed not only to succour his servants, and to deliver them from their calamities by ordinary means, but also to bring them from the grave, even after all hope of life is cut off; for *the gates of death* is a metaphorical expression, denoting the utmost perils which threaten destruction, or rather, which lay the grave open before us. In order, therefore, that neither the weight of the calamities which we presently endure, nor the fear of those which we see impending over us, may overwhelm our faith, or interrupt our prayers, let us call to our remembrance that the office of lifting up his people from the gates of death is not ascribed to God in vain.

14. *That I may recount.* David's meaning simply is, that he will celebrate the praises of God in all assemblies, and, wherever there is the greatest concourse of people, (for at that time it was the custom to hold assemblies at the gates of cities;) but, at the same time, there seems to be an allusion to the gates of death, of which he has just spoken, as if he had said, After I am delivered from the grave, I will do my endeavour to bear testimony, in the most public manner, to the goodness of God, manifested in my deliverance. As, however, it is not sufficient to utter the praises of God with our tongues, if they do not proceed from the heart, the Psalmist, in the last clause of the verse, expresses the inward

---

[1] " Or il faut noter que quand il ya humblement au recours a la misericorde de Dieu, c'est signe qu'il portoit doucement et patiemment la croix que Dieu luy avoir comme mise sur les espaules."—*Fr.* " But it ought to be observed, that, while he humbly betakes himself to the mercy of God, it is a sign that he bore, submissively and patiently, the cross which God had, as it were, laid upon his shoulders."

joy with which he would engage in this exercise, *And that I may rejoice in thy salvation;* as if he had said, I desire to live in this world for no other purpose than to rejoice in having been preserved by the grace of God. Under the name of daughter, as is well known, the Jews meant a people or city, but he here names the city from its principal part, namely, Sion.

> 15. *The heathen are sunk into the pit which they made; in the net which they have hid are their own feet taken.*
> 16. *Jehovah is known by executing judgment. The wicked is snared in the work of his own hands. Higgaion. Selah.*

15. *The heathen are sunk.* David being now raised up to holy confidence, triumphs over his enemies. In the first place, he says metaphorically, that they were taken in their own craftiness and snares. He next expresses the same thing without figure, that they were snared in their own wickedness. And he affirms that this happened not by chance, but was the work of God, and a striking proof of his judgment. When he compares his enemies to hunters or fowlers, it is not without having just ground for doing so. The wicked, it is true, often commit violence and outrage, yet in deceits and cunning artifices they always imitate their father Satan, who is the father of lies, and, therefore, whatever ingenuity they have, they employ it in practising wickedness and in devising mischief. As often, therefore, as wicked men cunningly plot our destruction, let us remember that it is no new thing for them to lay nets and snares for the children of God. At the same time, let us comfort ourselves from the reflection, that whatever they may attempt against us, the issue is not in their power, and that God will be against them, not only to frustrate their designs, but also to surprise them in the wicked devices which they frame, and to make all their resources of mischief to fall upon their own heads.

16. *The Lord is known in executing judgment.* The reading of the words literally is this, *The known Lord has done judgment.*

This manner of speech is abrupt, and its very brevity renders it obscure. It is therefore explained in two ways. Some explain it thus:—God begins then to be known when he punishes the wicked. But the other sense suits the passage better, namely, that it is a thing obvious and manifest to all that God executes the office of judge, as often as he ensnares the wicked in their own maliciousness. In short, whenever God turns back upon themselves whatever schemes of mischief they devise, David declares that in this case the divine judgment is so evident, that what happens can be ascribed neither to nature nor to fortune. If God, therefore, in this way manifestly display, at any time, the power of his hand, let us learn to open our eyes, that from the judgments which he executes upon the enemies of his Church our faith may be confirmed more and more. As to the word *Higgaion*, which properly signifies *meditation*, I cannot at present assign a better reason why it has been inserted than this, that David intended to fix the minds of the godly in meditation upon the judgments of God. The word *Selah* was intended to answer the same purpose, and as I have said before, regulated the singing in such a manner as to make the music correspond to the words and the sentiment.

17. *The wicked shall be turned into hell, and all the nations that forget God.*
18. *For the poor shall not always be forgotten ; the hope of the humble shall not perish for ever.*

17. *The wicked shall be turned into hell.* Many translate the verb in the optative mood, *Let the wicked be turned into hell*, as if it were an imprecation. But, in my judgment, David here rather confirms himself and all the godly with respect to the future, declaring that whatever the wicked may attempt, it will have a termination disastrous to themselves. By the word *turn* he means that the issue will be far otherwise than what they imagine; for there is implied in it a tacit contrast between the height of their presumption and the depth of their fall. As they have no fear of God, they exalt themselves above the clouds ; and then, as if they had

"made a covenant with death," according to the language of Isaiah, (ch. xxviii. 15,) they become so much the more arrogant and presumptuous. But when we see them raging without apprehension of danger, the prophet warns us that their madness carries them headlong, so that, at length, they fall into the grave, from which they thought themselves to be a great way off. Here, then, is described to us the sudden and unexpected change, by which God, when he pleases, restores to order things which were in confusion. When, therefore, we see the wicked flying aloft devoid of all fear, let us, by the eyes of faith, behold the grave which is prepared for them; and rest assured that the hand of God, although it is unseen, is very near, which can turn them back in the midst of their course in which they aim at reaching heaven, and make them tumble into hell in a moment. The meaning of the Hebrew word שְׁאוֹלָה, *sheolah*, is doubtful, but I have not hesitated to translate it *hell*.[1] I do not find fault with those who translate it *the grave*, but it is certain that the prophet means something more than common death, otherwise he would here say nothing else with respect to the wicked than what would also happen to all the faithful in common with them. Though then, he does not speak in express terms of eternal destruction, but only says, *They shall be turned into the grave*, yet, under the metaphor of *the grave*, he intimates that all the ungodly shall perish, and that the presumption with which, by every unlawful means, they raise themselves on high to trample righteousness under foot, and to oppress the innocent, shall bring upon them ruin and perdition. The faithful, also, it is true, descend into the grave, but not with such fearful violence as plunges them into it without hope of coming out again. So far is this from being the case, that even when shut up in the grave, they dwell already in heaven by hope.

18. *For the poor shall not always be forgotten.* The asser-

---

[1] "Le mot Hebrieu, pour lequel nous avons traduit *Enfer* signifie aussi Sepulchre; mais j'ay mieux aimé retenir ceste signification."—*Fr.* "The Hebrew word which we have translated *hell* also signifies *the grave*; but I have preferred to retain the former meaning of the word."

tion that God will not forsake the poor and afflicted for ever, is a confirmation of the preceding sentence. By it he intimates, that they may indeed seem to be forsaken for a time. Let us, therefore, remember that God has promised his assistance to us, not in the way of preventing our afflictions, but of at length succouring us after we have been long subdued under the cross. David speaks expressly of *hope* or *expectation*, thereby to encourage us to prayer. The reason why God seems to take no notice of our afflictions is, because he would have us to awaken him by means of our prayers; for when he hears our requests, (as if he began but then to be mindful of us,) he stretches forth his powerful hand to help us. David again repeats that this is not done immediately, in order that we may persevere in hoping well, even although our expectations may not be instantly gratified.

> 19. *Arise, O Jehovah; let not man*[1] *prevail: let the nations be judged in thy sight.*
> 20. *Put them in fear, O Jehovah; that the nations may know that they are men.*

19. *Arise, O Jehovah.* When David beseeches God to arise, the expression does not strictly apply to God, but it refers to external appearance and to our senses; for we do not perceive God to be the deliverer of his people except when he appears before our eyes, as it were sitting upon the judgment-seat. There is added a consideration or reason to induce God to avenge the injuries done to his people, namely, *that man may not prevail;* for when God arises, all the fierceness[2] of the ungodly must immediately fall down and give way. Whence is it that the wicked become so audaciously insolent, or have so great power to work mischief, if it is not because God is still, and gives them loose reins? But, as soon as he shows some token of his judgment, he immediately puts a stop to their proud tumults,[3] and breaks their strength and power with his nod alone.[4] We are taught, by this

---

[1] " L'homme mortel."—*Fr.* " Mortal man."
[2] " Toute la fierte et arrogance."—*Fr.* " All the pride and arrogance."
[3] " Leur rage et insolence."—*Fr.* " Their rage and insolence."
[4] " Solo nutu."*Lat.* "En faisant signe seulement du bout du doigt."—*Fr.*

manner of praying, that however insolently and proudly our enemies may boast of what they will do, yet they are in the hand of God, and can do no more than what he permits them; and farther, that God can doubtless, whenever he pleases, render all their endeavours vain and ineffectual. The Psalmist, therefore, in speaking of them, calls them *man*. The word in the original is אנוש, *enosh*, which is derived from a root signifying misery or wretchedness, and, accordingly, it is the same thing as if he had called them mortal or frail man. Farther, the Psalmist beseeches God to *judge the heathen before his face*. God is said to do this when he compels them, by one means or another, to appear before his judgment-seat. We know that unbelievers, until they are dragged by force into the presence of God, turn their backs upon him as much as they can, in order to exclude from their minds all thought of him as their Judge.

20. *Put them in fear, O Jehovah*. The Septuagint translates מורה, *morah*, [νομοθέτης,] *a lawgiver*, deriving it from ירה, *yarah*, which sometimes signifies *to teach*.[1] But the scope of the passage requires that we should understand it of fear or dread; and this is the opinion of all sound expositors. Now, it is to be considered of what kind of fear David speaks. God commonly subdues even his chosen ones to obedience by means of fear. But as he moderates his rigour towards them, and, at the same time, softens their stony hearts, so that they willingly and quietly submit themselves to him, he cannot be properly said to compel them by fear. With respect to the reprobate, he takes a different way of dealing. As their obduracy is inflexible, so that it is easier

[1] The Chaldee version reads *fear*, but the Syriac, Æthiopic, and Vulgate versions follow the Septuagint. The Arabic employs a word of nearly the same import, signifying *a doctor or teacher of the law*. In Coverdale's Bible it is, " O Lord, set a schoolmaster over them." Augustine and Jerome, who adopted the reading of the Septuagint, render the words, " Set, O Lord, a lawgiver over them;" and it was their opinion that *lawgiver* means antichrist, to whom God in his wrath gave dominion over the nations. According to others, lawgiver means Christ. Dr Horsley reads, " O Jehovah, appoint thou a teacher over them." Ainsworth and Dr Adam Clarke adopt the same rendering, and view the words as a prayer that the nations may learn humility and piety, that they may know their accountability to God, and become wise unto salvation.

to break than to bend them, he subdues their desperate obstinacy by force; not, indeed, that they are reformed, but, whether they will or no, an acknowledgment of their own weakness is extorted from them. They may gnash their teeth and boil with rage, and even exceed in cruelty wild beasts, but when the dread of God seizes upon them, they are thrown down with their own violence, and fall with their own weight. Some explain these words as a prayer that God would bring the nations under the yoke of David, and make them tributaries to his government; but this is a cold and forced explanation. The word *fear* comprehends in general all the plagues of God, by which is repulsed, as by the heavy blows of a hammer,[1] the rebellion of those who would never obey him except by compulsion.

There follows next the point to which the nations must be brought, namely, to acknowledge themselves to be mortal men. This, at first sight, seems to be a matter of small importance; but the doctrine which it contains is far from being trifling. What is man, that he dares of himself to move a finger? And yet all the ungodly run to excess as boldly and presumptuously as if there were nothing to hinder them from doing whatever they please. It is certainly through a distempered imagination that they claim to themselves what is peculiar to God; and, in short, they would never run to so great excess if they were not ignorant of their own condition. David, when he beseeches God to strike the nations with terror, that they *may know that they are men*,[2] does not mean that the ungodly will profit so much under the rods and chastisements of God as to humble themselves truly and from the heart; but the knowledge of which he speaks just means an experience of their own weakness. His language is as if he had said, Lord, since it is their ignorance of themselves which hurries them into their rage against me, make them actually to experience that their strength is not equal

---

[1] " Tous fleax de Dieu par lesquels est rembarre comme a grans coups de marteau."—*Fr.*

[2] The original word is אנוש, *enosh;* and therefore it is a prayer that they may know themselves to be but miserable, frail, and dying men. The word is in the singular number, but it is used collectively.

to their infatuated presumption, and after they are disappointed of their vain hopes, let them lie confounded and abased with shame. It may often happen that those who are convinced of their own weakness do not yet reform; but much is gained when their ungodly presumption is exposed to mockery and scorn before the world, that it may appear how ridiculous was the confidence which they presumed to place in their own strength. With respect to the chosen of God, they ought to profit under his chastisements after another manner. It becomes them to be humbled under a sense of their own weakness, and willingly to divest themselves of all vain confidence and presumption. And this will be the case if they remember that they are but men. Augustine has well and wisely said, that the whole humility of man consists in the knowledge of himself. Moreover, since pride is natural to all, God requires to strike terror into all men indiscriminately, that, on the one hand, his own people may learn to be humble, and that, on the other hand, the wicked, although they cease not to elevate themselves above the condition of man, may be put back with shame and confusion.

PSALM X.

David here complains, in his own name, and in the name of all the godly, that fraud, extortion, cruelty, violence, and all kind of injustice, prevailed every where in the world; and the cause which he assigns for this is, that ungodly and wicked men, being intoxicated with their prosperity, have shaken off all fear of God, and think they may do whatever they please with impunity. Accordingly, he earnestly beseeches God to help him, and to remedy his desperate calamities. In the close, he comforts himself and the rest of the faithful with the hope of obtaining deliverance in due time. This description represents, as in a mirror, a lively image of a widely corrupt and disorganised state of society. When, therefore, we see iniquity breaking out like a flood, that the strangeness of such a temptation may not shake the faith of the children of God and cause them to fall into despair, let them learn to look into this mirror. It tends greatly to lighten grief, to consider that nothing befalls us at this day which the Church of God has not experienced in the days of old ; yea, rather that we are just called to engage in the same conflicts with which David and the other holy patriarchs were exercised. Farther, the faithful are admonished to have recourse to God in such a confused state of things ; for unless they are convinced that it belongs to God to succour them, and to remedy such a state of matters, they will gain nothing by indulging in confused murmurings, and rending the air with their cries and complaints.

1. *Why standest thou afar off, O Jehovah? and winkest at seasonable times in trouble?*[1]
2. *The ungodly in his pride doth persecute the poor ;*[2] *let them be caught in the devices*[3] *which they imagine.*

1. *Lord, why standest thou afar off?* We here see how the prophet, seeking a remedy for his calamities, which were apparently past hope, directly addresses himself to God at the very commencement. And the rule which we should observe, when we are in trouble and sorrow, is this : We should seek comfort and solace in the providence of God ; for amidst our agitations, vexations, and cares, we ought to be fully persuaded that it is his peculiar office to give relief to the wretched and afflicted. It is in an improper sense, and by anthropathy,[4] that the Psalmist speaks of God as

[1] " Et te caches au temps *que sommes* en tribulation ?"—*Fr.* " And hidest thyself when we are in trouble ?"—*Heb.* " Aux opportunitez, ou, aux temps opportuns."—*Fr. marg.* " In opportunities, or, at seasonable times."

[2] " Ou, le poure est persecuté, ou, il brusle en l'orgueil des meschans." —*Fr. marg.* " Or, the poor is persecuted ; or, he burns in the pride of the wicked."

[3] Horsley reads " subtleties," and observes in a note, " I choose this ambiguous word ; being in doubt whether the petition against the wicked be that they may be ruined by their own stratagems against the righteous, or that they may be the dupes of their own atheistical speculations upon moral and religious subjects. It seems to me that the word מזמה, may signify either ' crafty tricks,' or ' refined theories,' and, in this latter sense, it is used in the fourth verse." Horsley considers this psalm as a general description of the oppression of the righteous by apostate spirits, atheists, and idolaters, who have all conspired against them, and not as referring to any particular calamity of the Jewish nation, or of any individual.

[4] " C'est quand nous attribuons à Dieu les passions, affections, et façons de faire des hommes."—*Fr. marg.* " That is, when we attribute to God the passions, affections, and manners of men."

standing afar off. Nothing can be hid from his eyes; but as God permits us to speak to him as we do to one another, these forms of expression do not contain any thing absurd, provided we understand them as applied to God, not in a strict sense, but only figuratively, according to the judgment which mere sense forms from the present appearance of things. It is possible that a righteous man may not check an injury which is done to a poor man before his eyes, because he is destitute of the power; but this cannot be the case with respect to God, who is always armed with invincible power. If, therefore, he act as if he took no notice, it is the same as if he withdrew himself afar off. The word תעלים, *taelim*, which signifies *to hide*, is explained in two ways. According to some, David here complains of God for hiding himself, as if he accounted the care of human affairs beneath him. Others understand it as meaning *to shut the eyes;* and this appears to me to be the more simple view. It is to be observed, that although David here complains that God kept himself afar off, he was, notwithstanding, fully persuaded of his presence with him, otherwise it would have been in vain to have called upon him for aid. The interrogation which he employs is to this effect: Lord, since it is thy prerogative to govern the world, and also to regulate it by thy righteousness as thou sustainest it by thy power, why is it that thou dost not more quickly show thyself a defender of thine own people against the arrogance and incredible pride of the ungodly? David, however, speaks thus not so much in the way of complaining, as to encourage himself in the confidence of obtaining what he desired. Through the infirmity of sense, he says, that it is unbecoming of God to cease so long from executing his office; and yet, at the same time, he fails not to yield to him the honour which is his due, and by his prayers he deposits into his bosom the great burden of trouble with which he was laden. The expression which follows, *at needful times,* relates to the same subject. Although God may not stretch forth his hand to take vengeance[1] at every moment, yet when he beholds the simple and inno-

---

[1] " Pour faire vengence."—*Fr.*

cent oppressed, it is not time for him to defer any longer. David briefly defines the fit time for putting the hand to the work to be when the faithful are in distress. Of this form of speech we have spoken in the preceding psalm, at the tenth verse.

2. *The ungodly in his pride, &c.* Before uttering his prayer against the ungodly, the Psalmist briefly sets forth their wickedness in cruelly vexing the afflicted, for no other reason but because they disdain and despise them, through the pride with which they are inflated. And their cruelty is not a little enhanced from this, that, forgetful of all humanity, they contemptuously triumph over the poor and afflicted, mocking them and inflicting injuries upon them.[1] Cruelty is, indeed, always proud, yea, rather, pride is the mother of all wrongs; for if a man did not through pride magnify himself above his neighbours, and through an overweening conceit of himself despise them, even common humanity would teach us with what humility and justice we ought to conduct ourselves towards each other. But David here intended to state that the only cause why the ungodly, whom he accuses, exercise their cruelty against the wretched and the needy, from whom they receive no provocation, is the pride and arrogance of their own spirits. Let every one, therefore, who desires to live justly and unblameably with his brethren, beware of indulging or taking pleasure in treating others disdainfully; and let him endeavour, above all things, to have his mind freed from the disease of pride. The word דלק, *dalak*, signifies *to suffer persecution*, as well as *to persecute;* and, therefore, some prefer translating the words, *The poor is persecuted in the pride of the ungodly.* They may also not improperly be rendered thus, *The poor burns in the pride of the ungodly,*[2] because this is the more common signification of

---

[1] "En se mocquant d'eux et les outrageant."—*Fr.*

[2] "דלק, *dalak*, signifies two things, to *persecute*, and *to be set on fire;* and though we render it in the former sense, and so apply it to רשע, *rasha, the wicked,* in the active tense,—*the wicked persecutes the poor,*—yet the ancient interpreters generally render it in the passive, and apply it to עני, *anay, the poor, that in the pride of the wicked he is set on fire,* that is, brought into great tribulation."—*Hammond.* The word used by the

the word. The pride of the wicked, like fire, devours the poor and afflicted.

3. *For the ungodly praiseth himself on account of the desire of his own soul; and the violent man blesseth himself; he despiseth Jehovah.*
4. *The ungodly, in the pride of his countenance,*[1] *inquireth not: all his devices say, There is no God.*

3. *For the ungodly praiseth himself.* This verse is variously explained. Literally the reading is, *For praiseth the wicked or ungodly;* and it is therefore necessary to supply some word, but what word is disputed.[2] Some translate the words, *ungodly* and *violent man,* in the accusative case, thus: *He praiseth the ungodly, and blesseth the violent man;* because they think it strange that after "praiseth" the sentence should end abruptly, without any thing being said of who or what was praised. But since it is quite common in Hebrew, when the agent and the subject are one and the same person, to express the word only once, while we repeat it in order to complete the sense,[3] the interpretation which I have followed appears to me the most proper, namely, that the ungodly man praises himself, and boasts of the desire of his soul, and blesses himself. Now, it may be asked, What is *this desire of soul?* It is usually understood in this sense, that the ungodly flatter and applaud themselves, while fortune smiles on them, and they obtain their wishes, and enjoy whatever they desire; just as David adds, a little after, that they abuse their prosperity, in attempting whatever comes into their fancy. But, in my opinion, *desire of soul* here denotes rather lust, and the intemperate gratification of passion and appetite; and thus the meaning is, that they indulge themselves with

---

Septuagint is $ἐμπυρίζεται$. There may be an allusion in the Hebrew word to the fires which persecutors have kindled for burning to death the confessors and martyrs of Christ.

[1] "In altitudine naris;"—literally, "In the height of his nose." This also is the literal rendering of the Hebrew text, "The nose and casting up of it signifies a proud, scornful, and sometimes an angry countenance."—*Ainsworth.*

[2] "Il y a mot à mot, Car louë le meschant et il y faut suppleer quelque petit mot: or, cela on y besongne diversement."—*Fr.*

[3] "On la repete pour parfaire le sense."—*Fr.*

delight in their depraved desires, and, despising the judgment of God, fearlessly absolve themselves from all guilt, maintain their innocence,[1] and justify their impiety. Moses uses a similar form of expression in Deut. xxix. 19, " I shall have peace, though I walk in the imagination of mine heart."

David, indeed, says a little after, that the ungodly abuse their prosperity, by flattering themselves; but here, in my judgment, he expresses something more weighty, namely, that they acquire praise from their presumptuousness, and glory in their wickedness; and this foolish confidence, or bold assurance, is the cause of their throwing off all restraint and breaking forth into every kind of excess. Accordingly, I interpret the words *praise* and *bless* as having the same meaning, just as the words, *ungodly* and *violent man*, are synonymous in this place, although they differ from each other as genus and species. With these statements agrees what is immediately added in the end of the verse, that these ungodly persons *despise God*. To translate the verb, *to blaspheme*, as has been done by some, or *to provoke to anger*, as has been done by others, is too remote from the scope of the passage. David rather teaches, that the cause of their careless indulgence in the gratification of their lusts, is their base contempt of God. He who duly reflects that God will be his judge, is so much alarmed by this reflection, that he dares not bless his soul while his conscience accuses him of guilt and of being given to the practice of sin.[2]

4. *The ungodly, in the pride of his countenance, &c.* Others translate the words, *The ungodly man, by reason of the violence of his anger*, or, *in the pride which he displays, does not inquire after God*. But this partly perverts the meaning, and partly weakens the force of what David intended to express. In the first place, the word *inquire*, which is here put absolutely, that is, without any noun which it governs, is, according to this translation, improperly limited to God. David simply means, that the ungodly, without examination, permit themselves to do any thing, or do not distinguish between

---

[1] " Ils s'osent bien absoudre et tenir pour innocens."—*Fr.*
[2] " Cependant qu'il se sent coulpable et adonne à mal faire."—*Fr.*

what is lawful and unlawful, because their own lust is their law, yea, rather, as if superior to all laws, they fancy that it is lawful for them to do whatever they please. The beginning of well-doing in a man's life is inquiry; in other words, we can only begin to do well when we keep ourselves from following, without choice and discrimination, the dictates of our own fancy, and from being carried away by the wayward propensities of our flesh. But the exercise of inquiring proceeds from humility, when we assign to God, as is reasonable, the place of judge and ruler over us. The prophet, therefore, very properly says, that the reason why the ungodly, without any regard or consideration, presume to do whatever they desire, is because, being lifted up with pride, they leave to God nothing whatever of the prerogative of a judge. The Hebrew word אף, *aph*, which we have translated *countenance*, I have no doubt is here taken in its proper and natural signification, and not metaphorically for *anger;* because haughty persons show their effrontery even by their countenance.

In the second clause, the prophet more severely, or, at least, more openly, accuses them, declaring that all their wicked imaginations show that they have no God. *All his devices say, There is no God.*[1] By these words I understand, that through their heaven-daring presumption, they subvert all piety and justice, as if there were no God sitting in heaven. Did they truly believe that there is a God, the fear of the judgment to come would restrain them. Not that they plainly and distinctly deny the existence of a God, but then they strip him of his power. Now, God would be merely like an idol, if, contented with an inactive existence, he should divest himself of his office as judge. Whoever, therefore, refuse to admit that the world is subject to the providence of God, or do not believe that his hand is stretched forth from on high to govern it, do as much as in them lies

[1] The sentence in the Hebrew text is elliptical, and hence it has been variously translated. Literally it is, *No God all his thoughts.* The Syriac version renders it, "There is no God in all his thoughts." The Septuagint reads, "Οὐκ ἔστιν ὁ θεὸς ἐνώπιον αὐτοῦ," "God is not before him." Mudge renders it, "No God is all his wicked politics;" Horsley, "No God is the whole of his philosophy;" and Fry, "'There is no Elohim' is all his thought."

to put an end to the existence of God. It is not, however, enough to have some cold and unimpressive knowledge of him in the head; it is only the true and heartfelt conviction of his providence which makes us reverence him, and which keeps us in subjection[1] to him. The greater part of interpreters understand the last clause as meaning generally, that all the thoughts of a wicked man tend to the denial of a God. In my opinion, the Hebrew word מזמות, *mezimmoth*, is here, as in many other places, taken in a bad sense for cunning and wicked thoughts,[2] so that the meaning, as I have noticed already, is this: Since the ungodly have the hardihood to devise and perpetrate every kind of wickedness, however atrocious, it is from this sufficiently manifest, that they have cast off all fear of God from their hearts.

5. *His ways are prosperous at all times; on high are thy judgments before him; he puffeth at all his enemies.*
6. *He saith in his heart, I shall not be moved from generation to generation, because he is not in adversity.*

There is a great diversity of opinion among interpreters respecting the first clause of this verse. The translators of the Septuagint version, thinking the word יָחִילוּ, *yachilu*, which is in the future tense, derived from the root חלל, *chalal*, which it is not, have rendered it, *his ways are defiled*.[3] But it is agreed among the Jewish expositors, that it is derived from the root חול, *chol*. Many among them, however, take it actively for *to put one in fear*, or *to put one to trouble*, as if it had been said, The ways of the ungodly are dreadful to the good, and torment them.[4] Some also apply the words to God, reading the sentence thus, *His ways come*, that is to say, *have their course*, or *prosper at all times*. This, however, in my judgment, is too forced. But as this word, in other texts of Scripture, means *to be prosperous*, I am surprised that there should be any difference of opinion among

---

[1] " Qui nous le fait avoir en reverence et nous tient là subjets."—*Fr.*
[2] " Pour meschantes et malicieuses pensees."—*Fr.* " Wicked and malicious thoughts."
[3] The Greek word which they use is Βεβηλουνται.
[4] Aben Ezra's rendering is, " His ways always cause terror."

the learned concerning this passage, when immediately, in the next clause, the prophet clearly shows that he is speaking of the prosperous condition of the ungodly, and the continued course of pleasure which intoxicates them. He not only complains of this their prosperity, but from it he aggravates their guilt, in that they take occasion, from the goodness of God, to harden themselves in their wickedness. I would, therefore, explain the verse thus: As they enjoy a continued course of prosperity, they dream that God is bound or plighted to them, and hence they put his judgments far from them; and if any man oppose them, they are confident they can immediately put him down, or dash him to pieces with a puff or breath. Now, we understand the simple meaning of the prophet to be, that the ungodly mock God, taking encouragement from his forbearance; as that base tyrant, Dionysius, because he had a prosperous voyage, after having plundered the temple of Proserpine,[1] boasted that God favoured the sacrilegious.[2] Hence it is, that they put far from them the judgments of God.

In the opinion of some, these words, *On high are thy judgments before him,* mean much the same thing as if the prophet had said, God treats them with too much clemency, and spares them; just as he elsewhere complains of their being exempted from the common afflictions of life. But this interpretation does not so well agree with the words; yea, it appears to be unnatural and forced. *The judgments of God* then are said *to be on high to the ungodly,* because, presuming upon the great distance of God from them,[3] they promise themselves not only a truce with death during their whole life, but also an everlasting covenant with it. We see how, by procrastinating the evil day, they harden themselves, and become more and more obstinate in evil;[4] yea, persuading themselves that God is shut up in heaven, as if they had nothing to do with him, they strengthen themselves in the hope

---

[1] " Apres qu'il eut pillé le temple de Proserpine."—*Fr.*
[2] Vale. lib. i. chap. 2.
[3] " Pource que se confians de la longue distance qui est entre Dieu et eux."—*Fr.*
[4] " Car nous voyons comme delayans le temps, il s'endurcissent et obstinent au mal de plus en plus."—*Fr.*

of escaping unpunished;[1] as we see them, in Isaiah, (chap. xxii. 13,) jesting at the threatenings of the prophets, saying, "Let us eat and drink, for to-morrow we shall die." When the prophets, in order to inspire the people with terror, denounced the dreadful vengeance of God, which was ready to be inflicted upon them, these wicked men cried out that it was all whims or idle stories. God therefore bitterly inveighs against them, because, when he called the people to mourning, ashes, and sackcloth, these mockers encouraged them to minstrelsy and feasting; and at length he swears, "As I live, surely this iniquity shall not be purged from you till ye die." The faithful, indeed, lift up their eyes to heaven to behold the judgments of God; and they are not less afraid of them than if they were just ready to fall upon their heads. The ungodly, on the contrary, despise them, and yet, in order not to be disturbed or tormented with the fear or apprehension of them, they would banish them into heaven; just as the Epicureans, although they did not presume avowedly to deny the existence of a God, yet imagined that he is confined to heaven, where he indulges himself in idleness, without taking any concern about what is done here below.[2] From this infatuation flows their presumptuous confidence of which David speaks, by which they assure themselves of being able to destroy, with a puff or blast alone, all who are enemies to them. The word פוּחַ, *phuach*, which sometimes signifies *to ensnare*, is here more properly taken for *to puff*, or *to blow out*.

The Psalmist confirms these statements in the next verse, where he tells us that the persons of whom he speaks are fully persuaded in their hearts that they are beyond all danger of change. *He saith in his heart, I shall not be moved from generation to generation.* The ungodly often pour forth proud language to this effect. David, however, only touches the hidden ulcer of their vile arrogance, which they cherish in their own breasts, and therefore he does not say what they

---

[1] "En l'esperance de jamais ne venir à conte."—*Fr.* "In the hope of never being called to account."
[2] "Font à croire qu'il est au ciel, où il se donne du bon temps sans se soucier de ce qu'il se fait yci bas."—*Fr.*

speak with their mouth, but what they persuade themselves of in their hearts. It may here be asked, Why does David blame in others what he professes concerning himself in so many places?[1] for trusting to the protection of God, he courageously triumphs over all dangers.[2] And surely it becomes the children of God effectually to provide for their safety, so that, although the world should a hundred times fall into ruins, they may have the comfortable assurance that they will remain unmoved. The answer to this question is easy, and it is this, The faithful promise themselves security in God, and no where else; and yet while they do this, they know themselves to be exposed to all the storms of affliction, and patiently submit to them. There is a very great difference between a despiser of God who, enjoying prosperity today, is so forgetful of the condition of man in this world, as through a distempered imagination to build his nest above the clouds, and who persuades himself that he shall always enjoy comfort and repose,[3]—there is a very great difference between him and the godly man, who, knowing that his life hangs only by a thread, and is encompassed by a thousand deaths, and who, ready to endure any kind of afflictions which shall be sent upon him, and living in the world as if he were sailing upon a tempestuous and dangerous sea, nevertheless, bears patiently all his troubles and sorrows, and comforts himself in his afflictions, because he leans wholly upon the grace of God, and entirely confides in it.[4] The ungodly man says, I shall not be moved, or I shall not shake for ever; because he thinks himself sufficiently strong and powerful to bear up against all the assaults which shall be made upon him. The faithful man says, What although I may happen to be moved, yea, even fall and sink into the lowest depths? my fall will not be fatal, for God will put his hand under me to sustain me. By

---

[1] Ps. iii. 7; xxiii. 4; xxvii. 3, &c.—*Fr.*
[2] "Il ose dire hardiment qu'il ne redoute nuls dangers et les desfie tous."—*Fr.* "He courageously declares that he is not afraid of any dangers, and defies them all."
[3] "Et se fait à croire qu'il sera tousjours à son aise et a repos."—*Fr.*
[4] "Toutesfois pource qu'il s'appuye du tout sur la grace de Dieu, et s'y confie, porte patiemment toutes molestes et ennuis et se console en ses afflictions."—*Fr.*

this, in like manner, we are furnished with an explanation of the different effects which an apprehension of danger has upon the good and the bad. Good men may tremble and sink into despondency, but this leads them to flee with all haste to the sanctuary of God's grace;[1] whereas the ungodly, while they are affrighted even at the noise of a falling leaf,[2] and live in constant uneasiness, endeavour to harden themselves in their stupidity, and to bring themselves into such a state of giddy frenzy, that being, as it were, carried out of themselves, they may not feel their calamities. The cause assigned for the confidence with which the prosperous ungodly man persuades himself that no change shall come upon him is, *because he is not in adversity.* This admits of two senses. It either means, that the ungodly, because they have been exempted from all calamity and misery during the past part of their life, entertain the hope of a peaceful and joyful state in the time to come; or it means, that through a deceitful imagination they exempt themselves from the common condition of men; just as in Isaiah, (chap. xxviii. 15,) they say, "When the overflowing scourge shall pass through, it shall not come upon us."

7. *His mouth is full of cursing, and deceit, and malice: under his tongue are mischief and iniquity.*
8. *He will sit in the ensnaring places of the villages; in his lurking places will he murder the innocent: his eyes will take their aim against the poor.*
9. *He will lie in wait secretly, as a lion in his den; he will lie in wait to catch the poor; he will catch the poor by drawing him into his net.*
10. *He will crouch low, and cast himself down, and then shall an army of the afflicted fall by his strengths.*[3]

7. *His mouth is full of cursing.* The scope of these four verses is this: If God intends to succour his servants, it is

[1] "Se retirent de bonne heure vers la grace de Dieu pour se mettre a sauvete comme en un lien de refuge et asseurance."—*Fr.* "Betake themselves with all haste to the grace of God, to put themselves in safety as in a place of refuge and security."

[2] "Au bruit des fueilles qui tombent des arbres."—*Fr.* "At the noise of leaves falling from the trees."

[3] "Ou, par ses forts, asçavoir membres."—*Fr.* "Or, by his strong members." That is, his teeth, or claws. The adjective for *strong*, in the ori-

now a proper time for doing so, inasmuch as the lawlessness of the ungodly has burst forth to the utmost possible excess. In the first place, he complains that their tongues are full of perjuries and deceits, and that they carry or hide mischief and wrongs, it being impossible to have any dealings with them in any matter without loss and damage. The word אלה, *alah*, which some render *cursing*, does not signify the execrations which they throw out against others, but rather those which they call down upon their own heads: for they do not scruple to utter the most awful imprecations against themselves, that thereby they may the better succeed in deceiving others. It is, therefore, not improperly rendered by some, *perjury*, for this word ought to be joined to the other two, *deceit and malice.* Thus the wicked are described as cursing or swearing falsely, so far as it contributes to forward their purposes of deceiving and doing injury. Hence follow mischief and injustice, because it is impossible for the simple, without suffering detriment, to escape their snares, which are woven of deceits, perjuries, and malice.

8. *He will sit in the ensnaring places of the villages.*[1] I have purposely avoided changing the verbs of the future tense into another tense, because they imply a continued act, and also because this Hebrew idiom has extended even to other languages. David, therefore, describes what ungodly men are accustomed to do. And, in the first place, he compares them to highwaymen, who lie in wait at the narrow parts of

ginal, is in the plural, and there is no substantive with which it agrees. We have examples of a similar ellipsis in other parts of Scripture. Thus in 2 Sam. xxi. 16, we have new, for a new sword; and in Psalm lxxiii. 10, full, for a full cup; and in Matth. x. 42, cold, for cold water.—*Poole's Annotations.*

[1] Horsley renders the eighth verse thus:

"He sitteth in ambush* in the villages in secret places;
He murdereth the innocent; his eyes are ever watching for the helpless."

And he has the following note: "Symmachus and St Jerome certainly read thus, ישב מארב בחצרים, and they both render מארב, as a participle. 'He sitteth prowling about the farm-houses.' This I take to be the true reading and the true rendering. The image is that of a beast of prey of the lesser order, a fox or a wolf, lying upon the watch about the farm-yard in the evening."

* Or, "he sitteth prowling about the farm-yard."

roads, and choose for themselves hiding-places from which they may fall upon travellers when off their guard. He says also, that *their eyes are bent or leering*,[1] by a similitude borrowed from the practice of dart-shooters, who take their aim with leering, or half shut eyes, in order to hit the mark the surer. Nor does he here speak of the common sort of highwaymen who are in the woods;[2] but he directs his language against those great robbers who hide their wickedness under titles of honour, and pomp, and splendour. The word חצרים, *chatserim*, therefore, which we have rendered *villages*, is by some translated *palaces*; as if David had said, they have converted their royal mansions into places of robbery, where they may cut the throats of their unhappy victims. But granting the word to have this allusion, I consider that it refers principally to the practice of robbers, to which there is a reference in the whole verse, and I explain it thus: Like as robbers lie in wait at the egresses of villages, so these persons lay their snares wherever they are.

In the next verse, he sets forth their cruelty in a light still more aggravated, by another comparison, saying, that they thirst for their prey *like lions in their dens*. Now, it is a step higher in wickedness to equal in cruelty wild beasts than to make havoc after the manner of robbers. It is worthy of remark, that he always joins deceits and snares with violence, in order the better to show how miserable the children of God would be, unless they were succoured by help from heaven. There is also added another similitude, which expresses more clearly how craft in catching victims is mingled with cruelty. *They catch them*, says he, but it is by *drawing them into their net*. By these words he means, that they not only rush upon them with open force and violence, but that, at the same time also, they spread their nets in order to deceive.

He again repeats all this in the tenth verse, giving a beautiful and graphic description of the very mien or gesture of

---

[1] Bishop Mant reads "peering eyes." "Concerning the word," says he, "which I have rendered *peering*, Parkhurst says that it is applied to winking or half closing the eyes in order to see more distinctly. The Septuagint and Vulgate translations, which mean *look at, behold*, give the general sense, but not the beautiful image expressed in the Hebrew."

[2] "Qui sont parmi les bois."—*Fr.*

such wicked men, just as if he set before our eyes a picture of them. *They crouch low,* says he, *and cast themselves down,*[1] that they may not, by their cruelty, frighten away their victims to a distance; for they would fain catch in their entanglements those whom they cannot hurt without coming close to them. We see how he joins these two things together, first snares or gins, and then sudden violence, as soon as the prey has fallen into their hands. For, by the second clause, he means, that whenever they see the simple to be fully in their power, they rush upon them by surprise with a savage violence, just as if a lion should furiously rise from his couch to tear in pieces his prey.[2] The obvious meaning of the Psalmist is, that the ungodly are to be dreaded on all sides, because they dissemble their cruelty, till they find those caught in their toils whom they wish to devour. There is some obscurity in the words, to which we shall briefly advert. In the clause which we have rendered *an army of the afflicted,* the Hebrew word חלכאים, *chelcaim, an army,* in the opinion of some, is a word of four letters.[3] Those, however, think more accurately who hold it to be compound, and equivalent to two words.[4] Although, therefore, the verb נפל, *naphal,* is in the singular number, yet the prophet, doubtless, uses חל כאים, *chel caim,* collectively, to denote a

---

[1] The allusion is to the practice of the lion, who, when he intends to seize upon his prey, crouches, or lies down, and gathers himself together, both to conceal himself, and that he may make the greater spring upon his prey when it comes within his reach, (Job xxxviii. 39, 40.)

[2] "Comme si un lion sortant de son giste se levoit furieusement pour mettre sa proye par pieces."—*Fr.* "As if a lion, issuing from his den, furiously raised himself to spring upon his prey, and to tear it in pieces." "When the lion," says Buffon, "leaps upon his prey, he gives a spring of ten or fifteen feet, falls on, seizes it with his fore-paws, tears it with his claws, and afterwards devours it with his teeth."

[3] Being the plural of חלכה, *chelcah,* which occurs three times in this psalm, namely, here and in the eighth and fourteenth verses, where it is rendered *poor.*

[4] Namely, חל כאים, *chel caim.* Those who adopt this reading observe, that according to the other view, the verb נפל, *naphal,* translated *may fall,* which is singular, is joined with a plural noun, חלכאים, *chelcaim,* but that, by dividing this last word into two, we get a singular nominative to the verb. Hammond, however, who adopts the first opinion, observes, "That it is an elegance, both in the Hebrew and Arabic, to use the verb singular with the nominative plural, especially when the verb is placed first, as here it is;" and, therefore, he denies the validity of that objection against the ordinary rendering.

great company of people who are afflicted by every one of these lions. I have rendered עֲצוּמִים, *atsumim, his strengths,* as if it were a substantive; because the prophet, doubtless, by this term, intends the talons and teeth of the lion, in which the strength of that beast chiefly consists. As, however, the word is properly an adjective in the plural number, signifying *strong,* without having any substantive with which it agrees, we may reasonably suppose that, by the talons and teeth of the lion, he means to express metaphorically a powerful body of soldiers. In short, the meaning is this: These wicked men hide their strength, by feigned humility and crafty courteous demeanour, and yet they will always have in readiness an armed band of satellites, or claws and teeth, as soon as an opportunity of doing mischief is presented to them.

11. *He hath said in his heart, God hath forgotten it : he hideth his face that he may never see it.*
12. *Arise, O Jehovah God, lift up thine hand : forget not the poor.*
13. *Why do the wicked despise God ? He saith in his heart, Thou wilt not require it.*

11. *He hath said in his heart.* The Psalmist again points out the source from which the presumption of the ungodly proceeds. Because God seems to take no notice of their wicked practices, they flatter themselves with the hope of escaping unpunished. As, however, they do not openly utter with their mouth the detestable blasphemy, that *God hath forgotten their conduct, and hath shut his eyes that he may never see it,* but hide their thoughts in the deep recesses of their own hearts, as Isaiah declares, (chap. xxix. 15;) the Psalmist uses the same form of expression which he used before, and which he repeats a little after the third time, namely, that the ungodly say to themselves, in their hearts, that God takes no concern whatever in the affairs of men. And it is to be observed, that the ungodly, when all things happen to them according to their wishes, form such a judgment of their prosperity as to persuade themselves that God is in a manner bound or obliged

to them.[1] Whence it comes to pass, that they live in a state of constant security,[2] because they do not reflect, that after God has long exercised patience towards them, they will undergo a solemn reckoning, and that their condemnation will be the more terrible, the greater the long-suffering of God.

12. *Arise, O Jehovah.* It is a disease under which men in general labour, to imagine, according to the judgment of the flesh, that when God does not execute his judgments, he is sitting idle, or lying at ease. There is, however, a great difference with respect to this between the faithful and the wicked. The latter cherish the false opinion which is dictated by the weakness of the flesh, and in order to soothe and flatter themselves in their vices, they indulge in slumbering, and render their conscience stupid,[3] until at length, through their wicked obstinacy, they harden themselves into a gross contempt of God. But the former soon shake from their minds that false imagination, and chastise themselves, returning of their own accord to a due consideration of what is the truth on this subject.[4] Of this we have here set before us a striking example. By speaking of God after the manner of men, the prophet declares that the same error which he has just now condemned in the despisers of God had gradually stolen in upon his own mind. But he proceeds at once to correct it, and resolutely struggles with himself, and restrains his mind from forming such conceptions of God, as would reflect dishonour upon his righteousness and glory. It is therefore a temptation to which all men are naturally prone, to begin to doubt of the providence of God, when his hand and judgment are not seen. The godly, however, differ widely from the wicked. The former, by means of faith, check this apprehension of the flesh; while the latter

---

[1] " Or il faut noter que les meschans voyans que tout leur vient à souchait font tellement estat de leur prosperite, qu'ils se font à croire que Dieu est aucunement obligé a eux."—*Fr.*

[2] " Qu'ils vivent sans crainte ne souci de l'advenir."—*Fr.* " That they live without any fear or concern about the future."

[3] " Et prenent plaisir à s'assopir et rendre leur conscience stupide, afin de se flatter en leurs vices."—*Fr.*

[4] " Retournans d'eux mesmes à bien considerer ce qui en est a la verite."—*Fr.*

indulge themselves in their froward imagination. Thus David, by the word *Arise*, does not so much stir up God, as he awakens himself, or endeavours to awaken himself, to hope for more of the assistance of God than he presently experienced. Accordingly, this verse contains the useful doctrine, that the more the ungodly harden themselves, through their slothful ignorance, and endeavour to persuade themselves that God takes no concern about men and their affairs, and will not punish the wickedness which they commit, the more should we endeavour to be persuaded of the contrary; yea, rather their ungodliness ought to incite us vigorously to repel the doubts which they not only admit, but studiously frame for themselves.

13. *Why doth the wicked despise God?* It is, indeed, superfluous to bring arguments before God, for the purpose of persuading him to grant us what we ask; but still he permits us to make use of them, and to speak to him in prayer, as familiarly as a son speaks to an earthly father. It should always be observed, that the use of praying is, that God may be the witness of all our affections; not that they would otherwise be hidden from him, but when we pour out our hearts before him, our cares are hereby greatly lightened, and our confidence of obtaining our requests increases. Thus David, in the present passage, by setting before himself how unreasonable and intolerable it would be for the wicked to be allowed to despise God according to their pleasure, thinking he will never bring them to an account,[1] was led to cherish the hope of deliverance from his calamities. The word which is here rendered *despise*, is the same as that which he had used before. Some translate it *to provoke*, and others *to blaspheme*. But the signification which I have preferred certainly agrees much better with the context; for when persons take from God the power and office of judging, this is ignominiously to drag him from his throne, and to degrade him, as it were, to the station of a private individual.[2]

[1] " A leur plaisir n'estimans pas que jamais il les amenast à conte."—*Fr.*
[2] " Au rang des hommes."—*Fr.* " To the rank of men."

Moreover, as David had a little before complained that the ungodly deny the existence of a God, or else imagine him to be constantly asleep, having no care about mankind, so now he complains to the same purpose that they say, *God will not require it.*

> 14. *Thou hast seen it; for thou considerest mischief and vexation,*[1] *that thou mayest take the matter into thine own hand: upon thee shall the poor leave, for thou wilt be the helper of the fatherless.*
> 15. *Break thou the arm of the wicked and the evil man; thou shalt seek his wickedness, and shalt not find it.*

14. *Thou hast seen it; for thou, &c.* Here David, suddenly kindled with a holy zeal, enters into conflict, and, armed with the shield of faith, courageously repels these execrable opinions; but as he could derive no advantage by making his appeal to men, he has recourse to God, and addresses him. As the ungodly, in the hope of enjoying unrestrained license in the commission of all kinds of wickedness, withdraw to the greatest possible distance from God,[2] and through the dictates of a perverse mind, imagine themselves to be far beyond his reach; so, on the contrary, the faithful ought carefully to keep themselves aloof from those wild opinions, which are afloat in the world, and with minds lifted upward, to speak to God as if present with them. Accordingly, David, in order to prevent himself from being overcome by the blasphemies of men, very properly turns away his attention from them. There is added a reason in confirmation of the first sentence of the verse, namely, because *God considers mischief and vexation.* Since it is the peculiar province of God to take cognisance of all wrongs, David concludes that it is impossible for God to shut his eyes when the ungodly are wrecklessly and without restraint committing their outrages. Moreover, he descends from the general to the particular, which ought to be attentively marked: for nothing is easier than to acknowledge in general terms that God exercises a care about the world, and the affairs of men; but it is very

---

[1] " Oppression."—*Fr.*
[2] " Se reculent le plus loin de Dieu qu'ils peuvent."—*Fr.*

difficult to apply this doctrine to its various uses in every-day life. And yet, all that the Scripture says concerning the power and righteousness of God will be of no advantage to us, and, as it were, only matter of meagre speculation,[1] unless every one apply these statements to himself, as his necessity may require. Let us therefore learn, from the example of David, to reason thus: that, since it belongs to God to take notice of all the mischief and injuries which are inflicted on the good and simple, He considers our trouble and sorrows even when he seems for a time to take no notice of them. The Psalmist also adds, that God does not look down from heaven upon the conduct of men here below as an idle and unconcerned spectator, but that it is his work to pass judgment upon it; for *to take the matter into his own hand*, is nothing else than duly and effectually to examine and determine it as a judge.

It is, however, our duty to wait patiently so long as vengeance is reserved in the hand of God, until he stretch forth his arm to help us. We see, therefore, the reason why it is immediately added, *Upon thee shall the poor leave*. By these words David means, that we ought to give the providence of God time to manifest itself. The godly, when they are afflicted, may with confidence cast their cares into his bosom, and commit themselves to his protection. They ought not, however, to be in haste for the accomplishment of their wishes; but, being now disburdened, they should take their breath till God manifestly declare that the fit time of interfering in their behalf is come. The man, therefore, *leaves upon God* who betakes himself to his protection, and who, fully persuaded of his faithfulness in keeping what is entrusted to him, quietly waits till the fit time of his deliverance come. Some read the verb passively, *The poor shall be left upon thee*. The first reading, however, is more correct, and it agrees with the rules of grammar; only it is a defective form of expression, inasmuch as the thing which the poor leaves is not expressed. But this defect is common in Hebrew; and there is no obscurity in the thing itself, namely, that, when the godly commit them-

---

[1] " Sera de nulle utilite et comme un speculation maigre."—*Fr.*

selves and their concerns to God by prayer, their prayers will not be in vain; for these two clauses are closely connected, *Upon thee shall the poor leave,* and, *Thou shalt be a helper to the fatherless.* By a metaphor he terms the person fatherless whom he had in the preceding clause called poor. And the verb being in the future tense denotes a continued act.

15. *Break thou the arm.* This form of expression just means breaking the power of the wicked. And it is not simply a prayer; it may also be regarded as a prophecy. As the ungovernable fury of our enemies very often makes us lose courage, as if there were no means by which it could be restrained, David, in order to support his faith, and preserve it from failing through the fears which presented themselves, sets before himself the consideration, that whenever it shall please God to break the power of the ungodly, he will bring to nothing both themselves and all their schemes. To make the meaning the more evident, the sentence may be explained in this way,—Lord, as soon as it shall seem good to thee to break the arm of the wicked, thou wilt destroy him in a moment, and bring to nought his powerful and violent efforts in the work of doing mischief. David, indeed, beseeches God to hasten his assistance and his vengeance; but, in the meantime, while these are withheld, he sustains himself by the consolatory reflection, that the ungodly cannot break forth into violence and mischief except in so far as God permits them; since it is in his power, whenever he ascends into the judgment-seat, to destroy them even with his look alone. And certainly, as the rising sun dissipates the clouds and vapours by his heat, and clears up the dark air, so God, when he stretches forth his hand to execute the office of a Judge, restores to tranquillity and order all the troubles and confusions of the world. The Psalmist calls the person of whom he speaks not only *wicked,* but *the wicked and the evil man,* and he does so, in my judgment, for the purpose of setting forth in a stronger light the greatness of the wickedness of the character which he describes. His words are as if he had said, Wicked men may even be frantic in their malice and im-

piety; but God can promptly and effectually remedy this evil whenever he pleases.

16. *Jehovah is King for ever and ever: the heathen are perished out of his land.*
17. *Thou hast heard the desire of the needy, O Jehovah: thou wilt direct* [1] *their hearts, and thine ear shall hear them.*
18. *To judge the fatherless and the poor, that the man who is of earth may no more terrify them.*

16. *Jehovah is King for ever and ever.* David now, as if he had obtained the desires of his heart, rises up to holy rejoicing and thanksgiving. When he calls God *King for ever and ever*, it is a token of his confidence and joy. By the title of *King*, he vindicates God's claim to the government of the world, and when he describes him as *King for ever and ever*, this shows how absurd it is to think to shut him up within the narrow limits of time. As the course of human life is short, even those who sway the sceptre over the greatest empires, being but mortal men, very often disappoint the expectations of their servants,[2] as we are taught in Psalm cxlvi. 3, 4, " Put not your trust in princes, nor in the son of man, in whom there is no help. His breath goeth forth, he returneth to his earth; in that very day his thoughts perish." Often the power of giving assistance to others fails them, and while they are delaying to give it, the opportunity slips away from them. But we ought to entertain more exalted and honourable conceptions of our heavenly King; for although he does not immediately execute his judgments, yet he has always the full and the perfect power of doing so. In short, he reigns, not for himself in particular; it is for us that he reigns for ever and ever. As this, then, is the duration of his reign, it follows that a long delay cannot hinder him from stretching forth his hand in due season to succour his people, even when they are, as it were, dead, or in a condition which, to the eye of sense and reason, is hopeless.—*The heathen are perished out of the land.* The meaning is, that the holy land was at length purged from the abominations and impurities with

---

[1] " Ou, fortifieras."—*Fr. marg.* " Or, thou wilt strengthen or establish."
[2] " Bien souvent frustrent leurs serviteurs de leur attente."—*Fr.*

which it had been polluted. It was a dreadful profanation, when the land which had been given for an inheritance to the people of God, and allotted to those who purely worshipped him, nourished ungodly and wicked inhabitants. By *the heathen* he does not mean foreigners, and such as did not belong to the race of Abraham according to the flesh,[1] but hypocrites, who falsely boasted that they belonged to the people of God, just as at this day many, who are Christians only in name, occupy a place in the bosom of the Church. It is no new thing for the prophets to call apostates, who have degenerated from the virtues and holy lives of their fathers, by the reproachful name of *heathen,* and to compare them not only to the uncircumcised, but also to the Canaanites, who were the most detestable among all the heathen. " Thy father was an Amorite, and thy mother an Hittite," (Ezek. xvi. 3.) Many other similar passages are to be met with in Scripture. David, therefore, in applying the dishonourable name of *heathen* to the false and bastard children of Abraham, gives God thanks for having expelled such a corrupt class out of his Church. By this example we are taught, that it is no new thing if we see in our own day the Church of God polluted by profane and irreligious men. We ought, however, to beseech God quickly to purge his house, and not leave his holy temple exposed to the desecration of swine and dogs, as if it were a dunghill.

17. *O Jehovah, thou hast heard the desire of the needy.* In these words the prophet confirms what I have just now said, that when hypocrites prevail in the Church, or exceed the faithful in number, we ought, unceasingly, to beseech God to root them out; for such a confused and shameful state of things ought surely to be matter of deep grief to all the true servants of God. By these words, also, the Holy Spirit assures us, that what of old God granted to the fathers in answer to their prayers, we at the present day will obtain, provided we have that anxious solicitude about the deliverance of the Church which we ought to entertain. The clause which

[1] " Et des personnes qui ne fussent de la race d'Abraham selon la chair."—*Fr.*

follows, *Thou wilt direct their hearts,* is variously interpreted by expositors. Some think it signifies the same thing as if it had been said, Thou wilt give success to their desires. According to others, the meaning is, Thou wilt frame and sanctify their hearts by thy grace, that they may ask nothing in prayer but what is right and according to the divine will, as Paul teaches us that the Holy Spirit " stirs up within us groanings which cannot be uttered," (Rom. viii. 26.) Both these expositions are perhaps too forced. David, in this clause, magnifies the grace of God in sustaining and comforting his servants in the midst of their troubles and distresses, that they may not sink into despondency,—in furnishing them with fortitude and patience,—in inspiring them with good hope,—and in stirring them up also to prayer. This is the import of the verb כין, *Kin,* which signifies not only *to direct,* but also *to establish.* It is a singular blessing which God confers upon us, when, in the midst of temptation, he upholds our hearts, and does not suffer them to recede from him, or to turn aside to any other quarter for support and deliverance. The meaning of the clause which immediately follows, *Thou wilt cause thine ear to hear,* is, that it is not in vain that God directs the hearts of his people, and leads them, in obedience to his command, to look to Himself, and to call upon him in hope and patience,—it is not in vain, because his ears are never shut against their groanings. Thus the mutual harmony between two religious exercises is here commended. God does not suffer the faith of his servants to faint or fail, nor does he suffer them to desist from praying; but he keeps them near him by faith and prayer, until it actually appear that their hope has been neither vain nor ineffectual. The sentence might, not improperly, be rendered thus: Thou shalt establish their heart, until thine ear hear them.

18. *That thou mayest judge.* Here the Psalmist applies the last sentence of the preceding verse to a special purpose, namely, to prevent the faithful, when they are unjustly oppressed, from doubting that God will at length take vengeance on their enemies, and grant them deliverance. By

these words he teaches us, that we ought to bear with patience and fortitude the crosses and afflictions which are laid upon us, since God often withholds assistance from his servants until they are reduced to extremity. This is, indeed, a duty of difficult performance, for we would all desire to be entirely exempted from trouble; and, therefore, if God does not quickly come to our relief, we think him remiss and inactive. But if we are anxiously desirous of obtaining his assistance, we must subdue our passion, restrain our impatience, and keep our sorrows within due bounds, waiting until our afflictions call forth the exercise of his compassion, and excite him to manifest his grace in succouring us.

That the man who is of earth may no more terrify them. David again commends the power of God in destroying the ungodly; and he does it for this purpose,—that in the midst of their tumultuous assaults we may have this principle deeply fixed in our minds, that God, whenever he pleases, can bring all their attempts to nothing. Some understand the verb ארץ, *arots*, which we have translated *to terrify*, as neuter, and read the words thus,—*that mortal man may be no more afraid.* But it agrees better with the scope of the passage to render it transitively, as we have done. And although the wicked prosper in their wicked course, and lift up their heads above the clouds, there is much truth in describing them as *mortal,* or *men liable to many calamities.* The design of the Psalmist is indirectly to condemn their infatuated presumption, in that, forgetful of their condition, they breathe out cruel and terrible threatenings, as if it were beyond the power of even God himself to repress the violence of their rage. The phrase, *of earth,* contains a tacit contrast between the low abode of this world and the height of heaven. For whence do they go forth to assault the children of God? Doubtless, from the earth, just as if so many worms should creep out of the crevices of the ground; but in so doing, they attack God himself, who promises help to his servants from heaven.

PSALM XI.

This psalm consists of two parts. In the first part, David recounts the severe assaults of temptation which he had encountered, and the state of distressing anxiety to which he had been reduced during the time of his persecution by Saul. In the second, he congratulates himself on the deliverance which God had granted him, and magnifies the righteousness of God in the government of the world.

¶ To the chief musician. A Psalm of David.

1. *In Jehovah do I put my trust : how then say ye to my soul, Flee ye into your mountain as a bird ?*
2. *Surely, behold ! the ungodly shall bend* [1] *their bow, they have fixed their arrows upon the string, to shoot secretly at the upright in heart.*
3. *Truly, the foundations are destroyed : what* [2] *hath the righteous One done ?*

1. *In Jehovah do I put my trust.* Almost all interpreters think that this is a complaint which David brings against his countrymen, that while seeking in every quarter for hiding-places, he could find nowhere even common humanity. And it is indeed true, that in the whole course of his wanderings, after betaking himself to flight to escape the cruelty of Saul, he could find no secure place of retreat, at least, none where he might continue for any length of time undisturbed. He might, therefore, justly complain of his own countrymen, in that none of them deigned to shelter him when he was a fugitive. But I think he has a respect to something higher. When all men were striving, as it were, with each other, to drive him to despair, he must, according to the weakness of the flesh, have been afflicted with great and almost overwhelming distress of mind; but fortified by faith, he confidently and stedfastly leaned on the promises of God,

---

[1] "Ont tendu l'arc."—*Fr.* "Have bent their bow."
[2] "Mais que ?"—*Fr.* "But what ?"

and was thus preserved from yielding to the temptations to which he was exposed. These spiritual conflicts, with which God exercised him in the midst of his extreme perils, he here recounts. Accordingly, as I have just now observed, the psalm should be divided into two parts. Before celebrating the righteousness of God, which he displays in the preservation of the godly, the Psalmist shows how he had encountered even death itself, and yet, through faith and an upright conscience, had obtained the victory. As all men advised him to leave his country, and retire into some place of exile, where he might be concealed, inasmuch as there remained for him no hope of life, unless he should relinquish the kingdom, which had been promised to him; in the beginning of the psalm, he opposes to this perverse advice the shield of his trust in God.

But before entering farther upon the subject, let us interpret the words. The word נוּד, *nud*, which we have rendered *to flee*, is written in the plural number, and yet it is read in the singular;[1] but, in my opinion, this is a corrupt reading. As David tells us that this was said to himself only, the Jewish doctors, thinking the plural number unsuitable, have taken it upon them to read the word in the singular. Some of them, wishing to retain the literal sense as it is called, perplex themselves with the question, why it is said, *Flee ye*, rather than *Flee thou;* and, at length, they have recourse to a very meagre subtilty, as if those who counselled him to betake himself to flight addressed both his soul and his body. But it was unnecessary labour to put themselves to so much trouble in a matter where there is no difficulty; for it is certain that those who counselled David did not say that he alone should flee, but that he

---

[1] Calvin's meaning is, that according to the Hebrew letters, the verb is in the plural number; but, according to the Hebrew punctuation, which regulates the reading, it is in the singular. Piscator, in his commentary on this passage, observes, "נוּדִי, *nudi*, according to the points, is singular and feminine, and refers to the soul of David; according to the letters it is plural, נוּדוּ, *nudu*, and refers to David and his associates. This last reading appears to me the most appropriate, both because it is followed by the relative in the plural number, and because it does not seem to be a proper or natural mode of expression, to speak of persons addressing the soul of another." The phrase, *to my soul*, however, may simply mean *to me*, a sense in which it is frequently used in Scripture.

should flee, together with all his attendants, who were in the same danger with himself. Although, therefore, they addressed themselves especially to David, yet they included his companions, who had a common cause with him, and were exposed to the like danger. Expositors, also, differ in their interpretation of what follows. Many render it *from your mountain*, as if it were מהרכם, *meharkem;* and, according to them, there is a change of person, because those who spoke to him must have said, *flee thou from* OUR *mountain.* But this is harsh and strained. Nor does it appear to me that they have any more reason on their side, when they say that Judea is here called mountain. Others think we should read הר כמו צפור, *har kemo tsippor*,[1] that is, *into the mountain as a bird*, without a pronoun.[2] But if we follow what I have said, it will agree very well with the scope of the passage to read thus, *Flee ye into your mountain,* for you are not permitted to dwell in your own country. I do not, however, think that any particular mountain is pointed out, but that David was sent away to the desert rocks wherever chance might lead him. Condemning those who gave him this advice, he declares that he depends upon the promise of God, and is not at all disposed thus to go away into exile. Such, then, was the condition of David, that, in his extreme necessity, all men repelled and chased him far away into desert places.

But as he seems to intimate that it would be a sign of distrust were he to place his safety in flight, it may be asked, whether or not it would have been lawful for him to flee; yea, we know that he was often forced to retire into exile, and

---

[1] This is the reading adopted by the Chaldee, Septuagint, and Vulgate versions. Hammond observes, that "where the Hebrew now reads, הרכם צפור, *harkem tsippor, To your mountain a sparrow,* all the ancient interpreters uniformly read, *To the mountain as a sparrow.*" Horsley translates the words, " Flee, sparrows, to your hill," and views the expression "as proverbial, denoting a situation of helplessness and danger, in which there was no hope of safety but in flight." The noun צפור *tsippor*, which he renders *sparrows*, is singular, and it is here construed with a plural verb and a plural pronoun. But he remarks, that as this word, like most names of animals in the Hebrew language, signifies either the individual or the species, it may here be used in the singular number for many individuals, and construed with plural verbs, adjectives, and pronouns.

[2] "Sans specifier à qui est ceste montagne."—*Fr.* "Without specifying whose mountain it is."

driven about from place to place, and that he even sometimes hid himself in caves. I answer, it is true he was unsettled like a poor fearful bird, which leaps from branch to branch,[1] and was compelled to seek for different bypaths, and to wander from place to place to avoid the snares of his enemies; yet still his faith continued so stedfast that he never alienated himself from the people of God. Others accounted him a lost man, and one whose affairs were in a hopeless condition, setting no more value upon him than if he had been a rotten limb,[2] yet he never separated himself from the body of the Church. And certainly these words, *Flee ye,* tended only to make him yield to utter despair. But it would have been wrong for him to have yielded to these fears, and to have betaken himself to flight, as if uncertain of what would be the issue. He therefore says expressly, that this *was spoken to his soul*, meaning that his heart was deeply pierced by such an ignominious rejection, since he saw (as I have said) that it tended only to shake and to weaken his faith. In short, although he had always lived innocently, as it became a true servant of God, yet these malignant men would have doomed him to remain for ever in a state of exile from his native country. This verse teaches us, that however much the world may hate and persecute us,[3] we ought nevertheless to continue stedfast at our post, that we may not deprive ourselves of a right to lay claim to the promises of God, or that these may not slip away from us; and that, however much and however long we may be harassed, we ought always to continue firm and unwavering in the faith of our having the call of God.

2. *Surely, behold! the ungodly.* Some think that this is added as the excuse made by those who desired David to save himself by flight. According to others, David expostulates with his countrymen, who saw death menacing him on

[1] " Je response que combien qu'il n'ait non plus este arresté qu'un poure oiselet craintif qui saute de branche en branche."—*Fr.*
[2] " Combien que les autres le tenissent pour un homme perdu et duquel les affaires estoyent hors d'espoir et qu'ils n'en feissent non plus de cas que d'un membre pourri."—*Fr.*
[3] " Nous deteste et poursuyve."—*Fr.*

all sides, and yet denied him shelter. But, in my judgment, he here continues his account of the trying circumstances in which he was placed. His design is not only to place before our view the dangers with which he was surrounded, but to show us that he was exposed even to death itself. He therefore says, that wherever he might hide himself, it was impossible for him to escape from the hands of his enemies. Now, the description of so miserable a condition illustrates the more strikingly the grace of God in the deliverance which he afterwards granted him. With respect to the words, *they have fixed their arrows upon the string, to* SHOOT SECRETLY, or *in darkness,* some understand them metaphorically of the attempts which David's enemies made to surprise him by craft and snares. I, however, prefer this interpretation, as being more simple,—that there was no place so hidden into which the darts of his enemies did not penetrate, and that, therefore, to whatever caves he could betake himself for concealment and shelter, death would follow him as his inseparable attendant.

3. *Truly, the foundations are destroyed.* Some translate the word השתות, *hashathoth,* by *nets,* a sense in which the Scripture in other places often uses this word; and their explanation of the words is, that the wicked and deceitful arts which the ungodly practised against David were defeated. If we admit this interpretation, the meaning of what he adds immediately after, *What hath the righteous one done?* will be, that his escape in safety was owing neither to his own exertion, nor to his own skill, but that, without putting forth any effort, and when, as it were, he was asleep, he had been delivered from the nets and snares of his enemies by the power of God. But the word *foundations* agrees better with the scope of the passage, for he evidently proceeds to relate into what straits he had been brought and shut up, so that his preservation was now to all appearance hopeless. Interpreters, however, who hold that *foundations* is the proper translation of the word, are not agreed as to the sense. Some explain it, that he had not a single spot on which to fix his foot; others, that covenants which ought to have stability, by being faithfully

kept, had been often shamefully violated by Saul. Some also understand it allegorically, as meaning that the righteous priests of God, who were the pillars of the land, had been put to death. But I have no doubt of its being a metaphor taken from buildings, which must fall down and become a heap of ruins when their foundations are undermined; and thus David complains, that, in the eyes of the world, he was utterly overthrown, inasmuch as all that he possessed was completely destroyed. In the last clause, he again repeats, that to be persecuted so cruelly was what he did not deserve: *What hath the righteous one done?* And he asserts his own innocence, partly to comfort himself in his calamities from the testimony of a good conscience, and partly to encourage himself in the hope of obtaining deliverance. That which encouraged him to trust in God was the belief which he entertained, that on account of the justice of his cause God was on his side, and would be favourable to him.

4. *Jehovah is in the palace of his holiness: Jehovah has his throne in heaven; his eyes behold,*[1] *and his eyelids consider the children of men.*

5. *Jehovah approves the righteous man; but his soul hateth the ungodly, and him who loveth iniquity.*

4. *Jehovah is in the palace of his holiness.* In what follows, the Psalmist glories in the assurance of the favour of God, of which I have spoken. Being destitute of human aid, he betakes himself to the providence of God. It is a signal proof of faith, as I have observed elsewhere, to take and to borrow, so to speak,[2] light from heaven to guide us to the hope of salvation, when we are surrounded in this world with darkness on every side. All men acknowledge that the world is governed by the providence of God; but when there comes some sad confusion of things, which disturbs their ease, and involves them in difficulty, there are few who retain in their minds the firm persuasion of this truth. But from the example of David, we ought to make such account

---

[1] The Septuagint has here the addition of Εις τον πενητα, "the afflicted one." "His eyes behold the afflicted one."

[2] "De prendre et par maniere de dire, emprunter lumiere du ciel."—*Fr.*

of the providence of God as to hope for a remedy from his judgment, even when matters are in the most desperate condition. There is in the words an implied contrast between heaven and earth; for if David's attention had been fixed on the state of things in this world, as they appeared to the eye of sense and reason, he would have seen no prospect of deliverance from his present perilous circumstances. But this was not David's exercise; on the contrary, when in the world all justice lies trodden under foot, and faithfulness has perished, he reflects that God sits in heaven perfect and unchanged, from whom it became him to look for the restoration of order from this state of miserable confusion. He does not simply say that God dwells in heaven; but that he reigns there, as it were, in a royal palace, and has his throne of judgment there. Nor do we indeed render to him the honour which is his due, unless we are fully persuaded that his judgment-seat is a sacred sanctuary for all who are in affliction and unrighteously oppressed. When, therefore, deceit, craft, treachery, cruelty, violence, and extortion, reign in the world; in short, when all things are thrown into disorder and darkness by injustice and wickedness, let faith serve as a lamp to enable us to behold God's heavenly throne, and let that sight suffice to make us wait in patience for the restoration of things to a better state. *The temple of his holiness*, or *his holy temple*, which is commonly taken for *Sion*, doubtless here signifies *heaven;* and that it does so is clearly shown by the repetition in the next clause, *Jehovah has his throne in heaven;* for it is certain David expresses the same thing twice.

His eyes behold. Here he infers, from the preceding sentence, that nothing is hidden from God, and that, therefore, men will be obliged to render up to him an account of all that they have done. If God reigns in heaven, and if his throne is erected there, it follows that he must necessarily attend to the affairs of men, in order one day to sit in judgment upon them. Epicurus, and such like him as would persuade themselves that God is idle, and indulges in repose in heaven, may be said rather to spread for him a couch on which to sleep,[1] than

---

[1] "Et se repose au ciel, luy font plustost une couche pour dormir."—*Fr.*

to erect for him a throne of judgment. But it is the glory of our faith that God, the Creator of the world, does not disregard or abandon the order which he himself at first established. And when he suspends his judgments for a time, it becomes us to lean upon this one truth—that he beholds from heaven; just as we now see David contenting himself with this consolatory consideration alone, that God rules over mankind, and observes whatever is transacted in the world, although his knowledge, and the exercise of his jurisdiction, are not at first sight apparent. This truth is still more clearly explained in what is immediately added in the fifth verse, that God distinguishes between the righteous and the unrighteous, and in such a way as shows that he is not an idle spectator; for he is said *to approve the righteous, and to hate the wicked.* The Hebrew word בחן, *bachan*, which we have rendered *to approve*, often signifies *to examine* or *try*. But in this passage I explain it as simply meaning, that God so inquires into the cause of every man as to distinguish the righteous from the wicked. It is farther declared, that God hates those who are set upon the infliction of injuries, and upon doing mischief. As he has ordained mutual intercourse between men, so he would have us to maintain it inviolable. In order, therefore, to preserve this his own sacred and appointed order, he must be the enemy of the wicked, who wrong and are troublesome to others. There is also here contrasted God's hatred of the wicked, and wicked men's *love of iniquity*, to teach us that those who please and flatter themselves in their mischievous practices gain nothing by such flatteries, and only deceive themselves.

6. *He will rain upon the ungodly snares, fire and brimstone, and a storm of whirlwinds: this is the portion of their cup.*
7. *For the righteous Jehovah loveth righteousness;*[1] *his countenance approveth the upright.*[2]

6. *He will rain upon the ungodly.* David now, in the last

---

[1] " Car le Seigneur *est* juste, et aime justice."—*Fr.* " For the Lord *is* righteous, and loveth righteousness."

[2] " La droiture."—*Fr.* " Uprightness." " Ou, le droiturier."—*Fr. marg.* " Or, the upright."

place, lays it down as a certain truth, that although God, for a time, may be still, and delay his judgments, yet the hour of vengeance will assuredly come. Thus we see how by degrees he rises up to the hope of a happy issue to his present affliction, and he uses his efforts to attain this, that the social and moral disorder, which he saw prevailing around him, might not weaken his faith. As the tribunal of God remains firm and immoveable, he, in the first place, sustains and comforts himself from the consideration, that God from on high beholds all that is done here below. In the next place, he considers what the office of judge requires, from which he concludes, that the actions of men cannot escape the inspection of God's omniscient eye, and that although he does not immediately punish their evil deeds, he hates all the wicked. Finally, he adds, that since God is armed with power, this hatred will not be in vain or ineffectual. Thus while God defers the infliction of punishment, the knowledge of his justice will have a powerful influence in maintaining our faith, until he actually show that he has never departed from his watch-tower, from which he beholds the actions of men.[1] He appropriately compares the punishments which God inflicts to rain. As rain is not constant, but the Lord sends it forth when he pleases; and, when the weather is calmest and most serene, suddenly raises a storm of hail or violent showers of rain; in like manner, it is here intimated that the vengeance which will be inflicted on the wicked will come suddenly, so that, when they shall be indulging in mirth, and intoxicated with their pleasures, and " when they shall say, Peace and safety, sudden destruction will come upon them."[2] At the same time, David here evidently alludes to the destruction of Sodom and Gomorrah. As the prophets, when they would promise the grace of God to the elect, remind them of the deliverance from Egypt, which God wrought in behalf of his ancient people, so when they would alarm the wicked, they threaten them with a destruction like that which befell Sodom and Gomorrah, and

---

[1] " De laquelle il contemple les faits des hommes."—*Fr.*

[2] " Et qu'ils diront paix et asseurance mort soudaine leur adviendra."—*Fr.*

they do so upon good grounds; since Jude, in his Epistle, tells us that these cities "are set forth for an example, suffering the vengeance of eternal fire," (verse 7.) The Psalmist, with much beauty and propriety, puts *snares*[1] before fire and brimstone. We see that the ungodly, while God spares them, fear nothing, but give themselves ample scope in their wayward courses, like horses let loose[2] in an open field; and then, if they see any adversity impending over them, they devise for themselves ways of escape: in short, they continually mock God, as if they could not be caught, unless he first entangle and hold them fast in his snares. God, therefore, begins his vengeance by snares, shutting up against the wicked every way of escape; and when he has them entangled and bound, he thunders upon them dreadfully and horribly, like as he consumed Sodom and the neighbouring cities with fire from heaven. The word וְלְעָפוֹת, *zilaphoth,* which we have rendered *whirlwinds,* is by some translated *kindlings*

---

[1] Horsley reads, "glowing embers." Lowth renders the word "live coals," and observes, that פחים, *pachim,* means *globes of fire,* or simply the *lightning.* "This," says he, "is certainly more agreeable to the context than snares. The root is *puach,* which, though it sometimes means *to ensnare,* yet more frequently means *to breathe forth,* or *emit,* fire, for instance. Ezekiel xxi. 31, ' In the fire of my wrath I will blow upon thee.' The Ammonites are spoken of as thrown into the furnace of the divine wrath: compare chap. xxii. 21, where almost the same words occur, except that the corresponding (and in this case synonymous) verb *napach* is made use of, whence *mapnach,* a bellows, Jer. vi. 29. In the same sense the verb *puach* is introduced, Prov. xxix. 8, ' Scorners will *inflame* a city.' From this explication of the root *puach,* the word *pach, a coal blown up,* is rightly derived."—*Sacred Poetry of the Hebrews,* vol. i. pp. 194, 195. Lowth also states, that the Orientals sometimes call the lightning *snares* or *chains,* probably from the continual corruscations of the lightning in its passage through the air, which seem to be connected with each other like a chain. Hengstenberg, however, opposes this exposition, and adopts and defends that which Calvin has given. "פחים," says he, "must here, according to most expositors, be taken as a figurative designation of *lightning,* which is alleged to be called also by the Arabians, in prose and poetry, by the name of *chains.* But it is a sufficient objection to this meaning, that פח does not signify *cord,* in general, but specially, gin, snare, trap." In proof of this, he quotes Psalm ix. 15; Job xviii. 9; xxii. 10; Isaiah xxiv. 17, 18; Prov. xxii. 5. "The expression, *that he will rain,"* says he, " can present no proper difficulty, as it simply points to the fulness of God's retributive judgments, noticed already by Luther, when he says, that by it ' the prophet indicates the great variety and multitude of the evils threatened.'"

[2] " Ainsi que des chevaux desbridez."—*Fr.*

or *burnings;* and by others, *commotions* or *terrors.*[1] But the context requires the interpretation which I have brought forward; for a tempest is raised by stormy winds, and then follow thunder and lightning.

The portion of their cup. By this expression he testifies that the judgments of God will certainly take effect, although ungodly men may delude themselves by deceitful flattery. This metaphor is frequently to be met with in the Scriptures. As the carnal mind believes nothing with greater difficulty than that the calamities and miseries which seem to be fortuitous, happen according to a just distribution from God, he represents himself under the character of a householder, who distributes to each member his portion or allowance. David, therefore, here intimates that there is certainly a reward laid up for the ungodly; that it will be in vain for them to resist, when the Lord shall reach to them the cup of his wrath to drink; and that the cup prepared for them is not such as they may sip drop by drop, but a cup, the whole of which they will be compelled to drink, as the prophet threatens, (Ezek. xxiii. 34,) " Thou shalt drink it off even to the dregs."

7. *For the righteous Jehovah loveth righteousness.* The Psalmist has just now reasoned from the office of God that he will punish the wicked, and now, from the nature of God, he concludes, that he will be the defender of the good and

---

[1] Dr Adam Clarke renders the words רוח זלעפות, *ruach zilaphoth*, "the spirit of terrors," and states, that "this may refer to the horribly suffocating Arabian wind called *Smum.*" Bishop Lowth translates the words, " a burning storm," upon which Michaelis observes, "This is an admirable image, and is taken from the school of nature. The wind *zilgaphoth*, which blows from the east, is very pestilential, and, therefore, almost proverbial among the Orientals. . . . . Many wonderful stories are related of its effects by the Arabians, and their poets feign that the wicked, in their place of eternal torment, are to breathe this pestiferous wind as their vital air."—*Lowth's Sacred Poetry*, vol. i. p. 193. Hengstenberg translates the words *wrath-wind*, and explains them as simply meaning the divine anger which breaks forth as a tempest; and observes, that the vehemence of the anger is denoted by the plural number. In opposition to the rendering *burning wind*, and to the opinion that there is an allusion to the Arabian *Samum*, he states, "The root, זעף, has, in Hebrew, the signification of *being angry*, no other; and that of *being hot*, is not once to be found in the dialects."

the upright. As he is righteous, David shows that, as the consequence of this, he must love righteousness, for otherwise he would deny himself. Besides, it would be a cold speculation to conceive of righteousness as inherent in God, unless, at the same time, we could come to the settled conclusion that God graciously owns whatever is his own, and furnishes evidence of this in the government of the world. Some think that the abstract term *righteousness* is put for *righteous persons*. But, in my opinion, the literal sense is here more suitable, namely, that righteousness is well pleasing to God, and that, therefore, he favours good causes. From this the Psalmist concludes, that the upright are the objects of his regard : *His countenance approveth the upright.* He had said a little before in a different sense, that God beholds the children of men, meaning that he will judge the life of every man; but here he means that God graciously exercises a special care over the upright and the sincere, takes them under his protection, and keeps them in perfect safety. This conclusion of the psalm sufficiently shows, that the scope of the whole of it was to make it manifest that all those who, depending upon the grace of God, sincerely follow after righteousness, shall be safe under his protection. The Psalmist himself was one of this number, and, indeed, the very chief of them. This last clause, *His countenance approveth the upright,* is, indeed, variously explained; but the true meaning, I have no doubt, is, that God has always a regard for the upright, and never turns away his eyes from them. It is a strained interpretation to view the words as meaning that the upright shall behold the face of God. But I will not stop to refute the opinions of other men.

PSALM XII.

David, deploring the wretched and forlorn condition of his people, and the utter overthrow of good order, beseeches God to afford them speedy relief. Then, in order to comfort both himself and all the godly, after having mentioned God's promise of assisting his people, he magnifies his faithfulness and constancy in performing his promises. From this he concludes, that at length God will deliver the godly, even when the world may be in a state of the greatest corruption.[1]

¶ To the chief musician upon the eighth. A song of David.

1. *Save me, O Jehovah ; for the merciful man hath failed, and the faithful are wasted away from among the children of men.*
2. *Every one speaketh deceit* [or *falsehood*] *with his neighbour; they speak with lips of flattery, with a double heart.*[2]

To the chief musician upon the eighth. With respect to the word *eighth*, there are two opinions among interpreters. According to some, it means a musical instrument; while others are rather inclined to think that it is a tune. But as it is of no great importance which of these opinions is adopted, I do not trouble myself much about this matter. The conjecture of some, that it was the beginning of a song, does not seem to me to be so probable as that it refers to the tune, and was intended to point out how the psalm was to be sung.[3] In the commencement David complains that the

---

[1] "Voire au temps mesmes qu'il n'y aura foy ni equite au monde."—*Fr.* "Even when there is neither faith nor equity in the world."

[2] Calvin's words literally rendered are, *with a heart and a heart*, and this is a very literal translation of the Hebrew words בלב ולב, *be-leb va-leb*. On the margin of the French version, he reads, "De cœur double," "*with a double heart*," which explains the meaning of the other phrase. "With a heart and a heart," is a form of expression which forcibly describes the character of deceitful men. "They seem to have *two hearts*," says Dr Adam Clarke, "*one* to speak fair words, and the *other* to invent mischief."

[3] "Et que c'est pour exprimer comment se devoit chanter le pseaume."—*Fr.*

land was so overspread with wicked men, and persons who had broken forth into the commission of every kind of wickedness, that the practice of righteousness and justice had ceased, and none was found to defend the cause of the good; in short, that there remained no longer either humanity or faithfulness. It is probable that the Psalmist here speaks of the time when Saul persecuted him, because then all, from the highest to the lowest, had conspired to destroy an innocent and an afflicted man. It is a thing very distressing to relate, and yet it was perfectly true, that righteousness was so utterly overthrown among the chosen people of God, that all of them, with one consent, from their hostility to a good and just cause, had broken forth into acts of outrage and cruelty. David does not here accuse strangers or foreigners, but informs us that this deluge of iniquity prevailed in the Church of God. Let the faithful, therefore, in our day, not be unduly discouraged at the melancholy sight of a very corrupt and confused state of the world; but let them consider that they ought to bear it patiently, seeing their condition is just like that of David in time past. And it is to be observed, that, when David calls upon God for succour, he encourages himself in the hope of obtaining it from this, that there was no uprightness among men; so that from his example we may learn to betake ourselves to God when we see nothing around us but black despair. We ought to be fully persuaded of this, that the greater the confusion of things in the world is, God is so much the readier to aid and succour his people,[1] and that it is then the most proper season for him to interpose his assistance.

1. *The merciful man hath failed.* Some think that this is a complaint that the righteous had been unjustly put to death; as if the Psalmist had said, Saul has cruelly cut off all who observed justice and faithfulness. But I would understand the words in a simpler sense, as meaning that there is no longer any beneficence or truth remaining among men. He has expressed in these two words in what true righteous-

---

[1] " Tant plus Dieu est prest d'aider et secourir les siens."—*Fr.*

ness consists. As there are two kinds of unrighteousness, violence and deceit; so men live righteously when, in their intercourse with each other, they conscientiously abstain from doing any wrong or injury to one another, and cultivate peace and mutual friendship; when they are neither lions nor foxes. When, however, we see the world in such a state of disorder as is here described, and are afflicted thereby, we ought to be careful not to howl with the wolves, nor to suffer ourselves to be carried away with the dissipation and overflowing flood of iniquity which we see prevailing around us, but should rather imitate the example of David.

2. *Every man speaketh deceit.* David in this verse sets forth that part of unrighteousness which is contrary to truth. He says that there is no sincerity or uprightness in their speech, because the great object upon which they are bent is to deceive. He next describes the manner in which they deceive, namely, that every man endeavours to ensnare his neighbour by *flattery.*[1] He also points out the fountain and first cause of this, *They speak with a double heart.* This doubleness of heart, as I may term it, makes men double and variable in their speech, in order thereby to disguise themselves in different ways,[2] or to make themselves appear to others different from what they really are. Hence the Hebrew word חלקות, *chalakoth,* which denotes flattery, is derived from a word which signifies *division.* As those who are resolved to act truthfully in their intercourse with their neighbours, freely and ingenuously lay open their whole heart; so treacherous and deceitful persons keep a part of their feeling hidden within their own breasts, and cover it with the varnish of hypocrisy and a fair outside; so that from their speech we cannot gather any thing certain with respect to their intentions. Our speech, therefore, must be sincere in order that it may be as it were a mirror, in which the uprightness of our heart may be beheld.

---

[1] Horsley reads "smooth lips." "Not smooth," says he, "with flattery, but with *glosing lies,* with ensnaring eloquence and specious arguments in support of the wretched cause which they espouse."

[2] "Pour se disguiser en diverses sortes."—*Fr.*

3. *Let Jehovah cut off all flattering lips, and the tongue that speaketh great* [or *proud*] *things :*
4. *Those who have said we will be strengthened by our tongues; our lips are in our own power : who is lord over us ?*

To his complaint in the preceding verse he now subjoins an imprecation, that God would cut off deceitful tongues. It is uncertain whether he wishes that deceitful men may be utterly destroyed, or only that the means of doing mischief may be taken from them; but the scope of the passage leads us rather to adopt the first sense, and to view David as desiring that God, by some means or other, would remove that plague out of the way. As he makes no mention of malice, while he inveighs so vehemently against their envenomed tongues, we hence conclude, that he had suffered much more injury from the latter than from the former; and certainly falsehood and calumnies are more deadly than swords and all other kind of weapons. From the second clause of the third verse it appears more clearly what kind of flatterers they were of whom mention was made in the preceding verse : *The tongue that speaketh great or proud things.* Some flatter in a slavish and fulsome manner, declaring that they are ready to do and suffer any thing which they possibly can for our benefit. But David here speaks of another kind of flatterers, namely, those who in flattering proudly boast of what they will accomplish, and mingle base effrontery and threatening with their deceitful arts. He does not, therefore, speak of the herd of mean conceited persons among the common people who make a trade of flattering, that they may live at other people's expense;[1] but he points his imprecation against the great calumniators of the court to which he was attached,[2] who not only insinuated

[1] " Il ne parle donc pas d'un tas de faquins du commun peuple, qui font estat de flatter pour avoir la lippee franche."—*Fr.*
[2] "The occasion on which this psalm was composed is not expressed, but it is a sad complaint of the corrupt manners of that age, (especially of the court of Saul, v. 3,) in which it was hard to find an honest plain-dealing man, in whom one might confide. Some think it aims partly at Doeg, and such like courtiers ; partly at the Ziphites, and such perfidious people in the country, who, promising him their friendship, (as Theodoret understands it,) would have most basely betrayed him unto Saul, his declared enemy."—*Bishop Patrick's Paraphrase on the Book of Psalms.*

themselves by gentle arts, but also lied designedly in boasting of themselves, and in the big and haughty discourse with which they overwhelmed the poor and simple.[1]

This the Psalmist confirms more fully in the following verse: *Who have said, we will be strengthened by our tongues.* Those must be possessed of great authority who think that, in the very falsehood to which they are addicted, they have enough of strength to accomplish their purposes, and to protect themselves. It is the utmost height of wickedness for persons to break out into such presumption, that they scruple not to overthrow all law and equity by their arrogant and boasting language; for, in doing this, it is just as if they openly declared war against God himself. Some read, *we will strengthen our tongues.* This reading is passable, in so far as the sense is concerned, but it scarcely agrees with the rules of grammar, because the letter ל, *lamed*, is added. Moreover, the sense which is more suitable is this: that the wicked persons spoken of being armed with their tongues, go beyond all bounds, and think they can accomplish by this means whatever they please; just as this set of men so deform every thing with their calumnies, that they would almost cover the sun himself with darkness.

> 5. Because of the spoiling[2] of the needy, because of the groaning of the poor, I will now arise, Jehovah will say ; I will set in safety him whom he snareth.[3]
> 6. The words of Jehovah are pure words : silver melted in an excellent crucible of earth, purified seven times.

5. *Because of the spoiling of the needy.* David now sets before himself as matter of consolation, the truth that God will not suffer the wicked thus to make havoc without end and measure. The more effectually to establish himself and others in the belief of this truth, he introduces God himself as speak-

---

[1] "Mais qui mentent à plaisir en se vantans et tenans propos braves et hautains, desquels ils accablent les poures et simples."—*Fr.*

[2] "Oppression."—*Fr.*

[3] "*Celuy* a qui *le meschant* tend des laqs."—*Fr.* "*Him* for whom *the wicked* lays snares."—*Heb.* "Il luy tend des laqs."—*Fr. marg.* "I will set in safety; he lays snares for him."

ing. The expression is more emphatic when God is represented as coming forward and declaring with his own mouth that he is come to deliver the poor and distressed. There is also great emphasis in the adverb *now*, by which God intimates that, although our safety is in his hand, and, therefore, in secure keeping, yet he does not immediately grant deliverance from affliction; for his words imply that he had hitherto been, as it were, lying still and asleep, until he was awakened by the calamities and the cries of his people. When, therefore, the injuries, the extortions, and the devastations of our enemies leave us nothing but tears and groans, let us remember that now the time is at hand when God intends to rise up to execute judgment. This doctrine should also serve to produce in us patience, and prevent us from taking it ill, that we are reckoned among the number of the poor and afflicted, whose cause God promises to take into his own hand.

With respect to the meaning of the second clause of the verse, expositors differ. According to some, *to set in safety*, means the same thing as *to give or bring safety*, as if the letter ב, *beth*, which signifies *in*, were superfluous. But the language rather contains a promise to grant to those who are unjustly oppressed, full restitution. What follows is attended with more difficulty. The word פוח, *phuach*, which we have rendered *to lay snares for*, sometimes signifies *to blow out*, or *to puff*,—at other times *to ensnare*, or *to lay snares for;* and sometimes, also, *to speak*. Those who think it is here put for *to speak* also differ among themselves with respect to the meaning. Some render it *God will speak to himself;* that is to say, God will determine with himself; but as the Psalmist had already declared the determination of God, this would be an unnecessary and vain repetition. Others refer it to the language of the godly, as if David introduced them speaking one to another concerning the faithfulness and stability of the promises of God; for with this word they connect the following sentence, *The words of the Lord are pure words, &c.* But this view is even more strained than the preceding. The opinion of others, who suppose, that to the determination of God *to arise*, there is subjoined the language which is addressed to the godly, is more admissible.

It would not be sufficient for God to determine with himself what he would do for our safety, if he did not speak to us expressly, and by name. It is only when God makes us to understand, by his own voice, that he will be gracious to us, that we can entertain the hope of salvation. God, it is true, speaks also to unbelievers, but without producing any good effect, seeing they are deaf; just as when he treats them with gentleness and liberality, it is without effect, because they are stupid, and devour his benefits without any sense of their coming from him. But as I perceive that under the word יאמר, *yomar, will say,* the promises of God may be suitably and properly comprehended, to avoid a repetition of the same thing, I adopt without hesitation the sense of the last clause, which I have given in the translation, namely, that God declares he will arise to restore to safety those who seem on all sides to be environed by the snares of their enemies, and even caught in them. The import of the language is this: The ungodly may hold the poor and afflicted entangled in their snares as a prey which they have caught; but I will set them in safety. If it should be replied, that the reading in the Hebrew is not *for whom,* but *for him,* I would observe, that it is no new thing for these words, *him, for him,* to be used instead of *whom* and *for whom.*[1] If any one prefer the sense of *puffing at,* I am not disposed greatly to oppose him. According to this reading, David would elegantly taunt the pride of the ungodly, who confidently imagine they can do any thing,[2] even with their breath, as we have seen in the tenth psalm, at the fifth verse.

6. *The words of Jehovah.* The Psalmist now declares, that God is sure, faithful, and stedfast in his promises. But the insertion by the way of this commendation of the word of God would be to no purpose, if he had not first called himself, and other believers, to meditate on God's pro-

---

[1] "Et quant à ce qu'on pourroit replicquer qu'il n'y a pas en l'Hebrieu A qui, mais Luy, ce n'est pas chose nouvelle que ces mots Le, Luy se prenent pour Qui et À qui."—*Fr.*
[2] "Qu'ils renverseront tout à souffler seulement."—*Fr.* "That they shall overthrow all simply by their breath."

mises in their afflictions. Accordingly, the order of the Psalmist is to be attended to, namely, that, after telling us how God gives to his servants the hope of speedy deliverance, even in their deepest distresses, he now adds, to support their faith and hope, that God promises nothing in vain, or for the purpose of disappointing man. This, at first sight, seems a matter of small importance; but if any person consider more closely and attentively how prone the minds of men are to distrust and ungodly doubtings, he will easily perceive how requisite it is for our faith to be supported by this assurance, that God is not deceitful, that he does not delude or beguile us with empty words, and that he does not magnify beyond all measure either his power or his goodness, but that whatever he promises in word he will perform in deed. There is no man, it is true, who will not frankly confess that he entertains the same conviction which David here records, *that the words of Jehovah are pure;* but those who while lying in the shade and living at their ease liberally extol by their praises the truth of God's word, when they come to struggle with adversity in good earnest, although they may not venture openly to pour forth blasphemies against God, often charge him with not keeping his word. Whenever he delays his assistance, we call in question his fidelity to his promises and murmur just as if he had deceived us. There is no truth which is more generally received among men than that God is true; but there are few who frankly give him credit for this when they are in adversity. It is, therefore, highly necessary for us to cut off the occasion of our distrust; and whenever any doubt respecting the faithfulness of God's promises steals in upon us, we ought immediately to lift up against it this shield, that the words of the Lord are pure. The similitude of *silver,* which the Psalmist subjoins, is indeed far below the dignity and excellence of so great a subject; but it is very well adapted to the measure of our limited and imperfect understanding. Silver, if thoroughly refined, is valued at a high price amongst us. But we are far from manifesting for the word of God, the price of which is inestimable, an equal regard; and its purity is of less account with us than that of a corruptible metal. Yea, a great many coin mere dross in their own brain, by which to efface or obscure the brightness which shines in the word of God. The word בַּעֲלִיל, *baälil*, which we have translated *crucible*, is interpreted by many *prince*, or *lord*, as if it were a simple word. According to them, the meaning would be, that the word of God is like the purest silver, from which the dross has been completely removed with the greatest art and care, not for common use, but for the service of a great lord or prince of some country. I, however, rather agree with others who consider that בַּעֲלִיל, *baälil*, is a word compounded of the letter בְּ, *beth*, which signifies *in*, and the noun עֲלִיל, *alil*, which signifies a clean or well polished vessel or crucible.

> 7. *Thou, O Jehovah, wilt keep them; thou wilt preserve him from this generation for ever.*
> 8. *The ungodly walk about on every side; when they are exalted, there is reproach to the children of men.*

7. *Thou, O Jehovah.* Some think that the language of the Psalmist here is that of renewed prayer; and they, therefore, understand the words as expressive of his desire, and translate them in the optative mood, thus, *Do thou, O Jehovah, keep them.*[1] But I am rather of opinion that David, animated with holy confidence, boasts of the certain safety of all the godly, of whom God, who neither can deceive nor lie, avows himself to be the guardian. At the same time, I do not altogether disapprove of the interpretation which views David as renewing his supplications at the throne of grace. Some give this exposition of the passage, *Thou wilt keep them,* namely, *thy words;*[2] but this does not seem

---

[1] "Que tu les gardes, Seigneur."—*Fr.*

[2] This is the view adopted by Hammond. He refers the *them* to the *words of the Lord* mentioned in the preceding verse, and the *him* following to the godly, or just man, and explains the verse thus: "Thou, O Lord, shalt keep, or perform, those words, thou shalt preserve the just man from this generation for ever." The Chaldee version reads, "Thou wilt keep the just;" the Septuagint, Vulgate, Arabic, and Æthiopic versions read, "Thou wilt keep us."

to me to be suitable.¹ David, I have no doubt, returns to speak of the poor, of whom he had spoken in the preceding part of the psalm. With respect to his changing the number, (for, he says first, *Thou wilt keep them,* and, next, *Thou wilt preserve him,*²) it is a thing quite common in Hebrew, and the sense is not thereby rendered ambiguous. These two sentences, therefore, *Thou wilt keep them,* and *Thou wilt preserve him,* signify the same thing, unless, perhaps, we may say that, in the second, under the person of one man, the Psalmist intends to point out the small number of good men. To suppose this is not unreasonable or improbable; and, according to this view, the import of his language is, Although only one good man should be left alive in the world, yet he would be kept in perfect safety by the grace and protection of God. But as the Jews, when they speak generally, often change the number, I leave my readers freely to form their own judgment. This, indeed, cannot be controverted, that by the word *generation,* or *race,* is denoted a great multitude of ungodly persons, and almost the whole body of the people. As the Hebrew word דור, *dor,* signifies as well the men who live in the same age, as the space of time itself, David, without doubt, here means that the servants of God cannot escape, and continue safe, unless God defend them against the malice of the whole people, and deliver them from the wicked and perverse men of the age in which they live. Whence we learn that the world, at that time, was so corrupt, that David, by way of reproach, puts them all, as it were, into one bundle. Moreover, it is of importance again to remember what we have already stated, that he does not here speak of foreign nations, but of the Israelites, and God's chosen people. It is well to mark this carefully, that we may not be discouraged by the vast multitude of the ungodly, if we should sometimes see an immense heap of chaff upon the barn-floor of the Lord, while only a few grains of corn lie hidden

---

¹ "Mais quant à ceux qui disent, Tu les garderas, asçavoir, Tes paroles; l'exposition ne me semble pas propre."—*Fr.*

² "Car il dit premierement, *Tu les garderas;* et puis, *Tu le preserveras.*"—*Fr.*

underneath. And then, however small may be the number of the good, let this persuasion be deeply fixed in our minds, that God will be their protector, and that for ever. The word לְעוֹלָם, *leolam*, which signifies *for ever*, is added, that we may learn to extend our confidence in God far into the future, seeing he commands us to hope for succour from him, not only once, or for one day, but as long as the wickedness of our enemies continues its work of mischief. We are, however, from this passage, at the same time, admonished that war is not prepared against us for a short time only, but that we must daily engage in the conflict. And if the guardianship which God exercises over the faithful is sometimes hidden, and is not manifest in its effects, let them wait in patience until he arise; and the greater the flood of calamities which overflows them, let them keep themselves so much the more in the exercise of godly fear and solicitude.

8. *The ungodly walk about on every side.* The Hebrew word סָבִיב, *sabib*, which we have translated *on every side*, signifies *a circuit*, or *a going round;* and, therefore, some explain it allegorically thus: the ungodly seize upon all the defiles or narrow parts of roads, in order to shut up or besiege the good on all sides; and others expound it even more ingeniously, thus: that they lay snares by indirect means, and by inventions full of art and deception. But I think the simple meaning is, that they possess the whole land, and range about through every part of it; as if the Psalmist had said, Wherever I turn my eyes, I see troops of them on every side. In the next clause he complains that mankind are shamefully and basely oppressed by their tyranny. This is the meaning, provided the clause is read as a distinct one by itself, separate from the preceding, a point about which interpreters differ, although this view seems to come nearer to the mind of the inspired writer. Some render the verse in one continuous sentence, thus: *The ungodly fly about every where, when the reproaches among the children of men* (that is to say, when the worthless and the refuse of men) *are exalted,* an exposition which is not unsuitable. It commonly happens, that as diseases flow from the head into the members, so

corruptions proceed from princes, and infect the whole people. As, however, the former exposition is more generally received, and the most learned grammarians tell us that the Hebrew word זלות, *zuluth,* which we have translated *reproach,* is a noun of the singular number, I have adopted the former exposition, not that I am dissatisfied with the latter, but because we must needs choose the one or the other.

PSALM XIII.

The subject of this psalm is almost the same as that of the preceding. David, being afflicted, not only with the deepest distress, but also feeling himself, as it were, overwhelmed by a long succession of calamities and multiplied afflictions, implores the aid and succour of God, the only remedy which remained for him; and, in the close, taking courage, he entertains the assured hope of life from the promise of God, even amidst the terrors of death.

¶ To the chief musician. A song of David.

1. *How long, O Jehovah, wilt thou forget me, for ever? how long wilt thou hide thy face from me?*
2. *How long shall I take counsel in my soul? and have sorrow in my heart daily? how long shall mine enemy be exalted over me?*

1. *How long, O Jehovah.* It is very true that David was so greatly hated by the generality of people, on account of the calumnies and false reports which had been circulated against him, that almost all men judged that God was not less hostile to him than Saul[1] and his other enemies were. But here he speaks not so much according to the opinion of others, as

[1] It was the opinion of Theodoret that this psalm was composed by David, not during his persecution by Saul, but when Absalom conspired against him; and the reason which he assigns for this opinion is, "that the trouble which Saul gave him was before his great sin, and so he was full of confidence; but that of Absalom was after it, which made him cry out in this doleful manner." —*Bishop Patrick's Paraphrase on the Book of Psalms.*

according to the feeling of his own mind, when he complains of being neglected by God. Not that the persuasion of the truth of God's promises was extinguished in his heart, or that he did not repose himself on his grace; but when we are for a long time weighed down by calamities, and when we do not perceive any sign of divine aid, this thought unavoidably forces itself upon us, that God has forgotten us. To acknowledge in the midst of our afflictions that God has really a care about us, is not the usual way with men, or what the feelings of nature would prompt; but by faith we apprehend his invisible providence. Thus, it seemed to David, so far as could be judged from beholding the actual state of his affairs, that he was forsaken of God. At the same time, however, the eyes of his mind, guided by the light of faith, penetrated even to the grace of God, although it was hidden in darkness. When he saw not a single ray of good hope to whatever quarter he turned, so far as human reason could judge, constrained by grief, he cries out that God did not regard him; and yet by this very complaint he gives evidence that faith enabled him to rise higher, and to conclude, contrary to the judgment of the flesh, that his welfare was secure in the hand of God. Had it been otherwise, how could he direct his groanings and prayers to him? Following this example, we must so wrestle against temptations as to be assured by faith, even in the very midst of the conflict, that the calamities which urge us to despair must be overcome; just as we see that the infirmity of the flesh could not hinder David from seeking God, and having recourse to him: and thus he has united in his exercise, very beautifully, affections which are apparently contrary to each other. The words, *How long, for ever?* are a defective form of expression; but they are much more emphatic than if he had put the question according to the usual mode of speaking, *Why for so long a time?* By speaking thus, he gives us to understand, that for the purpose of cherishing his hope, and encouraging himself in the exercise of patience, he extended his view to a distance, and that, therefore, he does not complain of a calamity of a few days' duration, as the effeminate and the cowardly are accustomed to do, who see only what is before their feet, and immediately succumb at the first assault. He teaches us, therefore, by his example, to stretch our view as far as possible into the future, that our present grief may not entirely deprive us of hope.

2. *How long shall I take counsel in my soul?* We know that men in adversity give way to discontent, and look around them, first to one quarter, and then to another, in search of remedies. Especially, upon seeing that they are destitute of all resources, they torment themselves greatly, and are distracted by a multitude of thoughts; and in great dangers, anxiety and fear compel them to change their purposes from time to time, when they do not find any plan upon which they can fix with certainty. David, therefore, complains, that while thinking of different methods of obtaining relief, and deliberating with himself now in one way, and now in another, he is exhausted to no purpose with the multitude of suggestions which pass through his mind; and by joining to this complaint the *sorrow* which he felt daily, he points out the source of this disquietude. As in severe sickness the diseased would desire to change their place every moment, and the more acute the pains which afflict them are, the more fitful and eager are they in shifting and changing; so, when sorrow seizes upon the hearts of men, its miserable victims are violently agitated within, and they find it more tolerable to torment themselves without obtaining relief, than to endure their afflictions with composed and tranquil minds. The Lord, indeed, promises to give to the faithful " the spirit of counsel," (Is. xi. 2;) but he does not always give it to them at the very beginning of any matter in which they are interested, but suffers them for a time to be embarrassed by long deliberation without coming to a determinate decision,[1] or to be perplexed, as if they were entangled among thorns, not knowing whither to turn,[2] or what course to take. Some explain the Hebrew word יוֹמָם, *yomam*, as meaning *all the day long*. But it seems to me,

---

[1] " Mais permet que pour un temps ils s'entortillent en de longs discours sans venir au poinct."—*Fr.*
[2] " Ne sçachans où se tourner."—*Fr.*

that by it is rather meant another kind of continuance, namely, that his sorrow returned, and was renewed every day. In the end of the verse he deplores another evil, that his adversaries triumph over him the more boldly, when they see him wholly enfeebled, and as it were wasted by continual languor. Now this is an argument of great weight in our prayers; for there is nothing which is more displeasing to God, and which he will less bear with, than the cruel insolence which our enemies display, when they not only feast themselves by beholding us in misery, but also rise up the higher against us, and treat us the more disdainfully, the more they see us oppressed and afflicted.

>   3. *Behold,* [or *look upon me,*] *answer me, O Jehovah my God; enlighten mine eyes, lest I sleep in death;*
>   4. *Lest my enemy say, I have prevailed against him; and those who afflict me rejoice if I should fall.*

3. *Look upon me, answer me.* As when God does not promptly afford assistance to his servants, it seems to the eye of sense that he does not behold their necessities, David, for this reason, asks God, in the first place, to look upon him, and, in the second place, to succour him. Neither of these things, it is true, is prior or posterior in respect of God; but it has been already stated in a preceding psalm, and we will have occasion afterwards frequently to repeat the statement, that the Holy Spirit purposely accommodates to our understanding the models of prayer recorded in Scripture. If David had not been persuaded that God had his eyes upon him, it would have availed him nothing to cry to God; but this persuasion was the effect of faith. In the meantime, until God actually puts forth his hand to give relief, carnal reason suggests to us that he shuts his eyes, and does not behold us. The manner of expression here employed amounts to the same thing as if he had put the mercy of God in the first place, and then added to it his assistance, because God then hears us, when, having compassion upon us, he is moved and induced to succour us. *To enlighten the eyes* signifies the same thing in the Hebrew language as to give the breath

of life, for the vigour of life appears chiefly in the eyes. In this sense Solomon says, (Prov. xxix. 13,) "The poor and the deceitful man meet together; the Lord lighteneth both their eyes." And when Jonathan fainted for hunger, the sacred history relates that his eyes were overcast with dimness; and again, that when he had tasted of the honeycomb, his eyes were enlightened, (1 Sam. xiv. 27.) The word *sleep*, as it is used in this passage, is a metaphor of a similar kind, being put for death. In short, David confesses, that unless God cause the light of life to shine upon him, he will be immediately overwhelmed with the darkness of death, and that he is already as a man without life, unless God breathe into him new vigour. And certainly our confidence of life depends on this, that although the world may threaten us with a thousand deaths, yet God is possessed of numberless means of restoring us to life.[1]

4. *Lest my enemy.* David again repeats what he had a little before said concerning the pride of his enemies, namely, how it would be a thing ill becoming the character of God were he to abandon his servant to the mockery of the ungodly. David's enemies lay, as it were, in ambush watching the hour of his ruin, that they might deride him when they saw him fall. And as it is the peculiar office of God to repress the audacity and insolence of the wicked, as often as they glory in their wickedness, David beseeches God to deprive them of the opportunity of indulging in such boasting. It is, however, to be observed, that he had in his conscience a sufficient testimony to his own integrity, and that he trusted also in the goodness of his cause, so that it would have been unbecoming and unreasonable had he been left without succour in danger, and had he been overwhelmed by his enemies. We can, therefore, with confidence pray for ourselves, in the manner in which David here does for himself, only when we fight under the standard of God, and are obedient to his orders, so

---

[1] "Toutesfois Dieu ha en main des moyens infinis de nous restablir en vie.'--*Fr.*

that our enemies cannot obtain the victory over us without wickedly triumphing over God himself.

> 5. *But I trust in thy goodness; my heart shall exult in thy salvation. I will sing unto the Lord, because he hath dealt bountifully with me.*[1]

The Psalmist does not as yet feel how much he has profited by praying; but depending upon the hope of deliverance, which the faithful promise of God enabled him to entertain, he makes use of this hope as a shield to repel those temptations with the terror of which he might be greatly distressed. Although, therefore, he is severely afflicted, and a multiplicity of cares urge him to despair, he, notwithstanding, declares it to be his resolution to continue firm in his reliance upon the grace of God, and in the hope of salvation. With the very same confidence ought all the godly to be furnished and sustained, that they may duly persevere in prayer. Whence, also, we gather what I have formerly adverted to, that it is by faith we apprehend the grace of God, which is hidden from and unknown to the understanding of the flesh. As the verbs which the Psalmist uses are not put in the same tense, different meanings may be drawn from the different tenses; but David, I have no doubt, here wishes to testify that he continued firm in the hope of the deliverance promised to him, and would continue so even to the end, however heavy the burden of temptations which might press upon him. Accordingly, the word *exult* is put in the future tense, to denote the continued exercise of the affection spoken of, and that no affliction shall ever shake out of his heart *the joy of faith.* It is to be observed, that he places the good-

---

[1] The Septuagint here add another line, namely, "Καὶ ψαλῶ τῷ ὀνόματι Κυρίου τοῦ ὑψίστου," "And I will sing to the name of Jehovah, the Most High." This line, which is the same with that which concludes the seventh psalm, has probably been lost in the Hebrew copy. "The conclusion of the psalm," says Lowth, "is manifestly defective; it ends with an odd hemistich wanting its correspondent. The LXX. have happily preserved it. . . . That it is not a double translation of the single hemistich, now in the Hebrew, is apparent from the difference of the latter Greek hemistich, which does not at all correspond with the words of the former."—*Dr Lowth in Merrick's note on this place.*

ness of God first in order, as being the cause of his deliverance,—*I will sing unto the Lord.* I translate this into the future tense. David, it is true, had not yet obtained what he earnestly desired, but being fully convinced that God was already at hand to grant him deliverance, he pledges himself to give thanks to him for it. And surely it becomes us to engage in prayer in such a frame of mind as at the same time to be ready to sing the praises of God; a thing which is impossible, unless we are fully persuaded that our prayers will not be ineffectual. We may not be wholly free from sorrow, but it is nevertheless necessary that this cheerfulness of faith rise above it, and put into our mouth a song on account of the joy which is reserved for us in the future, although not as yet experienced by us;[1] just as we see David here preparing himself to celebrate in songs the grace of God, before he perceives the issue of his troubles. The word גמל, *gamal*,[2] which others render *to reward*, signifies nothing else here than *to bestow a benefit from pure grace*, and this is its meaning in many other passages of Scripture. What kind of thanksgiving, I pray you to consider, would that be, to say that God rewarded and rendered to his servant due recompense? This is sufficient to refute the absurd and trifling sophism of those who wrest this passage to prove the merit of works. In short, the only thing which remains to be observed is, that David, in hastening with promptitude of soul to sing of God's benefits before he had received them, places the deliverance, which was then apparently at a distance, immediately before his eyes.

---

[1] " Qui ne nous est point encore presente."—*Fr.*

[2] גמל signifies " *to return, to requite, to recompense*, in whatever manner, whether evil for evil, good for evil, evil for good, or good for good." —*Parkhurst.* Those who argue from this passage for the merit of good works, make the argument to rest on the notion of retribution attached to the word. But although it uniformly meant *to reward*, no conclusive argument could here be drawn from this passage in support of that doctrine. What God bestows upon his people is sometimes called *a reward* in Scripture; not, however, because they can claim it as due to them by justice, but to express God's approbation of obedience, and the connection between obedience and happiness. Besides, גמל also means *to deal kindly with*, especially when applied to God, See Psalm cxix. 17, and cxlii. 8. The word has this meaning in Arabic; and that it is to be thus understood in the passage before us is supported by the ancient versions. The Septuagint reads εὐεργετήσαντι; and the Vulgate, *bona tribuit,* hath bestowed upon me good. The Arabic and Æthiopic adopt the same reading.

PSALM XIV.

In the beginning the Psalmist describes the wicked contempt of God into which almost the whole people had broken forth. To give the greater weight to his complaint, he represents God himself as uttering it. Afterwards he comforts himself and others with the hope of a remedy, which he assures himself God will very soon provide, although, in the meantime, he groans and feels deep distress at the disorder which he beholds.[1]

¶ To the chief musician of David.

1. *The fool hath said in his heart, There is no God; they have corrupted,*[2] *they have done abominable work; there is none that doeth good.*

MANY of the Jews are of opinion that in this psalm there is given forth a prediction concerning the future oppression of their nation: as if David, by the revelation of the Holy Spirit, bewailed the afflicted condition of the Church of God under the tyranny of the Gentiles. They therefore refer what is here spoken to the dispersed condition in which we see them at the present day, as if they were that precious heritage of God which the wild beasts devour. But it is very apparent, that in wishing to cover the disgrace of their nation, they wrest and apply to the Gentiles, without any just ground, what is said concerning the perverse children of Abraham.[3] We cannot certainly find a better qualified

---

[1] "Combien que cependant il gemisse et se sente angoisse du desordre qu'il veoit."—*Fr.*

[2] Calvin has here given a literal rendering of the Hebrew words, *They have corrupted*. Some suppose that *themselves* is to be understood, as in Ex. xxxii. 7; others, *their* ways, as in Gen. vi. 12: but the meaning which Calvin has attached to the phrase is, They have corrupted or perverted all good order.

[3] "Ce qui est dit de ceux qui à fausses enseignes serenomment enfans d'Abraham vivans autrement qu'il n'appartient."—*Fr.* "What is said of those who, according to false marks, call themselves the children of Abraham, while living a different life from what they ought."

interpreter than the Apostle Paul, and he applies this psalm expressly to the people who lived under the law, (Rom. iii. 19.) Besides, although we had not the testimony of this Apostle, the structure of the psalm very clearly shows that David means rather the domestic tyrants and enemies of the faithful than foreign ones; a point which it is very necessary for us to understand. We know that it is a temptation which pains us exceedingly, to see wickedness breaking forth and prevailing in the midst of the Church, the good and the simple unrighteously afflicted, while the wicked cruelly domineer according to their pleasure. This sad spectacle almost completely disheartens us; and, therefore, we have much need to be fortified from the example which David here sets before us: so that, in the midst of the greatest desolations which we behold in the Church, we may comfort ourselves with this assurance, that God will finally deliver her from them. I have no doubt that there is here described the disordered and desolate state of Judea which Saul introduced when he began to rage openly. Then, as if the remembrance of God had been extinguished from the minds of men, all piety had vanished, and with respect to integrity or uprightness among men, there was just as little of it as of godliness.

The fool hath said. As the Hebrew word נבל, *nabal*, signifies not only a fool, but also a perverse, vile, and contemptible person, it would not have been unsuitable to have translated it so in this place; yet I am content to follow the more generally received interpretation, which is, that all profane persons, who have cast off all fear of God and abandoned themselves to iniquity, are convicted of madness. David does not bring against his enemies the charge of common foolishness, but rather inveighs against the folly and insane hardihood of those whom the world accounts eminent for their wisdom. We commonly see that those who, in the estimation both of themselves and of others, highly excel in sagacity and wisdom, employ their cunning in laying snares, and exercise the ingenuity of their minds in despising and mocking God. It is therefore important for us, in the first place, to know, that however much the world applaud these crafty and scoffing characters, who allow themselves to indulge to any extent in wickedness, yet the Holy Spirit condemns them as being fools; for there is no stupidity more brutish than forgetfulness of God. We ought, however, at the same time, carefully to mark the evidence on which the Psalmist comes to the conclusion that they have cast off all sense of religion, and it is this: that they have overthrown all order, so that they no longer make any distinction between right and wrong, and have no regard for honesty, nor love of humanity. David, therefore, does not speak of the hidden affection of the heart of the wicked, except in so far as they discover themselves by their external actions. The import of his language is, How does it come to pass, that these men indulge themselves in their lusts so boldly and so outrageously, that they pay no regard to righteousness or equity; in short, that they madly rush into every kind of wickedness, if it is not because they have shaken off all sense of religion, and extinguished, as far as they can, all remembrance of God from their minds? When persons retain in their heart any sense of religion, they must necessarily have some modesty, and be in some measure restrained and prevented from entirely disregarding the dictates of their conscience. From this it follows, that when the ungodly allow themselves to follow their own inclinations, so obstinately and audaciously as they are here represented as doing, without any sense of shame, it is an evidence that they have cast off all fear of God.

The Psalmist says that they speak *in their heart.* They may not utter this detestable blasphemy, *There is no God,* with their mouths; but the unbridled licentiousness of their life loudly and distinctly declares that in their hearts, which are destitute of all godliness, they soothingly sing to themselves this song. Not that they maintain, by drawn out arguments or formal syllogisms, as they term them, that there is no God, (for to render them so much the more inexcusable, God from time to time causes even the most wicked of men to feel secret pangs of conscience, that they may be compelled to acknowledge his majesty and sovereign power;) but whatever right knowledge God instils into them they partly stifle it by their malice against him, and partly corrupt it, until religion in them becomes torpid, and at last dead. They may not plainly deny the existence of a God, but they imagine him to be shut up in heaven, and divested of his righteousness and power; and this is just to fashion an idol in the room of God. As if the time would never come when they will have to appear before him in judgment,[1] they endeavour, in all the transactions and concerns of their life, to remove him to the greatest distance, and to efface from their minds all apprehension of his majesty.[2] And when God is dragged from his throne, and divested of his character as judge, impiety has come to its utmost height; and, therefore, we must conclude that David has most certainly spoken according to truth, in declaring that those who give themselves liberty to commit all manner of wickedness, in the flattering hope of escaping with impunity, deny in their heart that there is a God. As the fifty-third psalm, with the exception of a few words which are altered in it, is just a repetition of this psalm, I will show in the proper places, as we proceed, the difference which there is between the two psalms. David here complains that they have done *abominable work;* but for the word *work*, the term there employed is *iniquity.* It should be observed that David does not speak of one work or of two; but as he had said, that they have perverted or *corrupted* all lawful order, so now he adds, that they have so polluted their whole life, as to make it abominable, and the proof of this which he adduces is, that they have no regard to uprightness in their dealings with one another, but have forgotten all humanity, and all beneficence towards their fellow-creatures.

---

[1] Some critics observe, that as יהוה, *Yehovah,* the name which denotes the infinite, self-existent essence of God, is not the word here employed, but אלהים, a name which they regard as referring to God as judge and governor of the world, the meaning of the first verse is not that the fool denies the existence of God, but only his providence and government of the world; that he persuades himself God has no concern about the actions of men, and that there will be no judgment to come; and, therefore, goes on in sin, in the hope of escaping with impunity.—See *Poole's Synopsis Criticorum.* The Targum paraphrases the words, "There is no God," thus, "There is no אלהים,*government* of God in the earth."

[2] "Et abolir de leurs esprits toute apprehension de sa majeste."—*Fr.*

2. *Jehovah looked down from heaven upon the children of men, to see whether there were any that did understand, and seek after God.*
3. *Every one of them has gone aside, they have altogether become putrid,* [or *rotten;*] *there is none that doeth good, not even one.*

2. *Jehovah looked down from heaven.* God himself is here introduced as speaking on the subject of human depravity, and this renders the discourse of David more emphatic than if he had pronounced the sentence in his own person. When God is exhibited to us as sitting on his throne to take cognisance of the conduct of men, unless we are stupified in an extraordinary degree, his majesty must strike us with terror. The effect of the habit of sinning is, that men grow hardened in their sins, and discern nothing, as if they were enveloped in thick darkness. David, therefore, to teach them that they gain nothing by flattering and deceiving themselves as they do, when wickedness reigns in the world with impunity, testifies that God looks down from heaven, and casts his eyes on all sides, for the purpose of knowing what is done among men. God, it is true, has no need to make inquisition or search; but when he compares himself to an earthly judge, it is in adaptation to our limited capacity, and to enable us gradually to form some apprehension of his secret providence, which our reason cannot all at once comprehend. Would to God that this manner of speaking had the effect of teaching us to summon ourselves before his tribunal; and that, while the world are flattering themselves, and the reprobate are trying to bury their sins in forgetfulness by their want of thought, hypocrisy, or shamelessness, and are blinded in their obstinacy as if they were intoxicated, we might be led to shake off all indifference and stupidity by reflecting on this truth, that God, notwithstanding, looks down from his high throne in heaven, and beholds what is going on here below!

To see if there were any that did understand. As the whole economy of a good and righteous life depends upon our being governed and directed by the light of understanding, David has justly taught us in the beginning of the psalm, that folly is the root of all wickedness. And in this clause he also very justly declares, that the commencement of integrity and uprightness of life consists in an enlightened and sound mind. But as the greater part misapply their intellectual powers to deceitful purposes, David immediately after defines, in one word, what true understanding is, namely, that it consists *in seeking after God;* by which he means, that unless men devote themselves wholly to God, their life cannot be well ordered. Some understand the word מַשְׂכִּיל, *maskil,* which we translated, *that did understand,* in too restricted a sense; whereas David declares that the reprobate are utterly destitute of all reason and judgment.

Every one of them has gone aside. Some translate the word סָר, *sar*, which is here used, *to stink*,[1] as if the reading were, *Every one of them emits an offensive odour,* that it may correspond in meaning with the verb in the next clause, which in Hebrew signifies *to become putrid* or *rotten.* But there is no necessity for explaining the two words in the same way, as if the same thing were repeated twice. The interpretation is more appropriate, which supposes that men are here condemned as guilty of a detestable revolt, inasmuch as they are estranged from God, or have departed far from him; and that afterwards there is pointed out the disgusting corruption or putrescence of their whole life, as if nothing could proceed from apostates but what smells rank of rottenness and infection. The Hebrew word סָר, *sar*, is almost universally taken in this sense. In the 53d Psalm, the word סָג, *sag,* is used, which signifies the same thing. In short, David declares that all men are so carried away by their capricious lusts, that nothing is to be found either of purity or integrity in their whole life. This, therefore, is defection so

---

[1] Hammond admits that the word סר, *sar,* means *to go aside,* or *to decline,* and that it is commonly applied to a way or path, declining from the right way, or going in a wrong way. But he thinks that the idea here is different, that it is taken from wine when it grows dead or sour, just as the word is used in this sense in Hosea iv. 18, סר סבאם, *sar sobim,* "Their drink is gone aside, or grown sour." He considers this view corroborated from the clause which immediately follows, נאלחו, *ne-elachu,* *they are become putrid,* which is derived from אלח, *alach, to be rotten* or *putrified,* referring properly to flesh which has become putrid. "Thus," says he, " the proportion is well kept between drink and meat, the one growing dead or sour, as the other putrifies and stinks, and then is good for nothing, but is thrown away."

complete, that it extinguishes all godliness. Besides, David here not only censures a portion of the people, but pronounces them all to be equally involved in the same condemnation. This was, indeed, a prodigy well fitted to excite abhorrence, that all the children of Abraham, whom God had chosen to be his peculiar people, were so corrupt from the least to the greatest.

But it might be asked, how David makes no exception, how he declares that not a righteous person remains, *not even one*, when, nevertheless, he informs us, a little after, that the poor and afflicted put their trust in God? Again, it might be asked, if all were wicked, who was that Israel whose future redemption he celebrates in the end of the psalm? Nay, as he himself was one of the body of that people, why does he not at least except himself? I answer: It is against the carnal and degenerate body of the Israelitish nation that he here inveighs, and the small number constituting the seed which God had set apart for himself is not included among them. This is the reason why Paul, in his Epistle to the Romans, chap. iii. 10, extends this sentence to all mankind. David, it is true, deplores the disordered and desolate state of matters under the reign of Saul. At the same time, however, he doubtless makes a comparison between the children of God and all who have not been regenerated by the Spirit, but are carried away according to the inclinations of their flesh.[1] Some give a different explanation, maintaining that Paul, by quoting the testimony of David, did not understand him as meaning that men are naturally depraved and corrupt; and that the truth which David intended to teach is, that the rulers and the more distinguished of the people were wicked, and that, therefore, it was not surprising to behold unrighteousness and wickedness prevailing so generally in the world. This answer is far from being satisfactory. The subject which Paul there reasons upon is not, what is the character of the greater part of men, but what is the character of all who are led and

---

[1] David speaks of all mankind, with the exception of the " people of God," and " the generation of the righteous," spoken of in verses 4, 5, who are opposed to the rest of the human race.

governed by their own corrupt nature. It is, therefore, to be observed, that when David places himself and the small remnant of the godly on one side, and puts on the other the body of the people, in general, this implies that there is a manifest difference between the children of God who are created anew by his Spirit, and all the posterity of Adam, in whom corruption and depravity exercise dominion. Whence it follows, that all of us, when we are born, bring with us from our mother's womb this folly and filthiness manifested in the whole life, which David here describes, and that we continue such until God make us new creatures by his mysterious grace.

4. *Have all the workers of iniquity no knowledge, who eat up my people as they eat bread? they call not upon the Lord.*[1]

This question is added to give a more amplified illustration of the preceding doctrine. The prophet had said that God observed from heaven the doings of men, and had found all of them gone out of the way; and now he introduces him exclaiming with astonishment, What madness is this, that they who ought to cherish my people, and assiduously perform to them every kind office, are oppressing and falling upon them like wild beasts, without any feeling of humanity? He attributes this manner of speaking to God, not because any thing can happen which is strange or unexpected to him, but in order the more forcibly to express his indignation. The Prophet Isaiah, in like manner, (chap. lix. 16,) when treating of almost the same subject, says, "And God saw that there was no man, and wondered that there was no intercessor." God, it is true, does not actually experience in himself such affections, but he represents himself as invested

---

[1] Calvin here reads *Dominus*, although the word in the Hebrew text is יהוה, *Yehovah*, which he almost uniformly retains. In the Septuagint, יהוה is always rendered by ὁ Κυριος, *the Lord*, which is equivalent to *Dominus*, and is expressive of dominion or property,—a word which implies a different idea from the name *Jehovah*, which denotes independent and eternal existence. The translators of the Septuagint used ὁ Κυριος for יהו, in accommodation to the scruples of the Jews, who directed אדני to be read wherever יהוה occurs.

with them, that we may entertain the greatest horror and
dread on account of our sins, when he declares them to
be of so monstrous a character, that he is as it were thrown
into agitation and disorder by them. And were we not
harder than the stones, our horror at the wickedness which
prevails in the world would make the hair of our head to
stand on end,[1] seeing God exhibits to us in his own person
such a testimony of the detestation with which he regards it.
Moreover, this verse confirms what I have said in the commencement, that David does not speak in this psalm of foreign
tyrants, or the avowed enemies of the church, but of the
rulers and princes of his people, who were furnished with
power and honour. This description would not apply to
men who were altogether strangers to the revealed will of
God; for it would be nothing wonderful to see those who
do not possess the moral law, the rule of life, devoting themselves to the work of violence and oppression. But the heinousness of the proceedings condemned is not a little aggravated from this circumstance, that it is the shepherds themselves, whose office it is to feed and to take care of the flock,[2]
who cruelly devour it, and who spare not even the people and
heritage of God. There is a similar complaint in Micah iii.
1-3, " And I said, Hear, I pray you, O heads of Jacob, and
ye princes of the house of Israel: Is it not for you to know
judgment? Who hate the good and love the evil; who pluck
off their skin from off them; and their flesh from off their
bones; who also eat the flesh of my people, and flay their skin
from off them," &c. If those who profess to know and to serve
God were to exercise such cruelty towards the Babylonians or
Egyptians, it would be a piece of injustice which could admit
of no excuse; but when they glut themselves with the blood
and flesh of the saints, as they devour bread, this is such
monstrous iniquity, that it may well strike both angels and
men with astonishment. Had such persons a particle of
sound understanding remaining in them, it would restrain
them from conduct so fearfully infatuated. They must, there-

[1] " Il faut que l'horreur des meschancetez qui regnent au monde nous
face dresser les cheveux en la teste."—*Fr.*

[2] " Desquels l'office est de paistre et governer le troupeau."—*Fr.*

fore, be completely blinded by the devil, and utterly bereft of reason and understanding, seeing they knowingly and willingly flay and devour the people of God with such inhumanity. This passage teaches us how displeasing to God, and how abominable is the cruelty which is exercised against the godly, by those who pretend to be their shepherds. In the end of the verse, where he says that *they call not upon the Lord*, he again points out the source and cause of this unbridled wickedness, namely, that such persons have no reverence for God. Religion is the best mistress for teaching us mutually to maintain equity and uprightness towards each other; and where a concern for religion is extinguished, then all regard for justice perishes along with it. With respect to the phrase, *calling upon God*, as it constitutes the principal exercise of godliness, it includes by synecdoche, (a figure of rhetoric, by which a part is put for the whole,) not only here, but in many other passages of Scripture, the whole of the service of God.

5. *There did they tremble with fear,*[1] *for God is in* [or *with*, or *for*[2]] *the generation of the righteous.*
6. *Ye deride the counsel of the poor, because Jehovah is his hope.*

5. *There did they tremble with fear.* The prophet now encourages himself and all the faithful with the best of all consolations, namely, that God will not forsake his people even to the end, but will at length show himself to be their defender. Some explain the adverb of place *there*, as meaning that God will take vengeance on the wicked in the

[1] It is the general opinion that this psalm was composed during the alarm and danger which were occasioned by Absalom's rebellion, and that this is a prediction of the failure of the conspiracy. But Calmet and Mudge refer the psalm to the captivity in Babylon, and the latter supposes that in this and the preceding verse there is an allusion to the great terror into which the heathen were thrown, in the midst of their impious carousals; which some refer to the scene which took place at Belshazzar's feast, when the hand was seen writing on the wall. There is, however, great uncertainty as to the occasions on which most of the psalms were composed; and those who have examined the different opinions of interpreters on this subject must be convinced of the difficulty of arriving at any thing like certainty in regard to it.

[2] "Avec ou pour."—*Fr. marg.*

presence of his saints, because they exercised their tyranny upon them. But I rather think that by this word there is expressed the certainty of their punishment,[1] as if the Psalmist pointed to it with the finger.[2] It may also intimate what we may gather from Psalm liii., that the judgment of God would come upon them suddenly, and when they were not thinking about it; for it is there added, *where no fear is*, or, *where no fear was*.[3] Expositors, I am aware, differ in their interpretation of these words. Some supply the word *equal* or *like*, and read, There is no fear equal to it. Others refer them to those secret alarms with which the ungodly are tormented, even when there may be no ground for apprehension. God threatens the transgressors of his law with such mental torment that they " shall flee when none pursueth them," (Lev. xxvi. 17, and Prov. xxviii. 1,) and that " the sound of a shaking leaf shall chase them," (Lev. xxvi. 36;) just as we see that they are themselves their own tormentors, and are agitated with mental trouble even when there is no external cause to create it. But I think the meaning of the prophet is different, namely, that when their affairs are in a state of the greatest tranquillity and prosperity, God will suddenly launch against them the bolts of his vengeance. " For when they shall say, Peace and safety, then sudden destruction cometh upon them," (1 Thess. v. 3.) The prophet, therefore, encourages and supports the faithful with this prospect, that the ungodly, when they think themselves free from all danger, and are securely celebrating their own triumphs, shall be overwhelmed with sudden destruction.

The reason of this is added in the last clause of the verse,

---

[1] Though punishment had not as yet been actually inflicted on the oppressors of the people of God, of whom the Psalmist had spoken in the preceding verse, he speaks of their punishment as if it had taken place. The reason of this manner of speaking concerning things future in prophetic poetry, Horsley explains to be this, " That a scene typical of futurity is presented to the prophet's imagination, and what he sees in that scene he speaks of as done."

[2] " The particle שׁ is used demonstratively, in reference to the scene which lies before the inspired poet's fancy. See there !"—*Horsley*.

[3] In the Septuagint version, to the words, *there were they in great fear*, there is added the words οὐ οὐκ ἦν ὁ φόβος, *where there was no fear*, the transcribers, perhaps, transferring it by memory from Psalm liii. 6, or the translators adding the words by way of paraphrase.

namely, because God is determined to defend the righteous, and to take in hand their cause: *For God is in the generation of the righteous.* Now, in order to preserve them safe, he must necessarily thunder in his wrath from heaven against their enemies, who unjustly oppress and waste them by violence and extortion.[1] There is, however, some ambiguity in the word דּוֹר, *dor,* which we have translated *generation.* As this noun in Hebrew sometimes signifies *an age,* or, *the course of human life,* the sentence might be explained as follows: Although God for a time may seem to take no notice of the wrongs inflicted upon his servants by the wicked, yet he is ever present with them, and exercises his grace towards them during their whole life. But it seems to me a more simple and natural exposition to interpret the clause thus: That God is on the side of the righteous, and takes their part, as we say,[2] so that דּוֹר, *dor,* will have the same signification here which the word *natio,* [nation,] sometimes has among the Latins.

In Psalm liii. 5, the Psalmist adds a sentence which does not occur in this psalm, *For God hath scattered the bones of him that besiegeth thee, thou shalt put them to shame; because God hath rejected them.* By these words the prophet explains more clearly how God protects the righteous, that it is by delivering them from the jaws of death, just as if one were to put to flight those who had laid siege to a town, and were to set at liberty its inhabitants, who before were in great extremity and quite shut up.[3] Whence it follows, that we must patiently bear oppression, if we desire to be protected and preserved by the hand of God, at the time of our greatest danger. The expression, *bones,* is used metaphorically for *strength* or *power.* The prophet particularly speaks of their power; for if the wicked were not possessed of riches, ammunition, and troops, which render them formidable, it would not appear, with sufficient evidence, that it is the hand of God which at length crushes them. The Psalmist next

---

[1] " Qui les foullent injustement et usent de violence et extorsion."—*Fr.*
[2] " Et tient leur parte, comme on dit."—*Fr.*
[3] " Ne plus ne moins que si quelqu'un mettoit en fuite ceux qui auroyent dressé le siege devant une ville, et mettoit en liberté les habitans d'icelle qui estoyent auparavant en grande extremité et bien enserrez."—*Fr.*

exhorts the faithful to a holy boasting, and bids them rest assured that an ignominious destruction hangs over the heads of the wicked. The reason of this is, because *God hath rejected them;* and if he is opposed to them, all things must ultimately go ill with them. As מאס, *maäs,* which we have translated *to reject,* sometimes signifies *to despise,* some render it thus,—*Because God hath despised them ;* but this, I think, does not suit the passage. It would be more appropriate to read,—*He hath rendered them contemptible,* or, *subjected them to disgrace and ignominy.* Whence it follows, that they only draw down upon themselves dishonour and infamy while they strive to elevate themselves, as it were, in despite of God.

6. *Ye deride the counsel of the poor.* He inveighs against those giants who mock at the faithful for their simplicity, in calmly expecting, in their distresses, that God will show himself to be their deliverer. And, certainly, nothing seems more irrational to the flesh than to betake ourselves to God when yet he does not relieve us from our calamities; and the reason is, because the flesh judges of God only according to what it presently beholds of his grace. Whenever, therefore, unbelievers see the children of God overwhelmed with calamities, they reproach them for their groundless confidence, as it appears to them to be, and with sarcastic jeers laugh at the assured hope with which they rely upon God, from whom, notwithstanding, they receive no sensible aid. David, therefore, defies and derides this insolence of the wicked, and threatens that their mockery of the poor and the wretched, and their charging them with folly in depending upon the protection of God, and not sinking under their calamities, will be the cause of their destruction. At the same time, he teaches them that there is no resolution to which we can come which is better advised than the resolution to depend upon God, and that to repose on his salvation, and on the assistance which he hath promised us, even although we may be surrounded with calamities, is the highest wisdom.

7. *Who shall give salvation* [or *deliverance*] *to Israel out of Sion? When Jehovah shall have brought back the captivity of his people, Jacob shall rejoice, and Israel shall be glad.*

David, after having laid down the doctrine of consolation, again returns to prayers and groanings. By this he teaches us, that although God may leave us for a long time to languish, yet we ought not to weary, or lose courage, but should always glory in him; and, again, that while our troubles continue, the most effectual solace we can have is often to return to the exercise of prayer. When he asks the question, *Who shall give salvation?* this does not imply, that he was looking either to the right hand or to the left, or that he turned away his eyes from God in search of another deliverer; he intends only to express the ardour of his desire, as if he had said, When will the time at length come when God will display his salvation, and make it fully manifest? By the word *Sion*, which he adds, he testifies that his hope is fixed on God; for Sion was the holy place from which God had promised to hear the prayers of his servants; and it was the dwelling-place of the ark of the covenant, which was an external pledge and symbol of the presence of God. He does not, therefore, doubt who would be the author of his salvation; but he asks, with a sorrowful heart, when at length that salvation will come forth which is to be expected from no other source than from God alone. The question may, however, be put, if this prayer refers to the time of Saul, how can Sion, with propriety, be named as being already the sanctuary of God? I will not deny that the Psalmist, by the spirit of prophecy, may have predicted what had not yet actually taken place; but I think it highly probable, that this psalm was not composed until the ark of the covenant had been placed on mount Sion. David, as we know, employed his leisure hours in committing to writing, for the benefit of posterity, events which had happened long before. Besides, by expressing his desire for the deliverance of Israel, we are taught that he was chiefly anxious about the welfare of the whole body of the Church, and that his thoughts were more occupied about this than about himself individually. This is worthy of being the more carefully marked when we consider, that, while our attention is engrossed with our own particular sorrows, we are in danger of almost entirely neglecting the welfare of our brethren. And yet the particular afflictions with which God visits each of us are intended to admonish us to direct our attention and care to the whole body of the Church, and to think of its necessities, just as we see David here including Israel with himself.

When the Lord shall have brought back the captivity of his people. In these words, David concludes, that God will not suffer the faithful to languish under continual sorrow, according as it is said in another psalm, (cxxvi. 5,) "They that sow in tears shall reap in joy." He doubtless aims at confirming and encouraging himself and all the godly to hope for the promised deliverance. He therefore says, in the first place, that although God may delay, or at least may not make so much haste as we would wish, he will, nevertheless, show himself to be the defender of his people, by redeeming them from captivity. And, in the next place, he assuages their sorrow, by setting forth that the issue of it will be joyful, seeing it will at length be turned into gladness. *The captivity*, of which he makes mention, is not the Babylonish, or the dispersion of his people among the heathen nations; it rather refers to an oppression at home, when the wicked exercise dominion like tyrants in the Church. We are, therefore, taught by these words, that when such furious enemies waste and destroy the flock of God, or proudly tread it under foot, we ought to have recourse to God, whose peculiar office it is to gather together his Israel from all places whither they have been dispersed. And the term *captivity*, which he employs, implies, that when the wicked overthrow at their pleasure all good and lawful order in the midst of the Church, it is converted into a Babylon or Egypt. Farther, although David defers the joy of the holy people to the time of their deliverance, yet the consolatory prospect of this should serve not only to moderate our grief, but also to mix and season it with joy.

PSALM XV.

This psalm teaches us upon what condition God made choice of the Jews to be his people, and placed his sanctuary in the midst of them. This condition was, that they should show themselves to be a peculiar and holy people, by leading a just and upright life.

¶ A Song of David.

1. *O Jehovah, who shall dwell in thy tabernacle? Who shall rest in the mountain of thy holiness?*
2. *He who walketh in integrity, and doeth righteousness, and who speaketh truth in his heart.*

1. *O Jehovah, who shall dwell in thy tabernacle?* As nothing is more common in the world than falsely to assume the name of God, or to pretend to be his people, and as a great part of men allow themselves to do this without any apprehension of the danger it involves, David, without stopping to speak to men, addresses himself to God, which he considers the better course; and he intimates, that if men assume the title of the people of God, without being so in deed and in truth, they gain nothing by their self-delusion, for God continues always like himself, and as he is faithful himself, so will he have us to keep faith with him in return. No doubt, he adopted Abraham freely, but, at the same time, he stipulated with him that he should live a holy and an upright life, and this is the general rule of the covenant which God has, from the beginning, made with his Church. The sum is, that hypocrites, who occupy a place in the temple of God, in vain pretend to be his people, for he acknowledges none as such but those who follow after justice and uprightness during the whole course of their life. David saw the temple crowded with a great multitude of men who all made a profession of the same religion, and presented themselves before God as to the outward ceremony; and, therefore, assuming the person

of one wondering at the spectacle, he directs his discourse to God, who, in such a confusion and medley of characters, could easily distinguish his own people from strangers.

There is a threefold use of this doctrine. In the first place, If we really wish to be reckoned among the number of the children of God, the Holy Ghost teaches us, that we must show ourselves to be such by a holy and an upright life; for it is not enough to serve God by outward ceremonies, unless we also live uprightly, and without doing wrong to our neighbours. In the second place, As we too often see the Church of God defaced by much impurity, to prevent us from stumbling at what appears so offensive, a distinction is made between those who are permanent citizens of the Church, and strangers who are mingled among them only for a time. This is undoubtedly a warning highly necessary, in order that when the temple of God happens to be tainted by many impurities, we may not contract such disgust and chagrin as will make us withdraw from it. By impurities I understand the vices of a corrupt and polluted life. Provided religion continue pure as to doctrine and worship, we must not be so much stumbled at the faults and sins which men commit, as on that account to rend the unity of the Church. Yet the experience of all ages teaches us how dangerous a temptation it is when we behold the Church of God, which ought to be free from all polluting stains, and to shine in uncorrupted purity, cherishing in her bosom many ungodly hypocrites, or wicked persons. From this the Catharists, Novatians, and Donatists, took occasion in former times to separate themselves from the fellowship of the godly. The Anabaptists, at the present day, renew the same schisms, because it does not seem to them that a church in which vices are tolerated can be a true church. But Christ, in Matth. xxv. 32, justly claims it as his own peculiar office to separate the sheep from the goats; and thereby admonishes us, that we must bear with the evils which it is not in our power to correct, until all things become ripe, and the proper season of purging the Church arrive. At the same time, the faithful are here enjoined, each in his own sphere, to use their endeavours that the Church of God may be purified from the corruptions which still exist within her. And this is the third use which we should make of this doctrine. God's sacred barn-floor will not be perfectly cleansed before the last day, when Christ at his coming will cast out the chaff; but he has already begun to do this by the doctrine of his gospel, which on this account he terms a fan. We must, therefore, by no means be indifferent about this matter; on the contrary, we ought rather to exert ourselves in good earnest, that all who profess themselves Christians may lead a holy and an unspotted life. But above all, what God here declares with respect to all the unrighteous should be deeply imprinted on our memory; namely, that he prohibits them from coming to his sanctuary, and condemns their impious presumption, in irreverently thrusting themselves into the society of the godly. David makes mention of *the tabernacle*, because the temple was not yet built. The meaning of his discourse, to express it in a few words, is this, that those only have access to God who are his genuine servants, and who live a holy life.

2. *He that walketh in integrity.* Here we should mark, that in the words there is an implied contrast between the vain boasting of those who are only the people of God in name, or who make only a bare profession of being so, which consists in outward observances, and this indubitable and genuine evidence of true godliness which David commends. But it might be asked, As the service of God takes precedence of the duties of charity towards our neighbours, why is there no mention here made of faith and prayer; for, certainly, these are the marks by which the genuine children of God ought to have been distinguished from hypocrites? The answer is easy: David does not intend to exclude faith and prayer, and other spiritual sacrifices; but as hypocrites, in order to promote their own interests, are not sparing in their attention to a multiplicity of external religious observances, while their ungodliness, notwithstanding, is manifested outwardly in the life, seeing they are full of pride, cruelty, violence, and are given to deceitfulness and extortion,—the Psalmist, for the purpose of discovering and drawing forth

into the light all who are of such a character, takes the marks and evidences of true and sincere faith from the second table of the law. According to the care which every man takes to practise righteousness and equity towards his neighbours, so does he actually show that he fears God. David, then, is not here to be understood as resting satisfied with political or social justice, as if it were enough to render to our fellow-men what is their own, while we may lawfully defraud God of his right; but he describes the approved servants of God, as distinguished and known by the fruits of righteousness which they produce. In the first place, he requires *sincerity;* in other words, that men should conduct themselves in all their affairs with singleness of heart, and without sinful craft or cunning. Secondly, he requires *justice;* that is to say, that they should study to do good to their neighbours, hurt nobody, and abstain from all wrong. Thirdly, he requires *truth* in their speech, so that they may speak nothing falsely or deceitfully. *To speak in the heart* is a strong figurative expression, but it expresses more forcibly David's meaning than if he had said *from the heart.* It denotes such agreement and harmony between the heart and tongue, as that the speech is, as it were, a vivid representation of the hidden affection or feeling within.

> 3. *He that slandereth not with his tongue, nor doeth evil to his companion, nor raiseth up a calumnious report against his neighbour.*

David, after having briefly set forth the virtues with which all who desire to have a place in the Church ought to be endued, now enumerates certain vices from which they ought to be free. In the first place, he tells them that they must not be *slanderers* or *detractors;* secondly, that they must restrain themselves from doing any thing mischievous and injurious to their neighbours; and, thirdly, that they must not aid in giving currency to calumnies and false reports. Other vices, from which the righteous are free, we shall meet with as we proceed. David, then, sets down calumny and detraction as the first point of injustice by which our neighbours are injured. If a good name is a treasure, more precious than all the riches of the world, (Prov. xxii. 1,) no greater injury can be inflicted upon men than to wound their reputation. It is not, however, every injurious word which is here condemned; but the disease and lust of detraction, which stirs up malicious persons to spread abroad calumnies. At the same time, it cannot be doubted that the design of the Holy Spirit is to condemn all false and wicked accusations. In the clause which immediately follows, the doctrine that the children of God ought to be far removed from all injustice, is stated more generally: *Nor doeth evil to his companion.* By the words *companion and neighbour,* the Psalmist means not only those with whom we enjoy familiar intercourse, and live on terms of intimate friendship, but all men, to whom we are bound by the ties of humanity and a common nature. He employs these terms to show more clearly the odiousness of what he condemns, and that the saints may have the greater abhorrence of all wrong dealing, since every man who hurts his neighbour violates the fundamental law of human society. With respect to the meaning of the last clause, interpreters are not agreed. Some take the phrase, *to raise up a calumnious report,* for *to invent,* because malicious persons raise up calumnies from nothing; and thus it would be a repetition of the statement contained in the first clause of the verse, namely, that good men should not allow themselves to indulge in detraction. But I think there is also here rebuked the vice of undue credulity, which, when any evil reports are spread against our neighbours, leads us either eagerly to listen to them, or at least to receive them without sufficient reason; whereas we ought rather to use all means to suppress and trample them under foot.[1] When any one is the bearer of invented falsehoods, those who reject them leave them, as it were, to fall to the ground; while, on the contrary, those who propagate and publish them from one person to another are, by an expressive form of speech, said to raise them up.

---

[1] " Et mettre sous le pied."—*Fr.*

4. *In his eyes the offcast* [or *reprobate*[1]] *is despised ; but he honoureth them that fear the Lord ; when he hath sworn to his own hurt, he changeth not.*

The first part of this verse is explained in different ways. Some draw from it this meaning, that the true servants of God are contemptible and worthless in their own estimation. If we adopt this interpretation, the copula *and*, which David does not express, must be supplied, making the reading thus, *He is vile and despised in his own eyes*. But besides the consideration, that, if this had been the sense, the words would probably have been joined together by the copula *and*, I have another reason which leads me to think that David had a different meaning. He compares together two opposite things, namely, to despise perverse and worthless characters, and to honour the righteous and those who fear God. In order that these two clauses may correspond with each other, the only sense in which I can understand what is here said about *being despised* is this, that the children of God despise the ungodly, and form that low and contemptuous estimate of them which their character deserves. The godly, it is true, although living a praiseworthy and virtuous life, are not inflated with presumption, but, on the contrary, are rather dissatisfied with themselves, because they feel how far short they are as yet of the perfection which is required. When, however, I consider what the scope of the passage demands, I do not think that we are here to view the Psalmist as commending humility or modesty, but rather a free and upright judgment of human character, by which the wicked, on the one hand, are not spared, while virtue, on the other, receives the honour which belongs to it; for flattery, which nourishes vices by covering them, is an evil not less pernicious than it is common. I indeed admit, that if the wicked are in authority, we ought not to carry our contempt of them the length of refusing to obey them in so far as a regard to our duty will permit; but, at the same time, we must beware of flattery and of accommodating ourselves to them, which would be to involve us in the same

---

[1] "Meschant, ou vilein et abominable."—*Note, Fr. marg.* " The wicked, or the vile and abominable."

condemnation with them. He who not only seems to regard their wicked actions with indifference, but also honours them, shows that he approves of them as much as it is in his power. Paul therefore teaches us, (Eph. v. 11,) that it is a species of fellowship with the unfruitful works of darkness when we do not reprove them. It is certainly a very perverse way of acting, when persons, for the sake of obtaining the favour of men, will indirectly mock God; and all are chargeable with doing this who make it their business to please the wicked. David, however, has a respect, not so much to persons as to wicked works. The man who sees the wicked honoured, and by the applause of the world rendered more obstinate in their wickedness, and who willingly gives his consent or approbation to this, does he not, by so doing, exalt vice to authority, and invest it with sovereign power? "But woe," says the prophet Isaiah, (ch. v. 20,) "unto them that call evil good, and good evil; that put darkness for light, and light for darkness."

Nor ought it to be regarded as a rude or violent manner of speaking, when David calls base and wicked persons *reprobates*, although they may be placed in an exalted and honourable station. If (as Cicero affirms, in his book entitled The Responses of the Aruspices) the inspectors of the entrails of the sacrifices, and other heathen soothsayers, applied to worthless and abandoned characters the term *rejected*, although they excelled in dignity and riches, why should not a prophet of God be permitted to apply the name of *degraded outcasts* to all who are rejected by God? The meaning of the Psalmist, to express it in a few words, is, that the children of God freely judge of every man's doings, and that for the purpose of obtaining the favour of men, they will not stoop to vile flattery, and thereby encourage the wicked in their wickedness.

What follows immediately after, namely, *to honour* the righteous and *those who fear God*, is no mean virtue. As they are often, as it were, the filth and the offscouring of all things in the estimation of the world, so it frequently happens that those who show them favour and sympathy, excite against themselves every where the hatred of the world.

The greater part of mankind, therefore, refuse the friendship of good men, and leave them to be despised, which cannot be done without grievous and heinous injury to God. Let us learn then not to value men by their estate or their money, or their transitory honours, but to hold in estimation godliness, or the fear of God. And certainly no man will ever truly apply his mind to the study of godliness who does not, at the same time, reverence the servants of God; as, on the other hand, the love we bear to them incites us to imitate them in sanctity of life.

When he hath sworn to his own hurt. The translation of the LXX. would agree very well with the scope of the passage, were it not that the points which are under the words in the Hebrew text will not bear such a sense.[1] It is, indeed, no proof of the inaccuracy of their rendering, that it does not agree with the points; for, although the Jews have always used the points in reading, it is probable that they did not always express them in writing. I, however, prefer following the commonly received reading. And the meaning is, that the faithful will rather submit to suffer loss than break their word. When a man keeps his promises, in as far as he sees it to be for his own advantage, there is in this no argument to prove his uprightness and faithfulness. But when men make a promise to each other, there is nothing more common than from some slight loss which the performance of it would occasion, to endeavour to find a pretext for breaking their engagements. Every one considers with himself what is for his own advantage, and if it puts him to inconvenience or trouble to stand to his promises, he is ingenious enough to imagine that he will incur a far greater loss than there is any

---

[1] "The LXX., instead of להרע, [lehara,] *to hurt,* seem to have read לרעה, [leharea,] *to his fellow,* for they render it, τῷ πλησίον αὐτου, *to his neighbour,* and so the Syriac, and Latin, and Arabic, and Æthiopic."—*Hammond.* This rendering agrees very well with the scope of the psalm, which relates to our dealing justly with our fellow-men; and it represents the good man as scrupulously performing the promissory oaths which he makes to his neighbour. But the ordinary reading, *he sweareth to his own hurt, and changeth not,* sets forth the moral integrity of the good man in a still more striking light, by describing him as performing his oath in the face of the greatest temptations to break it, when the performance of it may prove detrimental to his own interests; and this is no mean trial of a man's virtue.

reason to apprehend. It seems, indeed, a fair excuse when a man complains that, if he does not depart from his engagement, he will suffer great loss. Hence it is, that we generally see so much unfaithfulness among men, that they do not consider themselves bound to perform the promises which they have made, except in so far as it will promote their own personal interest. David, therefore, condemning this inconstancy, requires the children of God to exhibit the greatest stedfastness in the fulfilment of their promises. Here the question might be asked, If a man, having fallen into the hands of a highwayman, promise him a sum of money to save his life, and if, in consequence of this, he is let go, should he in that case keep his promise? Again, if a man has been basely deceived, in entering into a contract, is it lawful for him to break the oath which he shall have made in such an engagement? With respect to the highwayman, he who confers upon him money falls into another fault, for he supports at his own expense a common enemy of mankind to the detriment of the public welfare. David does not impose upon the faithful such an alternative as this, but only enjoins them to show a greater regard to their promises than to their own personal interests, and to do this especially when their promises have been confirmed by an oath. As to the other case, namely, when a person has sworn, from being deceived and imposed upon by wicked artifice, he ought certainly to hold the holy name of God in such veneration, as rather patiently to submit to loss than violate his oath. Yet it is perfectly lawful for him to discover or reveal the fraud which has been practised upon him, provided he is not led to do so by a regard to his own personal interest; and there is, besides, nothing to hinder him from peaceably endeavouring to compromise the matter with his adversary. Many of the Jewish expositors restrict this passage to vows, as if David exhorted the faithful to perform their vows when they have promised to humble and afflict themselves by fasting. But in this they are mistaken. Nothing is farther from his meaning than this, for he discourses here only of the second table of the law, and of the mutual rectitude which men should maintain in their dealings with one another.

5. *He putteth not out his money to usury, nor taketh bribes upon the innocent. He that doeth these things shall not be moved for ever.*

In this verse David enjoins the godly neither to oppress their neighbours by usury, nor to suffer themselves to be corrupted with bribes to favour unrighteous causes. With respect to the first clause, as David seems to condemn all kinds of usury in general, and without exception, the very name has been every where held in detestation. But crafty men have invented specious names under which to conceal the vice; and thinking by this artifice to escape, they have plundered with greater excess than if they had lent on usury avowedly and openly. God, however, will not be dealt with and imposed upon by sophistry and false pretences. He looks upon the thing as it really is. There is no worse species of usury than an unjust way of making bargains, where equity is disregarded on both sides. Let us then remember that all bargains in which the one party unrighteously strives to make gain by the loss of the other party, whatever name may be given to them, are here condemned. It may be asked, Whether all kinds of usury are to be put into this denunciation, and regarded as alike unlawful? If we condemn all without distinction, there is a danger lest many, seeing themselves brought into such a strait, as to find that sin must be incurred, in whatever way they can turn themselves, may be rendered bolder by despair, and may rush headlong into all kinds of usury, without choice or discrimination. On the other hand, whenever we concede that something may be lawfully done this way, many will give themselves loose reins, thinking that a liberty to exercise usury, without control or moderation, has been granted them. In the first place, therefore, I would, above all things, counsel my readers to beware of ingeniously contriving deceitful pretexts, by which to take advantage of their fellow-men, and let them not imagine that any thing can be lawful to them which is grievous and hurtful to others.

With respect to usury, it is scarcely possible to find in the world a usurer who is not at the same time an extortioner, and addicted to unlawful and dishonourable gain. Accordingly,

Cato[1] of old justly placed the practice of usury and the killing of men in the same rank of criminality, for the object of this class of people is to suck the blood of other men. It is also a very strange and shameful thing, that, while all other men obtain the means of their subsistence with much toil, while husbandmen fatigue themselves by their daily occupations, and artisans serve the community by the sweat of their brow, and merchants not only employ themselves in labours, but also expose themselves to many inconveniences and dangers,—that moneymongers should sit at their ease without doing any thing, and receive tribute from the labour of all other people. Besides, we know that generally it is not the rich who are exhausted by their usury,[2] but poor men, who ought rather to be relieved. It is not, therefore, without cause that God has, in Lev. xxv. 35, 36, forbidden usury, adding this reason, " And if thy brother be waxen poor and fallen in decay with thee, then thou shalt relieve him; take thou no usury of him or increase." We see that the end for which the law was framed was, that men should not cruelly oppress the poor, who ought rather to receive sympathy and compassion.[3] This was, indeed, a part of the judicial law which God appointed for the Jews in particular; but it is a common principle of justice which extends to all nations and to all ages, that we should keep ourselves from plundering and devouring the poor who are in distress and want. Whence it follows, that the gain which he who lends his money upon interest acquires, without doing injury to any one, is not to be included under

---

[1] " C'estoit un personnage Romain de grande reputation."—*Fr. marg.* " This was a Roman personage of great reputation."—See *Cicero de Officiis*, Lib. ii. cap. xxv.

[2] " Ce ne sont pas les riches lesquels on mange d'usures."—*Fr.* " It is not the rich whom they devour by usuries."

[3] " The Jews were prohibited by the law from taking usury or interest on money lent to their brethren, but not on what was lent to strangers; that is, foreigners of other countries, (Deut. xxiii. 20.) The manifest design of this prohibition was, to promote humane and fraternal sentiments in the bosoms of the Israelites towards each other. A more remote end seems also to have been aimed at, viz., to check the formation of a commercial character among the Jews, and to confine them as much as possible to those agricultural and private pursuits, which would seclude them from intercourse with the surrounding nations, as it was not very likely that a practice of this nature would be extended much among foreigners which was prohibited at home."—*Walford's New Translation of the Book of Psalms.*

the head of unlawful usury. The Hebrew word נשך, *neshek*, which David employs, being derived from another word, which signifies *to bite*, sufficiently shows that usuries are condemned in so far as they involve in them or lead to a license of robbing and plundering our fellow-men. Ezekiel, indeed, chapters xviii. 17, and xxii. 12, seems to condemn the taking of any interest whatever upon money lent; but he doubtless has an eye to the unjust and crafty arts of gaining, by which the rich devoured the poor people. In short, provided we had engraven on our hearts the rule of equity, which Christ prescribes in Matthew vii. 12, " Therefore, all things whatsoever ye would that men should do to you, do ye even so to them," it would not be necessary to enter into lengthened disputes concerning usury.

What next follows in the text properly applies to judges who, being corrupted by presents and rewards, pervert all law and justice. It may, however, be extended farther, inasmuch as it often happens, that even private individuals are corrupted by bribes to favour and defend bad causes. David, therefore, comprehends, in general, all those corruptions by which we are led away from truth and uprightness. Some think that what is here intended is the rapacity of judges in extorting money from the innocent who are accused, as the price of their deliverance, when they ought rather to have protected and assisted them gratuitously. But it appears from the passages similar to this in Ezekiel, which we have quoted, that the sense is different.

He who doeth these things. This conclusion warns us again, that all who thrust themselves into the sanctuary of God are not permanent citizens of " the holy Jerusalem which is above;"[1] but that hypocrites, and all who falsely assume the title of saints, shall at length be " cast out" with Ishmael whom they resemble. That which is ascribed in Psalm xlvi. to the whole Church, David here applies to every one of the faithful: *He shall not be moved for ever.* The reason of this which is there expressed is, because God dwells in the midst of Jerusalem. On the contrary, we know that he is far from the perfidious and the wicked, who approach him only with the mouth, and with feigned lips.

[1] " De la saincte Jerusalem celeste."—*Fr.*

PSALM XVI.

In the beginning David commends himself to the protection of God. He then meditates upon the benefits which he received from God, and thereby stirs himself up to thanksgiving. By his service, it is true, he could in no respect be profitable to God, but he, notwithstanding, surrenders and devotes himself entirely to him, protesting that he will have nothing to do with superstitions. He also states the reason of this to be, that full and substantial happiness consists in resting in God alone, who never suffers his own people to want any good thing.

¶ Mictam of David.

As to the meaning of the word *mictam*, the Jewish expositors are not of one mind. Some derive it from כתם, *catham*,[1] as if it were a golden crest or jewel. Others think it is the beginning of a song, which at that time was very common. To others it seems rather to be some kind of tune, and this opinion I am inclined to adopt.

1. *Keep* [or *guard*[2]] *me, O God ; for in thee do I trust.*[3]

THIS is a prayer in which David commits himself to the

---

[1] The word means *gold, the finest gold,* and those who understand it in this sense here, think the psalm receives this title to denote that it is fit to be written in letters of gold; and some conjecture that the psalms distinguished by this title were, on some occasion or other, thus written and hung up in the sanctuary. Others are of opinion that the word *mictam* is derived from כתם, *catham,* which signifies *to mark, to engrave,* to denote that the psalm is fit to be engraven on a valuable and durable pillar, to be preserved in everlasting remembrance. This is the meaning attached to the word by the Septuagint, which translates it στηλογραφία, an inscription on a pillar or monument. In either of these views the title cannot but be regarded as peculiarly appropriate to this sacred poem. "*As a sepulchral inscription,*" remarks Bishop Mant, "it might have been written on our Redeemer's tomb ; as *a triumphal monument,* it might have been sung by him in the region of departed spirits ; and in either, or in any sense, it may well be considered as a *golden* composition, as *apples of gold in network of silver,* invaluable in its subject, most pleasing in its structure." Calvin, however, considers the title as referring to the tune, and in this he is supported by Aben Ezra, who is of opinion that this and other strange words, which occur in the titles of the psalms, are the names of old melodies.

[2] "*Guard me.* The Hebrew word expresses the actions of those who watch over another's safety, as of guards attending their king, or a shepherd keeping his flock."—*Horsley.*

[3] "The Hebrew word חסיתי, *chasithi,* from חסה, *chasah,* denotes to betake one's self for refuge to any one, under whose protection he may be safe, as chickens under the wing of the hen."—*Buxtorff.*

protection of God. He does not, however, here implore the aid of God, in some particular emergency, as he often does in other psalms, but he beseeches him to show himself his protector during the whole course of his life, and indeed our safety both in life and in death depends entirely upon our being under the protection of God. What follows concerning *trust*, signifies much the same thing as if the Holy Spirit assured us by the mouth of David, that God is ready to succour all of us, provided we rely upon him with a sure and stedfast faith; and that he takes under his protection none but those who commit themselves to him with their whole heart. At the same time, we must be reminded that David, supported by this trust, continued firm and unmoved amidst all the storms of adversity with which he was buffeted.

2. *Thou shalt say unto Jehovah, Thou art my Lord, my welldoing extendeth not unto thee.*
3. *Unto the saints who are on the earth, and to the excellent; all my delight is in them.*

2. *Thou shalt say unto Jehovah.* David begins by stating that he can bestow nothing upon God, not only because God stands in no need of any thing, but also because mortal man cannot merit the favour of God by any service which he can perform to him. At the same time, however, he takes courage, and, as God accepts our devotion, and the service which we yield to him, David protests that he will be one of his servants. To encourage himself the more effectually to this duty he speaks to his own soul; for the Hebrew word which is rendered *Thou shalt say*, is of the feminine gender, which can refer only to the soul.[1] Some may prefer reading the word in the past tense, *Thou hast said*, which I think is unobjectionable, for the Psalmist is speaking of an affection which had a continued abode in his soul. The import of his language is, I am, indeed, fully convinced in my heart, and know assuredly, that God can derive no profit

[1] The word נפשי, *naphshi*, is commonly supposed to be understood, *Thou, my soul, shalt say*, or *hast said*. But all the ancient versions, except the Chaldee, read in the first person, *I have said*, and this is the reading in many MSS. The words, however, "Thou, my soul, hast said," are equivalent to "I have said."

or advantage from me; but notwithstanding this, I will join myself in fellowship with the saints, that with one accord we may worship him by the sacrifices of praise. Two things are distinctly laid down in this verse. The first is, that God has a right to require of us whatever he pleases, seeing we are wholly bound to Him as our rightful proprietor and Lord. David, by ascribing to him the power and the dominion of *Lord,* declares that both himself and all he possessed are the property of God. The other particular contained in this verse is, the acknowledgment which the Psalmist makes of his own indigence. *My well-doing extendeth not unto thee.* Interpreters expound this last clause in two ways. As עָלֶיךָ, *aleyka,* may be rendered *upon thee,* some draw from it this sense, that God is not brought under obligation, or in the least degree indebted to us, by any good deeds which we may perform to him; and they understand the term *goodness* in a passive sense, as if David affirmed that whatever goodness he received from God did not proceed from any obligation he had laid God under, or from any merit which he possessed. But I think the sentence has a more extensive meaning, namely, that let men strive ever so much to lay themselves out for God, yet they can bring no advantage to him. Our goodness extendeth not to him, not only because, having in himself alone an all-sufficiency, he stands in need of nothing,[1] but also because we are empty and destitute of all good things, and have nothing with which to show ourselves liberal towards him. From this doctrine, however, the other point which I have before touched upon will follow, namely, that it is impossible for men, by any merits of their own, to bring God under obligation to them, so as to make him their debtor. The sum of the discourse is, that when we come before God, we must lay aside all presumption. When we imagine that there is any good thing in us, we need not wonder if he reject us, as we thus take away from him a principal part of the honour which is his due. But, on

---

[1] The Septuagint reads, "Τῶν ἀγαθῶν μου οὐ χρείαν ἔχεις." "Thou hast no need of my goodness, [or good things."] The reading in Tyndale's Bible is, "My goods are nothing unto thee."

the contrary, if we acknowledge that all the services which we can yield him are in themselves things of nought, and undeserving of any recompense, this humility is as a perfume of a sweet odour, which will procure for them acceptance with God.

3. *Unto the saints who are on the earth.* Almost all are agreed in understanding this place, as if David, after the sentence which we have just now been considering, had added, The only way of serving God aright is to endeavour to do good to his holy servants. And the truth is, that God, as our good deeds cannot extend to him, substitutes the saints in his place, towards whom we are to exercise our charity. When men, therefore, mutually exert themselves in doing good to one another, this is to yield to God right and acceptable service. We ought, doubtless, to extend our charity even to those who are unworthy of it, as our heavenly Father "maketh his sun to rise on the evil and on the good," (Matth. v. 45;) but David justly prefers the saints to others, and places them in a higher rank. This, then, as I have said in the commencement, is the common opinion of almost all interpreters.[1] But although I do not deny that this doctrine is comprehended under the words of David, I think he goes somewhat farther, and intimates that he will unite himself with the devout worshippers of God, and be their associate or companion; even as all the children of God ought to be joined together by the bond of fraternal unity, that they may all serve and call upon their common Father with the same affection and zeal.[2] We thus see that David, after having confessed that he can find nothing in himself to bring to God, seeing he is indebted to him for every thing which he has, sets his affections upon the saints, because it is the will of God that, in this world, he should be magnified and exalted in the assembly of the just, whom he has adopted into his family for this end, that

---

[1] "Voyla donc (ainsi que j'ay commencé à dire) l'opinion commune, quasi de tous."—*Fr.*

[2] "D'un accord, et d'une mesme affection."—*Fr.* "With one accord, and with the same affection."

they may live together with one accord under his authority, and under the guidance of his Holy Spirit. This passage, therefore, teaches us that there is no sacrifice more acceptable to God than when we sincerely and heartily connect ourselves with the society of the righteous, and being knit together by the sacred bond of godliness, cultivate and maintain with them brotherly good-will. In this consists the communion of saints which separates them from the degrading pollutions of the world, that they may be the holy and peculiar people of God. He expressly speaks of *the saints who are on the earth,* because it is the will of God that, even in this world, there should be conspicuous marks, and as it were visible escutcheons,[1] of his glory, which may serve to conduct us to himself. The faithful, therefore, bear his image, that, by their example, we may be stirred up to meditation upon the heavenly life. For the same reason, the Psalmist calls them *excellent,* or honourable, because there is nothing which ought to be more precious to us than righteousness and holiness, in which the brightness of God's Spirit shines forth; just as we are commanded in the preceding psalm to prize and honour those who fear God. We ought, therefore, highly to value and esteem the true and devoted servants of God, and to regard nothing as of greater importance than to connect ourselves with their society; and this we will actually do if we wisely reflect in what true excellence and dignity consist, and do not allow the vain splendour of the world and its deceitful pomps to dazzle our eyes.

4. *Their sorrows shall be multiplied who offer to a stranger;*[2] *I will not taste*[3] *their libations*[4] *of blood, nor will I take their names in my lips.*

[1] "Et comme armoiries apparentes."—*Fr.*

[2] "A un Dieu estrange, et autre que le vray Dieu."—*Note, Fr. marg.* "That is, to a strange God, and another than the true God."

[3] In the Latin version, the word is "libabo," which means either *to taste,* or *to pour out in offering;* in the French version it is "gousteray," which means simply *to taste.* "The Gentiles used," says Poole, ("as diverse learned men have observed,) to offer, and sometimes to drink part of the blood of their sacrifices, whether of beasts or of men, as either of them were sacrificed."—*Annotations.*

[4] In the French version, the word is "sacrifices," on which Calvin has

The Psalmist now describes the true way of maintaining brotherly concord with the saints, by declaring that he will have nothing to do with unbelievers and the superstitious. We cannot be united into the one body of the Church under God, if we do not break off all the bonds of impiety, separate ourselves from idolaters, and keep ourselves pure and at a distance from all the pollutions which corrupt and vitiate the holy service of God. This is certainly the general drift of David's discourse. But as to the words there is a diversity of opinion among expositors. Some translate the first word of the verse עַצְבוֹת, *atsboth*, by *idols*,[1] and according to this rendering the meaning is, that after men in their folly have once begun to make to themselves false gods, their madness breaks forth without measure, until they accumulate an immense multitude of deities. As, however, this word is here put in the feminine gender, I prefer translating it *sorrows or troubles*, although it may still have various meanings. Some think it is an imprecation, and they read, *Let their sorrows be multiplied;* as if David, inflamed with a holy zeal, denounced the just vengeance of God against the superstitious. Others, whose opinions I prefer, do not change the tense of the verb, which in the Hebrew is future, *Their sorrows shall be multiplied;* but to me they do not seem to express, with sufficient clearness, what kind of sorrows David intends. They say, indeed, that wretched idolaters are perpetually adding to their new inventions, in doing which, they miserably torment themselves. But I am of

the following note on the margin :—" Le mot signifie proprement bruvages accoustumez en sacrifices."—" The word properly signifies the customary drinks in sacrifices."

[1] The Chaldee version reads, "their idols." The Septuagint reads, ἀσθένειαι αὐτῶν, "their weaknesses," or "afflictions;" and the Syriac and Arabic use a word of similar import. Bishop Patrick paraphrases the verse as follows :—" They multiply idols, (here in this place whither I am driven, 1 Sam. xxvi. 19,) and are zealous in the service of another God. But I will never forsake thee by partaking with them in their abominable sacrifices, (in which the blood of men is offered,) nor by swearing by the name of any of their false gods." " Dathe observes, that עצבת never signifies idols, the proper word being עצבים. See Gesenius and 1 Sam. xxxi. 9; 2 Sam. v. 21; Hosea iv. 17. The other versions of the Polyglott support the common interpretation, which is also approved by Dathe, Horsley, Berlin, and De Rossi."—*Roger's Book of Psalms, in Hebrew, Metrically Arranged*, vol. ii. p. 172.

opinion, that by this word there is, at the same time, denoted the end and issue of the pains which they take in committing it; it points out that they not only put themselves to trouble without any profit or advantage, but also miserably harass and busy themselves to accomplish their own destruction. As an incitement to him to withdraw himself farther from their company, he takes this as an incontrovertible principle, that, so far from deriving any advantage from their vain superstitions, they only, by their strenuous efforts in practising them, involve themselves in greater misery and wretchedness. For what must be the issue with respect to those miserable men who willingly surrender themselves as bond-slaves to the devil, but to be disappointed of their hope? even as God complains in Jeremiah, (chap. ii. 13,) "They have forsaken me the fountain of living waters, and hewed them out cisterns, broken cisterns, that can hold no water."

In the next clause there is also some ambiguity. The Hebrew word מהר, *mahar*, which we have translated *to offer*, in the conjugation *kal* signifies *to endow*, or *to give*. But as, in the conjugation *hiphil*, it is more frequently taken for *to run*, or *to make haste*,[1] many have preferred this latter meaning, and interpret the clause thus, that superstitious persons eagerly hasten after strange gods. And in fact we see them rushing into their idolatries with all the impetuosity and recklessness of madmen running in the fields;[2] and the prophets often upbraid them for this inconsiderate frenzy with which they are fired. I would, therefore, be much disposed to adopt this sense were it supported by the common usage of the language; but as grammarians

---

[1] Walford translates the verse thus:—
"They multiply their sorrows who hastily turn backward;
Their libations of blood will I not offer;
Nor will I take their names upon my lips."

And the sense which he attaches to the passage is, that David having in the preceding verse declared his delight in the righteous, here states that those who turn away from God and his truth augment their own sufferings; and affirms it to be his resolution to have no fellowship with them in their religious services, which were polluted and detestable, or in the intercourse of friendship by making mention of their names.

[2] "Et de faict, nous voyons de quelle impetuosite ils se jettent en leurs idolatries sans regarder à rien, tellement qu'il semble que ce soyent gens forcenez, qui courent à travers champs."—*Fr.*

observe that there is not to be found another similar passage in Scripture, I have followed, in my translation, the first opinion. In short, the sum of what the Psalmist says is this, That unbelievers, who lavish and squander away their substance upon their idols, not only lose all the gifts and offerings which they present to them, but also, by provoking the wrath of God against themselves, are continually increasing the amount of their miseries. Perhaps, also, the prophet has an allusion to the common doctrine of Scripture, that idolaters violate the promise of the spiritual marriage contracted with the true God, and enter into covenant with idols.[1] Ezekiel (chap. xvi. 33) justly upbraids the Jews, in that while the custom is for the lover to allure the harlot with presents, they, on the contrary, offered rewards to the idols to whom they prostituted and abandoned themselves. But the meaning which we have above given brings out the spirit of the passage, namely, that unbelievers, who honour their false gods by offering to them gifts, not only lose what is thus expended, but also heap up for themselves sorrows upon sorrows, because at last the issue will be miserable and ruinous to them.

I will not taste their libations of blood. By libations of blood some understand that there is a reference to sacrifices made of things acquired by murder or rapine. As, however, the prophet is not here inveighing against cruel and bloodthirsty men, but condemns, in general, all false and corrupt religious worship; and again, as he does not directly name sacrifices, but expressly speaks of the ceremony of taking the cup, and tasting a little of it, which was observed in offering sacrifices,[2] I have no doubt but that to this ceremony, as it was observed according to the law of God, he here tacitly opposes the drinking of blood in heathen sacrifices. We know that God, in order to teach his ancient people to hold in greater abhorrence murder and all cruelty,

---

[1] Horsley reads, " They shall multiply their sorrows [who] betroth themselves to another. That is, who go a whoring after other gods."

[2] " Mais touche nommément la ceremonie qu'on observoit es sacrifices asçavoir de prendre la coupe et en gouster un peu."—*Fr.* On the margin of the French version there is a reference to the Commentaries of Calvin upon Matth. xxvi. 26, and Gen. ix. 4.

forbade them to eat or to drink blood either in their common food or in sacrifices. On the contrary, the histories of the heathen nations bear testimony that the custom of tasting the blood in their sacrifices prevailed among them. David, therefore, protests, that he will not only keep himself uncontaminated by the corrupt and false opinions by which idolaters are seduced, but that he will also take care not to show outwardly any token of his complying with or approving them. In the same sense we are to understand what follows immediately after, *I will not take their names in my lips.* This implies that he will hold idols in such hatred and detestation, as to keep himself from naming them as from execrable treason against the majesty of heaven. Not that it is unlawful to pronounce their names, which we frequently meet with in the writings of the prophets, but David felt he could not otherwise more forcibly express the supreme horror and detestation with which the faithful ought to regard false gods. This is also shown by the form of expression which he employs, using the relative only, *their names,* although he has not expressly stated before that he is speaking of idols. Thus, by his example, he enjoins believers not only to beware of errors and wicked opinions, but also to abstain from all appearance of giving their consent to them. He evidently speaks of external ceremonies, which indicate either the true religion, or some perverse superstition. If, then, it is unlawful for the faithful to show any token of consenting to or complying with the superstitions of idolaters, Nicodemuses (who falsely call themselves by this name[1]) must not think to shelter themselves under the frivolous pretext that they have not renounced the faith, but keep it hidden within their hearts, when they join in the observance of the profane superstitions of the Papists. Some understand the words *strangers* and *their names,* as denoting the worshippers of false gods; but in my judgment David rather means the false gods themselves. The scope of his discourse is this: The earth is filled with an immense accumulation[2] of superstitions in every

---

[1] " Qui se nomment ainsi à tort."—*Fr.*
[2] " Quoy que la terre soit pleine d'un grand amas d'infinite de superstitions."—*Fr.*

possible variety, and idolaters are lavish beyond all bounds in ornamenting their idols; but the good and the holy will ever regard all their superstitious inventions with abhorrence.

> 5. *Jehovah is the portion of mine inheritance, and of my cup; thou sustainest my lot.*
> 6. *The lines have fallen to me in pleasant places; yea, I have a goodly heritage.*

5. *The Lord is the portion of mine inheritance.* Here the Psalmist explains his sentiments more clearly. He shows the reason why he separates himself from idolaters, and resolves to continue in the church of God, why he shuns, with abhorrence, all participation in their errors, and cleaves to the pure worship of God; namely, because he rests in the only true God as his portion. The unhappy restlessness of those blind idolaters[1] whom we see going astray, and running about as if stricken and impelled by madness, is doubtless to be traced to their destitution of the true knowledge of God. All who have not their foundation and trust in God must necessarily be often in a state of irresolution and uncertainty; and those who do not hold the true faith in such a manner as to be guided and governed by it, must be often carried away by the overflowing floods of errors which prevail in the world.[2] This passage teaches us, that none are taught aright in true godliness but those who reckon God alone sufficient for their happiness. David, by calling God *the portion of his lot,* and *his inheritance,* and *his cup,* protests that he is so fully satisfied with him alone, as neither to covet any thing besides him, nor to be excited by any depraved desires. Let us therefore learn, when God offers himself to us, to embrace him with the whole heart, and to seek in him only all the ingredients and the fulness of our happiness. All the superstitions which have ever prevailed in the world have undoubtedly proceeded from this source, that superstitious men have not been contented with possessing God

---

[1] " De ces aveugles d'idolatres."—*Fr.*

[2] " Transportez par les desbordemens impetueux des erreurs qui regnent au monde."—*Fr.*

alone. But we do not actually possess him unless "he is the portion of our inheritance;" in other words, unless we are wholly devoted to him, so as no longer to have any desire unfaithfully to depart from him. For this reason, God, when he upbraids the Jews who had wandered from him as apostates,[1] with having run about after idols, addresses them thus, " Let them be thine inheritance, and thy portion." By these words he shows, that if we do not reckon him alone an all-sufficient portion for us, and if we will have idols along with him,[2] he gives place entirely to them, and lets them have the full possession of our hearts. David here employs three metaphors; he first compares God to an inheritance; secondly, to a cup; and, thirdly, he represents him as He who defends and keeps him in possession of his inheritance. By the first metaphor he alludes to the heritages of the land of Canaan, which we know were divided among the Jews by divine appointment, and the law commanded every one to be content with the portion which had fallen to him. By the word *cup* is denoted either the revenue of his own proper inheritance, or by synecdoche, ordinary food by which life is sustained, seeing drink is a part of our nourishment.[3] It is as if David had said, God is mine both in respect of property and enjoyment. Nor is the third comparison superfluous. It often happens that rightful owners are put out of their possession because no one defends them. But while God has given himself to us for an inheritance, he has engaged to exercise his power in maintaining us in the safe enjoyment of a good so inconceivably great. It would be of little advantage to us to have once obtained him as ours, if he did not secure our possession of him against the assaults which Satan daily makes upon us. Some explain the third clause as if it had been said, *Thou art my ground in which my portion is situated;* but this sense appears to me to be cold and unsatisfactory.

6. *The lines*[4] *have fallen to me.* The Psalmist confirms

[1] " Qui s'estoyent destournez de lui comme apostats."—*Fr.*
[2] " Ains que no'vueillions avoir avec lui les idoles."—*Fr.*
[3] " D'autant que le bruvage est une partie de nostre nourriture."—*Fr.*
[4] The Hebrew is *measuring lines.* There is here an allusion to the

more fully what he had already said in the preceding verse with respect to his resting, with a composed and tranquil mind, in God alone; or rather, he so glories in God as nobly to despise all that the world imagines to be excellent and desirable without him. By magnifying God in such honourable and exalted strains, he gives us to understand that he does not desire any thing more as his portion and felicity. This doctrine may be profitable to us in many ways. It ought to draw us away not only from all the perverse inventions of superstition, but also from all the allurements of the flesh and of the world. Whenever, therefore, those things present themselves to us which would lead us away from resting in God alone, let us make use of this sentiment as an antidote against them, that we have sufficient cause for being contented, since he who has in himself an absolute fulness of all good has given himself to be enjoyed by us. In this way we will experience our condition to be always pleasant and comfortable; for he who has God as his portion is destitute of nothing which is requisite to constitute a happy life.

7. *I will magnify Jehovah, who giveth me counsel; even in the night my reins instruct me.*[1]

Last of all, David confesses that it was entirely owing to the pure grace of God that he had come to possess so great a good, and that he had been made a partaker of it by faith. It would be of no advantage to us for God to offer himself

ancient division of the land of Canaan among God's chosen people. This was done by lot, and the length and breadth of the portion of each tribe was ascertained by cords or measuring lines. Hence they came to signify the land so measured out.

[1] "My reins" is the literal rendering of the Hebrew text, and they denote the working of the thoughts and affections of the soul. "As common experience," says Parkhurst, "shows that the workings of the mind, particularly the passions of joy, grief, and fear, have a very remarkable effect on the *reins* or *kidneys*, so, from their retired situation in the body, and their being *hid* in fat, they are often used in Scripture to denote the most *secret working* of the soul and affections." "The reins or kidneys," says Walford, in a note on this passage, "are used to signify the interior faculties; and the divine speaker observes, that in seasons of solitude, his thoughts were instinctively employed in contemplating the heavenly discoveries that were communicated to him." In Tyndale's Bible the reading of the last clause is, "My reins also have *chastened me* in the night season." And Fry observes, that the word "יסר" signifies not so immediately *to instruct*, as *to chasten, correct*, or *discipline*."

freely and graciously to us, if we did not receive him by faith, seeing he invites to himself both the reprobate and the elect in common; but the former, by their ingratitude, defraud themselves of this inestimable blessing. Let us, therefore, know that both these things proceed from the free liberality of God; first, his being our inheritance, and next, our coming to the possession of him by faith. The *counsel* of which David makes mention is the inward illumination of the Holy Spirit, by which we are prevented from rejecting the salvation to which he calls us, which we would otherwise certainly do, considering the blindness of our flesh.[1] Whence we gather, that those who attribute to the free will of man the choice of accepting or rejecting the grace of God basely mangle that grace, and show as much ignorance as impiety. That this discourse of David ought not to be understood of external teaching appears clearly from the words, for he tells us that *he was instructed in the night* when he was removed from the sight of men. Again, when he speaks of this being done *in his reins*, he doubtless means secret inspirations.[2] Farther, it ought to be carefully observed, that, in speaking of the time when he was instructed, he uses the plural number, saying, it was done in the *nights*. By this manner of speaking, he not only ascribes to God the beginning of faith, but acknowledges that he is continually making progress under his tuition; and, indeed, it is necessary for God, during the whole of our life, to continue to correct the vanity of our minds, to kindle the light of faith into a brighter flame, and by every means to advance us higher in the attainments of spiritual wisdom.

> 8. *I have set Jehovah continually before me; because he is at my right hand, I shall not be moved.*
> 9. *Therefore my heart*[3] *is glad, my tongue rejoiceth; my flesh also dwelleth in confidence,* [or *in security.*]

8. *I have set Jehovah, &c.* The Psalmist again shows the

---

[1] " Ce qu'autrement nous ferions, veu l'aveuglement de nostre chair." —*Fr.*
[2] Calvin means that God taught David by secret inspirations.
[3] " כבוד, *kabod*, is the liver, which, like the heart, the reins, &c., is used for the mind, so that the sense is, I myself will rejoice."—*Walford.*

firmness and stability of his faith. To set God before us is nothing else than to keep all our senses bound and captive, that they may not run out and go astray after any other object. We must look to him with other eyes than those of the flesh, for we shall seldom be able to perceive him unless we elevate our minds above the world; and faith prevents us from turning our back upon him. The meaning, therefore, is, that David kept his mind so intently fixed upon the providence of God, as to be fully persuaded, that whenever any difficulty or distress should befall him, God would be always at hand to assist him. He adds, also, *continually*, to show us how he constantly depended upon the assistance of God, so that, amidst the various conflicts with which he was agitated, no fear of danger could make him turn his eyes to any other quarter than to God in search of succour. And thus we ought so to depend upon God as to continue to be fully persuaded of his being near to us, even when he seems to be removed to the greatest distance from us. When we shall have thus turned our eyes towards him, the masks and the vain illusions of this world will no longer deceive us.

Because he is at my right hand. I read this second clause as a distinct sentence from the preceding. To connect them together as some do in this way, *I have set the Lord continually before me, because he is at my right hand*, would give a meagre meaning to the words, and take away much of the truth which is taught in them, as it would make David to say, that he measured God's presence according to the experience he had of it; a mode of speaking which would not be at all becoming. I consider, therefore, the words, *I have set the Lord continually before me*, as a complete sentence, and David set the Lord before him for the purpose of constantly repairing to him in all his dangers. For his greater encouragement to hope well, he sets before himself what it is to have God's assistance and fatherly care, namely, that it implies his keeping firm and unmoved his own people with whom he is present. David then reckons himself secure against all dangers, and promises himself certain safety, because, with the eyes of faith, he beholds God as present with him. From this passage we are furnished with an argument which overthrows the fabrication of the Sorbonists,[1] *that the faithful are in doubt with respect to their final perseverance;* for David, in very plain terms, extends his reliance on the grace of God to the time to come. And, certainly, it would be a very miserable condition to be in, to tremble in uncertainty every moment, having no assurance of the continuance of the grace of God towards us.

9. *Therefore my heart is glad.* In this verse the Psalmist commends the inestimable fruit of faith, of which Scripture every where makes mention, in that, by placing us under the protection of God, it makes us not only to live in the enjoyment of mental tranquillity, but, what is more, to live joyful and cheerful. The principal, the essential part of a happy life, as we know, is to possess tranquillity of conscience and of mind; as, on the contrary, there is no greater infelicity than to be tossed amidst a multiplicity of cares and fears.

But the ungodly, however much intoxicated with the spirit of thoughtlessness or stupidity, never experience true joy or serene mental peace; they rather feel terrible agitations within, which often come upon them and trouble them, so much as to constrain them to awake from their lethargy. In short, calmly to rejoice is the lot of no man but of him who has learned to place his confidence in God alone, and to commit his life and safety to his protection. When, therefore, encompassed with innumerable troubles on all sides, let us be persuaded, that the only remedy is to direct our eyes towards God; and if we do this, faith will not only tranquillise our minds, but also replenish them with fulness of joy. David, however, not only affirms that he is glad inwardly; he also makes his *tongue,* yea, even his *flesh,* sharers of this joy. And not without cause, for true believers not only have this spiritual joy in the secret affection of their heart, but also manifest it by the tongue, inasmuch as they glory in God as He who protects them and secures their salvation. The word כבוד, *kabod,* properly signifies glory and excellence. I have, however, no doubt of its being here taken for *the tongue,*[2]

---
[1] The Doctors of the Sorbonne, a university in Paris.
[2] The reading of the Septuagint is, "γλωσσα μου," "my tongue."

as it is in Gen. xlix. 6; for otherwise the division which is obviously made in this verse of the person into three parts is not so distinct and evident. Farther, although the body is not free from inconveniences and troubles, yet as God defends and maintains not only our souls, but also our bodies, David does not speak groundlessly when he represents the blessing of dwelling in safety as extending to his flesh in common with his soul.

10. *For thou wilt not leave my soul in the grave; neither wilt thou make thy Holy One to see the pit.*[1]

The Psalmist goes on to explain still more fully the preceding doctrine, by declaring that as he is not afraid of death, there is nothing wanting which is requisite to the completion of his joy. Whence it follows, that no one truly trusts in God but he who takes such hold of the salvation which God has promised him as to despise death. Moreover, it is to be observed, that David's language is not to be limited to some particular kind of deliverance, as in Psalm xlix. 15, where he says, " God hath redeemed my soul from the power of the grave," and in other similar passages; but he entertains the undoubted assurance of eternal salvation, which freed him from all anxiety and fear. It is as if he had said, There will always be ready for me a way of escape from the grave, that I may not remain in corruption. God, in delivering his people from any danger, prolongs their life only for a

---

This is unquestionably the meaning. David uses the word *glory* for the organ by which God is glorified or praised. The Apostle Peter, in quoting this passage, (Acts ii. 26,) reads, " my tongue." See also Ps. xxxvi. 12.

[1] " The Hebrew word *shachath*," says Poole, " though sometimes, by a metonymy, it signifies the pit or place of corruption, yet properly and generally it signifies corruption or perdition. And so it must be understood here, although some of the Jews, to avoid the force of this argument, render it the pit. But in that sense it is not true, for whether it be meant of David, as they say, or of Christ, it is confessed that both of them did see the pit, that is, were laid in the grave." Hence he concludes that *corruption* is the proper rendering of the original word. The phrase, however, *to see the pit*, may not mean to be laid in the grave, but to continue in it for any length of time. The meaning which Calvin attaches to the word *pit* is substantially that which our English translators attached to the original word which they render *corruption*. Hengstenberg adopts and defends Calvin's rendering.

short time; but how slender and how empty a consolation would it be to obtain some brief respite, and to take breath for a short time, until death, coming at last, should terminate the course of our life,[1] and swallow us up without any hope of deliverance? Hence it appears that when David spake thus, he raised his mind above the common lot of mankind. As the sentence has been pronounced upon all the children of Adam, " Dust thou art, and unto dust shalt thou return," (Gen. iii. 19,) the same condition in this respect awaits them all without exception. If, therefore, Christ, who is the first-fruits of those who rise again, does not come forth from the grave, they will remain for ever under the bondage of corruption. From this Peter justly concludes, (Acts ii. 30,) that David could not have gloried in this manner but by the spirit of prophecy; and unless he had had a special respect to the Author of life, who was promised to him, who alone was to be honoured with this privilege in its fullest sense. This, however, did not prevent David from assuring himself of exemption from the dominion of death by right, seeing Christ, by his rising from the dead, obtained immortality not for himself individually, but for us all. As to the point, that Peter (Acts ii. 30) and Paul (xiii. 33) contend that this prophecy was fulfilled in the person of Christ alone,[2] the sense in which we must understand them is this, that he was wholly and perfectly exempted from the corruption of the grave, that he might call his members into his fellowship, and make them partakers of this blessing,[3] although by degrees, and each according to his measure. As the body of David, after death, was, in the course of time, reduced to dust, the apostles justly conclude that he was not exempted from corruption. It is the same with respect to all the faithful, not one of whom becomes a partaker of incorruptible life without being first subjected to corruption. From this it follows that the fulness of life which resides in

[1] " Jusqu'à ce que la mort finalement venant, rompist le cours de nos jours."—*Fr.*
[2] Thus we have the authority of two apostles for understanding the concluding part of this psalm as a prophecy of Christ's resurrection from the dead.
[3] " Et les faire venir a la participation de ce bien."—*Fr.*

the head alone, namely, in Christ, falls down upon the members only in drops, or in small portions. The question, however, may be asked, as Christ descended into the grave, was not he also subject to corruption? The answer is easy. The etymology or derivation of the two words here used to express the grave should be carefully attended to. The grave is called שְׁאוֹל, *sheol*, being as it were an insatiable gulf, which devours and consumes all things, and the pit is called שַׁחַת, *shachath*, which signifies *corruption*. These words, therefore, here denote not so much the place as the quality and condition of the place, as if it had been said, The life of Christ will be exempted from the dominion of the grave, inasmuch as his body, even when dead, will not be subject to corruption. Besides, we know that the grave of Christ was filled, and as it were embalmed with the life-giving perfume of his Spirit, that it might be to him the gate to immortal glory. Both the Greek and Latin Fathers, I confess, have strained these words to a meaning wholly different, referring them to the bringing back of the soul of Christ from hell. But it is better to adhere to the natural simplicity of the interpretation which I have given, that we may not make ourselves objects of ridicule to the Jews; and farther, that one subtilty, by engendering many others, may not involve us in a labyrinth. In the second clause mention is without doubt made of the body; and we know it to be a mode of speaking very common with David intentionally to repeat the same thing twice, making a slight variation as to words. It is true, we translate נֶפֶשׁ, *nephesh*, by *soul*, but in Hebrew it only signifies *the vital breath*, or *life itself*.

> 11. *Thou wilt make me to know the path of life; fulness of joy is in thy countenance, pleasures are at thy right hand for evermore.*

The Psalmist confirms the statement made in the preceding verse, and explains the way in which God will exempt him from the bondage of death, namely, by conducting and bringing him at length safely to the possession of eternal life. Whence we again learn what I have already observed, that this passage touches upon the difference which there is between true believers and aliens, or reprobates, with respect to their everlasting state. It is a mere cavil to say, that when David here speaks of *the path of life* being shown to him, it means the prolongation of his natural life. It is to form a very low estimate, indeed, of the grace of God to speak of him as a guide to his people in the path of life only for a very few years in this world. In this case, they would differ nothing from the reprobate, who enjoy the light of the sun in common with them. If, therefore, it is the special grace of God which he communicates to none but his own children, that David here magnifies and exalts, the showing of the way of life, of which he speaks, must undoubtedly be viewed as extending to a blessed immortality; and, indeed, he only knows the way of life who is so united to God that he lives in God, and cannot live without him.

David next adds, that when God is reconciled to us, we have all things which are necessary to perfect happiness. The phrase, *the countenance of God*, may be understood either of our being beheld by him, or of our beholding him; but I consider both these ideas as included, for his fatherly favour, which he displays in looking upon us with a serene countenance, precedes this joy, and is the first cause of it, and yet this does not cheer us until, on our part, we behold it shining upon us. By this clause David also intended distinctly to express to whom those *pleasures* belong, of which God has in his hand a full and an overflowing abundance. As there are with God pleasures sufficient to replenish and satisfy the whole world, whence comes it to pass that a dismal and deadly darkness envelopes the greater part of mankind, but because God does not look upon all men equally with his friendly and fatherly countenance, nor opens the eyes of all men to seek the matter of their joy in him, and no where else? *Fulness of joy* is contrasted with the evanescent allurements and pleasures of this transitory world, which, after having diverted their miserable votaries for a time, leave them at length unsatisfied, famished, and disappointed. They may intoxicate and glut themselves with pleasures to the greatest excess, but, instead of being satisfied, they rather become wearied of them through loathing; and, besides, the pleasures of this world vanish away like dreams. David, therefore, testifies that true and solid joy in which the minds of men may rest will never be found any where else but in God; and that, therefore, none but the faithful, who are contented with his grace alone, can be truly and perfectly happy.

PSALM XVII.

This psalm contains a mournful complaint against the cruel pride of David's enemies. He protests that he did not deserve to be persecuted with such inhumanity, inasmuch as he had given them no cause for exercising their cruelty against him. At the same time, he beseeches God, as his protector, to put forth his power for his deliverance. The inscription of the psalm does not refer to any particular time, but it is probable that David here complains of Saul and his associates.[1]

¶ *A prayer of David.*

1. *Hear my righteousness,*[2] *O Jehovah, attend to my cry; hearken to my prayer, which proceedeth not from deceitful lips.*
2. *Let my judgment* [or *judgment in my favour*] *come forth from the presence of thy countenance;*[3] *let thine eyes look upon my uprightness.*

1. *Hear my righteousness, O Jehovah.* The Psalmist begins

---

[1] This is the general opinion as to the occasion of the composition of this psalm. It is supposed that David, in representing his innocence of those things of which he was accused, refers to the charges brought against him of traitorously aspiring to the kingdom, and seeking the life of Saul, 1 Sam. xxiv. 9; and that therefore the persecutors and calumniators from whom he beseeches God to deliver him were Saul and his courtiers.

[2] The Vulgate, Æthiopic, and Arabic versions read "my righteousness," or "my right," as here and in our English version, meaning his righteous cause. The Septuagint, "Κυριε της δικαιοσυνης μου," "O Lord of my righteousness." Jerome reads, "Audi, Deus, justum," "Hear, O God, the just one," a reading which Horsley is inclined to adopt, viewing the Messiah as the speaker in this psalm. In the Syriac version the reading is, "Hear, O righteous Lord;" and this is followed by Bishop Horne, Dr Adam Clarke, and Dr Boothroyd.

[3] "'Let my sentence come forth from thy presence;' that is, be thou, O Jehovah, my judge in thine own person."—*Horsley.*

the psalm by setting forth the goodness of his cause. He does this because God has promised that he will not suffer the innocent to be oppressed, but will always, at length, succour them. Some explain the word *righteousness* as denoting *righteous prayer*, an interpretation which appears to me unsatisfactory. The meaning rather is, that David, confiding in his own integrity, interposes God as a Judge between himself and his enemies, to cognosce or determine in his cause. We have already seen, in a preceding psalm, that when we have to deal with wicked men, we may warrantably protest our innocence before God. As, however, it would not be enough for the faithful to have the approving testimony of a good conscience, David adds to his protestation earnest prayer. Even irreligious persons may often be able justly to boast of having a good cause; but as they do not acknowledge that the world is governed by the providence of God, they content themselves with enjoying the approbation of their own conscience, as they speak, and, gnawing the bit, bear the injuries which are done to them rather obstinately than stedfastly, seeing they do not seek for any consolation in faith and prayer. But the faithful not only depend upon the goodness of their cause, they also commit it to God that he may defend and maintain it; and whenever any adversity befalls them, they betake themselves to him for help. This, therefore, is the meaning of the passage; it is a prayer that God, who knew David to have done justly, and to have performed his duty without giving occasion to any to blame him,[1] and, therefore, to be unrighteously molested by his enemies, would graciously look upon him; and that he would do this especially, since, confiding in his aid, he entertained good hope, and, at the same time, prays to him with a sincere heart. By the words *cry* and *prayer* he means the same thing; but the word *cry*, and the repetition of what it denotes, by a different expression, serve to show his vehement, his intense earnestness of soul. Farther, as hypocrites talk loftily in commendation of themselves, and to show to others a token of the great confidence which they

---

[1] "Que David se soit porté justement et fait son devoir sans donner à aucun occasion de le blasmer."—*Fr.*

have in God, give utterance to loud cries, David protests concerning himself that he does not speak *deceitfully;* in other words, that he does not make use of his crying and prayer as a pretext for covering his sins, but comes into the presence of God with sincerity of heart. By this form of prayer the Holy Spirit teaches us, that we ought diligently to endeavour to live an upright and innocent life, so that, if there are any who give us trouble, we may be able to boast that we are blamed and persecuted wrongfully.[1] Again, whenever the wicked assault us, the same Spirit calls upon us to engage in prayer; and if any man, trusting to the testimony of a good conscience which he enjoys, neglects the exercise of prayer, he defrauds God of the honour which belongs to him, in not referring his cause to him, and in not leaving him to judge and determine in it. Let us learn, also, that when we present ourselves before God in prayer, it is not to be done with the ornaments of an artificial eloquence, for the finest rhetoric and the best grace which we can have before him consists in pure simplicity.

2. *From the presence of thy countenance.* Literally it is, *from before thy face,* or, *before thy face.* By these words David intimates that if God does not rise up as the vindicator of his cause, he will be overwhelmed with calumnies though innocent, and will be looked upon as a guilty and condemned person. The cognisance which God will take of his cause is tacitly set in opposition to the dark inventions of falsehood which were spread against him.[2] His language is as if he had said, I do not ask for any other judge but God, nor do I shrink from standing before his judgment-seat,[3] since I bring with me both a pure heart and a good cause. What he immediately adds with respect to God's *looking upon* his uprightness is of similar import. He does not mean to say that God is blind, but only beseeches him actually to show that he does not connive at the wickedness of men, and that it is not to him

---

[1] " Que nous sommes blasmez et persecutez a tort."—*Fr.*

[2] " Car la cognoissance que Dieu prendra de sa cause est tacitement mise à l'opposite des tenebres des mensonges qu'on semoit contre luy."—*Fr.*

[3] " Et qu'il ne refuse point de respondre devant le siege judicial d'iceluy."—*Fr.* " Nor do I refuse to answer before his judgment-seat."

a matter of indifference when he beholds those who have not the means of defending themselves[1] receiving evil treatment undeservedly. Some take the word *judgment* in too restricted a sense for the right to the kingdom which was promised to David, as if he petitioned to be placed on the royal throne by the power of God, inasmuch as he had been chosen by him to be king, and had also, in his name and by his authority, been anointed to this office by the hand of Samuel. The meaning which I attach to David's language is simply this, that being oppressed with many and varied wrongs, he commits himself to the protection and defence of God.

> 3. *Thou hast proved my heart; thou hast visited it by night; thou hast examined it, thou shalt find nothing; my thoughts shall not pass beyond my mouth.*[2]
> 4. *As for the works of men, by the word of thy lips I have taken heed of* [or *watched*] *the ways of the destroyer.*[3]

3. *Thou hast proved my heart.* Some are of opinion that in the three first verbs the past tense is put for the future. Others more correctly and more clearly resolve the words thus: If thou provest my heart, and visitest it by night, and examinest it thoroughly, there will not be found any deceit therein. But without making any change upon the words, they may be suitably enough explained in this way: Thou, Lord, who understandest all the secret affections and thoughts of my heart, even as it is thy peculiar prerogative to try men, knowest very well that I am not a double man, and do

---

[1] " Qui n'ont pas moyen de se defendre."—*Fr.*
[2] Great difference of opinion has prevailed among critics, as to the rendering and interpretation of this and the following verse. The third verse is rendered thus in Tyndale's Bible:—" Thou hast proved and visited mine heart in the night seasons, thou hast tried me in the fire, and hast found no wickedness in me; for I utterly purposed that my mouth should not offend." Geddes reads the third clause of the verse, " Thou hast smelted me, and found in me no dross;" and observes, that *smelted* is " a metaphor taken from the smelting of metals to purify them from extraneous matter."—*Geddes' New Translation of the Book of Psalms, with Notes.* The last clause of the third verse is added to the first clause of the fourth verse, in the Septuagint, Vulgate, Syriac, and Arabic versions, and the reading is thus:—" My mouth has not transgressed as to the evil designs of other men;" that is, I have not countenanced or approved of them by word.
[3] " Du violent."—*Fr.* " Of the violent."

not cherish any deceit within. What David intended to express is certainly very evident. As he was unjustly and falsely charged with crime, and could obtain neither justice nor humanity at the hands of men, he appeals to God, requesting he would become judge in the matter.[1] But not to do this rashly, he subjects himself to an impartial examination, seeing God, whose prerogative it is to search the secret recesses of the heart, cannot be deceived by the external appearance. The time when he declares God to have visited him is during *the night,* because, when a man is withdrawn from the presence of his fellow-creatures, he sees more clearly his sins, which otherwise would be hidden from his view; just as, on the contrary, the sight of men affects us with shame, and this is, as it were, a veil before our eyes, which prevents us from deliberately examining our faults. It is, therefore, as if David had said, O Lord, since the darkness of the night discovers the conscience more fully, all coverings being then taken away, and since, at that season, the affections, either good or bad, according to men's inclinations, manifest themselves more freely, when there is no person present to witness and pronounce judgment upon them; if thou then examinest me, there will be found neither disguise nor deceit in my heart.[2] Hence we conclude how great was David's integrity, seeing that, when purposely and leisurely taking account of his inmost thoughts, he presents himself so boldly, to be tried by the judgment of God. And he not only declares himself to be innocent of outward crimes, but also free from all secret malice. So far from cherishing malicious designs, while he covered them over with fair pretences, as his enemies alleged, he protests that his words were a frank and undisguised representation of what was passing in his heart: *My thought shall not pass beyond my mouth.* Our thought is said to pass beyond our mouth when, for the purpose of deceiving, the mind thinks differently from what the tongue expresses.[3] The word זמה,

[1] "Le requerant d'en vouloir estre le juge."—*Fr.*
[2] "Il ne sera trouve desguisement ne fraude quelconque en mon cœur."—*Fr.*
[3] This is the sense put upon this last clause by the learned Castellio, who translates it thus:—" Non deprehendes me aliud in pectore, aliud in

zimmah, which we have translated simply *thought,* may also be taken in a bad sense for deceitful and malicious devices.

4. *As for the works of men, by the word of thy lips.* Interpreters explain this verse in different senses. Some thinking that the letter ב, *beth,* which commonly signifies *in* or *by,* is taken for *against,* render it thus: As for the works of men which they practise against thy word. But I rather incline to the opinion of others who consider that there is here commended a right judgment of the actions of men which is formed according to the rule of the word of God. There are some shrewd and ingenious persons who carefully mark the works of men, but they do not judge of them according to the word of God. What we have as yet said does not, however, fully give us the sense of the passage. We must still consider what the Psalmist means when he speaks of *the paths of the destroyer.*[1] Some think he refers to the men of his own company, who, if he had not restrained them, would have instantly rushed like robbers to commit depredation; since being reduced to the greatest distress, and seeing no prospect of an alteration to the better in their affairs, they were become bold through despair; and we know how sharp a spur necessity is in goading men forward in any course. But this exposition seems to me to be forced, and therefore I rather refer the words to his enemies. Farther, there is a diversity of opinion among interpreters with respect to the meaning of the word *watched* or *observed.* Some understand it in this sense, that David had done his duty in strenuously opposing outrageous men, and those who were wickedly engaged in the work of disturbing the repose and tranquillity of their fellow-men.[2] Others understand it thus, that he was careful to distinguish between good and evil, or right and wrong,

ore habere." " Thou shalt not find me to have one thing in my breast and another in my mouth."

[1] Or, *the paths of the violent.* Literally of him who, by violent means, makes a breach in, or breaks down a wall or fence, the word פריץ, *pharits,* being derived from פרץ, *pharats, to break down,* or *break through.* It is referred by Calvin to the violent and wicked conduct of his enemies towards him.

[2] " De troubler le repos et la tranquillite des autres."—*Fr.*

that he might not be corrupted by bad examples,[1] but avoid them, and, on the contrary, practise those things which he saw to be agreeable to the word of God. But David, I have no doubt, had a different meaning, and intended to declare, that although wicked and malicious men provoked him to evil, he had, nevertheless, been always restrained by the word of God, so that he kept himself from exercising violence and inflicting injuries, or from rendering evil for evil.[2] He therefore tells us, that whatever may have been the works of men, he had been always so devoted to the word of God, and so hung, as it were, upon his mouth, that he could not think of allowing himself, when provoked by the injuries his enemies inflicted on him, to act towards them as they acted towards him. We know how severe a temptation it is, and how difficult to overcome, to disregard the manner in which men behave themselves towards us, and to consider only what God forbids or commands us. Even those who are naturally inclined to gentleness and humanity,[3] who desire to do good to all men, and wish to hurt nobody, whenever they are provoked, burst forth into a revengeful mood, carried away by a blind impetuosity; especially when we see all right and equity overthrown, the confusion so blinds us, that we begin to howl with the wolves. If, therefore, we would have a good rule for governing ourselves, when our enemies, by their mischievous actions, provoke us to treat them in a similar manner, let us learn, after the example of David, to meditate upon the word of God, and to keep our eyes fixed upon it. By this means our minds will be preserved from ever being blinded, and we shall always avoid the paths of wickedness, seeing God will not only keep our affections under restraint by his commandments, but will also train them to patience by his promises. He withholds us from doing evil to our neighbours,[4] not only by forbidding us, but by declaring, at the same time, that he will

---

[1] "Afin de n'estre point corrompu par mauvais exemples."—*Fr.*
[2] "*I have kept me from the paths, &c.*, or *observed the paths*, viz., so as to avoid them."—*Poole's Annotations.*
[3] "Car mesme ceux qui sont de nature enclins à debonnairete."—*Fr.*
[4] "De mal faire à nos prochains."—*Fr.*

take into his own hand the execution of vengeance on those who injure us,[1] he admonishes us to " give place unto wrath," (Rom. xii. 19.)

> 5. *Uphold my steps in thy paths, that the soles of my feet may not slide.*
> 6. *I have called upon thee, surely thou wilt hear me, O God; incline thine ear unto me, and hear my words.*

5. *Uphold my steps.* If we take *God's paths* for the precepts of his law, the sense will be evident, namely, that although David had spoken according to truth, in boasting of having, in the midst of the most grievous temptations which assailed him, constantly practised righteousness with a pure heart, yet, conscious of his own weakness, he commits himself to God to be governed by him, and prays for grace to enable him to persevere. His language is as if he had said, Since hitherto, under thy guidance, I have proceeded onward in the right path, I beseech thee, in like manner, to keep my steps from sliding with respect to the time to come. And certainly the more any one excels in grace,[2] the more ought he to be afraid of falling; for it is the usual policy of Satan to endeavour, even from the virtue and strength which God has given us,[3] to produce in us carnal confidence which may induce carelessness. I do not altogether reject this sense, but I think it more probable that David here beseeches God to bring his affairs to a prosperous issue, however dark the aspect of matters was at present. The import of his language is this, Lord, since thou seest that I walk in uprightness and sincerity of heart, govern thou me in such a manner as to make all men see that thou art my protector and guardian, and leave me not to be cast down at the will of my enemies. Thus, by *the paths of the Lord*, he will mean not the doctrine by which our life is regulated, but the power by which God upholds us, and the protection by which he preserves us. And he addresses God in this manner, not only because all events are in his hand, but because when he

---

[1] " Qu'il prendra en main la vengence contre ceux qui nous outragent."—*Fr.*

[2] " Et de faict, selon qu'un chacun a receu plus de graces."—*Fr.* " And certainly the more grace any one has received."

[3] " De la vertu et force que Dieu nous aura donnee."—*Fr.*

takes care of us all things in our lot go on prosperously. When he adds, *that the soles of my feet may not slide,* he refers to the many adverse events which threaten us every moment, and to the danger we are in of perishing, if not sustained by the hand of God.

6. *I have called upon thee, &c.* This verb being put in the past tense denotes a continued act; and, therefore, it includes the present time. The Hebrew word כי, *ki,* which we translate *surely,* often signifies *because,* and if it is so understood in this passage, the meaning will be, that David took encouragement to pray, because, depending upon the promise of God, he hoped that his prayers would not be in vain. But, perhaps, it may be thought preferable to change the tense of the verb as some do, so as to give this meaning, I will pray, because I have hitherto experienced that thou hast heard[1] my prayers. I have, however, chosen the exposition what appears to me the more simple. David, in my judgment, here encourages and animates himself to call upon God, from the confident hope of being heard, as if he had said, Since I call upon thee, surely, O God, thou wilt not despise my prayers. Immediately after he beseeches God to bestow upon him the blessings of which he told us he entertained an assured hope.

7. *Make marvellous thy mercies, O thou preserver of those who trust* [*in thee,*[2]] *from those that exalt themselves against thy right hand.*
8. *Keep me as the apple, the daughter of the eye ;*[3] *hide me in the shadow of thy wings.*
9. *From the face of the ungodly, who go about to destroy me ; and of mine enemies, who besiege* [or *encompass*] *my soul.*

7. *Make marvellous thy mercies.* As the word הפלה,

---

[1] The Septuagint renders the verb in the past tense, "Επηκουσας μου," "Thou hast heard me." The Syriac and Vulgate give a similar rendering. The verb, in the Hebrew, is in the future ; but it is a common thing in Hebrew to use the future tense for the past.

[2] These words are supplementary.

[3] "*The apple,* [or *pupil,*] *the daughter of the eye,* is the literal rendering of the Hebrew words, and thus they very powerfully set forth the beautiful image contained in them. Allusion is here made to the extreme care requisite for the preservation of so delicate an organ as the eye. Compare Prov. vii 2."—*French and Skinner's Translation of the Book of Psalms.*

haphleh, signifies sometimes *to make wonderful,* or *remarkable,* and sometimes *to separate and set apart,* both these senses will be very suitable to this passage. In Psalm xxxi. 19, the "goodness" of God is said to be "laid up" in store as a peculiar treasure "for them that fear him," that he may bring it forth at the proper season, even when they are brought to an extremity, and when all things seem to be desperate. If, then, the translation, *separate and set apart thy mercy,* is preferred, the words are a prayer that God would display towards his servant David the special grace which he communicates to none but his chosen ones. While God involves both the good and the bad in danger indiscriminately, he at length shows, by the different issue of things, in regard to the two classes, that he does not confusedly mingle the chaff and the wheat together, seeing he gathers his own people into a company by themselves, (Matth. iii. 12, and xxv. 32.) I, however, prefer following another exposition. David, in my judgment, perceiving that he could only be delivered from the perilous circumstances in which he was placed by singular and extraordinary means, betakes himself to the wonderful or miraculous power of God. Those who think he desires God to withhold his grace from his persecutors do too great violence to the scope of the passage. By this circumstance there is expressed the extreme danger to which David was exposed; for otherwise it would have been enough for him to have been succoured in the ordinary and common way in which God is accustomed daily to favour and to aid his own people. The grievousness of his distress, therefore, constrained him to beseech God to work miraculously for his deliverance. The title with which he here honours God, *O thou preserver of those who trust* [*in thee,*] serves to confirm him in the certain hope of obtaining his requests. As God takes upon him the charge of saving all who confide in him, David being one of their number, could upon good ground assure himself of safety and deliverance. Whenever, therefore, we approach God, let the first thought impressed on our minds be, that as he is not in vain called the preserver of those who trust in him, we have no reason whatever to be afraid of his not being ready to succour us, provided our faith continue firmly to rely upon his grace. And if every way of deliverance is shut up, let us also at the same time remember that he is possessed of wonderful and inconceivable means of succouring us, which serve so much the more conspicuously to magnify and manifest his power. But as the participle *trusting,* or *hoping,* is put without any additional word expressing the object of this trust or hope,[1] some interpreters connect it with the last words of the verse, *thy right hand,* as if the order of the words were inverted. They, therefore, resolve them thus, *O thou preserver of those who trust in thy right hand, from those who rise up against them.* As this, however, is harsh and strained, and the exposition which I have given is more natural, and more generally received,[2] let us follow it. To express, therefore, the meaning in one sentence, the Psalmist attributes to God the office of defending and preserving his own people from all the ungodly who rise up to assault them, and who, if it were in their power, would destroy them. And the ungodly are here said *to exalt themselves against the hand of God,* because, in molesting the faithful whom God has taken under his protection, they openly wage war against him. The doctrine contained in these words, namely, that when we are molested, an outrage is committed upon God in our person, is a very profitable one; for having once declared himself to be the guardian and protector of our welfare, whenever we are unjustly assailed, he puts forth his hand before us as a shield of defence.

The two similitudes which David has subjoined in the following verse, respecting *the apple of the eye,* and the little birds which the mother keeps *under her wings,*[3] are introduced for illustrating the same subject. God, to express the great care which he has of his own people, compares himself to a hen and other fowls, which spread out their wings to cherish and cover their young, and declares them to be no less dear to him than the apple of the eye, which is the

---

[1] Poole observes, that the Hebrew phrase for "them which trust," might be properly rendered without any supplement, "believers."

[2] Calvin's rendering is the same as that of the Septuagint, Vulgate, and Syriac versions.

[3] "Et des petis oiseaux que la mere tient *sous ses ailes.*"—*Fr.*

tenderest part of the body, is to man; it follows, therefore, that whenever men rise up to molest and injure the righteous, war is waged against him. As this form of prayer was put into the mouth of David by the Holy Spirit, it is to be regarded as containing in it a promise. We have here presented to our contemplation a singular and an astonishing proof of the goodness of God, in humbling himself so far, and in a manner so to speak, transforming himself, in order to lift up our faith above the conceptions of the flesh.

9. *From the face of the ungodly.* The Psalmist, by again accusing his enemies, intends to set forth his own innocence, as an argument for his obtaining the favour of God. At the same time, he complains of their cruelty, that God may be the more inclined to aid him. First, he says that they burn with an enraged desire to waste and to destroy him; secondly, he adds, that they *besiege him in his soul,* by which he means, that they would never rest satisfied until they had accomplished his death. The greater, therefore, the terror with which we are stricken by the cruelty of our enemies, the more ought we to be quickened to ardour in prayer. God, indeed, does not need to receive information and incitement from us; but the use and the end of prayer is, that the faithful, by freely declaring to God the calamities and sorrows which oppress them, and in disburdening them, as it were, into his bosom, may be assured beyond all doubt that he has a regard to their necessities.

10. *They have inclosed themselves in their own fat,*[1] *they have spoken proudly with their mouth.*
11. *They have now compassed me round about in our steps; they have fixed their eyes to cast down to the ground.*
12. *The likeness of him is as a lion that desireth to tear in pieces, and as a lion's whelp which lurketh in secret places.*

10. *They have inclosed themselves in their own fat.* If the

---

[1] Houbigant and Kennicott read עלי חבלמו סגרו, "They have closed their net upon me." Horsley and Fry adopt this reading. "But," says Rogers, "it receives no support from the ancient versions or MSS."

translation which is given by others is considered preferable, *They have inclosed their own fat*, the meaning will be quite the same. Some Jewish interpreters explain the words thus: that being stuffed with fat, and their throat being, as it were, choked with it, they were unable to speak freely; but this is a very meagre and unsatisfactory exposition. By the word *fat*, I think, is denoted the pride with which they were filled and swollen, as it were, with fatness. It is a very appropriate and expressive metaphor to represent them as having their hearts choked up with pride, in the manner in which corpulent persons are affected from the fat within them.[1] David complains of their being puffed up with their wealth and pleasures, and accordingly we see the ungodly, the more luxuriously they are pampered, conducting themselves the more outrageously and proudly. But I think there is described by the word *fat* an inward vice, namely, their being inclosed on all sides with arrogance and presumption, and their having become utter strangers to every feeling of humanity.[2] The Psalmist next declares that this is abundantly manifested in their language. In short, his meaning is, that inwardly they swell with pride, and that they take no pains to conceal it, as appears from the high swelling words to which they give utterance. When it is said, *They have spoken proudly with their mouth*, the word *mouth* is not a pleonasm, as it often is in other places; for David means, that with mouths widely opened they pour forth scornful

---

[1] " Comme les gens replets se trouvent saisis de leur graisse au dedans."—*Fr.*

" The sacred writers employ this term [fat] to signify a body pampered to excess by luxury and self-indulgence, Ps. lxxiii. 7; cxix. 70; Job xv. 27."—*French and Skinner's Translation of the Book of Psalms.* There may no doubt be a reference to the personal appearance and sensual indulgence of David's enemies. But something more is implied. " We know that in the figurative language of Scripture fatness denotes pride. This connection of ideas is still maintained in the East, where, when it is intended to indicate a proud man, he is said to be fat, or to look fat, whether really so or not."—*Illustrated Commentary upon the Bible.*

[2] Dr Geddes translates the clause, " Their hearts have they hardened." " Literally," says he, " they have closed their midriff;—shut out all compassion from their hearts." The Hebrew word which is rendered fat is explained by Gesenius, when used figuratively, as denoting a fat, that is, an unfeeling heart.

and contemptuous language, which bears testimony to the pride which dwells within them.

11. *They have now compassed me round about in our steps.* The Psalmist confirms what he has said before concerning the furious passion for doing mischief with which his enemies were inflamed. He says they were so cruelly bent on accomplishing his destruction, that in whatever way he directed or altered his course, they ceased not to follow close upon him. When he says *our steps,* he doubtless comprehends his own companions, although he immediately after returns to speak of himself alone; unless, perhaps, another reading is preferred, for some copies have סבבונו, *sebabunu, They have compassed us,* in the plural number. This, however, is not a matter of great importance. David simply complains, that unless God stretch forth his hand from heaven to deliver him, there now remains for him no way of escape, seeing his enemies, whenever he stirs his foot to avoid their fury, immediately pursue him, and watch all his steps. By the adverb *now,* he intimates not only that he is at present in very great danger, but also that at every moment his enemies, in whatever way he turns himself, pursue and press hard upon him. In the last clause, *They have fixed their eyes to cast down to the ground,* some consider David as comparing his enemies to hunters, who, with eyes fixed on the ground, are silently looking with eager desire for their prey. They, therefore, think that by the eyes fixed on the ground is denoted the gesture or attitude of David's adversaries, and certainly crafty and malicious men have their countenance often fixed on the ground. According to others, whose opinion is nearer the spirit of the passage, this form of expression signifies the continual and unwearied ardour by which the ungodly are impelled to turn all things upside down. *To fix their eyes,* therefore, is nothing else than to apply all their ingenuity, and put forth all their efforts. What follows, *to cast down to the ground,* is the same thing as to overthrow. The ungodly, as if they must necessarily fall, should the world continue to stand, would wish all

mankind thrown down or destroyed, and, therefore, they exert themselves to the utmost to bring down and ruin all men. This is explained more fully by the figurative illustration introduced in the following verse, where they are said to be *like lions and lions' whelps.*[1] But we ought always to keep this truth in remembrance, that the more proudly wicked men exercise their cruelty against us, the hand of God is so much the nearer to us to oppose itself to their savage fury; for to him alone belongs the praise of subduing and restraining these wild beasts who delight in shedding blood. David speaks of *dens,* or *secret lurking places,* because his enemies were deeply skilled in artful stratagem, and had various methods of doing mischief, while they had also at hand the power and means of executing them, so that it was difficult to resist them.

13. *Arise, O Jehovah, prevent* [or *go before*] *his face, lay him prostrate on the ground ;*[2] *deliver my soul from the ungodly man by thy sword:*
14. *From men by thy hand, O Jehovah, from men who are of long duration,* [or *who are from an age,*[3]] *whose portion is in life, whose belly thou fillest with thy secret goods ; their children are filled with them, and they leave the rest to their babes.*

13. *Arise, O Jehovah.* The more furiously David was persecuted by his enemies, he beseeches God the more earnestly to afford him immediate aid; for he uses the word *face* to denote the swift impetuosity of his adversary, to repress which there was need of the greatest haste. By these words, the Holy Spirit teaches us, that when death

---

[1] In the French version it is "lionceaux," "young lions." French and Skinner read "like a lion," and "like a young lion;" and observe, "The word translated 'young lion' signifies a lion in the vigour of youth, and fully capable of pursuing his prey."

[2] "The LXX. have happily expressed the exact import of the Hebrew word, 'Ὕπος κέλισον αὐτούς,' 'Make him sink upon his knees.'"—*Horsley.* Street reads, "Make them bend." Cocceius renders it, "Incurva illum," "Bend him," and explains the phrase thus:—"Fac, ut se demittat," &c.; *i. e.* "Make him to cast himself down, bend his stature, which is erect and inflexible like iron; that is to say, take away from him the power and the inclination of doing mischief."

[3] "A seculo."—*Lat.* "Dés un monde, ou un siecle."—*Fr. marg.* "From a world, or an age."

shows itself to be just at hand, God is provided with remedies perfectly prepared, by which he can effect our deliverance in a moment. The Psalmist not only attributes to God the office of delivering his people; he at the same time arms him with power to crush and break in pieces the wicked. He does not, however, wish them to be cast down farther than was necessary to their being humbled, that they might cease from their outrageous and injurious conduct towards him, as we may gather from the following clause, where he again beseeches God *to deliver his soul.* David would have been contented to see them continuing in the possession of their outward ease and prosperity, had they not abused their power by practising injustice and cruelty. Let us know then, that God consults the good of his people when he overthrows the ungodly, and breaks their strength; when he does this, it is for the purpose of delivering from destruction the poor innocents who are molested by these wretched men.[1] Some expositors read the passage thus, *From the ungodly man, who is thy sword,*[2] and also, *From the men who are thy hand;* but this does not seem to me to be a proper translation. I admit, that from whatever quarter afflictions come to us, it is the hand of God which chastises us, and that the ungodly are the scourges he employs for this purpose; and farther, that this consideration is very well fitted to lead us to exercise patience. But as this manner of speaking would here be somewhat harsh, and, at the same time, not very consistent with the prayer, I prefer adopting the exposition which re-

---

[1] " Qui sont molestez par ces malheureux."—*Fr.*

[2] " It may be questioned whether David, in this or the next clause, intended to represent wicked men as the sword and the hand of God; that is, the instruments which he employed to correct his servants; or whether his meaning was to pray that God would interpose his own hand and sword to defend him and punish his enemies. The latter sense is adopted by some interpreters; but as the former is a perfectly Scriptural sentiment, and requires the supposition of no ellipsis, it appears to me to be most likely what is intended. *Vide* Isa. x. 5."—*Walford.* Many of the most eminent critics, however, adopt the translation which Calvin has given, as Hammond, Houbigant, Ainsworth, Bishops Lowth, Horsley, Horne, and Hare, Dr Boothroyd, Dr Adam Clarke, Dathe, and Venema. The reading in Tyndale's Bible is, " Deliver my soul with thy sword from the ungodly."

presents David's words as a prayer that God would deliver him by his sword, and smite with his hand those men who, for too long a time, had been in possession of power and prosperity. He contrasts God's sword with human aids and human means of relief; and the import of his words is, If God himself does not come forth to take vengeance, and draw his sword, there remains for me no hope of deliverance.

14. *From men by thy hand, O Jehovah, from men who are from an age.* I connect these words thus: O Lord, deliver me by thy hand, or by thy heavenly aid, from men; I say from men whose tyranny has prevailed too long, and whom thou hast suffered to wallow too long in the filth and draff of their prosperity. This repetition is very emphatic; David's voice being stifled, as it were, with the indignation which he felt at seeing such villany continuing for so long a period, he stops all at once after uttering the first word, without proceeding farther in the sentence which he meant to express; then, after having recovered his breath, he declares what it is that so greatly distressed him. In the preceding verse he had spoken in the singular number; but now he gives us to understand that he had not only one enemy but many, and that those who were set against him were strong and powerful, so that he saw no hope of deliverance remaining for him except in the aid of God.

These words, *from world,* or *age,* (for such is the exact literal rendering,[1]) are expounded in different ways. Some understand them as meaning *men who have their time,* as if David intended to say that their prosperous condition would not be of long duration; but this does not appear to me to be the proper explanation. Others suppose he means by this expression such as are wholly devoted to the world, and whose whole attention and thoughts are absorbed in the things of earth; and, according to their opinion, David compares his enemies to brute beasts. In the same sense they explain what follows immediately after, *Their portion is in*

---

[1] " Ou siecle car il y a ainsi mot à mot."—*Fr.*

life, language which they consider as applied to them, because, being entirely destitute of the Spirit, and cleaving with their whole hearts to transitory good things, they think of nothing better than this world. For that in which each man places his felicity is termed his portion. As, however, the Hebrew word חלד, *cheled,* signifies *an age,* or *the course of a man's life,* David, I doubt not, complains that his enemies had lived and enjoyed prosperity longer than the ordinary term allotted to the life of man. The audacity and the outrages[1] committed by wicked men might be borne with for a short time, but when they wax wanton against God, it is very strange indeed to see them continuing stable in their prosperous condition. That this is the sense appears from the preposition מן, *min,* which we have translated *from,* by which David expresses that they were not sprung up only a few days before or lately, but that their prosperity, which should have vanished away in a moment, had lasted for a very long time. Such, then, is the meaning of the Psalmist, unless, perhaps, we may understand him as denominating them *of the world,* or *age,* because they bear the chief authority among men, and are exalted in honours and riches, as if this world had been made for them alone.

When he says, *Their portion is in life,* I explain it as meaning that they are exempted from all troubles, and abound in pleasures; in short, that they do not experience the common condition of other men; as, on the contrary, when a man is oppressed with adversities, it is said of him that his portion is in death. David therefore intimates, that it is not a reasonable thing that the ungodly should be permitted to gad about in joy and gaiety without having any fear of death, and to claim for themselves, as if by hereditary right, a peaceful and happy life.

What he adds immediately after, *Whose belly thou fillest with thy secret goods,* is of the same import. We see these persons not only enjoying, in common with other men, light, breath, food, and all other commodities of life, but we also see God often treating them more delicately and more bountifully

---

[1] " L'audace et les outrages."—*Fr.*

than others, as if he fed them on his lap, holding them tenderly like little babes, and fondling them more than all the rest of mankind.[1] Accordingly, by *the secret goods of God*, we are here to understand the rare and more exquisite dainties which he bestows upon them. Now, this is a severe temptation, if a man estimates the love and favour of God by the measure of earthly prosperity which he bestows; and, therefore, it is not to be wondered at, though David was greatly afflicted in contemplating the prosperous condition of ungodly men. But let us remember that he makes this holy complaint to console himself, and to mitigate his distress, not in the way of murmuring against God and resisting his will;—let us remember this, I say, that, after his example, we may learn also to direct our groanings to heaven. Some give a more subtile exposition of what is here called *God's secret goods*, viewing it as meaning the good things which the ungodly devour without thinking of or regarding him who is the author of them; or they suppose the good things of God to be called *secret*, because the reason why God pours them forth so abundantly upon the wicked is not apparent. But the exposition which I have given, as it is both simple and natural, so of itself it sufficiently disproves the others. The last point in this description is, that, by continual succession, these persons transmit their riches to their children and their children's children. As they are not among the number of the children of God, to whom this blessing is promised, it follows, that when they are thus fattened, it is for the day of slaughter which he hath appointed. The object which David therefore has in view in making this complaint is, that God would make haste to execute vengeance, seeing they have so long abused his liberality and gentle treatment.

---

[1] "Comme s'il les nourissoit en son giron, les tenant tendrement et mignardant plus que tout le reste."—*Fr.*

15. *But as for me, I shall behold thy face in righteousness : I shall be satisfied, when I shall awake, with thy image,* [or *likeness.*]

Having with anguish of heart declared before God the troubles which afflicted and tormented him, that he might not be overwhelmed with the load of temptations which pressed upon him, he now takes, as it were, the wings of faith, and rises up to a region of undisturbed tranquillity, where he may behold all things arranged and directed in due order. In the first place, there is here a tacit comparison between the well regulated state of things which will be seen when God by his judgment shall restore to order those things which are now embroiled and confused, and the deep and distressing darkness which is in the world, when God keeps silence, and hides his face. In the midst of those afflictions which he has recounted, the Psalmist might seem to be plunged in darkness from which he would never obtain deliverance.[1] When we see the ungodly enjoying prosperity, crowned with honours, and loaded with riches, they seem to be in great favour with God. But David triumphs over their proud and presumptuous boasting; and although, to the eye of sense and reason, God has cast him off, and removed him far from him, yet he assures himself that one day he will enjoy the privilege of familiarly beholding him. The pronoun *I* is emphatic, as if he had said, The calamities and reproaches which I now endure will not prevent me from again experiencing fulness of joy from the fatherly love of God manifested towards me. We ought carefully to observe, that David, in order to enjoy supreme happiness, desires nothing more than to have always the taste and experience of this great blessing that God is reconciled to him. The wicked may imagine themselves to be happy, but so long as God is opposed to them, they deceive themselves in indulging this imagination. *To behold God's face,* is nothing else than to have a sense of his fatherly favour, with which he not only causes us to rejoice by

---

[1] "Desquelles il n'y eust issue aucune."—*Fr.*

removing our sorrows, but also transports us even to heaven. By the word *righteousness*, David means that he will not be disappointed of the reward of a good conscience. As long as God humbles his people under manifold afflictions, the world insolently mocks at their simplicity, as if they deceived themselves, and lost their pains in devoting themselves to the cultivation and practice of purity and innocence.[1] Against such kind of mockery and derision David is here struggling, and in opposition to it he assures himself that there is a recompense laid up for his godliness and uprightness, provided he continue to persevere in his obedience to the holy law of God; as Isaiah, in like manner, (chap. iii. 10,) exhorts the faithful to support themselves from this consideration, that " it shall be well with the righteous: for they shall eat the fruit of their doings." We ought not, however, from this to think that he represents works as the cause of his salvation. It is not his purpose to treat of what constitutes the meritorious ground upon which he is to be received into the favour of God. He only lays it down as a principle, that they who serve God do not lose their labour, for although he may hide his face from them for a time, he causes them again in due season to behold his bright countenance[2] and compassionate eye beaming upon them.

I shall be satisfied. Some interpreters, with more subtility than propriety, restrict this to the resurrection at the last day, as if David did not expect to experience in his heart a blessed joy[3] until the life to come, and suspended every longing desire after it until he should attain to that life. I readily admit that this satisfaction of which he speaks will not in all respects be perfect before the last coming of Christ; but as the saints, when God causes some rays of the knowledge of his love to enter into their hearts, find great enjoyment in the light thus communicated, David justly calls this peace or joy of the Holy Spirit *satisfaction*. The un-

---

[1] " Comme s'ils s'abusoyent et perdoyent leurs peines en s'adonnant à purete et innocence."—*Fr.*

[2] " Il lui fait tousjours derechef contempler finalment son clair visage et son œil debonnaire."—*Fr.*

[3] " Comme si David remettoit à la vie à venir l'esperance de sentir en son cœur une joye heureuse."—*Fr.*

godly may be at their ease, and have abundance of good things, even to bursting, but as their desire is insatiable, or as they feed upon wind, in other words, upon earthly things, without tasting spiritual things, in which there is substance,[1] or being so stupified through the pungent remorse of conscience with which they are tormented, as not to enjoy the good things which they possess, they never have composed and tranquil minds, but are kept unhappy by the inward passions with which they are perplexed and agitated. It is therefore the grace of God alone which can give us contentment,[2] and prevent us from being distracted by irregular desires. David, then, I have no doubt, has here an allusion to the empty joys of the world, which only famish the soul, while they sharpen and increase the appetite the more,[3] in order to show that those only are partakers of true and substantial happiness who seek their felicity in the enjoyment of God alone. As the literal rendering of the Hebrew words is, *I shall be satisfied in the awaking of thy face;* or, *in awaking by thy face;* some, preferring the first exposition, understand by the awaking of God's face the breaking forth, or manifestation of the light of his grace, which before was, as it were, covered with clouds. But to me it seems more suitable to refer the word *awake* to David,[4] and to view it as meaning the same thing as to obtain respite from his sorrow. David had never indeed been overwhelmed with stupor; but after a lengthened period of fatigue, through the persecution of his enemies, he must needs have been brought into such a state as to appear sunk into a profound sleep. The saints do not sustain and repel all the assaults which are made upon them so courageously as not, by reason of

---

[1] " C'est à dire de choses terriennes, sans gouster les choses spirituelles esquelles il y a fermete."—*Fr.*

[2] " Qui nous puisse donner contentement."—*Fr.*

[3] " Lesquelles ne font qu'affamer et augmenter tousjours tout plus l'appetit."—*Fr.*

[4] The Chaldee version applies it to David, and reads, " When I shall awake, I shall be satisfied with the glory of thy countenance." But the Septuagint, the Vulgate, Arabic, and Æthiopic versions apply the verb, *awake* to *thy glory.* "'Εν τῳ ὀφθηναι την δοξαν σου," " At the appearing of thy glory," says the Septuagint. " Cum apparuerit gloria tua," " When thy glory shall appear," says the Vulgate.

the weakness of their flesh, to feel languid and feeble for a time, or to be terrified, as if they were enveloped in darkness. David compares this perturbation of mind to a sleep. But when the favour of God shall again have arisen and shone brightly upon him, he declares that then he will recover spiritual strength and enjoy tranquillity of mind. It is true, indeed, as Paul declares, that so long as we continue in this state of earthly pilgrimage, " we walk by faith, not by sight;" but as we nevertheless behold the image of God not only in the glass of the gospel, but also in the numerous evidences of his grace which he daily exhibits to us, let each of us awaken himself from his lethargy, that we may now be satisfied with spiritual felicity, until God, in due time, bring us to his own immediate presence, and cause us to enjoy him face to face.

PSALM XVIII.

We all know through what difficulties and almost insurmountable obstacles David came to the kingdom. Even to the time of Saul's death he was a fugitive, and, as it were, an outlaw, and wearily passed his life in fear, amidst many threatenings and dangers of death. After God had, with his own hand, placed him on the royal throne, he was immediately harassed with the tumults and insurrections of his own subjects, and the hostile faction being superior to him in power, he was often at the point of being completely overthrown. Foreign enemies, on the other hand, severely tried him even to his old age. These calamities he would never have surmounted had he not been aided by the power of God. Having therefore obtained many and signal victories, he does not, as irreligious men are accustomed to do, sing a song of triumph in honour of himself, but exalts and magnifies God the author of these victories, by a train of striking and appropriate epithets, and in a style of surpassing grandeur and sublimity. This psalm, therefore, is the first of those psalms in which David celebrates, in lofty strains, the wonderful grace which God had shown towards him, both in putting him in possession of the kingdom, and in afterwards maintaining him in it. He also shows that his reign was an image and type of the kingdom of Christ, to teach and assure the faithful that Christ, in spite of the whole world, and of all the resistance which it can make, will, by the stupendous and incomprehensible power of the Father, be always victorious.

¶ To the chief musician of David, the servant of Jehovah, who sung to Jehovah the words of this song in the day that Jehovah delivered him from the hand of all his enemies, and from the hand of Saul.

WE ought carefully to mark the particular time when this psalm was composed, as it shows us that David, when his affairs were brought to a state of peace and prosperity, was not intoxicated with extravagant joy like irreligious men, who, when they have obtained deliverance from their calamities, shake off from their minds the remembrance of God's benefits, and plunge themselves into gross and degrading pleasures, or erect their crests, and obscure the glory of God by their proud and vain boasting. David, as the sacred history relates, (2 Sam. xxii.,) sung this song to the Lord, when he was now almost spent with age, and when, being delivered from all his troubles, he enjoyed tranquillity. The inscription here agrees with that account, and, from what is there stated, we conclude, that it has not been improperly or incorrectly prefixed to this psalm. David points out the time when it was sung, namely, *after God had delivered him from all his enemies,* to show us that he was then in perfectly quiet possession of his kingdom, and that God had assisted him not once, nor against one kind of enemies only; seeing his conflicts were from time to time renewed, and the end of one war was the commencement of another; yea, many armies often rose up against him at the same time. Since the creation of the world, we will scarcely find another individual in it whom God has tried by so many and so varied afflictions. As Saul had persecuted him with more cruelty, and with greater fury and determination than all others, his name on that account is here expressly mentioned, although, in the preceding clause, the Psalmist had spoken in general terms of all his enemies. Saul is not put last, as if he had been one of his later enemies,[1] for his death had taken place

---

[1] "Car il ne faut pas penser qu'il soit mis en dernier lieu, comme celuy dont il fust plus fresche memoire, que de tous les autres."—*Fr.* "It is not necessary to suppose that Saul is put last, as he of whom he retained a fresher remembrance than of all his other enemies."

about thirty years previous to this time; and since that event David had discomfited many foreign enemies, and had also suppressed the rebellion of his own son Absalom. But, persuaded that it was a singular manifestation of the grace of God towards him, and eminently worthy of being remembered, that he had for so many years escaped from innumerable deaths, or rather that as many days as he had lived under the reign of Saul, God had wrought, as it were, so many miracles for his deliverance, he justly mentions and celebrates in particular his deliverance from the hands of this relentless enemy. By calling himself *the servant of God*, he doubtless intended to bear testimony to his call to be king, as if he had said, I have not rashly, and by my own authority, usurped the kingdom, but have only acted in obedience to the oracle of heaven. And, indeed, amidst the many storms which he had to encounter, it was a support highly necessary to be well assured in his own mind of having undertaken nothing but by the appointment of God; or rather, this was to him a peaceful haven, and a secure retreat in the midst of so many broils and strange calamities.[1] There is not a more wretched object than man in adversity, when he has brought himself into distress by acting according to the mere impulse of his own mind, and not by acting in obedience to the call of God. David, therefore, had a good reason for wishing it to be known that it was not ambition which impelled him to enter into those contests which were so painful and difficult for him to bear, and that he had not attempted any thing unlawful or by wicked means, but had always kept steadily in view the will of God, which served as a light to guide him in his path. This is a point which it is highly useful for us to know, in order that we may not expect to be exempted from all trouble, when we follow the call of God, but may rather prepare ourselves for a condition of warfare painful and disagreeable to our flesh. The name *servant*, therefore, in this passage, as in many others, relates to his public office; just as when the prophets and apostles call themselves the servants of God, they have a

[1] " Ou plustost ce luy avoit este un bon port et retraite seure au milieu de tant d'esclandres et calamitez estranges."—*Fr.*

reference to their official character. It is as if he had said, I am not a king of my own creation, but have been chosen by God to fill that high station. At the same time, we ought particularly to notice the humility of David, who, although distinguished by so many victories, and the conqueror of so many nations, and possessed of so great dignity and wealth, honours himself with no other title than this, *The servant of God;* as if he meant to show that he accounted it more honourable to have faithfully performed the duties of the office with which God had invested him, than to possess all the honours and excellence of the world.

1. *And he said, I will affectionately love thee,*[1] *O Jehovah, my strength.*
2. *Jehovah is my rock,*[2] *my fortress, and my deliverer; my God, my rock, I will trust in him: my shield, and the horn*[3] *of my salvation, my refuge.*

1. *And he said, &c.* I will not stop to examine too minutely the syllables, or the few words, in which this psalm differs from the song which is recorded in the twenty-second chapter of the Second Book of Samuel. When, however, we meet with any important difference, we shall advert to it in the proper place; and we find one in the remarkable sentence with which this psalm commences, *I*

---

[1] This is the rendering of the French version. The word in the Hebrew text, which is רחם, *racham*, is very expressive. "רחם," says Cocceius, "est intime ac medullitus cum motu omnium viscerum diligere;"—" is to love with the deepest and strongest affections of the heart, with the moving of all the bowels." Ainsworth reads, "I will dearly love thee;" Street, "I love thee exceedingly;" Bishop Horne, "With all the yearnings of affection I will love thee, O Jehovah;" and Dr Adam Clarke, "From my inmost bowels will I love thee, O Lord." The word, therefore, denotes the tenderness and intensity of David's emotions.

[2] The Hebrew word literally means *a cliff* or *crag;* and is a different word from the one which is translated *rock* in the following part of this verse. "The word סלע, *sela*," says Dr Adam Clarke, "signifies those craggy precipices which afforded shelter to men and animals; where the bees often made their nests, and whence honey was collected in great abundance. 'He made him to suck honey out of the rock,' Deut. xxxii. 13."

[3] The *horn* is the emblem of strength and power. The metaphor is taken from the bull and other powerful animals, who put forth their strength principally by the use of their horns.

will love thee affectionately, O Jehovah, my strength, which is omitted in the song in Samuel. As the Scripture does not use the verb רחם, *racham,* for *to love,* except in the conjugation *pihel,* and as it is here put in the conjugation *kal,* some of the Jewish expositors explain it as here meaning *to seek mercy;* as if David had said, Lord, since I have so often experienced thee to be a merciful God, I will trust to and repose in thy mercies for ever. And certainly this exposition would not be unsuitable, but I am unwilling to depart from the other, which is more generally received. It is to be observed, that love to God is here laid down as constituting the principal part of true godliness; for there is no better way of serving God than to love him. No doubt, the service which we owe him is better expressed by the word *reverence,* that thus his majesty may prominently stand forth to our view in its infinite greatness. But as he requires nothing so expressly as to possess all the affections of our heart, and to have them going out towards him, so there is no sacrifice which he values more than when we are bound fast to him by the chain of a free and spontaneous love; and, on the other hand, there is nothing in which his glory shines forth more conspicuously than in his free and sovereign goodness. Moses, therefore, (Deut. x. 12,) when he meant to give a summary of the law, says, "And now, Israel, what doth the Lord thy God require of thee but to love him?" In speaking thus, David, at the same time, intended to show that his thoughts and affections were not so intently fixed upon the benefits of God as to be ungrateful to him who was the author of them, a sin which has been too common in all ages. Even at this day we see how the greater part of mankind enjoy wholly at their ease the gifts of God without paying any regard to him, or, if they think of him at all, it is only to despise him. David, to prevent himself from falling into this ingratitude, in these words makes as it were a solemn vow, Lord, as thou art my strength, I will continue united and devoted to thee by unfeigned love.

2. *Jehovah is my rock, &c.* When David thus heaps together many titles by which to honour God, it is no useless

or unnecessary accumulation of words. We know how difficult it is for men to keep their minds and hearts stayed in God. They either imagine that it is not enough to have God for them, and, consequently, are always seeking after support and succour elsewhere, or, at the first temptation which assails them, fall from the confidence which they placed in him. David, therefore, by attributing to God various methods of saving his people, protests that, provided he has God for his protector and defender, he is effectually fortified against all peril and assault; as if he had said, Those whom God intends to succour and defend are not only safe against one kind of dangers, but are as it were surrounded by impregnable ramparts on all sides, so that, should a thousand deaths be presented to their view, they ought not to be afraid even at this formidable array.[1] We see, then, that the design of David here is not only to celebrate the praises of God, in token of his gratitude, but also to fortify our minds with a firm and stedfast faith, so that, whatever afflictions befall us, we may always have recourse to God, and may be fully persuaded that he has virtue and power to assist us in different ways, according to the different methods of doing us mischief which the wicked devise. Nor, as I have observed before, does David insist so much on this point, and express the same thing by different terms without cause. God may have aided us in one way, and yet whenever a new tempest arises, we are immediately stricken with terror, as if we had never experienced any thing of his aid. And those who in one trouble expect protection and succour from him, but who afterwards circumscribe his power, accounting it limited in other respects, act like a man who, upon going into battle, considers himself well secured as to his breast, because he has a breastplate and a shield to defend him, and yet is afraid of his head, because he is without a helmet. David, therefore, here furnishes the faithful with a complete suit of armour,[2] that they may feel that

---

[1] " Comme environnez de bons rempars de tous costez, tellement que mille morts, quand autant il s'en presenteroit à eux, ne leur doyvent point faire peur."—*Fr.*

[2] " Et pourtant David equippe yci les fideles de pied en cap comme on

they are in no danger of being wounded, provided they are shielded by the power of God. That such is the object he has in view, is apparent from the declaration which he makes of his confidence in God: *I will trust in him.* Let us, therefore, learn from his example, to apply to our own use those titles which are here attributed to God, and to apply them as an antidote against all the perplexities and distresses which may assail us; or rather, let them be deeply imprinted upon our memory, so that we may be able at once to repel to a distance whatever fear Satan may suggest to our mind. I give this exhortation, not only because we tremble under the calamities with which we are presently assailed, but also because we groundlessly conjure up in our own imaginations dangers as to the time to come, and thus needlessly disquiet ourselves by the mere creations of fancy. In the song, as recorded in 2 Sam. xxii. 3, instead of these words, *My God, my rock,* it is, *God of my rock.* And after the word *refuge,* there is, *My fortress, my saviour, thou shalt preserve me from violence;* words which make the sentence fuller, but the meaning comes to the same thing.

3. *I will call upon the praised Jehovah, and I shall be saved from mine enemies.*
4. *The cords*[1] *of death had compassed me about; the torrents of wickedness*[2] *had made me afraid.*
5. *The cords of the grave*[3] *had compassed me about; the snares of death had prevented me.*
6. *In my distress I called upon Jehovah, and cried to my God: and he heard my voice from his temple, and my cry came before him, even into his ears.*

3. *I will call upon the praised Jehovah.* Calling upon God, as has been observed elsewhere, frequently comprehends the whole of his service; but as the effect or fruit of prayer is particularly mentioned in what follows, this phrase in the

---

dit."—*Fr.* " David, therefore, here equips the faithful from head to foot, as we say."

[1] " Ou brisemens."—*Fr. marg.* " Or contritions."
[2] " Heb. de Belial."—*Fr. marg.* " Heb. of Belial."
[3] " Ou de corruption."—*Fr. marg.* " Or of corruption."

passage before us, I have no doubt, signifies to have recourse to God for protection, and to ask by prayer deliverance from him. David having said in the second verse, that he trusted in God, now subjoins this as an evidence of his trust; for every one who confides in God will earnestly beseech his aid in the time of need. He therefore declares, that he *will be saved*, and prove victorious over all *his enemies*, because he will have recourse to God for help. He calls God the *praised Jehovah*, not only to intimate that he is worthy of being praised, as almost all interpreters explain it, but also to point out, that, when he came to the throne of grace, his prayers would be mingled and interwoven with praises.[1] The scope of the passage seems to require that it be understood as meaning, that giving thanks to God for the benefits which he has received from him in times past, he will ask his assistance by renewed supplications. And certainly no man will ever invoke God in prayer freely and frankly unless he animate and encourage himself by the remembrance of the grace of God. Accordingly Paul, in Philip. iv. 6, exhorts the faithful "in every thing by prayer and supplication with thanksgiving, to make their requests known unto God," and to disburden their cares, as it were, into his bosom. All those whose prayers are not accompanied with the praises of God are chargeable with clamouring and complaining against him, when engaged in that solemn exercise.

4. *The cords*[2] *of death had compassed me about.* David now begins to recount the undoubted and illustrious proofs by which

---

[1] The word in the Hebrew text מְהֻלָּל, *mehullal*, literally signifies *praised*. The ancient versions view the word not as denoting that God is worthy to be praised, which is the meaning attached to it in our English version, but as referring to the Psalmist's resolution to praise God. The Septuagint reads, Αινων επικαλεσομαι Κυριον, "Praising I will call upon the Lord." The reading of the Vulgate is the same, "Laudans invocabo." The Chaldee reads, "In a song or hymn I pour out prayers unto the Lord;" and the Arabic, "I will praise the Lord, and call upon him." This is precisely the sense in which Calvin understands the words, "I will call upon the praised Jehovah."

[2] "Death is here personified under the semblance of a mighty conqueror, who binds his vanquished foes in strong fetters."—*Walford.*

he had experienced that the hand of God is sufficiently strong and powerful to repel all the dangers and calamities with which he may be assailed. And we need not wonder that those things which might have been described more simply, and in an unadorned style, are clothed in poetical forms of expression, and set forth with all the elegancies and ornaments of language. The Holy Spirit, to contend against and make an impression upon the wicked and perverse dispositions of men, has here furnished David with eloquence full of majesty, energy, and wonderful power, to awaken mankind to consider the benefits of God. There is scarcely any assistance God bestows, however evident and palpable it may be to our senses, which our indifference or proud disdain does not obscure. David, therefore, the more effectually to move and penetrate our minds, says that the deliverance and succour which God had granted him had been conspicuous in the whole frame-work of the world. This his intention it is needful for us to take into view, lest we should think that he exceeds due bounds in expressing himself in a style so remarkable for sublimity. The sum is, that, when in his distresses he had been reduced to extremity, he had betaken himself to God for help, and had been wonderfully preserved.

We shall now make a few observations with respect to the words. The Hebrew word חבלי, *chebley*, means *cords* or *sorrows*, or any deadly evil,[1] which consumes a man's health and strength, and which tends to his destruction. That the psalm may correspond with the song recorded in 2d Samuel, formerly referred to, I do not disapprove of this word being here taken for *contrition*, because the phrase there employed is משברי מות, *mishberey maveth*,[2] and the noun משברי, *mish-*

---

[1] "חבל, *chebel*," says Hammond, "signifies two things, a cord, and a pang of a woman's travail, and which it signifies must be resolved still by the context. Here, where it is joined with encompassing, it is most fitly to be understood in the former sense, because ropes or cords are proper for that turn, as for holding and keeping in when they are inclosed." The Chaldee understands the word in the other sense, and paraphrases the clause thus: "Distress hath compassed me as a woman in travail which hath not strength to bring forth, and is in danger of death." The Septuagint adopts the same view, reading, "ὠδῖνες θανάτου," "the pangs of death."

[2] Cocceius renders these words, "the waves of death;" and he observes,

berey, is derived from a verb which signifies to *break*. But as the metaphor taken from cords or snares agrees better with the verb *compass about*, the import of which is, that David was on all sides involved and entangled in the perils of death, I am disposed rather to adopt this interpretation. What follows concerning *torrents* implies that he had been almost overwhelmed by the violence and impetuosity of his enemies against him, even as a man who is covered over the head with floods of water is almost lost. He calls them *the torrents of Belial*, because it was wicked and perverse men who had conspired against him. The Hebrew word *Belial* has a wide signification. With respect to its etymology there are different opinions among expositors. Why Jerome has rendered it *without yoke*,[1] I know not. The more generally received opinion is, that it is compounded of these two words, בְּלִי, *beli, not*, and יַעַל, *yaäl*,[2] to denote that the wicked do not rise, in other words, ultimately gain nothing, and obtain no advantage by their infatuated course. The Jews certainly employed this word to designate every kind of detestable wickedness, and from this it is highly probable that David by it meant to describe his enemies, who basely and wickedly plotted his destruction.[3] If, however, any prefer translating the phrase, by *deadly torrents*, I am not disposed to oppose this rendering. In the following verse he again repeats, *that the corruptions or cords of the grave had compassed him about*. As the Hebrew word is the same which he had employed in the

---

that the word "waves," explains the verb "compassed me about." Death sent its sorrows thick upon him one after another, as the sea sends forth its waves, and with such violence that he was ready to be overwhelmed. The word מִשְׁבְּרֵי, *mishberey*, is applied both to the breaking forth of infants in the birth, (Is. xxxvii. 3; Hosea xiii. 13,) and to the waves of the sea, (Ps. xlii. 7.)—*Ainsworth*. Horsley translates the phrase, "The breakers of death." "The metaphor," says he, "is taken from those dangerous waves which our mariners call white breakers."

[1] Jerome doubtless derived the word from בְּלִי, *beli, not* or *without*, and עֹל, *ol, a yoke*, and thus the term *Belial* means those who shake off all restraint.

[2] Signifying to profit, or to gain advantage in any respect.

[3] "Belial is a compound term, significant of vileness and worthlessness. The 'floods of Belial' intend large bodies of men, who rush forward like impetuous torrents to overwhelm and destroy whatever opposes them."—*Walford*.

preceding verse, I have thought it proper to translate it *cords* here, as I have done there, not only because he uses a verb which signifies *to beset, to inclose,* or *to surround,* but also because he adds immediately after, *the snares of death,* which, in my opinion, is to be understood in the same sense. This, then, is the description of the dangerous circumstances into which he was brought, and it enhances and magnifies so much the more the glory of his deliverance. As David had been reduced to a condition so desperate that no hope of relief or deliverance from it was apparent, it is certain that he was delivered by the hand of God, and that it was not a thing effected by the power of man.

6. *In my distress, &c.* It was a very evident proof of uncommon faith in David, when, being almost plunged into the gulf of death, he lifted up his heart to heaven by prayer. Let us therefore learn, that such an example is set before our eyes, that no calamities, however great and oppressive, may hinder us from praying, or create an aversion to it. It was prayer which brought to David the fruits or wonderful effects of which he speaks a little after, and from this it appears still more clearly that his deliverance was effected by the power of God. In saying that he *cried,* he means, as we have observed elsewhere, the ardour and earnestness of affection which he had in prayer. Again, by calling God *his God,* he separates himself from the gross despisers of God, or hypocrites, who, when constrained by necessity, call upon the Divine Majesty in a confused and tumultuous manner, but do not come to God familiarly and with a pure heart, as they know nothing of his fatherly favour and goodness. When, therefore, as we approach to God, faith goes before to illumine the way, giving us the full persuasion that He is our Father, then is the gate opened, and we may converse freely with Him and he with us. David, by calling God his God, and putting him on his side, also intimates that God was opposed to his enemies; and this serves to show that he was actuated by true piety and the fear of God. By the word *temple* we are not here to understand the sanctuary as in many other places, but heaven; for the

description which immediately follows cannot be applied to the sanctuary. Accordingly, the sense is, that when David was forsaken and abandoned in the world, and all men shut their ears to his cry for help, God stretched forth his hand from heaven to save him.

> 7. *Then the earth shook and trembled; the foundations of the mountains were troubled, and were shaken, because he was wroth.*
> 8. *There went up a smoke by* [or *out of*] *his nostrils, and fire proceeding from his mouth devoured ; coals were kindled by it.*
> 9. *And he bowed the heavens and came down : and thick darkness was under his feet.*
> 10. *He rode also upon a cherub, and did fly ; and was carried upon the wings of the wind.*
> 11. *He made darkness his secret* [or *hiding*] *place ; his pavilion* [or *tent*] *round about him was dark waters, and the clouds of the skies.*

7. *Then the earth shook.* David, convinced that the aid of God, which he had experienced, was of such a character, that it was impossible for him to extol it sufficiently and as it deserved, sets forth an image of it in the sky and the earth, as if he had said, It has been as visible as the changes which give different appearances to the sky and the earth. If natural things always flowed in an even and uniform course, the power of God would not be so perceptible. But when he changes the face of the sky by sudden rain, or by loud thunder, or by dreadful tempests, those who before were, as it were, asleep and insensible, must necessarily be awakened, and be tremblingly conscious of the existence of a presiding God.[1] Such sudden and unforeseen changes manifest more clearly the presence of the great Author of nature. No doubt, when the sky is unclouded and tranquil, we see in it sufficient evidences of the majesty of God, but as men will not stir up their minds to reflect upon that majesty, until it come nearer to them, David, the more powerfully to affect us, recounts the sudden changes by which we are usually

---

[1] " Il faut necessairement que les gens qui auparavant estoyent comme endormis et stupides se resueillent et apprehendent qu'il y a un Dieu."— *Fr.*

moved and dismayed, and introduces God at one time clothed with a dark cloud,—at another, throwing the air into confusion by tempests,—now rending it by the boisterous violence of winds,—now launching the lightnings,—and anon darting down hailstones and thunderbolts. In short, the object of the Psalmist is to show that the God who, as often as he pleases, causes all parts of the world to tremble by his power, when he intended to manifest himself as the deliverer of David, was known as openly and by signs as evident as if he had displayed his power in all the creatures both above and beneath.

In the first place, he says, *The earth shook*, and nothing is more dreadful than an earthquake. Instead of the words, *the foundations of the mountains*, it is in the song, as recorded in 2d Samuel, *the foundations of the heavens;* but the meaning is the same, namely, that there was nothing in the world so settled and stedfast which did not tremble, and which was not removed out of its place. David, however, as I have already observed in the beginning, does not relate this as a piece of history, or as what had actually taken place, but he employs these similitudes for the purpose of removing all doubt, and for the greater confirmation of faith as to the power and providence of God; because men, from their slowness of understanding, cannot apprehend God except by means of external signs. Some think that these miracles were actually wrought, and performed exactly as they are here related; but it is not easy to believe this, since the Holy Spirit, in the narrative given of David's life, makes no mention whatever of such wonderful displays of divine power in his behalf. We cannot, however, justly censure or find fault with this hyperbolic manner of speaking, when we consider our slowness of apprehension, and also our depravity, to which I have just now called your attention. David, who was much more penetrating and quick of understanding than ordinary men, finding he could not sufficiently succeed in impressing and profiting people of sluggish and weak understandings by a simple manner of speaking, describes under outward figures the power of God, which he had discovered by means of faith, and the revelation of the Holy Spirit.

He doubtless hereby apprehended and knew more distinctly the omnipresent majesty of God, than the dull sort of common people perceive the hand of God in earthquakes, tempests, thunders, the gloomy lowerings of the heavens, and the boisterous winds. At the same time, it is proper to consider, that although God had, in a wonderful manner, displayed his grace in defending and maintaining David, many, nevertheless, thought that it was by his own skill, or by chance, or by other natural means, that all his affairs had come to a prosperous issue; and it was such stupidity or depravity as this which he saw in the men of his own time, that constrained him to mention and to summon together all parts of creation as witnesses for God. Some also justly and judiciously consider that, in the whole of this description, David has an allusion to the common deliverance of God's chosen people from Egypt. As God then designed and established that event to be a perpetual memorial, from which the faithful might learn that he was the guardian and protector of their welfare, so all the benefits which, from that period, he bestowed upon his people, either as a public body or as private individuals, were, so to speak, appendages of that first deliverance. Accordingly David, in other places as well as here, with the view of exalting the succour which God had granted to his people, sets forth that most memorable instance of the goodness of God towards the children of Israel, as if it were the archtype or original copy of the grace of God. And surely, while many, seeing him an exile from his country, held him in derision as a man expelled from the family of God, and many murmured that he had violently and unrighteously usurped the kingdom, he had good ground to include, under the deliverance which had been common to all the people, the protection and safety which God had afforded to himself; as if he had said, I have been wrongfully cast off as an alien or stranger, seeing God has sufficiently shown, in the deliverance which he has wrought for me, that by him I am owned and acknowledged to be a distinguished and valuable member of the Church. We see how the prophets, whenever they would inspire the people with the hope of salvation, call their thoughts back to the contemplation of that first covenant which had been confirmed by those miracles which were wrought in Egypt, in the passage through the Red Sea and in Mount Sinai. When he says, *The earth trembled, because he was wroth,* it is to be understood as referring to the ungodly. It is a form of speech which God often employs, to say, that, being inflamed with indignation, he arms himself to maintain the safety of his people against their persecutors.

8. *There went up a smoke by* [or *out of*] *his nostrils, &c.* The Hebrew word אף, *aph*, properly signifies *the nose,* or *the nostrils.* But as it is sometimes taken metaphorically for *wrath,* some translate it thus, *There went up a smoke in his wrath,* which, in my opinion, is not at all appropriate. David compares the mists and vapours which darken the air to the thick smoke which a man sends forth from his nostrils when he is angry. And when God, by his very breath, covers the heaven with clouds, and taking away from us the brightness of the sun and of all the stars, overwhelms us in darkness, by this we are very impressively taught how dreadful is his wrath. By the rendering which I have given, the figure here strikingly harmonizes with the one in the clause which immediately follows, namely, *that fire proceeding from his mouth consumed.* The Psalmist means, that God, without great labour or effort, as soon as he shall have sent forth a breath or blast from his nostrils, and opened his mouth, will kindle such a fire that its smoke will darken the whole world, and its intense heat devour it. What he adds, *Coals were kindled by it,* serves to distinguish this dreadful fire from a flame which blazes for a moment, and then is extinguished. *The bowing of the heavens,* denotes a time when the heavens are covered and obscured with clouds. When dense vapours occupy the middle of the air, the clouds seem to us to come down and to lie upon our heads. And not only so, but the majesty of God then approaching, as it were, nearer us, strikes us with dread dismay, and greatly distresses us, although before, when the sky was fair, agreeable, and tranquil, we took ample scope, and enjoyed ourselves with much gaiety. Again,

let us remember, that the Scripture, under these descriptions of a clouded and darkened sky, pourtray to us the anger of God. When the sky is clear and unclouded, it seems as if it were the pleasant and benignant countenance of God beaming upon us, and causing us to rejoice; whereas, on the other hand, when the atmosphere is troubled, we feel a depression of the animal spirits which constrains us to look sad, as if we saw God coming against us with a threatening aspect. At the same time, we are taught that no change takes place either in the atmosphere or in the earth, but what is a witness to us of the presence of God.

10. *He rode also upon a cherub.* The Psalmist having exhibited to us a sign of the wrath of God in the clouds, and in the darkening of the air, representing him as if he breathed out smoke[1] from his nostrils, and descended with a threatening countenance, to afflict men by the dreadful weight of his power; and having also represented lightnings and thunderbolts as flaming fire proceeding from his mouth,—he now introduces him as riding upon the winds and tempests, to take a survey of the whole world with rapid speed, or rather with the swiftness of flying. We meet with a similar description in Ps. civ. 3, where God is said to " walk upon the wings of the winds," and to send them forth in every direction as his swift messengers. David does not, however, simply represent God as the governor of the winds, who drives them by his power whithersoever he pleases; he at the same time tells us that he rides upon *a cherub,* to teach us that the very violence of the winds is governed by angels as God has ordained. We know that the angels were represented under the figure of the cherubim. David, therefore, I have no doubt, here intended to make an allusion to the ark of the covenant. In proposing for our consideration the power of God as manifested in the wonders of nature, he does it in such a manner as all the time to have an eye to the temple, where he knew God had made himself known in a peculiar manner to the children of Abraham. He therefore celebrates God not only

[1] " Tout ainsi que s'il jettoit une fureur par les narines."—*Fr.* " As if he cast forth fury from his nostrils."

as creator of the world, but as He who entered into covenant with Israel, and chose for himself a holy dwelling-place in the midst of that people. David might have called the angels by their common name, but he has expressly made use of a term which has a reference to the visible symbol of the ark, that true believers, in singing this psalm, might always have their minds directed to the service of God which was performed in the temple. What follows with respect to God's *dark pavilion* or *tent*, is a repetition of the preceding sentence in different words, namely, that when God covers the air with dark clouds, it is as if he spread a thick veil between him and men, to deprive them of the sight of his countenance,[1] just as if a king, incensed against his subjects, should retire into his secret chamber and hide himself from them. Those take a mistaken view of this verse who bring it forward to prove, in general, the hidden and mysterious character of the glory of God, as if David, with the view of restraining the presumption of human curiosity, had said that God is hidden in darkness in regard to men. God, it is true, is said to dwell "in the light which no man can approach unto," (1 Tim. vi. 16;) but the form of expression which David here employs, I have no doubt, ought to be restricted, according to the scope of the passage, to the sense which I have given.

12. *At the brightness which was before him, his clouds passed away; there was hail-storm and coals of fire.*
13. *Jehovah thundered in the heavens, and the Highest sent forth his voice; there was hail-storm and coals of fire.*
14. *He sent out his arrows, and scattered them,* [or *put them to flight;*] *he multiplied lightnings,[2] and put them into confusion.*

[1] " C'est comme s'il tendoit un voile espes entre luy et les hommes, afin de leur oster le regard de sa face."—*Fr.*
[2] In our English version it is, *He shot out lightnings.* The Hebrew word רבב, *rabab*, signifies both *to multiply* and *to shoot.* As the shooting of arrows is mentioned in the first clause of the verse, it may be presumed that it is the shooting of lightnings which is meant in the second clause, arrows and lightnings being contrasted. The reading of the Septuagint, Chaldee, Syriac, Vulgate, Arabic, and Æthiopic versions, however, is the same as that of Calvin,—*He multiplied lightnings.*

15. *The sources of the waters were seen, and the foundations of the world were disclosed at thy rebuke, O Jehovah! at the blast of the breath of thy nostrils.*[1]
16. *He sent from on high, he took me, and drew me out of great waters.*
17. *He delivered me from my strong enemy, and from my adversary; for they were too strong for me.*
18. *They had prevented me in the day of my calamity; but Jehovah was my support.*
19. *He brought me forth also into a large place; he delivered me, because he had a good will to me,* [or *because he loved me.*]

12. *At the brightness, &c.* The Psalmist again returns to the lightnings which, by dividing and as it were cleaving the clouds, lay open the heaven; and, therefore, he says, that the clouds of God (that is to say, those which he had set before him, in token of his anger, for the purpose of depriving men of the enjoyment of the light of his countenance) passed away *at the brightness which was before him.* These sudden changes affect us with a much more lively sense of the power and agency of God than natural phenomena which move on in one uniform course. He adds, that there followed *hail-storm and coals of fire;* for when the thunder separates and rends asunder the clouds, it either breaks out in lightnings, or the clouds resolve themselves into hail.

13. *Jehovah thundered.* David here repeats the same thing in different words, declaring that God thundered from heaven; and he calls the thunder *the voice of God,* that we may not suppose it is produced merely by chance or by natural causes, independent of the appointment and will of God. Philosophers, it is true, are well acquainted with the intermediate or secondary causes, from which the thunder proceeds, namely, that when the cold and humid vapours obstruct the dry and hot exhalations in their course upwards, a collision takes place, and by this, together with the noise of the clouds rushing against each other, is produced the rumbling thunder-peal.[2] But David, in describing the phenomena of the

---

[1] " Ou de ton ire."—*Fr. marg.* " Or at thy wrath."
[2] " De ce combat et aussi du bruit des nuees allans l'une contre l'autre, se fait un son."—*Fr.*

atmosphere, rises, under the guidance of the Holy Spirit, above the mere phenomena themselves, and represents God to us as the supreme governor of the whole, who, at his will, penetrates into the hidden veins of the earth, and thence draws forth exhalations; who then, dividing them into different sorts, disperses them through the air; who again collects the vapours together, and sets them in conflict with the subtile and dry heats, so that the thunder which follows seems to be a loud pealing voice proceeding from his own mouth. The song in 2d Samuel also contains the repetition to which we have referred in the commencement of our remarks on this verse; but the sense of this and the preceding verse, and of the corresponding verses in Samuel, are entirely similar. We should remember what I have said before, that David, under these figures, describes to us the dreadful power of God, the better to exalt and magnify the divine grace, which was manifested in his deliverance. He declares a little after, that this was his intention; for, when speaking of his enemies, he says, (verse 14,) that they *were scattered*, or *put to flight, by the arrows of God;* as if he had said, They have been overthrown, not by the hands or swords of men, but by God, who openly launched his thunderbolts against them. Not that he means to affirm that this happened literally, but he speaks in this metaphorical language, because those who were uninstructed and slow to acknowledge the power of God,[1] could not otherwise be brought to perceive that God was the author of his deliverance. The import of his words is, Whoever does not acknowledge that I have been preserved by the hand of God, may as well deny that it is God who thunders from heaven, and abolish his power which is manifested in the whole order of nature, and especially in those wonderful changes which we see taking place in the atmosphere. As God shoots lightnings as if they were arrows, the Psalmist has, in the first place, employed this metaphor; and then he has expressed the thing simply by its proper name.

---

[1] " Et tardifs à recognoistre la vertu de Dieu."—*Fr.*

15. *And the sources of the waters were seen.* In this verse, David doubtless alludes to the miracle which was wrought when the chosen tribes passed through the Red Sea. I have before declared the purpose for which he does this. As all the special benefits which God in old time conferred upon any of the children of Abraham as individuals, were so many testimonies by which he recalled to their remembrance the covenant which he had once entered into with the whole people, to assure them that he would always continue his grace towards them, and that one deliverance might be to them a token or pledge of their perpetual safety, and of the protection of God, David fitly conjoins with that ancient deliverance of the Church the assistance which God had sent from heaven to him in particular. As the grace which he declares God had shown towards him was not to be separated from that first deliverance, since it was, so to speak, a part and an appendage of it, he beholds, as it were at a glance, or in an instant, both the ancient miracle of the drying up of the Red Sea, and the assistance which God granted to himself. In short, God, who once opened up for his people a way through the Red Sea, and then showed himself to be their protector upon this condition, that they should assure themselves of being always maintained and preserved under his keeping, now again displayed his wonderful power in the defence and preservation of one man, to renew the remembrance of that ancient history. From this it appears the more evidently, that David, in using these apparently strange and exaggerated hyperboles, does not recite to us the mere creations of romance to please the fancy, after the manner of the heathen poets,[1] but observes the style and manner which God had, as it were, prescribed to his people. At the same time, we ought carefully to mark the reason already adverted to, which constrained him to magnify the grace of God in a style of such splendid imagery, namely, because the greater part of the people never made the grace of God the subject

---

[1] "En usant de ces hyperboles et similitudes qui semblent estranges et excessives ne nous recite pas des fables et contes faits à plaisir à la façon des Poëtes profanes."—*Fr.*

of serious consideration, but, either through wickedness or stupidity, passed over it with shut eyes. The Hebrew word אֲפִיקִים, *aphikim*, which I have rendered *sources*, properly signifies *the channels of rivers;* but David, in this passage, evidently means that the very springs or sources of the waters were laid open, and that thus it could be discerned whence proceeds the great and inexhaustible abundance of waters which supply the rivers, and by which they always continue to flow on in their course.

16. *He sent down from above.* Here there is briefly shown the drift of the sublime and magnificent narrative which has now passed under our review, namely, to teach us that David at length emerged from the profound abyss of his troubles, neither by his own skill, nor by the aid of men, but that he was drawn out of them by the hand of God. When God defends and preserves us wonderfully and by extraordinary means, he is said in Scripture language to send down succour from above; and this *sending* is set in opposition to human and earthly aids, on which we usually place a mistaken and an undue confidence. I do not disapprove of the opinion of those who consider this as referring to the angels, but I understand it in a more general sense; for by whatever means we are preserved, it is God who, having his creatures ready at his nod to do his will, appoints them to take charge of us, and girds or prepares them for succouring us. But, although every kind of aid comes from heaven, David, with good reason, affirms that God had stretched out his hand from on high to deliver him. In speaking thus, he meant to place the astonishing benefit referred to, by way of eminence, above others of a more common kind; and besides, there is in this expression a tacit comparison between the unusual exercise of the power of God here celebrated, and the common and ordinary means by which he succours his people. When he says, that *God drew him out of great waters,* it is a metaphorical form of expression. By comparing the cruelty of his enemies to impetuou torrents, by which he might have been swallowed up a hundred times, he expresses more clearly the greatness of the

danger; as if he had said, I have, contrary to the expectation of men, escaped, and been delivered from a deep abyss in which I was ready to be overwhelmed. In the following verse he expresses the thing simply and without a figure, declaring that he had been delivered from a *strong enemy*,[1] who mortally hated and persecuted him. The more to exalt and magnify the power of God, he directs our attention to this circumstance, that no strength or power of men had been able to prevent God from saving him, even when he was reduced to the greatest extremity of distress. As in the end of the verse there is the Hebrew particle כִּי, *ki*, which generally denotes the cause of what is predicated, almost all interpreters agree in explaining the verse thus: God has succoured me from above, because my enemies were so numerous and so strong that no relief was to be expected by the mere aid of men. From this we deduce a very profitable doctrine, namely, that the most seasonable time for God to aid his people is when they are unable to sustain the assaults of their enemies, or rather, when, broken and afflicted, they sink under their violence, like the wretched man who, having in a shipwreck lost all hope of being able to swim to the shore, sinks with great rapidity to the bottom of the deep. The particle כִּי, *ki*, however, might also be explained by the adversative particle *although*, in this way: Although the enemies of David were superior to him in number and power, he nevertheless was saved.

18. *They had prevented me in the day of my calamity*.[2] The Psalmist here confirms in different words the preceding sentence, namely, that he had been sustained by the aid of God, when there was no way of escaping by the power of man. He tells us how he had been besieged on all sides, and

---

[1] Bishop Patrick paraphrases the verse thus:—"He delivered me first from that mighty giant, Goliath, and then from Saul, whose power I was not able to withstand; and afterwards from the Philistines and Syrians, and many other nations, whose forces were far superior unto mine, and whose hatred instigated them to do all they could to destroy me."

[2] "They set their faces against me in the day of my calamity."— *Walford.*

that not by an ordinary siege, inasmuch as his enemies, in persecuting him, always molested him most in the time of his calamity. From this circumstance it is the more evident that he had obtained enlargement by no other means than by the hand of God. Whence proceeded so sudden a restoration from death to life, but because God intended to show that he has in his hand, and under his absolute control, the issues of death? In short, the Psalmist ascribes his deliverance to no other cause than the mere good pleasure of God, that all the praise might redound to him alone : *He delivered me, because he loved me,* or *had a good will to me.* In mentioning the good pleasure of God, he has a special respect to his own calling to be king. The point on which he principally insisted is, that the assaults which were made upon him, and the conflicts which he had to sustain, were stirred up against him for no other reason but because he had obeyed the call of God, and followed with humble obedience the revelation of his oracle. Ambitious and turbulent men, who are carried headlong by their unruly lusts, inconsiderately to attempt any thing, and who, by their rashness, involve themselves in dangers, may often accomplish their undertakings by vigorous and resolute efforts, but at length a reverse takes place, and they are stopt short in their career of success, for they are unworthy of being sustained and prospered by God, since, without having any warrant or foundation for what they do in his call, they would raise their insane structures even to heaven, and disturb all around them. In short, David testifies, by this expression, that the assistance of God had never failed him, because he had not thrust himself into the office of king of his own accord, but that when he was contented with his humble condition, and would willingly have lived in obscurity, in the sheep-cotes, or in his father's hut, he had been anointed by the hand of Samuel, which was the symbol of his free election by God to fill the throne.

20. *Jehovah rewarded me according to my righteousness; he recompensed me according to the cleanness of my hands.*
21. *For I have kept the ways of Jehovah, and have not wickedly departed from my God.*
22. *For all his judgments were before me, nor did I put away his statutes* [or *ordinances*] *from me.*
23. *I was also upright with him,*[1] *and kept myself from my iniquity.*
24. *Therefore Jehovah hath recompensed me according to my righteousness, according to the cleanness of my hands before his eyes.*

20. *Jehovah rewarded me.* David might seem at first sight to contradict himself; for, while a little before he declared that all the blessings which he possessed were to be traced to the good pleasure of God, he now boasts that God rendered to him a just recompense. But if we remember for what purpose he connects these commendations of his own integrity with the good pleasure of God, it will be easy to reconcile these apparently conflicting statements. He has before declared that God was the sole author and originator of the hope of coming to the kingdom which he entertained, and that he had not been elevated to it by the suffrages of men, nor had he rushed forward to it through the mere impulse of his own mind, but accepted it because such was the will of God. Now he adds, in the second place, that he had yielded faithful obedience to God, and had never turned aside from his will. Both these things were necessary; first, that God should previously show his favour freely towards David, in choosing him to be king; and next, that David, on the other hand, should, with an obedient spirit, and a pure conscience, receive the kingdom which God thus freely gave him; and farther, that whatever the wicked might attempt, with the view of overthrowing or shaking his faith, he should nevertheless continue to adhere to the direct course of his calling. Thus, then, we see that these two statements, so far from disagreeing with each other, admirably harmonize. David here represents God as if the president[2] of a combat, under whose

[1] "Envers ou devant luy."—*Note, Fr. marg.* "Towards or before him."
[2] *Agonotheta.* Calvin alludes to the ancient games and combats of Greece, the presidents of which were called *Agonothetæ*.

authority and conduct he had been brought forth to engage in the combats. Now that depended upon election, in other words, upon this, that God having embraced him with his favour, had created him king. He adds in the verses which immediately follow, that he had faithfully performed the duties of the charge and office committed to him even to the uttermost. It is not, therefore, wonderful if God maintained and protected David, and even showed, by manifest miracles, that he was the defender of his own champion,[1] whom he had, of his own free choice, admitted to the combat, and who he saw had performed his duty with all fidelity. We ought not, however, to think that David, for the sake of obtaining praise among men, has here purposely indulged in the language of vain boasting; we ought rather to view the Holy Spirit as intending by the mouth of David to teach us the profitable doctrine, that the aid of God will never fail us, provided we follow our calling, keep ourselves within the limits which it prescribes, and undertake nothing without the command or warrant of God. At the same time, let this truth be deeply fixed in our minds, that we can only begin an upright course of life when God of his good pleasure adopts us into his family, and in effectually calling, anticipates us by his grace, without which neither we nor any creature would give him an opportunity of bestowing this blessing upon us.[2]

There, however, still remains one question. If God rendered to David a just recompense, it may be said, does it not seem, when he shows himself liberal towards his people, that he is so in proportion as each of them has deserved? I answer, When the Scripture uses the word *reward* or *recompense*, it is not to show that God owes us any thing, and it is therefore a groundless and false conclusion to infer from this that there is any merit or worth in works. God, as a just judge, rewards every man according to his works, but he does it in such a manner, as to show that all men are indebted to him, while he himself is under obligation to no one. The reason

---

[1] *Athleta.* Those who exercised themselves with the view of contending for the prizes in the Grecian games and combats were called *Athletæ.*

[2] " Sans que nous ne creature quelconque luy en donnions occasion." —*Fr.*

is not only that which St Augustine has assigned, namely, that God finds no righteousness in us to recompense, except what he himself has freely given us, but also because, forgiving the blemishes and imperfections which cleave to our works, he imputes to us for righteousness that which he might justly reject. If, therefore, none of our works please God, unless the sin which mingles with them is pardoned, it follows, that the recompense which he bestows on account of them proceeds not from our merit, but from his free and undeserved grace. We ought, however, to attend to the special reason why David here speaks of God rewarding him according to his righteousness. He does not presumptuously thrust himself into the presence of God, trusting to or depending upon his own obedience to the law as the ground of his justification; but knowing that God approved the affection of his heart, and wishing to defend and acquit himself from the false and wicked calumnies of his enemies, he makes God himself the judge of his cause. We know how unjustly and shamefully he had been loaded with false accusations, and yet these calumnies did not so much bear against the honour and name of David as against the welfare and estate of the whole Church in common. It was indeed mere private spite which stirred up Saul, and drove him into fury against David, and it was to please the king that all other men were so rancorous against an innocent individual, and broke forth so outrageously against him; but Satan, there is no doubt, had a prime agency in exciting these formidable assaults upon the kingdom of David, and by them he endeavoured to accomplish his ruin, because in the person of this one man God had placed, and, as it were, shut up the hope of the salvation of the whole people. This is the reason why David labours so carefully and so earnestly to show and to maintain the righteousness of his cause. When he presents and defends himself before the judgment-seat of God against his enemies, the question is not concerning the whole course of his life, but only respecting one certain cause, or a particular point. We ought, therefore, to attend to the precise subject of his discourse, and what he here debates. The state of the matter is this: His adversaries charged him with many crimes;

first, of rebellion and treason, accusing him of having revolted from the king his father-in-law; in the second place, of plunder and robbery, as if, like a robber, he had taken possession of the kingdom; thirdly, of sedition, as if he had thrown the kingdom into confusion when it enjoyed tranquillity; and, lastly, of cruelty and many flagitious actions, as if he had been the cause of murders, and had prosecuted his conspiracy by many dangerous means and unlawful artifices. David, in opposition to these accusations, with the view of maintaining his innocence before God, protests and affirms that he had acted uprightly and sincerely in this matter, inasmuch as he attempted nothing without the command or warrant of God; and whatever hostile attempts his enemies made against him, he nevertheless always kept himself within the bounds prescribed by the Divine Law. It would be absurd to draw from this the inference that God is merciful to men according as he judges them to be worthy of his favour. Here the object in view is only to show the goodness of a particular cause, and to maintain it in opposition to wicked calumniators; and not to bring into examination the whole life of a man, that he may obtain favour, and be pronounced righteous before God. In short, David concludes from the effect and the issue, that his cause was approved of by God, not that one victory is always and necessarily the sign of a good cause, but because God, by evident tokens of his assistance, showed that he was on the side of David.

21. *For I have kept the ways of Jehovah.* He had spoken in the preceding verse of the cleanness of his hands, but finding that men judged of him perversely, and were very active in spreading evil reports concerning him,[1] he affirms that he had kept the ways of the Lord, which is equivalent to his appealing the matter to the judgment-seat of God. Hypocrites, it is true, are accustomed confidently to appeal to God in the same way; yea, there is nothing which they are more forward in doing than in dallying with the sacred name of God, and making it a cover to conceal their hypo-

---

[1] " Et que bien legerement on semoit de luy de mauvais bruits."—*Fr.*

crisy; but David brings forward nothing which men might not have certainly known to be true, if any regard to justice had existed among them. Let us, therefore, from his example, endeavour above all things to have a good conscience. And, in the second place, let us have the magnanimity to despise the false judgments of men, and to look up to heaven for the vindicator of our character and cause. He adds, *I have not wickedly departed from my God.* This implies, that he always aimed directly at the mark of his calling, although the ungodly attempted many things to overthrow his faith. The verb which he uses does not denote one fall only, but a defection which utterly removes and alienates a man from God. David, it is true, sometimes fell into sin through the weakness of the flesh, but he never desisted from following after godliness, nor deserted the service to which God had called him.

22. *For all his judgments were before me.* He now shows how he came to possess that unbending rectitude of character, by which he was enabled to act uprightly amidst so many and so grievous temptations, namely, because he always applied his mind to the study of the law of God. As Satan is daily making new assaults upon us, it is necessary for us to have recourse to arms, and it is meditation upon the Divine Law which furnishes us with armour to resist. Whoever, therefore, would desire to persevere in uprightness and integrity of life, let them learn to exercise themselves daily in the study of the word of God; for, whenever a man despises or neglects instruction, he easily falls into carelessness and stupidity, and all fear of God vanishes from his mind. I do not intend here to make any subtle distinction between these two words, *judgments* and *ordinances.* If, however, any person is inclined to make a distinction between them, the best distinction is to refer *judgments* to the second table of the law, and *ordinances,* or *statutes,* which in Hebrew are called חוּקוֹת, *chukoth,* to the duties of piety and the exercises immediately connected with the worship of God.

23. *I was also upright with him.* All the verbs in this

verse are put by David in the future tense, *I will be upright, &c.*, because he does not boast of one act only, or of a good work performed by fits and starts, but of steady perseverance in an upright course. What I have said before, namely, that David takes God for his judge, as he saw that he was wrongfully and unrighteously condemned by men, appears still more clearly from what he here says, "I have been upright with him." The Scriptures, indeed, sometimes speak in similar terms of the saints, to distinguish them from hypocrites, who content themselves with wearing the outward mask of religious observances; but it is to disprove the false reports which were spread against him that David thus confidently appeals to God with respect to them. This is still more fully confirmed by the repetition of the same thing which is made a little after, *According to the cleanness of my hands before his eyes.* In these words there is evidently a contrast between the eyes of God and the blinded or malignant eyes of the world; as if he had said, I disregard false and wicked calumnies, provided I am pure and upright in the sight of God, whose judgment can never be perverted by malevolent or other vicious and perverse affections. Moreover, the integrity which he attributes to himself is not perfection but sincerity, which is opposed to dissimulation and hypocrisy. This may be gathered from the last clause of the 23d verse, where he says, *I have kept myself from my iniquity.* In thus speaking, he tacitly acknowledges that he had not been so pure and free from sinful affections as that the malignity of his enemies did not frequently excite indignation within him, and gall him to the heart. He had therefore to fight in his own mind against many temptations, for as he was a man, he must have felt in the flesh on many occasions the stirrings of vexation and anger. But this was the proof of his virtue, that he imposed a restraint upon himself, and refrained from whatever he knew to be contrary to the word of God. A man will never persevere in the practice of uprightness and of godliness, unless he carefully keep himself from his iniquity.

25. With the merciful thou wilt deal mercifully,[1] with an upright man thou wilt show thyself upright.
26. With the pure[2] thou wilt be pure, and with the perverse thou wilt show thyself perverse.
27. For thou wilt save the afflicted people,[3] and wilt bring down the haughty eyes.[4]

25. *With the merciful, &c.* David here prosecutes the same subject. In considering the grace of God by which he had been delivered, he brings it forward as a proof of his integrity, and thus triumphs over the unfounded and disgraceful calumnies of his enemies. Hypocrites, I confess, are also accustomed to act in the same way; for prosperity and the success of their affairs so elates them that they are not ashamed proudly to vaunt themselves not only against men, but even against God. As such persons, however, openly mock God, when, by his long-suffering, he allures them to repentance, their wicked and unhappy presumption has no resemblance to the boasting by which we here see David encouraging himself. He does not abuse the forbearance and mercy of God by palliating or spreading a specious varnish over his iniquities, because God bears with them; but having, by the manifold aids he had received from God, experienced beyond doubt that he was merciful to him, he justly viewed them as evident testimonies of the divine favour towards him. And we ought to mark well this difference between the ungodly and the faithful, namely, that the former, intoxicated with prosperity, unblushingly boast of being acceptable to God, while yet they disregard him, and rather sacrifice to Fortune, and make it their God;[5] whereas the latter in their prosperity magnify the grace of God, from the deep sense of his grace with which their consciences

---

[1] "Tu te monstreras debonnaire envers le debonnaire."—*Fr.* "Towards the merciful thou wilt show thyself merciful."
[2] "Envers."—*Note, Fr. marg.* "That is, towards."
[3] Some read, *The humble people*, supposing that, as the contrast is between them and *proud looks*, humility rather than *suffering* is meant.
[4] This is the literal rendering of the Hebrew text. "The meaning obviously is, that the haughty themselves shall be humbled, however confident they may be."—*French and Skinner.*
[5] "Ils sacrifient plustost à Fortune, et en font leur Dieu."—*Fr.*

are affected. Thus David here boasts that God had succoured him on account of the justice of his cause. For, in the first place, we must adapt the words to the scope of the whole discourse, and view them as implying that God, in so often delivering an innocent man from death, when it was near him, showed, indeed, that he is merciful towards the merciful, and pure towards the pure. In the second place, we must view the words as teaching the general doctrine, that God never disappoints his servants, but always at length deals graciously with them, provided they wait for his aid with meekness and patience. To this purpose Jacob said, in Gen. xxx. 33, " God will make my righteousness to return upon me." The scope of the discourse is, that the people of God should entertain good hope, and encourage themselves to practise uprightness and integrity, since every man shall reap the fruit of his own righteousness.

The last clause of the 26th verse, where it is said, *With the perverse thou wilt show thyself perverse,* seems to convey a meaning somewhat strange, but it does not imply any thing absurd; yea, rather, it is not without good reason that the Holy Spirit uses this manner of speaking; for he designs thereby to awaken hypocrites and the gross despisers of God, who lull themselves asleep in their vices without any apprehension of danger.[1] We see how such persons, when the Scripture proclaims the sore and dreadful judgments of God, and when also God himself denounces terrible vengeance, pass over all these things, without giving themselves any trouble about them. Accordingly, this brutish, and, as it were, monstrous stupidity which we see in men, compels God to invent new forms of expression, and, as it were, to clothe himself with a different character. There is a similar sentence in Lev. xxvi. 21–24, where God says, " And if ye walk contrary unto [*or* perversely with] me, then will I also walk contrary unto [*or* perversely or roughly, *or* at random against] you ;" as if he had said, that their obstinacy and stubbornness would make him on his part forget his accustomed forbearance and gentleness, and cast himself recklessly or at random against

---

[1] " Qui s'endorment en leurs vices sans rien craindre."—*Fr.*

them.[1] We see, then, what the stubborn at length gain by their obduracy; it is this, that God hardens himself still more to break them in pieces, and if they are of stone, he causes them to feel that he has the hardness of iron. Another reason which we may assign for this manner of speaking is, that the Holy Spirit, in addressing his discourse to the wicked, commonly speaks according to their own apprehension. When God thunders in good earnest upon them, they transform him, through the blind terrors which seize upon them, into a character different from his real one, inasmuch as they conceive of nothing as entering into it but barbarity, cruelty, and ferocity. We now see the reason why David does not simply attribute to God the name and office of judge, but introduces him as armed with impetuous violence, for resisting and overcoming the perverse, according as it is said in the common proverb, A tough knot requires a stout wedge.

27. *For thou wilt save the afflicted people.* This verse contains the correction of a mistake into which we are very ready to fall. As experience shows that the merciful are often severely afflicted, and the sincere involved in troubles of a very distressing description, to prevent any from regarding the statement as false that God deals mercifully with the merciful, David admonishes us that we must wait for the end; for although God does not immediately run to succour the good, yet, after having exercised their patience for a time, he lifts them up from the dust on which they lay prostrate, and brings effectual relief to them, even when they were in despair. Whence it follows, that we ought only to judge by the issue how God shows himself merciful towards the merciful and pure towards the pure. If he did not keep his people in suspense and waiting long for deliverance from affliction, it could not be said that it is his prerogative to save the afflicted. And it is no small consolation, in the midst of our adversities, to know that God purposely delays to communicate his assist-

[1] " Comme s'il disoit que leur obstination et opiniastrete sera cause que luy de son costé oubliant sa moderation et douceur accoustumee, se jettera à tors et à travers contre eux."—*Fr.*

ance, which otherwise is quite prepared, that we may experience his goodness in saving us after we have been afflicted and brought low.[1] Nor ought we to reckon the wrongs which are inflicted upon us too bitter, since they excite God to show towards us his favour which bringeth salvation. As to the second clause of this verse, the reading is a little different in the song in the 2d Book of Samuel, where the words are, *Thine eyes are against the proud to cast them down.* But this difference makes no alteration as to the meaning, except that the Holy Spirit there more plainly threatens the proud, that, as God is on the watch to overthrow them, it is impossible for them to escape destruction. The substance of both places is this: The more the ungodly indulge in gratifying their own inclinations, without any fear of danger, and the more proudly they despise the afflicted poor who are under their feet, they are so much the nearer to destruction. Whenever, therefore, they cruelly break forth against us with mockery and contempt, let us know that there is nothing which prevents God from repelling their headstrong pertinacity, but that their pride is not yet come to its height.

28. *For thou shalt light my lamp, O Jehovah; my God shall enlighten my darkness.*
29. *For by thee[2] I shall break through the wedge[3] of a troop, and by my God I shall leap over a wall.*
30. *The way of God is perfect; the word of Jehovah is refined,* [or *purified;*] *he is a shield to all those who trust in him.*
31. *For who is God besides Jehovah? and who is strong except our God?*
32. *It is God who hath girded me with strength, and hath made my way perfect.*

28. *For thou shalt light my lamp.* In the song in Samuel, the form of the expression is somewhat more precise; for there it is said not that God lights our lamp, but that he himself is our lamp. The meaning, however, comes to the same thing, namely, that it was by the grace of God that David, who had

---

[1] "Afin de nous faire esprouver comment il sauve les affligez."—*Fr.*
[2] "Par ta vertu."—*Note, Fr. marg.* "That is, by thy power."
[3] *Cuneum.* A battalion or company of foot drawn up in the form of a wedge, the better to break the enemies' ranks.

been plunged in darkness, returned to the light. David does not simply give thanks to God for having lighted up a lamp before him, but also for having converted his darkness into light. He, therefore, acknowledges that he had been reduced to such extremity of distress, that he was like a man whose condition was forlorn and hopeless; for he compares the confused and perplexed state of his affairs to darkness. This, indeed, by the transference of material things to things spiritual, may be applied to the spiritual illumination of the understanding; but, at the same time, we must attend to the subject of which David treats, that we may not depart from the true and proper meaning. Now, as he acknowledges that he had been restored to prosperity by the favour of God, which was to him, as it were, a life-giving light, let us, after his example, regard it as certain that we will never have the comfort of seeing our adversities brought to an end, unless God disperse the darkness which envelops us, and restore to us the light of joy. Let it not, however, be distressing to us to walk through darkness, provided God is pleased to perform to us the office of a lamp. In the following verse, David ascribes his victories to God, declaring that, under his conduct, he *had broken through the wedges or phalanxes* of his enemies, and had taken by storm their fortified cities.[1] Thus we see that, although he was a valiant warrior, and skilled in arms, he arrogates nothing to himself. As to the tenses of the verbs, we would inform our readers once for all, that in this psalm David uses the past and the future tenses indifferently, not only because he comprehends different histories, but also because he presents to himself the things of which he speaks as if they were still taking place before his eyes, and, at the same time, describes a continued course of the grace of God towards him.

[1] The last clause, *By my God have I leaped over a wall*, is rendered by the Chaldee, " I will subdue fortified towers." Hammond renders it, " By my God I have taken a fort." In support of this view, he observes that the word שׁוּר, *shur*, from שׁוֹר, *shor, to look*, signifies both *a wall*, from which to observe the approach of the enemy, and *a watch-tower and fort;* that if we take שׁוּר, *shur*, as meaning a wall, the verb דָּלַג, *dalag*, will be rightly rendered to leap over; but if שׁוּר, *shur*, means a fort, then the verb will mean to seize on it suddenly, and will therefore be best translated *to take it.*

30. *The way of God is perfect.* The phrase, *The way of God,* is not here taken for his revealed will, but for his method of dealing towards his people. The meaning, therefore, is, that God never disappoints or deceives his servants, nor forsakes them in the time of need, (as may be the case with men who do not aid their dependants, except in so far as it contributes to their own particular advantage,) but faithfully defends and maintains those whom he has once taken under his protection. But we will never have any nearness to God, unless he first come near to us by his word; and, for this reason, David, after having asserted that God aids his people in good earnest, adds, at the same time, that *his word is purified.* Let us, therefore, rest assured that God will actually show himself upright towards us, seeing he has promised to be the guardian and protector of our welfare, and his promise is certain and infallible truth. That by *the word* we are not here to understand the commandments, but the promises of God, is easily gathered from the following clause, where it is said, *He is a shield to all those who trust in him.* It seems, indeed, a common commendation to say, that the word of God is pure, and without any mixture of fraud and deceit, like silver which is well refined and purified from all its dross. But our unbelief is the cause why God, so to speak, is constrained to use such a similitude, for the purpose of commending and leading us to form exalted conceptions of the stedfastness and certainty of his promises; for whenever the issue does not answer our expectation, there is nothing to which we are naturally more prone than forthwith to begin to entertain unhallowed and distrustful thoughts of the word of God. For a farther explanation of these words, we would refer our readers to our remarks on the 6th verse of the 12th Psalm.

31. *For who is God besides Jehovah?* David here, deriding the foolish inventions of men, who, according to their own fancy, make for themselves tutelary gods,[1] confirms what I

---

[1] " Qui se forgent à leur fantasie des dieux qui soyent leurs protecteurs et patrons."—*Fr.* " Who, according to their own fancy, make for themselves gods to be their protectors and patrons."

have said before, that he never undertook any thing but by the authority and command of God. If he had passed beyond the limits of his calling, he could not with such confidence have said that God was on his side. Besides, although in these words he opposes to the true God all the false gods invented by men, his purpose, at the same time, is to overthrow all the vain hopes in which the world is wrapped up, and by which it is carried about, and prevented from resting in God. The question which David here treats of is not the bare title and name of *God*, but he declares that whatever assistance we need we should seek it from God, and from no other quarter, because he alone is endued with power: *Who is strong except our God?* We should, however, attend to the design of David, which I have first adverted to, namely, that, by confidently representing God as opposed to all his enemies, and as the leader, under whose standard he had valiantly fought against them, he means to affirm that he had attempted nothing according to his own fancy, or with an evil and condemning conscience.

32. *It is God who hath girded.* This is a metaphor taken either from the belt or girdle of a warrior, or from the reins, in which the Scripture sometimes places a man's vigour or strength. It is, therefore, as if he had said, I, who would otherwise have been feeble and effeminate, have been made strong and courageous by the power of God. He afterwards speaks of the success itself with which God had favoured him; for it would not be enough for persons to have prompt and active courage, nor even to excel in strength, if their undertakings were not at the same time crowned with a prosperous issue. Irreligious men imagine that this proceeds from their own prudence, or from fortune; but David ascribes it to God alone: *It is God who hath made my way perfect.* The word *way* is here to be understood of the course of our actions, and the language implies, that whatever David undertook, God, by his blessing, directed it to a successful issue.

33. *Making my feet like hinds'*¹ *feet, and he hath set me upon my high places.*
34. *Teaching my hands to war: and a bow of steel*² *will be broken by my arms.*
35. *Thou hast also given me the shield of thy salvation; and thy right hand hath holden me up, and thy clemency hath increased me.*
36. *Thou hast enlarged my steps under me, and my feet have not staggered.*

David, having taken many strongholds which, on account of their steep and difficult access, were believed to be impregnable, extols the grace of God in this particular. When he says that God had given him feet like *hinds' feet,* he means that he had given him unusual swiftness, and such as does not naturally belong to men. The sense, therefore, is, that he had been aided by God in an extraordinary manner, so that like a roe he climbed with amazing speed over inaccessible rocks. He calls the strongholds, which, as conqueror, he had obtained by right of war, *his high places;* for he could justly boast that he took possession of nothing which belonged to another man, inasmuch as he knew that he had been called to occupy these fortresses by God. When he says that *his hands* had been taught and framed *to war,* he confesses that he had not acquired his dexterity in fighting by his own skill, nor by exercise and experience, but had obtained it as a gift through the singular goodness of God. It is true in general, that strength and skill in war proceed only from a secret virtue communicated by God; but David immediately after shows that he had been furnished with greater strength for

---

[1] "Faisant, ascavoir, me donnant legerete de pieds."—*Note, Fr. marg.* "Making, namely, giving me swiftness of feet."

[2] It should be *brass,* and not *steel.* "A bow of *steel,*" says Dr Adam Clarke, "is out of the question. In the days of David, it is not likely that the method of making *steel* was known. The method of making *brass* out of *copper* was known at a very early period of the world; and the ancients had the art of *hardening* it, so as to work it into the most efficient swords." Horsley reads, "Thou hast made my arms like a brazen bow." This is also the reading of the Septuagint, Vulgate, Jerome, and all the versions. But the reading of Calvin, which is that of our English version, seems preferable, and is more expressive. To bend a strong bow was anciently considered a proof of great strength, much more to compress it so as to break it. To bend a bow of *brass* is still more expressive, and still more so to do it by the *arms* without requiring the assistance of the foot, which was then usually employed in making that effort.

carrying on his wars than what men commonly possess, inasmuch as his arms were sufficiently strong *to break even bows of brass in pieces.* True, he had by nature a vigorous and powerful bodily frame; but the Scripture describes him as a man of low stature, and the similitude itself which he here uses implies something surpassing the natural strength of man. In the following verse, he declares that it was by the grace of God alone that he had escaped, and been kept in perfect safety: *Thou hast also given me the shield of thy salvation.* By the phrase, *the shield of God's salvation,* he intimates, that if God had not wonderfully preserved him, he would have been exposed unprotected to many deadly wounds; and thus God's shield of salvation is tacitly opposed to all the coverings and armour with which he had been provided. He again ascribes his safety to the free goodness of God as its cause, which he says *had increased him,* or more and more carried him forward in the path of honour and success; for, by the word *increase,* he means a continuation and an unintermitted and ever growing augmentation of the tokens of the divine favour towards him.

By *the enlargement of his steps,* he intimates that God had opened up to him an even and an accommodating pathway through places to which there was before no means of access; for there is in the words an implied contrast between a large and spacious place and a narrow spot, out of which a person cannot move his foot. The meaning is, that when David was reduced to the greatest distress, and saw no way of escape, God had graciously brought him out of his straits and difficulties. This is a lesson which may be highly useful for correcting our distrust. Unless we see before us a beautiful and pleasant plain, in which the flesh may freely enjoy itself, we tremble as if the earth would sink under our feet. Let us, therefore, remember, that the office of enlarging our ways and making them level belongs to God, and is here justly ascribed to him. In short, the Psalmist subjoins the effect of this instance of the grace of God towards him, namely, that *his feet had not staggered* or *slipped;* in other words, no resistance, adversity, or calamity, which had befallen him, had been able to deprive him of courage, or cast him into despair.

37. *I will pursue my enemies, and will overtake them ; nor will I return till I have consumed them.*
38. *I have afflicted* [or *smitten*] *them, so that they were not able to rise ; they have fallen under my feet.*
39. *Thou hast girded me with strength*[1] *for the war ; thou hast bowed down my enemies under me.*
40. *And thou hast given me the neck of my enemies, and those who hated me I have destroyed.*[2]

The point on which David insists so much is, that of showing from the effect or issue, that all his victories were to be traced to the favour of God ; and from this it follows that his cause was good and just. God, no doubt, sometimes grants successes even to the ungodly and wicked; but he at length shows by the issue, that he was all the while opposed to them and their enemy. It is his servants alone who experience such tokens of his favour as he showed towards David, and he intends by these to testify that they are approved and accepted by him. We are apt to think that David here speaks too much after the manner of a soldier, in declaring that he will not cease from the work of slaughter until he has destroyed all his enemies ; or rather that he has forgotten the gentleness and meekness which ought to shine in all true believers, and in which they should resemble their heavenly Father; but as he attempted nothing without the command of God, and as his affections were governed and regulated by the Holy Spirit, we may be assured that these are not the words of a man who was cruel, and who took pleasure in shedding blood, but of a man who faithfully executed the judgment which God had committed to him. And, indeed, we know that he was so distinguished for gentleness of disposition as to abhor the shedding of even a single drop of blood, except in so far as duty and the necessity of his office required. We must, therefore, take into consideration David's vocation, and also his pure zeal, which was free from all perturbation of the flesh. Moreover, it should be particularly attended to, that the Psalmist here calls those his

---

[1] "To be *well girt* was to be *well armed* in the Greek and Latin idioms, as well as in the Hebrew."—*Dr Geddes.*
[2] In the French version it is, "Tu les as destruits ;"—" Thou hast destroyed them."

enemies whose indomitable and infatuated obstinacy merited and called forth such vengeance from God. As he represented the person of Christ, he inflicted the punishment of death only on those who were so inflexible that they could not be reduced to order by the exercise of a mild and humane authority; and this of itself shows, that there was nothing in which he more delighted than to pardon those who repented and reformed themselves. He thus resembled Christ, who gently allures all men to repentance, but breaks in pieces, with his iron rod, those who obstinately resist him to the last. The sum of these verses is, that David, as he fought under the authority of God, being chosen king by him, and engaging in no undertaking without his warrant, was assisted by him, and rendered invincible against the assaults of all his enemies, and enabled even to discomfit vast and very powerful armies. Farther, let us remember, that under this type there is shadowed forth the invincible character and condition of the kingdom of Christ, who, trusting to, and sustained by, the power of God, overthrows and destroys his enemies, —who, in every encounter, uniformly comes off victorious,— and who continues king in spite of all the resistance which the world makes to his authority and power. And as the victories secured to him involve a security of similar victories to us, it follows that there is here promised us an impregnable defence against all the efforts of Satan, all the machinations of sin, and all the temptations of the flesh. Although, therefore, Christ can only obtain a tranquil kingdom by fighting, let us not on that account be troubled, but let it be enough to satisfy us, that the hand of God is always ready to be stretched forth for its preservation. David was, for a time, a fugitive, so that it was with difficulty he could save his life, by taking shelter in the dens of wild beasts; but God, at length, made his enemies turn their backs, and not only put them to flight, but also delivered them over to him, that he might pursue and utterly discomfit them. In like manner, our enemies for a time may be, as it were, just ready to put the knife to our throat[1] to destroy us, but God,

---

[1] "Comme tous prests à nous mettre le cousteau sur la gorge."—*Fr.*

at length, will make them not only to flee before us, but also to perish in our presence, as they deserve. At the same time, let us remember what kind of warfare it is to which God is calling us, against what kind of persons he will have us to contend, and with what armour he furnishes us, that it may suffice us to have the devil, the flesh, and sin overthrown and placed under our feet by his spiritual power. With respect to those to whom he has given the power of the sword, he will also defend them, and not suffer them to be unrighteously opposed, provided they reign under Christ, and acknowledge him as their head. As to the words, interpreters almost unanimously render the beginning of the 40th verse, *My enemies have turned the back*, a phrase of the same import as, *They have been put to flight;* but as the Hebrew word ערף, *oreph*, properly signifies *the head or neck*, we may very suitably view the words as meaning that God gave David the neck of his enemies, inasmuch as he delivered them into his hands to be slain.

41. *They shall cry, but there shall be no saviour for them; even unto Jehovah, but he shall not answer them.*
42. *And I will beat* [or *grind*] *them small as the dust which is driven by the wind;*[1] *as the mire of the streets I will tread them under foot.*
43. *Thou shalt deliver me from the contentions of the people; thou shalt make me the head of the nations; a people whom I have not known shall serve me.*
44. *At the hearing of the ear,*[2] *they shall obey me; the children of strangers*[3] *shall lie to me.*[4]
45. *The children of strangers shall lose their courage, and tremble out of their places of concealment.*

41. *They shall cry, &c.* The change of the tense in the verb from the past to the future does not break the conti-

---

[1] " Qui est jette par le vent."—*Fr.*
[2] " Si tost que le bruit de mon nom viendra à leurs aureilles."—*Note, Fr. marg.* " That is, as soon as the fame of my name reaches their ears."
[3] " Les peuples estranges."—*Note, Fr. marg.* " That is, strange peoples, or foreign nations."
[4] " Feront semblant d'estre des miens s'humilians de crainte."—*Note, Fr. marg.* " That is, shall feign to be my servants, [or submission to me,] humbling themselves through fear."

nuity of the narration; and, therefore, the words should be explained thus: Although they cried to God, yet their prayers were rejected by him. He pursues the same subject which it was his object to illustrate before, namely, that it was at length manifest from the issue that his enemies falsely boasted of having the support and countenance of God, who showed that he had turned away from them. It is true, that when their affairs continued to go on prosperously, they sometimes received such applause and commendation, that it was commonly believed that God was favourable to them, while, at the same time, he seemed to be opposed to David, who, although he cried night and day to him, found it of no avail. But after God had sufficiently tried the patience of his servant, he cast them down, and disappointed them of their vain hope; yea, rather he would not deign to hear their prayers. We now perceive the design of David in these words. As the ungodly had long wickedly abused the name of God, by pretending that he favoured their unjust proceedings, the Psalmist derides their vain boasting, in which they were completely disappointed. It is to be observed, that he here speaks of hypocrites, who never call upon God in sincerity and truth. For this promise shall never fail, " The Lord is nigh unto all them that call upon him, to all that call upon him in truth," (Ps. cxlv. 18.) David does not, therefore, say that his enemies were repulsed when they had recourse to God with sincere affection of heart, but only when, with their accustomed effrontery, they thought that God was, so to speak, bound to conduct and advance their wicked enterprises. When the ungodly, in the extremity of their distress, pour forth prayers, and when, cast down with fear, and trembling with the dread of impending evils, they show an appearance of humility, they, notwithstanding, do not change their purpose, so as truly to repent and amend the evil of their ways. Besides, instead of being influenced by faith, they are actuated by presumption and hardness of heart, or they pour forth their complaints in doubt, rather for the purpose of murmuring against God, than of familiarly and confidently placing their trust in him. From this passage we may gather a profitable warning, namely, that all who treat the afflicted poor with cruel mockery, and who proudly thrust back those who come to them as humble suppliants, will experience that God is deaf to their prayers. We are farther taught by the following verse, that after God has cast off the ungodly, he leaves them to be treated with every kind of indignity, and gives them up to be trampled under foot, as *the mire of the streets.* He not only declares, that when the proud and the cruel cry to him in their affliction, he will shut his ears against their cry; but he also threatens, that, in the course of his retributive providence, they shall be treated in the same manner in which they treat others.

43. *Thou shalt deliver me from the contentions of the people.* David states, in a few words, that he had experienced the assistance of God in all variety of ways. He was in great danger from the tumults which sometimes arose among his own subjects, if God had not wonderfully allayed them, and subdued the fierceness of the people. It also happened, contrary to the general expectation, that David, as is stated in the second clause of the verse, was victorious far and wide, and overthrew the neighbouring nations who had a little before discomfited all Israel by their forces. It was an astonishing renovation of things, when he not only suddenly restored to their former estate the people of Israel, who had been greatly reduced by defeat and slaughter, but also made his tributaries the neighbouring nations, with whom before, on account of their hostility to the nation of Israel, it was impossible to live in peace. It would have been much to see the kingdom, after having sustained so grievous a calamity, still surviving, and after having again collected strength recovering its former state; but God, contrary to all expectation, conferred upon the people of Israel more than this; he enabled them even to subdue those who before had been their conquerors. David makes mention of both these; he tells us, in the first place, that when the people rose up in tumult against him, it was none other but God who stilled these commotions which took place within the kingdom; and, in the second place, that it was under the authority, and by the conduct and power of God, that powerful nations

were subjected to him, and that the limits of the kingdom, which, in the time of Saul, had been weak and half broken, were greatly enlarged. Hence it is evident that David was assisted by God, not less with respect to his domestic affairs, that is to say, within his own kingdom, than against foreign enemies. As the kingdom of David was a type under which the Holy Spirit intended to shadow forth to us the kingdom of Christ, let us remember that, both in erecting and preserving it, it is necessary for God not only to stretch forth his arm and fight against avowed enemies, who from without rise up against him, but also to repress the tumults and strifes which may take place within the Church. This was clearly shown in the person of Christ from the beginning. In the first place, he met with much opposition from the infatuated obstinacy of those of his own nation. In the next place, the experience of all ages shows that the dissensions and strifes with which hypocrites rend and mangle the Church, are not less hurtful in undermining the kingdom of Christ, (if God do not interpose his hand to prevent their injurious effects,) than the violent efforts of his enemies. Accordingly God, to advance and maintain the kingdom of his own Son, not only overthrows before him external enemies, but also delivers him from domestic contentions; that is to say, from those within his kingdom, which is the Church.[1] In the song in 2d Samuel, instead of these words, *Thou hast made me the head of the nations*, the word employed is תשמרני, *tishmereni*, which signifies *to keep* or *guard*, and is therefore to be understood in this sense, that David will be securely, and for a long time, maintained in possession of the kingdom. He knew how difficult it is to keep under discipline and subjection those who have not been accustomed to the yoke; and, accordingly, nothing is of more frequent occurrence than for kingdoms which have been lately acquired by conquest to be shaken with fresh commotions. But David, in the song in Samuel, declares that God, having elevated him to such a high degree of power as to make him the head of the nations, will also maintain him in

---

[1] "C'est à dire au dedans de son royaume qui est l'Eglise."—*Fr.*

the possession of the sovereignty he had been pleased to confer upon him.

A people whom I have not known shall serve me. The whole of this passage strongly confirms what I have just now touched upon, that the statements here made are not to be restricted to the person of David, but contain a prophecy respecting the kingdom of Christ which was to come. David, it is true, might have boasted that nations, with whose manners and dispositions he was only very imperfectly acquainted, were subject to him; but it is nevertheless certain, that none of the nations which he conquered were altogether unknown to him, nor removed at so great a distance as to render it difficult for him to acquire some knowledge of them. The conquests of David, therefore, and the submission of the people to him, were only an obscure figure in which God has exhibited to us some faint representation of the boundless dominion of his own Son, whose kingdom extends "from the rising of the sun, even unto the going down of the same," (Mal. i. 11,) and comprehends the whole world.

44. *At the simple fame of my name they shall obey me.* This is of the same import with the last clause of the preceding verse. Although David, by his victories, had acquired such reputation and renown, that many laid down their arms and came voluntarily to surrender themselves to him; yet, as they also had been subdued through the dread of the power of his arms, which they saw their neighbours had experienced to their smart, it cannot be said, properly speaking, that at the simple fame of the name of David they submitted themselves to him. This applies more truly to the person of Christ, who, by means of his word, subdues the world to himself, and, at the simple hearing of his name, makes those obedient to him who before had been rebels against him. As David was intended to be a type of Christ, God subjected to his authority distant nations, and such as before had been unknown to Israel in so far as familiar intercourse was concerned. But that was only a prelude, and, as it were, preparatory to the dominion promised to Christ, the boundaries of which must be extended to the uttermost ends of the earth. In like manner, David

had acquired to himself so great a name by arms and warlike prowess, that many of his enemies, subdued by fear, submitted themselves to him. And in this God exhibited a type of the conquest which Christ would make of the Gentiles, who, by the preaching of the Gospel alone, were subdued, and brought voluntarily to submit to his dominion; for the obedience of faith in which the dominion of Christ is founded "cometh by hearing," (Rom. x. 17.)

The children of strangers shall lie to me. Here there is described what commonly happens in new dominions acquired by conquest, namely, that those who have been vanquished pay homage with great reverence to their conqueror; but it is by a feigned and forced humility. They obey in a slavish manner, and not willingly or cheerfully. This is evidently the sense. Some interpreters, indeed, give a different explanation of the word *lie,* viewing David as meaning by it that his enemies had either been disappointed in their expectation, or that, in order to escape the punishment which they were afraid he might inflict upon them, they had lied in declaring that they had never devised any thing hostile against him; but it appears to me, that this does not sufficiently express what David intended. In my opinion, therefore, the words *to lie* are here to be understood generally as in other places, for *to be humbled after a slavish manner.* The Hebrew word כחש, *cachash,* here used, which signifies *to lie,* is sometimes to be understood metaphorically for *to be humbled, to submit to, to take upon one's self the yoke of subjection;*[1] but still in a feigned and servile manner. Those whom he terms the *children of the stranger,* or *of strangers,* are the nations who did not belong to the people of Israel, but who, previous to their being conquered by him, formed a distinct and an independent community by themselves. This also we see fulfilled in Christ, to whom many come with apparent humility; not, however, with true affection, but with a double and false heart, whom, on that account, the Holy Spirit fitly terms *strangers.* They are, indeed, mingled among the chosen people, but they

---

[1] The Syriac version reads, " They shall submit themselves to me;" meaning a forced, and so a feigned and hypocritical subjection.

are not united to the same body with them by a true faith, and, therefore, ought not to be accounted children of the Church. It is very true that all the Gentiles, when in the beginning they were called into the Church, were strangers; but when they began to entertain new feelings and new affections towards Christ, they who before were "strangers and foreigners" became "fellow-citizens with the saints, and of the household of God," (Eph. ii. 19.)

What is added immediately after, (verse 45,) *the children of strangers shall fade away; they shall tremble[1] from within their places of concealment,* serves to place, in a still more striking light, the great fame and formidable name which we have said David had acquired. It is no ordinary sign of reverence when those who are protected in hiding-places, and shut up within steep fortifications, are so stricken with terror as to come forth of their own accord and surrender themselves. As fear made the enemies of David to come forth from their places of concealment, to meet him with submission, so the Gospel strikes the unbelieving with such fear, as compels them to yield obedience to Christ. Such is the power of prophecy, that is to say, the preaching of the word, as Paul testifies in 1 Cor. xiv. 24, that, convincing the consciences of men, and making manifest the secrets of their hearts, it causes those who before were rebels to prostrate themselves with fear, and to give glory to God.

[1] The Hebrew word חרג, *charag*, signifies both *to be moved* and *to tremble*, and combining both ideas, *to move fearfully.* The last appears to be the view which Calvin attaches to the word. "Fear shall cause them to be afraid, and come forth of their secret holes and holds, to seek pardon."—*Note, Bassandyne's Bible.*

Walford reads,

"The sons of the stranger lose their strength;
Through alarm they quit their strongholds."

Street reads,

"Foreign nations are confounded, and they shudder within their fortresses."

46. Let Jehovah live,[1] and blessed be my strength :[2] *and let the God of my salvation be exalted;*
47. The God who giveth me vengeance, and subdueth peoples [or nations] under me.
48. My deliverer from my enemies; yea, thou hast lifted me up from those who had risen up against me; thou hast delivered me from the man of violence.
49. Therefore will I praise thee, O Jehovah, among the heathen, and will sing to thy name.
50. He worketh great deliverances for his king, and showeth mercy to David, his anointed, and to his seed for ever.

46. *Let Jehovah live.* If it is thought proper to adopt this reading, which is in the optative mood, expressing a wish *that God might live,* the manner of expression may seem somewhat strange; but it may be alleged in defence of it, that it is a metaphor borrowed from the custom of men, who not only use this manner of speaking when they wish well to any one, but likewise utter it with loud and applauding acclamation, when they intend to receive their princes with due honour. According to this view, it would be an expression in which praise is ascribed to God, and suitable for a triumphal song.[3] It may, however, be very properly considered as a simple affirmation, in which David declares that *God lives,* in other words, that he is endued with sovereign power. Farther, the life which David attributes to God is not to be restricted to the being or essence of God, but is rather to be understood of the evidence of it deducible from his works, which manifest to us that he liveth. Whenever he withdraws the working of his power from before our eyes, the sense and cognizance of the truth, " God liveth," also evanishes from our minds. He is, therefore, said *to live,* inasmuch as he shows, by evident proofs of his power, that it is he who preserves and upholds the world. And as David had known, by experience, this life of God, he celebrates it with praises and thanksgiving. If we read the first clause in the present tense, *The Lord liveth,* the copula *and,* which

---

[1] " Ou, le Seigneur vit."—*Fr. marg.* " Or, Jehovah lives."
[2] " Celuy qui me donne force."—*Note, Fr. marg.* " That is, he who giveth me strength."
[3] " Ainsi ce seroit un mot tendant à louër Dieu et convenable à un cantique de triomphe."—*Fr.*

follows, has the force of an inference; and, accordingly, the words should be resolved thus:—*Jehovah liveth, and, therefore, blessed be my strength.* The epithet, *My strength,* and the other which occurs in verse 48th, *My deliverer,* confirm what I have already stated, that God does not simply live in himself, and in his secret place, but displays his vital energy in the government of the whole world. The Hebrew word, צוּרִי, *tsuri,* which we have translated *my strength,* is here to be understood in a transitive sense for *Him* who bestows strength.

47. *The God who giveth me vengeance.* The Psalmist again attributes to God the victories which he had obtained. As he could never have expected to obtain them unless he had been confident that he would receive the aid of God, so now he acknowledges God to be the sole author of them. That he may not seem carelessly to bestow upon him, as it were, in passing, only a small sprinkling of the praise of his victories, he repeats, in express terms, that he had nothing but what God had given him. In the first place, he acknowledges that power was given him from above, to enable him to inflict on his enemies the punishment which they deserved. It may seem at first sight strange that God should arm his own people to execute vengeance; but as I have previously shown you, we ought always to remember David's vocation. He was not a private person, but being endued with royal power and authority, the judgment which he executed was enjoined upon him by God. If a man, upon receiving injury, breaks forth to avenge himself, he usurps the office of God; and, therefore, it is rash and impious for private individuals to retaliate the injuries which have been inflicted upon them. With respect to kings and magistrates, God, who declares that vengeance belongeth to him, in arming them with the sword, constitutes them the ministers and executioners of his vengeance. David, therefore, has put the word *vengeance* for the just punishments which it was lawful for him to inflict by the commandment of God, provided he was led under the influence of a zeal duly regulated by the Holy Spirit, and not under the influence of the impetuosity of the

flesh. Unless this moderation is exemplified in performing the
duties of their calling, it is in vain for kings to boast that God
has committed to them the charge of taking vengeance;
seeing it is not less unwarrantable for a man to abuse, according to his own fancy and the lust of the flesh, the sword
which he is allowed to use, than to seize it without the command of God. The Church militant, which is under the
standard of Christ, has no permission to execute vengeance,
except against those who obstinately refuse to be reclaimed.
We are commanded to endeavour to overcome our enemies
by doing them good, and to pray for their salvation. It
becomes us, therefore, at the same time, to desire that they
may be brought to repentance, and to a right state of mind,
until it appear beyond all doubt that they are irrecoverably
and hopelessly depraved. In the meantime, in regard to
vengeance, it must be left to God, that we may not be carried headlong to execute it before the time. David next
concludes, from the perils and distresses in which he had
been involved, that if he had not been preserved by the hand
of God, he could not in any other way have escaped in
safety: *My deliverer from my enemies; yea, thou hast lifted
me up from those who had risen up against me.* The sense in
which we are to understand *the lifting up* of which he speaks
is, that he was wonderfully raised up above the power and
malice of his enemies that he might not sink under their violence, and that they might not be victorious over him.

49. *Therefore will I praise thee, O Jehovah!* In this verse
he teaches us that the blessings God had conferred upon him,
of which he had spoken, are worthy of being celebrated with
extraordinary and unusual praises, that the fame of them
might reach even the heathen. There is in the words an
implied contrast between the ordinary worship of God which
the faithful were then accustomed to perform in the temple,
and this thanksgiving of which David speaks, which could
not be confined within so narrow limits. The meaning,
therefore, is, O Lord, I will not only give thee thanks in the
assembly of thy people, according to the ritual which thou
hast appointed in thy law, but thy praises shall extend to

a greater distance, even as thy grace towards me is worthy of being recounted through the whole world. Moreover, from these words we conclude that this passage contains a prophecy concerning the kingdom of Christ, which was to come. Unless the heathen had been allured into the fellowship of the chosen people, and united into one body with them, to praise God among them would have been to sing his praises among the deaf, which would have been foolish work and lost labour. Accordingly, Paul very properly and suitably proves from this text, that the calling of the Gentiles was not a thing which happened by chance, or at a venture, (Rom. xv. 9.) We shall afterwards see in many places that the Church is appointed to be the sacred dwelling-place for showing forth the praises of God. And, therefore, the name of God could not have been rightly and profitably celebrated elsewhere than in Judea, until the ears of the Gentiles were opened, which was done when God adopted them, and called them to himself by the gospel.

50. *He worketh great deliverances, &c.* This concluding verse clearly shows why God had exercised such goodness and liberality towards David, namely, because he had anointed him to be king. By calling himself *God's king*, David testifies that he had not rashly rushed into that office, nor was thrust into it by conspiracies and wicked intrigues, but, on the contrary, reigned by lawful right, inasmuch as it was the will of God that he should be king. This he proves by the ceremony of anointing; for God, in anointing him by the hand of Samuel, had asserted his right to reign not less than if he had visibly stretched forth his hand from heaven to place and establish him on the royal throne. This election, he says, was confirmed by a continued series of great deliverances; and from this it follows, that all who enter on any course without having the call of God, are chargeable with avowedly making war against him. At the same time, he attributes these deliverances to the goodness of God as their cause, to teach us, that that kingdom was founded purely and simply upon the good pleasure of God. Farther, from the concluding sentence of the psalm, it appears, as I have said before, that David does not here so much recount

by way of history the singular and varied instances of the grace of God which he had personally experienced, as predict the everlasting duration of his kingdom. And it is to be observed, that by the word *seed* we are not to understand all his descendants indiscriminately; but we are to consider it as particularly referring to that successor of David of whom God had spoken in 2 Samuel vii. 12, promising that he would be a father to him. As it had been predicted that his kingdom would continue as long as the sun and the moon should shine in the heavens, the prophecy must necessarily be viewed as descending to him who was to be king not for a time, but for ever. David, therefore, commends his seed to us, as honoured by that remarkable promise, which fully applies neither to Solomon nor to any other of his successors, but to the only begotten Son of God; as the apostle, in his Epistle to the Hebrews, (chap. i. 4,) teaches us, that this is a dignity in which he excels the angels. In conclusion, we shall then only duly profit in the study of this psalm, when we are led by the contemplation of the shadow and type to him who is the substance.

PSALM XIX.

David, with the view of encouraging the faithful to contemplate the glory of God, sets before them, in the first place, a mirror of it in the fabric of the heavens, and in the exquisite order of their workmanship which we behold; and, in the second place, he recalls our thoughts to the Law, in which God made himself more familiarly known to his chosen people. Taking occasion from this, he continues to discourse at considerable length on this peculiar gift of Heaven, commending and exalting the use of the Law. Finally, he concludes the psalm with a prayer.

¶ To the chief musician. A song of David.

1. *The heavens declare the glory of God; and the expanse*[1] *proclaims the works of his hands.*

[1] " L'entour du ciel et de l'air."—*Note, Fr. marg.* " That is, the cope or vault of the heaven and of the air." Bishop Mant reads also *expanse*,

2. *Day unto day uttereth speech, and night unto night publishes knowledge.*[1]

3. *There is no language and no speech [where] their voice is not heard.*

4. *Their writing has gone forth through all the earth, and their words to the end of the world: he hath set in them a tabernacle for the sun.*

5. *And he goeth forth as a bridegroom out of his chamber: he rejoiceth as a strong man to run his race.*

6. *His going forth is from the end of the heavens, and his circuit is to their utmost limits, and none is hidden from his heat.*

1. *The heavens declare the glory of God.*[2] I have already said, that this psalm consists of two parts, in the first of which David celebrates the glory of God as manifested in his works; and, in the other, exalts and magnifies the knowledge of God which shines forth more clearly in his word. He only makes mention of the heavens; but, under this part of creation, which is the noblest, and the excellency of which is more conspicuous, he doubtless includes by synecdoche the whole fabric of the world. There is certainly nothing so obscure or contemptible, even in the smallest corners of the earth, in which some marks of the power and wisdom of God may not be seen; but as a more distinct image of him is engraven on the heavens, David has particularly selected them for contemplation, that their splendour might lead us to contemplate all parts of the world. When a man, from beholding and contemplating the heavens, has been brought to acknowledge God, he will learn also to reflect upon and to admire his wisdom and power as displayed on the face of

---

which he considers more correct than *firmament*. "The latter word," says he, "is adopted from the Greek version; but the Hebrew word is derived from a verb, signifying *to spread abroad, stretch forth, extend, expand.* The proper rendering therefore is, 'expanse,' agreeably to other passages of Scripture which speak of the Creator as '*stretching out* the heavens as a curtain, and spreading them out as a tent to dwell in.' (See Ps. civ. 2; Is. xl. 22.) 'The expanse of heaven' is a frequent phrase with Milton, as with other poets."

[1] "Un jour desgorge propos à *l'autre* jour, et la nuict declare science à l'autre nuict."—*Fr.* "One day uttereth speech to *another* day, and the night declares knowledge to another night."

[2] Dr Geddes has remarked, in reference to this psalm, that "no poem ever contained a finer argument against Atheism, nor one better expressed."

the earth, not only in general, but even in the minutest plants. In the first verse, the Psalmist repeats one thing twice, according to his usual manner. He introduces the heavens as witnesses and preachers of the glory of God, attributing to the dumb creature a quality which, strictly speaking, does not belong to it, in order the more severely to upbraid men for their ingratitude, if they should pass over so clear a testimony with unheeding ears. This manner of speaking more powerfully moves and affects us than if he had said, The heavens *show* or *manifest* the glory of God. It is indeed a great thing, that in the splendour of the heavens there is presented to our view a lively image of God; but, as the living voice has a greater effect in exciting our attention, or at least teaches us more surely and with greater profit than simple beholding, to which no oral instruction is added, we ought to mark the force of the figure which the Psalmist uses when he says, that the heavens by their preaching declare the glory of God.

The repetition which he makes in the second clause is merely an explanation of the first. David shows how it is that the heavens proclaim to us the glory of God, namely, by openly bearing testimony that they have not been put together by chance, but were wonderfully created by the supreme Architect. When we behold the heavens, we cannot but be elevated, by the contemplation of them, to Him who is their great Creator; and the beautiful arrangement and wonderful variety which distinguish the courses and station of the heavenly bodies, together with the beauty and splendour which are manifest in them, cannot but furnish us with an evident proof of his providence. Scripture, indeed, makes known to us the time and manner of the creation; but the heavens themselves, although God should say nothing on the subject, proclaim loudly and distinctly enough that they have been fashioned by his hands: and this of itself abundantly suffices to bear testimony to men of his glory. As soon as we acknowledge God to be the supreme Architect, who has erected the beauteous fabric of the universe, our minds must necessarily be ravished with wonder at his infinite goodness, wisdom, and power.

2. *Day unto day uttereth speech.* Philosophers, who have more penetration into those matters than others, understand how the stars are arranged in such beautiful order, that notwithstanding their immense number there is no confusion; but to the ignorant and unlettered, the continual succession of days is a more undoubted proof of the providence of God. David, therefore, having spoken of the heavens, does not here descend from them to other parts of the world; but, from an effect more sensible and nearer our apprehension, he confirms what he has just now said, namely, that the glory of God not only shines, but also resounds in the heavens. The words may be variously expounded, but the different expositions which have been given of them make little difference as to the sense. Some explain them thus, that no day passes in which God does not show some signal evidence of his power. Others are of opinion that they denote the augmentations of instruction and knowledge,—that every succeeding day contributes something new in proof of the existence and perfections of God. Others view them as meaning that the days and nights talk together, and reason concerning the glory of their Creator; but this is a somewhat forced interpretation. David, I have no doubt, here teaches, from the established alternations of days and nights, that the course and revolutions of the sun, and moon, and stars, are regulated by the marvellous wisdom of God. Whether we translate the words *Day after day,* or *one day to another day,* is of little consequence; for all that David means is the beautiful arrangement of time which the succession of days and nights effects. If, indeed, we were as attentive as we ought to be, even one day would suffice to bear testimony to us of the glory of God, and even one night would be sufficient to perform to us the same office. But when we see the sun and the moon performing their daily revolutions,—the sun by day appearing over our heads, and the moon succeeding in its turn,—the sun ascending by degrees, while at the same time he approaches nearer us, —and afterwards bending his course so as to depart from us by little and little;—and when we see that by this means the

length of the days and nights is regulated, and that the variation of their length is arranged according to a law so uniform, as invariably to recur at the same points of time in every successive year, we have in this a much brighter testimony to the glory of God. David, therefore, with the highest reason, declares, that although God should not speak a single word to men, yet the orderly and useful succession of days and nights eloquently proclaims the glory of God, and that there is now left to men no pretext for ignorance; for, since the days and nights perform towards us so well and so carefully the office of teachers, we may acquire, if we are duly attentive, a sufficient amount of knowledge under their tuition.

3. *There is no language nor speech* [*where*] *their voice is not heard.* This verse receives two almost contrary interpretations, each of which, however, has the appearance of probability. As the words, when rendered literally, read thus—*No language, and no words, their voice is not heard*—some connect the third and fourth verses together, as if this sentence were incomplete without the clause which follows in the beginning of the fourth verse, *Their writing has gone forth through all the earth*, &c. According to them, the meaning is this :—The heavens, it is true, are mute, and are not endued with the faculty of speech; but still they proclaim the glory of God with a voice sufficiently loud and distinct. But if this was David's meaning, what need was there to repeat three times that they have not articulate speech? It would certainly be spiritless and superfluous to insist so much upon a thing so universally known. The other exposition, therefore, as it is more generally received, seems also to be more suitable. In the Hebrew tongue, which is concise, it is often necessary to supply some word; and it is particularly a common thing in that language for the relatives to be omitted, that is to say, the words *which, in which,* &c., as here, *There is no language, there is no speech,* [*where*[1]]

---

[1] Both Calvin and the translators of our English version appear to have followed the Septuagint and Vulgate versions in inserting the word *where*, which is not in the Hebrew text.

their voice is not heard.[1] Besides, the third negation, בְּלִי, *beli*,[2] rather denotes an exception to what is stated in the preceding members of the sentence, as if it had been said, The difference and variety of languages does not prevent the preaching of the heavens and their language from being heard and understood in every quarter of the world. The difference of languages is a barrier which prevents different nations from maintaining mutual intercourse, and it makes him who in his own country is distinguished for his eloquence, when he comes into a foreign country either dumb or, if he attempt to speak, barbarous. And even although a man could speak all languages, he could not speak to a Grecian and a Roman at the same time; for as soon as he began to direct his discourse to the one, the other would cease to understand him. David, therefore, by making a tacit comparison, enhances the efficacy of the testimony which the heavens bear to their Creator. The import of his language is, Different nations differ from each other as to language; but the heavens have a common language to teach all men without distinction, nor is there any thing but their own carelessness to hinder even those who are most strange to each other, and who live in the most distant parts of the world, from profiting, as it were, at the mouth of the same teacher.

4. *Their writing has gone forth, &c.* Here the inspired writer declares how the heavens preach to all nations indiscriminately, namely, because men, in all countries and in all parts of the earth, may understand that the heavens are set before their eyes as witnesses to bear testimony to the glory of God. As the Hebrew word קָו, *kav*, signifies sometimes *a line*, and some-

---

[1] "C'est asçavoir ces mots, Lequel, Laquelle, &c., comme yci Il n'y a langage, il n'y a paroles *esquelles* la voix d'iceux ne soit ouye."—*Fr.*

[2] בְּלִי, *beli*, commonly signifies *not*; but it is also often used for all sort of exclusive particles, *without, besides, unless.* Hence Grotius renders it here *without.* As בַּל, *bal*, means in Arabic *but*, and as the Arabic is just a dialect of the Hebrew, Hammond concludes that this may have been its meaning among the Jews; and therefore proposes to render the verse thus:—"Not speech, nor words, but, or notwithstanding, [בְּלִי, *beli*,] their voice is, or has been heard."

times *a building*, some deduce from it this meaning, that the fabric of the heavens being framed in a regular manner, and as it were by line, proclaims the glory of God in all parts of the world. But as David here metaphorically introduces the splendour and magnificence of the heavenly bodies, as preaching the glory of God like a teacher in a seminary of learning, it would be a meagre and unsuitable manner of speaking to say, that the line of the heavens goes forth to the uttermost ends of the earth. Besides, he immediately adds, in the following clause, that *their words* are every where heard; but what relation is there between words and the beauty of a building? If, however, we render קו, *kav, writing*, these two things will very well agree, first, that the glory of God is written and imprinted in the heavens, as in an open volume which all men may read; and, secondly, that, at the same time, they give forth a loud and distinct voice, which reaches the ears of all men, and causes itself to be heard in all places.[1] Thus we are taught, that the language of which mention has been made before is, as I may term it, a visible language, in other words, language which addresses itself to the sight; for it is to the eyes of men that the heavens speak, not to their ears; and thus David justly compares the beautiful order and arrangement, by which the heavenly bodies are distinguished, to a writing. That the Hebrew word קו, *kav*, signifies a line in writing,[2] is sufficiently evident from Isaiah xxviii. 10, where God, comparing the Jews to children who are not yet of sufficient age to make great proficiency, speaks thus: " For precept must be upon precept, precept upon precept; line upon line, line upon line; here a little, and there a little." In my judgment, therefore, the meaning is, that the glory of God is not written in small obscure letters, but richly engraven in large and bright characters, which all men may read, and read with the greatest ease.

---

[1] " Et se fait ouir en tous endroits."—*Fr.*

[2] The reading in the English Geneva Bible is, " Their line is gone forth through all the earth, and their words unto the ends of the world." The marginal note in explanation of this is, " The heavens are as a line of great capital letters to show unto us God's glory."

Hitherto I have explained the true and proper meaning of the inspired writer. Some have wrested this part of the psalm by putting upon it an allegorical interpretation; but my readers will easily perceive that this has been done without reason. I have shown in the commencement, and it is also evident from the scope of the whole discourse, that David, before coming to the law, sets before us the fabric of the world, that in it we might behold the glory of God. Now, if we understand the heavens as meaning the apostles, and the sun Christ, there will be no longer place for the division of which we have spoken; and, besides, it would be an improper arrangement to place the gospel first and then the law. It is very evident that the inspired poet here treats of the knowledge of God, which is naturally presented to all men in this world as in a mirror; and, therefore, I forbear discoursing longer on that point. As, however, these allegorical interpreters have supported their views from the words of Paul, this difficulty must be removed. Paul, in discoursing upon the calling of the Gentiles, lays down this as an established principle, that, " Whoever shall call upon the name of the Lord, shall be saved;" and then he adds, that it is impossible for any to call upon him until they know him by the teaching of the gospel. But as it seemed to the Jews to be a kind of sacrilege that Paul published the promise of salvation to the Gentiles, he asks whether the Gentiles themselves had not heard? And he answers, by quoting this passage, that there was a school open and accessible to them, in which they might learn to fear God, and serve him, inasmuch as " the writing[1] of the heavens has gone forth *through all the earth, and their words unto the ends of the world,*" (Rom. x. 18.) But Paul could not at that time have said with truth, that the voice of the gospel had been heard through the whole world from the mouth of the apostles, since it had scarcely as yet reached even a few countries. The preaching of the other apostles certainly had not then extended to far distant parts of the world, but was confined within the boundaries

---

[1] Paul reads, " their sound," quoting from the Septuagint, the version of the Old Testament then chiefly used, and it employs here the word φθόγγος.

of Judea. The design of the apostle it is not difficult to
comprehend. He intended to say that God, from ancient
times, had manifested his glory to the Gentiles, and that this
was a prelude to the more ample instruction which was one
day to be published to them. And although God's chosen
people for a time had been in a condition distinct and separate from that of the Gentiles, it ought not to be thought
strange that God at length made himself known indiscriminately to both, seeing he had hitherto united them to himself
by certain means which addressed themselves in common
to both; as Paul says in another passage, that when God,
" in times past, suffered all nations to walk in their own ways,
he nevertheless left not himself without a witness," (Acts
xiv. 16, 17.) Whence we conclude, that those who have
imagined that Paul departed from the genuine and proper
sense of David's words are grossly mistaken. The reader
will understand this still more clearly by reading my commentaries on the above passage of St Paul.

He hath set in them a tabernacle [or *pavilion*] *for the sun.*
As David, out of the whole fabric of the world, has especially
chosen the heavens, in which he might exhibit to our view
an image of God, because there it is more distinctly to be
seen, even as a man is better seen when set on an elevated
stage; so now he shows us the sun as placed in the highest
rank, because in his wonderful brightness the majesty
of God displays itself more magnificently than in all the
rest. The other planets, it is true, have also their motions,
and as it were the appointed places within which they run
their race,[1] and the firmament, by its own revolution,
draws with it all the fixed stars, but it would have been
lost time for David to have attempted to teach the secrets
of astronomy to the rude and unlearned; and therefore
he reckoned it sufficient to speak in a homely style, that he
might reprove the whole world of ingratitude, if, in beholding the sun, they are not taught the fear and the knowledge
of God. This, then, is the reason why he says that a tent
or pavilion has been erected for the sun, and also why he

---

[1] " Quasi stadia."—*Lat.* " Comme des lices ordonnees dedans les
quelles elles font leurs courses."—*Fr.*

says, that he goes forth from one end of the heaven, and quickly passes to the other and opposite end. He does not here discourse scientifically (as he might have done, had he spoken among philosophers) concerning the entire revolution which the sun performs, but, accommodating himself to the rudest and dullest, he confines himself to the ordinary appearances presented to the eye, and, for this reason, he does not speak of the other half of the sun's course, which does not appear in our hemisphere. He proposes to us three things to be considered in the sun,—the splendour and excellency of his form,—the swiftness with which he runs his course,—and the astonishing power of his heat. The more forcibly to express and magnify his surpassing beauty and, as it were, magnificent attire, he employs the similitude of a bridegroom. He then adds another similitude, that of a valiant man who enters the lists as a racer to carry off the prize of the course. The swiftness of those who in ancient times contended in the stadium, whether on chariots or on foot, was wonderful; and although it was nothing when compared with the velocity with which the sun moves in his orbit, yet David, among all that he saw coming under the ordinary notice of men, could find nothing which approached nearer to it. Some think that the third clause, where he speaks of the heat of the sun, is to be understood of his vegetative heat, as it is called; in other words, that by which the vegetating bodies which are in the earth have their vigour, support, and growth.[1] But I do not think that this sense suits the passage. It is, indeed, a wonderful work of God, and a signal evidence of his goodness, that the powerful influence of the sun penetrating the earth renders it fruitful. But as the Psalmist says, that *no man* or *nothing is hidden from his heat*, I am rather inclined to understand it of the violent heat which scorches men and other living creatures as well as plants and trees. With respect to the enlivening heat of the sun, by which we feel ourselves to be invigorated, no man desires to avoid it.

---

[1] "Aucuns l'entendent de sa chaleur vegetative, qu'on appelle, c'est à dire par laquelle ces choses basses ont vigueur, sont maintenues, et prenent accroissement."—*Fr.*

7. *The law of the Lord*[1] *is perfect, restoring the soul; the testimony of Jehovah is faithful,* [or *true,*] *instructing the babe*[2] *in wisdom.*
8. *The statutes of Jehovah are right, rejoicing the heart; the commandment of the Lord*[3] *is pure, enlightening the eyes.*
9. *The fear of Jehovah is clean, enduring for ever; the judgments of Jehovah are truth, and justified together.*

7. *The law of the Lord.* Here the second part of the psalm commences. After having shown that the creatures, although they do not speak, nevertheless serve as instructors to all mankind, and teach all men so clearly that there is a God, as to render them inexcusable, the Psalmist now turns towards the Jews, to whom God had communicated a fuller knowledge of himself by means of his word. While the heavens bear witness concerning God, their testimony does not lead men so far as that thereby they learn truly to fear him, and acquire a well-grounded knowledge of him; it serves only to render them inexcusable. It is doubtless true, that if we were not very dull and stupid, the signatures and proofs of Deity which are to be found on the theatre of the world, are abundant enough to incite us to acknowledge and reverence God; but as, although surrounded with so clear a light, we are nevertheless blind, this splendid representation of the glory of God, without the aid of the word, would profit us nothing, although it should be to us as a loud and distinct proclamation sounding in our ears. Accordingly, God vouchsafes to those whom he has determined to call to salvation special grace, just as in ancient times, while he gave to all men without exception evidences of his existence in his works, he communicated to the children of Abraham alone his Law, thereby to furnish them with a more certain and intimate knowledge of his majesty. Whence it follows, that the Jews are bound by a double tie to serve God. As the Gentiles, to whom God has spoken only by the dumb crea-

---

[1] Here our author uses Dominus, but in the Hebrew text it is יהוה, *Yehovah.*
[2] In Tyndale's Bible the reading is, "And giveth wisdom even unto babes." *Babes* is the word employed in most of the versions.
[3] In the Hebrew text it is יהוה, *Yehovah.*

tures, have no excuse for their ignorance, how much less is their stupidity to be endured who neglect to hear the voice which proceeds from his own sacred mouth? The end, therefore, which David here has in view, is to excite the Jews, whom God had bound to himself by a more sacred bond, to yield obedience to him with a more prompt and cheerful affection. Farther, under the term *law*, he not only means the rule of living righteously, or the Ten Commandments, but he also comprehends the covenant by which God had distinguished that people from the rest of the world, and the whole doctrine of Moses, the parts of which he afterwards enumerates under the terms *testimonies, statutes*, and other names. These titles and commendations by which he exalts the dignity and excellence of the Law would not agree with the Ten Commandments alone, unless there were, at the same time, joined to them a free adoption and the promises which depend upon it; and, in short, the whole body of doctrine of which true religion and godliness consists. As to the Hebrew words which are here used, I will not spend much time in endeavouring very exactly to give the particular signification of each of them, because it is easy to gather from other passages, that they are sometimes confounded or used indifferently. עֵדוּת, *eduth*, which we render *testimony*, is generally taken for the covenant, in which God, on the one hand, promised to the children of Abraham that he would be their God, and on the other required faith and obedience on their part. It, therefore, denotes the mutual covenant entered into between God and his ancient people. The word פִּקּוּדִים, *pikkudim*, which I have followed others in translating *statutes*, is restricted by some to ceremonies, but improperly in my judgment: for I find that it is every where taken generally for ordinances and edicts. The word מִצְוָה, *mitsvah*, which follows immediately after, and which we translate *commandment*, has almost the same signification. As to the other words, we shall consider them in their respective places.

The first commendation of the law of God is, that it is *perfect*. By this word David means, that if a man is duly instructed in the law of God, he wants nothing which is requisite to perfect wisdom. In the writings of heathen authors there are no doubt to be found true and useful sentences scattered here and there; and it is also true, that God has put into the minds of men some knowledge of justice and uprightness; but in consequence of the corruption of our nature, the true light of truth is not to be found among men where revelation is not enjoyed, but only certain mutilated principles which are involved in much obscurity and doubt. David, therefore, justly claims this praise for the law of God, that it contains in it perfect and absolute wisdom. As *the conversion of the soul,* of which he speaks immediately after, is doubtless to be understood of its *restoration,* I have felt no difficulty in so rendering it. There are some who reason with too much subtilty on this expression, by explaining it as referring to the repentance and regeneration of man. I admit that the soul cannot be restored by the law of God, without being at the same time renewed unto righteousness; but we must consider what is David's proper meaning, which is this, that as the soul gives vigour and strength to the body, so the law in like manner is the life of the soul. In saying that the soul is restored, he has an allusion to the miserable state in which we are all born. There, no doubt, still survive in us some small remains of the first creation; but as no part of our constitution is free from defilement and impurity, the condition of the soul thus corrupted and depraved differs little from death, and tends altogether to death. It is, therefore, necessary that God should employ the law as a remedy for restoring us to purity; not that the letter of the law can do this of itself, as shall be afterwards shown more at length, but because God employs his word as an instrument for restoring our souls.

When the Psalmist declares, *The testimony of Jehovah is faithful,* it is a repetition of the preceding sentence, so that *the integrity* or *perfection of the law,* and *the faithfulness* or *truth of his testimony,* signify the same thing; namely, that when we give ourselves up to be guided and governed by the word of God, we are in no danger of going astray, since this is the path by which he securely guides his own people to salvation. *Instruction in wisdom* seems here to be added as the commencement of the restoration of the soul. Understanding is the most excellent endowment of the soul; and David teaches us that it is to be derived from the law, for we are naturally destitute of it. By the word *babes,* he is not to be understood as meaning any particular class of persons, as if others were sufficiently wise of themselves; but by it he teaches us, in the first place, that none are endued with right understanding until they have made progress in the study of the law. In the second place, he shows by it what kind of scholars God requires, namely, those who are fools in their own estimation, (1 Cor. iii. 18,) and who come down to the rank of children, that the loftiness of their own understanding may not prevent them from giving themselves up, with a spirit of entire docility, to the teaching of the word of God.

8. *The statutes of Jehovah are right.* The Psalmist at first view may seem to utter a mere common-place sentiment when he calls the statutes of the Lord *right.* If we, however, more attentively consider the contrast which he no doubt makes between the rectitude of the law and the crooked ways in which men entangle themselves when they follow their own understandings, we will be convinced that this commendation implies more than may at first sight appear. We know how much every man is wedded to himself, and how difficult it is to eradicate from our minds the vain confidence of our own wisdom. It is therefore of great importance to be well convinced of this truth, that a man's life cannot be ordered aright unless it is framed according to the law of God, and that without this he can only wander in labyrinths and crooked bypaths. David adds, in the second place, *that God's statutes rejoice the heart.* This implies that there is no other joy true and solid but that which proceeds from a good conscience; and of this we become partakers when we are certainly persuaded that our life is pleasing and acceptable to God. No doubt, the source from which true peace of conscience proceeds is faith, which freely reconciles us to God. But to the saints who serve God with true affection of heart there arises unspeakable joy also, from the knowledge that they do not labour in his service in vain, or without hope of

recompense, since they have God as the judge and approver of their life. In short, this joy is put in opposition to all the corrupt enticements and pleasures of the world, which are a deadly bait, luring wretched souls to their everlasting destruction. The import of the Psalmist's language is, Those who take delight in committing sin procure for themselves abundant matter of sorrow; but the observance of the law of God, on the contrary, brings to man true joy. In the end of the verse, the Psalmist teaches that *the commandment of God is pure, enlightening the eyes.* By this he gives us tacitly to understand that it is only in the commandments of God that we find the difference between good and evil laid down, and that it is in vain to seek it elsewhere, since whatever men devise of themselves is mere filth and refuse, corrupting the purity of the life. He farther intimates that men, with all their acuteness, are blind, and always wander in darkness, until they turn their eyes to the light of heavenly doctrine. Whence it follows, that none are truly wise but those who take God for their conductor and guide, following the path which he points out to them, and who are diligently seeking after the peace which he offers and presents by his word.

But here a question of no small difficulty arises; for Paul seems entirely to overthrow these commendations of the law which David here recites. How can these things agree together: that the law restores the souls of men, while yet it is a dead and deadly letter? that it rejoices men's hearts, and yet, by bringing in the spirit of bondage, strikes them with terror? that it enlightens the eyes, and yet, by casting a veil before our minds, excludes the light which ought to penetrate within? But, in the first place, we must remember what I have shown you at the commencement, that David does not speak simply of the precepts of the Moral Law, but comprehends the whole covenant by which God had adopted the descendants of Abraham to be his peculiar people; and, therefore, to the Moral Law—the rule of living well—he joins the free promises of salvation, or rather Christ himself, in whom and upon whom this adoption was founded. But Paul, who had to deal with persons who perverted and abused the law, and separated it from the grace and the Spirit of Christ, refers to the ministry of Moses viewed merely by itself, and according to the letter. It is certain, that if the Spirit of Christ does not quicken the law, the law is not only unprofitable, but also deadly to its disciples. Without Christ there is in the law nothing but inexorable rigour, which adjudges all mankind to the wrath and curse of God. And farther, without Christ, there remains within us a rebelliousness of the flesh, which kindles in our hearts a hatred of God and of his law, and from this proceed the distressing bondage and awful terror of which the Apostle speaks. These different ways in which the law may be viewed, easily show us the manner of reconciling these passages of Paul and David, which seem at first view to be at variance. The design of Paul is to show what the law can do for us, taken by itself; that is to say, what it can do for us when, without the promise of grace, it strictly and rigorously exacts from us the duty which we owe to God; but David, in praising it as he here does, speaks of the whole doctrine of the law, which includes also the gospel, and, therefore, under the law he comprehends Christ.

9. *The fear of Jehovah is clean.* By the *fear of God* we are here to understand the way in which God is to be served; and therefore it is taken in an active sense for the doctrine which prescribes to us the manner in which we ought to fear God. The way in which men generally manifest their fear of God, is by inventing false religions and a vitiated worship; in doing which they only so much the more provoke his wrath. David, therefore, here indirectly condemns these corrupt inventions, about which men torment themselves in vain,[1] and which often sanction impurity; and in opposition to them he justly affirms, that in the keeping of the law there is an exemption from every thing which defiles. He adds, that *it endures for ever;* as if he had said, This is the treasure of everlasting happiness. We see how mankind, without well thinking what they are doing, pursue, with impetuous

---

[1] " Apres lesquelles les hommes se tormentent en vain."—*Fr.*

and ardent affections, the transitory things of this world; but, in thus catching at the empty shadow of a happy life, they lose true happiness itself. In the second clause, by calling the commandments of God *truth*, David shows that whatever men undertake to do at the mere suggestion of their own minds, without having a regard to the law of God as a rule, is error and falsehood. And, indeed, he could not have more effectually stirred us up to love, and zealously to live according to the law, than by giving us this warning, that all those who order their life, without having any respect to the law of God, deceive themselves, and follow after mere delusions. Those who explain the word *judgments*, as referring only to the commandments of the second table, are, in my opinion, mistaken: for David's purpose was to commend, under a variety of expressions, the advantages which the faithful receive from the law of God. When he says, *They are justified together*, the meaning is, They are all righteous from the greatest to the least, without a single exception. By this commendation he distinguishes the law of God from all the doctrines of men, for no blemish or fault can be found in it, but it is in all points absolutely perfect.

10. *More to be desired are they than gold, yea, than much fine gold; sweeter also than honey, and the droppings of honeycombs.*[1]
11. *Moreover, by them is thy servant made circumspect; and in the keeping of them there is great reward.*

10. *More to be desired are they than gold.* The Psalmist now exalts the law of God both on account of its price and sweetness. This commendation depends on the commendations given in the preceding verses; for the many and great advantages which he has just now enumerated, ought justly to make us account heavenly truth the highest and most excellent treasure, and to despise, when compared with it, all the gold and silver of the world. Instead of the word *fine gold*, which the Latins have called *Aurum obryzum*,[2]

---

[1] "Et ce qui distille des rais de miel."—*Fr.*
[2] "Lequel les Latins ont nommé *Aurum obryzum*."—*Fr.*

some render the Hebrew word *a jewel,* or *precious stones,*[1] but the other translation is more generally received, namely, *fine gold,* that is, gold which is pure and well refined in the furnace; and there are many passages of Scripture by which this rendering is confirmed.[2] The Hebrew word פָז, *paz,* is derived from פָזַה, *pazah,* which signifies *to strengthen;*[3] from which we may conjecture that the Psalmist does not mean the gold of any particular country, as if one should say the gold of Ophir, but gold completely refined and purified by art. So far is פָז, *paz,* from being derived from the name of a country, that, on the contrary, it appears from Jer. x. 9, that the land of Uphaz took its name from this Hebrew word, because it had in it mines of the finest gold. As to the origin of the word *obrizum,* which the Latins have used, we cannot say any thing with certainty, except that, according to the conjecture of Jerome, it signifies *brought from the land of Ophir,* as if it had been said, *aurum Ophrizum.* In short, the sense is, that we do not esteem the law as it deserves, if we do not prefer it to all the riches of the world. If we are once brought thus highly to prize the law, it will serve effectually to deliver our hearts from an immoderate desire of gold and silver. To this esteem of the law there must be added love to it, and delight in it, so that it may not only subdue us to obedience by constraint, but also allure us by its sweetness; a thing which is impossible, unless, at the same time, we have mortified in us the love of carnal pleasures, with which it is not wonderful to see us enticed and ensnared, so long as we reject, through a vitiated taste, the righteousness of God. From this we may again deduce another evidence, that David's discourse is not to be understood simply of the commandments, and of the dead letter, but that he comprehends, at the same time, the promises by

---

[1] The rendering of the Septuagint is, λιθον τιμιον, *precious stone;* and in Psalm cxix. 127, they translate the same Hebrew word τοπαζιον, *a topaz,* which is a precious stone. This last Greek word, according to Hesychius, is derived from the Hebrew word פז, *paz.*

[2] The word is evidently used for *fine gold* in Psalm xxi. 3, and Job xxviii. 17.

[3] Or *to consolidate:* and hence פז, *paz,* means *solid gold,* or *gold well purified:* for the more it is purified, it is the more solid, and consequently of greater weight and value.

which the grace of God is offered to us. If the law did nothing else but command us, how could it be loved, since in commanding it terrifies us, because we all fail in keeping it?[1] Certainly, if we separate the law from the hope of pardon, and from the Spirit of Christ, so far from tasting it to be sweet as honey, we will rather find in it a bitterness which kills our wretched souls.

11. *Moreover, by them is thy servant made circumspect.* These words may be extended generally to all the people of God; but they are properly to be understood of David himself, and by them he testifies that he knew well, from his own experience, all that he had stated in the preceding verses respecting the law. No man will ever speak truly and in good earnest of heavenly truth, but he who has it deeply fixed in his own heart. David therefore acknowledges, that whatever prudence he had for regulating and framing his life aright, he was indebted for it to the law of God. Although, however, it is properly of himself that he speaks, yet by his own example he sets forth a general rule, namely, that if persons wish to have a proper method for governing the life well, the law of God alone is perfectly sufficient for this purpose; but that, on the contrary, as soon as persons depart from it, they are liable to fall into numerous errors and sins. It is to be observed that David, by all at once turning his discourse to God, appeals to him as a witness of what he had said, the more effectually to convince men that he speaks sincerely and from the bottom of his heart. As the Hebrew word זהר, *zahar*, which I have translated *made circumspect*, signifies *to teach*, as well as *to be on one's guard*, some translate it in this place, *Thy servant is taught*, or *warned*, by the commandments of the law. But the sentence implies much more, when it is viewed as meaning that he who yields himself to God to be governed by him is made circumspect and cautious, and, therefore, this translation seems to me to be preferable.

In the second clause the Psalmist declares, that whoever

---

[1] " Veu qu'en commandant elle nous espouante, à cause que nous defaillons tous en l'observation d'icelle?'—*Fr.*

yield themselves to God to observe the rule of righteousness which he prescribes, do not lose their labour, seeing he has in reserve for them a great and rich reward: *In keeping of them there is great reward.* It is no mean commendation of the law when it is said, that in it God enters into covenant with us, and, so to speak, brings himself under obligation to recompense our obedience. In requiring from us whatever is contained in the law, he demands nothing but what he has a right to; yet such is his free and undeserved liberality, that he promises to his servants a reward, which, in point of justice, he does not owe them. The promises of the law, it is true, are made of no effect; but it is through our fault: for even he who is most perfect amongst us comes far short of full and complete righteousness; and men cannot expect any reward for their works until they have perfectly and to the full satisfied the requirements of the law. Thus these two doctrines completely harmonize: first, that eternal life shall be given as the reward of works to him who fulfils the law in all points; and, secondly, that the law notwithstanding denounces a curse against all men, because the whole human family are destitute of the righteousness of works. This will presently appear from the following verse. David, after having celebrated this benefit of the law—that it offers an abundant reward to those who serve God—immediately changes his discourse, and cries out, *Who can understand his errors?* by which he pronounces all men liable to eternal death, and thus utterly overthrows all the confidence which men may be disposed to place in the merit of their works. It may be objected, that this commendation, *In the keeping of thy commandments there is great reward,* is in vain ascribed to the law, seeing it is without effect. The answer is easy, namely, that as in the covenant of adoption there is included the free pardon of sins, upon which depends the imputation of righteousness, God bestows a recompense upon the works of his people, although, in point of justice, it is not due to them. What God promises in the law to those who perfectly obey it, true believers obtain by his gracious liberality and fatherly goodness, inasmuch as he accepts for perfect righteousness their holy desires and earnest endeavours to obey.

12. *Who can understand his errors?*[1] *Cleanse thou me from my secret sins.*
13. *Keep back thy servant also from presumptuous sins,*[2] *that they may not have dominion over me; then shall I be upright and clean from much wickedness.*[3]
14. *Let the words of my mouth, and the meditations of my heart, be acceptable in thy sight, O Jehovah, my strength and my redeemer.*

12. *Who can understand his errors?* This exclamation shows us what use we should make of the promises of the law, which have a condition annexed to them. It is this: As soon as they come forth, every man should examine his own life, and compare not only his actions, but also his thoughts, with that perfect rule of righteousness which is laid down in the law. Thus it will come to pass, that all, from the least to the greatest, seeing themselves cut off from all hope of reward from the law, will be constrained to flee for refuge to the mercy of God. It is not enough to consider what the doctrine of the law contains; we must also look into ourselves, that we may see how far short we have come in our obedience to the law. Whenever the Papists hear this promise, "He who doeth these things shall live in them," (Lev. xviii. 5,) they do not hesitate at once to connect eternal life with the merit of their works, as if it were in their own power to fulfil the law, of which we are all transgressors, not only in one point, but in all its parts. David, therefore, being involved as it were in a labyrinth on all sides, acknowledges with astonishment that he is over-

---

[1] "*Ses* fautes."—*Fr.* "*His* faults." "Erreurs ou ignorances."—*Fr. marg.* "Errors or ignorances."

[2] The word which our author uses denotes literally *arrogances* or *proudnesses;* and this is also the literal rendering of the Hebrew word here used. Calvin has the following note on the margin of the French version, explanatory of *arrogances,* "Pechez commis par contumace et rebellion." "That is, sins committed obstinately and rebelliously."

[3] *From much wickedness.* This translation conveys the precise meaning of what David intended. He was afraid of incurring accumulated guilt. In our English translation it is "the great transgression," on which Walford remarks, "The insertion of the definite article 'the' is not authorised by the original, and leads to a supposition which is incorrect, that some definite crime, such as 'the sin against the Holy Ghost,' is intended."

whelmed under a sense of the multitude of his sins. We ought then to remember, in the first place, that as we are personally destitute of the righteousness which the law requires, we are on that account excluded from the hope of the reward which the law has promised; and, in the next place, that we are guilty before God, not of one fault or of two, but of sins innumerable, so that we ought, with the bitterest sorrow, to bewail our depravity, which not only deprives us of the blessing of God, but also turns to us life into death. This David did. There is no doubt that when, after having said that God liberally offers a reward to all who observe his law, he cried out, *Who can understand his errors?* it was from the terror with which he was stricken in thinking upon his sins. By the Hebrew word שגיאות, *shegioth*, which we have translated *errors*, some think David intends lesser faults; but in my judgment he meant simply to say, that Satan has so many devices by which he deludes and blinds our minds, that there is not a man who knows the hundredth part of his own sins. The saints, it is true, often offend in lesser matters, through ignorance and inadvertence; but it happens also that, being entangled in the snares of Satan, they do not perceive even the grosser faults which they have committed. Accordingly, all the sins to the commission of which men give themselves loose reins, not being duly sensible of the evil which is in them, and being deceived by the allurements of the flesh, are justly included under the Hebrew word here used by David, which signifies *faults* or *ignorances*.[1] In summoning himself and others before the judgment-seat of God, he warns himself and them, that although their consciences do not condemn them, they are not on that account absolved; for God sees far more clearly than men's consciences, since even those who look most attentively into themselves, do not perceive a great part of the sins with which they are chargeable.

After making this confession, David adds a prayer for

[1] " Dont à bon droict tous les pechez ausquels les hommes se laschent la bride, pource qu'ils ne sentent pas à bon escient le mal qui y est, et sont deceus par les allechemens de la chair, sont nommez du mot Hebrieu duquel David use yci qui signifie Fautes ou Ignorances."—*Fr.*

pardon, *Cleanse thou me from my secret sins*. The word *cleanse* is to be referred not to the blessing of regeneration, but to free forgiveness; for the Hebrew verb נקה, *nakah*, here used, comes from a word which signifies *to be innocent*. The Psalmist explains more clearly what he intended by the word *errors*, in now calling them *secret sins;* that is to say, those with respect to which men deceive themselves, by thinking that they are no sins, and who thus deceive themselves not only purposely and by expressly aiming at doing so, but because they do not enter into the due consideration of the majesty of the judgment of God. It is in vain to attempt to justify ourselves under the pretext and excuse of ignorance. Nor does it avail any thing to be blind as to our faults, since no man is a competent judge in his own cause. We must, therefore, never account ourselves to be pure and innocent until we are pronounced such by God's sentence of absolution or acquittal. The faults which we do not perceive must necessarily come under the review of God's judgment, and entail upon us condemnation, unless he blot them out and pardon them; and if so, how shall he escape and remain unpunished who, besides these, is chargeable with sins of which he knows himself to be guilty, and on account of which his own conscience compels him to judge and condemn himself? Farther, we should remember that we are not guilty of one offence only, but are overwhelmed with an immense mass of impurities. The more diligently any one examines himself, the more readily will he acknowledge with David, that if God should discover our secret faults, there would be found in us an abyss of sins so great as to have neither bottom nor shore, as we say;[1] for no man can comprehend in how many ways he is guilty before God. From this also it appears, that the Papists are bewitched, and chargeable with the grossest hypocrisy, when they pretend that they can easily and speedily gather all their sins once a year into a bundle. The decree of the Lateran Council commands every one to confess all his sins once every year, and at the same time declares that there is no hope

---

[1] " Il se trouvera en nous un tel abysme de pechez, qu'il n'y aura no fond ne rive, comme on dit."—*Fr.*

of pardon but in complying with that decree. Accordingly, the blinded Papist, by going to the confessional, to mutter his sins into the ear of the priest, thinks he has done all that is required, as if he could count upon his fingers all the sins which he has committed during the course of the whole year; whereas, even the saints, by strictly examining themselves, can scarcely come to the knowledge of the hundredth part of their sins, and, therefore, with one voice unite with David in saying, *Who can understand his errors?* Nor will it do to allege that it is enough if each performs the duty of reckoning up his sins to the utmost of his ability. This does not diminish, in any degree, the absurdity of this famous decree.[1] As it is impossible for us to do what the law requires, all whose hearts are really and deeply imbued with the principle of the fear of God must necessarily be overwhelmed with despair, so long as they think themselves bound to enumerate all their sins, in order to their being pardoned; and those who imagine they can disburden themselves of their sins in this way must be persons altogether stupid. I know that some explain these words in a different sense, viewing them as a prayer, in which David beseeches God, by the guidance of his Holy Spirit, to recover him from all his errors. But, in my opinion, they are to be viewed rather as a prayer for forgiveness, and what follows in the next verse is a prayer for the aid of the Holy Spirit, and for success to overcome temptations.

13. *Keep back thy servant also from presumptuous sins.* By *presumptuous sins* he means known and evident transgressions,[2] accompanied with proud contempt and obstinacy. By the word *keep back*, he intimates, that such is the natural propensity of the flesh to sin, that even the saints themselves would immediately break forth or rush headlong into it, did not God, by his own guardianship and protection, keep them back. It is to be observed, that while he calls himself *the servant of God*, he nevertheless acknowledges that he had

---

[1] "Cela ne diminue en rien l'absurdité de ce beau decret."—*Fr.*
[2] That is, known and evident to the person committing them. He sins against knowledge.

need of the bridle, lest he should arrogantly and rebelliously break forth in transgressing the law of God. Being regenerated by the Spirit of God, he groaned, it is true, under the burden of his sins; but he knew, on the other hand, how great is the rebellion of the flesh, and how much we are inclined to forgetfulness of God, from which proceed contempt of his majesty and all impiety. Now, if David, who had made so much progress in the fear of God, was not beyond the danger of transgressing, how shall the carnal and unrenewed man, in whom innumerable lusts exercise dominion, be able to restrain and govern himself by his own free will? Let us learn, then, even although the unruliness of our wayward flesh has been already subdued by the denial of ourselves, to walk in fear and trembling; for unless God restrain us, our hearts will violently boil with a proud and insolent contempt of God. This sense is confirmed by the reason added immediately after, *that they may not have dominion over me.* By these words he expressly declares, that unless God assist him, he will not only be unable to resist, but will be wholly brought under the dominion of the worst vices. This passage, therefore, teaches us not only that all mankind are naturally enslaved to sin, but that the faithful themselves would become the bond-slaves of sin also, if God did not unceasingly watch over them to guide them in the path of holiness, and to strengthen them for persevering in it. There is also another useful lesson which we have here to attend to, namely, that we ought never to pray for pardon, without, at the same time, asking to be strengthened and fortified by the power of God for the time to come, that temptations, in future, may not gain advantage over us. And although we may feel in our hearts the incitements of concupiscence goading and distressing us, we ought not, on that account, to become discouraged. The remedy to which we should have recourse is to pray to God to restrain us. No doubt, David could have wished to feel in his heart no stirrings of corruption; but knowing that he would never be wholly free from the remains of sin, until at death he had put off this corrupt nature, he prays to be armed with the grace of the Holy Spirit for the combat, that iniquity might not reign victorious over him. In the end of the verse there are two things to be observed. David, in affirming that *he shall then be upright and clean from much wickedness,* attributes, in the first place, the honour of preserving him innocent to the spiritual assistance of God; and depending upon it, he confidently assures himself of victory over all the armies of Satan. In the second place, he acknowledges, that unless he is assisted by God, he will be overwhelmed with an immense load, and plunged as it were into a boundless abyss of wickedness: for he says, that aided by God, he will be clear not of one fault or of two, but of many. From this it follows, that as soon as we are abandoned by the grace of God, there is no kind of sin in which Satan may not entangle us. Let this confession of David then quicken us to earnestness in prayer; for in the midst of so many and various snares, it does not become us to fall asleep or to be indolent. Again, let the other part of the Psalmist's exercise predominate in our hearts—let us boast with him, that although Satan may assault us by many and strong armies, we will nevertheless be invincible, provided we have the aid of God, and will continue, in despite of every hostile attempt, to hold fast our integrity.

14. *Let the words of my mouth, and the meditation of my heart.* David asks still more expressly to be fortified by the grace of God, and thus enabled to live an upright and holy life. The substance of the verse is this: I beseech thee, O God, not only to keep me from breaking forth into the external acts of transgression, but also to frame my tongue and my heart to the obedience of thy law. We know how difficult it is, even for the most perfect, so to bridle their words and thoughts, as that nothing may pass through their heart or mouth which is contrary to the will of God; and yet this inward purity is what the law chiefly requires of us. Now, the rarer this virtue—the rarer this strict control of the heart and of the tongue is, let us learn so much the more the necessity of our being governed by the Holy Spirit, in order to regulate our life uprightly and honestly. By the word *acceptable,* the Psalmist shows that the only rule of

living well is for men to endeavour to please God, and to be approved of him. The concluding words, in which he calls God *his strength and his redeemer,* he employs to confirm himself in the assured confidence of obtaining his requests.

PSALM XX.

This psalm contains a common prayer of the Church in behalf of the King of Israel, that God would succour him in danger; and in behalf of his kingdom, that God would maintain it in safety, and cause it to prosper : for in the person of David the safety and well-being of the whole community centred. To this there is added a promise, that God will preside over that kingdom of which he was the founder, and so effectually watch over it as to secure its continual preservation.

¶ To the chief musician. A Psalm of David.

1. *May Jehovah hear thee in the day of trouble! may the name of the God of Jacob defend thee!*
2. *May he send thee help from his sanctuary, and sustain thee out of Sion!*

THE inscription shows that the psalm was composed by David; but though he was its author, there is no absurdity in his speaking of himself in the person of others. The office of a prophet having been committed to him, he with great propriety prepared this as a form of prayer for the use of the faithful. In doing this, his object was not so much to commend his own person, by authoritatively issuing a royal ordinance enjoining upon the people the use of this prayer, as to show, in the exercise of his office as a teacher, that it belonged to the whole Church to concern itself, and to use its endeavours that the kingdom which God had erected might continue safe and prosperous. Many interpreters view this prayer as offered up only on one particular occasion; but in this I cannot agree. The occasion of its composition at first may have arisen from some particular battle which was about to be fought, either against the Ammonites, or against some other enemies of Israel. But the design of the Holy Spirit, in my judgment, was to deliver to the Church a common form of prayer, which, as we may gather from the words, was to be used whenever she was threatened with any danger. God commands his people, in general, to pray for kings, but there was a special reason, and one which did not apply to any other kingdom, why prayer was to be made in behalf of this kingdom; for it was only by the hand of David and his seed that God had determined to govern and maintain his people. It is particularly to be noticed, that under the figure of this temporal kingdom, there was described a government far more excellent, on which the whole joy and felicity of the Church depended. The object, therefore, which David had expressly in view was, to exhort all the children of God to cherish such a holy solicitude about the kingdom of Christ, as would stir them up to continual prayer in its behalf.

1. *May Jehovah hear thee, &c.* The Holy Spirit, by introducing the people as praying that God would answer the prayers of the king, is to be viewed as at the same time admonishing kings that it is their duty to implore the protection of God in all their affairs. When he says, *In the day of trouble*, he shows that they will not be exempted from troubles, and he does this that they may not become discouraged, if at any time they should happen to be in circumstances of danger. In short, the faithful, that the body may not be separated from the head, further the king's prayers by their common and united supplications. *The name of God* is here put for *God himself*, and not without good reason; for the essence of God being incomprehensible to us, it behoves us to trust in him, in so far as his grace and power are made known to us. From his name, therefore, proceeds confidence in calling upon him. The faithful desire that the king may be protected and aided by God, whose name was called upon among *the sons of Jacob*. I cannot agree with those who think that mention is here made of that patriarch, because God exercised him with various afflictions, not unlike those with which he tried his servant David. I am rather of

opinion that, as is usual in Scripture, the chosen people are denoted by the term *Jacob*. And from this name, *the God of Jacob,* the faithful encourage themselves to pray for the defence of their king; because it was one of the privileges of their adoption to live under the conduct and protection of a king set over them by God himself. Hence we may conclude, as I have said before, that under the figure of a temporal kingdom there is described to us a government much more excellent.[1] Since Christ our King, being an everlasting priest, never ceases to make intercession with God, the whole body of the Church should unite in prayer with him;[2] and farther, we can have no hope of being heard except he go before us, and conduct us to God.[3] And it serves in no small degree to assuage our sorrows to consider that Jesus Christ, when we are afflicted, accounts our distresses his own, provided we, at the same time, take courage, and continue resolute and magnanimous in tribulation; which we should be prepared to do, since the Holy Spirit here forewarns us that the kingdom of Christ would be subject to dangers and troubles.

2. *May he send thee help.* That is to say, may he succour thee out of mount Sion, where he commanded the ark of the covenant to be placed, and chose for himself a dwelling-place. The weakness of the flesh will not suffer men to soar up to heaven, and, therefore, God comes down to meet them, and by the external means of grace shows that he is near them. Thus the ark of the covenant was to his ancient people a pledge of his presence, and the sanctuary an image of heaven. But as God, by appointing mount Sion to be the place where the faithful should continually worship him, had joined the kingdom and priesthood together, David, in put-

---

[1] " Et de là il nous convient recueillir ce que j'ay dit, que sous la figure d'un regne temporel nous est descrit un gouvernement bien plus excellent."—*Fr.*

[2] As the people of Israel here unite in prayer with and for the monarch of Israel, whom we may picture to our minds as repairing to the tabernacle to offer sacrifices, where this animated ode was sung by the priests and people.

[3] " Si non qu'il marche devant, et nous conduise à Dieu."—*Fr.*

ting into the lips of the people a prayer for help out of Sion, doubtless had an eye to this sacred bond of union. Hence I conjecture that this psalm was composed by David in his old age, and about the close of his life. Some think he spake of Sion by the Spirit of prophecy before it had been appointed that the ark should be placed there; but this opinion seems strained, and to have little probability.

3. *May he remember all thy offerings; and make thy holocaust* [or *burnt-sacrifice*] *fat !*[1] *Selah.*
4. *May he grant thee according to thy heart, and fulfil all thy counsel !*
5. *That we may rejoice in thy salvation,* [or *safety :*] *and set up a banner in the name of our God, when Jehovah shall fulfil all thy petitions.*

3. *May he remember.* I understand the word *remember* as meaning *to have regard to,* as it is to be understood in many other places; just as *to forget* often signifies *to neglect,* or *not to deign to regard, nor even to behold,* the object to which it is applied. It is, in short, a prayer that God would actually show that the king's sacrifices were acceptable to him. Two kinds of them are here mentioned; first, the מנחה, *mincha,* mentioned in the first clause of the verse, which was the appointed accompaniment of all sacrifices, and which was also sometimes offered by itself; and, secondly, the holocaust, or whole burnt-sacrifice. But under these two kinds David intended to comprehend, by synecdoche, all sacrifices; and under sacrifices he comprehends requests and prayers. We know that whenever the fathers prayed under the law, their hope of obtaining what they asked was founded upon their sacrifices; and, in like manner, at this day our prayers are acceptable to God only in so far as Christ sprinkles and sanctifies them with the perfume of his own sacrifice. The faithful, therefore, here desire that the solemn prayers of the king, which were accompanied with sacrifices and oblations, might

---

[1] That is, May he accept it! The best and fattest of the flocks and herds were, according to the Mosaic injunction, to be offered to God, and were consequently the sacrifices he most approved of.

have their effect in the prosperous issue of his affairs. That this is the meaning may be gathered still more clearly from the following verse, in which they commend to God the desires and counsels of the king. But as it would be absurd to ask God to grant foolish and wicked desires, it is to be regarded as certain, that there is here described a king who was neither given to ambition, nor inflamed with avarice, nor actuated by the desire of whatever the unruly passions might suggest, but wholly intent on the charge which was committed to him, and entirely devoted to the advancement of the public good; so that he asks nothing but what the Holy Spirit dictated to him, and what God, by his own mouth, commanded him to ask.

5. *That we may rejoice in thy salvation.* This verse may be explained in two other ways, besides the sense it bears according to the translation which I have given. Some consider it to be a prayer, as if it had been said, Lord, make us to rejoice. Others think that the faithful, after having finished their prayer, encourage themselves to entertain good hope;[1] or rather, being already inspired with an assured hope of success, they begin to sing, so to speak, of the victory, even as it is usual with David to intermingle such kind of rejoicings with his prayers, thereby to stir up himself to continue with the more alacrity in prayer. But upon considering the whole more carefully, my opinion is, that what is meant to be expressed is the effect or fruit which would result from the bestowment of the grace and favour of God, for which the people prayed; and, therefore, I have thought it necessary to supply the particle *that*, in the beginning of the verse. The faithful, as an argument to obtain the favour of God towards their king, set forth the joy which they would all experience in common, in seeing it exercised towards him, and the thanksgiving which they would with one accord render for it. The import of their language is, It is not for the preservation and welfare of one man that we are solicitous; it is for the safety and well-being of the whole Church. The expression, *In thy salvation*, may be referred to God as well

---

[1] Reading, " We will rejoice in thy salvation, and in the name of our God will we set up our banners."

as to the king; for the salvation which God bestows is often called *the salvation of God;* but the context requires that it should be rather understood of the king. The people lived "under the shadow of the king," to use the words of Jeremiah, (Lam. iv. 20;) and, therefore, the faithful now testify, that as long as he is safe and in prosperity, they will all be joyful and happy. At the same time, to distinguish their joy from the heathen dancings and rejoicings, they declare that they will set up their banners in the name of God; for the Hebrew word דגל, *dagal,* here used, means *to set* or *lift up a banner.* The meaning is, that the faithful, in grateful acknowledgment of the grace of God, will celebrate his praises and triumph in his name.

6. *Now I know that Jehovah hath saved his anointed; he will hear him from the heavens of his sanctuary, in the mightiness of the salvation of his right hand.*[1]
7. *Some trust*[2] *in chariots, and some in horses; but we will remember the name of Jehovah our God.*
8. *They are bowed down and are fallen; but we are risen and are erect.*
9. *Save, O Jehovah! let the king hear us in the day that we call upon him.*

6. *Now I know.* Here there follows grateful rejoicing, in which the faithful declare that they have experienced the goodness of God in the preservation of the king. To this there is at the same time added a doctrine of faith, namely,

---

[1] "Ou éspuissances le salut de sa dextre."—*Fr. marg.* "In mightiness the salvation of his right hand." The rendering which Horsley gives is this: "In powers [or in strengths] salvation of his right hand;" and he views this clause as a complete sentence by itself. He explains it thus :—" In all situations of power and strength, whatever a man's natural means of deliverance may be, his preservation must be the work of God's right hand." "This seems," says he, "to be the best exposition of this line, which is a clause by itself, not a part of the preceding sentence; ישע is a noun substantive, the subject of the verb substantive understood. The chariots and horses mentioned in the next verse are exposive of גברת in this line, and all that follows of this psalm is an amplification of this general sentiment."
[2] In the Hebrew text there is here an ellipsis, the reading being, "Some in chariots, and some in horses," &c. All the ancient versions read the words as they are in the Hebrew text, without supplying any verb. Calvin does the same in his Latin version; but in the French he supplies the verb "Se foyent," "trust," the same supplement as that which is made in our English version.

that God showed by the effect that he put forth his power in maintaining the kingdom of David, because it was founded upon his calling. The meaning is, It appears from certain experience, that God is the guardian of the kingdom which he himself set up, and of which he is the founder. For David is called Messiah, or *anointed,* that the faithful might be persuaded that he was a lawful and sacred king, whom God had testified, by outward anointing, to be chosen by himself. Thus, then, the faithful ascribe to the grace of God the deliverance which had been wrought for David from the greatest dangers, and at the same time, particularly mention the cause of this to be, that God had determined to protect and defend him who, by his commandment, had been anointed king over his people. They confirm still more clearly their hope, with respect to the future, in the following clause : *God will hear him out of heaven.* I do not translate the verb which is here used into the past tense, but retain the future : for I have no doubt, that from the experience which God had already given them of his goodness, they concluded that it would be hereafter exercised in the continual preservation of the kingdom. Here the Psalmist makes mention of another *sanctuary,*[1] namely, a heavenly. As God then graciously vouchsafed to descend among the Israelites, by the ark of the covenant, in order to make himself more familiarly known to them; so, on the other hand, he intended to draw the minds of his people upwards to himself, and thereby to prevent them from forming carnal and earthly conceptions of his character, and to teach them that he was greater than the whole world. Thus, under the visible sanctuary, which was made with hands, there is set forth the fatherly goodness of God, and his familiarity with his people ; while, under the heavenly sanctuary, there is shown his infinite power, dominion, and majesty. The words, *In the mightiness of the salvation,* mean *his mighty salvation,* or *his saving power.* Thus, in the very expression there is a transposing of the words. The sense comes to this : May God by his wonderful power, preserve the king who was anointed

---

[1] Different from " the sanctuary" mentioned in verse second.

by his commandment! The Holy Spirit, who dictated this prayer, saw well that Satan would not suffer David to live in peace, but would put forth all his efforts to oppose him, which would render it necessary for him to be sustained by more than human power. I do not, however, disapprove of the other exposition which I have marked on the margin, according to which the faithful, for their greater encouragement, set before themselves this truth, that the salvation of God's right hand is in mightiness; in other words, is sufficiently strong to overcome all impediments.

7. *Some trust in chariots.* I do not restrict this to the enemies of Israel, as is done by other interpreters. I am rather inclined to think that there is here a comparison between the people of God and all the rest of the world. We see how natural it is to almost all men to be the more courageous and confident the more they possess of riches, power, and military forces. The people of God, therefore, here protest that they do not place their hope, as is the usual way with men, in their military forces and warlike apparatus, but only in the aid of God. As the Holy Spirit here sets the assistance of God in opposition to human strength, it ought to be particularly noticed, that whenever our minds come to be occupied by carnal confidence, they fall at the same time into a forgetfulness of God. It is impossible for him, who promises himself victory by confiding in his own strength, to have his eyes turned towards God. The inspired writer, therefore, uses the word *remember*, to show, that when the saints betake themselves to God, they must cast off every thing which would hinder them from placing an exclusive trust in him. This remembrance of God serves two important purposes to the faithful. In the first place, however much power and resources they may possess, it nevertheless withdraws them from all vain confidence, so that they do not expect any success except from the pure grace of God. In the second place, if they are bereft and utterly destitute of all succour, it notwithstanding so strengthens and encourages them, that they call upon God both with confidence and constancy. On the other hand, when un-

godly men feel themselves strong and powerful, being blinded with pride, they do not hesitate boldly to despise God; but when they are brought into circumstances of distress, they are so terrified as not to know what to become. In short, the Holy Spirit here recommends to us the remembrance of God, which, retaining its efficacy both in the want and in the abundance of power, subdues the vain hopes with which the flesh is wont to be inflated. As the verb נזכיר, *nazkir*, which I have translated *we will remember*, is in the conjugation *hiphil*, some render it transitively, *we shall cause to remember*. But it is no new thing in Hebrew for verbs to be used as neuter which are properly transitive; and, therefore, I have adopted the exposition which seems to me the most suitable to this passage.

8. *They are bowed down.* It is probable that there is here pointed out, as it were with the finger, the enemies of Israel, whom God had overthrown, when they regarded no event as less likely to happen. There is contained in the words a tacit contrast between the cruel pride with which they had been lifted up for a time when they audaciously rushed forward to make havoc of all things on the one hand, and the oppression of the people of God on the other. The expression, *to rise*, is applied only to those who were before sunk or fallen; and, on the other hand, the expression, *bowed down and fallen*, is with propriety applied to those who were lifted up with pride and presumption. The prophet therefore teaches by the event, how much more advantageous it is for us to place all our confidence in God than to depend upon our own strength.

9. *Save, O Jehovah! &c.* Some read in one sentence, *O Jehovah! save the king;*[1] perhaps because they think it wrong to attribute to an earthly king what is proper to God only,—to be called upon, and to hear prayer. But if we turn our eyes towards Christ, as it becomes us to do, we

---

[1] This is the reading of the Septuagint. Its words are, Κυριε σωσον τον βασιλεα. The reading of the Vulgate is the same. Calvin's rendering, which is also that of our English version, agrees with the masoretical punctuation; but the Septuagint has followed a different pointing.

will no longer wonder that what properly belongs to him is attributed in a certain sense to David and his successors, in so far as they were types of Christ. As God governs and saves us by the hand of Christ, we must not look for salvation from any other quarter. In like manner, the faithful under the former economy were accustomed to betake themselves to their king as the minister of God's saving grace. Hence these words of Jeremiah, (Lam. iv. 20,) " The breath of our nostrils, the anointed of the Lord, of whom we said, Under his shadow we shall live among the heathen." Whenever, therefore, God promises the restoration of his church, he sets forth a symbol or pledge of its salvation in the kingdom. We now see that it is not without very good reason that the faithful are introduced asking succour from their king, under whose guardianship and protection they were placed, and who, as the vicegerent of God, presided over them; as the Prophet Micah says, (chap. ii. 13,) " Their king shall pass before them, and the Lord on the head of them;" by which words he intimates, that their king will be as it were a mirror in which they may see reflected the image of God. To return to the present passage:—The expression, *Save, O Jehovah,* is elliptical, but it has greater emphasis than if the object for which salvation is sought had been mentioned; for by this means David shows that this salvation belongs in common to the whole body of the church. In Psalm cxviii. 25, there is a prayer in the same words, and it is certain that it is the very same prayer. In short, this is a prayer, that God, by blessing the king, would show himself the Saviour of the whole people. In the last clause of the verse there is expressed the means of this salvation. The people pray that the king may be furnished with power from God to deliver them whenever they are in distress, and cry to him for help : *Let the king hear us in the day that we call upon him.* God had not promised that his people would be saved in any other way than by the hand and conduct of the king whom he had given them. In the present day, when Christ is now manifested to us, let us learn to yield him this honour—to renounce all hope of salvation from any other quarter, and to trust to that salvation only which he shall bring to us from God his Father. And of this we shall then only become partakers when, being all gathered together into one body, under the same Head, we shall have mutual care one of another, and when none of us will have his attention so engrossed with his own advantage and individual interest, as to be indifferent to the welfare and happiness of others.

PSALM XXI.

This psalm contains a public and solemn thanksgiving for the prosperous and happy condition of the king. Its subject is almost the same with that of the preceding.[1] In the former there was set forth a common form of prayer, which was designed to excite in the whole people earnest concern for the preservation of their head. In this it is shown that the safety and prosperity of the king ought to produce public and general rejoicing through the whole realm, inasmuch as God by this means intended to preserve the whole body in safety. But, above all, it was the design of the Holy Spirit here to direct the minds of the faithful to Christ, who was the end and perfection of this kingdom, and to teach them that they could not be saved except under the head which God himself had appointed over them.

¶ To the chief musician. A psalm of David.

1. *The king will rejoice in thy strength, O Jehovah! and in thy salvation how greatly will he rejoice!*
2. *Thou hast given him the desire of his heart, and hast not denied him the request of his lips. Selah.*
3. *For thou wilt prevent him with blessings of good, thou wilt set a crown of gold upon his head.*[2]

1. *The king will rejoice in thy strength, O Jehovah!* David could have given thanks to God in private for the victories and

---

[1] " What was anticipated in the preceding psalm, the present poem appears to celebrate as having been achieved."—*Drake's Harp of Judah.*
[2] The Hebrew word is פז, *paz,* denoting fine gold, the purest gold, the same word which is used in Psalm xix. 10.

other signal favours which he had received from him; but it was his intention to testify not only that it was God who elevated him to the throne, but also that whatever blessings God had conferred upon him redounded to the public good, and the advantage of all the faithful. In the beginning of the psalm the believing Israelites express their firm persuasion that God, who had created David to be king, had undertaken to defend and maintain him. It therefore appears that this psalm, as well as the preceding, was composed for the purpose of assuring the faithful that the goodness of God in this respect towards David would be of long duration, and permanent; and it was necessary, in order to their being established in a well-grounded confidence of their safety, to hope well of their king, whose countenance was as it were a mirror of the merciful and reconciled countenance of God. The sense of the words is: Lord, in putting forth thy power to sustain and protect the king, thou wilt preserve him safe; and, ascribing his safety to thy power, he will greatly rejoice in thee. The Psalmist has doubtless put *strength* and *salvation* for *strong and powerful succour*, intimating, that the power of God in defending the king would be such as would preserve and protect him against all dangers.

In the second verse there is pointed out the cause of this joy. The cause was this: that God had heard the prayers of the king, and had liberally granted him whatever he desired. It was important to be known, and that the faithful should have it deeply impressed on their minds, that all David's successes were so many benefits conferred upon him by God, and at the same time testimonies of his lawful calling. And David, there is no doubt, in speaking thus, testifies that he did not give loose reins to the desires of the flesh, and follow the mere impulse of his appetites like worldly men, who set their minds at one time upon this thing, and at another time upon that, without any consideration, and just as they are led by their sensual lusts; but that he had so bridled his affections as to desire nothing save what was good and lawful. According to the infirmity which is natural to men, he was, it is true, chargeable with some vices, and even fell shamefully on two occasions; but the habitual administration of his kingdom was such that it was easy to see that the Holy Spirit presided over it. But as by the Spirit of prophecy the Psalmist had principally an eye to Christ, who does not reign for his own advantage, but for ours, and whose desire is directed only to our salvation, we may gather hence the very profitable doctrine, that we need entertain no apprehension that God will reject our prayers in behalf of the church, since our heavenly King has gone before us in making intercession for her, so that in praying for her we are only endeavouring to follow his example.

3. *For thou wilt prevent him.* The change of the tense in the verbs does not break the connection of the discourse; and, therefore, I have, without hesitation, translated this sentence into the future tense, as we know that the changing of one tense into another is quite common in Hebrew. Those who limit this psalm to the last victory which David gained over foreign nations, and who suppose that the crown of which mention is here made was the crown of the king of the Ammonites, of which we have an account in sacred history, give, in my judgment, too low a view of what the Holy Spirit has here dictated concerning the perpetual prosperity of this kingdom. David, I have no doubt, comprehended his successors even to Christ, and intended to celebrate the continual course of the grace of God in maintaining his kingdom through successive ages. It was not of one man that it had been said, " I will be his father, and he shall be my son," (2 Sam. vii. 14;) but this was a prophecy which ought to be extended from Solomon to Christ, as is fully established by the testimony of Isaiah, (chap. ix. 6,) who informs us that it was fulfilled when the Son was given or manifested. When it is said, *Thou wilt prevent him,* the meaning is, that such will be the liberality and promptitude of God, in spontaneously bestowing blessings, that he will not only grant what is asked from him, but, anticipating the requests of the king, will load him with every kind of good things far beyond what he had ever expected. By *blessings* we are to understand abundance or plenteousness. Some translate the Hebrew word טוב, *tob, goodness;*[1] but with this I

[1] Reading " blessings of goodness ;" that is, the best or most excellent blessings.

cannot agree. It is to be taken rather for *the beneficence* or *the free gifts of God.* Thus the meaning will be, The king shall want nothing which is requisite to make his life in every respect happy, since God of his own good pleasure will anticipate his wishes, and enrich him with an abundance of all good things. The Psalmist makes express mention of *the crown*, because it was the emblem and ensign of royalty; and he intimates by this that God would be the guardian of the king, whom he himself had created. But as the prophet testifies, that the royal diadem, after lying long dishonoured in the dust, shall again be put upon the head of Christ, we come to the conclusion, that by this song the minds of the godly were elevated to the hope of the eternal kingdom, of which a shadow only, or an obscure image, was set forth in the person of the successors of David. The doctrine of the everlasting duration of the kingdom of Christ is, therefore, here established, seeing he was not placed upon the throne by the favour or suffrages of men, but by God, who, from heaven, set the royal crown upon his head with his own hand.

4. *He asked life from thee, and thou hast given him length of days for ever and ever.*
5. *His glory is great in thy salvation: thou hast put upon him splendour and beauty.*[1]
6. *For thou hast set him to be blessings for ever: thou hast gladdened him with joy before thy countenance,* [or, *in thy presence.*]

4. *He asked life from thee.* This verse confirms what I have formerly said, that this psalm is not to be limited to the person of any one man. David's life, it is true, was prolonged to an advanced period, so that, when he departed from this world, he was an old man, and full of days; but the course of his life was too short to be compared to this *length of days*, which is said to consist of many ages. Even

---

[1] *Splendour and beauty.* " Parkhurst observes, that the two words thus translated are often joined in Scripture. The former seems to denote the *splendour* or *glory* itself; the latter the *ornament, beauty,* or *majesty,* resulting from that glory."—*Bishop Mant.*

if we reckon the time from the commencement of David's reign to the captivity of Babylon, this length of days will not be made up and completed in all David's successors. David, therefore, without doubt, comprehends the Eternal King. There is here a tacit comparison between the beginnings of this kingdom, which were obscure and contemptible, or rather which were fraught with the most grievous perils, and which bordered on despair; and the incredible glory which followed, when God, exempting it from the common lot of other kingdoms, elevated it almost above the heavens. For it is no ordinary commendation of this kingdom, when it is said, that it shall endure as long as the sun and moon shall shine in the heavens, (Ps. lxxii.) David, therefore, in saying that *he asked life,* tacitly points to the distressed circumstances to which he had often been reduced; and the meaning is, Lord, since the time thou hast called thy servant to the hope of the kingdom by thy holy anointing, his condition has been such that he has accounted it a singular blessing to be rescued from the jaws of death; but now, he has not only, by thy grace, escaped in safety the dangers which threatened his life: thou hast also promised that his kingdom will be continued for many ages in his successors. And it serves not a little to magnify the grace of God, that he vouchsafed to confer on a poor and miserable man, who was almost at the point of death, not only his life,— when, amidst the dangers which threatened it, he tremblingly asked merely its preservation,—but also the inestimable honour of elevating him to the royal dignity, and of transmitting the kingdom to his posterity for ever. Some expound the verse thus:—Thou hast given him the life which he asked, even to the prolonging of his days for ever and ever. But this seems to me a cold and strained interpretation. We must keep in view the contrast which, as I have said, is here made between the weak and contemptible beginnings of the kingdom, and the unexpected honour which God conferred upon his servant, in calling the moon to witness that his seed should never fail. The same has been exemplified in Christ, who, from contempt, ignominy, death, the grave, and despair, was raised up by his Father to the sovereignty of heaven, to sit at the Father's right hand for ever, and at length to be the judge of the world.

5. *His glory is great.* By these words the people intimate that their king, through the protection which God afforded him, and the deliverances which he wrought for him, would become more renowned than if he had reigned in peace with the applause of all men, or had been defended by human wealth and human strength, or, finally, had continued invincible by his own power and policy; for thereby it appeared the more clearly that he had only attained to the royal dignity by the favour, conduct, and commandment of God. The believing Israelites, therefore, leave it to heathen kings to ennoble themselves by their own achievements, and to acquire fame by their own valour; and they set more value upon this, that God graciously showed himself favourable towards their king,[1] than upon all the triumphs of the world. At the same time, they promise themselves such assistance from God as will suffice for adorning the king with majesty and honour.

6. *For thou hast set him to be blessings for ever.* Some explain these words simply thus, That God had chosen David to be king, in order to pour upon him his blessings in rich abundance. But it is evident that something more is intended by this manner of speaking. It implies, that the king had such an exuberant abundance of all good things, that he might justly be regarded as a pattern of the greatness of the divine beneficence; or that, in praying, his name would be generally used to serve as an example of how the suppliant wished to be dealt with. The Jews were accustomed to speak of those being set to be a curse, who were rendered so detestable, and on whom the dreadful vengeance of God had been inflicted with such severity, that their very names served for cursing and direful imprecations. On the other hand, they were accustomed to speak of those being set to be a blessing, whose names we propose in our prayers as an

---

[1] " Que la grace de Dieu se monstre favorable envers leur Roy."—*Fr.*

example of how we desire to be blessed; as if a man for instance should say, May God graciously bestow upon thee the same favour which he vouchsafed to his servant David! I do not reject this interpretation, but I am satisfied with the other, which views the words as implying that the king, abounding in all kind of good things, was an illustrious pattern of the liberality of God. We must carefully mark what is said immediately after concerning joy: *Thou hast gladdened him with joy before thy countenance.*[1] The people not only mean that God did good to the king, seeing he looked upon him with a benignant and fatherly eye, but they also point out the proper cause of this joy, telling us that it proceeded from the knowledge which the king had of his being the object of the Divine favour. It would not be enough for God to take care of us, and to provide for our necessities, unless, on the other hand, he irradiated us with the light of his gracious and reconciled countenance, and made us to taste of his goodness, as we have seen in the 4th Psalm, "There be many that say, Who will show us any good? Lord, lift thou up the light of thy countenance upon us, and we shall be saved." And without all doubt, it is true and solid happiness to experience that God is so favourable to us that we dwell as it were in his presence.

7. *For the king trusteth in Jehovah, and through the goodness of the Most High, he shall not be moved.*
8. *Thy hand shall find out all thy enemies, thy right hand shall find out those that hate thee.*
9. *Thou shalt put them as it were into a furnace of fire, in the time of thy anger; Jehovah*[2] *in his wrath shall overwhelm them, and the fire shall consume them.*
10. *Thou wilt destroy their fruit from the earth, and their seed from among the children of men.*

7. *For the king trusteth.* Here again the pious Israelites glory that their king shall be established, because he relies

---

[1] Walford reads this clause—"Thou hast made him glad with the joy of thy presence."
[2] This is rendered according to the pointing in the French version. According to the pointing in the Latin version, *Jehovah* is joined to the preceding clause thus:—" In the time of thy anger, O Jehovah!"

upon God; and they express at the same time how he relies upon him, namely, by hope or trust. I read the whole verse as one sentence, so that there is but one principal verb, and explain it thus :—The king, as he places by faith his dependence on God and his goodness, will not be subject to the disasters which overthrow the kingdoms of this world. Moreover, as we have said before, that whatever blessings the faithful attribute to their king, belong to the whole body of the Church, there is here made a promise, common to all the people of God, which may serve to keep us tranquil amidst the various storms which agitate the world. The world turns round as it were upon a wheel, by which it comes to pass, that those who were raised to the very top are precipitated to the bottom in a moment; but it is here promised, that the kingdom of Judah, and the kingdom of Christ of which it was a type, will be exempted from such vicissitude. Let us remember, that those only have the firmness and stability here promised, who betake themselves to the bosom of God by an assured faith, and relying upon his mercy, commit themselves to his protection. The cause or the ground of this hope or trust is at the same time expressed, and it is this,—that God mercifully cherishes his own people, whom he has once graciously received into his favour.

8. *Thy hand shall find.* Hitherto the internal happiness of the kingdom has been described. Now there follows, as it was necessary there should, the celebration of its invincible strength against its enemies. What is said in this verse is of the same import as if the king had been pronounced victorious over all his enemies. I have just now remarked, that such a statement is not superfluous; for it would not have been enough for the kingdom to have flourished internally, and to have been replenished with peace, riches, and abundance of all good things, had it not also been well fortified against the attacks of foreign enemies. This particularly applies to the kingdom of Christ, which is never without enemies in this world. True, it is not always assailed by

open war, and there is sometimes granted to it a period of respite; but the ministers of Satan never lay aside their malice and desire to do mischief, and therefore they never cease to plot and to endeavour to accomplish the overthrow of Christ's kingdom. It is well for us that our King, who lifts up his hand as a shield before us to defend us, is stronger than all. As the Hebrew word מצא, *matsa*, which is twice repeated, and which we have translated, *to find*, sometimes signifies *to suffice*; and, as in the first clause, there is prefixed to the word כל, *kal*, which signifies *all*, the letter ל, *lamed*, which signifies *for*, or *against*, and which is not prefixed to the Hebrew word which is rendered *those that hate thee;* some expositors, because of this diversity, explain the verse as if it had been said, Thy hand shall be able for all thine enemies, thy right hand shall find out those that hate thee. Thus the sentence will ascend by degrees,— Thy hand shall be able to withstand, thy right hand shall lay hold upon thy enemies, so that they shall not escape destruction.

9. *Thou shalt put them as it were into a furnace of fire.*[1] The Psalmist here describes a dreadful kind of vengeance, from which we gather, that he does not speak of every kind of enemies in general, but of the malicious and frantic

---

[1] French and Skinner's translation of these words is the same, and so also is that of Rogers. This last author observes, "The common interpretation, *Thou shalt make them like a fiery oven*, &c., is not very intelligible. I consider כתנור as put by ellipsis for כבתנור, *Thou shalt place them as it were* [in] *a furnace of fire.*"—(Rogers' Book of Psalms, in Hebrew, metrically arranged, vol. ii. p. 178.) Poole takes the same view. Calvin, however, in his French version, gives a translation much the same as that of our English version: "Tu les rendras comme une fournaise de feu en temps de ta cholere." "Thou shalt make them like a furnace of fire, in the time of thy anger." This is exactly the rendering of Horsley, in which he is followed by Walford. "It describes," says the learned prelate, "the smoke of the Messiah's enemies perishing by fire, ascending like the smoke of a furnace. 'The smoke of their torment shall ascend for ever and ever.'" "How awfully grand," says Bishop Mant, "is that description of the ruins of the cities of the plain, as the prospect struck on Abraham's eye on the fatal morning of their destruction: 'And he looked toward Sodom and Gomorrah, and toward all the land of the plain, and beheld, and, lo! the smoke of the country went up as the smoke of a furnace.'"

despisers of God, who, after the manner of the giants[1] of old, rise up against his only begotten Son. The very severity of the punishment shows the greatness of the wickedness. Some think that David alludes to the kind of punishment which he inflicted upon the Ammonites, of which we have an account in the sacred history; but it is more probable that he here sets forth metaphorically the dreadful destruction which awaits all the adversaries of Christ. They may burn with rage against the Church, and set the world on fire by their cruelty, but when their wickedness shall have reached its highest pitch, there is this reward which God has in reserve for them, that he will cast them into his burning furnace to consume them. In the first clause, the king is called an avenger; in the second, this office is transferred to God; and in the third, the execution of the vengeance is attributed to fire; which three things very well agree. We know that judgment has been committed to Christ, that he may cast his enemies headlong into everlasting fire; but it was of importance distinctly to express that this is not the judgment of man but of God. Nor was it less important to set forth how extreme and dreadful a kind of vengeance this is, in order to arouse from their torpor those who, unapprehensive of danger, boldly despise all the threatenings of God. Besides, this serves not a little for the consolation of the righteous. We know how dreadful the cruelty of the ungodly is, and that our faith would soon sink under it, if it did not rise to the contemplation of the judgment of God. The expression, *In the time of thy wrath*, admonishes us that we ought patiently to bear the cross as long as it shall please the Lord to exercise and humble us under it. If, therefore, he does not immediately put forth his power to destroy the ungodly, let us learn to extend our hope to the time which our heavenly Father has appointed in his eternal purpose for the execution of his judgment, and when our King, armed with his terrible power, will come forth to execute vengeance. While he now seems to take no notice, this does not imply that he has forgotten either himself or us. On the contrary,

---

[1] The allusion is to the fabulous giants of heathen mythology, who waged war against heaven.

he laughs at the madness of those who go on in the commission of every kind of sin without any fear of danger, and become more presumptuous day after day. This laughter of God, it is true, brings little comfort to us; but we must, nevertheless, complete the time of our condition of warfare till "the day of the Lord's vengeance" come, which, as Isaiah declares, (chap. xxxiv. 8,) shall also be "the year of our redemption." It does not seem to me to be out of place to suppose, that in the last clause, there is denounced against the enemies of Christ a destruction like that which God in old time sent upon Sodom and Gomorrah. That punishment was a striking and memorable example above all others of the judgment of God against all the wicked, or rather it was, as it were, a visible image upon earth of the eternal fire of hell which is prepared for the reprobate: and hence this similitude is frequently to be met with in the sacred writings.

10. *Thou shalt destroy their fruit from the earth.* David amplifies the greatness of God's wrath, from the circumstance that it shall extend even to the children of the wicked. It is a doctrine common enough in Scripture, that God not only inflicts punishment upon the first originators of wickedness, but makes it even to overflow into the bosom of their children.[1] And yet when he thus pursues his vengeance to the third and fourth generation, he cannot be said indiscriminately to involve the innocent with the guilty. As the seed of the ungodly, whom he has deprived of his grace, are accursed, and as all are by nature children of wrath, devoted to everlasting destruction, he is no less just in exercising his severity towards the children than towards the fathers. Who can lay any thing to his charge, if he withhold from those who are unworthy of it the grace which he communicates to his own children? In both ways he shows how dear and precious to him is the kingdom of Christ; first, in extending his mercy to the children of the righteous even to a thousand

---

[1] " Mais qu'il le fait mesme regorger au sein des enfans d'iceux."—*Fr.* See Isaiah lxv. 6, 7.

generations; and, secondly, in causing his wrath to rest upon the reprobate, even to the third and fourth generation.

> 11. *For they have spread out*[1] *evil against thee; they have devised a stratagem against thee, which they could not accomplish.*
> 12. *For*[2] *thou wilt set them as a butt; thou wilt prepare thy bowstrings to shoot against their faces.*
> 13. *Raise thyself, O Jehovah! in thy strength; then we will sing, and celebrate in psalms thy power.*

11. *For they have spread out.* In this verse David shows that the ungodly had deserved the awful ruin which he predicted would befall them, since they had not only molested a mortal man, but had also rushed forth in the fury of their pride to make war against God himself. No man, as has been stated in our exposition of the second psalm, could offer violence to the kingdom of Israel, which was consecrated in the person of David, by the commandment of God, without making foul and impious war against God. Much more when persons directly attack the kingdom of Christ to overthrow it, is the majesty of God violated, since it is the will of God to reign in the world only by the hand of his Son. As the Hebrew word נטה, *natah,* which we have translated *to spread out,* also sometimes signifies *to turn aside,* it may not unsuitably be here rendered either way. According to the first view the meaning is, that the wicked, as if they had spread out their nets, endeavoured to subject to themselves the power of God. According to the second the meaning is, that for the purpose of hindering, and as it were swallowing up his power,[3] they turned aside their malice, so as to make it bear against it, just like a man who, having dug a great ditch, turned aside the course of some torrent to make it fall within it. The Psalmist next declares, that they *devised a stratagem,* or device, which would fail of its accomplishment. By these words he rebukes the foolish arrogance of those who, by making war against God, manifest a reck-

---

[1] "Ou, ont décliné."—*Fr.* "Or, have turned aside."
[2] This verse explains the reason why they could not accomplish what they had devised.
[3] "Pour icelle empescher et comme engloutir."—*Fr.*

lessness and an audacity which will undertake any thing, however daring.

12. *For thou wilt set them as a butt.* As the Hebrew word שכם, *shekem*, which we have rendered *a butt*, properly signifies *a shoulder*, some understand it in that sense here, and explain the sentence thus: Their heads shall be smitten with heavy blows, so that having their bodies bended, their shoulders shall appear sticking out. According to these interpreters, the subjugation of the enemies of God is here metaphorically pointed out. But there is another explanation which is more generally received even among the Jewish expositors, namely, that God will shut them up in some corner, and there keep them from doing mischief;[1] and they take this view, because the Hebrew word שכם, *shekem*, is often used to denote a *corner*, *quarter*, or *place*. As, however, the sacred writer, in the clause immediately following, represents God as furnished with a bow, ready to shoot his arrows directly in their faces, I have no doubt that, continuing his metaphor, he compares them to a butt, or mound of earth, on which it is customary to plant the mark which is aimed at, and thus the sense will flow very naturally thus: Lord, thou wilt make them as it were a butt against which to shoot thine arrows.[2] The great object which the Psalmist has in view is doubtless to teach us to exercise patience, until God, at the fit time, bring the ungodly to their end.

---

[1] Kimchi and others read, "Thou wilt put them into a corner;" which has been understood in this sense, "Thou wilt thrust them into a corner, and then direct thine arrows against their faces."—See *Poole's Synopsis Criticorum.*

[2] This is the view taken by Ainsworth, Castellio, Cocceius, Diodati, Dathe, Horsley, and Fry. Horsley translates the verse thus:—

"Truly thou shalt make them a butt for thine arrows :[*]
Thou shalt take a steady aim against them."

"I take," says he, " כון, [the word which he translates *a steady aim,*] to be a technical term of archery, to express the act of taking aim at a particular object." In our English version it is, "Therefore thou shalt make them turn their backs." In defence of this sense of שכם, *shekem*, see *Merrick's Annotations.* Gesenius takes the word in the same sense.

[*] Literally, "thy bow-strings."

13. *Raise thyself, O Jehovah!* The psalm is at length concluded with a prayer, which again confirms that the kingdom which is spoken of is so connected with the glory of God, that his power is reflected from it. This was no doubt true with respect to the kingdom of David; for God in old time displayed his power in exalting him to the throne. But what is here stated was only fully accomplished in Christ, who was appointed by the heavenly Father to be King over us, and who is at the same time God manifest in the flesh. As his divine power ought justly to strike terror into the wicked, so it is described as full of the sweetest consolation to us, which ought to inspire us with joy, and incite us to celebrate it with songs of praise and thanksgivings.

PSALM XXII.

David complains in this psalm, that he is reduced to such circumstances of distress that he is like a man in despair. But after having recounted the calamities with which he was so severely afflicted, he emerges from the abyss of temptations, and gathering courage, comforts himself with the assurance of deliverance. At the same time, he sets before us, in his own person, a type of Christ, who he knew by the Spirit of prophecy behoved to be abased in marvellous and unusual ways[1] previous to his exaltation by the Father. Thus the psalm, in the two parts of which it consists, explains that prophecy of Isaiah, (chap. liii. 8,) "He was taken from prison and from judgment: and who shall declare his generation?"

¶ To the chief musician. Upon the hind of the morning. A psalm of David.

This inscription is obscure; but interpreters have needlessly perplexed themselves in seeking after I know not what sublime mystery in a matter of small importance. Some are of opinion that the word אילת, *ayeleth*, means *the morning star*;[2] others that it denotes *strength*;[3] but it is

---

[1] "En toutes les sortes qu'il est possible de penser."—*Fr.* "In every way which it is possible to conceive."

[2] And this title they say is prefixed to the psalm, because the whole of it is concerning Christ the morning star.

[3] Those who render it *strength* derive the word from איל, *eyl, strength*, and

more correctly rendered *hind*. As it is evident, from the testimony of the apostles, that this psalm is a prophecy concerning Christ, the ancient interpreters thought that Christ would not be sufficiently dignified and honoured unless, putting a mystical or allegorical sense upon the word *hind*, they viewed it as pointing out the various things which are included in a sacrifice. Those, also, who prefer translating the original words, אילת השחר, *ayeleth hashachar, the dawn of the day* or *morning*,[1] have endeavoured to do the same thing. But as I find no solidity in these subtleties, it will be better to take that view of the title which is more simple and natural. I think it highly probable that it was the beginning of some common song; nor do I see how the inscription bears any relation to the subject-matter of the psalm. From the tenor of the whole composition, it appears that David does not here refer merely to one persecution, but comprehends all the persecutions which he suffered under Saul. It is, however, uncertain whether he composed this psalm when he peaceably enjoyed his kingdom, or in the time of his affliction; but there is no doubt that he here describes the thoughts which passed through his mind in the midst of his troubles, perplexities, and sorrows.

1. *My God! my God! why hast thou forsaken me? Why art thou far from my help, and from the words of my roaring?*
2. *O my God! I cry in the day-time,[2] but thou hearest not: and in the night-season, and there is no silence to me.*

1. *My God!* The first verse contains two remarkable sentences, which, although apparently contrary to each other, are yet ever entering into the minds of the godly together. When the Psalmist speaks of being forsaken and cast off by God, it seems to be the complaint of a man in despair; for can a man have a single spark of faith remaining in him, when he believes that there is no longer any succour for him in God? And yet, in calling God twice his own God, and depositing his groanings into his bosom, he makes a very distinct confession of his faith. With this inward conflict the godly must necessarily be exercised whenever God withdraws from them the tokens of his favour, so that, in whatever direction they turn their eyes, they see nothing but the dark-

observe, that the cognate word in verse 20, אילותי, *eyaluthi*, is rendered by the Septuagint την βοηθειαν μου, *my aid* or *strength*. By *the strength of the morning* they understand the dawning of the day.

[1] This is the sense in which Lightfoot understands the words.
[2] "Mon Dieu, je crie *tout* le jour."—*Fr.* "O my God, I cry *all* the day."

ness of night. I say, that the people of God, in wrestling with themselves, on the one hand discover the weakness of the flesh, and on the other give evidence of their faith. With respect to the reprobate, as they cherish in their hearts their distrust of God, their perplexity of mind overwhelms them, and thus totally incapacitates them for aspiring after the grace of God by faith. That David sustained the assaults of temptation, without being overwhelmed, or swallowed up by it, may be easily gathered from his words. He was greatly oppressed with sorrow, but notwithstanding this, he breaks forth into the language of assurance, *My God! my God!* which he could not have done without vigorously resisting the contrary apprehension[1] that God had forsaken him. There is not one of the godly who does not daily experience in himself the same thing. According to the judgment of the flesh, he thinks he is cast off and forsaken by God, while yet he apprehends by faith the grace of God, which is hidden from the eye of sense and reason; and thus it comes to pass, that contrary affections are mingled and interwoven in the prayers of the faithful. Carnal sense and reason cannot but conceive of God as being either favourable or hostile, according to the present condition of things which is presented to their view. When, therefore, he suffers us to lie long in sorrow, and as it were to pine away under it, we must necessarily feel, according to the apprehension of the flesh, as if he had quite forgotten us. When such a perplexing thought takes entire possession of the mind of man, it overwhelms him in profound unbelief, and he neither seeks, nor any longer expects, to find a remedy. But if faith come to his aid against such a temptation, the same person who, judging from the outward appearance of things, regarded God as incensed against him, or as having abandoned him, beholds in the mirror of the promises the grace of God which is hidden and distant. Between these two contrary affections the faithful are agitated, and, as it were, fluctuate, when Satan, on the one hand, by exhibiting to their view

---

[1] " Ce qu'il ne pouvoit faire si non en resistant vivement à la apprehension contraire."—*Fr.*

the signs of the wrath of God, urges them on to despair, and endeavours entirely to overthrow their faith; while faith, on the other hand, by calling them back to the promises, teaches them to wait patiently and to trust in God, until he again show them his fatherly countenance.

We see then the source from which proceeded this exclamation, *My God! my God!* and from which also proceeded the complaint which follows immediately after, *Why hast thou forsaken me?* Whilst the vehemence of grief, and the infirmity of the flesh, forced from the Psalmist these words, *I am forsaken of God;* faith, lest he should when so severely tried sink into despair, put into his mouth a correction of this language, so that he boldly called God, of whom he thought he was forsaken, his God. Yea, we see that he has given the first place to faith. Before he allows himself to utter his complaint, in order to give faith the chief place, he first declares that he still claimed God as his own God, and betook himself to him for refuge. And as the affections of the flesh, when once they break forth, are not easily restrained, but rather carry us beyond the bounds of reason, it is surely well to repress them at the very commencement. David, therefore, observed the best possible order in giving his faith the precedency—in expressing it before giving vent to his sorrow, and in qualifying, by devout prayer, the complaint which he afterwards makes with respect to the greatness of his calamities. Had he spoken simply and precisely in these terms, Lord, why forsakest thou me? he would have seemed, by a complaint so bitter, to murmur against God; and besides, his mind would have been in great danger of being embittered with discontent through the greatness of his grief. But, by here raising up against murmuring and discontent the rampart of faith, he keeps all his thoughts and feelings under restraint, that they may not break beyond due bounds. Nor is the repetition superfluous when he twice calls God *his God;* and, a little after, he even repeats the same words the third time. When God, as if he had cast off all care about us, passes over our miseries and groanings as if he saw them not, the conflict with this species of temptation is arduous and painful, and therefore David the more strenuously exerts himself in seeking the confirmation of his faith. Faith does not gain the victory at the first encounter, but after receiving many blows, and after being exercised with many tossings, she at length comes forth victorious. I do not say that David was so courageous and valiant a champion as that his faith did not waver. The faithful may put forth all their efforts to subdue their carnal affections, that they may subject and devote themselves wholly to God; but still there is always some infirmity remaining in them. From this proceeded that halting of holy Jacob, of which Moses makes mention in Gen. xxxii. 24; for although in wrestling with God he prevailed, yet he ever after bore the mark of his sinful defect. By such examples God encourages his servants to perseverance, lest, from a consciousness of their own infirmity, they should sink into despair. The means therefore which we ought to adopt, whenever our flesh becomes tumultuous, and, like an impetuous tempest, hurries us into impatience, is to strive against it, and to endeavour to restrain its impetuosity. In doing this we will, it is true, be agitated and sorely tried, but our faith will, nevertheless, continue safe, and be preserved from shipwreck. Farther, we may gather from the very form of the complaint which David here makes, that he did not without cause redouble the words by which his faith might be sustained. He does not simply say that he *was forsaken* by God, but he adds, that God *was far from his help,* inasmuch as when he saw him in the greatest danger, he gave him no token to encourage him in the hope of obtaining deliverance. Since God has the ability to succour us, if, when he sees us exposed as a prey to our enemies, he nevertheless sits still as if he cared not about us, who would not say that he has drawn back his hand that he may not deliver us? Again, by the expression, *the words of my roaring,* the Psalmist intimates that he was distressed and tormented in the highest degree. He certainly was not a man of so little courage as, on account of some slight or ordinary affliction, to howl in this manner like a brute beast.[1]

---

[1] " Et de faict, il n'estoit point de si petit courage, que pour quelque

We must therefore come to the conclusion, that the distress was very great which could extort such roaring from a man who was distinguished for meekness, and for the undaunted courage with which he endured calamities.

As our Saviour Jesus Christ, when hanging on the cross, and when ready to yield up his soul into the hands of God his Father, made use of these very words, (Matth. xxvii. 46,) we must consider how these two things can agree, that Christ was the only begotten Son of God, and that yet he was so penetrated with grief, seized with so great mental trouble, as to cry out that God his Father had forsaken him. The apparent contradiction between these two statements has constrained many interpreters to have recourse to evasions for fear of charging Christ with blame in this matter.[1] Accordingly, they have said that Christ made this complaint rather according to the opinion of the common people, who witnessed his sufferings, than from any feeling which he had of being deserted by his Father. But they have not considered that they greatly lessen the benefit of our redemption, in imagining that Christ was altogether exempted from the terrors which the judgment of God strikes into sinners. It was a groundless fear to be afraid of making Christ subject to so great sorrow, lest they should diminish his glory. As Peter, in Acts ii. 24, clearly testifies that " it was not possible that he should be holden of the pains of death," it follows that he was not altogether exempted from them. And as he became our representative, and took upon him our sins, it was certainly necessary that he should appear before the judgment-seat of God as a sinner. From this proceeded the terror and dread which constrained him to pray for deliverance from death ; not that it was so grievous to him merely to depart from this life; but because there was before his eyes the curse of God, to which all who are sinners are exposed. Now, if during his first conflict " his sweat was as it were great drops of

---

mal leger il hurlast ainsi comme une beste brute."—*Fr.* " The original word [for *roaring*] properly denotes the roaring of a lion, and is often applied to the deep groaning of men in sickness. See among other places, Ps. xxxii. 3 ; xxxviii. 9."—*Bishop Mant.*

[1] " Pour crainte de charger Christ de ce blasme."—*Fr.*

blood," and he needed an angel to comfort him, (Luke xxii. 43,) it is not wonderful if, in his last sufferings on the cross, he uttered a complaint which indicated the deepest sorrow. By the way, it should be marked, that Christ, although subject to human passions and affections, never fell into sin through the weakness of the flesh; for the perfection of his nature preserved him from all excess. He could therefore overcome all the temptations with which Satan assailed him, without receiving any wound in the conflict which might afterwards constrain him to halt. In short, there is no doubt that Christ, in uttering this exclamation upon the cross, manifestly showed, that although David here bewails his own distresses, this psalm was composed under the influence of the Spirit of prophecy concerning David's King and Lord.

2. *O my God! I cry in the day-time.* In this verse the Psalmist expresses the long continuance of his affliction, which increased his disquietude and weariness. It was a temptation even still more grievous, that his crying seemed only to be lost labour; for, as our only means of relief under our calamities is in calling upon God, if we derive no advantage from our prayers, what other remedy remains for us? David, therefore, complains that God is in a manner deaf to his prayers. When he says in the second clause, *And there is no silence to me*, the meaning is, that he experienced no comfort or solace, nothing which could impart tranquillity to his troubled mind. As long as affliction pressed upon him, his mind was so disquieted, that he was constrained to cry out. Here there is shown the constancy of faith, in that the long duration of calamities could neither overthrow it, nor interrupt its exercise. The true rule of praying is, therefore, this, that he who seems to have beaten the air to no purpose, or to have lost his labour in praying for a long time, should not, on that account, leave off, or desist from that duty. Meanwhile, there is this advantage which God in his fatherly kindness grants to his people, that if they have been disappointed at any time of their desires and expectations, they may make known to God their perplexities and distresses, and unburden them, as it were, into his bosom.

3. Yet thou art holy, who inhabitest the praises of Israel.
4. Our fathers trusted in thee: they trusted, and thou didst deliver them.
5. They cried unto thee, and were delivered: they trusted in thee, and were not confounded.
6. But I am a worm, and not a man; the scorn of men, and the contempt of the people.
7. All those who see me mock at me: they thrust out the lip, and shake the head.
8. " He has committed," say they, " his cause unto [or, devolved his cause upon] Jehovah:[1] let him deliver him, let him deliver him,[2] seeing he delights in him."

3. *Yet thou art holy.* In the Hebrew, it is properly, *And thou art holy:* but the copula ו, *vau,* ought, without doubt, to be rendered by the adversative particle *yet.* Some think that the eternal and immutable state of God is here set in opposition to the afflictions which David experienced;[3] but I cannot subscribe to this opinion. It is more simple and natural to view the language as meaning, that God has always shown himself gracious to his chosen people. The subject here treated is not what God is in heaven, but what he has shown himself to be towards men. It may be asked, whether David, in these words, aggravates his complaint, by insinuating that he is the only person who obtains nothing from God? or whether, by holding up these words as a shield before him, he repels the temptation with which he was assailed, by exhibiting to his view this truth, that God is the continual deliverer of his people? I admit that this verse is an additional expression of the greatness of David's grief; but

[1] In the Hebrew it is, " He rolled [himself] upon God." In the Latin version our author reads, " Devolvit ad Jehovam;" and in the French, " Il a remis *disent-ils,* au Seigneur *son affaire.*"
[2] *Let him deliver him, let him deliver him.* This repetition is also the rendering adopted by Street, and it is approved by Poole. "The same thing," says Poole, " is twice repeated, to show both the vehemence of their hatred and their confidence of success against him."
[3] As ישב, *yashab,* not only signifies *to inhabit,* but also *to remain* or *continue,* (see Psalm cii. 13,) Hammond thinks this last is the meaning here, and renders the word, " But thou remainest or continuest to be holy, O thou, the praises of, or who art the praises of Israel, that is, the object of all their praises; or more simply, But thou remainest holy, the praises of Israel."

I have no doubt, that in using this language he seeks from it a remedy against his distrust. It was a dangerous temptation to see himself forsaken by God; and, accordingly, lest by continually thinking upon it, he should nourish it, he turned his mind to the contemplation of the constant evidences afforded of the grace of God, from which he might encourage himself, in the hope of obtaining succour. He, therefore, not only meant to ask how it was that God, who had always dealt mercifully with his people, should now, forgetting as it were his own nature, thus leave a miserable man without any succour or solace; but he also takes a shield with which to defend himself against the fiery darts of Satan. He calls God *holy*, because he continues always like himself. He says that he *inhabiteth the praises of Israel;* because, in showing such liberality towards the chosen people, as to be continually bestowing blessings upon them, he furnished them with matter for continued praise and thanksgiving. Unless God cause us to taste of his goodness by doing us good, we must needs become mute in regard to the celebration of his praise. As David belonged to the number of this chosen people, he strives, in opposition to all the obstacles which distrust might suggest as standing in the way, to cherish the hope that he shall at length be united to this body to sing along with them the praises of God.

4. *Our fathers trusted in thee.* Here the Psalmist assigns the reason why God sitteth amidst the praises of the tribes of Israel. The reason is, because his hand had been always stretched forth to preserve his faithful people. David, as I have just now observed, gathers together the examples of all past ages, in order thereby to encourage, strengthen, and effectually persuade himself, that as God had never cast off any of his chosen people, he also would be one of the number of those for whom deliverance is securely laid up in the hand of God. He therefore expressly declares that he belongs to the offspring of those who had been heard, intimating by this, that he is an heir of the same grace which they had experienced. He has an eye to the covenant by which God had adopted the posterity of Abraham to be his peculiar people. It would

be of little consequence to know the varied instances in which God has exercised his mercy towards his own people, unless each of us could reckon himself among their number, as David includes himself in the Church of God. In repeating three times that the fathers had obtained deliverance by *trusting*, there is no doubt that with all modesty he intends tacitly to intimate that he had the same hope with which they were inspired, a hope which draws after it, as its effect, the fulfilment of the promises in our behalf. In order that a man may derive encouragement from the blessings which God has bestowed upon his servants in former times, he should turn his attention to the free promises of God's word, and to the faith which leans upon them. In short, to show that this confidence was neither cold nor dead, David tells us, at the same time, that *they cried unto God*. He who pretends that he trusts in God, and yet is so listless and indifferent under his calamities that he does not implore his aid, lies shamefully. By prayer, then, true faith is known, as the goodness of a tree is known by its fruit. It ought also to be observed, that God regards no other prayers as right but those which proceed from faith, and are accompanied with it. It is therefore not without good reason that David has put the word *cried* in the middle between these words, *They trusted in thee, they trusted,* in the fourth verse, and these words, *They trusted in thee,* in the fifth verse.

6. *But I am a worm, and not a man.* David does not murmur against God as if God had dealt hardly with him; but in bewailing his condition, he says, in order the more effectually to induce God to show him mercy, that he is not accounted so much as a man. This, it is true, seems at first sight to have a tendency to discourage the mind, or rather to destroy faith; but it will appear more clearly from the sequel, that so far from this being the case, David declares how miserable his condition is, that by this means he may encourage himself in the hope of obtaining relief. He therefore argues that it could not be but that God would at length stretch forth his hand to save him; to save him, I say, who was so severely afflicted, and on the brink of despair. If God has had com-

passion on all who have ever been afflicted, although afflicted only in a moderate degree, how could he forsake his servant when plunged in the lowest abyss of all calamities? Whenever, therefore, we are overwhelmed under a great weight of afflictions, we ought rather to take from this an argument to encourage us to hope for deliverance, than suffer ourselves to fall into despair. If God so severely exercised his most eminent servant David, and abased him so far that he had not a place even among the most despised of men, let us not take it ill, if, after his example, we are brought low. We ought, however, principally to call to our remembrance the Son of God, in whose person we know this also was fulfilled, as Isaiah had predicted, (ch. liii. 3;) "He is despised and rejected of men; a man of sorrows, and acquainted with grief: and we hid as it were our faces from him; he was despised, and we esteemed him not." By these words of the prophet we are furnished with a sufficient refutation of the frivolous subtlety of those who have philosophised upon the word *worm*, as if David here pointed out some singular mystery in the generation of Christ; whereas his meaning simply is, that he had been abased beneath all men, and, as it were, cut off from the number of living beings. The fact that the Son of God suffered himself to be reduced to such ignominy, yea, descended even to hell, is so far from obscuring, in any respect, his celestial glory, that it is rather a bright mirror from which is reflected his unparalleled grace towards us.

7. *All those who see me mock at me, &c.*[1] This is an explanation of the preceding sentence. He had said that he was an object of scorn to the lowest of men, and, as it were, to the refuse of the people. He now informs us of the igno-

---

[1] Bishop Horsley reads these words, "All who see me insult [me] with gestures of derision:" and says, "I can no otherwise render the verb לעג, than by this periphrasis." Bishop Mant translates the whole verse thus:

"All who to slaughter see me led,
Deride my state distrest;
They curl the lip, they shake the head,
They point the taunting jest:"

And observes, "The distinctness and colouring of the prophetic picture here are as striking to the imagination, as the subject is painful to the heart."

miny with which he had been treated,—that not content with opprobrious language, they also showed their insolence by their very gesture, both by shooting out their lips,[1] and by shaking their heads. As the words which we render *they thrust out the lip*, is, in the Hebrew, *they open with the lip*,[2] some explain them as meaning *to rail*. But this view does not appear to me to be appropriate; for the letter ב, *beth*, which signifies *with*, is here superfluous, as it often is in the Hebrew. I have therefore preferred rendering the original words, *they thrust out the lip;* which is the gesture of those who mock openly and injuriously. The reproachful language which follows was much more grievous when they alleged against him that God, who he openly avowed was his father, was turned away from him. We know that David, when he saw himself unjustly condemned of the world, was accustomed to support and console himself with the assurance, that since he had the approving testimony of a good conscience, he had God in heaven for his guardian, who was able to execute vengeance upon his revilers.[3] But now, all who saw him reproached him, that with vain arrogance he had groundlessly boasted of the succour he would receive from God. Where is that God, say they, on whom he leaned? Where is that love to which he trusted? Satan has not a more deadly dart for wounding the souls of men than when he endeavours to dislodge hope from our minds, by turning the promises of God into ridicule. David's enemies, however, do not simply say that his prayers were in vain, and that the love of God of which he boasted was fallacious; but they indirectly charge him with being a hypocrite, in that he falsely pretended to be one of the children of God, from whom he was altogether estranged.

How severe a temptation this must have been to David every man may judge from his own experience. But by the remedy he used he afforded a proof of the sincerity of his confidence: for unless he had had God as the undoubted

---

[1] "To protrude the lower lip is, in the East, considered a very strong indication of contempt. Its employment is chiefly confined to the lower orders."—*Illustrated Commentary upon the Bible.*

[2] בשפה, *besaphah*, *with the lip*.

[3] "Qu'il avoit Dieu au ciel pour garent qui sçavoit bien faire la vengence de ses mesdisans."—*Fr.*

witness and approver of the sincerity of his heart, he would never have dared to come before him with this complaint. Whenever, therefore, men charge us with hypocrisy, let it be our endeavour that the inward sincerity of our hearts may answer for us before God. And whenever Satan attempts to dislodge faith from our minds, by biting detraction and cruel derision, let this be our sacred anchor,—to call upon God to witness it, and that, beholding it, he may be pleased to show his righteousness in maintaining our right, since his holy name cannot be branded with viler blasphemy than to say that those who put their trust in him are puffed up with vain confidence, and that those who persuade themselves that God loves them deceive themselves with a groundless fancy. As the Son of God was assailed with the same weapon, it is certain that Satan will not be more sparing of true believers who are his members than of him. They ought, therefore, to defend themselves from this consideration—that although men may regard them as in a desperate condition, yet, if they commit to God both themselves and all their affairs, their prayers will not be in vain. By the verb, גֹּל, *gol*, which is rendered *to commit*, the nature and efficacy of faith are very well expressed, which, reposing itself upon the providence of God, relieves our minds from the burdens of the cares and troubles with which they are agitated.

9. *Surely thou didst draw me forth from the womb, and thou didst cause me to confide upon the breasts of my mother.*[1]
10. *I was cast upon thee*[2] *from the womb: thou art my God from my mother's belly.*
11. *Depart not far from me, for distress is near, and there is none to help me.*

9. *Surely thou.* David again here raises a new fortress, in order to withstand and repel the machinations of Satan.

---

[1] "Qui m'as donné asseurance, lorsque je succoye les mammelles de ma mere."—*Note, Fr. marg.* "That is, thou gavest me confidence whilst I sucked the breasts of my mother."
[2] "Abandonné entre tes mains."—*Note, Fr. marg.* "That is, left among thy hands." Poole, applying this to Christ, says, "I was like one forsaken by his parent, and cast wholly upon thy providence. I had no father upon earth; and my mother was poor and helpless."

He briefly enumerates the benefits which God had bestowed upon him, by which he had long since learned that he was his father. Yea, he declares that even before he was born God had shown towards him such evidence of his fatherly love, that although now overwhelmed with the darkness of death, he might upon good ground venture to hope for life from him. And it is the Holy Spirit who teaches the faithful the wisdom to collect together, when they are brought into circumstances of fear and trouble, the evidences of the goodness of God, in order thereby to sustain and strengthen their faith. We ought to regard it as an established principle, that as God never wearies in the exercise of his liberality, and as the most exuberant bestowment cannot exhaust his riches, it follows that, as we have experienced him to be a father from our earliest infancy, he will show himself the same towards us even to extreme old age. In acknowledging that he was *taken from the womb* by the hand of God, and that *God had caused him to confide upon the breasts of his mother*, the meaning is, that although it is by the operation of natural causes that infants come into the world, and are nourished with their mother's milk, yet therein the wonderful providence of God brightly shines forth. This miracle, it is true, because of its ordinary occurrence, is made less account of by us. But if ingratitude did not put upon our eyes the veil of stupidity, we would be ravished with admiration at every childbirth in the world. What prevents the child from perishing, as it might, a hundred times in its own corruption, before the time for bringing it forth arrives, but that God, by his secret and incomprehensible power, keeps it alive in its grave? And after it is brought into the world, seeing it is subject to so many miseries, and cannot stir a finger to help itself, how could it live even for a single day, did not God take it up into his fatherly bosom to nourish and protect it? It is, therefore, with good reason said, that the infant *is cast upon him;* for, unless he fed the tender little babes, and watched over all the offices of the nurse, even at the very time of their being brought forth, they are exposed to a hundred deaths, by which they would be suffocated in an instant. Finally, David concludes that God was *his God.* God, it is true, to all appearance, shows the like goodness which is here celebrated even to the brute creation; but it is only to mankind that he shows himself to be a father in a special manner. And although he does not immediately endue babes with the knowledge of himself, yet he is said *to give them confidence,* because, by showing in fact that he takes care of their life, he in a manner allures them to himself; as it is said in another place, " He giveth to the beast his food, and to the young ravens which cry," (Ps. cxlvii. 9.) Since God anticipates in this manner, by his grace, little infants before they have as yet the use of reason, it is certain that he will never disappoint the hope of his servants when they petition and call upon him. This is the argument by which David struggled with, and endeavoured to overcome temptation.

11. *Depart not far from me.* Here he employs another argument to induce God to show him mercy, alleging that he is sorely pressed and hemmed in by the greatest distress. He doubtless set before his eyes the office which the Scriptures every where attribute to God of succouring the miserable, and of being the more ready to help us the more we are afflicted. Even despair itself, therefore, served as a ladder to elevate his mind to the exercise of devout and fervent prayer. In like manner, the feeling we have of our afflictions should excite us to take shelter under the wings of God, that by granting us his aid, he may show that he takes a deep interest in our welfare.

12. *Strong bulls have encompassed me; the bulls of Bashan have beset me round.*
13. *They have opened their mouth against me, as a ravening and a roaring lion.*
14. *I am poured out like water, and all my bones are disjointed: my heart is like wax; it is melted in the midst of my bowels.*
15. *My strength is dried up like a potsherd, and my tongue cleaveth to my jaws; and thou hast brought me to the dust of death.*
16. *For dogs have encompassed me; the assembly of the wicked have surrounded me: they have pierced my hands and my feet.*

12. *Strong bulls have encompassed me.* The Psalmist now

complains of the cruelty and barbarous rage of his enemies; and he compares them first to bulls, secondly to lions, and thirdly to dogs. When the anger of bulls is kindled, we know how fierce and terrible they are. The lion, also, is a cruel beast, and dreadful to mankind. And the eager and fierce boldness with which dogs, when once they are irritated, rush upon a man to do him injury, is well known. In short, David's enemies were so blood-thirsty and cruel, that they more resembled wild beasts than men. He calls them not simply *bulls*, but *strong bulls*. Instead of rendering the original word רבים, *rabbim, strong*, as we have done, some would render it *many:* with which I cannot agree. David, it is true, was assailed by great hosts of enemies; but it appears, from the second clause of the verse, that what is here described is their strength, and not their number. He there terms them *the bulls of Bashan;* meaning by that expression, well-fed bulls, and, consequently, large and strong: for we know that the hill of Bashan was distinguished for rich and fat pastures.[1]

14. *I am poured out like water.* Hitherto he has informed us that being surrounded by wild beasts, he was not far from death, as if he had been at the point of being devoured every moment. He now bewails, in addition to this, his inward distress; from which we learn that he was not stupid or insensible in dangers. It could have been no ordinary fear which made him almost pine away, by which his bones were disjointed, and his heart poured out like water. We see, then, that David was not buffeted with the waves of affliction like a rock which cannot be moved, but was agitated within by sore troubles and temptations, which, through the infirmity of the flesh, he would never have been able to sustain had he not been aided by the power of the Spirit of God. How these sufferings are applicable to Christ I have informed you a little before. Being a real man, he was truly subject to the infirmities of our flesh, only without the taint of sin. The perfect purity of his nature did not extinguish the

---

[1] "The bull is known to be a fierce animal, and those of Bashan, from its luxuriant pastures, were uncommonly so."—*Dr Geddes.*

human affections; it only regulated them, that they might not become sinful through excess. The greatness of his griefs, therefore, could not so weaken him as to prevent him, even in the midst of his most excruciating sufferings, from submitting himself to the will of God, with a composed and peaceful mind. Now, although this is not the case with respect to us, who have within us turbulent and disorderly affections, and who never can keep them under such restraint as not to be driven hither and thither by their impetuosity, yet, after the example of David, we ought to take courage; and when, through our infirmity, we are, as it were, almost lifeless, we should direct our groanings to God, beseeching him that he would be graciously pleased to restore us to strength and vigour.[1]

15. *My strength is dried up.* He means the vigour which is imparted to us by the radical moisture, as physicians call it. What he adds in the next clause, *My tongue cleaveth to my jaws,* is of the same import. We know that excessive grief not only consumes the vital spirits, but also dries up almost all the moisture which is in our bodies. He next declares, that in consequence of this, he was adjudged or devoted to the grave: *Thou hast brought me to the dust of death.* By this he intimates, that all hope of life was taken from him; and in this sense Paul also says, (2 Cor. i. 9,) that " he had received the sentence of death in himself." But David here speaks of himself in hyperbolical language, and he does this in order to lead us beyond himself to Christ. The dreadful encounter of our Redeemer with death, by which there was forced from his body blood instead of sweat; his descent into hell, by which he tasted of the wrath of God which was due to sinners; and, in short, his emptying himself, could not be adequately expressed by any of the ordinary forms of speech. Moreover, David speaks of death as those who are in trouble are accustomed to speak of it, who, struck with fear, can think of nothing but of their being reduced to dust and to destruction. Whenever the minds of the saints are

[1] "A ce qu'il luy plaise nous remettre sus, et nous rendre force et vigueur."—*Fr.*

surrounded and oppressed with this darkness, there is always some unbelief mixed with their exercise, which prevents them from all at once emerging from it to the light of a new life. But in Christ these two things were wonderfully conjoined, namely, terror, proceeding from a sense of the curse of God; and patience, arising from faith, which tranquillized all the mental emotions, so that they continued in complete and willing subjection to the authority of God. With respect to ourselves, who are not endued with the like power, if at any time, upon beholding nothing but destruction near us, we are for a season greatly dismayed, we should endeavour by degrees to recover courage, and to elevate ourselves to the hope which quickens the dead.

16. *They have pierced my hands and my feet.* The original word, which we have translated *they have pierced*, is כארי, *caäri*, which literally rendered is, *like a lion*. As all the Hebrew Bibles at this day, without exception, have this reading, I would have had great hesitation in departing from a reading which they all support, were it not that the scope of the discourse compels me to do so, and were there not strong grounds for conjecturing that this passage has been fraudulently corrupted by the Jews. With respect to the Septuagint version, there is no doubt that the translators had read in the Hebrew text, כארו, *caäru*, that is the letter ו, *vau*, where there is now the letter י, *yod*.[1] The Jews prate much about the literal sense being purposely and deliberately over-

---

[1] This word has created much discussion. In the Hebrew Bible, the *kethib* or *textual* reading is, כארי, *caäri*, *like a lion;* the *keri*, or *marginal* reading, is כארו, *caäru,* " *they pierced,*" from כרה, *carah*, *to cut, dig,* or *pierce.* Both readings are supported by MSS. There is, however, no ground to doubt that the genuine reading is, כארו, *caäru.* As the Septuagint here reads ωρυξαν, *they pierced,* the translators, doubtless, considered that the correct reading of the Hebrew text was כארו, *caäru.* The Vulgate, Syriac, Arabic, and Æthiopic, give a similar rendering. All the Evangelists also quote and apply the passage to the crucifixion of Christ. Besides, the other reading, כארי, *caäri, as a lion*, renders the passage unintelligible. The Chaldee version has combined both the ideas of *pierced* and *as a lion,* reading, " Biting, as a lion, my hands and my feet." Our author supposes that the text has been fraudulently corrupted by the Jews, who have intentionally changed כארו, *caäru,* into כארי, *caäri.* But there is no necessity for supposing that there has been any fraud in the case. In the process of transcription, the change might have been made unintentionally,

thrown, by our rendering the original word by *they have pierced:* but for this allegation there is no colour of truth whatever. What need was there to trifle so presumptuously in a matter where it was altogether unnecessary? Very great suspicion of falsehood, however, attaches to them, seeing it is the uppermost desire of their hearts to despoil the crucified Jesus of his escutcheons, and to divest him of his character as the Messiah and Redeemer. If we receive this reading as they would have us to do, the sense will be enveloped in marvellous obscurity. In the first place, it will be a defective form of expression; and to complete it, they say it is necessary to supply the verb *to surround* or *to beset.* But what do they mean by *besetting the hands and the feet?* Besetting belongs no more to these parts of the human body than to the whole man. The absurdity of this argument being discovered, they have recourse to the most ridiculous old wives' fables, according to their usual way, saying, that the lion, when he meets any man in his road, makes a circle with his tail before rushing upon his prey: from which it is abundantly evident that they are at a loss for arguments to support their view.

Again, since David, in the preceding verse, has used the similitude of a lion, the repetition of it in this verse would be superfluous. I forbear insisting upon what some of our expositors have observed, namely, that this noun, when it has prefixed to it the letter כ, *caph*, which signifies *as*, the word denoting similitude, has commonly other points than those which are employed in this passage. My object, however, is not here to labour to convince the Jews who in controversy are in the highest degree obstinate and opinionative. I only intend briefly to show how wickedly they endeavour to perplex Christians on account of the different reading which occurs in this place. When they object, that by the appointment of the law no man was fastened with nails to a cross, they betray in this their gross ignor-

---

by the substitution of the letter י, *yod*, for the letter ו, *vau*, which i so nearly resembles. Walford observes, "that the present reading [כארי, *caäri*] is quite satisfactory, if it be taken as a participle plural in regim., and be translated, 'Wounders of my hands and my feet.'"

ance of history, since it is certain that the Romans introduced many of their own customs and manners into the provinces which they had conquered. If they object that David was never nailed to a cross, the answer is easy, namely, that in bewailing his condition, he has made use of a similitude, declaring that he was not less afflicted by his enemies than the man who is suspended on a cross, having his hands and feet pierced through with nails. We will meet a little after with more of the same kind of metaphors.

17. *I will number all my bones ; they look and stare upon me.*
18. *They part my garments among them, and cast the lot upon my vesture.*
19. *Be not thou then, O Jehovah! far from me. O thou! who art my strength, make haste to help me.*
20. *Deliver my soul from the sword; my only one*[1] *from the hand* [or *power*] *of the dog.*
21. *Save me from the mouth of the lion, and hear me from the horns of the unicorns.*[2]

17. *I will number.* The Hebrew word עצמות, *atsmoth*, which signifies *bones*, is derived from another word, which signifies *strength;* and, therefore, this term is sometimes applied to friends, by whose defence we are strengthened, or to arguments and reasons which are, as it were, the sinews and the strength of the defence of a cause. Some, therefore, put this meaning upon the passage,—I will profit nothing by reckoning up all my arguments in self-vindication; for my enemies are fully determined to destroy me by some means or other, whether fair or foul, without having any regard to the dictates of justice. Others explain it thus: Although I should gather together all the aids which might seem to be capable of affording me succour, they would avail me nothing. But the exposition which is more generally received seems to me to be also the more simple and natural, and, therefore, I embrace it the more readily. It is this—that David complains that his body was so lean and wasted, that

---

[1] " Asçavoir, vie, qui est seule."—*Note, Fr. marg.* " Namely, my life, which is alone."

[2] " Et me respon, en me sauvant des cornes des licornes."—*Fr.* " And answer me, *by saving* me from the horns of the unicorns."

the bones appeared protruding from all parts of it; for he adds immediately after, that his enemies took pleasure in seeing him in so pitiable a condition. Thus the two clauses of the verse are beautifully connected together. The cruelty of his enemies was so insatiable, that beholding a wretched man wasted with grief, and as it were pining away, they took pleasure in feeding their eyes with so sad a spectacle.

What follows in the next verse concerning his garments is metaphorical. It is as if he had said, that all his goods were become a prey to his enemies, even as conquerors are accustomed to plunder the vanquished, or to divide the spoil among themselves, by casting lots to determine the share which belongs to each. Comparing his ornaments, riches, and all that he possessed, to his garments, he complains that, after he had been despoiled of them, his enemies divided them among themselves, as so much booty, accompanied with mockery of him; and by this mockery the villany of their conduct was aggravated, inasmuch as they triumphed over him, as if he had been a dead man. The Evangelists quote this place to the letter, as we say, and without figure; and there is no absurdity in their doing so. To teach us the more certainly that in this psalm Christ is described to us by the Spirit of prophecy, the heavenly Father intended that in the person of his Son those things should be visibly accomplished which were shadowed forth in David. Matthew, (chap. viii. 16, 17,) in narrating that the paralytic, the blind, and the lame, were healed of their diseases, says, that this was done "that it might be fulfilled which was spoken by Esaias the prophet, saying, Himself took our infirmities, and bear our sicknesses;" although the prophet, in that place, sets before us the Son of God in the character of a spiritual physician. We are extremely slow and backward to believe; and it is not wonderful, that, on account of our dulness of apprehension, a demonstration of the character of Christ, palpable to our senses, has been given us,[1] which might have the effect of arousing the sluggishness of our understandings.

[1] "Il nous a esté faite une demonstration si grossiere, qu'on la pouvoit taster au doigt."—*Fr.* "There has been given us a demonstration so palpable, that it might be touched with the finger."

19. *Be not thou, then, far from me, O Jehovah!* We must keep in mind all that David has hitherto related concerning himself. As his miseries had reached the utmost height, and as he saw not even a single ray of hope to encourage him to expect deliverance, it is a wonderful instance of the power of faith, that he not only endured his afflictions patiently, but that from the abyss of despair he arose to call upon God. Let us, therefore, particularly mark, that David did not pour out his lamentations thinking them to be in vain, and of no effect, as persons who are in perplexity often pour forth their groanings at random. The prayers which he adds sufficiently show that he hoped for such an issue as he desired. When he calls God *his strength*, by this epithet he gives a more evident proof of his faith. He does not pray in a doubting manner; but he promises himself the assistance which the eye of sense did not as yet perceive. By *the sword*, by *the hand of the dog*, by *the mouth of the lion*, and by *the horns of the unicorns*, he intimates that he was presently exposed to the danger of death, and that in many ways. Whence we gather, that although he utterly fainted in himself when thus surrounded by death, he yet continued strong in the Lord, and that the spirit of life had always been vigorous in his heart. Some take the words *only soul*, or *only life*, for *dear* and *precious;*[1] but this view does not appear to me to be appropriate. He rather means, that, amidst so many deaths he found no help or succour in the whole world; as in Psalm xxxv. 17, the words, *only soul*,[2] are used in the same sense for a person who is alone and destitute of all aid and succour. This will appear more clearly from Psalm xxv. 16, where David, by calling himself poor and alone, doubtless complains that he was completely deprived of friends, and forsaken of the whole world. When it is said in the end of the 21st verse, *Answer me*, or, *Hear me from the horns of the unicorns*, this Hebrew manner of speaking may seem strange and obscure to our ears, but the sense is not at all ambiguous. The cause is only put instead of the effect; for our deliverance is the consequence or

---

[1] That is, my life, which is dear and precious to me.
[2] " La vie esseulee."—*Fr.* " Life deserted or left alone."

effect of God's hearing us. If it is asked how this can be applied to Christ, whom the Father did not deliver from death? I answer, in one word, that he was more mightily delivered than if God had prevented him from falling a victim to death, even as it is a much greater deliverance to rise again from the dead than to be healed of a grievous malady. Death, therefore, did not prevent Christ's resurrection from at length bearing witness that he had been heard.

22. *I will declare thy name to my brethren: in the midst of the assembly will I praise thee.*
23. *[Saying,[1]] Ye who fear Jehovah, praise him : all ye the seed of Jacob, glorify him ; and fear him, all ye the seed of Israel.*
24. *For he hath not despised nor disdained the poor; nor hath he hidden his face from him ; and when he cried unto him he heard him.*

22. *I will declare thy name.*[2] David, in promising that when he is delivered he will not be ungrateful, confirms what I have previously stated, that he had never been so cast down by temptation as not to take courage to resist it. How could he be putting himself in readiness, as he is doing here, to offer to God the sacrifice of thanksgiving, if he had not beforehand entertained the assured hope of deliverance? Should we even grant that this psalm was composed after David had actually obtained what he desired, there is no doubt that what he afterwards put into writing formed the meditations and reflections which had passed through his mind during the time of his heavy afflictions. It ought to be particularly noticed, that it is no ordinary token of gratitude which he promises, but such as God required for rare blessings ; namely, that the faithful should come into his sanctuary, and there bear solemn testimony to the grace which they had received. The design of public and solemn thanksgiving is, that the faithful may employ themselves

---

[1] "*Disant.*"—*Fr.*

[2] The second part of the psalm here commences. There is a transition from language of the deepest anguish to that of exalted joy and gratitude. The suffering Messiah here contemplates the blessed results of his sufferings.

in all variety of ways, in serving and honouring God, and that they may encourage one another to act in the same manner. We know that God's wonderful power shone forth in the protection of David; and that not only by one miracle, but by many. It is, therefore, not wonderful that he brings himself under obligation, by a solemn vow, to make open and public profession of his piety and faithfulness towards God. By *his brethren* he means the Israelites; and he gives them this appellation, not only because he and they were both descended from the same parentage, but rather because the religion which they had in common, as a sacred bond, kept them united to one another by a spiritual relationship. The apostle, (Heb. ii. 12,) in applying this verse to Christ, argues from it, that he was a partaker of the same nature with us, and joined to us by a true fellowship of the flesh, seeing he acknowledges us as his brethren, and vouchsafes to give us a title so honourable. I have already repeatedly stated, (and it is also easy to prove it from the end of this psalm,) that under the figure of David, Christ has been here shadowed forth to us. The apostle, therefore, justly deduces from this, that under and by the name of *brethren*, the right of fraternal alliance with Christ has been confirmed to us. This, no doubt, to a certain extent, belongs to all mankind, but the true enjoyment thereof belongs properly to genuine believers alone. For this reason Christ himself, with his own mouth, limits this title to his disciples, saying, " Go to my brethren, and say unto them, I ascend unto my Father and your Father, and to my God and your God," (John xx. 17.) The ungodly, by means of their unbelief, break off and dissolve that relationship of the flesh, by which he has allied himself to us, and thus render themselves utter strangers to him by their own fault. As David, while he comprehended under the word *brethren* all the offspring of Abraham, immediately after (verse 23) particularly addresses his discourse to the true worshippers of God; so Christ, while he has broken down " the middle wall of partition" between Jews and Gentiles, and published the blessings of adoption to all nations, and thereby exhibited himself to them as a brother, retains in the degree of brethren none but true believers.

23. *Ye who fear Jehovah.* Here, again, the Psalmist expresses more distinctly the fruit of public and solemn thanksgiving, of which I have spoken before, declaring, that by engaging in this exercise, every man in his own place invites and stirs up the church by his example to praise God. He tells us, that the end for which he will praise the name of God in the public assembly is to encourage his brethren to do the same. But as hypocrites commonly thrust themselves into the church, and as on the barn-floor of the Lord the chaff is mingled with the wheat, he addresses himself expressly to the godly, and those who *fear* God. Impure and wicked men may sing the praises of God with open mouth, but assuredly, they do nothing else than pollute and profane his holy name. It were, indeed, an object much to be desired, that men of all conditions in the world would, with one accord, join in holy melody to the Lord. But as the chief and most essential part of this harmony proceeds from a sincere and pure affection of heart, none will ever, in a right manner, celebrate the glory of God, except the man who worships him under the influence of holy fear. David names, a little after, *the seed of Jacob and Israel,* having a reference to the common calling of the people; and certainly, he put no obstacle in the way to hinder even all the children of Abraham from praising God with one accord. But as he saw that many of the Israelites were bastard and degenerate, he distinguishes true and sincere Israelites from them; and at the same time shows that God's name is not duly celebrated, unless where there is true piety and the inward fear of God. Accordingly, in his exhortation he again joins together the praises of God and reverence towards him. *Fear him, ye seed of Israel,* says he; for all the fair faces which hypocrites put on in this matter are nothing but pure mockery. The fear which he recommends is not, however, such as would frighten the faithful from approaching God, but that which will bring them truly humbled into his sanctuary, as has been stated in the fifth psalm. Some may be surprised to find David addressing an exhortation to praise God,[1] to those whom he had previously

---

[1] It is "praise God," both in the Latin and French versions; but the train of thought seems to require that it should be "fear God."

commended for doing so. But this is easily explained, for even the holiest men in the world are never so thoroughly imbued with the fear of God as not to have need of being continually incited to its exercise. Accordingly, the exhortation is not at all superfluous when, speaking of those who fear God, he exhorts them to stand in awe of him, and to prostrate themselves humbly before him.

24. *For he hath not despised.* To rejoice in one another's good, and to give thanks in common for each other's welfare, is a branch of that communion which ought to exist among the people of God, as Paul also teaches, (2 Cor. i. 11,) "That for the gift bestowed upon us by the means of many persons, thanks may be given by many on our behalf." But this statement of David serves another important purpose—it serves to encourage every man to hope that God will exercise the same mercy towards himself. By the way, we are taught from these words that the people of God ought to endure their afflictions patiently, however long it shall please the Lord to keep them in a state of distress, that he may at length succour them, and lend them his aid when they are so severely tried.

25. *My praise shall proceed from thee*[1] *in the great assembly; I will pay my vows in the presence of them that fear him.*
26. *The poor shall eat and be satisfied; they shall praise Jehovah that seek him: your heart shall live for ever.*
27. *All the ends of the earth shall remember, and turn to Jehovah; and all the tribes of the Gentiles shall prostrate themselves before his face.*
28. *For the kingdom is Jehovah's, that he may be the governor among the nations.*
29. *All the fat ones of the earth shall eat and worship: all those who are going down to the dust shall bow before him; and he who quickeneth not his own soul,* [*or he who is unable to keep himself alive.*]

25. *My praise shall proceed from thee.* I do not reject the other translation; but in my opinion, the Hebrew manner of

[1] "A te laus mea."—*Lat.* "Ma louange *proviendra* de toy."—*Fr.* "Ou, ma louange sera de toy."—*Fr. marg.* "Or, my praise shall be of thee."

expression here requires this sense—that David will take the matter of his song of praise from God. Accordingly, I supply the verb *shall proceed,* or *shall flow,*—*My praise shall proceed or flow from thee;* and he made this statement in order to testify that he owed his deliverance entirely to God. We know that there are many who, under pretence of praising God, trumpet forth their own praises, and those of their friends, and leaving God in the back-ground, take occasion from one thing or another to celebrate their own triumphs. The Psalmist repeats what he had touched upon a little before, that he will show the tokens of his gratitude in a public manner, in order thereby to edify others. He adds, that among these tokens will be the solemn exercise of godliness enjoined by the law: *I will pay my vows in the presence of them that fear him.* In important affairs, and when threatened with imminent danger, it was a common practice among God's ancient people to vow a peace-offering, and after having obtained the object of their desire, they performed their vow. As David, therefore, belonged to the number of the saints, he conformed himself, as it became him, to that common and understood regulation of the Church. The vows which he promises to pay are those which he intimates he had made in his extreme distress, and he prepares himself to perform them with a noble and cheerful heart, yea, with a heart full of confidence. Now, although it behoved him to perform this solemn act of religion in the presence of the whole assembly without distinction, he again confesses it to be his desire, that all who should be present there to witness it should be the true worshippers of God. Thus, although it may not be in our power to cleanse the Church of God, it is our duty to desire her purity. The Papists, by wresting this passage to support their false and deceitful vows, show themselves so stupid and so ridiculous, that it is unnecessary to spend much time in refuting them. What resemblance is there between these childish fooleries, with which according to their own imagination they attempt to appease God, and this holy testimony of gratitude, which not only a true sense of religion and the fear of God suggested to the fathers, but which God himself has commanded and ratified in his law? Yea, how can they have the face to equal their foolish and infamous superstitions to the most precious of all sacrifices— the sacrifice of thanksgiving? even as the Scriptures testify, that the principal part of the service of God consists in this, that true believers publicly and solemnly acknowledge that he is the author of all good things.

26. *The poor shall eat.* The Psalmist has a reference to the custom which was at that time prevalent among the Jews, of feasting on their sacrifices, as is very well known. He here promises this feast, in order to exercise and prove his charity. And surely that is a pleasant and an acceptable oblation to God to which compassion and mercy are joined. Without these, the ceremonies by which men profess to worship God, with all their pomp and magnificence, vanish into smoke. David does not, however, simply promise to bestow upon the poor and the hungry something for the mere nourishment of the body. He declares that they shall be partakers of this feast for another purpose, namely, that matter of comfort being ministered to them, joy might be restored to their hearts and flourish afresh. For they saw in that feast, as in a mirror, the goodness of God set forth to all who are in affliction, which might assuage with wonderful consolation the grief arising from all their calamities. The Psalmist therefore adds, *They shall praise Jehovah that seek him.* The abundant repast of which they had partaken ought, no doubt, to have incited them to give thanks to God; but what is particularly meant is, praising God for that deliverance in grateful commemoration of which the sacrifice was offered. This appears still more clearly from the last clause of the verse: *Your heart shall live for ever.* One meal could not have sufficed to make their hearts live for ever. It was rather the hope which they entertained of having ready succour from God which did this; for all the faithful justly reckoned the deliverance of this one man as a deliverance wrought for themselves in particular. Whence it follows, that, in the peace-offerings, the praises of God were so celebrated, as that genuine worshippers also exercised their hope

in them. Farther, as hypocrites content themselves with merely going through the bare and lifeless ceremony, the Psalmist restricts the right performance of this exercise to true and holy Israelites: *They shall praise Jehovah that seek him;* and to seek God is the certain mark of genuine godliness. Now, if the fathers under the law had their spiritual life renewed and invigorated by their holy feasts, this virtue will show itself much more abundantly at this day in the holy supper of Christ, provided those who come to partake of it seek the Lord truly, and with their whole heart.

27. *All the ends of the earth shall remember.* This passage, beyond all doubt, shows that David stops not at his own person, but that under himself, as a type, he describes the promised Messiah. For even then, it ought to have been a well-known point, that he had been created king by God, that the people might be united together and enjoy a happy life under one head; and this was at length completely fulfilled in Christ. David's name, I admit, was great and renowned among the neighbouring nations; but what was the territory which they occupied in comparison of the whole world? Besides, the foreign nations whom he had subdued had never been converted by him to the true worship of God. That forced and slavish submission, therefore, which the heathen nations had been brought by conquest to yield to an earthly king, was very different from the willing obedience of true godliness by which they would be recovered from their miserable wanderings, and gathered to God. Nor does the Psalmist mean an ordinary change, when he says, that the nations shall return to God, after having become well acquainted with his grace. Moreover, by uniting them to the fellowship of the holy feast, he manifestly grafts them into the body of the Church. Some explain these words, *They shall remember,* as meaning, that upon the restoration of the light of faith to the Gentiles, they should then come to remember God, whom they had for a time forgotten;[1] but this seems to me too

[1] As it is not said what they should remember, some commentators explain it thus: That they shall remember, with penitence, their sins; and, particularly, their idolatry. Others, that they shall remember the goodness and mercy of God, through Christ, to a lost world. And others, that

refined, and far from the meaning. I allow that the conversion or return of which mention is here made, implies that they had previously been alienated from God by wicked defection; but this remembrance simply means that the Gentiles, awakened by the signal miracles wrought by God, would again come to embrace the true religion, from which they had fallen away. Farther, it is to be observed, that the true worship of God proceeds from the knowledge of him; for the language of the Psalmist implies, that those shall come to prostrate themselves before God, in humble adoration, who shall have profited so far in meditation upon his works, as that they shall have no more desire proudly and contemptuously to break forth against him.

This sense is more fully confirmed by the reason[1] which is added in the following verse, (28,) *The kingdom is Jehovah's, that he may rule over the nations.* Some explain these words thus :—It is not to be wondered at if the Gentiles should be constrained to yield honour to God, by whom they were created, and by whose hand they are governed, although he has not entered into a covenant of life with them. But I reject this as a meagre and unsatisfactory interpretation. This passage, I have no doubt, agrees with many other prophecies which represent the throne of God as erected, on which Christ may sit to superintend and govern the world. Although, therefore, the providence of God is extended to the whole world, without any part of it being excepted, yet let us remember that he then, in very deed, exercises his authority, when having dispelled the darkness of ignorance, and diffused the light of his word, he appears conspicuous on his throne. We have such a description of his kingdom by the prophet Isaiah, (chap. ii. 4,) " He shall judge among the nations, and shall rebuke many people." Moreover, as God had not subdued the world to himself, prior to the time when those who before were unconquerable were subdued to a willing obedience by the preaching of the gospel, we may

they shall remember God whom they had forgotten, worshipping, instead of him, wood and stones. This last seems to be the view to which Calvin refers.

[1] The reason why the Gentiles shall remember, and turn to the Lord.

conclude that this conversion was effected only under the management and government of Christ. If it is objected, that the whole world has never yet been converted, the solution is easy. A comparison is here made between that remarkable period in which God suddenly became known every where, by the preaching of the gospel, and the ancient dispensation, when he kept the knowledge of himself shut up within the limits of Judea. Christ, we know, penetrated with amazing speed, from the east to the west, like the lightning's flash, in order to bring into the Church the Gentiles from all parts of the world.

29. *All the fat ones of the earth shall eat and worship.* Lest it should be thought inconsistent that now the fat ones of the earth are admitted as guests to this banquet, which David seemed immediately before to have appointed only for the poor, let us remember that the first place was given to the poor, because to them principally comfort was set forth in the example of David. Yet it was necessary, in the second place, that the rich and the prosperous should be called to the feast, that they might not think themselves excluded from the participation of the same grace. They are not, it is true, urged, by the pressure of present calamities, to seek comfort for grief, but they have need of a remedy to prevent them from intoxicating themselves with their delights, and to excite them rather to lay up their joy in heaven. Again, since they also are subject to a variety of troubles, their abundance will be a curse to them, provided it keep their minds down to the earth. The amount of the Psalmist's statement is, that this sacrifice will be common as well to those who are sound, lusty, and in opulent circumstances, as to those who are lean, poor, and half dead from the want of food; that the former, laying aside their pride, may humble themselves before God, and that the latter, though they may be brought low, may lift up their minds by spiritual joy to God, the author of all good things, as James (chap. i. 9, 10) admonishes both classes, in these words, " Let the brother of low degree rejoice in that he is exalted; but the rich in that he is made low." Now, if God, under the law, joined the full with the hungry, the

noble with the mean, the happy with the wretched, much more ought this to take place at the present day under the gospel. When, therefore, the rich hear that food is offered to them elsewhere than in earthly abundance, let them learn to use the outward good things which God has bestowed upon them for the purposes of the present life, with such sobriety as that they may not be disgusted with spiritual food, or turn away from it, through loathing. So long as they wallow in their own filth, they will never long for this food with a holy desire; and although they may have it at hand, they will never take pleasure in tasting it.[1] Farther, as those who are fat must become lean, in order that they may present themselves to God to be fed and nourished, so David endeavours to inspire the famished with assured and undaunted confidence, lest their poverty should hinder them from coming to the banquet. Yea, he invites even the dead to come to the feast, in order that the most despised, and those who, in the estimation of the world, are almost like putrefying carcases, may be encouraged and emboldened to present themselves at the holy table of the Lord. The change which the Psalmist makes in the number, from the plural to the singular, in the end of the verse, somewhat obscures the sense; but the meaning undoubtedly is, that those who seem already to be reduced to dust, and whose restoration from death to life is, as it were, despaired of, shall be partakers of the same grace with him.

30. *Their seed shall serve him, and shall be registered to the Lord*[2] *for a generation.*
31. *They shall come, and shall declare his righteousness to a people that shall be born, because he hath done it.*

30. *Their seed shall serve him.* The more to exalt the greatness of the benefit, he declares that it will be of such a character that posterity will never forget it. And he shows how it will come to be perpetuated, namely, because the conversion of the world, of which he has spoken, will not be for

---

[1] " Et encores qu'ils les ayent à main, ils ne pourront prendre plaisir à les savourer."—*Fr.*

[2] The Hebrew word here is אדני, *Adonai.*

a short time only but will continue from age to age. Whence we again conclude, that what is here celebrated is not such a manifestation of the glory of God to the Gentile nations as proceeds from a transitory and fading rumour, but such as will enlighten the world with its beams, even to the end of time. Accordingly, the perpetuity of the Church is here abundantly proved, and in very clear terms: not that it always flourishes or continues in the same uniform course through successive ages, but because God, unwilling that his name should be extinguished in the world, will always raise up some sincerely to devote themselves to his service. We ought to remember that this seed, in which the service of God was to be preserved, is the fruit of the incorruptible seed; for God begets and multiplies his Church only by means of his word.

The expression, *To be registered to the Lord for a generation*, is explained in two ways. Some take the Hebrew word דור, *dor*, for *a succession of ages*, and explain the clause thus: They shall be registered to the Lord age after age. Others take it for *generation*, in the sense in which the word *natio* [nation] is used in the Latin tongue. As both these senses suit very well, and come almost to the same thing, I leave my readers at liberty to choose between them. I am, however, I admit, rather inclined to the opinion, that by this word is designated God's chosen people and peculiar nation, which may be accounted the heritage of God. Farther, as the name *Jehovah*, which is expressive of God's essence, is not here used as it is a little before, but the word *Adonai*, I do not disapprove of the opinion of those who think that Christ is here expressly invested with authority over[1] the Church, that he may register all who shall give in their names as on the side of God his Father. And, indeed, as our heavenly Father has committed all his chosen ones to the protection and guardianship of his own Son, he acknowledges as his people none but those who belong to the flock of Christ.

31. *They shall come, and shall declare.* The Psalmist here

[1] The Hebrew word *Adonai* is derived from a verb which signifies *to direct, rule, judge;* and it therefore signifies *director, ruler, judge.*

confirms what I have previously stated, that since the fathers will transmit the knowledge of this benefit to their children, as it were from hand to hand, the name of God will be always renowned. From this we may also deduce the additional truth, that it is by the preaching of the grace of God alone that the Church is kept from perishing. At the same time, let it be observed, that care and diligence in propagating divine truth are here enjoined upon us, that it may continue after we are removed from this world. As the Holy Spirit prescribes it as a duty incumbent on all the faithful to be diligent in instructing their children, that there may be always one generation after another to serve God, the sluggishness of those who have no scruple of conscience in burying the remembrance of God in eternal silence, a sin with which those are virtually chargeable who neglect to speak of him to their children, and who thus do nothing to prevent his name from utterly perishing, is condemned as involving the greatest turpitude. The term *righteousness,* in this place, refers to the faithfulness which God observes in preserving his people, of which we have a memorable example in the deliverance of David. In defending his servant from the violence and outrage of the wicked, he proved himself to be righteous. Hence we may learn how dear our welfare is to God, seeing he combines it with the celebration of the praise of his own righteousness. If then the righteousness of God is illustriously manifested in this, that he does not disappoint us of our hope, nor abandon us in dangers, but defends and keeps us in perfect safety, there is no more reason to fear that he will forsake us in the time of our need, than there is reason to fear that he can forget himself. We must, however, remember that it is not for any particular succour afforded to one individual, but it is for the redemption of the human race, that the celebration of the praise of God is required from us in this passage. In short, the Holy Spirit, by the mouth of David, recommends to us the publication of Christ's resurrection. In the end of this psalm some commentators resolve the particle כִּי, *ki, because,* into the pronoun אֲשֶׁר, *asher, which,* as if it had been said, *The righteousness which he hath done.* But the sentence will be fuller if we read, *because,* and explain the passage thus: They shall come, and shall declare his righteousness, because God shall have given proof, or demonstration, of his righteousness—shall have afforded evidence by the effect, or the deed itself, that he is the faithful guardian of his own people.

PSALM XXIII.

This psalm is neither intermingled with prayers, nor does it complain of miseries for the purpose of obtaining relief; but it contains simply a thanksgiving, from which it appears that it was composed when David had obtained peaceable possession of the kingdom, and lived in prosperity, and in the enjoyment of all he could desire. That he might not, therefore, in the time of his great prosperity, be like worldly men, who, when they seem to themselves to be fortunate,[1] bury God in forgetfulness, and luxuriously plunge themselves into their pleasures, he delights himself in God, the author of all the blessings which he enjoyed. And he not only acknowledges that the state of tranquillity in which he now lives, and his exemption from all inconveniences and troubles, is owing to the goodness of God; but he also trusts that through his providence he will continue happy even to the close of his life, and for this end that he may employ himself in his pure worship.

A Psalm of David.

1. *Jehovah is my shepherd, I shall not want.*[2]
2. *He maketh me to lie down in pastures of grass; he leadeth me to gently flowing waters.*[3]
3. *He restoreth my soul: he leadeth me by the paths of righteousness for his name's sake.*
4. *Though I should walk in the valley of the shadow of death, I will fear no evil: for thou art with me; thy staff and thy crook comfort me.*

1. *Jehovah is my shepherd.* Although God, by his benefits,

---

[1] "Lesquels ayans le vent à gré, comme on dit."—*Fr.* "Who having the wind to their mind, as we say."

[2] "Le Seigneur est mon pasteur, *parquoy* je n'auray faute *de rien.*"—*Fr.* "The Lord is my shepherd, *therefore* I shall not want *any thing.*"

[3] "Il me mene aux eaux quoyes."—*Fr.* "He leadeth me to the quiet [or peaceful] waters."

gently allures us to himself, as it were by a taste of his fatherly sweetness, yet there is nothing into which we more easily fall than into a forgetfulness of him, when we are in the enjoyment of peace and comfort. Yea, prosperity not only so intoxicates many, as to carry them beyond all bounds in their mirth, but it also engenders insolence, which makes them proudly rise up and break forth against God. Accordingly, there is scarcely a hundredth part of those who enjoy in abundance the good things of God, who keep themselves in his fear, and live in the exercise of humility and temperance, which would be so becoming.[1] For this reason, we ought the more carefully to mark the example which is here set before us by David, who, elevated to the dignity of sovereign power, surrounded with the splendour of riches and honours, possessed of the greatest abundance of temporal good things, and in the midst of princely pleasures, not only testifies that he is mindful of God, but calling to remembrance the benefits which God had conferred upon him,[2] makes them ladders by which he may ascend nearer to Him. By this means he not only bridles the wantonness of his flesh, but also excites himself with the greater earnestness to gratitude, and the other exercises of godliness, as appears from the concluding sentence of the psalm, where he says, "I shall dwell in the house of Jehovah for a length of days." In like manner, in the xviiith psalm, which was composed at a period of his life when he was applauded on every side, by calling himself the servant of God, he showed the humility and simplicity of heart to which he had attained, and, at the same time, openly testified his gratitude, by applying himself to the celebration of the praises of God.

Under the similitude of a shepherd, he commends the care which God, in his providence, had exercised towards him. His language implies that God had no less care of him than a shepherd has of the sheep who are committed to his charge. God, in the Scripture, frequently takes to himself the name, and puts on the character of a shepherd, and this is no mean

[1] " Qui se contiene en la crainte de Dieu se selon la modestie et temperance qui seroit requise."—*Fr.*
[2] " Mais rememorant les benefices qu'il reçoit de luy."—*Fr.*

token of his tender love towards us. As this is a lowly and homely manner of speaking, He who does not disdain to stoop so low for our sake, must bear a singularly strong affection towards us. It is therefore wonderful, that when he invites us to himself with such gentleness and familiarity, we are not drawn or allured to him, that we may rest in safety and peace under his guardianship. But it should be observed, that God is a shepherd only to those who, touched with a sense of their own weakness and poverty, feel their need of his protection, and who willingly abide in his sheepfold, and surrender themselves to be governed by him. David, who excelled both in power and riches, nevertheless frankly confessed himself to be a poor sheep, that he might have God for his shepherd. Who is there, then, amongst us, who would exempt himself from this necessity, seeing our own weakness sufficiently shows that we are more than miserable if we do not live under the protection of this shepherd? We ought to bear in mind, that our happiness consists in this, that his hand is stretched forth to govern us, that we live under his shadow, and that his providence keeps watch and ward over our welfare. Although, therefore, we have abundance of all temporal good things, yet let us be assured that we cannot be truly happy unless God vouchsafe to reckon us among the number of his flock. Besides, we then only attribute to God the office of a Shepherd with due and rightful honour, when we are persuaded that his providence alone is sufficient to supply all our necessities.[1] As those who enjoy the greatest abundance of outward good things are empty and famished if God is not their shepherd; so it is beyond all doubt that those whom he has taken under his charge shall not want a full abundance of all good things. David, therefore, declares that he is not afraid of wanting any thing, because God is his Shepherd.

2. *He maketh me to lie down in pastures of grass.* With respect to the words, it is in the Hebrew, *pastures*, or *fields of grass*, for *grassy and rich grounds*. Some, instead of trans-

---

[1] "Que sa seule providence est suffisante pour nous administrer toutes nos necessitez."—*Fr.*

lating the word נאות, *neoth*, which we have rendered *pastures*, render it *shepherds' cots* or *lodges*. If this translation is considered preferable, the meaning of the Psalmist will be, that sheep-cots were prepared in rich pasture grounds, under which he might be protected from the heat of the sun. If even in cold countries the immoderate heat which sometimes occurs is troublesome to a flock of sheep, how could they bear the heat of the summer in Judea, a warm region, without sheepfolds? The verb רבץ, *rabats, to lie down,* or *repose,* seems to have a reference to the same thing. David has used the phrase, *the quiet waters,* to express gently flowing waters; for rapid streams are inconvenient for sheep to drink in, and are also for the most part hurtful. In this verse, and in the verses following, he explains the last clause of the first verse, *I shall not want.* He relates how abundantly God had provided for all his necessities, and he does this without departing from the comparison which he employed at the commencement. The amount of what is stated is, that the heavenly Shepherd had omitted nothing which might contribute to make him live happily under his care. He, therefore, compares the great abundance of all things requisite for the purposes of the present life which he enjoyed, to meadows richly covered with grass, and to gently flowing streams of water; or he compares the benefit or advantage of such things to sheep-cots; for it would not have been enough to have been fed and satisfied in rich pasture, had there not also been provided waters to drink, and the shadow of the sheep-cot to cool and refresh him.

3. *He restoreth my soul.* As it is the duty of a good shepherd to cherish his sheep, and when they are diseased or weak to nurse and support them, David declares that this was the manner in which he was treated by God. *The restoring of the soul,* as we have translated it, or *the conversion of the soul,* as it is, literally rendered, is of the same import as *to make anew,* or *to recover,* as has been already stated in the xixth psalm, at the seventh verse. By *the paths of righteousness,* he means easy and plain paths.[1] As he still

[1] Walford adopts and defends this view. His reading is, "He leadeth

continues his metaphor, it would be out of place to understand this as referring to the direction of the Holy Spirit. He has stated a little before that God liberally supplies him with all that is requisite for the maintenance of the present life, and now he adds, that he is defended by him from all trouble. The amount of what is said is, that God is in no respect wanting to his people, seeing he sustains them by his power, invigorates and quickens them, and averts from them whatever is hurtful, that they may walk at ease in plain and straight paths. That, however, he may not ascribe any thing to his own worth or merit, David represents the goodness of God as the cause of so great liberality, declaring that God bestows all these things upon him *for his own name's sake.* And certainly his choosing us to be his sheep, and his performing towards us all the offices of a shepherd, is a blessing which proceeds entirely from his free and sovereign goodness, as we shall see in the sixty-fifth psalm.

4. *Though I should walk.* True believers, although they dwell safely under the protection of God, are, notwithstanding, exposed to many dangers, or rather they are liable to all the afflictions which befall mankind in common, that they may the better feel how much they need the protection of God. David, therefore, here expressly declares, that if any adversity should befall him, he would lean upon the providence of God. Thus he does not promise himself continual pleasures; but he fortifies himself by the help of God courageously to endure the various calamities with which he might be visited. Pursuing his metaphor, he compares the care which God takes in governing true believers to a shepherd's staff and crook, declaring that he is satisfied with this as all-sufficient for the protection of his life. As a sheep, when it wanders up and

---

me in straight paths." "This version," says he, "may perhaps prove not altogether agreeable to the feelings of the reader, in consequence of his being accustomed to a different expression in the English Bible. But the consistency of the imagery requires the alteration; as otherwise, we have an incongruous mixture of physical and moral figures. A careful shepherd leads his sheep to verdant pastures, conducts them near peaceful waters, affords them the means of refreshment when wearied, and guides them away from rugged and tortuous paths to such as are direct and easy."

down through a dark valley, is preserved safe from the attacks of wild beasts and from harm in other ways, by the presence of the shepherd alone, so David now declares that as often as he shall be exposed to any danger, he will have sufficient defence and protection in being under the pastoral care of God.

We thus see how, in his prosperity, he never forgot that he was a man, but even then seasonably meditated on the adversities which afterwards might come upon him. And certainly, the reason why we are so terrified, when it pleases God to exercise us with the cross, is, because every man, that he may sleep soundly and undisturbed, wraps himself up in carnal security. But there is a great difference between this sleep of stupidity and the repose which faith produces. Since God tries faith by adversity, it follows that no one truly confides in God, but he who is armed with invincible constancy for resisting all the fears with which he may be assailed.[1] Yet David did not mean to say that he was devoid of all fear, but only that he would surmount it so as to go without fear wherever his shepherd should lead him. This appears more clearly from the context. He says, in the first place, *I will fear no evil;* but immediately adding the reason of this, he openly acknowledges that he seeks a remedy against his fear in contemplating, and having his eyes fixed on, the staff of his shepherd: *For thy staff and thy crook comfort me.* What need would he have had of that consolation, if he had not been disquieted and agitated with fear? It ought, therefore, to be kept in mind, that when David reflected on the adversities which might befall him, he became victorious over fear and temptations, in no other way than by casting himself on the protection of God. This he had also stated before, although a little more obscurely, in these words, *For thou art with me.* This implies that he had been afflicted with fear. Had not this been the case, for what purpose could he desire the presence of God?[2] Besides, it is not against the

---

[1] "Celuy qui est armé d'une constance invincible pour resister à toutes les frayeurs qui peuvent survenir."—*Fr.*
[2] "Car s'il n'y eust point eu de crainte, à quel propos desireroit il la presence de Dieu?"—*Fr.*

common and ordinary calamities of life only that he opposes the protection of God, but against those which distract and confound the minds of men with the darkness of death. For the Jewish grammarians think that צַלְמָוֶת, *tsalmaveth*, which we have translated *the shadow of death*, is a compound word, as if one should say *deadly shade*.[1] David here makes an allusion to the dark recesses or dens of wild beasts, to which when an individual approaches he is suddenly seized at his first entrance with an apprehension and fear of death. Now, since God, in the person of his only begotten Son, has exhibited himself to us as our shepherd, much more clearly than he did in old time to the fathers who lived under the Law, we do not render sufficient honour to his protecting care, if we do not lift our eyes to behold it, and keeping them fixed upon it, tread all fears and terrors under our feet.[2]

5. *Thou wilt prepare a table before me in the presence of my persecutors : thou wilt anoint my head with oil; my cup overflows.*
6. *Surely goodness and mercy will follow me all the days of my life ; and I shall dwell in the house of Jehovah for a length of days.*

5. *Thou wilt prepare.* These words, which are put in the future tense, here denote a continued act. David, therefore, now repeats, without a figure, what he has hitherto declared, concerning the beneficence of God, under the similitude of a shepherd. He tells us that by his liberality he is supplied with all that is necessary for the maintenance of this life. When he says, *Thou preparest a table before me,* he means that God furnished him with sustenance without trouble or difficulty on his part, just as if a father should stretch forth his hand to give food to his child. He enhances this benefit from the additional consideration, that although many mali-

---

[1] "The original, בגיא צלמות, is very emphatic, ' In or through the valley of death-shade.' This expression seems to denote imminent danger, (Jer. ii. 6,) sore affliction, (Psal. xliv. 19,) fear and terror, (Psal. cvii. 10, 14 ; Job xxiv. 17,) and dreadful darkness, (Job x. 21, 22.")—*Morison's Commentary on the Psalms.*

[2] "Si non qu'eslevans là nos yeux et les y ayans fichez, nous foullions aux pieds craintes et espouantemens."—*Fr.*

cious persons envy his happiness, and desire his ruin, yea, endeavour to defraud him of the blessing of God; yet God does not desist from showing himself liberal towards him, and from doing him good. What he subjoins concerning *oil*, has a reference to a custom which then prevailed. We know that in old time, ointments were used at the more magnificent feasts, and no man thought he had honourably received his guests if he had not perfumed them therewith. Now, this exuberant store of *oil*, and also this overflowing *cup*, ought to be explained as denoting the abundance which goes beyond the mere supply of the common necessaries of life; for it is spoken in commendation of the royal wealth with which, as the sacred historian records, David had been amply furnished. All men, it is true, are not treated with the same liberality with which David was treated; but there is not an individual who is not under obligation to God by the benefits which God has conferred upon him, so that we are constrained to acknowledge that he is a kind and liberal Father to all his people. In the meantime, let each of us stir up himself to gratitude to God for his benefits, and the more abundantly these have been bestowed upon us, our gratitude ought to be the greater. If he is ungrateful who, having only a coarse loaf, does not acknowledge in that the fatherly providence of God, how much less can the stupidity of those be tolerated, who glut themselves with the great abundance of the good things of God which they possess, without having any sense or taste of his goodness towards them? David, therefore, by his own example, admonishes the rich of their duty, that they may be the more ardent in the expression of their gratitude to God, the more delicately he feeds them. Farther, let us remember, that those who have greater abundance than others are bound to observe moderation not less than if they had only as much of the good things of this life as would serve for their limited and temperate enjoyment. We are too much inclined by nature to excess; and, therefore, when God is, in respect of worldly things, bountiful to his people, it is not to stir up and nourish in them this disease. All men ought to attend to the rule of Paul, which is laid down in Philip. iv. 12, that they " may know both how to be abased, and how to abound." That want may not sink us into despondency, we need to be sustained by patient endurance; and, on the other hand, that too great abundance may not elate us above measure, we need to be restrained by the bridle of temperance. Accordingly, the Lord, when he enriches his own people, restrains, at the same time, the licentious desires of the flesh by the spirit of continence, so that, of their own accord, they prescribe to themselves rules of temperance. Not that it is unlawful for rich men to enjoy more freely the abundance which they possess than if God had given them a smaller portion; but all men ought to beware, (and much more kings,) lest they should be dissolved in voluptuous pleasures. David, no doubt, as was perfectly lawful, allowed himself larger scope than if he had been only one of the common people, or than if he had still dwelt in his father's cottage, but he so regulated himself in the midst of his delicacies, as not at all to take pleasure in stuffing and fattening the body. He knew well how to distinguish between the table which God had prepared for him and a trough for swine. It is also worthy of particular notice, that although David lived upon his own lands, the tribute money and other revenues of the kingdom, he gave thanks to God just as if God had daily given him his food with his own hand. From this we conclude that he was not blinded with his riches, but always looked upon God as his householder, who brought forth meat and drink from his own store, and distributed it to him at the proper season.

6. *Surely goodness and mercy.* Having recounted the blessings which God had bestowed upon him, he now expresses his undoubted persuasion of the continuance of them to the end of his life. But whence proceeded this confidence, by which he assures himself that the beneficence and mercy of God will accompany him for ever, if it did not arise from the promise by which God is accustomed to season the blessings which he bestows upon true believers, that they may not inconsiderately devour them without having any taste or relish for them? When he said to himself before, that even amidst the darkness of death he would keep his eyes fixed

in beholding the providence of God, he sufficiently testified that he did not depend upon outward things, nor measured the grace of God according to the judgment of the flesh, but that even when assistance from every earthly quarter failed him, his faith continued shut up in the word of God. Although, therefore, experience led him to hope well, yet it was principally on the promise by which God confirms his people with respect to the future that he depended. If it is objected that it is presumption for a man to promise himself a continued course of prosperity in this uncertain and changing world, I answer, that David did not speak in this manner with the view of imposing on God a law; but he hoped for such exercise of God's beneficence towards him as the condition of this world permits, with which he would be contented. He does not say, My cup shall be always full, or, My head shall be always perfumed with oil; but in general he entertains the hope that as the goodness of God never fails, he will be favourable towards him even to the end.

I will dwell in the house of Jehovah. By this concluding sentence he manifestly shows that he does not confine his thoughts to earthly pleasures or comforts; but that the mark at which he aims is fixed in heaven, and to reach this was his great object in all things. It is as if he had said, I do not live for the mere purpose of living, but rather to exercise myself in the fear and service of God, and to make progress daily in all the branches of true godliness. He makes a manifest distinction between himself and ungodly men, who take pleasure only in filling their bellies with luxuriant fare. And not only so, but he also intimates that to live to God is, in his estimation, of so great importance, that he valued all the comforts of the flesh only in proportion as they served to enable him to live to God. He plainly affirms, that the end which he contemplated in all the benefits which God had conferred upon him was, that he might dwell in the house of the Lord. Whence it follows, that when deprived of the enjoyment of this blessing, he made no account of all other things; as if he had said, I would take no pleasure in earthly comforts, unless I at the same time belonged to the flock of God, as he also writes in another place, " Happy is that people that is in such a case : yea, happy is that people whose God is the Lord," (Psalm cxliv. 15.) Why did he desire so greatly to frequent the temple, but to offer sacrifices there along with his fellow-worshippers, and to improve by the other exercises of religion in meditation upon the celestial life? It is, therefore, certain that the mind of David, by the aid of the temporal prosperity which he enjoyed, was elevated to the hope of the everlasting inheritance. From this we conclude, that those men are brutish who propose to themselves any other felicity than that which arises from drawing near to God.

PSALM XXIV.

As God stands related to all mankind as their Creator and Governor, David, from this consideration, magnifies the special favour which God manifested towards the children of Abraham, in choosing them to be his peculiar people, in preference to the rest of mankind, and in erecting his sanctuary as his house that he might dwell among them. He shows, at the same time, that although the sanctuary was open to all the Jews, God was not near to all of them, but only to those who feared and served him in sincerity, and who had cleansed themselves from the pollutions of the world, in order to devote themselves to holiness and righteousness. Moreover, as the grace of God was more clearly manifested after the temple was built, he celebrates that grace in a strain of splendid poetry, to encourage true believers with the more alacrity to persevere in the exercise of serving and honouring him.

A Psalm of David.

1. *The earth is Jehovah's, and the fulness thereof ;*[1] *the world, and they that dwell therein:*
2. *For he hath founded it upon the seas, and established it upon the floods.*
3. *Who shall ascend unto the hill of Jehovah ? who shall stand in his holy place ?*

[1] " Son contenu."—*Note, Fr. marg.* " That is, its contents."

4. *He who is clean of hands, and pure of heart; who hath not lifted up his soul to vanity, nor sworn deceitfully.*

1. *The earth is Jehovah's.* We will find in many other places the children of Abraham compared with all the rest of mankind, that the free goodness of God, in selecting them from all other nations, and in embracing them with his favour, may shine forth the more conspicuously. The object of the beginning of the psalm is to show that the Jews had nothing of themselves which could entitle them to approach nearer or more familiarly to God than the Gentiles. As God by his providence preserves the world, the power of his government is alike extended to all, so that he ought to be worshipped by all, even as he also shows to all men, without exception, the fatherly care he has about them. But since he preferred the Jews to all other nations, it was indispensably necessary that there should be some sacred bond of connection between him and them, which might distinguish them from the heathen nations. By this argument David invites and exhorts them to holiness. He tells them that it was reasonable that those whom God had adopted as his children, should bear certain marks peculiar to themselves, and not be altogether like strangers. Not that he incites them to endeavour to prejudice God against others, in order to gain his exclusive favour; but he teaches them, from the end or design of their election, that they shall then have secured to them the firm and peaceful possession of the honour which God had conferred upon them above other nations, when they devote themselves to an upright and holy life.[1] In vain would they have been collected together into a distinct body, as the peculiar people of God, if they did not apply themselves to the cultivation of holiness. In short, the Psalmist pronounces God to be the King of the whole world, to let all men know that, even by the law of nature, they are bound to serve him. And by declaring that he made a covenant of salvation with a small portion of man-

[1] " Qu'adonc ils entreront en ferme et paisible possession de l'honneur que Dieu leur a fait par dessus les autres nations."—*Fr.*

kind, and by the erection of the tabernacle, gave the children of Abraham the symbol of his presence, thereby to assure them of his dwelling in the midst of them, he teaches them that they must endeavour to have purity of heart and of hands, if they would be accounted the members of his sacred family.

With respect to the word *fulness*, I admit that under it all the riches with which the earth is adorned are comprehended, as is proved by the authority of Paul; but I have no doubt that the Psalmist intends by the expression men themselves, who are the most illustrious ornament and glory of the earth. If they should fail, the earth would exhibit a scene of desolation and solitude, not less hideous than if God should despoil it of all its other riches. To what purpose are there produced so many kinds of fruit, and in so great abundance, and why are there so many pleasant and delightful countries, if it is not for the use and comfort of men?[1] Accordingly, David explains, in the following clause, that it is principally of men that he speaks. It is his usual manner to repeat the same thing twice, and here *the fulness of the earth*, and *the inhabitants of the world*, have the same meaning. I do not, however, deny that the riches with which the earth abounds for the use of men, are comprehended under these expressions. Paul, therefore, (1 Cor. x. 26,) when discoursing concerning meats, justly quotes this passage in support of his argument, maintaining that no kind of food is unclean, because "the earth is the Lord's, and the fulness thereof."

2. *For he hath founded it upon the seas.* The Psalmist here confirms the truth, that men are rightfully under the authority and power of God, so that in all places and countries they ought to acknowledge him as King. And he confirms it from the very order manifested in the creation; for the wonderful providence of God is clearly reflected in the whole face of the earth. In order to prove this, he brings forward the

---

[1] " Car à quelle fin font produits des fruits de tant de sortes, et en telle abondance, et qu'il y a tant de lieux de plaisance, si non pour l'usage et commodite des hommes?"—*Fr.*

proof of it, which is most evident. How is it that the earth appears above the water, but because God purposely intended to prepare a habitation for men? Philosophers themselves admit, that as the element of the water is higher than the earth, it is contrary to the nature of the two elements,[1] for any part of the earth to continue uncovered with the waters, and habitable. Accordingly, Job (chap. xxviii. 11, 25) extols, in magnificent terms, that signal miracle by which God restrains the violent and tempestuous ragings of the sea, that it may not overwhelm the earth, which, if not thus restrained, it would immediately do, and produce horrible confusion. Nor does Moses forget to mention this in the history of the creation. After having narrated that the waters were spread abroad so as to cover the whole earth, he adds, that by an express command of God they retired into one place, in order to leave empty space for the living creatures which were afterwards to be created, (Gen. i. 9.) From that passage we learn that God had a care about men before they existed, inasmuch as he prepared for them a dwelling-place and other conveniences; and that he did not regard them as entire strangers, seeing he provided for their necessities, not less liberally than the father of a family does for his own children. David does not here dispute philosophically concerning the situation of the earth, when he says, that *it has been founded upon the seas.* He uses popular language, and adapts himself to the capacity of the unlearned. Yet this manner of speaking, which is taken from what may be judged of by the eye, is not without reason. The element of earth, it is true, in so far as it occupies the lowest place in the order of the sphere, is beneath the waters; but the habitable part of the earth is above the water, and how can we account for it, that this separation of the water from the earth remains stable, but because God has put the waters underneath, as it were for a foundation? Now, as from the creation of the world, God extended his fatherly care to all mankind, the prerogative of honour, by which the Jews

---

[1] " C'est contre la nature des deux elemens."—*Fr.*

excelled all other nations, proceeded only from the free and sovereign choice by which God distinguished them.

3. *Who shall ascend unto.* It being very well known that it was of pure grace that God erected his sanctuary, and chose for himself a dwelling-place among the Jews, David makes only a tacit reference to this subject.[1] He insists principally on the other point contained in the verse, that of distinguishing true Israelites from the false and bastards. He takes the argument by which he exhorts the Jews to lead a holy and righteous life from this, that God had separated them from the rest of the world, to be his peculiar inheritance. The rest of mankind, it is true, seeing they were created by him, belong to his empire; but he who occupies a place in the church is more nearly related to him. All those, therefore, whom God receives into his flock he calls to holiness; and he lays them under obligations to follow it by his adoption. Moreover, by these words David indirectly rebukes hypocrites, who scrupled not falsely to take to themselves the holy name of God, as we know that they are usually lifted up with pride, because of the titles which they take without having the excellencies which these titles imply, contenting themselves with bearing only outside distinctions;[2] yea, rather he purposely magnifies this singular grace of God, that every man may learn for himself, that he has no right of entrance or access to the sanctuary, unless he sanctify himself in order to serve God in purity. The ungodly and wicked, it is true, were in the habit of resorting to the tabernacle; and, therefore, God, by the Prophet Isaiah, (chap. i. 12,) reproaches them for coming unworthily into his courts, and wearing the pavement thereof. But David here treats of those who may lawfully enter into God's sanctuary. The house of God being holy, if any rashly, and without a right,

---

[1] " Il n'en fait yci que bien petite mention et comme en passant."—*Fr.* " He here only slightly adverts to this subject, and as it were in passing."

[2] " Comme nous sçavons que c'est leur coustume de s'eslever par orgueil à cause des titres qu'ils prenent sans avoir l'effect, se contentans de porter seulement les marques par dehors."—*Fr.*

rush into it, their corruption and abuse are nothing else but polluting it. As therefore they do not go up thither lawfully, David makes no account of their going up; yea, rather, under these words there is included a severe rebuke, of the conduct of wicked and profane men, in daring to go up into the sanctuary, and to pollute it with their impurity. On this subject I have spoken more fully on the 15th psalm. In the second part of the verse he seems to denote perseverance, as if he had said, Who shall go up into the hill of Sion, to appear and stand in the presence of God? The Hebrew word קום, *kum*, it is true, sometimes signifies *to rise up*, but it is generally taken for *to stand*, as we have seen in the first psalm. And although this is a repetition of the same idea, stated in the preceding clause, it is not simply so, but David, by expressing the end for which they ought to go up, illustrates and amplifies the subject; and this repetition and amplification we find him often making use of in other psalms. In short, how much soever the wicked were mingled with the good in the church, in the time of David, he declares how vain a thing it is to make an external profession unless there be, at the same time, truth in the inward man. What he says concerning the tabernacle of the covenant must be applied to the continual government of the church.

4. *He who is clean of hands, and pure of heart.* Under the purity of the hands and of the heart, and the reverence of God's name, he comprehends all religion, and denotes a well ordered life. True purity, no doubt, has its seat in the heart, but it manifests its fruits in the works of the hands. The Psalmist, therefore, very properly joins to a pure heart the purity of the whole life; for that man acts a ridiculous part who boasts of having a sound heart, if he does not show by his fruits that the root is good. On the other hand, it will not suffice to frame the hands, feet, and eyes, according to the rule of righteousness, unless purity of heart precede outward continence. If any man should think it absurd that the first place is given to the hands, we answer without hesitation, that effects are often named before their causes, not

that they precede them in order, but because it is sometimes advantageous to begin with things which are best known. David, then, would have the Jews to bring into the presence of God pure hands, and these along with an unfeigned heart. *To lift up,* or *to take his soul,* I have no doubt is here put for *to swear.* It is, therefore, here required of the servants of God, that when they swear, they do it with reverence and in good conscience;[1] and, under one particular, by synecdoche, is denoted the duty of observing fidelity and integrity in all the affairs of life. That mention is here made of oaths, appears from the words which immediately follow, *And hath not sworn deceitfully,* which are added as explanatory of what goes before. As, however, there is a twofold reading of the Hebrew word for *soul,* that is to say, as it may be read, *my soul,* or *his soul,* on account of the point *hirek,* some Jewish commentators read, *Who hath not lifted up my soul to vanity,*[2] and understand the word *my* as spoken of God, an exposition which I reject as harsh and strained. It is a manner of speaking which carries in it great emphasis, for it means, that those who swear offer their souls as pledges to God. Some, however, may perhaps prefer the opinion, that *to lift up the soul,* is put for *to apply it to lying,* an interpretation to the adoption of which I have no great objection, for it makes little difference as to the sense. A question may here be raised—it may be asked, why David does not say so much as one word concerning faith and calling upon God. The reason of this is easily explained. As it seldom happens that a man behaves himself uprightly and innocently towards his

---

[1] " Par ainsi il est yci requis des serviteurs de Dieu, que quand ils jurent, ce soit avec reverence et en bonne conscience."—*Fr.*

[2] The textual reading is נפשו, *naphshiv,* ʾ*is soul;* the marginal reading is נפשי, *naphshi, my soul.* But the textual reading, from its clearness and simplicity, is, without doubt, the correct one. " The points," says Hammond, " direct to render נַפְשׁוֹ, *my soul,* and so the interlinear reads *animam meam, my soul* or *life,* as if it were נַפְשִׁי, making God the speaker of this verse, and then it is God's life or soul. But the text writing ', not ', and the context agreeing with it, the punctuation must, in reason, give place; and, accordingly, all the ancient interpreters appear to have read it נפשו, *his soul,* meaning by that *his own soul,* or the *soul of the swearer.*"

brethren, unless he is so endued with the true fear of God as to walk circumspectly before him, David very justly forms his estimate of the piety of men towards God by the character of their conduct towards their fellow-men. For the same reason, Christ (Matth. xxiii. 23) represents "judgment, mercy, and faith," as the principal points of the law; and Paul calls "charity" at one time "the end of the law," (1 Tim. i. 5,) and at another "the bond of perfection," (Col. iii. 14.)

> 5. *He shall receive blessing from Jehovah, and righteousness from the God of his salvation.*
> 6. *This is the generation of them that seek him, of them that seek thy face, O Jacob!*[1] *Selah.*

5. *He shall receive blessing.* The more effectually to move the minds of the Israelites, David declares that nothing is more desirable than to be numbered among the flock of God, and to be members of the church. We must here consider that there is an implied contrast between true Israelites and those of them who were degenerate and bastards. The more license the wicked give themselves, the more presumptuous are they in pretending to the name of God, as if he were under obligation to them, because they are adorned with the same outward symbols or badges as true believers. Accordingly, the demonstrative pronoun *this,* in the following verse, is of great weight, for it expressly excludes all that bastard generation which gloried only in the mask of external ceremonies. And in this verse, when he speaks of *blessing,* he intimates that it is not those who boast of being the servants of God, while they have only the name, who shall be partakers of the promised blessing, but those only who answer to their calling with their whole heart, and without hypocrisy. It is, as we have already observed, a very powerful inducement to godliness and an upright life, when the faithful are assured that they do not lose their labour in following righteousness, since God has in reserve for them a blessing which cannot fail them. The word *righteousness* may be explained two ways.

---

[1] "*Asçavoir,* Jacob."—*Fr.* "*Namely,* Jacob."

It either means all the benefits of God, by which he proves himself to be righteous and faithful towards his people in keeping his promises to them, or it denotes the fruit or reward of the believer's righteousness. Indeed, David's meaning is abundantly manifest. He intends to show on the one hand, that it is not to be expected that the fruit or reward of righteousness will be bestowed on those who unrighteously profane God's sacred worship; and on the other hand, that it is impossible for God to disappoint his true worshippers; for it is his peculiar office to give evidence of his righteousness by doing them good.

6. *This is the generation.* I have just now observed, that by the demonstrative pronoun *this*, the Psalmist erazes from the catalogue of the servants of God all counterfeit Israelites, who, trusting only to their circumcision and the sacrifices of beasts, have no concern about offering themselves to God; and yet, at the same time, they rashly thrust themselves into the church. Such persons may pretend to have delight in the service of God, by often coming to his temple, but they have no other design than to withdraw themselves from him as far as they can. Now, as nothing was more common in the mouths of each of them than to say, that they all belonged to the holy seed, the Psalmist has limited the name of holy generation to the true observers of the law; as if he had said, All who have sprung from Abraham, according to the flesh, are not, on that account, his legitimate children. It is, no doubt, truly said in many other places, as we shall see in Psalm xxvii., that those sought the face of God who, to testify their godliness, exercised themselves in the ceremonies before the ark of the covenant; that is to say, if they were brought thither by a pure and holy affection. But as hypocrites seek God externally in a certain way, as well as true saints, while yet they shun him by their windings and false pretences,[1] David here declares that God is not sought in truth unless there go before a zealous cultivation of holiness and righteousness. To give the sentence

[1] " Lequel toutesfois ils fuyent par leurs destours et faux semblans."—*Fr.*

greater emphasis, he repeats it, using the second person, and addressing his discourse to God.[1] It is as if he summoned before the judgment-seat of God hypocrites, who account it nothing falsely to use the name of God before the world; and he thus teaches us, that whatever they may say in their empty talk among men, the judgment of God will be a very different matter. He adds the word *Jacob*, for the confirmation of the same doctrine, putting it for those who were descended from Jacob; as if he had said, Although circumcision distinguishes all the seed of Jacob according to the flesh from the Gentiles, yet we can only distinguish the chosen people by the fear and reverence of God, as Christ said, " Behold an Israelite indeed, in whom is no guile!" (John i. 47.)

7. *Lift up your heads, O ye gates! and be ye lifted up, ye everlasting doors! and the King of glory shall enter in.*
8. *Who is this King of glory? Jehovah strong and mighty, Jehovah mighty in battle.*
9. *Lift up your heads, O ye gates! be ye lifted up, ye everlasting doors! and the King of glory shall enter in.*
10. *Who is this King of glory? Jehovah of hosts, he is the King of glory. Selah.*

7. *Lift up your heads, O ye gates!* The magnificent and splendid structure of the temple, in which there was more outward majesty than in the tabernacle, not being yet erected, David here speaks of the future building of it. By doing this, he encourages the pious Israelites to employ themselves more willingly, and with greater confidence, in the ceremonial observances of the law. It was no ordinary token of the goodness of God that he condescended to dwell in the midst of them by a visible symbol of his presence, and was willing that his heavenly dwelling-place should be seen upon earth. This doctrine ought to be of use to us at this day; for it is an instance of the inestimable grace of God, that so far as the infirmity of our flesh will permit, we are lifted up even to God by the exercises of religion. What is the design of

[1] He first says, " That seek *him*," and next, " That seek *thy* face."

the preaching of the word, the sacraments, the holy assemblies, and the whole external government of the church, but that we may be united to God? It is not, therefore, without good reason that David extols so highly the service of God appointed in the law, seeing God exhibited himself to his saints in the ark of the covenant, and thereby gave them a certain pledge of speedy succour whenever they should invoke him for aid. God, it is true, " dwelleth not in temples made with hands," nor does he take delight in outward pomp; but as it was useful, and as it was also the pleasure of God, that his ancient people, who were rude, and still in their infancy, should be lifted up to him by earthly elements, David does not here hesitate to set forth to them, for the confirmation of their faith, the sumptuous building of the temple, to assure them that it was not a useless theatre; but that when they rightly worshipped God in it, according to the appointment of his word, they stood as it were in his presence, and would actually experience that he was near them. The amount of what is stated is, that in proportion as the temple which God had commanded to be built to him upon mount Sion, surpassed the tabernacle in magnificence, it would be so much the brighter a mirror of the glory and power of God dwelling among the Jews. In the meantime, as David himself burned with intense desire for the erection of the temple, so he wished to inflame the hearts of all the godly with the same ardent desire, that, aided by the rudiments of the law, they might make more and more progress in the fear of God. He terms the *gates, everlasting*, because the promise of God secured their continual stability. The temple excelled in materials and in workmanship, but its chief excellence consisted in this, that the promise of God was engraven upon it, as we shall see in Psalm cxxxii. 14, " This is my rest for ever." In terming the gates *everlasting*, the Psalmist, at the same time, I have no doubt, makes a tacit contrast between the tabernacle and the temple. The tabernacle never had any certain abiding place, but being from time to time transported from one place to another, was like a wayfaring man. When, however, mount Sion was chosen, and the temple built, God then began to have there a certain and fixed place of abode. By the coming of Christ, that visible shadow vanished, and it is therefore not wonderful that the temple is no longer to be seen upon mount Sion, seeing it is now so great as to occupy the whole world. If it is objected, that at the time of the Babylonish captivity the gates which Solomon had built were demolished, I answer, God's decree stood fast, notwithstanding that temporary overthrow; and by virtue of it, the temple was soon after rebuilt; which was the same as if it had always continued entire. The Septuagint has from ignorance corrupted this passage.[1] The Hebrew word ראשים, *rashim*, which we have rendered *heads*, is no doubt sometimes taken metaphorically for *princes;* but the word *your*, which is here annexed to it, sufficiently shows that we cannot draw from it another sense than this—that the gates lift up their heads; otherwise we must say, Your princes. Some, therefore, think that kings and magistrates are here admonished of their duty, which is to open up the way, and give entrance to God. This is a plausible interpretation, but it is too much removed from the design and words of the prophet. Above all, from the natural sense of the words, we may perceive how foolishly and basely the Papists have abused this passage for the confirmation of the gross and ridiculous notion by which they introduce Christ as knocking at the gate of the infernal regions, in order to obtain admission.[2] Let us, therefore, learn from this, to handle the holy word of God with sobriety and reverence, and to hold Papists in detestation, who, as it were, make sport of corrupting

---

[1] The Septuagint reads, "Αρατε πύλας οἱ ἄρχοντες ὑμῶν;" which may be rendered, "Ye princes, lift up your gates." The reading of the Vulgate is similar: "Attollite portas principes vestras:" and so is that of the Arabic and Æthiopic. But that rendering, as Calvin justly observes, is inadmissible; for in the Hebrew text, the affix כם, *kem*, *your*, is joined to ראשי, *rashey*, *heads*, and not to שערים, *shearim*, *gates*. Although, however, the reading of the Septuagint may be translated as above, "Ye princes, lift up your gates," Hammond thinks it more probable, that the translators intended οἱ ἄρχοντες ὑμῶν, *your princes*, to represent ראשיכם, *rashekem*, *your heads*, inverting, by mistake, the construction of the sentence, so as to give this reading, "Your heads, or princes, lift up the gates," instead of, "Ye gates, lift up your heads."

[2] "Par lesquels ils introduissent Christ frappant à la porte pour entrer és enfers."—*Fr.*

and falsifying it in this manner, by their execrable impieties.[1]

8. *Who is this King of glory?* &c. The praises by which the power of God is here magnified are intended to teach the Jews that he did not sit idle in his temple, but took up his abode in it, in order to show himself ready to succour his people. It is to be observed, that there is great weight both in the interrogation, and in the repetition of the same sentence. The prophet assumes the person of one who wonders thereby to express with greater effect that God comes armed with invincible power to maintain and save his people, and to keep the faithful in safety under his shadow. We have already said, that when God is spoken of as dwelling in the temple, it is not to be understood as if his infinite and incomprehensible essence had been shut up or confined within it; but that he was present there by his power and grace, as is implied in the promise which he made to Moses, " In all places where I record my name, I will come unto thee, and I will bless thee," (Exod. xx. 24.) That this was no vain and empty promise, but that God truly dwelt in the midst of the people, is what the faithful experienced who sought him not superstitiously, as if he had been fixed to the temple, but made use of the temple and of the service which was performed in it for elevating their hearts to heaven. The amount of what is stated is, that whenever the people should call upon God in the temple, it would manifestly appear, from the effect which would follow, that the ark of the covenant was not a vain and an illusory symbol of the presence of God, because he would always stretch forth his omnipotent arm for the defence and protection of his people. The repetition teaches us that true believers cannot be too constant and diligent in meditation on this subject. The Son of God, clothed with our flesh, has now shown himself to be *King of glory* and *Lord of hosts*, and he is not entered into his temple only by shadows and figures, but really and in very deed, that he may dwell in the midst of us. There is,

---

[1] " Qui comme sacrileges execrables tienent pour jeu de la corrompre et falsifier en ceste sorte."—*Fr.*

therefore, nothing to hinder us from boasting that we shall be invincible by his power. Mount Sion, it is true, is not at this day the place appointed for the sanctuary, and the ark of the covenant is no longer the image or representation of God dwelling between the cherubim; but as we have this privilege in common with the fathers, that, by the preaching of the word and the sacraments, we may be united to God, it becomes us to use these helps with reverence; for if we despise them by a detestable pride, God cannot but at length utterly withdraw himself from us.

PSALM XXV.

This psalm consists of meditations mingled with prayers. Being rudely treated, and grievously distressed, by the cruelty of his enemies, David, in order to obtain assistance from God, first acknowledges that God had justly made use of this as a means of chastising and punishing him for his sins; and, therefore, he prays for their forgiveness, that he may at once enjoy assurance of the divine favour, and obtain deliverance. He then implores the aid of the Holy Spirit, that, sustained by it, he might, even in the midst of so many temptations, continue in the fear of God. And in various places he intermingles meditation, as the means of stirring up himself to increased confidence in God, and of withdrawing his thoughts from the allurements of the world.

A Psalm of David.

1. *Unto thee, O Jehovah! I have lifted up my soul*
2. *O my God! I have put my trust in thee; let me not be ashamed; let not mine enemies rejoice over me.*
3. *Yea, none of those that wait on thee shall be ashamed; but they shall be ashamed that deal falsely without cause.*

1. *Unto thee, O Jehovah! &c.* The Psalmist declares at the very outset, that he is not driven hither and thither, after the manner of the ungodly, but that he directs all his desires and prayers to God alone. Nothing is more incon-

sistent with true and sincere prayer to God, than to waver and gaze about as the heathen do, for some help from the world; and at the same time to forsake God, or not to betake ourselves directly to his guardianship and protection. Those who imagine that David here declares that he had devoted himself entirely to God, as if he had offered up himself in sacrifice, do not properly understand the import of the passage. The meaning rather is, that in order to strengthen the hope of obtaining his request, he declares, what is of the greatest importance in prayer, that he had his hope fixed in God, and that he was not ensnared by the allurements of the world, or prevented from lifting up his soul fully and unfeignedly to God. In order, therefore, that we may pray aright to God, let us be directed by this rule—not to distract our minds by various and uncertain hopes, nor to depend on worldly aid, but to yield to God the honour of lifting up our hearts to him in sincere and earnest prayer. Moreover, although the verb is properly rendered, *I will lift up*, yet I have followed other interpreters in changing it into the past tense, *I have lifted up*. By the future tense, however, David denotes a continued act.

2. *O my God! I have put my trust in thee.* By this verse we learn, (what will appear more clearly afterwards,) that David had to do with men; but as he was persuaded that his enemies were, as it were, the scourges of God, he with good reason asks that God would restrain them by his power, lest they should become more insolent, and continue to exceed all bounds. By the word *trust* he confirms what he had just said of the lifting up of his soul to God; for the term is employed either as descriptive of the way in which the souls of the faithful are lifted up, or else faith and hope are added as the cause of such an effect, namely, the lifting up of the soul. And, indeed, these are the wings by which our souls, rising above this world, are lifted up to God. David, then, was carried upward to God with the whole desire of his heart, because, trusting to his promises, he thereby hoped for sure salvation. When he asks *that God would not suffer him to be put to shame*, he offers up a prayer,

which is taken from the ordinary doctrine of Scripture, namely, that they who trust in God shall never be ashamed. The reason which is added, and which he here pleads, to induce God to have pity upon him, ought also to be noticed. It is this, that he might not be exposed to the derision of his enemies, whose pride is no less hurtful to the feelings of the godly than it is displeasing to God.

3. *Yea, none of those, &c.* If these words should be explained in the form of a desire, as if David had said, Let none who wait on thee be put to shame,[1] then, in this verse, he continues his prayer, and extends to all the faithful in common what he had spoken of himself alone. But I am rather inclined to understand the words in a different sense, and to view them as meaning that David shows the fruit of divine grace which should proceed from his deliverance. And there is peculiar force in the word *yea;* for as he knew that he was seen by many, and that the report of his confidence in God was widely spread, his meaning is, that what shall be done in his person shall extend far and wide, as an example to others, and shall have the effect of reviving and animating all the children of God, on the one hand, and of casting to the ground the arrogance of the wicked, on the other. The words might also be understood in another sense, namely, that David, for the strengthening of his faith, sets before himself a promise which God frequently makes in his word. But the sense in which I have interpreted them seems to be more suitable. By the wicked *that deal falsely without cause,* he no doubt means especially his enemies. Accordingly, he declares that when he is delivered he will not enjoy exclusively the benefit of it; but that its fruit shall extend to all true believers; just as on the other hand, the faith of many would have been shaken if he had been forsaken of God. In the last clause of the verse, which he puts in opposition to the first, he argues that when the wicked lie confounded, it redounds to the glory of God, because the vaunting in which they indulge in their prosperity is an open mockery of God, while, in despite of his

---

[1] " Que tous ceux qui s'attendent à toy ne soyent point confus."—*Fr.*

judgment, they break forth more boldly in doing evil. When he adds, *without cause*, it only tends to show the aggravated nature of the offence. The wickedness of a man is always the more intolerable, when, unprovoked by wrongs, he sets himself, of his own accord, to injure the innocent and blameless.

4. *O Jehovah! make me to know thy ways, and teach me thy paths.*
5. *Lead me in thy truth, and teach me : for thou art the God of my salvation : I have waited for thee all the day.*
6. *Remember, O Jehovah! thy tender mercies and thy loving-kindnesses, for they have been from everlasting.*
7. *Remember not the sins of my youth, nor my transgressions : according to thy compassion, and for the sake of thy goodness, O Jehovah! do thou remember me.*

4. *O Jehovah! make me to know thy ways.* By *the ways of the Lord*, David sometimes means, as we have seen in another place, the happy and prosperous issue of affairs, but more frequently he uses this expression to denote the rule of a holy and righteous life. As the term *truth* occurs in the immediately following verse, the prayer which he offers up in this place is, in my opinion, to this effect : Lord, keep thy servant in the firm persuasion of thy promises, and do not suffer him to turn aside to the right hand or to the left. When our minds are thus composed to patience, we undertake nothing rashly or by improper means, but depend wholly upon the providence of God. Accordingly, in this place David desires not merely to be directed by the Spirit of God, lest he should err from the right way, but also that God would clearly manifest to him his truth and faithfulness in the promises of his word, that he might live in peace before him, and be free from all impatience.[1] If any one would rather take the words in a general sense, as if David committed himself wholly to God to be governed by him, I do not object to it. As, however, I think it probable, that, under the name of *truth* in the next verse, he explains what he means by the ways and paths of God, of which he here speaks, I have no hesitation in referring the prayer to this circumstance, namely, that David, afraid of yielding to the feeling of impatience, or the desire

---

[1] "Et sans estre troublé d'impatience."—*Fr.*

of revenge, or some extravagant and unlawful impulse, asks that the promises of God may be deeply impressed and engraven on his heart. For I have said before, that as long as this thought prevails in our minds, that God takes care of us, it is the best and most powerful means for resisting temptations. If, however, by *the ways and paths of God,* any would rather understand his doctrine, I, nevertheless, still hold this as a settled point, that in the language of the Psalmist there is an allusion to those sudden and irregular emotions which arise in our minds when we are tossed by adversity, and by which we are precipitated into the devious and deceitful paths of error, till they are in due time subdued or allayed by the word of God. Thus the meaning is, Whatever may happen, suffer me not, O Lord, to fall from thy ways, or to be carried away by a wilful disobedience to thy authority, or any other sinful desire; but rather let thy truth preserve me in a state of quiet repose and peace, by an humble submission to it. Moreover, although he frequently repeats the same thing, asking that God would make him to know his ways, and teach him in them, and lead him in his truth, there is no redundancy in these forms of speech. Our adversities are often like mists which darken the eyes; and every one knows from his own experience how difficult a thing it is, while these clouds of darkness continue, to discern in what way we ought to walk. But if David, so distinguished a prophet and endued with so much wisdom, stood in need of divine instruction, what shall become of us if, in our afflictions, God dispel not from our minds those clouds of darkness which prevent us from seeing his light? As often, then, as any temptation may assail us, we ought always to pray that God would make the light of his truth to shine upon us, lest, by having recourse to sinful devices, we should go astray, and wander into devious and forbidden paths.

At the same time, we ought to observe the argument which David here employs to enforce his prayer. By calling God *the God of his salvation,* he does so in order to strengthen his hope in God for the future, from a consideration of the benefits which he had already received from him; and then he repeats the testimony of his confidence towards God. Thus the first part of the argument is taken from the nature of God himself, and the duty which, as it were, belongs to him; that is to say, because he engages to maintain the welfare of the godly, and aids them in their necessities, on this ground, that he will continue to manifest the same favour towards them even to the end. But as it is necessary that our confidence in God should correspond to his great goodness towards us, David alleges it, at the same time, in connection with a declaration of his perseverance. For, by the expression *all the day*, or *every day*, he signifies that with a fixed and untiring constancy he depended upon God alone. And, doubtless, it is the property of faith always to look to God, even in the most trying circumstances, and patiently to wait for the aid which he has promised. That the recollection of the divine blessings may nourish and sustain our hope, let us learn to reflect upon the goodness which God has already manifested towards us, as we see that David did in making this the ground of his confidence, that he had found in his own personal experience God to be the author of salvation.

6. *Remember, O Jehovah!* From this it appears, in the first place, that David was grievously afflicted and tried, so much so that he had lost all sense of God's mercy: for he calls upon God to remember for him his favour, in such a manner as if he had altogether forgotten it. This, therefore, is the complaint of a man suffering extreme anguish, and overwhelmed with grief. We may learn from this, that although God, for a time, may withdraw from us every token of his goodness, and, apparently regardless of the miseries which afflict us, should, as if we were strangers to him, and not his own people, forsake us, we must fight courageously, until, set free from this temptation, we cordially present the prayer which is here recorded, beseeching God, that, returning to his former manner of dealing, he would again begin to manifest his goodness towards us, and to deal with us in a more gracious manner. This form of prayer cannot be used with propriety, unless when God is hiding

his face from us, and seems to take no interest at all in us. Moreover David, by having recourse to the mercy or compassion and goodness of God, testifies that he trusts not to his own merit as any ground of hope. He who derives every thing from the fountain of divine mercy alone, finds nothing in himself entitled to recompense in the sight of God. But as the intermission which David had experienced was an obstacle which prevented his free access to God, he rises above it, by the very best remedy—the consideration, that although God, who from his very nature is merciful, may withdraw himself, and cease for a time to manifest his power, yet he cannot deny himself; that is to say, he cannot divest himself of the feeling of mercy which is natural to him, and which can no more cease than his eternal existence. But we must firmly maintain this doctrine, that God has been merciful even from the beginning, so that if at any time he seem to act with severity towards us, and to reject our prayers, we must not imagine that he acts contrary to his real character, or that he has changed his purpose. Hence we learn for what end it is that the Scriptures every where inform us, that in all ages God has regarded his servants with a benignant eye, and exercised his mercy towards them.[1] This, at least, we ought to regard as a fixed and settled point, that although the goodness of God may sometimes be hidden, and as it were buried out of sight, it can never be extinguished.

7. *Remember not the sins of my youth.* As our sins are like a wall between us and God, which prevents him from hearing our prayers, or stretching forth his hand to help us, David now removes this obstruction. It is indeed true, in general, that men pray in a wrong way, and in vain, unless they begin by seeking the forgiveness of their sins. There is no hope of obtaining any favour from God unless he is reconciled to us. How shall he love us unless he first freely reconcile us to himself? The right and proper order of prayer therefore is, as I have said, to ask, at the very outset, that God would par-

---

[1] " Et usé de douceur envers eux."—*Fr.*

don our sins. David here acknowledges, in explicit terms, that he cannot in any other way become a partaker of the grace of God than by having his sins blotted out. In order, therefore, that God may be mindful of his mercy towards us, it is necessary that he forget our sins, the very sight of which turns away his favour from us. In the meantime, the Psalmist confirms by this more clearly what I have already said, that although the wicked acted towards him with cruelty, and persecuted him unjustly, yet he ascribed to his own sins all the misery which he endured. For why should he ask the forgiveness of his sins, by having recourse to the mercy of God, but because he acknowledged, that by the cruel treatment he received from his enemies, he only suffered the punishment which he justly merited? He has, therefore, acted wisely in turning his thoughts to the first cause of his misery, that he may find out the true remedy; and thus he teaches us by his example, that when any outward affliction presses upon us, we must entreat God not only to deliver us from it, but also to blot out our sins, by which we have provoked his displeasure, and subjected ourselves to his chastening rod. If we act otherwise, we shall follow the example of unskilful physicians, who, overlooking the cause of the disease, only seek to alleviate the pain, and apply merely adventitious remedies for the cure. Moreover, David makes confession not only of some slight offences, as hypocrites are wont to do, who, by confessing their guilt in a general and perfunctory manner, either seek some subterfuge, or else extenuate the enormity of their sin; but he traces back his sins even to his very childhood, and considers in how many ways he had provoked the wrath of God against him. When he makes mention of the sins which he had committed in his youth, he does not mean by this that he had no remembrance of any of the sins which he had committed in his later years; but it is rather to show that he considered himself worthy of so much the greater condemnation.[1] In the first place, considering that he had not begun only of late to commit sin, but that he had for a long time heaped up sin upon sin, he bows himself, if we

---

[1] " Redevable de tant plus grande condemnation."—*Fr.*

may so speak, under the accumulated load ; and, in the second place, he intimates, that if God should deal with him according to the rigour of law, not only the sins of yesterday, or of a few days, would come into judgment against him, but all the instances in which he had offended, even from his infancy, might now with justice be laid to his charge. As often, therefore, as God terrifies us by his judgments and the tokens of his wrath, let us call to our remembrance, not only the sins which we have lately committed, but also all the transgressions of our past life, proving to us the ground of renewed shame and renewed lamentation. Besides, in order to express more fully that he supplicates a free pardon, he pleads before God only on the ground of his mere good pleasure; and therefore he says, *According to thy compassion do thou remember me.* When God casts our sins into oblivion, this leads him to behold us with fatherly regard. David can discover no other cause by which to account for this paternal regard of God, but that he is good, and hence it follows that there is nothing to induce God to receive us into his favour but his own good pleasure. When God is said to remember us according to his mercy, we are tacitly given to understand that there are two ways of remembering which are entirely opposite; the one when he visits sinners in his wrath, and the other when he again manifests his favour to those of whom he seemed for a time to take no account.

8. *Good and upright is Jehovah ; therefore will he teach sinners in t he way.*
9. *He will guide the poor in judgment, and will teach the poor*[1] *his way.*
10. *All the ways of Jehovah are mercy and truth, to those who keep his covenant and his testimony.*
11. *For thy name's sake, O Jehovah! be thou merciful to mine iniquity, for it is great.*

8. *Good and upright is Jehovah.* Pausing for a little, as it were in the prosecution of his prayer, he exercises his thoughts in meditation upon the goodness of God, that he

---

[1] " Humbles."—*Fr.* " Humble."

may return with renewed ardour to prayer. The faithful feel that their hearts soon languish in prayer, unless they are constantly stirring themselves up to it by new incitements; so rare and difficult a thing is it to persevere stedfastly and unweariedly in this duty. And, indeed, as one must frequently lay on fuel in order to preserve a fire, so the exercise of prayer requires the aid of such helps, that it may not languish, and at length be entirely extinguished. David, therefore, desirous to encourage himself to perseverance, speaks to himself, and affirms that God is *good and upright,* that, gathering new strength by meditating on this truth, he may return with the more alacrity to prayer. But we must observe this consequence—that as God is good and upright, he stretches forth his hand *to sinners* to bring them back again into *the way.* To attribute to God an uprightness which he may exercise only towards the worthy and the meritorious, is a cold view of his character, and of little advantage to sinners, and yet the world commonly apprehends that God is good in no other sense. How comes it to pass that scarcely one in a hundred applies to himself the mercy of God, if it is not because men limit it to those who are worthy of it? Now, on the contrary, it is here said, that God gives a proof of his uprightness when he shows to transgressors the way; and this is of the same import as to call them to repentance, and to teach them to live uprightly. And, indeed, if the goodness of God did not penetrate even to hell, no man would ever become a partaker of it. Let the Papists then boast as they please of their imaginary preparations, but let us regard this as a sure and certain doctrine, that if God do not prevent men by his grace, they shall all utterly perish. David, therefore, here commends this preventing grace, as it is called, which is manifested either when God in calling us at first renews, by the Spirit of regeneration, our corrupt nature, or when he brings us back again into the right way, after we have gone astray from him by our sins. For since even those whom God receives for his disciples are here called sinners, it follows that he renews them by his Holy Spirit, that they may become docile and obedient.

9. *He will guide the poor in judgment.* The Psalmist here specifies the second manifestation of his grace which God makes towards those who, being subdued by his power, and brought under his yoke, bear it willingly, and submit themselves to his government. But never will this docility be found in any man, until the heart, which is naturally elated and filled with pride, has been humbled and subdued. As the Hebrew word ענוים, *anavim,* denotes the *poor* or *afflicted,* and is employed in a metaphorical sense, to denote *the meek and humble,* it is probable that David, under this term, includes the afflictions which serve to restrain and subdue the frowardness of the flesh, as well as the grace of humility itself; as if he had said, When God has first humbled them, then he kindly stretches forth his hand to them, and leads and guides them throughout the whole course of their life. Moreover, some understand these terms, *judgment* and *way of the Lord,* as denoting a righteous and well ordered manner of life. Others refer them to the providence of God, an interpretation which seems more correct, and more agreeable to the context, for it is immediately added, *All the ways of Jehovah are mercy and truth.* The meaning therefore is, that those who are truly humbled in their hearts, and brought to place their confidence in God, shall experience how much care he has for his children,[1] and how well he provides for their necessities. The terms, *judgment* and *way of the Lord,* therefore, are simply of the same import in this place as his government, in the exercise of which he shows that he, as a kind father, has a special interest in the welfare of his children, by relieving them when they are oppressed, raising them up when cast down, cheering and comforting them when sorrowful, and succouring them when afflicted. We perceive, then, by what order God proceeds in the manifestation of his grace towards us. First, he brings us again into the way when we are wandering and going astray from him, or rather, when we are already fugitives and exiles from him, he restrains our frowardness; and whereas we were before froward and rebellious, he now subdues us to the obedience of

---

[1] " Quel soin il ha de ses enfans."—*Fr.*

his righteousness: and, secondly, after he has afflicted and tried us, he does not forsake us; but after he has moulded and trained us by the cross to humility and meekness, he still shows himself to be a wise and provident father in guiding and directing us through life.

10. *All the ways of Jehovah.* This verse is erroneously interpreted by those who think that the doctrine of the law is here described as true and sweet, and that those who keep it feel it indeed to be so, as if this passage were of the same import as that which was spoken by Jesus Christ, (Matth. xi. 30,) "My yoke is easy, and my burden is light." Such an interpretation is not only strained, but may also be easily disproved by many similar passages in which the expression, *The ways of the Lord*, is taken in a passive signification, for the paternal manner in which he acts towards those who are his people, in defending and cherishing them; nay, even for his whole conduct in the government and direction of the affairs of this world. The amount of what is said is, that God acts in such a manner towards his people, as that, in all respects, they may find from experience that he is merciful and faithful. David is not here speaking of the character in which God acts towards mankind in general, but what his own children find him to be. We have already seen in Ps. xviii. 26, that he is stern and severe towards the obstinate and rebellious; and even though he act with kindness towards them, in mercifully exercising forbearance towards them notwithstanding their iniquity, yet we find, that so far from seeking their full enjoyment in him, and trusting to his promises, they have no sense of his goodness. Nay, as soon as any adversity befalls them, they either become passionate and fretful, accuse God of acting cruelly towards them, or else complain that he is deaf to their prayers; and when they enjoy prosperity, they despise and neglect him, and as much as they are able flee from his presence. David, therefore, in speaking of the *mercy* and *faithfulness* of God, justly describes them as a treasure peculiar to the godly; as if he had said, We have no reason to be afraid that God will deceive us if we persevere in his covenant. These words,

covenant and *testimony*, are of the same import, unless that the second is added as an explanation of the first. They comprehend the whole doctrine of the law, by which God enters into covenant with his chosen people.

11. *For thy name's sake, O Jehovah!* As in the original text the copulative *and* is inserted between the two clauses of this verse, some think that the first clause is incomplete, and that some word ought to be supplied; and then they read these words, *Be thou merciful to mine iniquity, &c.*, as a distinct sentence by itself. And thus, according to their opinion, the sense would be, Lord, although I have not fully kept thy covenant, yet do not on that account cease to show thy kindness towards me; and that mine iniquity may not prevent thy goodness from being extended towards me, do thou graciously pardon it. But I am rather of the opinion of others, who consider that the copulative is here, as it is in many other places, superfluous, so that the whole verse may form one connected sentence. As to the tense of the verb, there is also a diversity of opinion among interpreters. Some render it in the past tense thus, *Thou hast been merciful*, as if David here renders thanks to God because he had pardoned his sin. But the other interpretation, which is the one more generally received, is also the most correct, namely, that David, in order to obtain pardon, again resorts to the mercy of God as his only refuge. The letter ו, *vau*, which is equivalent to *and*, has often the force of changing the tense in the Hebrew verbs, so that the future tense is often taken in the sense of the optative. Moreover, I connect this verse with the preceding one in this way: The prophet, having reflected upon this, that God is kind and faithful to those who serve him, now examines his own heart, and acknowledges that he cannot be accounted of their number, unless God grant unto him the forgiveness of his sins; and, therefore, he betakes himself to prayer for pardon: as in Ps. xix. 13, after having spoken of the reward which is laid up for the faithful who keep the law, he instantly exclaims, "Who can understand his errors?" Accordingly, although David is not ignorant that God promises liberally to bestow

upon those who keep his covenant every thing which pertains to a life of happiness, yet, at the same time, considering how far he is as yet from the perfect righteousness of the law, he does not rest his confidence upon it, but seeks a remedy for the manifold offences of which he feels himself to be guilty. And thus, in order that God may reckon us of the number of his servants, we ought always to come to him, entreating him, after the example of David, in his fatherly loving-kindness, to bear with our infirmities, because, without the free remission of our sins, we have no reason to expect any reward of our works. At the same time, let it be observed, that in order to show more distinctly that he depends entirely upon the free grace of God, he expressly says, *for thy name's sake;* meaning by this, that God, as often as he vouchsafes to pardon his people, does so from no other cause than his own good pleasure; just as he had said a little before, in the same verse, *for thy goodness' sake.* He was also constrained, by a consideration of the magnitude of his offence, to call upon the name of God: for he immediately adds, by way of confession, *because mine iniquity is great,* or *manifold,* (for the word רב, *rab,* may be translated in both ways;) as if he had said, My sins are, indeed, like a heavy burden which overwhelms me, so that the multitude or enormity of them might well deprive me of all hope of pardon; but, Lord, the infinite glory of thy name will not suffer thee to cast me off.

12. *Who is the man that feareth Jehovah? he will teach him in the way that he should choose.*
13. *His soul shall dwell in good, and his seed shall inherit the earth.*
14. *The counsel*[1] *of Jehovah is towards them that fear him, that he may make known his covenant to them.*
15. *Mine eyes are continually towards Jehovah, for he will bring my feet out of the net.*

12. *Who is the man.* By again recalling to his mind the character in which God manifests himself towards his servants, he derives new strength and courage. For we have said,

---

[1] " Ou, secret."—*Fr.* " Or, secret."

that nothing more readily occurs than a relaxation in earnest and attentive prayer, unless it be sustained by the recollection of God's promises. There can, however, be no doubt, that David both accuses himself, and by entertaining a better hope, takes encouragement to continue in the fear of God. In the first place, by intimating that men are destitute of right understanding and sound judgment, because they yield not themselves to be governed by God with reverence and fear, he imputes it to his own indolence, that by reason of the darkness of his mind, he had wandered so far astray after his own lusts; and yet, on the other hand, he promises himself the guidance and direction of the Holy Spirit, if he only yield himself wholly to God, and show that he is willing to learn. Moreover, the interrogatory style of speaking, which he here employs, seems designed to show how few there are who fear God: for, although all men in general pray, and manifest some appearance of piety, yet where is there one among so many who is really in earnest? Instead of this, almost all men indulge themselves in their own drowsiness. The fear of God, therefore, is very rare; and on this account it is that the world, for the most part, continues destitute of the Spirit of counsel and wisdom.

Some interpreters render the word *choose* in the present tense, instead of the future, *shall choose;* as if it had been said, that God shows the way which he approves, and in which he wishes men to walk. With this interpretation I cannot agree; for, in my judgment, the word *choose* rather refers to every individual; as if it had been said, Provided we are disposed to fear God, he will not be wanting on his part, but will always direct us by the Spirit of wisdom to choose the right way. When we are called upon to adopt some particular course in life, we find ourselves as it were placed between two ways, and know not which of them to follow;[1] nay, in almost all our affairs we are held in suspense and doubt, unless God appear to show us the way. David therefore says, that although men know not what is right, and what they ought to choose, yet provided they

---

[1] " Ne sçachans lequel prendre."—*Fr.*

submit to God with pious docility of mind, and are willing to follow him, he will always manifest himself towards them as a sure and faithful guide. As, however, the fear of God is not naturally in us, it were foolish for any man to argue from this place, that God does not begin to take care of men until, by their own previous efforts, they insinuate themselves into his favour, that he may aid them in their pious endeavours. David has just declared, that this grace comes directly from God, when he says that God teaches the transgressors: and now he adds, in the second place, that after men have once been subdued and moulded to meekness of spirit, God still takes them under his charge, guiding and directing them till they are able, by the illumination of the Holy Spirit, to know what is their duty.

13. *His soul shall dwell in good.* If the supreme felicity of man consists in undertaking or attempting nothing except by the warrant of God, it follows that it is also a high and incomparable benefit to have him for our conductor and guide through life, that we may never go astray. But, in addition to this, an earthly blessing is here promised, in which the fruit of the preceding grace is distinctly shown, as Paul also teaches, (1 Tim. iv. 8,) "Godliness is profitable unto all things, having promise of the life that now is, and of that which is to come." The sum is, that those who truly serve God are not only blessed as to spiritual things, but are also blessed by him as to their condition in the present life. It is indeed true, that God does not always deal with them according to their desires, and that the blessings which they would wish do not always flow in a certain and uniform manner. On the contrary, it often happens that they are tossed with sickness and trouble, whilst the wicked enjoy prosperity. But we must know, that as often as God withdraws his blessing from his own people, it is for the purpose of awakening them to a sense of their condition, and discovering to them how far removed they still are from the perfect fear of God. And yet, in so far as it is expedient for them, they now enjoy the blessings of God, so that, in comparison of worldly men, and the despisers of God, they

are truly happy and blessed, because, even in their greatest
poverty, they never lose the assurance that God is present
with them; and being sustained by this consolation, they
enjoy peace and tranquillity of mind. It is indeed true,
that all our miseries proceed from this one source—that
by our sins we prevent the divine blessing from flowing
down in a uniform course upon us; and yet, amidst such
a state of confusion, his grace never ceases to shine forth,
so that the condition of the godly is always better than that
of others: for although they are not satiated with good things,
yet they are continually made to experience a sense of the
fatherly favour of God. And to this I am willing to refer
the word *soul*, namely, that, in the reception of the gifts of
God, they do not devour them without feeling a sense of
their sweetness, but really relish them, so that the smallest
competency is of more avail to satisfy them than the greatest abundance is to satisfy the ungodly. Thus, according
as every man is contented with his condition, and cheerfully
cherishes a spirit of patience and tranquillity, his soul is said
to dwell in good. Some interpreters apply this word *to dwell* or
abide to the time of death; but this interpretation is more
subtle than solid. The inspired penman rather speaks, as we
have already said, of the condition of the present life.[1] He
adds, in the second place, by way of illustration, that the
posterity of the faithful *shall inherit the land;*[2] and from this
it follows, that God continues to extend his favour towards
them. Hence we may again infer, that the death of God's
servants does not imply their utter destruction, and that
they do not cease to exist when they pass out of this world,
but continue to live for ever. It would be absurd to suppose
that God would totally deprive of life those for whose sake
he does good even to others. As to what is here said, that

---

[1] Horsley refers the words to the blessedness of a future state. He reads, "His soul shall rest in bliss;" and has the following note :—" תלין, *pernoctavit*. The words seem to allude to the happy state of the good man's departed soul, while his posterity prosper in the present world."

[2] That is, the land of Canaan, which God promised to perpetuate to the obedient Israelites and their posterity. "It was promised and given," says Poole, "as an earnest of the whole covenant of grace and all its promises, and, therefore, is synecdochically put for all of them. The sense is, his seed shall be blessed."

the children of the saints shall inherit the land, it has been touched upon elsewhere, and it will be shown still more fully on the thirty-seventh Psalm, in what respects, and how this is accomplished.

14. *The counsel of Jehovah.* The Psalmist here confirms what he had just said in a preceding verse, namely, that God will faithfully discharge the office of a teacher and master to all the godly; and, after his usual manner, he repeats the same sentiment twice in the same verse: for the *covenant of God* is nothing else than his *secret* or *counsel.* By the use of the term *secret,* he means to magnify and extol the excellency of the doctrine which is revealed to us in the law of God. However much worldly men, through the pride and haughtiness of their hearts, despise Moses and the prophets, the faithful nevertheless acknowledge, that in the doctrine which they contain, the secrets of heaven, which far surpass the comprehension of man, are revealed and unfolded. Whoever, therefore, desires to derive instruction from the law, let him regard with reverence and esteem the doctrine which it contains. We are, farther, by this place admonished to cultivate the graces of meekness and humility, lest, in reliance upon our own wisdom, or trusting to our own understanding, we should attempt, by our own efforts, to comprehend those mysteries and secrets, the knowledge of which David here declares to be the prerogative of God alone. Again, since the fear of the Lord is said to be the beginning, and as it were the way that leads to a right understanding of his will, (Ps. cxi. 10,) according as any one desires to increase in faith, so also let him endeavour to advance in the fear of the Lord. Moreover, when piety reigns in the heart, we need have no fear of losing our labour in seeking God. It is indeed true, that the covenant of God is a secret which far exceeds human comprehension; but as we know that he does not in vain enjoin us to seek him, we may rest assured that all those who endeavour to serve him with an upright desire will be brought, by the teaching of the Holy Spirit, to the knowledge of that heavenly wisdom which is appointed for their salvation. But, in the meantime, David indirectly rebukes those who falsely and groundlessly

boast that they are interested in the covenant of God, while they rest merely in the letter of the law, and have no saving impressions of the fear of God. God, it is true, addresses his word indiscriminately to the righteous and the wicked; but men do not comprehend it, unless they have sincere piety; just as Isaiah, chap. xxix. 11, says, that as regards the ungodly, the law is like " a book that is sealed." And, therefore, it is no wonder that there is here made a distinction between those who truly serve God, and to whom he makes known his secret, and the wicked or hypocrites. But when we see David in this confidence coming boldly to the school of God, and leading others along with him, let us know, as he clearly shows, that it is a wicked and hateful invention to attempt to deprive the common people of the Holy Scriptures, under the pretence of their being a hidden mystery; as if all who fear him from the heart, whatever their state or condition in other respects may be, were not expressly called to the knowledge of God's covenant.

15. *Mine eyes are continually towards Jehovah.* David here speaks of his own faith, and of its perseverance, not in the way of boasting, but to encourage himself in the hope of obtaining his requests, so that he might give himself the more readily and cheerfully to prayer. As the promise is made to all who trust in God, that they shall not be disappointed of their hope, and that they shall never be put to shame, the saints often make this their shield of defence. Meanwhile, David shows to others, by his own example, the right manner of prayer, telling them that they should endeavour to keep their thoughts fixed upon God. As the sense of sight is very quick, and exercises an entire influence over the whole frame, it is no uncommon thing to find all the affections denoted by the term *eyes*. The reason which immediately follows shows still more plainly, that in the mind of David hope was associated with desire; as if he had said, That in resting his confidence in the help of God, he did so, not in doubt or uncertainty, but because he was persuaded that he would be his deliverer. The pronoun *He,* it ought to be observed, is also emphatic. It shows that David did not gaze around him in every direction, after the

manner of those who, being in uncertainty, devise for themselves various methods of deliverance and salvation, but that he was contented with God alone.

16. *Have respect unto me, and pity me, for I am alone and poor.*
17. *The troubles of my heart are enlarged; bring thou me out of my distresses.*
18. *Look upon mine affliction and my trouble,*[1] *and take away all my sins.*
19. *Behold mine enemies, for they are increased; and they hate me with a violent*[2] *hatred.*
20. *Preserve my soul, and deliver me, that I may not be ashamed; for I have put my trust in thee.*
21. *Let integrity and uprightness preserve me, for I have waited upon thee.*
22. *Do thou, O God! redeem Israel from all his troubles.*

16. *Have respect unto me.* As the flesh is ever ready to suggest to our minds that God has forgotten us, when he ceases to manifest his power in aiding us, David here follows the order which nature dictates, in asking God to have respect unto him, as if he had altogether neglected him before. Now, it appears to me that the words might be explained thus: Have respect unto me, in order to pity me. He accounts it at once the cause and the source of his salvation to be regarded of God; and then he adds the effect of it: for as soon as God, of his own good pleasure, shall vouchsafe to regard us, his hand also will be ready to help us. Again, in order to excite the compassion of God, he sets forth his own misery, expressly stating that he is *alone*, that is to say, *solitary;*[3] and then he describes himself as *poor*. There can be no doubt that, in speaking thus, he alludes to the promises in which God declares that he will be always present with the afflicted and oppressed, to aid and help them.

17. *The troubles of my heart are enlarged.* In this verse

---

[1] "Mon souci et travail."—*Fr. marg.* "My care and labour."
[2] "C'est, cruelle."—*Note, Fr. marg.* "That is, cruel."
[3] The Hebrew word here used is יחיד, *yachid, unus, one,* which is not unfrequently put, as in this place, for a *solitary* and *desolate* person. David was now deserted, desolate, and destitute of all help. The word is used in the same sense in Ps. xxii. 20, and xxxv. 17.

he acknowledges not only that he had to contend outwardly with his enemies and the troubles which they occasioned him, but that he was also afflicted inwardly with sorrow and anguish of heart. It is also necessary to observe the manner of expression which he here employs, and by which he intimates that the weight and number of his trials had accumulated to such an extent that they filled his whole heart, even as a flood of waters bursting every barrier, and extending far and wide, covers a whole country. Now, when we see that the heart of David had sometimes been wholly filled with anguish, we need no longer wonder if at times the violence of temptation overwhelm us; but let us ask with David, that even whilst we are as it were at the point of despair, God would succour us.

18. *Look upon mine affliction.* By repeating these complaints so frequently, he plainly shows that the calamities with which he was assailed were not some slight and trivial evils. And this ought to be carefully marked by us, so that when trials and afflictions shall have been measured out to us after the same manner, we may be enabled to lift up our souls to God in prayer; for the Holy Spirit has set before our view this representation, that our minds may not fail us under the multitude or weight of afflictions. But in order to obtain an alleviation of these miseries, David again prays that his sins may be pardoned, recalling to his recollection what he had already stated, that he could not expect to enjoy the divine favour, unless he were first reconciled to God by receiving a free pardon. And, indeed, they are very insensible who, contented with deliverance from bodily affliction, do not search out the evils of their own hearts, that is to say, their sins, but as much as in them lies rather desire to have them buried in oblivion. To find a remedy, therefore, to his cares and sorrows, David begins by imploring the remission of his sins, because, so long as God is angry with us, it must necessarily follow, that all our affairs shall come to an unhappy termination; and he has always just ground of displeasure against us so long as our sins continue, that is to

say, until he pardons them.[1] And although the Lord has various ends in view in bringing his people under the cross, yet we ought to hold fast the principle, that as often as God afflicts us, we are called to examine our own hearts, and humbly to seek reconciliation with him.

19. *Behold mine enemies.* In this verse David complains of the number and cruelty of his enemies, because the more the people of God are oppressed, the more is he inclined to aid them; and in proportion to the magnitude of the danger by which they are surrounded, he assists them the more powerfully. The words, *hatred of violence,*[2] are here to be understood of a cruel and sanguinary hatred. Now, as the rage of David's enemies was so great, that nothing short of his death would satisfy them, he calls upon God to become the guardian and protector of his life; and from this it may be inferred, as I have already said, that he was now placed in extreme danger. The clause which immediately follows, *That I may not be ashamed,* may be understood in two ways. Some retain the future tense, *I shall not be ashamed,* as if David felt assured that he was already heard by God, and as the reward of his hope promised himself a gracious answer to his prayers. I am rather inclined to the opposite opinion— to consider these words as still forming a part of his prayer. The amount of what is stated therefore is, that as he trusts in God, he prays that the hope of salvation which he had formed might not be disappointed. There is nothing better fitted to impart a holy ardour to our prayers, than when we are able to testify with sincerity of heart that we confide in God. And, therefore, it behoves us to ask with so much the greater care, that he would increase our hope when it is small, awaken it when it is dormant, confirm it when it is wavering, strengthen it when it is weak, and that he would even raise it up when it is overthrown.

21. *Let integrity and uprightness preserve me.* Some are of

---

[1] " Cependant que nos pechez demeurent c'est à dire jusques à ce qu'il les pardonne."
[2] The Hebrew words literally rendered are, " With hatred of violence."

opinion, that in these words David simply prays that he may be preserved from all mischief, on the ground that he had conducted himself inoffensively towards others, and had abstained from all deceit and violence. Others make the words to contain a twofold subject of prayer, and understand them as including at the same time a desire that God would bestow upon him a sincere and upright purpose of heart; and all this lest he should break forth into revenge, and other unlawful means of preserving his life. Thus the meaning would be: Lord, although my flesh may urge me to seek relief from whatever quarter it may appear, and mine enemies also may constrain me to it by their importunity, yet do thou subdue within me every sinful passion, and every perverse desire, so that I may always exercise over my mind a pure and entire control; and let integrity and uprightness suffice as two powerful means of preserving me. We prefer the first interpretation, because he immediately subjoins a proof of his integrity. Whosoever waits upon God with a meek and quiet spirit, will rather suffer any thing which men can inflict, than allow himself to contend unrighteously with his enemies. In my opinion, therefore, David protests that such was the rectitude of his behaviour amongst men, that the persecution of his enemies was wholly unmerited and unjust; and being conscious of having given no offence to any, he calls upon God as the protector of his innocence. But as he has already, in three different places, acknowledged that he was justly visited with affliction, it may seem strange that he should now glory in his integrity. This apparent inconsistency has already been explained in another place, where we have shown that the saints, in respect of themselves, always come into the presence of God with humility, imploring his forgiveness: and yet this does not prevent them from setting forth before him the goodness of their cause, and the justice of their claims. At the same time, in saying that he *trusted* in God, he only states what indeed is essentially necessary; for, in undertaking our defence, it is not enough that we have justice on our side, unless depending upon his promises, we rely with confidence upon his protection. It often happens, that men of firmness and prudence, even when their cause is good, do not always succeed in its defence, because they confide in their own understanding, or rely upon fortune. In order, therefore, that God may become the protector and defender of our innocence, let us first conduct ourselves uprightly and innocently towards our enemies, and then commit ourselves entirely to his protection.

22. *Do thou, O God! redeem Israel.* By this conclusion David shows of what character the enemies were of whom he complained. From this it would appear that they were domestic enemies, who, like some disease raging within the bowels, were now the cause of trouble and vexation to the people of God. By the word *redeem*, which he here employs, we may infer that the Church was at that time oppressed with hard bondage; and, therefore, I have no doubt that in this psalm he alludes to Saul and others who reigned with him in a tyrannical manner. At the same time, he shows that he has respect not merely to his own benefit, but that he comprehends in his prayer the state of the whole realm, just as the mutual communion and connection which subsist among the saints require that every individual, deeply affected by a sense of the public calamities which befall the Church at large, should unite with all the others in lamentation before God. This contributed in no small degree to confirm the faith of David, when, regarding himself as in all things connected with the whole body of the faithful, he considered that all the afflictions and wrongs which he endured were common to himself with them. And we ought to regard it as of the greatest importance, that in accordance with this rule, every one of us, in bewailing his private miseries and trials, should extend his desires and prayers to the whole Church.

PSALM XXVI.

This psalm, for the most part, is similar to the preceding. The prophet, oppressed with numerous wrongs, and finding no succour in the world, implores the aid of God, entreating him to undertake the cause of a man unrighteously afflicted, and to assert his innocence. And as his contest was with hypocrites, he appeals to the judgment of God, sharply reproving them for making a false profession of God's name. In the conclusion, as if he had obtained his wish, he promises a sacrifice of praise to God for his deliverance.

¶ A Psalm of David.

1. *Judge me, O Jehovah! because I have walked in mine integrity, and trusted in Jehovah, I shall not stumble.*
2. *Prove me, O Jehovah! and try me; search my reins and my heart.*
3. *For thy goodness is before mine eyes: I have therefore walked in thy truth.*
4. *I have not sat with vain men, neither will I walk with deceitful men.*

1. *Judge me, O Jehovah!* I have just said, that David betakes himself to the judgment of God, because he found neither equity nor humanity among men. The Hebrew word which is rendered *to judge,* signifies to undertake the cognisance of a cause. The meaning here, therefore, is as if David called upon God to be the defender of his right.[1] When God leaves us for a time to the injuries and petulance of our enemies, he seems to neglect our cause; but when he restrains them from assailing us at their pleasure, he clearly demonstrates that the defence of our cause is the object of his care. Let us, therefore, learn from the example of David, when we are destitute of man's aid, to

---

[1] Hammond renders the original word, "Plead for, or defend me;" and Green, "Vindicate me." The word denotes both the act of a judge and of an advocate. This last view agrees very well with the scope of the psalm, which, from the strong assertions of innocence with which it abounds, appears to have been written by David in vindication of himself from various crimes which had been alleged against him; although the particular events to which it refers are not indicated.

have recourse to the judgment-seat of God, and to rely upon his protection. The clause which follows is variously explained by interpreters. Some read it in connection with the first clause, *Judge me, O Jehovah! because I have walked in mine integrity;* but others refer it to the last clause, *Because I have walked in mine integrity, therefore I shall not stumble.* In my opinion, it may be properly connected with both. As it is the proper work of God to maintain and defend righteous causes, the Psalmist, in constituting him his defender, summons him as the witness of his integrity and trust, and thus conceives the hope of obtaining his aid. If, on the other hand, any one thinks that the clauses should be separated, it seems most probable that this sentence, *Judge me, O Lord!* should be read by itself; and then that the second prayer should follow, *that God would not allow him to stumble, because he had behaved himself inoffensively and uprightly, &c.* But there is a force in the possessive pronoun *my,* which interpreters have overlooked. For David does not simply aver that he had been upright, but that he had constantly proceeded in an upright course, without being driven from his purpose, however powerful the devices by which he had been assailed. When wicked men attack us with a view to overwhelm us, either by force or fraud, we know how difficult it is to preserve always the same fortitude. We place our hope of victory in endeavouring resolutely and vigorously to oppose force to force, and art to art. And this is a temptation which so much the more affects honest and steady men, who are otherwise zealous to do well, when the cruelty of their enemies compels them to turn aside from the right path. Let us, therefore, learn from the example of David, even when an opportunity of injuring our enemies is offered us, and when by various methods they force and provoke us, to remain firm in our course, and not suffer ourselves to be diverted in any manner from persevering in the path of our integrity.

2. *Prove me,*[1] *O Jehovah!* The more that David observed

---

[1] The primary signification of the Hebrew word צרף, *tsaraph,* is to try, as the refiner tries his gold by dissolving and melting it. In this sense it is used in Ps. lxvi. 10, "Thou hast tried us as silver is tried."

himself basely and undeservedly pursued with calumnies, the more powerfully was he excited by the vehemence of his grief fearlessly to assert his rectitude. Nor does he merely clear himself of outward sins; he glories also in the uprightness of his heart, and the purity of its affections, tacitly comparing himself, at the same time, with his enemies. As they were gross hypocrites, proudly boasting of their reverence for God, he lays open before him their shameless effrontery and hardihood. This protestation, too, shows how intimately acquainted he was with himself, when he durst offer to submit the whole recesses of his heart to the examination of God. It is to be observed, however, that it was the wickedness of his enemies which forced him to commend himself so much. Had he not been unjustly condemned by men, he would have humbly deprecated such an examination, as he well knew, notwithstanding his zeal to act aright, that he was far from perfection. But when he felt himself to be falsely accused, the injustice and cruelty of men emboldened him to appeal to God's judgment-seat without hesitation. And as he knew that an external appearance of innocence was of no avail there, he brings forward the honest uprightness of his heart. The distinction which some make here, that *the heart* signifies the higher affections, and *the reins* those that are sensual (as they term them) and more gross, is more subtle than solid. We know that the Hebrews understood by the term *reins* that which is most secret in men. David, therefore, conscious of his innocence, offers the whole man to the examination of God; not like careless, or rather stupid men, who, flattering themselves, imagine that they will deceive God with their pretences. It is evident, on the contrary, that he had honestly and thoroughly searched himself, before he presented himself with such confidence in the divine presence. And this we must especially bear in mind, if we would desire to obtain the approbation of God, that when unjustly persecuted, we must not only abstain from retaliation, but also persevere in a right spirit.

3. *For thy goodness is before mine eyes.* This verse may be viewed as one sentence, or divided into two parts, but with

almost the same sense. If the former reading is adopted, both the verbs will be emphatic, after this manner: "Because thy goodness, O Lord, has been ever before mine eyes, and I have trusted in thy faithfulness, I have restrained all wicked lusts in my heart, lest, provoked by the malice of mine enemies, I should be forced to retaliate." By this interpretation there would be the rendering of a cause. The other exposition, also, is not unsuitable, namely, "Because thy goodness has been before mine eyes, I have walked in the truth which thou commandest." In this case the conjunction, as is common among the Hebrews, is superfluous. But although this exposition is allied to the former, I would rather prefer one less remote from the words. As it is a rare and difficult virtue, not only to refrain one's self from wicked actions, when greatly tempted thereto, but also to preserve integrity of heart; the prophet declares in what manner he pursued his course in the midst of such powerful temptations, telling us that it was by setting the goodness of God, which so carefully preserves his servants, before his eyes, lest, declining to evil practices, he might deprive himself of his protection; and by confiding in his faithfulness, he possessed his soul in patience, firmly persuaded that God would never forsake his faithful people who trusted in him. And certainly, had he not relied upon the goodness of God, he could not have so constantly prosecuted the path of integrity amidst such numerous and such severe assaults. It is, indeed, a remarkable difference between the children of God and worldly men, that the former, in the hope of a favourable issue at the Lord's hand, rely upon his word, and are not driven by restlessness to mischievous practices; while the latter, although they maintain a good cause, yet because they are ignorant of the providence of God, are hurried hither and thither; follow unlawful counsels; betake themselves to craftiness; and, in short, have no other object than to overcome evil with evil. Whence, accordingly, their miserable and sorrowful, and often their tragical ends, but because, despising the favour of God, they give themselves up to cunning and deceit? In short, David was steady in preserving his uprightness, because he had resolved that God should be his guide. In the first place, therefore, he mentions his *goodness,* and afterwards he adds, his *truth,* because his goodness, which enables us to walk with unyielding courage in the midst of all temptations, is only known to us by his promises.

4. *I have not sat with vain men.* He again declares the very great dissimilarity which existed between him and his adversaries. For the contrast is always to be observed, that wicked men, by all the harm and mischief they wrought against him, could never drive him from the path of rectitude. This verse might likewise be joined with the former, as if completing the sentence, in this way, That David, by confiding in the favour of God, had withdrawn himself from deceivers. The words, *sitting* and *walking,* denote *sharing in counsel and fellowship in working,* according to what is said in the first psalm. David denies that he had any intercourse with vain and deceitful men. And certainly the best remedy to recall and save us from the assembly of the wicked is to fix our eyes upon God's goodness; for he who walks in the confidence of God's protection, committing all events to his providence, will never imitate their deceitfulness. Those whom he denominates in the first clause, *men of vanity,* he soon after terms נעלמים, *naälamim,* that is, *close and wrapped up in craftiness.*[1] For in this consists the vanity of dissimulation, that deceitful men conceal in their hearts another thing than that which their tongues declare. It is, however, absurd to derive this word from עלם, *alam, to play,* for it is out of place here to compare their impostures to children's play. I confess, indeed, that those who give themselves to craftiness are mockers; but why have recourse to such a forced exposition, when it is plain that the word shows the source from which all lying and deceit proceed? Thus faith, which steadily looks to God's promises, is aptly opposed to all the crooked and iniquitous counsels in which unbelief involves us as often as we ascribe not proper honour to the guardianship of God. David teaches, by his own example, that we have not the

---

[1] Horsley renders the word, "Those who seek concealment." In like manner, the Chaldee paraphrases it, "They that hide themselves that they may do evil."

slightest cause to fear that our integrity will make us a prey to the ungodly, when God promises us safety under his hand. The children of God, indeed, are prudent, but their prudence is altogether different from that of the flesh. Under the guidance and government of the Holy Spirit, they take every necessary precaution against snares, but in such a manner as not to practise any craftiness.

> 5. *I hate the assembly of transgressors, and I will not sit with the wicked.*
> 6. *I will wash my hands in purity,*[1] *and will encompass thine altar, O Jehovah!*
> 7. *That 1 may make men to hear the voice of thy praise, and tell them of all thy wonderful works.*

5. *I hate the assembly.* The Psalmist protests again how greatly he abhorred the ungodly. Formerly he denied that he had any fellowship with them; now he still more explicitly declares that he fled from their company with loathing, for that is the meaning of the phrase, *I hate.* It is indeed true, that the wicked are everywhere hated; but how few withdraw themselves from them, that they may not imitate their vices! David asserts both; he tells us that he hated their society, and that he had no communion with them, from which it appears that he warred not so much with their persons as with their evil doings. He mentions also as another qualification, that he shunned the wicked in such a manner as not on that account to forsake the congregation of God, or withdraw himself from the company of those with whom he was commanded by divine appointment to associate. Many err in this way grievously; imagining when they see the evil mingled with the good, that they will be infected with pollution, unless they immediately withdraw themselves from the whole congregation. This preciseness drove the Donatists of old, and prior to them the Cathari and the Novatians, into mischievous schisms. In our own times, too, the Anabaptists, from a similar conceit, have separated themselves from the sacred assemblies, because they reckoned them not so free from all defilement as could have been wished. Moreover,

[1] " Innocence."—*Fr. marg*

the Donatists made themselves a laughing-stock in a certain process, by tenaciously clinging to mere words. When an assembly was held to settle dissensions, and they were invited by the president of the meeting, with a view to do honour to them, to take a seat, they replied, they would stand, because it was not lawful to " sit with the wicked." Why then, wittily replied Augustine, did your conscience permit you to come in amongst us? for the one is written as well as the other, *I will not go in to the wicked, neither will I sit with the ungodly.* David, therefore, prudently moderates his zeal, and while separating himself from the ungodly, ceases not to frequent the temple, as the divine commandment and the order prescribed in the law required. When he denominates them *the assembly* of the ungodly, we may unquestionably conclude, that their number was not few; nay, it is probable that they flaunted about at that time, as if they alone were exalted above the people of God, and were lords over them: yet this did not prevent David from coming as usual to the sacrifices. Public care, indeed, is to be used that the Church be not defiled by such wickedness, and every man ought privately to endeavour, in his own place, that his remissness and forbearance do not cherish the disorders which these vices occasion. Although, however, this strictness should not be exercised with that care which is necessary, there is nothing in this to hinder any of the faithful from piously and holily remaining in the fellowship of the Church. It is to be observed, in the meantime, that what retained David, was his communion with God and with sacred things.

6. *I will wash my hands in purity.* Referring, in these words, to the ordinary use of the sacrifices, he makes a distinction between himself and those who professed to offer the same divine worship, and thrust themselves forward in the services of the sanctuary, as if they alone had the sole right to perform them. As David, therefore, and these hypocrites were one in this respect, that they entered the sanctuary, and surrounded the sacred altar together, he proceeds to show that he was a true worshipper, declaring, that he not only diligently attended to the external rites, but came to worship

God with unfeigned devotion. It is obvious that he alludes to the solemn rite of washing which was practised under the law.[1] He, accordingly, reproves the gross superstition of hypocrites, who, in seeking only the purification of water, neglected true purification; whereas it was God's design, in the appointment of the outward sign, to put men in mind of their inward pollution, and thus to encourage them to repentance. The outward washing alone, instead of profiting hypocrites, kept them at a greater distance from God. When the Psalmist, therefore, says, *I will wash my hands in innocence*, he intimates that they only gather more pollution and filth by their washings. The Hebrew word נקיון, *nikkayon*, signifies the cleanness of any thing, and is figuratively used for *innocence*. We thus see, that as hypocrites derive no moral purity whatever from their washings, David mocks at the labour with which they vainly toil and torment themselves in such rites. However high, therefore, the wicked may be exalted in the Church, and though crowds of them should fill our sanctuaries, let us, after the example of David, celebrate the outward profession of our faith in such a manner as not deceitfully to substitute its external rites in the room of true devotion. Thus shall we be pure and free from all stain of wickedness. Moreover, as the people were not permitted to touch the altar, David uses the word *encompass*.[2]

7. *That I may make men to hear, &c.* In these words, he shows that he referred the sacrifices to their proper use

---

[1] The washing of the hands in solemn protestation of innocence, on particular occasions, was enjoined by the Mosaic ritual, and was common among the Jews, Deut. xxi. 6, 7. It was in common use among them before prayer; and the priests, in particular, were not to perform any sacred office in the sanctuary until they had poured water from the laver, which was set in the temple for that purpose, and washed their hands, Exod. xl. 30-33.

[2] Mudge conjectures that the expression, *encompass*, is probably taken from the custom of forming a ring round the altar at the time of worship. And Goodwyn informs us, that at the feast of tabernacles the people, on the seventh day, encompassed the altar seven times, carrying branches of palm trees in their hands in remembrance of the overthrow of Jericho, and singing hosannas.—*Moses and Aaron*, p. 132. David, however, may refer to the practice of the priests, who, when they offered sacrifices, went round about the altar; and his meaning may simply be, that as the priests first washed their hands, and then performed their sacred office at the altar; so he deeply felt the necessity of personal purity, in order to his engaging in the service of God.

and design, which hypocrites were far from doing. They neither know, nor do they consider, for what purpose God appointed the services of worship, but think it sufficient to thrust themselves into the divine presence with the pomp and form of their dissimulation. David, therefore, wishing to distinguish spiritual worship from that which is fictitious and counterfeit, affirms that he came into the sanctuary to set forth the praise of God's name. There is, however, a synecdoche in his words, as only one kind of worship is mentioned, although, in offering the sacrifices, the exercise of repentance and faith was required, as well as the giving of thanks. But as the ultimate design of the sacrifices, or at least their principal object, was to celebrate the goodness of God in thus acknowledging his blessings, there was no impropriety in comprehending the other parts of worship under this. Thus, in Ps. l. 14, the sacrifice of praise is preferred to all external ceremonies, as if the whole of devotion consisted in it alone. Likewise in Ps. cxvi. 12, it is said, "What shall I render unto the Lord for all his benefits? I will take the cup of salvation, and call upon the name of the Lord." Moreover, that he may the better commend the acknowledged power of God, and more impressively extol his benefits, David employs the phrase *wondrous;* as if he had said, that it was in no ordinary way that God had helped him.

8. *O Jehovah! I have loved the habitation of thy house,*[1] *and the dwelling-place of thy glory.*
9. *Gather not my soul with wicked men, nor my life with bloody men.*[2]
10. *For in their hands is maliciousness, and their right hand is full of bribes.*
11. *But I will walk in mine integrity: redeem me, and be merciful to me.*

8. *O Jehovah! I have loved, &c.* In this verse he confirms what he had said before, that he came not into the sanctuary in a careless manner, but with serious devotion. Irreligious

---

[1] *The habitation of thy house*—a Hebraism for *the house which thou inhabitest.* This name was given to the tabernacle, 1 Sam. ii. 29, 32, and afterwards to Solomon's temple, 2 Chron. xxxvi. 15.
[2] Heb. *men of blood.* See Psalm v. 7.

men, although they often resort to the sacred assemblies, frequent them merely as lurking places, where they may escape the eye of God. On the contrary, the truly pious and pure in heart resort to them, not for the sake of vain ostentation, but as they are sincerely bent on seeking God, they willingly and affectionately employ the helps which he there affords them; and the advantage which they derive from them creates love to them in their hearts, and longings after them. This declaration farther shows, that however David excelled others in faith, yet he was not without fear lest the violence of his enemies might deprive him of the ordinary means of instruction which God had conferred on his Church. He felt his need of the Church's common discipline and order, and he therefore anxiously laboured to retain his enjoyment of them. From this we infer the impious pride of those who look with contempt on the services of religion as unnecessary, although David himself could not live without them. Another consideration, indeed, existed in those days, I confess, while the law, like a schoolmaster, held the ancient people in a state of servitude compared with ours. Our case, however, is one with theirs in this respect, that the weakness of our faith requires help as well as theirs. And as God for this purpose has appointed the sacraments, as well as the whole order of the Church, woe to the pride of those who recklessly desert the services which we perceive to have been held in such high esteem by the pious servants of God. The Hebrew word מעון, *me-on*, according to some, is derived from a word[1] which signifies *an eye;* and they translate it *comeliness,* or *appearance.* This is the translation of the Septuagint.[2] But as the word is almost every where used to signify *a dwelling-place,* which is more simple, I prefer to retain it. The sanctuary is called *God's house,* and *the dwelling-place of his glory;* and we know how frequently expressions of this kind are employed in Scripture to bear testimony to the presence of God. Not that God either dwelt in a tent, or wished to confine the minds of his people to earthly symbols; but it was needful to remind the faithful of God's present goodness,

---

[1] Namely, עין, *ayin.*
[2] The word which it employs is εὐπρέπεια.

that they might not think they sought him in vain, as we have elsewhere already said. Now, that God's glory may dwell among us, it is necessary that a lively image of it should shine forth in word and sacraments. From this it follows, that the temples which are reckoned such among Papists are only filthy brothels of Satan.

9. *Gather not my soul with wicked men.* Having now affirmed his innocence, he has recourse again to prayer, and calls upon God to defend him. At first sight, indeed, it appears strange to pray that God would not involve a righteous man in the same destruction with the wicked; but God, with paternal indulgence, allows this freedom in prayer, that his people may themselves in this way correct their anxieties, and overcome the fears with which they are tempted. David, when he conceived this supplication, in order to free himself from anxiety and fear, placed before his eyes the righteous judgment of God, to whom nothing is more abhorrent than to mingle good and bad together without distinction. The Hebrew word אסף, *asaph,* sometimes signifies *to gather together,* and sometimes *to destroy.* In this place, I am of opinion it signifies to *gather into a heap,* as was wont to be the case in a confused slaughter. This was the objection stated by Abraham, (Gen. xviii. 25,) "That be far from thee to do after this manner, to slay the righteous with the wicked: and that the righteous should be as the wicked, that be far from thee." Let us remember, therefore, that these forms of prayer are dictated by the Holy Spirit, in order that the faithful may unhesitatingly assure themselves that God still sits in inquisition upon every man's case, in order to give righteous judgment at last. In the second clause, instead of the phrase, *wicked men,* he uses *bloody men,* amplifying what he had said. For although many wicked men rush not all at once to murder, yet in process of time they harden themselves to cruelty; nor does Satan allow them to rest until he precipitate them into deeds of blood.

10. *For in their hands is maliciousness.* The Hebrew word זמה, *zimmah,* signifies properly *an inward stratagem,* or *device.*

But here it is not improperly applied to *the hands,* because David wished to intimate, that the wicked, of whom he was speaking, not only secretly imagined deceits, but also vigorously executed with their hands the malice which their hearts devised. When he farther says, *Their right hands are full of bribes,* we may infer from this, that it was not the common people whom he pointed out for observation, but the nobility themselves, who were most guilty of practising this corruption. Although the common and baser sort of men may be hired for reward, and suborned as agents in wickedness, yet we know that bribes are offered chiefly to judges, and other great men who are in power; and we likewise know, that at the time referred to here the worst of men bore sway. It was no wonder, therefore, that David complained that justice was exposed to sale. We are farther admonished by this expression, that those who delight in gifts can scarcely do otherwise than sell themselves to iniquity. Nor is it in vain, unquestionably, that God declares that " gifts blind the eyes of the wise, and pervert the hearts of the righteous," (Deut. xvi. 19.)

11. *But I will walk in mine integrity.* In this repetition there is to be remarked a circumstance which more clearly illustrates David's righteousness; namely, that, in the midst of so many temptations, he steadily held on his way. He saw many become suddenly rich by gifts, as we still see those who sit at the helm of affairs accumulating to themselves, in a very brief space, a great abundance of wealth, building sumptuous palaces, and extending their lands far and wide. As no allurements could induce him to imitate their example in this, he gave a proof of rare and heroic virtue. He therefore affirms with truth, that although the world accounted them happy, he had not been seduced from his wonted integrity, that thus it might appear that he ascribed more to the providence of God than to evil practices. He, therefore, beseeches God *to redeem him,* because, being oppressed with wrongs, and tempted in various ways, he relied only on God, trusting that he would deliver him. From this we may conclude, that he was at this time reduced to great straits. He

adds, *Be merciful to me,* by which he shows that this deliverance flows from the grace of God, as its true source; and we have already seen that the cause is often put for the effect.

12. *My foot hath stood in uprightness :*[1] *in the congregations will I bless thee, O Jehovah!*

This verse may be explained in two ways. Some are of opinion that David declares how carefully he had studied uprightness among men; but I rather think that he celebrates the grace of God towards him, and, at the same time, vows his gratitude. By the use of the metaphor, therefore, he tells us that he was preserved in safety. And as he knew that it was the hand of God alone which enabled him to stand, he therefore addresses himself to the exercise of praise and thanksgiving. Nor does he merely say, that he will acknowledge in private the goodness of God bestowed upon him, but in public also, that the assemblies of God's people may be witnesses of it. It is highly necessary that every one should publicly celebrate his experience of the grace of God, as an example to others to confide in him.[2]

PSALM XXVII.

In this psalm, David rehearses the desires and meditations with which he had exercised himself in the midst of his great dangers. The thanksgivings which he mingles with them show that it was composed after his deliverance. It is also probable that he repeats at once the prayers which had exercised his thoughts in his different meditations. Hence it is to be seen here with what invincible fortitude of soul the holy man was endued, that he might overcome the most grievous assaults of his enemies. His wonderful piety shines forth in this, that he wished to live for no other purpose than to serve God: nor could he be turned aside from this purpose by any anxiety or trouble.

[1] " C'est, en lieu plain et droict; c'est a dire, seur."—*Fr. marg.* "That is, in a plain and straight; that is to say, sure place."

[2] " Qu'elle soit celebree publiquement; afin qu'elle serue d'exemple aux autres pour se confermer en Dieu."—*Fr.*

¶ *A Psalm of David.*

1. *Jehovah is my light and my salvation, whom shall I fear? Jehovah is the strength of my life, of whom shall I be afraid?*
2. *When the wicked came upon me to eat up my flesh, when my oppressors and mine enemies came upon me, they stumbled and fell.*
3. *Though armies should encamp against me, my heart shall not fear; though war should rise against me, in this will I be confident.*

1. *Jehovah is my light.* This commencement may be understood as meaning that David, having already experienced God's mercy, publishes a testimony of his gratitude. But I rather incline to another meaning, namely, that, perceiving the conflict he had to wage with the sharpest temptations, he fortifies himself beforehand, and as it were brings together matter for confidence : for it is necessary that the saints earnestly wrestle with themselves to repel or subdue the doubts which the flesh is so prone to cherish, that they may cheerfully and speedily betake themselves to prayer. David, accordingly, having been tossed with various tempests, at length recovers himself, and shouts triumphantly over the troubles with which he had been harassed, rejoicing that whenever God displays his mercy and favour, there is nothing to be feared. This is farther intimated by the accumulation of terms which he employs, when he calls God not only *his light*, but *his salvation*, and *the rock* or *strength of his life*. His object was, to put a threefold shield, as it were, against his various fears, as sufficient to ward them off. The term *light*, as is well known, is used in Scripture to denote joy, or the perfection of happiness. Farther, to explain his meaning, he adds that God was *his salvation* and *the strength of his life*, as it was by his help that he felt himself safe, and free from the terrors of death. Certainly we find that all our fears arise from this source, that we are too anxious about our life, while we acknowledge not that God is its preserver. We can have no tranquillity, therefore, until we attain the persuasion that our life is sufficiently guarded, because it is protected by his omnipotent power. The interrogation, too, shows how highly David esteemed the Divine protection, as he thus boldly

exults against all his enemies and dangers. Nor assuredly do we ascribe due homage to God, unless, trusting to his promised aid, we dare to boast of the certainty of our safety. Weighing, as it were, in scales the whole power of earth and hell, David accounts it all lighter than a feather, and considers God alone as far outweighing the whole.

Let us learn, therefore, to put such a value on God's power to protect us as to put to flight all our fears. Not that the minds of the faithful can, by reason of the infirmity of the flesh, be at all times entirely devoid of fear; but immediately recovering courage, let us, from the high tower of our confidence, look down upon all our dangers with contempt. Those who have never tasted the grace of God tremble because they refuse to rely on him, and imagine that he is often incensed against them, or at least far removed from them. But with the promises of God before our eyes, and the grace which they offer, our unbelief does him grievous wrong, if we do not with unshrinking courage boldly set him against all our enemies. When God, therefore, kindly allures us to himself, and assures us that he will take care of our safety, since we have embraced his promises, or because we believe him to be faithful, it is meet that we highly extol his power, that it may ravish our hearts with admiration of himself. We must mark well this comparison, What are all creatures to God? Moreover, we must extend this confidence still farther, in order to banish all fears from our consciences, like Paul, who, when speaking of his eternal salvation, boldly exclaims, "If God be for us, who can be against us?" (Rom. viii. 34.)

2. *When the wicked, &c.* There is no reason for translating this sentence, as some interpreters do, into the future tense.[1] But while we retain the past tense which the prophet employs, the words may be explained in a twofold manner. The mean-

[1] The rendering of the learned Castellio is, "Si invadant——offensuri sunt atque casuri;"—"If they invade me——they shall stumble and fall." The Hebrew verbs for "stumble" and "fall" are indeed in the *past tense;* but in the prophetic writings it is often used for the future. There does not, however, as Calvin remarks, appear to be any necessity for translating the verbs into the future tense in this passage, in which David may be considered as contemplating the past evidences of the goodness of God towards him, and from them taking encouragement with respect to the future.

ing either is, that David celebrates the victory which he had obtained by the blessing of God; or there is a reference to the manner in which he had encouraged himself to hope the best, even in the midst of his temptations, namely, by thinking of God's former favours. The latter is the exposition which I prefer. They both, however, amount to the same thing, and imply that David had no reason henceforth to doubt of God's assistance when he considered his former experience; for nothing is of greater use to confirm our faith, than the remembrance of those instances in which God has clearly given us a proof not only of his grace, but of his truth and power. I connect this verse, accordingly, with the following one. In the former, David recalls to mind the triumphs which, by God's help, he had already obtained; and from this he concludes, that by what hosts soever he may be environed, or whatever mischief his enemies may devise against him, he would fearlessly stand up against them. The Hebrew word קרב, *karab*, signifies *to approach;* but here it refers to the irruption that David's enemies made upon him when they assaulted him. Some translate it *to fight*, but this translation is flat. To testify his innocence, he calls them *wicked* or *froward*, and by saying that they *came upon him to eat up his flesh*,[1] he expresses their savage cruelty.

3. *Though armies should encamp.* He infers from his former experience, as I have already mentioned, that whatever adversity may befall him, he ought to hope well, and to have no misgivings about the divine protection, which had been so effectually vouchsafed to him in his former need. He had asserted this, indeed, in the first verse, but now, upon farther proof of it, he repeats it. Under the terms, *camps* and *armies*, he includes whatever is most formidable in the world: as if he had said, Although all men should conspire for my destruction, I will disregard their violence, because the power of God, which I know is on my side, is far above theirs. But when he declares, *My heart shall not fear*, this does not imply that he would be entirely devoid of fear,—for that would have

---

[1] French and Skinner read, "to devour my flesh;" and observe, that "this image is taken from a wild beast. Compare Ps. iii. 7, and Ps. xxii. 13."

been more worthy of the name of insensibility than of virtue; but lest his heart should faint under the terrors which he had to encounter, he opposed to them the shield of faith. Some transfer the word translated *in this* to the following verse, meaning that he was confident that he would dwell in God's house; but I am of opinion that it belongs rather to the preceding doctrine. For then does faith bring forth its fruit in due season, when we remain firm and fearless in the midst of dangers. David, therefore, intimates, that when the trial comes, his faith will prove invincible, because it relies on the power of God.

> 4. *One thing have I desired of Jehovah, this will I follow after; that I may dwell in the house of Jehovah all the days of my life, to behold the beauty of Jehovah, and diligently to survey his temple.*
> 5. *For he shall hide me in his tent in the day of evil:*[1] *he shall hide me in the secret place of his tent; he shall set me up upon a rock.*
> 6. *And now shall he lift up my head above mine enemies who surround me: and I will offer sacrifices of joy in his tabernacle; I will sing and praise Jehovah.*

4. *One thing have I desired.* Some consider this as a prophecy of the perpetuity of David's kingdom, on which not only his own personal happiness depended, but also the happiness of his whole people; as if he had said, I am so well contented with this singular proof of God's favour, that I can think on nothing else night and day. In my opinion, however, it appears a simpler interpretation to view the words as meaning, that although David was banished from his country, despoiled of his wife, bereft of his kinsfolk; and, in fine, dispossessed of his substance, yet he was not so desirous for the recovery of these, as he was grieved and afflicted for his banishment from God's sanctuary, and the loss of his sacred privileges. Under the word *one*, there is an implied antithesis, in which David, disregarding all other interests, displays his intense affection for the service of God; so that it was bitterer to him to be an exile from the sanctuary, than to be

---

[1] " C'est, d'adversite."—*Note, Fr. marg.* " That is, of adversity."

denied access to his own house. That David desired only one thing, therefore, namely, to dwell in the house of the Lord, must be read in one sentence. For there is no probability that he means by this some secret wish which he suppressed, seeing he distinctly proclaims what it was that chiefly troubled him. He adds, too, steadiness of purpose, declaring that he will not cease to reiterate these prayers. Many may be seen spurring on with great impetuosity at first, whose ardour, in process of time, not only languishes, but is almost immediately extinguished. By declaring, therefore, that he would persevere in this wish during his whole life, he thereby distinguishes between himself and hypocrites.

We must, however, observe by what motive David was so powerfully stimulated. " Surely," some may say, "he could have called on God beyond the precincts of the temple. Wherever he wandered as an exile, he carried with him the precious promise of God, so that he needed not to put so great a value upon the sight of the external edifice. He appears, by some gross imagination or other, to suppose that God could be enclosed by wood and stones." But if we examine the words more carefully, it will be easy to see, that his object was altogether different from a mere sight of the noble building and its ornaments, however costly. He speaks, indeed, of the beauty of the temple, but he places that beauty not so much in the goodliness that was to be seen by the eye, as in its being the celestial pattern which was shown to Moses, as it is written in Exod. xxv. 40, " And look that thou make them after this pattern which was showed thee in the mount." As the fashion of the temple was not framed according to the wisdom of man, but was an image of spiritual things, the prophet directed his eyes and all his affections to this object. Their madness is, therefore, truly detestable who wrest this place in favour of pictures and images, which, instead of deserving to be numbered among temple ornaments, are rather like dung and filth, defiling all the purity of holy things. We should now consider, whether the faithful are to be likeminded under the Christian or Gospel dispensation.[1] I own,

---

[1] " Sous le regne de Christ."—*Fr.*

indeed, that we are in very different circumstances from the ancient fathers; but so far as God still preserves his people under a certain external order, and draws them to him by earthly instructions, temples have still their beauty, which deservedly ought to draw the affections and desires of the faithful to them. The Word, sacraments, public prayers, and other helps of the same kind, cannot be neglected, without a wicked contempt of God, who manifests himself to us in these ordinances, as in a mirror or image.

5. *For he shall hide me in his tent.* Here the Psalmist promises himself that his prayer would not be in vain. Although he is deprived of the visible sanctuary for a time, he doubts not that, wherever he may be, he shall experience the protecting power of God. And he alludes to the temple, because it was a symbol to the faithful of the divine presence; as if he had said, that in making the request which he mentioned he by no means lost his labour; for every one who shall seek God sincerely, and with a pure heart, shall be safely concealed under the wings of his protection. The figure of the temple, he therefore affirms, was not an unmeaning one, for there God, so to speak, spread forth his wings to gather true believers under his protection. From this he concludes, that as he had no greater desire than to flee for refuge under these wings, there would be a shelter ready for him in times of adversity, under the divine protection, which, under the figure of *a rock*, he tells us, would be impregnable like towers, which, for the sake of strength, were wont to be built, in ancient times, in lofty places. Although he was, therefore, at this time, environed by enemies on every side, yet he boasts that he shall overcome them. It is, indeed, a common form of speech in the Scriptures to say, that those who are oppressed with grief walk with a bowed down back and dejected countenance, while, on the other hand, they lift up their heads when their joyfulness is restored. Thus David spake, Psalm iii. 4, " Thou, Lord, art the lifter up of mine head." But because besieging is here put in opposition to this, he meant to say, that in that divine refuge he would be as it were lifted on high, so that he might fear-

lessly disregard the darts of his enemies, which might have otherwise pierced him. And in hoping for victory, though he was reduced to such straits as threatened instant death, he gives us a remarkable proof of his faith; by which we are taught not to measure the aid of God by outward appearances or visible means, but even in the midst of death to hope for deliverance from his powerful and victorious hand.

6. *And I will offer sacrifices of triumph*[1] *in his tabernacle.* By making a solemn vow of thanksgiving, after he shall have been delivered from dangers, he confirms himself again in the hope of deliverance. The faithful under the Law, we know, were wont, by a solemn rite, to pay their vows, when they had experienced any remarkable blessing from God. Here, therefore, David, though in banishment, and prohibited from approaching the temple, boasts that he would again come to the altar of God, and offer the sacrifice of praise. It appears, however, that he tacitly sets the holy rejoicing and songs, in which he promises to give thanks to God, in opposition to the profane triumphings of the world.

7. *Hear, O Jehovah! my voice, with which I cry unto thee; have mercy upon me, and answer me.*
8. *My heart said to thee,*[2] *Seek ye my face; therefore,*[3] *thy face, O Jehovah! will I seek.*
9. *Hide not thy face from me; cast not away thy servant in thy wrath: thou hast been my strength; leave me not, neither forsake me utterly, O God of my salvation!*

7. *Hear, O Jehovah! my voice.* The Psalmist returns again to prayer, and in doing so, he declares with what armour he was furnished to break through his temptations. By the word *cry*, he expresses his vehemence, as I have elsewhere said, that he may thereby move God the sooner to help him.

---

[1] " Sacrificia jubili."—*Lat.* " Sacrifice de triomphe."—*Fr.* Ainsworth reads, " Sacrifices of shouting, or of triumph, of joyful sounding and alarm." " This," says he, " hath respect to the law which appointed over the sacrifices trumpets to be sounded, Numb. x. 10, whose chiefest, most loud, joyful, and triumphant sound was called *trughnah,* [or תרועה, *truah,* the word here used,] ' triumph,' ' alarm,' or ' jubilation,' Numb. x. 5-7."

[2] " Ou dit de toy."—*Fr. marg.* " Or said of or concerning thee."

[3] " Pourtant."—*Fr.*

For the same purpose, also, he a little after mentions his misery, because the more the faithful are oppressed, the more does their very need induce God to extend his favour towards them.

8. *My heart said to thee.* The change of person in the verbs has occasioned a variety of interpretations of this verse. But whoever closely examines David's design will perceive that the text runs perfectly well. As it becomes us not rashly to rush into the presence of God, until he first calls us, David first tells us, that he carefully considered how gently and sweetly God prevents his people, by spontaneously inviting them to seek his face; and then, recovering his cheerfulness, he declares he would come wheresoever God may call him. The sense of the Hebrew word לך, *leka*, is somewhat ambiguous. It may mean the same thing as *tibi, to thee,* in Latin. But as the Hebrew letter ל, *lamed,* is often used for the preposition *of,* or *concerning,* it may properly enough be translated, *My heart hath said of thee;* an exposition to which the majority of interpreters incline. More probably, however, in my opinion, it denotes a mutual conversation between God and the prophet. I have just said, that no one can believingly rise to seek God until the way is first opened by God's invitation, as I have elsewhere shown from the prophet's declaration, " I will say, It is my people; and they shall say, The Lord is my God," (Zech. xiii. 9.) David accordingly says, that in this way the door was opened for him to seek God: he brings forward this promise, and thus responds, as it were, to God.[1] And, certainly, if this symphony does not precede, no man will conduct aright the chorus of the invitation. As soon, therefore, as we hear God presenting himself to us, let us cordially reply, Amen; and let us think with ourselves of his promises, as if they were familiarly addressed to us. Thus

---

[1] Calvin's meaning appears to be this :—God has given us in his word that gracious command or invitation, " Seek ye my face," inviting us to seek him by prayer and the other exercises of religion. Now, when David says, " My heart said to thee, Seek ye my face," he means that his heart reminded God of his command or invitation ; and by this he encouraged himself to seek God's face, which he expresses his resolution to do in the following clause, " Thy face, O Jehovah! will I seek."

true believers have no need to seek any subtle artifice or tedious circuits to introduce themselves into God's favour, since this preface prepares so easy a way for them, "However unworthy we are to be received by thee, O Lord, yet thy commandment, by which thou enjoinest upon us to come to thee, is sufficient encouragement to us." The voice of God, therefore, ought to resound in our hearts, like an echo in hollow places, that from this mutual concord there may spring confidence to call upon him.

The term, *face*, is commonly explained to mean *help* or *succour;* as if it had been said, Seek me. But I am persuaded that the allusion here is also to the sanctuary, and that David refers to the mode of manifestation in which God was wont to render himself in some degree visible. No doubt, it is unlawful to form any gross or carnal idea of him, but as he appointed the ark of the covenant to be a token of his presence, it is, without any impropriety, every where denominated his face. It is indeed true, that we are far from God so long as we abide in this world, because faith is far removed from sight; but it is equally true, that we now see God as in a mirror, and darkly, (1 Cor. xiii. 12,) until he shall openly show himself to us at the last day. Under this word, therefore, I am persuaded, are represented to us those helps by which God raises us to his presence, descending from his inconceivable glory to us, and furnishing us on earth with a vision of his heavenly glory. But as it is according to his own sovereign pleasure that God vouchsafes us to look upon him, (as he does in Word and sacraments,) it becomes us steadily to fix our eyes on this view, that it may not be with us as with the Papists, who, by means of the wildest inventions, wickedly transform God into whatever shapes please their fancy, or their brains have conceived.

9. *Hide not thy face from me.* The Psalmist elegantly continues the same form of speech, but with a different meaning. *The face of God* is now employed to describe the sensible effects of his grace and favour: as if it had been said, Lord, make me truly to experience that thou hast been near to me, and let me clearly behold thy power in saving

me. We must observe the distinction between the theoretical knowledge derived from the Word of God and what is called the experimental knowledge of his grace. For as God shows himself present in operation, (as they usually speak,) he must first be sought in his Word. The sentence which follows, *Cast not away thy servant in thine anger*, some Jewish interpreters expound in too forced a manner to mean, Suffer not thy servant to be immersed in the wicked cares of this world, which are nothing but anger and madness. I, however, prefer to translate the Hebrew word נטה, *natah*, as many translate it, *to turn away from*, or *to remove*. Their meaning is more probable who interpret it, Make not thy servant to decline to anger. When a person is utterly forsaken by God, he cannot but be agitated within by murmuring thoughts, and break forth into the manifestations of vexation and anger. If any one think that David now anticipates this temptation, I shall not object, for he was not without reason afraid of impatience, which weakens us and makes us go beyond the bounds of reason. But I keep to the first exposition, as it is confirmed by the two words which follow; and thus the term *anger* imports a tacit confession of sin; because, although David acknowledges that God might justly cast him off, he deprecates his anger. Moreover, by recalling to mind God's former favours, he encourages himself to hope for more, and by this argument he moves God to continue his help, and not to leave his work imperfect.

10. *When my father and mother shall forsake me, Jehovah will take me up.*
11. *Teach me thy way, O Jehovah! and lead me in the right path, because of mine adversaries.*
12. *Give me not up to the desire[1] of mine oppressors : for false witnesses have risen up against me, and he who bringeth forth violence.*

10. *When my father and my mother shall forsake me.* As it appears from the sacred history, that Jesse, so far as his opportunity admitted, performed his duty to his son David, some are of opinion that the nobles and councillors are here

---

[1] " C'est, plaisir."—*Fr. marg.* " That is, will or pleasure."

mentioned allegorically; but this is not suitable. Nor is it with any reason that they urge this scruple. David does not complain that he was unnaturally betrayed by his father or mother; but by this comparison he magnifies the grace of God, declaring, that he would ever find him ready to help him, although he might be forsaken of all men. The Hebrew particle כִּי, *ki*, for the most part, signifies *for*, but it is also known to be often employed for the adverb of time, *when*. David, therefore, meant to intimate, that whatever benevolence, love, zeal, attention, or service, might be found among men, they are far inferior to the paternal mercy with which God encircles his people. The highest degree of love among men, it is true, is to be found in parents who love their children as their own bowels. But God advances us higher, declaring, by the prophet Isaiah, that though a mother may forget the child of her womb, he would always be mindful of us, (Isaiah xlix. 15.) In this degree does David place him, so that he who is the source of all goodness far surpasses all mortals, who are naturally malevolent and niggardly. It is, however, an imperfect mode of speech, like that in Isaiah lxiii. 16, "Doubtless, thou art our Father, though Abraham be ignorant of us, and Israel acknowledge us not." The purport of the whole is this : However inclined by nature earthly parents are to help their children, nay, though they should endeavour to cherish them with the greatest ardour of affection, yet should affection be wholly extinguished in the earth, God would fulfil the duty both of father and mother to his people. From which it follows, that we basely undervalue the grace of God, if our faith rise not above all the affections of nature ; for sooner shall the laws of nature be overturned a hundred times, than God shall fail his people.

11. *Teach me thy way, O Jehovah!* Many think that David here requests that God would guide him by his Spirit, lest he should surpass his enemies in acting violently and wickedly. This doctrine is, no doubt, very useful, but it does not seem to agree with the scope of the passage. It is a simpler interpretation, in my opinion, to consider that David desires, in order to escape the snares and violence of his enemies,

that God would extend to him his hand, and safely conduct him, so as to give a happy issue to his affairs. He sets *the right path* in opposition to the difficulties and impediments which are in places which are rough, and of difficult access, to overcome which he was unequal, unless God undertook the office of a guide to lead him. But he who thus desires to commit himself to the safeguard and protection of God,[1] must first renounce crafty and wicked devices. We must not expect that God, who promises to grant a happy issue only to the single in heart, and those who trust in his faithfulness, will bless crooked and wicked counsels.

12. *Give me not up to the desire of mine oppressors.* The Hebrew noun נֶפֶשׁ, *nephesh*, signifies *lust, will,* or *desire;* and the language of David implies, Deliver me not up to the pleasure or lust of mine enemies, and thus he intimates, that they greedily gaped for his destruction. God delivers his people in two ways; either by appeasing the cruelty of the wicked, and rendering them meek; or, if he permit them to burn with fury, by restraining their power and violence, so that they desire and endeavour in vain to do mischief. The Psalmist afterwards adds, that he is persecuted both with slanders and false accusations, and also by open violence; for when he says, that they *bring forth violence*,[2] he means that they speak of nothing but of war and slaughter. We thus see that the holy man was miserably oppressed on every side. Even his integrity, which we know to have been singular, could not free him from bitter and deadly calumnies, and he was at the same time overwhelmed by the violence and force of his enemies. If the ungodly, therefore, should at any time rise against us, not only with menaces and cruel violence, but to give the semblance of justice to their enmity, should slander us with lies, let us remember the example of David, who was assaulted in both ways; nay, let us recall to mind that Christ the Son of God suffered no less injury from

---

[1] "En la sauvegarde et protection de Dieu."—*Fr.*
[2] Hammond renders the words "*breathers* or *speakers of injury* or *rapine;* חמס, signifying *injury* or *rapine,* and יפח, *to breathe* or *speak.*" Ainsworth reads, "He that breatheth or puffeth out violent wrong."

lying tongues than from violence.[1] Moreover, this prayer was dictated for our comfort, to intimate that God can maintain our innocence, and oppose the shield of his protection to the cruelty of our enemies.

13. *Unless I had believed to see the goodness of Jehovah in the land of the living* ———.[2]
14. *Wait thou on Jehovah; be of good courage, and he shall strengthen thine heart: wait thou also on Jehovah.*

13. *Unless I had believed to see the goodness of Jehovah.* It is generally agreed among interpreters, that this sentence is incomplete. Some, however, are of opinion, that the Hebrew particle לולא, *lulë*, is used for the purpose of affirmation, as if it were a species of oath; the Hebrews being accustomed to swear elliptically; for breaking off in the middle of the discourse and leaving it imperfect, they supplied an imprecation, namely, that God would punish them in case they perjured themselves. But the greater number give a different interpretation, namely, that David intimates that he was supported solely by faith, otherwise he had perished a hundred times. The meaning which they elicit, accordingly, is, Had I not relied on the promise of God, and been assuredly persuaded that he would safely preserve me, and had I not continued firm in this persuasion, I had utterly perished: There was no other remedy. Some understand by *the land of the living*, the heavenly inheritance; but this interpretation is forced,

---

[1] "De glaives et autre tels efforts."—*Fr.* "From the sword and other such weapons."

[2] In the Hebrew this verse is elliptical, as Calvin here translates it. In the French version he supplies the ellipsis, by adding to the end of the verse the words, "C'estoit fait de moy," "I had perished." In our English version, the words, "I had fainted," are introduced as a supplement in the beginning of the verse. Both the supplement of Calvin, and that of our English version, which are substantially the same, doubtless explain the meaning of the passage; but they destroy the elegant abrupt form of the expression employed by the Psalmist, who breaks off in the middle of his discourse without completing the sentence, although what he meant to say is very evident. "Unless I had believed to see the goodness of the Lord in the land of the living ——— What! what, alas! should have become of me!"—*Dr Adam Clarke.* As, however, לולא, *lulë*, which is rendered *unless*, is omitted by the ancient versions and several MSS., some consider it an interpolation, and translate the verse without an ellipsis. Thus Walford renders it: "I have believed that I shall behold the goodness of Jehovah in the land of the living."

and disagrees with the usual style of Scripture. When Hezekiah laments in his song recorded in Isaiah xxxviii. 11, that he had no hope of seeing God "in the land of the living," he means, without all doubt, the present life, as he immediately adds, "I shall behold man no more with the inhabitants of the world." A similar form of speech occurs also in another place, (Jer. xi. 19.) David then believed that he would still enjoy the goodness of God in this world, although he was now deprived of all experience of his favour, and could see no spark of light. From the darkness of death, therefore, he promises himself a view of the divine favour, and by this persuasion his life is sustained, although, according to the judgment of carnal reason, it was past recovery and lost. It is to be observed, however, that David does not rashly go beyond the divine promise. It is true that "godliness is profitable unto all things, having promise of the life that now is, and of that which is to come," (1 Tim. iv. 8;) but he would have never dared to entertain this persuasion had he not been informed by a special revelation, and assuredly promised a successor, who should always sit upon his throne, (Psalm cxxxii. 11, 12.) He was, therefore, justly persuaded that he would not die till this promise was fulfilled. Lest any man, therefore, by an unwarranted imitation of his example, should overleap the boundaries of faith, it is necessary to understand what was peculiar to him, and did not belong to us. In general, however, we ought all to hope that, although God may not openly work deliverance for us, or show us his favour in a visible manner, he will, nevertheless, be always merciful to us, even in the present life.

14. *Wait thou on Jehovah.* It may be doubted whether David, having in the preceding verses spoken of himself, here addresses his discourse to others, and exhorts them by his own example to fortitude and persevering patience, as he does in the conclusion of Psalm xxxi. 19, where, after speaking concerning himself particularly, he makes a transition, and addresses himself to all the godly. But as he speaks here in the singular number, and uses no mark to show that he directs his discourse to others, it is in my opinion pro-

bable that he applies it to himself, the more to encourage his confidence in God, lest at any time his heart should faint.[1] As he was conscious of his weakness, and knew that his faith was the great means of preserving him safe, he seasonably strengthens himself for the future. Under the word *waiting*, too, he puts himself in mind of new trials, and sets before his eyes the cross which he must bear. We are then said to wait on God, when, withdrawing his grace from us, he suffers us to languish under afflictions. David, therefore, having got through one conflict, prepares himself to encounter new ones. But as nothing is more difficult than to give God the honour of relying upon him, when he hides himself from us, or delays his assistance, David stirs himself up to collect strength; as if he had said, If fearfulness steal upon thee; if temptation shake thy faith; if the feelings of the flesh rise in tumult, do not faint; but rather endeavour to rise above them by an invincible resolution of mind. From this we may learn, that the children of God overcome, not by sullenness, but by patience, when they commit their souls quietly to God; as Isaiah says, "In quietness and in confidence shall be your strength," (Isaiah xxx. 15.) As David did not feel himself equal to great and difficult efforts, he borrows strength from God by prayer. Had he said no more than *Act like a man*,[2] he would have appeared to allege the motions of his own free-will, but as he immediately adds, by way of correction, that God would be at hand *to strengthen his heart*, he plainly enough shows, that when the saints strive vigorously, they fight in the strength of another, and not in their own. David does not, like the Papists, put his own efforts into the van, and afterwards supplicate for divine aid, but having done his own duty, although he knew that he was destitute of strength in himself, he requests that his deficiency

---

[1] "A ce que sa foy ne soit jamais esbranler."—*Fr.* "That his faith might never be shaken."

[2] Calvin here seems to use the Septuagint version. What he renders in the text, "Be of good courage," is rendered by the Septuagint "$\mathit{\dot{\alpha}\nu\delta\rho\dot{\iota}\zeta ov}$," "Be manly, or act like a man." The Vulgate reads, "viriliter age," following the Septuagint, as it generally does. Paul uses the same phraseology in 1 Cor. xvi. 13. "These," says Ainsworth, "are the words of encouragement against remissness, fear, faintness of heart, or other infirmities."

may be supplied by the grace of the Holy Spirit. And as he knew that the war must be continued during his whole life, and that new conflicts would daily arise, and that the troubles of the saints are often protracted for a long period, he again repeats what he had said about waiting on God: *Wait thou alone on Jehovah.*

PSALM XXVIII.

After being delivered by God's help from great dangers, David, in this psalm, according to his custom, first records the vows that he had made in the midst of his difficulties, and then his thanksgivings and praises to God, to induce others to follow his example. It is probable that he speaks of his persecutions by Saul.

¶ A Psalm of David.

1. *Unto thee, O Jehovah! will I cry; O my strength! hold not thy peace from me; lest, shouldst thou be silent to me, I become like them that go down to the grave.*
2. *Hear the voice of my prayers when I cry to thee, when I lift up my hands to the sanctuary of thy holiness.*

1. *Unto thee, O Jehovah! will I cry.* The Psalmist begins by declaring that he would betake himself to the help of God alone, which shows both his faith and his sincerity. Although men labour every where under a multitude of troubles, yet scarcely one in a hundred ever has recourse to God. Almost all having their consciences burdened with guilt, and having never experienced the power of divine grace which might lead them to betake themselves to it, either proudly gnaw the bit or fill the air with unavailing complaints, or, giving way to desperation, faint under their afflictions. By calling God *his strength*, David more fully shows that he confided in God's assistance, not only when he was in the shade and in peace, but also when he was exposed to the severest temptations. In comparing himself to the dead, too, he in-

timates how great his straits were, although his object was not merely to point out the magnitude of his danger, but also to show that when he needed succour, he looked not here and there for it, but relied on God alone, without whose favour there remained no hope for him. It is, therefore, as if he had said, I am nothing if thou leavest me; if thou succourest me not, I perish. It is not enough for one who is in such a state of affliction to be sensible of his misery, unless, convinced of his inability to help himself, and renouncing all help from the world, he betake himself to God alone. And as the Scriptures inform us that God answers true believers when he shows by his operations that he regards their supplications, so the word *silent* is set in opposition to the sensible and present experience of his aid, when he appears, as it were, not to hear their prayers.

2. *Hear the voice of my prayers when I cry to thee.* This repetition is a sign of a heart in anguish. David's ardour and vehemence in prayer are also intimated by the noun signifying *voice*, and the verb signifying *to cry*. He means that he was so stricken with anxiety and fear, that he prayed not coldly, but with burning, vehement desire, like those who, under the pressure of grief, vehemently cry out. In the second clause of the verse, by synecdoche, the thing signified is indicated by the sign. It has been a common practice in all ages for men to lift up their hands in prayer. Nature has extorted this gesture even from heathen idolaters, to show by a visible sign that their minds were directed to God alone. The greater part, it is true, contented with this ceremony, busy themselves to no effect with their own inventions; but the very lifting up of the hands, when there is no hypocrisy and deceit, is a help to devout and zealous prayer. David, however, does not say here that he lifted his hands to heaven, but to *the sanctuary*, that, aided by its help, he might ascend the more easily to heaven. He was not so gross, or so superstitiously tied to the outward sanctuary, as not to know that God must be sought spiritually, and that men then only approach to him when, leaving the world, they penetrate by faith to celestial glory. But remembering that he was a man, he would not neglect this aid

afforded to his infirmity. As the sanctuary was the pledge or token of the covenant of God, David beheld the presence of God's promised grace there, as if it had been represented in a mirror; just as the faithful now, if they wish to have a sense of God's nearness to them, should immediately direct their faith to Christ, who came down to us in his incarnation, that he might lift us up to the Father. Let us understand, then, that David clung to the sanctuary with no other view than that by the help of God's promise he might rise above the elements of the world, which he used, however, according to the appointment of the Law. The Hebrew word דְּבִיר, *debir*, which we have rendered *sanctuary*,[1] signifies the inner-room of the tabernacle or temple, or the most holy place, where the ark of the covenant was contained, and it is so called from the answers or oracles which God gave forth from thence, to testify to his people the presence of his favour among them.

> 3. *Draw me not away with wicked men, nor with the workers of iniquity, who speak peace to their neighbours, while malice is in their hearts.*
> 4. *Give them according to their works, and according to the wickedness of their doings ; give them according to the work of their hands ; render them their reward.*
> 5. *Because they regard not the doings of Jehovah, neither the work of his hands, let him destroy them, and not build them up.*

3. *Draw me not away with wicked men.* The meaning is, that in circumstances so dissimilar, God should not mingle the righteous with the wicked in the same indiscriminate destruction.[2] Undoubtedly, too, in speaking of his enemies, he indirectly asserts his own integrity. But he did not pray in this manner, because he thought that God was indiscriminately and unreasonably angry with men; he reasons rather from

---

[1] דְּבִיר, *debir*, is derived from דבר, *dabar*, *to speak*.
[2] The verb משׁך, *mashak*, here rendered *draw*, " signifies," as Hammond observes, " both to draw and apprehend," and may " be best rendered here, *Seize not on me*, as he that seizeth on any to carry or drag him to execution. The Septuagint, after having literally rendered the Hebrew by Μὴ συνελκύσῃς τὴν ψυχήν μου, *draw not my soul together with*, &c., add, Κίαν μὴ συναπολέσῃς, με, &c., *and destroy me not together with*," &c. Calvin here evidently takes the same view; though he does not express it in the form of criticism.

the nature of God, that he ought to cherish good hope, because it was God's prerogative to distinguish between the righteous and the wicked, and to give every one his due reward. By *the workers of iniquity*, he means man wholly addicted to wickedness. The children of God sometimes fall, commit errors, and act amiss in one way or other, but they take no pleasure in their evil doings; the fear of God, on the contrary, stirs them up to repentance. David afterwards defines and enlarges upon the wickedness of those whom he describes; for, under pretence of friendship they perfidiously deceived good men, professing one thing with their tongue, while they entertained a very different thing in their hearts. Open depravity is easier to be borne with than this craftiness of the fox, when persons put on fair appearances in order to find opportunity of doing mischief.[1] This truth, accordingly, admonishes us that those are most detestable in God's sight, who attack the simple and unwary with fair speeches as with poison.

4. *Give them according to their works.* Having thus requested God to have a regard to his innocence, the Psalmist thunders forth a curse against his enemies. And the accumulation of words shows that he had groaned long and grievously under the burden before he broke forth to desire such vengeance. He intimates that the wicked of whom he speaks had transgressed not once, nor for a short time, nor in one way, but that they had proceeded so far in their constant evil doings, that their audacity was no longer to be endured. We know how troublesome and grievous a temptation it is to see the ungodly proceeding without measure or end, as if God connived at their wickedness. David, therefore, wearied as it were with continual forbearing, and fainting under the burden, implores God, at length, to restrain the wantonness of his enemies, who of late ceased not to heap wickedness upon wickedness. Thus we perceive that there is nothing superfluous in this verse, when to *works* he adds *the wickedness of their doings*, and *the work of their hands*,

[1] " Que ceste finesse de renard, quand on use de beaux semblans pour avoir occasion de nuire."—*Fr.*

and thrice petitions that they may receive the *reward* which they have deserved. Add to this, that he at the same time bears testimony to his own faith, to which boasting hypocrites often compel the children of God, while by their deceit and cavils, they impose upon the judgments of the world. We see how men who are distinguished for wickedness, not content with impunity themselves, cannot abstain from oppressing the innocent by false accusations, just as the wolf, desirous of making a prey[1] of the lambs, according to the common proverb, accused them of troubling the water. David is therefore compelled by this exigency to call upon God for protection. Here again occurs the difficult question about praying for vengeance, which, however, I shall despatch in few words, as I have discussed it elsewhere. In the first place, then, it is unquestionable, that if the flesh move us to seek revenge, the desire is wicked in the sight of God. He not only forbids us to imprecate evil upon our enemies in revenge for private injuries, but it cannot be otherwise than that all those desires which spring from hatred must be disordered. David's example, therefore, must not be alleged by those who are driven by their own intemperate passion to seek vengeance. The holy prophet is not inflamed here by his own private sorrow to devote his enemies to destruction; but laying aside the desire of the flesh, he gives judgment concerning the matter itself. Before a man can, therefore, denounce vengeance against the wicked, he must first shake himself free from all improper feelings in his own mind. In the second place, prudence must be exercised, that the heinousness of the evils which offend us drive us not to intemperate zeal, which happened even to Christ's disciples, when they desired that fire might be brought from heaven to consume those who refused to entertain their Master, (Luke ix. 54.) They pretended, it is true, to act according to the example of Elias; but Christ severely rebuked them, and told them that they knew not by what spirit they were actuated. In particular, we must observe this general rule, that we cordially desire and labour for the welfare of the whole human race. Thus

---

[1] " Voulant devorer les agneaux."—*Fr.*

it will come to pass, that we shall not only give way to
the exercise of God's mercy, but shall also wish the conversion of those who seem obstinately to rush upon their own
destruction. In short, David, being free from every evil
passion, and likewise endued with the spirit of discretion
and judgment, pleads here not so much his own cause as
the cause of God. And by this prayer, he farther reminds
both himself and the faithful, that although the wicked may
give themselves loose reins in the commission of every
species of vice with impunity for a time, they must at length
stand before the judgment-seat of God.

5. *Because they regard not the doings of Jehovah.* In this
verse he lays open the root of impiety, declaring that the
ungodly are so bold to do mischief, because, while they are
thus indulging their hatred, and perpetrating every species of
wickedness, they think that they have nothing to do with God.
And when conscience stings them, they soothe themselves
with false hopes, and at last stubbornly harden themselves into
insensibility. First, being intoxicated with prosperity, they
flatter themselves that God is their friend, while he has no
regard for those good men who are overwhelmed with so
many afflictions; and, next, they persuade themselves that
the world is governed by chance, thus blinding themselves in
the midst of the clear light of day. In this manner, David's
adversaries, willingly ignorant that God had appointed him
to be king, emboldened themselves to persecute him. He
therefore complains of their gross ignorance of this, just as
Isaiah (chap. v. 20) brings the same complaint, in general
terms, against all the ungodly of his days. This doctrine,
then, has a twofold use. First, it is no small consolation to
the children of God to be persuaded, while they are unrighteously vexed, that by the providence of God they are thus
profitably exercised to patience; and that while the affairs
of this world are all in a state of disturbance and confusion,
God nevertheless sits supreme in heaven conducting and
governing all things.[1] In the second place, this is a very
proper curb to subdue the passions of our flesh, that we may

---

[1] " Conduisant et gouvernant toutes choses."—*Fr.*

not, like the Andabates,[1] contend in the dark, and with shut eyes, as if God saw not and cared not about what is done here below. Let us, therefore, learn carefully to consider that the judgments which God executes are just so many proofs of his righteousness in governing mankind, and that although all things should be huddled together in confusion, the eye of faith should be directed to heaven, to consider God's secret judgments. And as God never ceases, even in the midst of the greatest darkness, to give some tokens of his providence, it is inexcusable indolence not to attend to them. This perverseness the prophet aggravates, by repeating again, *the works of God's hands.* He thus intimates, that the ungodly, by recklessly pursuing their course, trample under foot whatever of God's works they may meet with to check their madness.

Let him destroy them, and not build them up. Some are of opinion that the first part of this verse is the nominative in the room of a substantive to the verbs in the last clause; as if David had said, This brutal madness shall destroy them; but the name of God should rather be supplied, and then the context will run excellently. As the verbs, however, in the Hebrew are in the future tense,[2] the sentence may be explained as meaning that David now assures himself of the destruction of the reprobates for which he had lately prayed. I do not reject this interpretation; but, in my opinion, the words are just a continuance of his petitions. In this way, he prays that the wicked may be overthrown, so as not to rise again, or recover their former state. The expression, *Let him destroy them, and not build them up,* is a common figure of speech among the Hebrews, according to what Malachi says concerning Edom, "Thus saith the Lord of Hosts, They shall build, but I shall throw down," (chap. i. 4.) Lest we should be struck, therefore, with an incurable plague, let us learn to awake our minds to the consideration

---

[1] " C'estoyent certains peuples ou escrimeurs qui souloyent ainsi combattre. Voyez les Chiliades d'Erasme."—*Note, Fr. marg.* "These were certain people or fencers, who were wont to fight in this manner. See the Chiliades of Erasmus."

[2] " He will destroy them, and not build them up."

of God's works, that we may be taught to fear him, to persevere in patience, and to advance in godliness.

> 6. *Blessed be Jehovah, for he hath heard the voice of my supplication.*
> 7. *Jehovah is my strength and my shield, my heart hath trusted in him, and I have been helped : therefore shall my heart rejoice, and with my song will I praise him.*
> 8. *Jehovah is their strength ; and he is also the strength of the salvations* [or *deliverances*] *of his anointed.*

6. *Blessed be Jehovah, who hath heard.* This is the second part of the psalm in which the prophet begins to give thanks to God. We have already seen how he employed himself in prayer in the midst of his dangers ; and now by this thanksgiving he teaches us that his prayers were not in vain. Thus he confirms by his own example, that God is ready to bring help to his people whenever they seek him in truth and sincerity. He declares the same truth more fully in the next verse, calling God *his strength* and *his shield;* for he was persuaded that God had heard him from this, that he had been wonderfully preserved. He adds, that he had been *helped* in respect of his confidence and hope; for it often comes to pass, that those who call upon God, notwithstanding come short of his grace through their own unbelief. Thirdly, he says that he will add to his joy a testimony of his gratitude. Wicked men and hypocrites flee to God when they are overwhelmed with difficulties, but as soon as they escape from them, forgetting their deliverer, they rejoice with frantic mirth. In short, David trusted not in vain, since he truly found by experience that God possesses ever present power to preserve his servants ; and that this was matter of true and solid joy to him, that he found God ever favourable to him. On this account, likewise, he promises that he would be mindful of God, and grateful to him. And undoubtedly, when God spreads cheerfulness through our hearts, it is to open our mouths to sing his praises.

8. *Jehovah is their strength.* By way of explanation, he repeats what he had said before, that God had been his

strength; namely, because he had blessed his armies. David had indeed employed the hand and labour of men, but to God alone he ascribes the victory. As he knew that whatever help he had obtained from men proceeded from God, and that his prosperous success flowed likewise from his gratuitous favour, he discerned his hand in these means, as palpably as if it had been stretched forth from heaven. And surely it is passing shameful, that human means, which are only the instruments of God's power, should obscure his glory; although there is no sin more common. It is a manner of speaking which has great weight, when, speaking of his soldiers, he uses only the pronoun *their*, as if he pointed to them with the finger. The second clause assigns the reason of the other. He declares that himself and his whole army were endued with victorious valour from heaven, because he fought under the standard of God. This is the meaning of the word *anointed;* for, had not God appointed him king, and freely adopted him, he would not have favoured him any more than he did Saul. By this means, in extolling solely the power of God which advanced him to the kingdom, he attributes nothing to his own policy or power. In the meantime, we may learn, that when one is satisfied of the lawfulness of his calling, this doctrine encourages him to entertain good hope with respect to the prosperous issue of his affairs. In particular, it is to be observed, as we have briefly noticed in another place, that the fountain whence all the blessings God bestows upon us flows is, that he hath chosen us in Christ. David employs *salvations* or *deliverances* in the plural number, because he had been often and in various ways preserved. The meaning, therefore, is, that from the time when God had anointed him by the hand of Samuel, he never ceased to help him, but delivered him in innumerable ways, until he had accomplished the work of his grace in him.

9. *Save thy people, and bless thine inheritance; feed them, and lift them up for ever.*

In this verse he shows that it was not so much his own welfare as the welfare of the whole Church which was the object of his concern, and that he neither lived nor reigned for himself, but for the common good of the people. He well knew that he was appointed king for no other end. In this he declares himself to be a type of the Son of God, of whom, when Zechariah (chap. ix. 9) predicts that he would come "having salvation," there is no doubt that he promises nothing to him apart from his members, but that the effects of this salvation would diffuse themselves throughout his whole body. By this example, accordingly, he prescribes a rule to earthly kings, that, devoting themselves to the public good, they should only desire to be preserved for the sake of their people.[1] How very far otherwise it is, it is needless to say. Blinded with pride and presumption they despise the rest of the world, just as if their pomp and dignity raised them altogether above the common state of man. Nor is it to be wondered at, that mankind are so haughtily and contumeliously trampled under foot of kings, since the greatest part cast off and disdain to bear the cross of Christ.[2] Let us therefore remember that David is like a mirror, in which God sets before us the continual course of his grace. Only we must be careful, that the obedience of our faith may correspond to his fatherly love, that he may acknowledge us for his people and inheritance. The Scriptures often designate David by the name of a shepherd; but he himself assigns that office to God, thus confessing that he is altogether unfit for it,[3] save only in as far as he is God's minister.

PSALM XXIX.

David, that he may humble all men before God, from the highest to the lowest, celebrates his terrible power in the various wonders of nature,

---

[1] "Que tout la prosperite qu'ils se souhaitent soit à cause du peuple." —*Fr.* "That all the prosperity they desire should be for the sake of the people."

[2] "Veu que la plus grand part rejette et desdaigne de porter le joug de Christ."—*Fr.*

[3] "Qu'il n'en est pas digne."—*Fr.* "That he is not worthy of it."

which he affirms are not less fitted to arouse us to give glory to God, than if he were to assert his empire and majesty with his own voice. After he has struck fear into the proud, who are reluctant to yield, and addressed an exhortation to them accompanied by a gentle reproof, he sweetly invites the faithful voluntarily to fear the Lord.

¶ A Psalm of David.

1. *Give unto Jehovah, ye sons of the mighty, give unto Jehovah glory and strength.*
2. *Give unto Jehovah the glory of his name ;*[1] *worship before Jehovah in the brightness of his sanctuary.*
3. *The voice of Jehovah is upon the waters ; the God of glory thundereth ; Jehovah is upon the great waters.*
4. *The voice of Jehovah is in strength, the voice of Jehovah is in beauty.*

1. *Give unto Jehovah, ye sons of the mighty.* It was no doubt David's design to lead all men to worship and reverence God; but as it is more difficult to reduce great men, who excel in rank, to order, he expressly addresses himself to them. It is obvious, that the LXX, in giving the translation, *sons of rams,*[2] were led into a mistake by the affinity of the Hebrew words.[3] About the signification of the word, indeed, the Jewish commentators are all agreed ; but when they proceed to speak of its meaning, they pervert and obscure it by the most chilling comments. Some

---

[1] " C'est, digne de son nom."—*Note, Fr. marg.* " That is, worthy of his name."

[2] The entire reading of the verse in the Septuagint is, " Ἐνέγκατε τῷ Κυρίῳ υἱοὶ Θεοῦ, ἐνέγκατε τῷ Κυρίῳ υἱοὺς κριῶν." " Bring to the Lord, ye sons of God, bring to the Lord young rams." Thus the LXX., as is not unusual in other places, render the words for " Ye sons of the mighty" twice ; first, in the vocative case, addressing them, Ὑιοὶ Θεου, *Ye sons of God,* and then in the accusative case, υἱοὺς κριῶν, *young rams,* being apparently doubtful which was the correct rendering, and, therefore, putting down both. The Vulgate, Arabic, and Æthiopic, exactly follow them. Jerome also reads, " Afferte Domino filios arietum ;" although he does not give a double translation of the original words. But the correct rendering, we have no doubt, is, " Ye sons of the mighty ;" which is just a Hebrew idiomatic expression for " Ye mighty ones," or, " Ye princes ;" and to them the inspired writer addresses an invitation to acknowledge and worship God from the manifestation of his majesty and power in the wonders of nature.

[3] The Hebrew word which Calvin renders " mighty," is אלים, *elim,* a word which means *gods.* The Hebrew word אילים, *eylim,* which means *rams,* nearly resembles it, having only an additional י, *yod,* and this letter is often cut off in nouns.

expound it of the angels,[1] some of the stars; and others will have it, that by the great men who are referred to are meant the holy fathers. But David only intended to humble the princes of this world, who, being intoxicated with pride, lift up their horns against God. This, accordingly, is the reason why he introduces God, with a terrific voice, subduing by thunders, hail-storms, tempests, and lightnings, these stubborn and stiff-necked giants, who, if they are not struck with fear, refuse to stand in awe of any power in heaven. We see, therefore, why, passing by others, he directs his discourse particularly to the sons of the mighty. The reason is, because there is nothing more common with them than to abuse their lofty station by impious deeds, while they madly arrogate to themselves every divine prerogative. At least that they may modestly submit themselves to God, and, mindful of their frailty, place their dependence upon his grace, it is necessary, as it were, to compel them by force. David, therefore, commands them *to give strength unto Jehovah*, because, deluded by their treacherous imaginations, they think that the power which they possess is supplied to them from some other quarter than from heaven. In short, he exhorts them to lay aside their haughtiness, and their false opinion about their own strength, and to glorify God as he deserves. By *the glory of God's name*, (ver. 2,) he means that which is worthy of his majesty, of which the great men of this world are wont to deprive him. The repetition, also, shows that they must be vehemently urged ere a proper acknowledgment be extorted from them. By *the brightness of God's sanctuary*[2] is to be understood, not heaven as some think, but the tabernacle of the covenant, adorned with the symbols of the divine glory, as is evident from the context. And the

---

[1] The Chaldee paraphrases it thus:—" The assembly of angels, sons of God," meaning by God *angels*.

[2] This translation conveys a somewhat different meaning from that of our English version; but it is supported by several critics. Green reads, "In his beautiful sanctuary;" and Fry, "Worship Jehovah with holy reverence," or, " Worship Jehovah in the glorious places of the sanctuary." "Where the Hebrews read בהדרת," says Hammond, "*in the glory* or *beauty* of *holiness*, from הדר, *to honour*, or *beautify*, the LXX. read, ἐν αὐλῇ ἁγίᾳ αὐτοῦ, *in his holy court*, as if it were from חדר, *penetrale, thalamus, area, a closet*, a marriage-chamber, a court; and so the Latin and Syriac follow them, and the Arabic, *in his holy habitation*."

prophet designedly makes mention of this place, in which the true God had manifested himself, that all men, bidding adieu to superstition, should betake themselves to the pure worship of God. It would not be sufficient to worship any heavenly power, but the one and unchangeable God alone must be worshipped, which cannot come to pass until the world be reclaimed from all foolish inventions and services forged in the brains of men.

3. *The voice of Jehovah is upon the waters.* David now rehearses the wonders of nature which I have previously referred to; and well indeed does he celebrate the power of God as well as his goodness, in his works. As there is nothing in the ordinary course of nature, throughout the whole frame of heaven and earth, which does not invite us to the contemplation of God, he might have brought forward, as in Psalm xix. 1, the sun and the stars, and the whole host of heaven, and the earth with its riches; but he selects only those works of God which prove not only that the world was at first created by him, and is governed by his power, but which also awaken the torpid, and drag them, as it were, in spite of themselves, humbly to adore him; as even Horace was compelled, though he was not only a heathen poet, but an Epicurean, and a vile contemner of Deity, to say of himself in one of his Odes,—(Lib. I. Ode xxxiv.)

> " A fugitive from heaven and prayer,
>   I mocked at all religious fear,
>   Deep scienced in the mazy lore
>   Of mad philosophy ; but now
>   Hoist sail, and back my voyage plough
>   To that blest harbour which I left before.
>
> " For, lo! that awful heavenly Sire,
>   Who frequent cleaves the clouds with fire,
>   Parent of day, immortal Jove ;
>   Late through the floating fields of air,
>   The face of heaven serene and fair,
>   His thund'ring steeds, and winged chariot drove," &c.[1]

Experience, too, tells us that those who are most daring in

[1] Dr Francis' Translation of Horace.

their contempt of God are most afraid of thunderings, storms, and such like violent commotions. With great propriety, therefore, does the prophet invite our attention to these instances which strike the rude and insensible with some sense of the existence of a God,[1] and rouse them to action, however sluggish and regardless they are. He says not that the sun rises from day to day, and sheds abroad his life-giving beams, nor that the rain gently descends to fertilize the earth with its moisture; but he brings forward thunders, violent tempests, and such things as smite the hearts of men with dread by their violence. God, it is true, speaks in all his creatures, but here the prophet mentions those sounds which rouse us from our drowsiness, or rather our lethargy, by the loudness of their noise. We have said, that this language is chiefly directed to those who, with stubborn recklessness, cast from them, as far as they can, all thought of God. The very figures which he uses sufficiently declare, that David's design was to subdue by fear the obstinacy which yields not willingly otherwise. Thrice he repeats that God's voice is heard in great and violent tempests, and in the subsequent verse he adds, that it is full of power and majesty.

5. *The voice of Jehovah breaketh the cedars; I say, Jehovah breaketh the cedars of Lebanon.*
6. *And he maketh Lebanon to skip like a calf, and Sirion like a young unicorn.*
7. *The voice of Jehovah striketh out* [or *heweth out*] *flames of fire.*
8. *The voice of Jehovah maketh the wilderness to quake, the voice of Jehovah maketh the wilderness of Kadesh to tremble.*

5. *The voice of Jehovah breaketh the cedars.* We see how the prophet, in order to subdue the stubbornness of men, shows, by every word, that God is terrible. He also seems to rebuke, in passing, the madness of the proud, and of those who swell with vain presumption, because they hearken not to the voice of God in his thunders, rending the air with his

---

[1] " Qui contraignent les barbares et gens esbestez sentir qu'il y a un Dieu."—*Fr.* " Which constrain the rude and insensible to feel that there is a God."

lightnings, shaking the lofty mountains, prostrating and overthrowing the loftiest trees. What a monstrous thing is it, that while all the irrational portion of the creation tremble before God, men alone, who are endued with sense and reason, are not moved! Moreover, though they possess genius and learning, they employ enchantments to shut their ears against God's voice, however powerful, lest it should reach their hearts. Philosophers think not that they have reasoned skilfully enough about inferior causes, unless they separate God very far from his works. It is a diabolical science, however, which fixes our contemplations on the works of nature, and turns them away from God. If any one who wished to know a man should take no notice of his face, but should fix his eyes only on the points of his nails, his folly might justly be derided. But far greater is the folly of those philosophers, who, out of mediate and proximate causes, weave themselves vails, lest they should be compelled to acknowledge the hand of God, which manifestly displays itself in his works. The Psalmist particularly mentions *the cedars of Lebanon*, because lofty and beautiful cedars were to be found there. He also refers to *Lebanon* and *Mount Hermon*, and to *the wilderness of Kadesh*,[1] because these places were best known to the Jews. He uses, indeed, a highly poetical figure, accompanied with a hyperbole, when he says, *that Lebanon skips like a calf at God's voice*, and *Sirion* (which is also called Mount Hermon[2]) *like a unicorn*, which, we know, is one of the swiftest animals. He also alludes to the terrific noise of thunder, which seems almost to shake the mountains to their foundations. Similar is the figure, when he says, *the Lord striketh out flames of fire*, which is done when the vapours, being struck, as it were, with his hammer, burst forth into lightnings and thunderbolts. Aristotle, in his book on Meteors, reasons very shrewdly about these things, in so far as relates to proximate causes, only that he omits the chief

---

[1] That is, the wilderness of Zin, Numb. xxxiii. 36. It is described in Deut. i. 19, as the "great and terrible wilderness." The Israelites passed through this wilderness in their way from Egypt to the promised land, Numb. xiii. 27. It received its name from the city of Kadesh, by which it lay, Numb. xx. 1, 16.

[2] The Sidonians applied to Hermon the name of Sirion, Deut. iii. 9.

point. The investigation of these would, indeed, be both a profitable and pleasant exercise, were we led by it, as we ought, to the Author of Nature himself. But nothing is more preposterous than, when we meet with mediate causes, however many, to be stopped and retarded by them, as by so many obstacles, from approaching God;[1] for this is the same as if a man were to remain at the very rudiments of things during his whole life, without going farther. In short, this is to learn in such a manner that you can never know any thing. That shrewdness alone, therefore, is worthy of praise, which elevates us by these means even to heaven, in order that not a confused noise only may strike our ears, but that the voice of the Lord may penetrate our hearts, and teach us to pray and serve God. Some expound the Hebrew word יחיל, *yachil,* which we have translated *to tremble,* in another way, namely, that *God maketh the wilderness of Kadesh to travail in birth,*[2] because of the manifold wonders which were wrought in it as the Israelites passed through it. But this sense I object to, as far too subtle and strained. David appears rather to refer to the common feelings of men; for as wildernesses are dreadful of themselves, they are much more so when they are filled with thunders, hail, and storms. I do not, however, object that the wilderness may be understood, by synecdoche, to mean the wild beasts which lodge in it; and thus the next verse, where hinds are mentioned, may be considered as added by way of exposition.

9. *The voice of Jehovah maketh the hinds to bring forth, and discovereth* [or *maketh bare*] *the forests, and in his temple every one speaketh of his praise.*

10. *Jehovah sitteth upon the flood; Jehovah, I say, sitteth King for ever.*

11. *Jehovah will give strength to his people; Jehovah will bless his people with peace.*

9. *The voice of Jehovah maketh the hinds to bring forth.*[3]

---

[1] " D'approcher de Dieu."—*Fr.*
[2] " Fait avortir."—*Fr.* " To miscarry or prove abortive."
[3] Bishop Lowth reads, " Maketh the oaks to tremble," (Lectures on Hebrew Poetry, vol. ii. p. 253,) in which he is followed by Dimock, Green,

A tacit comparison, as I have said, is here made. It is worse than irrational, it is monstrous, that men are not moved at God's voice, when it has such power and influence on wild beasts. It is base ingratitude, indeed, in men not to perceive his providence and government in the whole course of nature; but it is a detestable insensibility that at least his unusual and extraordinary works, which compel even wild beasts to obey him, will not teach them wisdom. Some interpreters think that *hinds* are mentioned, rather than other beasts, on account of their difficulty in bringing forth their young; which I disapprove not. *The voice of the Lord* is also said *to discover* or *make bare the forests*, either because there is no covering which can prevent it from penetrating into the most secret recesses and caverns; or, because lightnings, rains, and stormy winds, beat off the leaves and make the trees bare. Either sense is appropriate.

In his temple. God's voice fills the whole world, and spreads itself to its farthest limits; but the prophet declares that his glory is celebrated only in his church, because God not only speaks intelligibly and distinctly there, but also there gently allures the faithful to himself. His terrible

---

Secker, Horsley, Fry, and others. But Dathe, Berlin, De Rossi, Dr Adam Clarke, Rogers, &c., adhere to the common interpretation, in which they are supported by all the ancient versions, except the Syriac, which seems to favour the view of Lowth. A main argument of Lowth and those who follow him in support of his rendering is, that the common translation, which supposes the passage to relate to *the hinds bringing forth their young*, agrees very little with the rest of the imagery either in nature or dignity; whereas the oak struck with lightning is a far nobler image, and one which falls in more naturally with the scattering of a forest's foliage under the action of a storm. But Rogers justly observes, that "we are not warranted in altering the Hebrew text, because the oriental imagery which we meet with does not correspond with our ideas of poetical beauty and grandeur," (Book of Psalms in Hebrew, metrically arranged, vol. ii. p. 186.) With respect to the sense conveyed by the common reading, it may be observed, that hinds bring forth their young with great difficulty and pain, " bowing themselves, bruising their young ones, and casting out their sorrows," (Job xxxix. 4, 6;) and it therefore heightens the description given of the terrific character of the thunder-storm, when the thunder, which is here called the voice of God, is represented as causing, through the terror which it inspires, the hinds in their pregnant state prematurely to drop their young; although, according to our ideas of poetical imagery, this may not accord so well with the other images in the passage, nor appear so beautiful and sublime as the image of the oaks trembling at the voice of Jehovah.

voice, which thunders in various ways in the air, strikes upon the ears, and causes the hearts of men to beat in such a manner, as to make them shrink from rather than approach him: not to mention that a considerable portion turn a deaf ear to its sound in storms, rains, thunder, and lightnings. As men, therefore, profit not so much in this common school as to submit themselves to God, David wisely says especially that the faithful sing the praises of God in his temple, because, being familiarly instructed there by his fatherly voice, they devote and consecrate themselves wholly to his service. No man proclaims the glory of God aright but he who worships him willingly. This may be understood likewise as a complaint, in which David reproves the whole world of being silent in so far as the glory of God is concerned,[1] and laments, that although his voice resounds through all regions, yet his praises are no where sung but in his temple alone. He appears, however, after the example of all the godly, to exhort the whole of mankind to praise God's name, and designedly to erect a temple as a receptacle for his glory, for the purpose of teaching us, that in order truly to know God, and praise him as is his due, we need another voice than that which is heard in thunders, showers, and storms in the air, in the mountains, and in the forests; for if he teach us not in plain words, and also kindly allure us to himself, by giving us a taste of his fatherly love, we will continue dumb. It is the doctrine of salvation alone, therefore, which cheers our hearts and opens our mouths in his praises, by clearly revealing to us his grace, and the whole of his will. It is from thence that we must learn how we ought to praise him. We may also unquestionably see that at that time there was nothing of the light of godliness in the whole world, except in Judea. Even philosophers, who appeared to approach nearest to the knowledge of God, contributed nothing whatever that might truly glorify him. All that they say concerning religion is not only frigid, but for the most part insipid. It is therefore in his word alone that there shines forth the truth which may lead us to true piety, and to fear and serve God aright.[2]

[1] "Etant que touche la gloire de Dieu."—*Fr.*
[2] "Pour le craindre et servir comme il appartient."—*Fr.*

10. *Jehovah sitteth upon the flood.* Some think that David here alludes to that memorable instance of God's vengeance, when he drowned the world at once by the flood,[1] and thus testified to all ages that he is the judge of mankind. I agree to this in part, but extend his meaning still farther. In my opinion, he prosecutes the former subject, putting us in mind that those floods, which still threaten destruction to the earth, are controlled by the providence of God in such a way, as to make it evident that it is he alone who governs all things at all times.[2] David, therefore, mentions this among other proofs of God's power, that even when the elements appear to be mingled and confounded together by the utmost fury of the weather, God controls and moderates these commotions from his throne in heaven. He accordingly adds, for the sake of explanation, *God sits King for ever.*

11. *Jehovah will give strength to his people.* He returns to his former doctrine, namely, that although God exhibits his visible power to the view of the whole world indiscriminately, yet he exerts it in a peculiar manner in behalf of his elect people. Moreover, he here describes him in a very different manner from what he did formerly; that is to say, not as one who overwhelms with fear and dread those to whom he speaks, but as one who upholds, cherishes, and strengthens them. By the word *strength* is to be understood the whole condition of man. And thus he intimates that every thing necessary to the preservation of the life of the godly depends entirely upon the grace of God. He amplifies this by the word *bless;* for God is said *to bless with peace* those whom he treats liberally and kindly, so that nothing is awanting to the prosperous course of their life, and to their complete happiness. From this we may learn, that we ought to stand in awe of the majesty of God, in such a manner as, notwith-

---

[1] "Par le deluge."—*Fr.* This is the view taken of the passage by the ancient versions. "God," says the Chaldee, "in the generation of the deluge sat in judgment." The Septuagint reads, "God shall make the deluge to be inhabited," or "make the world habitable after it;" the Syriac, "God called back the deluge;" and the Arabic, "God restrained the deluge." Ainsworth reads, "Jehovah sat at the flood," and explains it as meaning "Noah's flood."

[2] "Que c'est luy seul qui gouverne toutes choses en tout temps."—*Fr.*

standing, to hope from him all that is necessary to our prosperity; and let us be assuredly persuaded, that since his power is infinite, we are defended by an invincible fortress.

PSALM XXX.

David having been delivered from great danger, not only renders thanks to God apart by himself, but at the same time invites and exhorts all the pious to perform the same duty. He then confesses that he had flattered himself too confidently in his prosperity, and that his security had justly been chastised. In the third place, having briefly expressed his sorrow, he returns again to thanksgiving.

¶ *A psalm sung at the dedication of David's house.*

Interpreters doubt whether this psalm was composed by David, or by some of the prophets after the return of the Jews from the Babylonish captivity; for *house* means, in their opinion, *the temple.* But as the title expressly mentions David's name, it is more probable that it is David's private house which is here spoken of. Moreover, the supposition entertained by some, that when he was about to dedicate his palace, he was seized with heavy sickness, is founded upon no solid reason. We may rather conjecture from what is stated in sacred history, that as soon as he had built his royal palace, he dwelt in it quietly and at his ease. He said to the prophet Nathan, that he felt ashamed comfortably "to dwell within an house of cedar," while "the ark of God dwelt under curtains," (2 Sam. vii. 2.) Besides, to restrict that to sickness which is here spoken generally concerning some kind of danger, is altogether groundless. It is more probable, that Absalom being dead, and his faction extinguished, and the fatal commotion which they had raised put down, David celebrated the divine favour toward him, as one who had returned from exile to his former station in his kingdom. For he mentions that he was chastised by God's hand, because, exulting too much in his happy estate, and almost intoxicated with it, he falsely and foolishly promised himself entire freedom from adversity. Moreover, when he began to inherit the magnificent and royal palace, of which I have just spoken, his kingdom was yet scarcely restored to peace. It was not yet time, therefore, for forgetfulness of human frailty to creep upon him, which might provoke the wrath of God, and expose him to dangers which might bring him to the very verge of destruction. It is not unreasonable, therefore, to suppose, that in this psalm he celebrates God's favour to him in restoring him to his former state. It was necessary again to dedicate his house, which had been defiled by the incestuous whoredoms of Absalom, and other wickednesses; and under this word seems to be denoted a double blessing, both his restoration to life and to his kingdom: as if he had said, that after settling the public affairs of his kingdom, he sung this song, and solemnly dedicated his house to God that he might live in his own family. But it must be briefly observed concerning this ceremony of the law, that as we are very slow and cold in thinking of God's benefits, this exercise was enjoined upon his ancient people, that they might understand that there is no pure and lawful use of any thing without thanksgiving to God. As by offering the first-fruits to God, therefore, they acknowledged that they received the increase of the whole year from him, in like manner, by consecrating their houses to God, they declared that they were God's tenants, confessing that they were strangers, and that it was he who lodged and gave them a habitation there.[1] If a levy for war, therefore, took place, this was a just cause of exemption, when any one alleged that he had not yet dedicated his house.[2] Besides, they were at the same time admonished by this ceremony, that every one enjoyed his house aright and regularly, only when he so regulated it that it was as it were a sanctuary of God, and that true piety and the pure worship of God reigned in it. The types of the law have now ceased, but we must still keep to the doctrine of Paul, that whatever things God appoints for our use, are still "sanctified by the word of God and prayer," (1 Tim. iv. 4, 5.)

1. *I will extol thee, O Jehovah! for thou hast lifted me up,*[3] *and hast not made my foes to rejoice over me.*
2. *O Jehovah my God! I have cried to thee, and thou hast healed me.*
3. *O Jehovah! thou hast brought up my soul from the grave; thou hast quickened me from among those who go down*[4] *into the pit.*

1. *I will extol thee, O Jehovah!* As David had been brought, as it were, from the grave to the life-giving air, he promises to extol the name of God. It is God who lifts us up with his own hand when we have been plunged into a profound

---

[1] " Se recognoissans estrangers, et que c'estoit luy qui les y logeoit et leur bailloit demeurance."—*Fr.*
[2] " Quand l'homme allegoit qu'il n'avoit encores dedié sa maison."—*Fr.*
[3] Ainsworth reads, "Thou hast drawn up me," which he explains to mean, "drawn as out of a pit of waters;" "for," says he, "this word is used for 'drawing of waters,' Exod. ii. waters signifying troubles." "דליתני, *Thou hast drawn me up as it were out of a dungeon.*"—*Rogers' Book of Psalms.*
[4] "D'entre ceux que descendent."—*Fr.*

gulf; and therefore it is our duty, on our part, to sing his praises with our tongues. By *the foes* who, he says, obtained no matter of rejoicing over him, we may understand both domestic and foreign enemies. Although wicked and evil disposed persons flattered him with servile adulation, they at the same time cherished secret hatred against him, and were ready to insult him as soon as an opportunity should occur. In the second verse, he concludes that he was preserved by the favour of God, alleging in proof of this, that when he was at the very point of death he directed his supplications to God alone, and that he immediately felt that he had not done so in vain. When God hears our prayers, it is a proof which enables us to conclude with certainty that he is the author of our salvation, and of the deliverance which we obtain. As the Hebrew word רפא, *rapha*, signifies *to heal*, interpreters have been led, from this consideration, to restrict it to sickness. But as it is certain, that it sometimes signifies *to restore*, or *to set up again*, and is moreover applied to an altar or a house when they are said to be repaired or rebuilt, it may properly enough mean here any deliverance. The life of man is in danger in many other ways than merely from disease; and we know that it is a form of speech which occurs every where in the Psalms, to say that David was restored to life whenever the Lord delivered him from any grievous and extreme danger. For the sake of amplification, accordingly, he immediately adds, *Thou hast brought up my soul from the grave.* He reckoned that he could not sufficiently express in words the magnitude of the favour which God had conferred upon him, unless he compared the darkness of that period to a grave and pit, into which he had been forced to throw himself hastily, to protect his life by hiding, until the flame of insurrection was quenched. As one restored to life, therefore, he proclaims that he had been marvellously delivered from present death, as if he had been restored to life after he had been dead. And assuredly, it appears from sacred history, how completely he was overwhelmed with despair on every side.

4. *Sing unto Jehovah, O ye who are his meek ones! and acknowledge the memorial of his holiness.*[1]

5. *For his anger is only for a moment,*[2] *but life*[3] *is in his favour; weeping will lodge in the evening, and rejoicing shall come in the morning.*

4. *Sing unto Jehovah.* The better to testify his gratitude, David calls upon all the saints to join with him in singing the praises of God; and under one class he describes the whole body. As he had been preserved beyond all expectation, and by this instance had been instructed concerning God's continual and infinite goodness towards all the godly, he breaks forth into this exhortation, in which he includes the general deliverance of the whole church as well as his own. He rehearses not only what God had been to himself, but also how bountifully and promptly he is accustomed to assist his people. In short, confirmed by one particular instance, he turns his thoughts to the general truth. The meaning of the Hebrew term חסידים, *chasidim,* which we have translated *meekness,* by which David often describes the faithful, has been already shown in the sixteenth Psalm. Their heavenly adoption ought to excite them to the exercise of beneficence, that they may imitate their Father's disposition, "who maketh his sun to rise on the evil and on the good," (Matth. v. 45.) There is nothing in which men resemble God more truly than in doing good to others. *The memorial of his holiness,* in the second clause of the verse, may refer to the tabernacle; as if David had exhorted all the children of God to go before the ark of the covenant, which was the memorial of God's presence. The Hebrew letter ל,[4] *lamed,* often denotes a place. I readily subscribe, however, to their opinion, who think that *memorial* signifies the same thing as *name;* for God has assuredly rendered himself worthy of remembrance by his works, which are a bright representation of his glory, the sight of which should stir us up to praise him.

[1] "Ou chantez afin qu'il soit memoire."—*Fr. marg.* "Or sing, that he may be remembered."
[2] Literally, "There is but a moment in his anger;" and this is also the literal rendering of the Hebrew.
[3] "C'est, un long temps."—*Note, Fr. marg.* "That is, a long time."
[4] לזכר, *lezeker,* at the memorial.

5. *For his anger is only for a moment.* It is beyond all controversy that *life* is opposed here to *for a moment*, and consequently signifies long continuance, or the constant progress of time from day to day. David thus intimates that if God at any time chastise his people, he not only mitigates the rigour of their punishment, but is immediately appeased, and moderates his anger; whereas he prolongs his kindness and favour for a long time. And, as I have already observed, he chose rather to couch his discourse in general terms, than to speak particularly of himself, that the godly might all perceive that this continued manifestation of God's favour belongs to them. We are hereby taught, however, with how much meekness of spirit, and with what prompt obedience he submitted his back to God's rod. We know that from the very first bloom of youth, during almost his whole life, he was so tried by a multiplied accumulation of afflictions, that he might have been accounted miserable and wretched above all other men; yet in celebrating the goodness of God, he acknowledges that he had been lightly afflicted only for a short period, and as it were in passing. Now, what inspired him with so great meekness and equanimity of mind was, that he put a greater value upon God's benefits, and submitted himself more quietly to the endurance of the cross, than the world is accustomed to do. If we are prosperous, we devour God's blessings without feeling that they are his, or, at least, we indolently allow them to slip away; but if any thing sorrowful or adverse befall us, we immediately complain of his severity, as if he had never dealt kindly and mercifully with us. In short, our own fretfulness and impatience under affliction makes every minute an age; while, on the other hand, our repining and ingratitude lead us to imagine that God's favour, however long it may be exercised towards us, is but for a moment. It is our own perversity, therefore, in reality, which hinders us from perceiving that God's anger is but of short duration, while his favour is continued towards us during the whole course of our life. Nor does God in vain so often declare that he is merciful and gracious to a thousand generations, long-suffering, slow to anger, and ready to forgive. And as what he says by the prophet Isaiah has

a special reference to the kingdom of Christ, it must be daily fulfilled, " For a small moment have I afflicted thee, but with everlasting mercies will I gather thee," (Isa. liv. 7.) Our condition in this world, I confess, involves us in such wretchedness, and we are harassed by such a variety of afflictions, that scarcely a day passes without some trouble or grief. Moreover, amid so many uncertain events, we cannot be otherwise than full of daily anxiety and fear. Whithersoever, therefore, men turn themselves, a labyrinth of evils surrounds them. But however much God may terrify and humble his faithful servants, with manifold signs of his displeasure, he always besprinkles them with the sweetness of his favour to moderate and assuage their grief. If they weigh, therefore, his *anger* and his *favour* in an equal balance, they will always find it verified, that while the former is but for a moment, the latter continues to the end of life; nay, it goes beyond it, for it were a grievous mistake to confine the favour of God within the boundaries of this transitory life. And it is unquestionably certain,[1] that none but those whose minds have been raised above the world by a taste of heavenly life really experience this perpetual and uninterrupted manifestation of the divine favour, which enables them to bear their chastisements with cheerfulness. Paul, accordingly, that he may inspire us with invincible patience, refers to this in 2 Cor. iv. 17, " For our light affliction, which is but for a moment, worketh for us a far more exceeding and eternal weight of glory, while we look not at the things which are seen, but at the things which are not seen." In the meantime, it is to be observed that God never inflicts such heavy and continued chastisements on his people, without frequently mitigating them, and sweetening their bitterness with some consolation. Whoever, therefore, directs his mind to meditation upon the heavenly life, will never faint under his afflictions, however long continued ; and, comparing them with the exceeding great and manifold favours of God towards him, he will put such honour on the latter as to judge that God's goodness, in his estimation, outweighs his displeasure a hundred-fold. In the second clause, David

---

[1] " Et de faict, c'est un poinct tout resolu."—*Fr.*

repeats the same thing figuratively: *Weeping will lodge in the evening, and rejoicing shall come in the morning.* He does not simply mean, that the affliction would be only for one night, but that if the darkness of adversity should fall upon the people of God, as it were, in the evening, or at the setting of the sun, light would soon after arise upon them, to comfort their sorrow-stricken spirits. The amount of David's instruction is, that were we not too headstrong, we would acknowledge that the Lord, even when he appears to overwhelm us for a time with the darkness of affliction, always seasonably ministers matter of joy, just as the morning arises after the night.

6. *And in my tranquillity*[1] *I had said, I shall never be moved.*
7. *O Jehovah! in thy good pleasure thou hast established strength to my mountain: thou hast hidden thy face, I have been terrified.*
8. *O Jehovah! I cried to thee, and to my Lord*[2] *I made my supplication.*
9. *What profit is there in my blood, when I go down into the pit?*[3] *Shall the dust praise thee? shall it declare thy truth?*
10. *Hear, O Jehovah! and have mercy upon me: O Jehovah! be thou my helper.*

6. *And in my tranquillity I had said.* This is the confession which I formerly mentioned, in which David acknowledges that he had been justly and deservedly punished for his foolish and rash security, in forgetting his mortal and mutable condition as a man, and in setting his heart too much on prosperity. By the term *tranquillity*, he means the quiet and flourishing state of his kingdom. Some translate the Hebrew word שַׁלְוָה, *shiluah*, which we have rendered *tranquillity*, by *abundance*, in which sense it is often used in other places; but the word *tranquillity* agrees better with the context; as if David had said, When fortune smiled upon me on

---

[1] "C'est, en ma prosperite."—*Note, Fr. marg.* "That is, in my prosperity."

[2] Our author here uses *Dominus;* but in the Hebrew it is יהוה, *Yehovah*

[3] The Septuagint has "Εἰς διαφθοράν," "to corruption." The rendering of Jerome is the same, "In corruptionem."

every side, and no danger appeared to occasion fear, my
mind sunk as it were into a deep sleep, and I flattered myself that my happy condition would continue, and that things
would always go on in the same course. This carnal confidence frequently creeps upon the saints when they indulge
themselves in their prosperity, and so to speak, wallow upon
their dunghill.[1] Hence Jeremiah (chap. xxxi. 18) compares
himself to a wild bullock before the Lord tamed him and
accustomed him to the yoke. This may at first sight appear
to be but a small crime, yet we may gather from its punishment how much it is displeasing to God : nor will we wonder at this when we consider the root from which it springs
and the fruits which it bears. As deaths innumerable continually hover before our eyes, and as there are so many
examples of change to awaken us to fear and caution, those
must be bewitched with devilish pride who persuade themselves that their life is privileged above the common lot of
the world. They see the whole earth jumbled together in
undistinguishing variety, and its individual parts in a manner tossed hither and thither ; and yet, as if they did not
belong to the human race, they imagine that they shall
always continue stable and liable to no changes. Hence
that wantonness of the flesh, with which they so licentiously
indulge their lusts; hence their pride and cruelty, and
neglect of prayer. How indeed should those flee to God,
who have no sense of their need to instigate or move them to
that ? The children of God have also a pious security of their
own, which preserves their minds in tranquillity amidst the
troublesome storms of the world ; like David, who, although
he had seen the whole world made to shake, yet leaning
upon the promise of God, was bound to hope well concerning the continuance of his kingdom. But although the
faithful, when raised aloft on the wings of faith, despise
adversity, yet, as they consider themselves liable to the
common troubles of life, they lay their account with enduring
them,—are every hour prepared to receive wounds,—shake
off their sluggishness, and exercise themselves in the warfare

[1] " Qu'ils se mignardent en leur prosperité, et par maniere de dire, crou-
pissent sur leur fumier."—*Fr.*

to which they know that they were appointed,—and with humility and fear put themselves under God's protection; nor do they consider themselves safe anywhere else than under his hand. It was otherwise with David, who, when ensnared by the allurements of his prosperous state, promised himself unbroken tranquillity not from the word of God but from his own feelings. The same thing also occurred to the pious King Hezekiah, who, although lately afflicted with a sore disease, as soon as all was well and according to his wish, was hurried by the vanity of the flesh to pride and vain boasting, (2 Chron. xxxii. 24.) By this we are taught to be on our guard when in prosperity, that Satan may not bewitch us with his flatteries. The more bountifully God deals with any one, the more carefully ought he to watch against such snares. It is not, indeed, probable that David had become so hardened as to despise God and defy all misfortunes, like many of the great men of this world, who, when immersed among their luxuries and surfeitings, insolently scoff at all God's judgments; but an effeminate listlessness having come over his mind, he became more lukewarm in prayer, nor did he depend on the favour of God; in short, he put too much confidence in his uncertain and transitory prosperity.

7. *O Jehovah! of thy good pleasure.* This verse describes the difference which exists between the confidence which is founded upon the word of God and the carnal security which springs from presumption. True believers, when they rely upon God, are not on that account neglectful of prayer. On the contrary, looking carefully at the multitude of dangers by which they are beset, and the manifold instances of human frailty which pass before their eyes, they take warning from them, and pour out their hearts before God. The prophet now failed in duty as to this matter; because, by anchoring himself on his present wealth and tranquillity, or spreading his sails to the prosperous winds, he depended not on the free favour of God in such a manner as to be ready at any time to resign into his hands the blessings which he had bestowed upon him. The contrast should be

observed between that confidence of stability which arises from the absence of trouble, and that which rests upon the gracious favour of God. When David says that *strength was established to his mountain,* some interpreters expound it of mount Zion. Others understand by it a stronghold or fortified tower, because in old time fortresses were usually built upon mountains and lofty places. I understand the word metaphorically to signify a solid support, and therefore readily admit that the prophet alludes to mount Zion. David thus blames his own folly, because he considered not, as he ought to have done, that there was no stability in the nest which he had formed for himself, but in God's good will alone.

Thou hast hidden thy face. Here he confesses, that, after he was deprived of God's gifts, this served to purge his mind as it were by medicine from the disease of perverse confidence. A marvellous and incredible method surely, that God, by hiding his face, and as it were bringing on darkness, should open the eyes of his servant, who saw nothing in the broad light of prosperity. But thus it is necessary that we be violently shaken, in order to drive away the delusions which both stifle our faith and hinder our prayers, and which absolutely stupify us with a soothing infatuation. And if David had need of such a remedy, let us not presume that we are endued with so good a state of heart as to render it unprofitable for us to be in want, in order to remove from us this carnal confidence, which is as it were a diseased repletion which would otherwise suffocate us. We have, therefore, no reason to wonder, though God often hides his face from us, when the sight of it, even when it shines serenely upon us, makes us so wretchedly blind.

8. *O Jehovah! I cried unto thee.* Now follows the fruit of David's chastisement. He had been previously sleeping profoundly, and fostering his indolence by forgetfulness; but being now awakened all on a sudden with fear and terror, he begins to cry to God. As the iron which has contracted rust cannot be put to any use until it be heated again in the fire, and beaten with the hammer, so in like manner, when carnal security has once got the mastery, no one can give himself

cheerfully to prayer, until he has been softened by the cross, and thoroughly subdued. And this is the chief advantage of afflictions, that while they make us sensible of our wretchedness, they stimulate us again to supplicate the favour of God.

9. *What profit is there in my blood?* Some explain the verse after this manner : What will it avail me to have lived, unless thou prolongest my life till I shall have finished the course of my vocation ? But this exposition seems too strained, especially as the term *blood* here signifies *death*, not *life:* as if David had said, What profit wilt thou derive from my death ? This interpretation is farther confirmed by the following clause, where he complains that his lifeless body will then be useless for celebrating the praises of God. And he seems expressly to mention the *truth* of God, to intimate that it would be unsuitable to the character of God to take him out of the world by an untimely death, before God had accomplished the promise which he had made to him concerning his future heir. As there is a mutual relation between God's promises and our faith, truth is, as it were, the medium by which God openly shows that he does not merely make liberal promises to us in words, to feed us with empty hopes, and afterwards to disappoint us. Moreover, to obtain a longer life, David draws an argument from the praises of God, to celebrate which we are born and nourished : as if he had said, For what purpose hast thou created me, O God! but that through the whole course of my life I may be a witness and a herald of thy grace to set forth the glory of thy name ? But my death will cut short the continuance of this exercise, and reduce me to eternal silence. A question, however, arises here, Does not, it may be said, the death of true believers glorify God as well as their life ? We answer, David speaks not simply of death, but adds a circumstance which I have already treated of in the sixth Psalm. As God had promised him a successor, the hope of living longer being taken from him, he had good reason to be afraid lest this promise should be frustrated by his death, and was therefore compelled to exclaim, *What profit is there in my blood?* It highly concerned the glory of God that he should be preserved alive, until by

obtaining his desire, he should be able to bear witness to God's faithfulness in completely fulfilling his promise to him. By inquiring in the end of the verse, *Shall the dust praise thee?* he does not mean that the dead are altogether deprived of power to praise God, as I have already shown in the sixth Psalm. If the faithful, while encumbered with a burden of flesh, exercise themselves in this pious duty, how should they desist from it when they are disencumbered, and set free from the restraints of the body? It ought to be observed, therefore, that David does not professedly treat of what the dead do, or how they are occupied, but considers only the purpose for which we live in this world, which is this, that we may mutually show forth to one another the glory of God. Having been employed in this exercise to the end of our life, death at length comes upon us and shuts our mouth.

10. *Hear, O Jehovah!* In this clause the Psalmist softens and corrects his former complaint; for it would have been absurd to expostulate with God like one who despaired of safety, and to leave off in this fretful temper. Having asked, therefore, with tears, what profit God would derive from his death, he encourages himself to a more unconstrained manner of prayer, and, conceiving new hope, calls upon God for mercy and help. He puts God's favour, however, in the first place, from whom alone he could expect the help which he implored.

11. *Thou hast turned my mourning into dancing; thou hast loosed my sackcloth, and girded me with gladness.*
12. *That my glory may sing praise to thee, and not be silent: O Jehovah my God! I will set forth thy praise for ever.*

11. *Thou hast turned my mourning into dancing.* David concludes the psalm as he had begun it, with thanksgiving. He affirms that it was by the help and blessing of God that he had escaped safe; and he then adds, that the final object of his escape was, that he might employ the rest of his life in celebrating the praises of God. Moreover, he shows us that

he was not insensible or obdurate under his afflictions, but mourned in heaviness and sorrow; and he also shows that his very mourning had been the means of leading him to pray to God to deprecate his wrath. Both these points are most worthy of our observation, in order, first, that we may not suppose that the saints are guilty of stoical insensibility, depriving them of all feeling of grief; and, secondly, that we may perceive that in their mourning they were exercised to repentance. This latter he denotes by the term *sackcloth*. It was a common practice among the ancients to clothe themselves with sackcloth when mourning,[1] for no other reason, indeed, than that like guilty criminals, they might approach their heavenly Judge, imploring his forgiveness with all humility, and testifying by this clothing their humiliation and dissatisfaction with themselves.[2] We know also that the orientals were addicted beyond all others to ceremonies. We perceive, therefore, that David, although he patiently submitted himself to God, was not free from grief. We also see that his sorrow was "after a godly sort," as Paul speaks, (2 Cor. vii. 10;) for to testify his penitence he clothed himself with sackcloth. By the term *dancing*, he does not mean any wanton or profane leaping, but a sober and holy exhibition of joy like that which sacred Scripture mentions when David conveyed the ark of the covenant to its place, (2 Sam. vi. 16.) If we may conjecture, however, we may gather from this, that the great danger of which David speaks in this psalm is by some improperly restricted to sickness, as it was very improbable that he would put on sackcloth when he was confined to a sick-bed. This, indeed, would not be a sufficient reason of itself, but in a doubtful case, as this is, it is not destitute of force. David

---

[1] This custom was not confined to the Israelites. It was practised also among the heathen nations. An instance of this is recorded in Jonah iii. 5-8. It appears from Plutarch, that this was also sometimes practised among the Greeks. The Hebrew word for *sackcloth* is שק, *sak;* and it is remarkable that the word *sak* exists in various languages, denoting the same thing. It shows the unaffected character of real sorrow, leading men to neglect the adorning of their persons, when we find several nations manifesting it by wearing the same dismal garb, and employing a word of the same sound to express it.

[2] "Ne monstrant qu'abjection et desplaisance d'eux-mesmes."—*Fr.*

therefore means, that, laying aside his mourning apparel, he returned from a state of heaviness and sorrow to joy; and this he ascribes to the grace of God alone, asserting that he had been his deliverer.

12. *That my glory may sing praise to thee.* In this verse he more fully expresses his acknowledgment of the purpose for which God had preserved him from death, and that he would be careful to render him a proper return of gratitude. Some refer the word *glory* to the body, and some to the soul, or the higher powers of the mind. Others, as the pronoun *my*, which we have supplied, is not in the Hebrew text, prefer to translate it in the accusative case, supplying the word *every man*, in this way: *That every man may celebrate thy glory;* as if the prophet had said, This is a blessing worthy of being celebrated by the public praises of all men. But as all these interpretations are strained, I adhere to the sense which I have given. The Hebrew word כבוד, *kebod*, which signifies *glory*, it is well known, is sometimes employed metaphorically to signify *the tongue*, as we have seen in Psalm xvi. 9. And as David adds immediately after, *I will celebrate thy praise for ever*, the context demands that he should particularly speak of his own duty in this place. His meaning, therefore, is, O Lord, as I know that thou hast preserved me for this purpose, that thy praises may resound from my tongue, I will faithfully discharge this service to thee, and perform my part even unto death. *To sing, and not be silent*, is a Hebrew *amplification;* as if he had said, My tongue shall not be mute, or deprive God of his due praise; it shall, on the contrary, devote itself to the celebration of his glory.

PSALM XXXI.

David, having been delivered from some great danger, or rather from many dangers, first relates the prayers which he had offered up to God amidst the terrors of death. He then subjoins his thanksgiving, which is no ordinary one; for he celebrates his deliverance at great length, and exhorts all the saints to be of good hope, as they had in him a most excellent and memorable example of God's goodness.

¶ To the chief musician. A psalm of David.

1. *In thee, O Jehovah! have I put my trust, let me not be ashamed for ever: deliver me in thy righteousness.*
2. *Incline thine ear unto me, deliver me speedily; be unto me a strong rock, a house of defence to save me.*
3. *For thou art my rock and my fortress: and for thy name's sake thou wilt lead and guide me.*[1]
4. *Pluck me out of the net which they have hidden for me; for thou art my strength.*

1. *In thee, O Jehovah! have I put my trust.* Some are of opinion that this psalm was composed by David, after he had most unexpectedly escaped out of the wilderness of Maon; to which I do not object, although it is only a doubtful conjecture. Certainly he celebrates one or more of the greatest of his dangers. In the commencement he tells us what kind of prayer he offered in his agony and distress; and its language breathes affection of the most ardent nature. He takes it for a ground of hope that he trusted in the Lord, or continued to trust in him; for the verb in the past tense seems to denote a continued act. He held it as a principle, that the hope which depends upon God cannot possibly be disappointed. Meanwhile, we see how he brings forward nothing but faith alone; promising himself deliverance only because he is persuaded that he will be saved by the help and favour

---

[1] " Ou, adresse moy et conduy."—*Fr. marg.* " Or, do thou direct and guide me."

of God. But as this doctrine has been expounded already, and will yet occur oftener than once, it is sufficient at present to have glanced at it. Oh! that all of us would practise it in such a manner as that, whenever we approach to God, we may be able with David to declare that our prayers proceed from this source, namely, from a firm persuasion that our safety depends on the power of God. The particle signifying *for ever* may be explained in two ways. As God sometimes withdraws his favour, the meaning may not unsuitably be, Although I am now deprived of thy help, yet cast me not off utterly, or for evermore. Thus David, wishing to arm himself with patience against his temptations, would make a contrast between these two things,—being in distress for a time, and remaining in a state of confusion.[1] But if any one choose rather to understand his words in this way, " Whatever afflictions befall me, may God be ready to help me, and ever and anon stretch forth his hand to me, as the case requires," I would not reject this meaning any more than the other. David desires to be *delivered in the righteousness of God*, because God displays his righteousness in performing his promise to his servants. It is too much refinement of reasoning to assert that David here betakes himself to the righteousness which God freely bestows on his people, because his own righteousness by works was of no avail. Still more out of place is the opinion of those who think that God preserves the saints according to his righteousness; that is to say, because having acted so meritoriously, justice requires that they should obtain their reward. It is easy to see from the frequent use of the term in The Psalms, that God's righteousness means his faithfulness, in the exercise of which he defends all his people who commit themselves to his guardianship and protection. David, therefore, confirms his hope from the consideration of the nature of God, who cannot deny himself, and who always continues like himself.

2. *Incline thine ear unto me.* These words express with how much ardour David's soul was stimulated to pray. He

[1] " Feroit une antithese entre ces deux choses, Estre en destresse pour un temps, et demeurer confus."—*Fr.*

affects no splendid or ornate language, as rhetoricians are wont to do; but only describes in suitable figures the vehemence of his desire. In praying that he may be delivered *speedily* there is shown the greatness of his danger, as if he had said, All will soon be over with my life, unless God make haste to help me. By the words, *house of defence, fortress,* and *rock,* he intimates, that, being unable to resist his enemies, his hope rests only on the protection of God.

3. *For thou art my rock.* This verse may be read as one sentence, thus: As thou art like a tower for my defence, for thy name's sake direct and guide me during my whole life. And thus the conjunction, as in many similar cases, would be superfluous. But I rather prefer a different sense, namely, that David, by interjecting this reflection, encourages himself not only to earnestness in prayer, but also in the confident hope of obtaining his requests. We know, at all events, that it is usual with him to mingle such things in his prayers as may serve to remove his doubts, and to confirm his assurance. Having, therefore, expressed his need, he assures himself, in order to encourage and animate himself, that his prayer shall certainly have a happy answer. He had formerly said, *Be thou my strong rock and fortress;* and now he adds, *Assuredly thou art my rock and my fortress:* intimating, that he did not throw out these words rashly, like unbelievers, who, although they are accustomed to ask much from God, are kept in suspense by the dread of uncertain events. From this he also draws another encouragement, that he shall have God for his guide and governor during the whole course of his life. He uses two words, *lead* and *guide,* to express the same thing, and this he does (at least so I explain it) on account of the various accidents and unequal vicissitudes by which the lives of men are tried: as if he had said, Whether I must climb the steep mountain, or struggle along through rough places, or walk among thorns, I trust that thou wilt be my continual guide. Moreover, as men will always find in themselves matter for doubt, if they look to their own merits,[1] David expressly asks that God may be

---

[1] " Si les hommes regardent à leur dignite."—*Fr.*

induced to help him *for his own name's sake*, or from regard to his own glory, as, properly speaking, there is no other thing which can induce him to aid us. It must therefore be remembered, that *God's name*, as it is opposed to all merit whatever, is the only cause of our salvation. In the next verse, under the metaphor of a *net*, he appears to designate the snares and artifices with which his enemies encompassed him. We know that conspiracies were frequently formed against his life, which would have left him no room for escape; and as his enemies were deeply skilled in policy, and hating him with an inconceivable hatred, were eagerly bent on his destruction, it was impossible for him to be saved from them by any human power. On this account he calls God *his strength;* as if he had said, He alone is sufficient to rend asunder all the snares with which he sees his afflicted people entangled.

5. *Into thy hand I commit my spirit, for thou hast redeemed me, O Jehovah! God of truth.*
6. *I hate all that give heed to lying vanities; but I have trusted in Jehovah.*
7. *I will be glad and rejoice in thy goodness, because thou hast regarded my affliction: thou hast known my soul in distresses.*
8. *And thou hast not shut me up in the hand of mine enemy:* [1] *thou hast set my feet in a large place.*

5. *Into thy hand I commit my spirit.* David again declares his faith to God, and affirms that he had such high thoughts of his providence, as to cast all his cares upon it. Whoever commits himself into God's hand and to his guardianship, not only constitutes him the arbiter of life and death to him, but also calmly depends on him for protection amidst all his dangers. The verb is in the future tense, "I will commit," and it unquestionably denotes a continued act, and is therefore fitly translated into the present tense. It is also to be

[1] Dr Geddes observes, that this is the literal translation of the Hebrew words; "but," says he, "as negative propositions in Hebrew are often equivalent in sense to opposite positives, I deemed it better to use an equivalent as more agreeable to what precedes and follows." His rendering is, "Rescued me from the hand of mine enemy."

observed, that no man can possibly commit his life to God with sincerity, but he who considers himself exposed to a thousand deaths, and that his life hangs by a thread, or differs almost nothing from a breath which passes suddenly away. David being thus at the point of despair, leaves nothing to himself to do but this—to go on his way, trusting in God as the keeper and governor of his life. It is marvellous, that, although many things distress us all, scarcely one in a hundred is so wise as to commit his life into God's hand. Multitudes live from day to day as merry and careless as if they were in a quiet nest, free from all disturbance; but as soon as they encounter any thing to terrify them, they are ready to die for anguish. It thus happens that they never betake themselves to God, either because they deceive themselves with vain delusions, flattering themselves that all will yet be well,[1] or because they are so stricken with dread and stupified with amazement, that they have no desire for his fatherly care. Farther, as various tempests of grief disturb us, and even sometimes throw us down headlong, or drag us from the direct path of duty, or at least remove us from our post, the only remedy which exists for setting these things at rest is to consider that God, who is the author of our life, is also its preserver. This, then, is the only means of lightening all our burdens, and preserving us from being swallowed up of over-much sorrow. Seeing, therefore, that God condescends to undertake the care of our lives, and to support them, although they are often exposed to various sorts of death, let us learn always to flee to this asylum; nay, the more that any one is exposed to dangers, let him exercise himself the more carefully in meditating on it. In short, let this be our shield against all dangerous attacks—our haven amidst all tossings and tempests—that, although our safety may be beyond all human hope, God is the faithful guardian of it; and let this again arouse us to prayer, that he would defend us, and make our deliverance sure. This confidence will likewise make every man forward to discharge his duty with alacrity, and constantly and fearlessly to struggle on-

---

[1] "Se faisans à croire que de leur faict ce ne sera que triomphe."—*Fr.*

ward to the end of his course. How does it happen that so many are slothful and indifferent, and that others perfidiously forsake their duty, but because, overwhelmed with anxiety, they are terrified at dangers and inconveniences, and leave no room for the operation of the providence of God?

To conclude, whoever relies not on the providence of God, so as to commit his life to its faithful guardianship, has not yet learned aright what it is to live. On the other hand, he who shall entrust the keeping of his life to God's care, will not doubt of its safety even in the midst of death. We must therefore put our life into God's hand, not only that he may keep it safely in this world, but also that he may preserve it from destruction in death itself, as Christ's own example has taught us. As David wished to have his life prolonged amidst the dangers of death, so Christ passed out of this transitory life that his soul might be saved in death. This is a general prayer, therefore, in which the faithful commit their lives to God, first, that he may protect them by his power, so long as they are exposed to the dangers of this world; and, secondly, that he may preserve them safe in the grave, where nothing is to be seen but destruction. We ought farther to assure ourselves, that we are not forsaken of God either in life or in death; for those whom God brings safely by his power to the end of their course, he at last receives to himself at their death. This is one of the principal places of Scripture which are most suitable for correcting distrust. It teaches us, first, that the faithful ought not to torment themselves above measure with unhappy cares and anxieties; and, secondly, that they should not be so distracted with fear as to cease from performing their duty, nor decline and faint in such a manner as to grasp at vain hopes and deceitful helps, nor give way to fears and alarms; and, in fine, that they should not be afraid of death, which, though it destroys the body, cannot extinguish the soul. This, indeed, ought to be our principal argument for overcoming all temptations, that Christ, when commending his soul to his Father, undertook the guardianship of the souls of all his people. Stephen, therefore, calls upon him to be his keeper, saying, "Lord Jesus, receive my spirit,"

(Acts vii. 59.) As the soul is the seat of life, it is on this account, as is well known, used to signify life.

Thou hast redeemed me. Some translate the past tense here into the future; but, in my opinion, without any reason. For it is evident to me, that David is here encouraging himself to continued confidence in God, by calling to remembrance the proofs of his favour which he had already experienced.[1] It is no small encouragement to us for the future, to be assuredly persuaded that God will watch over our life, because he hath been our deliverer already. Hence the epithet by which David recognises God. He calls him *true* or *faithful*, because he believes that he will continue the same to him for ever that he has already been. Accordingly, this is as it were a bond by which he joins to the former benefits which God had conferred upon him confidence in prayer, and the hope of aid for the time to come: as if he had said, Lord, thou who art ever the same, and changest not thy mind like men, hast already testified in very deed that thou art the defender of my life: now, therefore, I commit my life, of which thou hast been the preserver, into thy hands. What David here declares concerning his temporal life, Paul transfers to eternal salvation. " I know," says he, " whom I have believed, and am persuaded that he is able to keep that which I have committed to him," (2 Tim. i. 12.) And surely, if David derived so much confidence from temporal deliverance, it is more than wicked and ungrateful on our part, if the redemption purchased by the blood of Christ does not furnish us with invincible courage against all the devices of Satan.

6. *I hate all that give heed to lying vanities.* In order the better to express that his faith was firmly fixed on God, he affirms that he was free from the vile affections which usually turn away our minds from God, and under which unbelievers for the most part labour. For we know that by contrasting things which are opposite, a subject is better illustrated. To restrict the Hebrew word הבל, *hebel*, which we have rendered

[1] Horsley, while his translation is similar to that of Calvin, " Thou hast delivered me," takes a somewhat different view of the meaning. " *Thou hast, i. e.,* Thou most surely wilt.—The thing is as certain as if it were done."

vanities, to magical arts, as some interpreters do, is absurd.[1] I confess, indeed, that the Orientals were so much addicted to these impostures, that it was a common evil among them. But as the devices by which Satan ensnares the minds of men, and the allurements by which he draws them away from God, are innumerable, it is not at all probable that the prophet mentions one species only. Whatever vain hopes, therefore, we form to ourselves, which may draw us off from our confidence in God, David generally denominates *vanities,* yea, *false* or *lying vanities,* because, although they feed us for a time with magnificent promises, in the end they beguile and disappoint us. He affirms, therefore, that casting away the vanities which men usually invent to support their hopes, he relies solely on God. And as men not only intoxicate themselves personally with the deceitful allurements of the world, but in this respect also deceive one another, the prophet expressly declares, with a view that we may carefully avoid them, unless we wish to be wilfully entangled in their dangerous toils, that he hated all who involved themselves in such lies. The second clause, *I have trusted in Jehovah,* must be read in connection with the first, because it both assigns the cause of his hatred of lying vanities, and shows that it is impossible for men to have any true faith in God, unless they abhor whatever would draw them away from him.

7. *I will be glad and rejoice in thy goodness.* Here is inserted a thanksgiving, although many are rather of opinion that David's prayer is suspended, and that he makes a vow, when he shall be delivered from present danger. But as no condition is annexed, I am rather inclined to think that stopping all at once in the middle of his prayer, he promises

---

[1] Hammond considers "vanities" as referring to the practice of superstitiously having recourse to auguries and divinations for advice and direction, a practice which prevailed among the heathen, when they met with any difficulty or danger. To the responses of augury they showed the greatest regard; although they were deceived and disappointed in the confidence which they reposed in them. David declares that he detested all such practices, and trusted for aid to God alone. French and Skinner, by *lying vanities,* understand *idols.* "Idols," says Walford, "are often thus denominated; though the term is not to be confined to this sense, as all the pursuits of iniquity may be justly comprehended under it.—*Vide* Deut. xxxii. 21; Jonah ii. 8."

himself a deliverance, for which he will have abundant matter for giving thanks. Nor is it to be wondered at that different feelings are mingled in the psalms in which David has set forth his own temptations, as well as the resistance which his faith made to them, considering also that when he sung the praises of God, after having already obtained deliverance from him, he embraces different periods in his song, as he here says, *that God had regarded his affliction,* intimating by this the effect of the assistance which God had afforded him. And that he may the better confirm this, he adds, *that he had not been delivered into the hands of his enemies:* in which words there is an implied antithesis, namely, that when he was encompassed on every side by severe afflictions, he was marvellously delivered by God. This is also farther intimated by the following sentence, *Thou hast set my feet in a large place,*[1] which denotes a sudden and unexpected change.

9. *Have mercy upon me, O Jehovah! for I am in trouble: mine eye, my soul, and my belly, are consumed by reason of anger.*
10. *For my life is wasted by reason of grief, and my years with groaning: my strength faileth in my sorrow, and my bones are consumed.*
11. *I was a reproach by reason of all mine enemies, yea, exceedingly to my neighbours, and a fear to my acquaintances; and they who saw me abroad fled from me.*
12. *I am forgotten as one dead, I am become like a broken vessel.*
13. *For I have heard the railing of many,*[2] *and fear encloseth me on every side, while they consult together against me, and plot to take away my life.*

9. *Have mercy upon me, O Jehovah!* To move God to succour him, he magnifies the greatness of his misery and grief by the number of his complaints; not that God needs arguments to persuade him, but because he allows the faithful to deal familiarly with him, that they may disburden themselves of their cares. The greater the number of afflic-

---

[1] "There is a contrast in the expression between the straits to which he had been confined, and the freedom which was now bestowed upon him." — *Walford.*

[2] "Ou, des grans." — *Fr. marg.* "Or, of the great."

tions with which they are oppressed, the more do they encourage themselves, while bewailing them before God, in the hope of obtaining his assistance. These forms of expression may seem hyperbolical, but it is obvious that it was David's purpose to declare and set forth what he had felt in his own person. First, he says that *his eyes, his soul, and his belly, were consumed with grief.* From this it appears that it was neither lightly nor for a short time that he was thus tormented and vexed by these calamities. Indeed, he was endued with so much meekness of spirit that he would not allow himself to be excited easily, and by a slight circumstance, nor vexed by immoderate sorrow. He had also been for a long time inured to the endurance of troubles. We must, therefore, admit that his afflictions were incredibly severe, when he gave way to such a degree of passion. By the word *anger,* too, he shows that he was not at all times of such iron-like firmness, or so free from sinful passion, as that his grief did not now and then break forth into an excess of impetuosity and keenness. Whence we infer that the saints have often a severe and arduous conflict with their own passions; and that although their patience has not always been free from peevishness, yet by carefully wrestling against it, they have at last attained this much, that no accumulation of troubles has overwhelmed them. By *life* some understand the vital senses, an interpretation which I do not altogether reject. But I prefer to explain it as simply meaning, that, being consumed with grief, he felt his life and his years sliding away and failing. And by these words again, David bewails not so much his pusillanimity of mind as the grievousness of his calamities; although he was by no means ashamed to confess his infirmity, for which he was anxiously seeking a remedy. When he says, that *his strength failed under his sorrow,* some interpreters prefer reading, *under his iniquity;* and I confess that the Hebrew word עון, *on,* bears both significations,[1] nay, more

---

[1] "The word עון," says Hammond, "as it signifies *sin,* so it signifies also the punishment of sin, Isa. liii. 6, 11;" and in this last sense this critic here understands it, that it may be connected with *grief* and *sighing,* which are mentioned in the preceding clause, and may express those miseries which David's sins had brought upon him. " עון," observes Rogers, "signifies here and in some other places, *affliction,* the punishment or conse-

frequently it signifies *an offence* or *a fault*. But as it is sometimes used for *punishment*, I have chosen the sense which appears most agreeable to the context. And although it is true that David was accustomed to ascribe the afflictions which he at any time suffered to his own fault, yet, as he is only recounting his miseries here, without mentioning the cause of them, it is probable that, according to his usual manner, he expresses the same thing twice by different words.

11. *I was a reproach by reason of all mine enemies.* Others translate thus —*more than mine enemies,* and as the Hebrew letter מ, *mem,* is often used as a sign of comparison, they interpret this clause to mean that David's friends and acquaintances reproached him more than all his enemies. But, in my opinion, he intended to express a different idea, namely, that as he was everywhere hated, and his enemies had induced almost the whole realm to take part with them against him, he had an evil name even among his friends and neighbours; just as popular opinion, like a violent tempest, usually carries all before it. I suppose, therefore, that the Hebrew copula ו, *vau,* is used for the sake of amplification, to show that David was an object of detestation, not only to strangers to whom he was formerly unknown, but also to his principal friends. He adds, likewise, that *when they saw him abroad they fled from him.* By the adverb, *abroad,* he means to say, that they did not think the miserable man worthy of a near approach to them; nay, that they fled from the very sight of him, at however great a distance, lest the contagion of his misery should reach them, and because they reckoned it would be injurious and disgraceful to them to show him any sign of friendship.

12. *I am forgotten as one dead.* The Psalmist still pursues the same idea, and complains that he was as completely blotted out of all men's remembrance as if he had been dead.

quence of sin; see Gen. iv. 13; 1 Sam. xxviii. 10; 2 Kings vii. 9," &c.—*Book of Psalms in Hebrew, metrically arranged,* vol. ii. p. 188. The Septuagint reads, *in poverty* or *affliction,* in which it is followed by the Syriac and Vulgate.

The memory of some men after their death flourishes for a time among survivors, but it more frequently vanishes; for there is no longer any intercourse between the quick and the dead, nor can the living be of any farther service to the dead. David illustrates this idea by the metaphor of *a broken vessel*,[1] which denotes utter contempt and meanness; as if he had said, that he was accounted no longer worthy of any place or respect. He adds, in fine, that he was railed upon by the multitude, and agitated with terrors. I would, however, prefer translating the Hebrew word רבּים, *rabbim*, by *the great*,[2] rather than by *many*. When great men, who are often as powerful in judgment as in authority, slander and defame us as wicked persons, this adds to the indignity with which we are treated, because, whatever they say in condemnation of us has the effect of prejudicing the common people against us. It will therefore be very suitable to understand the words as meaning that David was ignominiously condemned by the whole order of the nobility; and thus the innocence of this afflicted man was thrown into the shade by their greatness. This interpretation is confirmed by what immediately follows: *Fear encloseth me on every side*,[3] *while they consult together against me*. As he is still speaking of the same persons, it is certain that this language applies more appropriately to the nobles than to the common people. Moreover, we see that the primary object of the wicked in the deceitful counsels by which they conspired to destroy David, was to create among the whole people hatred against him as a wicked and reprobate, man. We also see that while they mangled his reputation, they did it in such a manner as that they covered their

---

[1] "I am become like a broken vessel;" that is, utterly neglected as being worthless.

[2] Horsley takes the same view. He reads, "the mighty."

[3] "*Fearfulness on every side*, or *terror round about*. In Heb., *magor missabib*, which name Jeremiah gave to Pashur the priest, signifying that he 'should be a terror to himself and to all his friends,' Jer. xx. 3, 4."— Ainsworth. Horsley reads,

"Truly I heard the angry muttering of the mighty,
Of them that are the general dread."

On this he has the following note: " מסביב מגור. I take this to be a phrase describing the mighty, whose malignant threats against him he overheard, as persons universally dreaded for their power and their cruelty."

wickedness under the appearance of grave and considerate procedure, in consulting among themselves to destroy him as a man who no longer ought to be tolerated on the earth. It is not to be wondered at, therefore, that his mind was wounded, as we have just seen, by so many and so sharp temptations.

14. *Yet have I trusted in thee, O Jehovah! I have said, Thou art my God.*
15. *My times are in thy hand; deliver me from the hand of mine enemies, and from them that persecute me.*
16. *Make thy face to shine upon thy servant; preserve me in thy goodness.*
17. *O Jehovah! let me not be ashamed; for I have called on thee: let the wicked be ashamed, let them be silent in the grave.*
18. *Let lying lips be put to silence, which speak a hard* [or *grievous*] *thing against the just, in pride and scorn.*

14. *Yet have I trusted in thee, O Jehovah!* The rendering properly is, *And I have trusted in thee;* but the Hebrew copulative particle ו, *vau, and,* is used here instead of the adversative particle *yet,* or *nevertheless.* David, setting the stedfastness of his faith in opposition to the assaults of the temptations of which he has made mention, denies that he had ever fainted, but rather maintains, on the contrary, that he stood firm in his hope of deliverance from God. Nor does this imply that he boasted of being so magnanimous and courageous that he could not be overthrown through the infirmity of the flesh. However contrary to one another they appear, yet these things are often joined together, as they ought to be, in the same person, namely, that while he pines away with grief, and is deprived of all strength, he is nevertheless supported by so strong a hope that he ceases not to call upon God. David, therefore, was not so overwhelmed in deep sorrow, and other direful sufferings, as that the hidden light of faith could not shine inwardly in his heart; nor did he groan so much under the weighty load of his temptations, as to be prevented from arousing himself to call upon God. He struggled through many obstacles to be able to make the confession which he here makes. He next defines the manner

of his faith, namely, that he reflected with himself thus—that God would never fail him nor forsake him. Let us mark his manner of speech: *I have said, Thou art my God*. In these words he intimates that he was so entirely persuaded of this truth, that God was his God, that he would not admit even a suggestion to the contrary. And until this persuasion prevails so as to take possession of our minds, we shall always waver in uncertainty. It is, however, to be observed, that this declaration is not only inward and secret —made rather in the heart than with the tongue—but that it is directed to God himself, as to him who is the alone witness of it. Nothing is more difficult, when we see our faith derided by the whole world, than to direct our speech to God only, and to rest satisfied with this testimony which our conscience gives us, *that he is our God*. And certainly it is an undoubted proof of genuine faith, when, however fierce the waves are which beat against us, and however sore the assaults by which we are shaken, we hold fast this as a fixed principle, that we are constantly under the protection of God, and can say to him freely, *Thou art our God*.

15. *My times are in thy hand*. That he might the more cheerfully commit the preservation of his person to God, he assures us, that, trusting to his divine guardianship, he did not trouble himself about those casual and unforeseen events which men commonly dread. The import of his language is, Lord, it is thy prerogative, and thou alone hast the power, to dispose of both my life and my death. Nor does he use the plural number, in my opinion, without reason; but rather to mark the variety of casualties by which the life of man is usually harassed. It is a cold exposition to restrict the phrase, *my times*, to the time which he had to live, as if David meant no more than that his time or his days on earth were in God's hand. On the contrary, I am of opinion that, while he mused on the various revolutions and manifold dangers which continually hang over us, and the manifold unlooked-for events which from time to time happen, he nevertheless confidently reposed upon the providence of God, which he believed to be, according to the common

saying, the arbiter both of good and of evil fortune. In the first clause we see that he not only denominates God the governor of the world in general, but also affirms that his life is in his hand; and not only so, but that to whatever agitations it might be subjected, and whatever trials and vicissitudes might befall him, he was safe under his protection. On this he founds his prayer, that God would preserve and *deliver him from the hand of his enemies.*

16. *Make thy face to shine upon thy servant.* We have said formerly, and we shall see in many instances hereafter, that this form of speech is taken from the common apprehension of men, who think that God regards them not, unless he really show his care of them by its effects. According to the judgment of sense, afflictions hide his countenance, just as clouds obscure the brightness of the sun. David therefore supplicates that God, by affording him immediate assistance, would make it evident to him that he enjoyed his grace and favour, which it is not very easy to discern amidst the darkness of afflictions. Now, God is said to lift the light of his countenance upon us in two ways; either when he opens his eyes to take care of our affairs, or when he shows to us his favour. These two things are indeed inseparable, or rather, the one depends upon the other. But by the first mode of speech, we, according to our carnal conceptions, attribute to God a mutability which, properly speaking, does not belong to him: whereas the second form of speech indicates, that our own eyes, rather than the eyes of God, are shut or heavy when he seems to have no regard to our afflictions. By the word *preserve* David explains what he meant by the former expression; but as there was at that time no way of safety apparent to him, he encourages himself to hope for it by setting before him *the goodness of God.*

17. *O Jehovah! let me not be ashamed.* In these words, the Psalmist continues his prayer, and to strengthen his hopes, he contrasts himself with his enemies; for it would have been more than absurd to permit those who by their wickedness so openly provoked the wrath of God to escape

with impunity, and that one who was innocent and relied upon God should be disappointed and made a laughing-stock. Here, accordingly, we perceive what the Psalmist's comparison implies. Moreover, instead of speaking of his hope or trust, he now speaks of his calling upon God, saying, *I have called on thee;* and he does this with good reason, for he who relies on the providence of God must flee to him with prayers and strong cries. *To be silent in the grave,* implies that death, when it befalls the ungodly, restrains and prevents them from doing farther injury. This silence is opposed both to their deceitful and treacherous devices, and to their outrageous insolence. In the very next verse, therefore, he adds, *Let lying lips be put to silence,* which, in my opinion, includes both their craftiness, and the false pretences and calumnies by which they endeavour to accomplish their designs, and also the vain boasting in which they indulge themselves. For he tells us that *they speak with harshness and severity against the righteous, in pride and scorn;* because it was their froward conceit, which almost always begets contempt, that made David's enemies so bold in lying. Whoever proudly arrogates to himself more than is his due, will almost necessarily treat others with contempt.

19. *O how great is thy goodness which thou hast hidden*[1] *for them that fear thee! which thou hast performed for them that trust in thee before the sons of men!*
20. *Thou shalt hide them in the secret* [or, *in the hiding-place*] *of thy countenance from the pride of man; thou shalt hide them as in a tent from the strife of tongues.*
21. *Blessed be Jehovah! for he hath made wonderful his goodness towards me, as in a fortified city.*

19. *O how great is thy goodness which thou hast hidden for them that fear thee!* In this verse the Psalmist exclaims that God is incomprehensibly good and beneficent towards his servants. *Goodness* here means those divine blessings which are the effects of it. The interrogatory form of the sentence

---

[1] " C'est, reservee."—*Fr. marg.* "That is, laid up."

has a peculiar emphasis; for David not only asserts that God is good, but he is ravished with admiration of the goodness which he had experienced. It was this experience, undoubtedly, which caused him break out into the rapturous language of this verse; for he had been marvellously and unexpectedly delivered from his calamities. By his example, therefore, he enjoins believers to rise above the apprehension of their own understanding, in order that they may promise themselves, and expect far more from the grace of God than human reason is able to conceive. He says that the goodness of God is *hidden* for his servants, because it is a treasure which is peculiar to them. It, no doubt, extends itself in various ways to the irreligious and unworthy, and is set before them indiscriminately; but it displays itself much more plenteously and clearly towards the faithful, because it is they alone who enjoy all God's benefits for their salvation. God " maketh his sun to rise on the evil and on the good," (Matth. v. 45,) and shows himself bountiful even to the irrational creation; but he declares himself a Father, in the true and full sense of the term, to those only who are his servants. It is not without reason, therefore, that the goodness of God is said to be hidden for the faithful, whom alone he accounts worthy of enjoying his favour most intimately and tenderly. Some give a more subtle interpretation of the phrase, *the goodness of God is hidden*, explaining it as meaning that God, by often exercising his children with crosses and afflictions, hides his favour from them, although, at the same time, he does not forget them. It is more probable, however, that it should be understood of a treasure which God has set apart and laid up in store for them, unless perhaps we choose to refer it to the experience of the saints, because they alone, as I have said, experience in their souls the fruit of divine goodness; whereas brutish stupidity hinders the wicked from acknowledging God as a beneficent Father, even while they are devouring greedily his good things. And thus it comes to pass, that while the goodness of God fills and overspreads all parts of the world, it is notwithstanding generally unknown. But the mind of the sacred writer will be more clearly perceived from the contrast which exists between the faithful and those who are strangers to God's love. As a provident man will regulate his liberality towards all men in such a manner as not to defraud his children or family, nor impoverish his own house, by spending his substance prodigally on others; so God, in like manner, in exercising his beneficence to aliens from his family, knows well how to reserve for his own children that which belongs to them as it were by hereditary right; that is to say, because of their adoption.[1] The attempt of Augustine to prove from these words that those who unbelievingly dread God's judgment have no experience of his goodness, is most inappropriate. To perceive his mistaken view of the passage, it is only necessary to look to the following clause, in which David says that God makes the world to perceive that he exercises inestimable goodness towards those who serve him, both in protecting them and in providing for their welfare. Whence we learn, that it is not of the everlasting blessedness which is reserved for the godly in heaven that the Psalmist here speaks, but of the protection and other blessings which belong to the preservation of the present life; which he declares to be so manifest that even the ungodly themselves are forced to become eye-witnesses of them. The world, I admit, passes over all the works of God with its eyes shut, and is especially ignorant of his fatherly care of the saints; still it is certain that there shine forth such daily proofs of it, that even the reprobate cannot but see them, except in so far as they willingly shut their eyes against the light. David, therefore, speaks according to truth, when he declares that God gives evidences of his goodness to his people *before the sons of men,* that it may be clearly seen that they do not serve him unadvisedly or in vain.[2]

20. *Thou shalt hide them in the secret of thy countenance.* In this verse the Psalmist specially commends the grace of God, because it preserves and protects the faithful against all harm. As Satan assiduously and by innumerable means

---

[1] " C'est à dire, à cause de leur adoption."—*Fr.*
[2] " *Before the sons of men, i.e.* openly, so that the world must acknowledge 'there is a reward for the righteous man.' Compare Psalm lviii. 11."
—*French and Skinner.*

opposes their welfare, and as the greater part of the world is at deadly war with them, they must be exposed to many dangers. Unless God, therefore, protected them by his power, and came from time to time to their aid, their condition would be most miserable. The Psalmist makes an allusion to *the hiding* which he had just mentioned, and although the metaphor may, at first sight, appear somewhat harsh, it very aptly expresses, that provided the Lord take care of them, the faithful are perfectly safe under his protection alone. By this eulogium, therefore, he sublimely extols the power of divine Providence, because it alone suffices to ward off every species of evil, and while it shines upon the godly, it blinds the eyes of all the wicked, and weakens their hands.[1] In the opinion of some, the Psalmist, when he speaks of *the secret of God's countenance*, refers to the sanctuary, an interpretation which I do not altogether reject, although it does not appear to me sufficiently solid. Again, he says that God hides the faithful from *the pride of man and the strife of tongues*, because, if God restrain not the wicked, we know that they have the audacity to break forth with outrageous violence against the truly godly; but however unbridled their lust and insolence may be, God preserves his people from harm, by wondrously covering them with the brightness of his countenance. Some translate the Hebrew word רִכְסִים, *rikasim*, *conspiracies*,[2] others *perversities*, but without any reason; nor, indeed, does the etymology of the word admit of it, for it comes from a root which signifies *to lift up*, or *to elevate*. To *pride* is added *the strife of tongues*, because God's children have cause to fear not only the inhuman deeds of their enemies, but also their still more wicked and violent calumnies, as David himself more than enough experienced. And as our innocence ought to be justly dearer to us than our life, let us learn to cultivate uprightness in such a manner as that, trusting to God's protection, we may disregard every false calumny. And let us always remember that it is God's

---

[1] "Et que quand elle luit sur les fideles, ses rayons sont pour esblouir les yeux de tous les iniques, et affoiblir leur mains."—*Fr.*

[2] This is the reading adopted by Walford. "מרכסי à, רכס, *colligavit*: hence 'bands,' 'conspiracies.'"

peculiar prerogative to vindicate his people from all unjust reproaches.

21. *Blessed be Jehovah!* These general truths the Psalmist here proceeds to apply to his own circumstances, and he declares that the goodness of God in preserving his life was wondrously displayed. As he speaks of aid which had been suddenly and unexpectedly afforded him in very desperate circumstances, those interpreters judge aright who here supply *as*, the mark of similitude,[1] in this way, *as in a fortified city*. David lay open to every blow, and had been exposed to every sort of injury, and he boasts that in his nakedness and destitution the assistance of God had been of greater service to him than a city well fortified, or an impregnable fortress would have been.

22. *And I said in my fear*,[2] *I am cast out of thy sight: yet truly thou hast heard the voice of my supplications when I cried unto thee.*
23. *O love Jehovah, all ye his meek ones! Jehovah preserveth the faithful, and plentifully*[3] *recompenseth him who behaveth himself proudly.*
24. *Be of good courage, and he shall strengthen your heart, all ye who hope in Jehovah.*

22. *And I said in my fear.* David here confesses that for his distrust he deserved to be deserted by God and left to perish. It is true that to confess this before men he felt to be a shameful thing; but that he may the more fully illustrate the grace of God to him, he hesitates not to publish the shame of his fault. He repeats almost the same acknowledgment in Psalm cxvi. 11, "I said in my haste, All men are liars." I am aware that the Hebrew word חפז, *chaphaz*, is explained by some as meaning *flight;* as if David, in fleeing from death,

---

[1] "The particle of similitude is wanting in Hebrew, as is not uncommon. The intention of the Psalmist is evidently to describe by a metaphor his signal deliverance, as if he had been guarded by invincible fortifications."—*Walford.*
[2] "Ou, perturbation; ou, hastivete."—*Fr. marg.* "Or, perturbation; or, haste."
[3] "Ou, par excellence."—"Or, excellently."—*Fr. marg.*

because he was unable to make resistance, was stricken with this fear. But I refer it rather to his trouble of mind. Whether, therefore, we translate it *haste* or *fear*, it means that he had been, as it were, carried headlong to entertain the thought that he was neglected by God. And this haste is opposed to calm and deliberate consideration; for although David was stricken with fear, he did not faint under the trial, and this persuasion did not continue fixed in his mind. For we know that the faithful are often disquieted by fears and the heat of impatience, or driven headlong as it were by their too hasty or precipitate wishes, but afterwards they come to themselves. That David's faith had never been overthrown by this temptation appears from the context, for he immediately adds, *that God had heard the voice of his supplications;* but if his faith had been extinguished, he could not have brought his mind earnestly to engage in prayer, and therefore this complaint was only a lapse of the tongue uttered in haste. Now if peevish hastiness of thought could drive this holy prophet of God, a man who was adorned with so many excellencies, to despair, how much reason have we to fear, lest our minds should fail and fatally ruin us? This confession of David, as we have already observed, serves to magnify the grace of God; but at the same time he sufficiently shows, in the second clause of the verse, that his faith, although severely shaken, had not been altogether eradicated, because he ceased not meanwhile to pray. The saints often wrestle in this manner with their distrust, that partly they may not despond, and that partly they may gather courage and stimulate themselves to prayer. Nor does the weakness of the flesh, even when they are almost overthrown, hinder them from showing that they are unwearied and invincible champions before God. But although David stoutly resisted temptation, he nevertheless acknowledges himself unworthy of God's grace, of which he in some measure deprived himself by his doubt. For the Hebrew particle אכן, *aken*, is here to be understood adversatively and rendered *yet*, intimating that David had been preserved without any desert of his own, inasmuch as God's immeasurable goodness strove with his unbelief. But as it is a sign of affirmation in Hebrew, I have thought proper to translate it, *Yet truly*. I have no doubt that he opposes his language to the various temptations with which, it is probable, his mind had been driven hither and thither.

23. *O love Jehovah, all ye his meek ones!* In my opinion, the Psalmist does not here exhort the saints to fear and reverence God, as many think, but encourages them to confide in him; or, in other words, to devote themselves wholly to him, to put all their hope in him, and to rely entirely upon him, without seeking to any other. Whence is it that our own fond devices delight us, but because we do not delight in God so much as we ought, and because our affections do not cleave to him? This love of God, therefore, comprehends in it all the desires of the heart. By nature, all men greatly desire to be in a prosperous or happy state; but while the greater number are fascinated by the allurements of the world, and prefer its lies and impostures, scarcely one in a hundred sets his heart on God. The reason which immediately follows confirms this interpretation; for the inspired Psalmist exhorts *the meek* to love God, because he *preserves the faithful*, which is as if he had desired them to rest satisfied with his guardianship, and to acknowledge that in it they had sufficient succour.[1] In the meantime, he admonishes them to keep a good conscience, and to cultivate uprightness, since God promises to preserve only such as are upright and faithful. On the other hand, he declares that he *plentifully recompenses the proud*, in order that when we observe them succeeding prosperously for a time, an unworthy emulation may not entice us to imitate them, and that their haughtiness, and the outrage they commit, while they think they are at liberty to do what they please, may not crush and break our spirits. The amount of the whole is this, Although the ungodly flatter themselves, while they proceed in their wickedness with impunity, and believers are harassed with many fears and dangers, yet devote yourselves to God, and rely upon his grace, for he will always defend the faithful,

---

[1] " Et recognoistre qu'en icelle ils ont assez de secours."—*Fr.*

and reward the proud as they deserve. Concerning the meaning of the Hebrew word עַל־יֶתֶר, *al-yether*, which we have rendered *plentifully*,[1] interpreters are not agreed. Some translate it *pride*, meaning that to those who behave themselves proudly, God will render according to their pride; others translate it *to overflowing*, or *beyond measure*, because יֶתֶר, *yether*, signifies in Hebrew *residue* or *remnant;* instead of which I have translated it *plentifully*. Some understand it as extending to their children and children's children, who shall remain the residue of their seed. Besides, as the same word is frequently used for *excellence*,[2] I have no doubt that the prophet elegantly rebukes the proud, who imagine that their fancied excellence is not only a shield to them, but an invincible fortress against God. As their groundless authority and power blind, or rather bewitch them, so that they vaunt themselves intemperately and without measure against those who are lowly and feeble, the prophet elegantly says that there is a reward in store for them proportioned to the haughtiness with which they are puffed up.

24. *Be of good courage.* This exhortation is to be understood in the same way as the preceding; for the stedfastness which the Psalmist here enjoins is founded on the love of God of which he had spoken, when renouncing all the enticements of the world, we embrace with our whole hearts the defence and protection which he promises to us. Nor is his exhortation to courage and firmness unnecessary; because, when any one begins to rely on God, he must lay his account with and arm himself for sustaining many assaults from Satan. We are first, then, calmly to commit ourselves to the protection and guardianship of God, and to endeavour to have the experience of his goodness pervading our whole minds. Secondly, thus furnished with steady firmness and unfailing

---

[1] Literally, "with plenty."

[2] The word גאה, *gaäh*, from which גאוה, *gaävah*, which we have rendered *proudly*, is derived, signifies *elatus est, eminuit;* and גאוה, *gaävah*, "is sometimes taken in a bad sense for *pride* or *arrogance*, as in Ps. x. 2; and sometimes in a good sense for *splendour, magnificence, strength, excellence*. In the latter sense it is used of God, Ps. lxviii. 35, *His height*, or *excellence and strength, are in the clouds.*"—*Hammond.*

strength, we are to stand prepared to sustain every day new conflicts. As no man, however, is able of himself to sustain these conflicts, David urges us to hope for and ask the spirit of fortitude from God, a matter particularly worthy of our notice. For hence we are taught, that when the Spirit of God puts us in mind of our duty, he examines not what each man's ability is, nor does he measure men's services by their own strength, but stimulates us rather to pray and beseech God to correct our defects, as it is he alone who can do this.

PSALM XXXII.

David having largely and painfully experienced what a miserable thing it is to feel God's hand heavy on account of sin, exclaims that the highest and best part of a happy life consists in this, that God forgives a man's guilt, and receives him graciously into his favour. After giving thanks for pardon obtained, he invites others to fellowship with him in his happiness, showing, by his own example, the means by which this may be obtained.

¶ A Psalm of David giving instruction.

The title of this psalm gives some idea of its subject. Some think that the Hebrew word משכיל, *maskil*, which we have rendered *giving instruction*,[1] is taken from verse 7th;[2] but it is more accurate to consider it as a title given to the psalm in accordance with its whole scope and subject-matter. David, after enduring long and dreadful torments, when God was severely trying him, by showing him the tokens of his wrath, having at length obtained favour, applies this evidence of the divine goodness for his own benefit, and the benefit of the whole Church, that from it he may teach himself and them what constitutes the chief point of salvation. All men must necessarily be either in miserable torment, or, which is worse, forgetting themselves and God, must continue

---

[1] "Pour lequel nous avons traduit, Donnant instruction."—*Fr.*
[2] Where it is said, "I will instruct thee and teach thee."

in deadly lethargy, until they are persuaded that God is reconciled towards them. Hence David here teaches us that the happiness of men consists only in the free forgiveness of sins, for nothing can be more terrible than to have God for our enemy; nor can he be gracious to us in any other way than by pardoning our transgressions.

1. *Blessed are they whose iniquity is forgiven, and whose transgression is covered.*
2. *Blessed is the man to whom Jehovah imputeth no sin, and in whose spirit there is no guile.*

1. *Blessed are they whose iniquity is forgiven.* This exclamation springs from the fervent affection of the Psalmist's heart as well as from serious consideration. Since almost the whole world turning away their thoughts from God's judgment, bring upon themselves a fatal forgetfulness, and intoxicate themselves with deceitful pleasures; David, as if he had been stricken with the fear of God's wrath, that he might betake himself to Divine mercy, awakens others also to the same exercise, by declaring distinctly and loudly that those only are blessed to whom God is reconciled, so as to acknowledge those for his children whom he might justly treat as his enemies. Some are so blinded with hypocrisy and pride, and some with such gross contempt of God, that they are not at all anxious in seeking forgiveness, but all acknowledge that they need forgiveness; nor is there a man in existence whose conscience does not accuse him at God's judgment-seat, and gall him with many stings. This confession, accordingly, that all need forgiveness, because no man is perfect, and that then only is it well with us when God pardons our sins, nature herself extorts even from wicked men. But in the meantime, hypocrisy shuts the eyes of multitudes, while others are so deluded by a perverse carnal security, that they are touched either with no feelings of Divine wrath, or with only a frigid feeling of it.

From this proceeds a twofold error: first, that such men make light of their sins, and reflect not on the hundredth part of their danger from God's indignation; and, secondly, that they invent frivolous expiations to free themselves from guilt and to purchase the favour of God. Thus in all ages it has been everywhere a prevailing opinion, that although all men are infected with sin, they are at the same time adorned with merits which are calculated to procure for them the favour of God, and that although they provoke his wrath by their crimes, they have expiations and satisfactions in readiness to obtain their absolution. This delusion of Satan is equally common among Papists, Turks, Jews, and other nations. Every man, therefore, who is not carried away by the furious madness of Popery, will admit the truth of this statement, that men are in a wretched state unless God deal mercifully with them by not laying their sins to their charge. But David goes farther, declaring that the whole life of man is subjected to God's wrath and curse, except in so far as he vouchsafes of his own free grace to receive them into his favour; of which the Spirit who spake by David is an assured interpreter and witness to us by the mouth of Paul, (Rom. iv. 6.) Had Paul not used this testimony, never would his readers have penetrated the real meaning of the prophet; for we see that the Papists, although they chant in their temples, " Blessed are they whose iniquities are forgiven," &c., yet pass over it as if it were some common saying and of little importance. But with Paul, this is the full definition of the righteousness of faith; as if the prophet had said, Men are then only blessed when they are freely reconciled to God, and counted as righteous by him. The blessedness, accordingly, that David celebrates utterly destroys the righteousness of works. The device of a partial righteousness with which Papists and others delude themselves is mere folly; and even among those who are destitute of the light of heavenly doctrine, no one will be found so mad as to arrogate a perfect righteousness to himself, as appears from the expiations, washings, and other means of appeasing God, which have always been in use among all nations. But yet they do not hesitate to obtrude their virtues upon God, just as if by them they had acquired of themselves a great part of their blessedness.

David, however, prescribes a very different order, namely, that in seeking happiness, all should begin with the principle, that God cannot be reconciled to those who are worthy of eternal destruction in any other way than by freely pardoning them, and bestowing upon them his favour. And justly does he declare that if mercy is withheld from them, all men must be utterly wretched and accursed; for if all men are naturally prone only to evil, until they are regenerated, their whole previous life, it is obvious, must be hateful and loathsome in the sight of God. Besides, as even after regeneration, no work which men perform can please God unless he pardons the sin which mingles with it, they must be excluded from the hope of salvation. Certainly nothing will remain for them but cause for the greatest terror. That the works of the saints are unworthy of reward because they are spotted with stains, seems a hard saying to the Papists. But in this they betray their gross ignorance in estimating, according to their own conceptions, the judgment of God, in whose eyes the very brightness of the stars is but darkness. Let this therefore remain an established doctrine, that as we are only accounted righteous before God by the free remission of sins, this is the gate of eternal salvation; and, accordingly, that they only are blessed who rely upon God's mercy. We must bear in mind the contrast which I have already mentioned between believers who, embracing the remission of sins, rely upon the grace of God alone, and all others who neglect to betake themselves to the sanctuary of Divine grace.

Moreover, when David thrice repeats the same thing, this is no vain repetition. It is indeed sufficiently evident of itself that the man must be blessed whose iniquity is forgiven; but experience teaches us how difficult it is to become persuaded of this in such a manner as to have it thoroughly fixed in our hearts. The great majority, as I have already shown you, entangled by devices of their own, put away from them, as far as they can, the terrors of conscience and all fear of Divine wrath. They have, no doubt, a desire to be reconciled to God; and yet they shun the sight of him, rather than seek his grace sincerely and with all their hearts. Those, on the other hand, whom God has truly awakened so as to be affected with a lively sense of their misery, are so constantly agitated and disquieted that it is difficult to restore peace to their minds. They taste indeed God's mercy, and endeavour to lay hold of it, and yet they are frequently abashed or made to stagger under the manifold assaults which are made upon them. The two reasons for which the Psalmist insists so much on the subject of the forgiveness of sins are these,—that he may, on the one hand, raise up those who are fallen asleep, inspire the careless with thoughtfulness, and quicken the dull; and that he may, on the other hand, tranquillise fearful and anxious minds with an assured and steady confidence. To the former, the doctrine may be applied in this manner: "What mean ye, O ye unhappy men! that one or two stings of conscience do not disturb you? Suppose that a certain limited knowledge of your sins is not sufficient to strike you with terror, yet how preposterous is it to continue securely asleep, while you are overwhelmed with an immense load of sins!" And this repetition furnishes not a little comfort and confirmation to the feeble and fearful. As doubts are often coming upon them, one after another, it is not sufficient that they are victorious in one conflict only. That despair, therefore, may not overwhelm them amidst the various perplexing thoughts with which they are agitated, the Holy Spirit confirms and ratifies the remission of sins with many declarations.

It is now proper to weigh the particular force of the expressions here employed. Certainly the remission which is here treated of does not agree with satisfactions. God, in lifting off or taking away sins, and likewise in covering and not imputing them, freely pardons them. On this account the Papists, by thrusting in their satisfactions and works of supererogation as they call them, bereave themselves of this blessedness. Besides, David applies these words to complete forgiveness. The distinction, therefore, which the Papists here make between the remission of the punishment and of the fault, by which they make only half a pardon, is not at all to the purpose. Now, it is necessary to consider to whom this happiness belongs, which may be easily gathered from the circumstance of the time. When David was taught that he was blessed through the mercy of God alone, he was not an alien from the church of God; on the contrary, he had profited above many in the fear and service of God, and in holiness of life, and had exercised himself in all the duties of godliness. And even after making these advances in religion, God so exercised him, that he placed the alpha and omega of his salvation in his gratuitous reconciliation to God. Nor is it without reason that Zacharias, in his song, represents "the knowledge of salvation" as consisting in knowing "the remission of sins," (Luke i. 77.) The more eminently that any one excels in holiness, the farther he feels himself from perfect righteousness, and the more clearly he perceives that he can trust in nothing but the mercy of God alone. Hence it appears, that those are grossly mistaken who conceive that the pardon of sin is necessary only to the beginning of righteousness. As believers are every day involved in many faults, it will profit them nothing that they have once entered the way of righteousness, unless the same grace which brought them into it accompany them to the last step of their life. Does any one object, that they are elsewhere said to be blessed "who fear the Lord," "who walk in his ways," "who are upright in heart," &c., the answer is easy, namely, that as the perfect fear of the Lord, the perfect observance of his law, and perfect uprightness of heart, are nowhere to be found, all that the Scripture anywhere says, concerning blessedness, is founded upon the free favour of God, by which he reconciles us to himself.

2. *In whose spirit there is no guile.* In this clause the Psalmist distinguishes believers both from hypocrites and from senseless despisers of God, neither of whom care for this happiness, nor can they attain to the enjoyment of it. The wicked are, indeed, conscious to themselves of their guilt, but still they delight in their wickedness; harden themselves in their impudence, and laugh at threatenings; or, at least, they indulge themselves in deceitful flatteries, that they may not be constrained to come into the presence of God. Yea, though they are rendered unhappy by a sense of their misery, and harassed with secret torments, yet with perverse forgetfulness they stifle all fear of God. As for hypocrites, if their conscience as any time stings them, they soothe their pain with ineffectual remedies: so that if God at any time cite them to his tribunal,

they place before them I know not what phantoms for their
defence; and they are never without coverings whereby they
may keep the light out of their hearts. Both these classes of
men are hindered by inward guile from seeking their happiness
in the fatherly love of God. Nay more, many of them rush
frowardly into the presence of God, or puff themselves up with
proud presumption, dreaming that they are happy, although
God is against them. David, therefore, means that no man
can taste what the forgiveness of sins is until his heart is first
cleansed from guile. What he means, then, by this term,
guile, may be understood from what I have said. Whoever
examines not himself, as in the presence of God, but, on the
contrary, shunning his judgment, either shrouds himself in
darkness, or covers himself with leaves, deals deceitfully both
with himself and with God. It is no wonder, therefore, that
he who feels not his disease refuses the remedy. The two
kinds of this guile which I have mentioned are to be particularly attended to. Few may be so hardened as not to be
touched with the fear of God, and with some desire of his
grace, and yet they are moved but coldly to seek forgiveness.
Hence it comes to pass, that they do not yet perceive what
an unspeakable happiness it is to possess God's favour.
Such was David's case for a time, when a treacherous security stole upon him, darkened his mind, and prevented him
from zealously applying himself to pursue after this happiness.
Often do the saints labour under the same disease. If, therefore, we would enjoy the happiness which David here proposes
to us, we must take the greatest heed lest Satan, filling our
hearts with guile, deprive us of all sense of our wretchedness,
in which every one who has recourse to subterfuges must
necessarily pine away.

> 3. *When I kept silence, my bones wasted away, and when I cried
>   out all the day.*
> 4. *For day and night thy hand was heavy upon me; and my green-
>   ness was turned into the drought of summer.*

3. *When I kept silence, my bones wasted away.* Here David
confirms, by his own experience, the doctrine which he had
laid down; namely, that when humbled under the hand of

God, he felt that nothing was so miserable as to be deprived of his favour: by which he intimates, that this truth cannot be rightly understood until God has tried us with a feeling of his anger. Nor does he speak of a mere ordinary trial, but declares that he was entirely subdued with the extremest rigour. And certainly, the sluggishness of our flesh, in this matter, is no less wonderful than its hardihood. If we are not drawn by forcible means, we will never hasten to seek reconciliation to God so earnestly as we ought. In fine, the inspired writer teaches us by his own example, that we never perceive how great a happiness it is to enjoy the favour of God, until we have thoroughly felt from grievous conflicts with inward temptations, how terrible the anger of God is. He adds, that whether he was silent, or whether he attempted to heighten his grief by his crying and roaring,[1] his bones waxed old; in other words, his whole strength withered away. From this it follows, that whithersoever the sinner may turn himself, or however he may be mentally affected, his malady is in no degree lightened, nor his welfare in any degree promoted, until he is restored to the favour of God. It often happens that those are tortured with the sharpest grief who gnaw the bit, and inwardly devour their sorrow, and keep it enclosed and shut up within, without discovering it, although afterwards they are seized as with sudden madness, and the force of their grief bursts forth with the greater impetus the longer it has been restrained. By the term *silence*, David means neither insensibility nor stupidity, but that feeling which lies between patience and obstinacy, and which is as much allied to the vice as to the virtue. For his bones were not consumed with age, but with the dreadful torments of his mind. His silence, however, was not the

---

[1] The translation of this verse in our English Bible is, "When I kept silence, my bones waxed old through my roaring all the day long;" on which Street observes, "I must own I do not understand how a man can be said *to keep silence* who *roars* all the day long." Accordingly, instead of *When I kept silence*, he reads, *While I am lost in thought;* observing, that "the verb חרש, in the Hiphil conjugation, signifies *to ponder, to consider, to be deep in thought.*" But according to the translation and exposition of Calvin, there is no inconsistency between the first and the second clause of the verse. To avoid the apparent contradiction of being at once *silent* and yet *roaring* all the day long, Dr Boothroyd, instead of *roaring*, reads *pangs*.

silence of hope or obedience, for it brought no alleviation of his misery.

4. *For day and night thy hand was heavy upon me.* In this verse he explains more fully whence such heavy grief arose; namely, because he felt the hand of God to be sore against him. The greatest of all afflictions is to be so heavily pressed with the hand of God, that the sinner feels he has to do with a Judge whose indignation and severity involve in them many deaths, besides eternal death. David, accordingly, complains that his moisture was dried up, not merely from simply meditating on his sore afflictions, but because he had discovered their cause and spring. The whole strength of men fails when God appears as a Judge and humbles and lays them prostrate by exhibiting the signs of his displeasure. Then is fulfilled the saying of Isaiah, (chap. xl. 7,) " The grass withereth, the flower fadeth, because the Spirit of the Lord bloweth upon it." The Psalmist, moreover, tells us, that it was no common chastisement by which he had been taught truly to fear the divine wrath; for the hand of the Lord ceased not to be heavy upon him both day and night. From a child, indeed, he had been inspired with the fear of God, by the secret influence of the Holy Spirit, and had been taught in true religion and godliness by sound doctrine and instruction. And yet so insufficient was this instruction for his attainment of this wisdom, that he had to be taught again like a new beginner in the very midst of his course. Yea, although he had now been long accustomed to mourn over his sins, he was every day anew reduced to this exercise: which teaches us, how long it is ere men recover themselves when once they have fallen; and also how slow they are to obey until God, from time to time, redouble their stripes, and increase them from day to day. Should any one ask concerning David, whether he had become callous under the stripes which he well knew were inflicted on him by the hand of God, the context furnishes the answer; namely, that he was kept down and fettered by perplexing griefs, and distracted with lingering torments, until he was well subdued and made meek, which is the first sign of seeking a remedy. And this again teaches us, that it is

not without cause that the chastisements by which God seems to deal cruelly with us are repeated, and his hand made heavy against us, until our fierce pride, which we know to be untameable, unless subdued with the heaviest stripes, is humbled.

> 5. *I have acknowledged my sin unto thee, and mine iniquity have I not hid. I said, I will confess against myself to Jehovah my wickedness; and thou didst remit the guilt[1] of my sin. Selah.*
> 6. *Therefore shall every one that is meek pray unto thee in the time of finding thee; so that in a flood of many waters,[2] they shall not come nigh unto him.*
> 7. *Thou art my hiding-place; thou shalt preserve me from trouble; thou shalt compass me about with songs of deliverance. Selah.*

5. *I have acknowledged my sin unto thee.* The prophet now describes the issue of his misery, in order to show to all the ready way of obtaining the happiness of which he makes mention. When his feeling of divine wrath sorely vexed and tormented him, his only relief was unfeignedly to condemn himself before God, and humbly to flee to him to crave his forgiveness. He does not say, however, that his sins merely came to his remembrance, for so also did the sins of Cain and Judas, although to no profit; because, when the consciences of the wicked are troubled with their sins, they cease not to torment themselves, and to fret against God: yea, although he forces them unwillingly to his bar, they still eagerly desire to hide themselves. But here there is described a very different method of acknowledging sin; namely, when the sinner willingly betakes himself to God, building his hope of salvation not on stubbornness or hypocrisy, but on supplication for pardon. This voluntary confession is always conjoined with faith; for otherwise the sinner will continually seek lurking-places where he may hide himself from God. David's words clearly show that he came unfeignedly and cordially into the presence of God, that he might conceal nothing. When he tells us that *he acknowledged his sin*, and *did not hide it*, the latter

---

[1] "Ou, peine."—*Fr. marg.* "Or, punishment."
[2] "De grandes eaux."—*Fr.* "Of great waters."

clause is added, according to the Hebrew idiom, for the sake of amplification. There is no doubt, therefore, that David, when he appeared before God, poured out all his heart. Hypocrites, we know, that they may extenuate their evil doings, either disguise or misrepresent them; in short, they never make an honest confession of them, with an ingenuous and open mouth. But David denies that he was chargeable with this baseness. Without any dissimulation he made known to God whatever grieved him; and this he confirms by the words, *I have said.* While the wicked are dragged by force, just as a judge compels offenders to come to trial, he assures us that he came deliberately and with full purpose of mind; for the term, *said,* just signifies that he deliberated with himself. It therefore follows, that he promised and assured himself of pardon through the mercy of God, in order that terror might not prevent him from making a free and an ingenuous confession of his sins.

The phrase, *upon myself,* or *against myself,* intimates that David put away from him all the excuses and pretences by which men are accustomed to unburden themselves, transferring their fault, or tracing it to other people. David, therefore, determined to submit himself entirely to God's judgment, and to make known his own guilt, that being self-condemned, he might as a suppliant obtain pardon.

And thou didst remit the guilt of my sin. This clause is set in opposition to the grievous and direful agitations by which he says he was harassed before he approached by faith the grace of God. But the words also teach, that as often as the sinner presents himself at the throne of mercy, with ingenuous confession, he will find reconciliation with God awaiting him. In other words, the Psalmist means that God was not only willing to pardon him, but that his example afforded a general lesson that those in distress should not doubt of God's favour towards them, so soon as they should betake themselves to him with a sincere and willing mind. Should any one infer from this, that repentance and confession are the cause of obtaining grace, the answer is easy; namely, that David is not speaking here of the cause but of the manner in which the sinner becomes reconciled to God. Confession, no doubt, intervenes, but we must go beyond this, and consider that it is faith which, by opening our hearts and tongues, really obtains our pardon. It is not admitted that every thing which is necessarily connected with pardon is to be reckoned amongst its causes. Or, to speak more simply, David obtained pardon by his confession, not because he merited it by the mere act of confessing, but because, under the guidance of faith, he humbly implored it from his judge. Moreover, as the same method of confession ought to be in use among us at this day, which was formerly employed by the fathers under the law, this sufficiently refutes that tyrannical decree of the Pope, by which he turns us away from God, and sends us to his priests to obtain pardon.

6. *Therefore shall every one that is meek pray unto thee.* Here the Psalmist expressly states that whatever he has hitherto set forth in his own person belongs in common to all the children of God. And this is to be carefully observed, because, from our native unbelief, the greater part of us are slow and reluctant to appropriate the grace of God. We may also learn from this, that David obtained forgiveness, not by the mere act of confession, as some speak, but by faith and prayer. Here he directs believers to the same means of obtaining it, bidding them betake themselves to prayer, which is the true sacrifice of faith. Farther, we are taught, that in David God gave an example of his mercy, which may not only extend to us all, but may also show us how reconciliation is to be sought. The words, *every one,* serve for the confirmation of every godly person; but the Psalmist at the same time shows, that no one can obtain the hope of salvation but by prostrating himself as a suppliant before God, because all without exception stand in need of his mercy.

The expression, *The time of finding,* which immediately follows, some think, refers to the ordinary and accustomed hours of prayer; but others more accurately, in my opinion, compare it[1] with that place in Isaiah, (chap. lv. 6,) where it

---

[1] In the Septuagint version it is rendered, "In the time of finding favour;" in the Arabic, "In a time of hearing;" and in the Syriac, "In an acceptable time."

is said, "Seek ye the Lord while he may be found, call ye upon him while he is near." It is never out of season, indeed, to seek God, for every moment we need his grace, and he is always willing to meet us. But as slothfulness or dulness hinders us from seeking him, David here particularly intimates the critical seasons when believers are stimulated by a sense of their own need to have recourse to God. The Papists have abused this place to warrant their doctrine, that we ought to have advocates in heaven to pray for us;[1] but the attempt to found an argument in support of such a doctrine from this passage is so grossly absurd that it is unworthy of refutation. We may see from it, however, either how wickedly they have corrupted the whole Scripture, or with what gross ignorance they blunder in the plainest matters.

In the flood of many waters. This expression agrees with that prophecy of Joel, (chap. ii. 32,) "Whosoever shall call on the name of the Lord, shall be delivered." The meaning is, that although the deep whirlpools of death may compass us round on every side, we ought not to fear that they shall swallow us up; but rather believe that we shall be safe and unhurt, if we only betake ourselves to the mercy of God. We are thus emphatically taught that the godly shall have certain salvation even in death, provided they betake themselves to the sanctuary of God's grace. Under the term *flood* are denoted all those dangers from which there appears no means of escape.

At last the Psalmist gives himself to thanksgiving, and although he uses but few words to celebrate the divine favour, there is, notwithstanding, much force in his brevity. In the first place, he denies that there is any other haven of safety but in God himself. Secondly, he assures himself that God will be his faithful keeper hereafter; for I willingly retain the future tense of the verb, though some, without any reason, translate it into the past. He is not, however, to be understood as meaning that he conceived himself safe from future tribulations, but he sets God's guardianship over against them. Lastly, whatever adversity may befall him, he is per-

[1] "Qu'ils nous faut avoir des advocats au ciel qui prient pour nous." —*Fr.*

suaded that God will be his deliverer. By the word *compass*, he means manifold and various kinds of deliverance; as if he had said, that he should be under obligation to God in innumerable ways, and that he should, on every side, have most abundant matter for praising him. We may observe in the meantime, how he offers his service of gratitude to God, according to his usual method, putting *songs of deliverance* instead of *help*.

8. *I will instruct thee, and teach thee in the way that thou mayest walk: I will counsel thee with mine eye.*[1]

9. *Be not like the horse or mule, which have no understanding: thou shalt bind his jaw with bit and bridle, lest they kick against* [or *become obstreperous against* or *obstinately disobey*] *thee.*[2]

10. *Many sorrows shall be to the wicked: but the man who hopeth in Jehovah, mercy shall surround him.*

11. *Be glad in Jehovah, and rejoice, ye righteous: sing all ye that are upright in heart.*

8. *I will instruct thee, and teach thee.* That his exhortation may have the greater force, the divine speaker directs his discourse to every man individually; for the doctrine which is spoken penetrates the mind more readily, when every man applies it particularly to himself. When the way of salvation is here shown to the children of God, the greatest care must be taken that no man depart from it in the slightest degree. We may also learn from this place, that we are reconciled to God upon condition that every man endeavour

---

[1] " Ou, te guideray de mon œil."—*Fr. marg.* " Or, I will guide thee with mine eye."

[2] This verse in the Hebrew is very elliptical and obscure. Hence, besides the translation of Calvin, which agrees very well with the scope of the passage, various other translations have been given of it. In our English Bible, the last clause is rendered, "lest they come near unto thee," that is, to attack thee. But this is evidently an incorrect translation. This is not the common practice of these animals, which are timid, and not ferocious; bits and bridles are not used for the purpose of keeping them away from us, but of subduing, guiding, and making them subservient to our will; and were this the sense, the figure would be inappropriate, since the object of the Psalmist is to induce men to approach God. The clause, therefore, is rendered by many critics, " Or they will not come nigh unto thee;" that is, they will flee from thee. The Hebrew for this last phrase is, " There is not a coming to thee."

to make his brethren partakers of the same benefit. David, the more strongly to mark his care about them, describes it by *the sight of the eye.*[1] By the way it should be observed, that those who are solicitous about our welfare are appointed by the Lord as guides of our way, from which it appears how great is the paternal solicitude which he has about us.

9. *Be not like the horse or mule.* David now briefly explains the amount of the counsel which he formerly said he would give. He exhorts all to learn with quietness, to lay aside stubbornness, and to put on the spirit of meekness. There is much wisdom, too, in the advice which he gives to the godly to correct their hardihood; for if we were as attentive to God's corrections as we ought, every one would eagerly hasten to seek his favour. Whence is so much slowness to be found in all, but that we are either stupid or refractory? By likening the refractory, therefore, to brute beasts, David puts them to shame, and at the same time declares that it will avail them nothing to "kick against the pricks." Men, says he, know how to tame the fierceness of horses by bridles and bits; what then do they think God will do when he finds them intractable?

10. *Many sorrows shall be to the wicked.* Without a figure he here declares what will be the condition of the rebellious and stiff-necked.[2] He mentioned before that God wanted not bridles and bits with which to restrain their frowardness; and now he adds, that there would be no end or measure of their miseries until they were utterly consumed. Although

---

[1] Most commentators consider Jehovah as the person speaking in this verse. Calvin, however, views David as the speaker. In this opinion he is followed by Walford. "In Psalm li. 13," says this critic, "written about the same time and on the same occasion, David urges as a reason why God should restore to him the joy of his salvation, that he might be enabled to teach transgressors his ways, and that sinners might be converted to him. So in the passage before us, he addresses himself to sinners, and says, 'I will instruct thee, and teach thee the way in which thou shalt go.'"

[2] Fry reads, "Many are the wounds of the refractory;" on which he has the following note:—"We perceive in this place the exact idea of יטו, in its allusion to the restive, disobedient, unyielding, ungovernable mule or horse. It is opposed to חםב, *to confide in, to yield to,* or *succumb,* as the gentle beast fully confides and yields himself to the management of his guide."

God, therefore, may spare us for a time, yet let this denunciation fill us with fear, and preserve us from hardening ourselves, because we are as yet unpunished; nor let our prosperity, which is cursed by God, so deceive us as to close our minds against reflecting on those unseen sorrows which he threatens against all the wicked. And as the Psalmist has told us, on the one hand, that God is armed with innumerable plagues against the wicked, so he adds, on the other hand, that he is furnished with infinite goodness, with which he can succour all who are his. The sum is, that there is no other remedy for our afflictions but to humble ourselves under God's hand, and to found our salvation on his mercy alone; and that those who rely on God shall be blessed in all respects, because, on whatever side Satan may assault them, there will the Lord oppose him, and shield them with his protecting power.

11. *Be glad in Jehovah.* After teaching how ready and accessible true happiness is to all the godly, David, with much reason, exhorts them to gladness. He commands them to rejoice in the Lord, as if he had said, There is nothing to prevent them from assuring themselves of God's favour, seeing he so liberally and so kindly offers to be reconciled to them. In the meantime, we may observe that this is the incomparable fruit of faith which Paul likewise commends, namely, when the consciences of the godly being quiet and cheerful, enjoy peace and spiritual joy. Wherever faith is lively, this holy rejoicing will follow. But since the world's own impiety prevents it from participating in this joy, David, therefore, addresses the righteous alone, whom he denominates *the upright in heart,* to teach us that the external appearance of righteousness which pleases men is of no avail in the sight of God. But how does he call those righteous, whose whole happiness consists in the free mercy of God not imputing their sins to them? I answer, that none others are received into favour but those who are dissatisfied with themselves for their sins, and repent with their whole heart; not that this repentance merits pardon, but because faith can never be separated from the spirit of regeneration. When they have begun to devote themselves to God, he accepts the upright disposition of their

hearts equally as if it were pure and perfect; for faith not only reconciles a man to God, but also sanctifies whatever is imperfect in him, so that by the free grace of God, he becomes righteous who could never have obtained so great a blessing by any merit of his own.

PSALM XXXIII.

David, or whoever was the author of this psalm, in order to excite believers to praise God, founds his argument upon the general providence of God, by which he sustains, protects, and governs the whole world. Afterwards he celebrates God's paternal kindness towards his chosen people, showing at the same time how necessary it is that the godly should be cherished by his special care.

1. *Rejoice in Jehovah, ye righteous; praise is comely*[1] *for the upright.*
2. *Praise Jehovah upon the harp; sing unto him upon the viol, and an instrument of ten strings.*
3. *Sing a new song to him; sing loudly with joyfulness:*
4. *For the word of Jehovah is right; and all his works are in faithfulness.*[2]

1. *Rejoice in Jehovah, ye righteous.* Here the inspired writer addresses believers or the righteous by name, because they alone are capable of proclaiming the glory of God. Unbelievers, who have never tasted his goodness, cannot praise him from the heart, and God has no pleasure in his name being pronounced by their unholy tongues. But the context shows more distinctly why this exhortation is suitable for believers only. Many, accordingly, expound the latter clause, *Praise is comely for the upright,* as meaning, that if the ungodly or hypocrites attempt this exercise, it will turn to the reproach and dishonour of God rather than to his praise; nay, more,

---

[1] " Ou, digne d'estre aimee par les," &c.—*Fr. marg.* " Or, is worthy of being loved by them."
[2] " Fideles, c'est, fermes et permanentes."—*Fr. marg.* " Faithful, that is, firm and permanent."

that they only profane his holy name. It is, no doubt, very true, as I have already remarked, that God creates for himself a church in the world by gracious adoption, for the express purpose, that his name may be duly praised by witnesses suitable for such a work. But the real meaning of the clause, *Praise is comely for the upright,* is, that there is no exercise in which they can be better employed. And, assuredly, since God by his daily benefits furnishes them with such matter for celebrating his glory, and since his boundless goodness, as we have elsewhere seen, is laid up as a peculiar treasure for them, it were disgraceful and utterly unreasonable for them to be silent in the praises of God. The amount of the matter is, that the principal exercise in which it becomes the righteous to be employed is to publish among men the righteousness, goodness, and power of God, the knowledge of which is implanted in their minds. Following other interpreters, I have translated the clause, *Praise is comely,* but the word rendered *comely* may also be properly rendered *desirable,* if we view it as derived from the Hebrew word אוה, *avah,* which signifies to *wish* or *desire.* And certainly, when God allures believers so sweetly, it is proper that they employ themselves in celebrating his praises with their whole hearts. It is also to be observed, that when the prophet, after having in the first clause used the appellation, *the righteous,* immediately adds the words, *the upright,* which comprehend the inward integrity of the heart, he defines what true righteousness is, or in what it consists.

2. *Praise Jehovah upon the harp.* It is evident that the Psalmist here expresses the vehement and ardent affection which the faithful ought to have in praising God, when he enjoins musical instruments to be employed for this purpose. He would have nothing omitted by believers which tends to animate the minds and feelings of men in singing God's praises. The name of God, no doubt, can, properly speaking, be celebrated only by the articulate voice; but it is not without reason that David adds to this those aids by which believers were wont to stimulate themselves the more to this exercise; especially considering that he was speaking to God's ancient people. There is a distinction, however, to be observed

here, that we may not indiscriminately consider as applicable to ourselves, every thing which was formerly enjoined upon the Jews. I have no doubt that playing upon cymbals, touching the harp and the viol, and all that kind of music, which is so frequently mentioned in the Psalms, was a part of the education; that is to say, the puerile instruction of the law: I speak of the stated service of the temple. For even now, if believers choose to cheer themselves with musical instruments, they should, I think, make it their object not to dissever their cheerfulness from the praises of God. But when they frequent their sacred assemblies, musical instruments in celebrating the praises of God would be no more suitable than the burning of incense, the lighting up of lamps, and the restoration of the other shadows of the law. The Papists, therefore, have foolishly borrowed this, as well as many other things, from the Jews. Men who are fond of outward pomp may delight in that noise; but the simplicity which God recommends to us by the apostle is far more pleasing to him. Paul allows us to bless God in the public assembly of the saints only in a known tongue, (1 Cor. xiv. 16.) The voice of man, although not understood by the generality, assuredly excels all inanimate instruments of music; and yet we see what St Paul determines concerning speaking in an unknown tongue.[1] What shall we then say of chanting, which fills the ears with nothing but an empty sound? Does any one object, that music is very useful for awakening the minds of men and moving their hearts? I own it; but we should always take care that no corruption creep in, which might both defile the pure worship of God and involve men in superstition. Moreover, since the Holy Spirit expressly warns us of this danger by the mouth of Paul, to proceed beyond what we are there warranted by him is not only, I must say, unadvised zeal, but wicked and perverse obstinacy.

3. *Sing unto him a new song.* As the Psalmist afterwards treats of the mighty works of God, and particularly concerning the preservation of the Church, it is not wonderful that he exhorts the righteous to sing a new, that is, a rare and

---

[1] "Et neant moins nous voyons ce que Sainct Paul en determine."—*Fr.*

choice song. The more closely and diligently that believers consider the works of God, the more will they exert themselves in his praises. It is no common song, therefore, which he exhorts them to sing, but a song corresponding to the magnificence of the subject. This is also the meaning of the second clause, in which he urges them *to sing loudly.* In this sense, I understand the Hebrew word היטיב, *heytib*, although others refer it rather to the proper setting of the notes.

4. *For the word of Jehovah is right.* As I have just remarked, the Psalmist first sets forth God's general providence by which he governs the whole world; and he tells us that he so exerts his power in the whole course of his operations, that the most perfect equity and faithfulness shine forth everywhere. Some will have the terms *word* and *work* to be synonymous; but I think there is a distinction, and that *word* means the same thing as *counsel* or *ordinance,* while *work* signifies the effect or execution of his counsel. I grant that here the same subject is repeated in different words, as is the case in other places; but a slight variation will be found in such repetitions, that the same thing may be expressed in various ways. The amount of what is stated is, that whatever God appoints and commands is right; and whatever he brings to pass in actual operation is faithful and true. Meanwhile, it ought to be observed, that the term *word* is not to be understood of doctrine, but of the method by which God governs the world.

5. *He loveth righteousness and judgment : the earth is full of the goodness of Jehovah.*
6. *By the word of Jehovah were the heavens established ; and all the host of them by the spirit* [1] *of his mouth.*
7. *He gathered together the waters of the sea as into a heap; he hath laid up the deeps in treasures.*
8. *Let all the earth fear Jehovah; let the inhabitants of the world stand in awe of him:*
9. *For he spake, and it was ; he commanded, and it stood.*

5. *He loveth righteousness and judgment.* This is a confir-

---

[1] " C'est, le soufle, le vent."—*Note, Fr. marg.* " That is, the breath."

mation of the preceding verse, and intimates to us that God of his own nature loves righteousness and equity. It therefore follows, that froward affections cannot hurry him, after the manner of men, to evil devices. At first sight, indeed, this appears but a common commendation of God, and of small importance, because all confess that he observes the most perfect rule of righteousness in all his works. Why then, may some one say, has a new song just been spoken of, as if it had been about some unusual matter? We answer, in the first place, because it is too obvious how wickedly a great part of the world shut their eyes to God's righteousness, while they either carelessly overlook innumerable proofs of his providence, or imagine that they happen by chance. But there is often a worse fault than this; namely, that if our wishes are not gratified, we instantly murmur against God's righteousness; and although the maxim, "God doeth all things righteously," is in every man's mouth, yet scarcely one in a hundred firmly believes it in his heart, otherwise, as soon as this truth is pronounced, "Thus it pleaseth God," every man would obediently submit himself to God's will. Now, as men in adversity are with the utmost difficulty brought to this point—to acknowledge that God is just, and as, in prosperity, they soon fall from the acknowledgment of it, it is not to be wondered at that the prophet, in order to persuade men that God is an upright governor, affirms that he loveth righteousness. Whoever, therefore, has thoroughly embraced this doctrine, let him know that he has profited much.

Others explain this to mean, that God loveth righteousness in men. This, indeed, is true; but it is far from the sense of the text, because the design of the Holy Spirit here is to maintain the glory of God in opposition to the poison of ungodliness, which is deeply seated in many hearts. In the second clause of the verse, the Psalmist commends another part of God's excellence, namely, that *the earth is full of his goodness.* The righteousness of God ought justly to incite us to praise him, but his goodness is a more powerful motive; because, the more experience which any man has of his beneficence and mercy, the more strongly is he influenced to worship him.

Farther, the discourse is still concerning all the benefits of God which he scatters over the whole human race. These, the inspired writer declares, meet us wherever we turn our eyes.

6. *By the word of Jehovah.* That he may stir us up to think more closely of God's works, he brings before us the creation of the world itself; for until God be acknowledged as the Creator and Framer of the world, who will believe that he attends to the affairs of men, and that the state of the world is controlled by his wisdom and power? But the creation of the world leads us by direct consequence to the providence of God. Not that all men reason so justly, or are endued with so sound a judgment, as to conclude that the world is at this day maintained by the same divine power which was once put forth in creating it: on the contrary, the great majority imagine that he is an idle spectator in heaven of whatever is transacted on earth. But no man truly believes that the world was created by God unless he is also firmly persuaded that it is maintained and preserved by him. Wisely and properly, therefore, does the prophet carry us back to the very origin of the world, in order to fix in our minds the certainty of God's providence in the continual order of nature. By the figure synecdoche, he uses the term *heavens* for the whole fabric of the world, because, as I have elsewhere remarked, the sight of the heavens more than all the other parts of creation transports us with admiration. He therefore immediately adds, *And all the host of them,* by which phraseology, according to the usual method of Scripture, he means the stars and planets; for if the heavens were destitute of this ornament, they would in a manner be empty. In saying that the heavens were created by *the word of God,* he greatly magnifies his power, because by his nod alone,[1] without any other aid or means, and without much time or labour,[2] he created so noble and magnificent a work. But

---

[1] "Par son simple vouloir et commandement."—*Fr.* "Simply by his will and commandment."

[2] "Sans aussi y employer beaucoup de temps ou travail."—*Fr.*

although the Psalmist sets *the word of God* and *the breath of his mouth* in opposition both to all external means, and to every idea of painful labour on God's part, yet we may truly and certainly infer from this passage, that the world was framed by God's Eternal Word, his only begotten Son. Ancient interpreters have, with considerable ingenuity, employed this passage as a proof of the eternal Deity of the Holy Spirit against the Sabellians. But it appears from other places, particularly from Isaiah xi. 4, that by *the breath of the mouth* is meant nothing else but *speech*. For it is there said concerning Christ, "He shall smite the earth with the rod of his mouth, and with the breath of his lips shall he slay the wicked." As powerful and effective speech is there allegorically denominated *the rod of his mouth;* so in like manner, for another purpose it is denominated in the immediately succeeding clause *the breath of his mouth*, to mark the difference that exists between God's speech and the empty sounds which proceed from the mouths of men. In proving the Divinity of the Holy Spirit, therefore, I durst not press this text against Sabellius. Let us account it sufficient that God has formed the heavens by his Word in such a manner as to prove the eternal Deity of Christ. Should any object that these divine persons would not appear distinct if the terms *Word* and *Breath* are synonymous; I answer, that the term *breath* is not employed here simply as in other places, in which there is evidently a distinction made between the *Word* and the *Spirit ;* but *the breath of his mouth* is used figuratively for the very utterance of speech; as if it had been said, As soon as God uttered the breath of his mouth, or proclaimed in word what he wished to be done, the heavens were instantly brought into existence, and were furnished, too, with an inconceivable number and variety of stars. It is indeed true that this similitude is borrowed from men; but the Scriptures often teach in other places, that the world was created by that Eternal Word, who, being the only begotten Son of God, appeared afterwards in flesh.

7. *He gathered together the waters of the sea as into a*

heap.[1] Here the Psalmist does not speak of all that might have been said of every part of the world, but under one department he comprehends all the rest. He celebrates, however, a signal and remarkable miracle which we see in looking on the surface of the earth; namely, that God gathers together the element of water, fluid and unstable as it is, into a solid heap, and holds it so at his pleasure. Natural philosophers confess, and experience openly proclaims, that the waters occupy a higher place than the earth. How is it then that, as they are fluid and naturally disposed to flow, they do not spread abroad and cover the earth, and how is it that the earth, which is lower in position, remains dry? In this we certainly perceive that God, who is ever attentive to the welfare of the human race, has inclosed the waters within certain invisible barriers, and keeps them shut up to this day; and the prophet elegantly declares that they stand still at God's commandment, as if they were a heap of firm and solid matter. Nor is it without design that the Holy Spirit, in various passages, adduces this proof of divine power, as in Jer. v. 22, and Job xxxviii. 8.

In the second part of the verse, he seems to repeat the same idea, but with amplification. God not only confines the immense mass of waters in the seas, but also hides them, by a mysterious and incomprehensible power, in the very bowels of the earth. Whoever will compare the elements among themselves, will reckon it contrary to nature that the bottomless depths, or the immeasurable gulfs of waters, whose native tendency is rather to overwhelm the earth, should lie hid under it. That so many hollow channels and gulfs, accordingly, should not swallow up the earth every moment, affords another magnificent display of divine power; for although now and then some cities and fields are engulfed, yet the body of the earth is preserved in its place.

[1] In Genesis i. 9 we read, "God said, Let the waters under the heavens be gathered together into one place, and let the dry land appear: and it was so." The Psalmist here probably has a reference to that passage, as in the 9th verse there is evidently an imitation of the style in which God is described in the first chapter of Genesis as performing the work of creation.

8. *Let all the earth fear Jehovah.* The Psalmist concludes that there is just reason why the whole world should reverently submit itself to the government of God, who gave it being, and who also preserves it. *To fear Jehovah, and to stand in awe of him,* just means to do honour to, and to reverence his mighty power. It is a mark of great insensibility not to bow at God's presence, from whom we have our being, and upon whom our condition depends. The prophet alludes to both these things, affirming that the world appeared as soon as God spake, and that it is upheld in being by his commandment; for it would not have been enough for the world to have been created in a moment, if it had not been supported in existence by the power of God. He did not employ a great array of means in creating the world, but to prove the inconceivable power of his word, he ordered that so soon as he should as it were pronounce the word, the thing should be done.[1] The word *command,* therefore, confirms what I formerly said, that his speech was nothing else than a nod, or wish, and that *to speak* implies the same thing as to command. It is proper, however, to understand that in this nod, or command, the eternal wisdom of God displayed itself.

10. *Jehovah scattereth the counsel of the nations, and bringeth to nought the imaginations of the people.*[2]
11. *The counsel of Jehovah shall stand for ever, and the thoughts of his heart from age to age.*[3]
12. *Blessed are the people whose God is Jehovah, the people whom he hath chosen for his inheritance.*

10. *Jehovah scattereth the counsel of the nations.* After briefly touching upon the creation of the world, the Psalmist returns to his former subject, namely, to show that the events

[1] "Il a commandé que si tost qu'il auroit comme prononcé le mot, la chose aussi se trouvast faire."—*Fr.*

[2] The Septuagint here adds a sentence which is not in the Hebrew, namely, "Καὶ ἀθετεῖ βουλὰς ἀρχόντων,"—" And frustrates the counsels of princes." The Vulgate, Arabic, and Æthiopic, copying from the Septuagint, have the same addition. But it is not in the Chaldee and Syriac versions, which agree with our Hebrew Bibles; and from this we are led to conclude that the translators of the Greek version have added this by way of paraphrase; a liberty which we find them using in other places.

[3] Heb. *To generation and generation.*

which daily come to pass are undoubted proofs of the providence of God. And lest any man should be surprised, that he should exhibit God as an adversary to men, scattering their counsels rather than establishing and bringing them to a happy issue, he selects an instance which had the greatest power to comfort the saints. We know how many things men continually venture upon and contrive against all law and justice, and how they endeavour by their devices to turn the world upside down, that they may tyrannically acquire power to trample upon the good and simple. What creatures then would be more miserable than we, if men, possessed of such a variety of wicked affections, were permitted to act with unlicensed wantonness towards us? But when God declares from heaven to us, that it is his work to dash in pieces their devices, and to bring their determinations to nought, there is no reason why we should not keep ourselves quiet, even when they bestir themselves most tumultuously. God is, therefore, said to overthrow the counsels of men, not because he professedly delights in frustrating them, but to check their wantonness; for they would immediately throw all things into confusion were they to succeed according to their wishes: yea, as in outraging equity, and vexing the upright and innocent, they fail not to fight against God himself, it is very necessary to consider that God's power and protection is set in opposition to their fury. And as the great majority of men, despising all modesty, rush headlong into indiscriminate licentiousness, the prophet speaks not only of individual men, but of whole nations; in other words, he affirms, that however men may conspire among themselves, and determine to attempt this or that with great hosts, yet shall their purposes be brought to nought, because it is as easy for God to scatter multitudes as to restrain a few. But although it is God's design in this place to fortify us with good hope against the boldness of the wicked, he warns us, at the same time, to undertake nothing without his command and guidance.

11. *The counsel of Jehovah.* The prophet extols the infinite power of God in such a manner as that he may build up our faith in its greatness; for he does not here commend

a counsel of God which is hidden in heaven, and which he would have us to honour and revere at a distance. But as the Lord everywhere in Scripture testifies that he loveth righteousness and truth; that he cares for the righteous and good; and that he is ever inclined to succour his servants when they are wrongfully oppressed;—the prophet means, that all this shall remain sure and stedfast. Thus he declares for what end God bringeth to nought the counsels of the nations, namely, because without discrimination they run headlong into the violation of all order.

In the first place, then, let us learn to look at God's counsel in the glass of his word; and when we have satisfied ourselves that he has promised nothing but what he has determined to perform, let us immediately call to mind the stedfastness of which the prophet here speaks. And as many, or rather whole, nations sometimes endeavour to impede its course by innumerable hinderances, let us also remember the preceding declaration, that when men have imagined many devices, it is in God's power, and often his pleasure, to bring them to nought. The Holy Spirit unquestionably intended to have our faith exercised in this practical knowledge; otherwise what he here says of the counsel of God would be but cold and fruitless. But when we shall have once persuaded ourselves of this, that God will defend his servants who call upon his name, and rid them of all dangers; whatever mischief the wicked may practise against them, their endeavours and attempts shall in nowise terrify us, because, so soon as God sets himself in opposition to their machinations, no craft on their part will be able to defeat his counsel.

12. *Blessed are the people whose God is Jehovah.* This verse excellently agrees with the preceding, because it would profit us little to observe what is said of the stability of God's counsel if that counsel referred not to us. The prophet, therefore, in proclaiming that they are blessed whom God receives into his protection, reminds us that the counsel which he had just mentioned is not a secret which remains always hidden in God, but is displayed in the existence and protection of the Church, and may there be beheld. Thus we see,

that it is not those who coldly speculate about the power of God, but those alone who apply it to their own present benefit, who rightly acknowledge God as the Governor of the world. Moreover, when the Psalmist places all our blessedness in this, that *Jehovah is our God,* in touching upon the fountain of divine love towards us, he comprehends, in one word, whatever is wont to be desired to make life happy. For when God condescends to undertake the care of our salvation, to cherish us under his wings, to provide for our necessities, to aid us in all our dangers, all this depends on our adoption by him. But lest it should be thought that men obtain so great a good by their own efforts and industry, David teaches us expressly that it proceeds from the fountain of God's gracious electing love that we are accounted the people of God. It is indeed true, that, in the person of Adam, men were created at first for the very purpose that they should be the sons of God; but the estrangement which followed upon sin deprived us of that great blessing. Until God, therefore, freely adopt us, we are all by nature wretched, and we have no other entrance to or means of attaining happiness but this, that God, of his own good pleasure, should choose us who are altogether unworthy. It appears, accordingly, how foolishly they corrupt this passage, who transfer to men what the prophet here ascribes to God, as if men would choose God for their inheritance. I own, indeed, that it is by faith that we distinguish the true God from idols; but this principle is always to be held fast, that we have no interest in him at all unless he prevent us by his grace.

13. *Jehovah looked down from heaven; he beheld the children of Adam.*
14. *From the dwelling-place of his throne he looked on all the inhabitants of the earth.*
15. *He who fashioned their hearts altogether,*[1] *who understandeth all their works.*
16. *A king is not saved for the multitude of his host, nor a giant delivered for the greatness of his strength.*

[1] " C'est, sans en excepter un."—*Note, Fr. marg.* " That is, without a single exception."

17. *A horse is a deceitful thing for safety,*[1] *and will not deliver by the greatness of his strength.*

13. *Jehovah looked down from heaven.* The Psalmist still proceeds with the same doctrine, namely, that human affairs are not tossed hither and thither fortuitously, but that God secretly guides and directs all that we see taking place. Now he here commends God's inspection of all things, that we on our part may learn to behold, and to contemplate with the eye of faith, his invisible providence. There are, no doubt, evident proofs of it continually before our eyes; but the great majority of men, notwithstanding, see nothing of them, and, in their blindness, imagine that all things are under the conduct of a blind fortune. Nay, the more plenteously and abundantly that he sheds his goodness upon us, the less do we raise our thoughts to him, but preposterously settle them down immoveably on the external circumstances which surround us. The prophet here rebukes this base conduct, because no greater affront can be offered to God than to shut him up in heaven in a state of idleness. This is the same as if he were to lie buried in a grave. What kind of life would God's life be, if he neither saw nor took care of any thing? Under the term *throne*, too, the sacred writer shows, from what is implied in it, what an absurd infatuation it is to divest God of thought and understanding. He gives us to understand by this word, that heaven is not a palace in which God remains idle and indulges in pleasures, as the Epicureans dream, but a royal court, from which he exercises his government over all parts of the world. If he has erected his throne, therefore, in the sanctuary of heaven, in order to govern the universe, it follows that he in no wise neglects the affairs of earth, but governs them with the highest reason and wisdom.

15. *He who fashioned their hearts altogether.* It appears that this is added for the express purpose of assuredly persuading believers, that, however the wicked might craftily, deceitfully, and by secret stratagems, attempt to withdraw

---

[1] " Heb. est mensonge à salut."—*Fr. marg.* " Heb. is a lie for safety."

themselves from God's sight, and hide themselves in caverns, yet his eyes would penetrate into their dark hiding-places. And the Psalmist argues from the very creation that God cannot but bring men's devices and doings into reckoning and judgment; because, though each man has intricate recesses concealed in his bosom, so that there is a wonderful diversity of different minds in this respect, and this great variety creates a most confounding obscurity; yet the eyes of God cannot be dazzled and darkened, so that he may not be a competent judge and take cognizance of his own work. By the adverb *together,* therefore, he does not mean that the hearts of men were formed at the same moment of time; but that all of them were fashioned even to one, and without a single exception; so that those manifest great folly who attempt to hide, or to withdraw the knowledge of their hearts from him who framed them. The discourse may also be understood as meaning, that men cannot, by the erring devices of their own thoughts, diminish the authority of God over them, so that he may not govern by his secret providence the events which seem to them to happen by chance. We see, indeed, how, in forming their vain hopes, they despoil God of his power, and transfer it to the creatures, at one time to this object, and at another time to that, conceiving that they have no need of his aid, so long as they are furnished with outward means and helps to protect themselves.

It therefore follows, *A king is not saved for the multitude of his host, &c.* By this the inspired writer means to teach us, that the safety of men's lives depends not upon their own strength, but upon the favour of God. He names particularly *kings* and *giants* rather than others; because, as they are not of the common class of men, but of a higher condition, they appear to themselves to be beyond the reach of all danger from darts, and if any adversity befall them, they promise themselves an easy deliverance from it. In short, intoxicated with a presumptuous confidence of their own strength, they scarcely think themselves mortal. They are still more hardened in this pride by the foolish admiration of the common people, who stand amazed at the greatness of their power. If, therefore, neither a king is saved by his troops, nor a giant by his strength, when they are exposed to danger, in vain do mankind neglect the providence of God, and look around them for human help. From this it follows, that the condition, both of the strong and the weak, is miserable, until they learn to rely on the protection of God.

17. *A horse is a deceitful thing for safety.* In this verse, the Psalmist, by the figure synecdoche under the name of *horse,* is to be understood as meaning any kind of help. The sense is, that in general those who conceive that their life is well protected by earthly means, are commonly disappointed at the very crisis of danger, and are miserably beguiled to their utter undoing, so that God therein clearly shows them their folly. It is true, that kings are not armed with the sword in vain, nor is the use of horses superfluous, nor are the treasures and resources which God furnishes to defend men's lives unnecessary, provided a right method of employing them be observed. But as the greater part of men the more they are surrounded with human defences, withdraw themselves the farther from God, and by a false imagination persuade themselves that they are in a haven safe from all disturbance, God acts most justly in disappointing this madness. This is the reason why his gifts often pass away without effect, because the world, by separating them from the giver, is also justly deprived of his blessing.

18. *Behold, the eye of Jehovah is upon them that fear him, upon those who hope in his mercy;*
19. *To deliver their souls from death, and to give them life in the time of famine.*

18. *Behold, the eye of Jehovah is upon them that fear him.* Having shown that what men account their best defences often profit them nothing, or rather are utterly worthless, when men depend upon them; the Psalmist now shows, on the other hand, that believers, although they are neither men of great power nor of great wealth, are nevertheless sufficiently protected by God's favour alone, and shall be safe for ever. His meaning is not a little illustrated by this comparison, that kings and giants derive no aid from their

invincible strength, while God supports the life of the saints in famine and dearth, as really as if he were to restore life to them when dead. We consequently understand better why the prophet lays low all the strength of the world; not, surely, that men should lie prostrate, or be so heart-broken as to pine away in despair; but that, laying aside their pride, they should fix their thoughts on God alone, and persuade themselves that their life depends on his protection. Moreover, in saying that the eye of God is bent upon them that fear him to save them, he expresses more than if he had said that his hand and power were sufficient to preserve them. A doubt might creep into the minds of the weak, whether God would extend this protection to every individual; but when the Psalmist introduces him as keeping watch and ward, as it were, over the safety of the faithful, there is no reason why any one of them should tremble, or hesitate with himself a moment longer, since it is certain that God is present with him to assist him, provided he remain quietly under his providence. From this, also, it appears still more clearly how truly he had said a little before, that *the people are blessed whose God is Jehovah,* because, without him, all the strength and riches which we may possess will be vain, deceitful, and perishing; whereas, with a single look he can defend his people, supply their wants, feed them in a time of famine, and preserve them alive when they are appointed to death. The whole human race, no doubt, are maintained by the providence of God; but we know that his fatherly care is specially vouchsafed to none but his own children, that they may feel that their necessities are truly regarded by him.

Again, when it is affirmed, that God, in times of famine and dearth, has remedies in readiness to preserve the lives of the godly, we are taught that the faithful only pay due honour to his providence when they allow not their hearts to despond in the extremest indigence; but, on the contrary, raise their hopes even from the grave. God often suffers his servants to be hungry for a time that he may afterwards satiate them, and he overspreads them with the darkness of death that he may afterwards restore them to the light of life. Yea, we only begin to place our trust firmly in him when death comes to present itself before our eyes; for, until we have known by experience the vanity of the aids of the world, our affections continue entangled in them, and wedded to them. The Psalmist characterises believers by two marks, which comprehend the whole perfection of our life. The first is, that we reverently serve the Lord; and the second, that we depend upon his grace. Hypocrites may loudly boast of their faith, but they have never tasted even a little of the divine goodness, so as to be induced to look to him for what they need. On the contrary, when the faithful give themselves with their whole heart to the service and fear of God, this affection springs from faith; or rather the principal part of right worship, which the faithful render to God, consists in this, that they depend upon his mercy.

20. *Our soul waiteth upon Jehovah, he is our help and our shield.*
21. *Surely our heart shall rejoice in him, because*[1] *we will trust in his holy name.*
22. *Let thy mercy be upon us, O Jehovah! according as we have trusted in thee.*

20. *Our soul waiteth upon Jehovah.* What the Psalmist has hitherto spoken concerning God's providence, and particularly concerning that faithful guardianship by which he protects his people, he has spoken not so much from himself as from the mouth of the Holy Spirit. He now, therefore, in the name of the whole Church, raises his song to declare that there is nothing better than to commit our welfare to God. Thus we see that the fruit of the preceding doctrine is set forth to all true believers, that they may unhesitatingly cast themselves with confidence, and with a cheerful heart, upon the paternal care of God. In this matter, the Psalmist declares nothing concerning himself in particular, but unites the whole of the godly with him in the acknowledgment of the same faith. There is an emphasis in the word *soul* which should be attended to; for, although this is a common mode of speech among the Hebrews, yet it expresses earnest affec-

---

[1] " Ou, certes."—*Fr. marg.* " Or, certainly."

tion; as if believers should say, We sincerely rely upon God with our whole heart, accounting him our shield and help.

21. *Surely our heart shall rejoice in him.* As the particle כִּי, *ki*, which is twice employed in this verse, has various meanings in Hebrew, it may be understood in a twofold sense here. If we expound it affirmatively in both clauses, the sense will be, that believers glory both in their joy and in their hope. Nor do I think it improper that these two should be referred to distinctly in the same context thus: Surely God shall always be our joy; surely his holy name shall be like an impregnable fortress for our refuge. Whence is it that believers continue perseveringly to call upon God, but because, satisfied with his favour, they have always, amidst their sorrows and griefs, this comfort, which is sufficient to maintain their cheerfulness? Justly, therefore, do believers affirm, in the first place, that their heart rejoices in the Lord; because, freed from wandering after the fascinations of the world, they neither waver nor hesitate at every change of fortune, but place the whole felicity of their life in enjoying the free and paternal favour of God. They afterwards add, in the second place, that *they trust in his holy name.* If any one, however, choose to understand the particle כִּי, *ki*, as meaning *because*, assigning a cause or reason, the sense will be no less properly and elegantly expressed in this way: Because our hope is fixed on God, he will be equally ready on his part to minister to us continual matter of joy. And experience undoubtedly proves, that when men are overwhelmed with sorrow, and pine away with care, grief, and anxiety, it is that they may receive the recompense of their folly; seeing that there is nothing to which they are led with more difficulty, than to set their hopes on God alone, and not to exult in their own deceitful imaginations, with which they please themselves.

22. *Let thy mercy be on us, O Jehovah!* At length the psalm concludes with a prayer, which the sacred writer offers in the name of all the godly, that God would make them feel from the effect that they have not relied on the divine good-

ness in vain. In the meantime, the Spirit, by dictating to us this rule of prayer by the mouth of the prophet, teaches us, that the gate of divine grace is opened for us when salvation is neither sought nor hoped for from any other quarter. This passage gives us another very sweet consolation, namely, that if our hope faint not in the midst of our course, we have no reason to fear that God will fail to continue his mercy towards us, without intermission, to the end of it.

PSALM XXXIV.

¶ A Psalm of David, when he changed his countenance before Abimelech, who banished him from his presence, and he departed from him.

David gives thanks to God for a signal deliverance, and takes occasion from it to celebrate his perpetual grace towards all the saints, and to exhort them both to trust in him, and to the study of godliness; affirming, that the only way to pass through life happily, is to walk holily and harmlessly in the world, in the service and fear of God. It is obvious from the title what particular instance of God's favour he here celebrates. When he was driven to King Achish, as recorded in 1 Sam. xxvii. 2,[1] whom, with the exception of Saul, he accounted the deadliest of all his enemies, it was not probable that he would ever be able to make his escape from him. The only means, therefore, he had of saving his life was to feign himself mad by frothing at the mouth, looking fiercely, and disfiguring his countenance. Nor is this to be wondered at; for Achish, being disappointed of the confident hope of victory which he had, and attributing to David alone both the loss which he had sustained and the dishonour which he had received, burned with implacable hatred against him. In allowing him to escape, therefore, contrary to his own expectation, and the expectation of all other men, David acknowledges that there had been exhibited a memorable instance of God's favour towards him, which may be serviceable for the general instruction of the whole Church. Instead of Achish,[2] Abimelech is here employed; and it is probable that the latter name had been the common

---

[1] It should be 1 Sam. xxi. 11, 12.
[2] Achish may have been his particular name, while Abimelech was the common title of the Kings of Gath. The word *Abimelech* signifies *Father—King.*

designation of the monarchs of the Philistines, as Pharaoh was the common name of the monarchs of Egypt, and Cæsar that of the Roman Emperors, which was borrowed from the name of Julius Cæsar, who had first seized the imperial power among the Romans. We know that many ages before David was born, the kings who reigned in Gerar in the time of Abraham were called Abimelech. It is not, therefore, to be wondered at, that this name should be handed down from age to age among their posterity, and become the common name of all the kings of Palestine. The Hebrew word טעם, taäm, which I have translated *countenance*, signifies also *tasting, understanding*,[1] and therefore might be pertinently interpreted in this manner, that he appeared foolish and without taste. The verb from which it is derived properly signifies *to taste*, and therefore is often transferred to reason, understanding, and all the senses. Accordingly, David having feigned himself mad, the term *understanding* is very appropriate. Now, although he escaped by this subtle device, he doubts not that he was delivered by the hand of God; nor does he ascribe the praise of his safety to the pretence of madness, but rather acknowledges that the cruelty of his enemy had been softened by the secret influence of God, so that he who formerly burned with rage against him had been pacified by an artifice. Certainly it was not to be expected that Achish would have driven away in contempt from him so brave a man, whom he had found a dangerous enemy to his whole kingdom, and from whom he had suffered such severe losses. This gives rise to the question, Whether David feigned himself mad under the guidance of the Holy Spirit? For by his appearing to connect together these two things,—the pretence of madness and the happy result of this pretence, it might be inferred that the same Spirit by whom this psalm was dictated suggested this stratagem[2] to the mind of David, and directed him in deceiving King Achish. I answer, that although God sometimes delivers his people, while at the same time they err in choosing the means, or even fall into sin in adopting them, yet there is nothing inconsistent in this. The deliverance, therefore, was the work of God, but the intermediate sin, which is on no account to be excused, ought to be ascribed to David. In this way Jacob obtained the blessing by the favour and good pleasure of God; and yet the subtlety of the mother, with which the obtaining of it was mixed up, was, we know, sinful on her part. It may then sometimes happen that the event shall be brought to pass by the Spirit of God, and yet the saints whom he may employ as instruments shall swerve from the path of duty. It would therefore be

---

[1] Ainsworth reads, *His behaviour*, or *his sense, reason;* and observes, that it is "properly *the taste*, as in verse 9, Job vi. 6, and often elsewhere, which is used both for one's inward sense or reason, and outward gesture and demeanour, (as the Gr. here translateth it, *face*,) because by it a man is discerned and judged to be wise or foolish, as meats are discerned by the taste."

[2] "Luy meit aussi au cœur ceste finesse."—*Fr.*

a superfluous task to endeavour to exculpate David, who is rather to be blamed, because, by not committing his life entirely to God, he exposed himself and the grace of the Spirit, by whom he was governed, to the derision of the ungodly. I would not positively assert it, but there appears in this deception some token of infirmity. If it should be said that David here magnifies the grace of God, because by changing his countenance and his speech he escaped death, I again reply, that David expressly mentions this circumstance, in order to render the grace of God still more illustrious, in that his fault was not laid to his charge.

1. *I will bless Jehovah at all times: his praise shall always be in my mouth.*
2. *My soul shall make her boast in Jehovah: the humble shall hear of it, and be glad.*
3. *Magnify Jehovah with me, and let us exalt his name together.*
4. *I sought Jehovah, and he answered me, and delivered me from all my fears.*
5. *They shall look to him, and shall flow to him; and their faces shall not be ashamed.*
6. *This poor man cried, and Jehovah heard him, and delivered him from all his troubles.*

1. *I will bless Jehovah at all times.*[1] David here extols the greatness of God, promising to keep in remembrance during his whole life the goodness which he had bestowed upon him. God assists his people daily, that they may continually employ themselves in praising him; yet it is certain that the blessing which is said to be worthy of everlasting remembrance is distinguished by this mark from other benefits which are ordinary and common. This, therefore, is a rule which should be observed by the saints—they should often call into remembrance whatever good has been bestowed upon them by God; but if at any time he should display his power more illustriously in preserving them from some danger, so much the more does it become them earnestly to testify their gratitude. Now if by one benefit alone God lays us under obligation to himself all our life, so that we may never lawfully cease from setting forth his praises, how much more

---

[1] "That is, in all circumstances; in every posture of my affairs."—*Horsley.*

when he heaps upon us innumerable benefits?[1] In order to distinguish the praise which he had before said would be continually in his mouth from the empty sound of the tongue, in which many hypocrites boast, he adds, in the beginning of the second verse, that it would proceed from the heart.

2. *My soul shall make her boast in Jehovah.* The term *soul* in this place signifies not the vital spirit, but the seat of the affections; as if David had said, I shall always have ground of boasting with my whole heart in God alone, so that I shall never suffer myself to fall into forgetfulness of so great a deliverance. In the second clause he specifies this as the fruit of his thanksgiving, that the afflicted and miserable shall derive from it ground of hope. The Hebrew word עֲנָוִים, *anavim*, which we have rendered *humble*, signifies not all the afflicted[2] in general, but those who, being humbled and subdued by afflictions, instead of breathing the spirit of pride, are cast down, and ready to abase themselves to the very dust. These, he says, shall be partakers of his joy; but not, as some have coldly explained it, simply from a feeling of sympathy, but because, being persuaded that in the example of David, God had given them a general testimony of his grace, their hearts would recover from sorrow, and would be lifted up on high. Accordingly, he says that this joy shall spring from hope, because, having received a pledge of their deliverance, they shall cheerfully have recourse to God.

3. *Magnify Jehovah with me.* The Psalmist shows still another fruit which would be the result of his giving thanks to God, namely, that he shall induce others by his example to the same exercise of devotion; nay more, he calls upon all the godly to unite with him in this exercise, inviting and exhorting them heartily and with one consent to extol the Lord. Let us therefore learn, from the many instances in

---

[1] "Quand il ne cesse de nous bien-faire?"—*Fr.* "When he never ceases from doing us good?"

[2] The word עֲנָוִים, *anavim*, may also be rendered *the afflicted.* Our author in his exposition combines both the ideas of *humble* and *afflicted.*

which God may have given helps to any of his people, to abound in hope; and when each recites the personal benefits which he has received, let all be animated unitedly and in a public manner to give praise to God. We give thanks publicly to God, not only that men may be witnesses of our gratitude, but also that they may follow our example.

4. *I sought Jehovah, and he answered me.* The Psalmist here explains more plainly and more fully what he had said concerning joy. In the first place, he tells us that his prayers had been heard. This he applies to all the godly, that, encouraged by a testimony so precious, they might stir themselves up to prayer. What is implied in *seeking God* is evident from the following clause. In some places it is to be understood in a different sense, namely, to bend the mind in earnest application to the service of God, and to have all its thoughts directed to him. Here it simply means to have recourse to him for help; for it immediately follows that God answered him; and he is properly said to answer prayer and supplication. By *his fears* the Psalmist means, taking the effect for the cause, the dangers which sorely disquieted his mind; yet doubtless he confesses that he had been terrified and agitated by fears. He did not look upon his dangers with a calm and untroubled mind, as if he viewed them at a distance and from some elevated position, but being grievously tormented with innumerable cares, he might justly speak of his fears and terrors. Nay more, by the use of the plural number, he shows that he had been greatly terrified not only in one way, but that he had been distracted by a variety of troubles. On the one hand, he saw a cruel death awaiting him; while on the other, his mind may have been filled with fear, lest Achish should send him to Saul for his gratification, as the ungodly are wont to make sport to themselves of the children of God. And since he had already been detected and betrayed once, he might well conclude, even if he should escape, that the hired assassins of Saul would lay wait for him on all sides. The hatred too which Achish had conceived against him, both for the death of Goliath and the destruction of his own

army, might give rise to many fears; especially considering that his enemy might instantly wreak his vengeance upon him, and that he had good reason to think that his cruelty was such as would not be appeased by subjecting him to some mild form of death.[1] We ought to mark this particularly, in order that, if at any time we are terrified because of the dangers which surround us, we may not be prevented by our effeminacy from calling upon God. Even David, who is known to have surpassed others in heroism and bravery, had not such a heart of iron as to repel all fears and alarms, but was sometimes greatly disquieted and smitten with fear.

5. *They shall look to him, and shall flow to him.* I have already intimated, that this verse and the following should be read in connection with the preceding verse. In relating his own experience, David has furnished an example to others, that they should freely and without fear approach God in order to present their prayers before him. Now, he says that they shall come, and this too with a happy issue. The first two verbs are expressed in the past time in the Hebrew; but I have, notwithstanding, no doubt that the sentence ought to be explained thus: When they shall have looked to him, and flowed to him, their faces shall not be ashamed. I have therefore translated them in the future tense. David is not relating things which had happened, but is commending the fruit of the favour which had been manifested to himself. Some interpreters, I know, refer the words *to him* to David,[2] because immediately after he speaks of himself in the third person. Others with greater propriety explain it of God himself. A difference of opinion also exists as to the Hebrew verb נָהֲרוּ, *naharu*, which some, supposing it to be derived from the root אוֹר, *or*, render *to be enlightened*.[3] But,

---

[1] " Et qu'il avoit bien occasion de penser que la cruaute d'iceluy ne se pourroit pas appaiser à le faire mourir de quelque legere mort."—*Fr.*

[2] Those who take this view explain the words as meaning that the humble or afflicted, upon looking to David, saw how graciously God had dealt with him, and were enlightened, revived, and encouraged. They also consider, as Calvin himself does, the humble or afflicted as the persons who speak in the sixth verse, where, pointing as it were with the finger to David, they say, " This poor man cried," &c.

[3] This is the rendering adopted by Horsley, who understands by the

in my opinion, the natural signification of the word appears very appropriate to this place; as if he had said, There shall now be a mirror set forth, in which men may behold the face of God serene and merciful; and therefore the poor and afflicted shall henceforth dare to lift up their eyes to God, and to resort to him with the utmost freedom, because no uncertainty shall any longer retard them or render them slothful. If, however, any one should prefer the word *enlighten*, the meaning will be, They who formerly languished in darkness shall lift up their eyes to God, as if a light had suddenly appeared unto them, and they who were cast down and overwhelmed with shame, shall again clothe their countenances with cheerfulness. But as the meaning in either case is substantially the same, I am not much disposed to contend which of the two interpretations ought to be preferred.

6. *This poor man cried, and Jehovah heard him.* David here introduces all the godly speaking of himself, the more emphatically to express how much weight there is in his example to encourage them. This poor man, say they, cried; therefore God invites all the poor to cry to him. They contemplate in David what belongs to the common benefit of all the godly; for God is as willing and ready at this day to hear all the afflicted who direct their sighs, wishes, and cries, to him with the same faith, as he was at that time to hear David.

expression the illumination of the soul by the light of Divine truth. He reads the verb in the imperative mood, and his translation of the entire verse is as follows :

" Look towards him, and thou shalt be enlightened;
And your faces shall never be ashamed."

This reading is sanctioned by the Septuagint. It supposes two alterations on the text. First, that instead of הִבִּיטוּ, *hibitu, they looked*, we should read הַבִּיטוּ, *habitu, look ye;* and this last reading is supported by several of Dr Kennicott's and De Rossi's MSS. The other alteration is, that instead of פְּנֵיהֶם, *upeneyhem, their faces*, we should read וּפְנֵיכֶם, *upeneykem, your faces*. Poole, in defence of reading *your* instead of *their*, observes, "that the change of persons is very frequent in this book."

7. *The angel of Jehovah encampeth*[1] *round about them that fear him, and will deliver them.*

8. *Taste and see that Jehovah is good: blessed is the man who trusteth in him.*

9. *Fear Jehovah, ye his saints, for there is no want to them that fear him.*

10. *The young lions are destitute and famished: but they who fear Jehovah shall not want any good thing.*

7. *The angel of Jehovah encampeth round about them that fear him.* David here discourses in general of God's fatherly favour towards all the godly; and as the life of man is exposed to innumerable dangers, he at the same time teaches us that God is able to deliver them. The faithful especially, who are as sheep in the midst of wolves, beset as it were with death in every form, are constantly harassed with the dread of some approaching danger. David therefore affirms, that the servants of God are protected and defended by angels. The design of the Psalmist is to show, that although the faithful are exposed to many dangers, yet they may rest assured that God will be the faithful guardian of their life. But in order to confirm them the more in this hope, he adds at the same time, and not without reason, that those whom God would preserve in safety he defends by the power and ministration of angels. The power of God alone would indeed be sufficient of itself to perform this; but in mercy to our infirmity he vouchsafes to employ angels as his ministers. It serves not a little for the confirmation of our faith to know that God has innumerable legions of angels who are always ready for his service as often as he is pleased to aid us; nay, more, that the angels too, who are called principalities and powers, are ever intent upon the preservation of our life, because they know that this duty is intrusted to them. God is indeed designated with propriety the wall of his Church, and every kind of fortress and place of defence[2] to

---

[1] This description seems to have been suggested by Jacob's vision of angels, recorded in Gen. xxxii. 1, 2, "And Jacob went on his way, and the *angels* of God met him. And when Jacob saw them he said, This is God's *host;* and he called the name of that place Mahanaim," (*i. e., encampments.*)

[2] "Toute sorte de forteresse et lieu de defense."—*Fr.*

her; but in accommodation to the measure and extent of our present imperfect state, he manifests the presence of his power to aid us through the instrumentality of his angels. Moreover, what the Psalmist here says of one angel in the singular number, ought to be applied to all the other angels: for they are distinguished by the general appellation of "ministering spirits, sent forth to minister to them who shall be the heirs of salvation," (Heb. i. 14;) and the Scriptures in other places teach us, that whenever it pleases God, and whenever he knows it to be for their benefit, many angels are appointed to take care of each of his people, (2 Kings vi. 15; Psalm xci. 11; Luke xvi. 22.) The amount then of what has been said is, that however great the number of our enemies and the dangers by which we are surrounded may be, yet the angels of God, armed with invincible power, constantly watch over us, and array themselves on every side to aid and deliver us from all evil.

8. *Taste and see that Jehovah is good.* In this verse the Psalmist indirectly reproves men for their dulness in not perceiving the goodness of God, which ought to be to them more than matter of simple knowledge. By the word *taste* he at once shows that they are without taste; and at the same time he assigns the reason of this to be, that they devour the gifts of God without relishing them, or through a vitiated loathing ungratefully conceal them. He, therefore, calls upon them to stir up their senses, and to bring a palate endued with some capacity of tasting, that God's goodness may become known to them, or rather, be made manifest to them. The words literally rendered are, *Taste and see, for the Lord is good;* but the particle כִּי, *ki, for,* is taken exegetically. David's meaning, therefore, is, that there is nothing on the part of God to prevent the godly, to whom he particularly speaks in this place, from arriving at the knowledge of his goodness by actual experience. From this it follows, that they also are infected with the common malady of dulness. This doctrine is confirmed by the promise immediately added, *Blessed is the man who trusteth in him;* for God never disappoints the expectations of those who seek his favour.

Our own unbelief is the only impediment which prevents him from satisfying us largely and bountifully with abundance of all good things.

9. *Fear Jehovah, ye his saints.* Here the people of God are exhorted to the pursuit of holiness and righteousness, that they may open up a channel for divine blessings. We know that men are accustomed to provide for their wants, by resorting to fraud, plunder, and even to wrongful violence. Nor is it possible but that the faithful must feel some stirrings of a desire to imitate the wicked, and envy them in some degree in their prosperity, so that they permit themselves sometimes to howl among the wolves. And although they voluntarily abstain from all wrongful violence, yet the common way of living among those around them carries them away like a tempest; and, in the meantime, they think that the plea of necessity is sufficient to excuse them. David represses, as with a bridle, these temptations, promising that all will be well with the people of God, provided they keep themselves in the fear of God, which he opposes to all wicked and deceitful counsels; because the greater part of men reckon those to be fools who aim at simplicity, since in so doing they do not consult their own interests and profit. While, therefore, ungodly men are afraid of poverty, and carnal reason urges them to attempt whatever their fancy may suggest for keeping themselves from it, David here testifies that God takes care of the godly, so that he never suffers them to be in want. Let no fear or distrust, says he, withdraw you from the pursuit of what is right, because God never forsakes those who walk righteously before him. The Psalmist, therefore, bids them yield to God the honour of expecting more from him alone than the wicked expect from their deceitful traffic and unlawful practices. Moreover, as iniquity rages with unbridled fury everywhere throughout the world, he calls expressly upon the saints to be on their guard, because he would be of no service to the promiscuous multitude. It is a sentiment contrary to the generally received opinion among men, that while the integrity of the good and simple is exposed to the will of the wicked, there should yet be greater security in integrity than in all the resources of fraud

and injustice. There is, therefore, no inconsistency in his admonishing the saints who, of their own accord, are endeavouring to walk uprightly, not to depart from the fear of God; for we know how easily the light of piety may be obscured and extinguished, when there appears no hope of living happily and prosperously, except in the pursuit of the world and its enticing pleasures.

The Psalmist illustrates this doctrine by a very apposite comparison, namely, that God provides every thing necessary for his people, and relieves their wants, whilst the lions, which surpass in ferocity all the wild beasts of the earth, prowl about in a famishing condition for their prey. Some think, that under the name of *lions*, those men who are addicted to violence and plunder are metaphorically described; but this, in my opinion, is too refined. David simply asserts, that those who guard against all unrighteousness should profit more by so doing than by rapine and plunder; because the Lord feeds his people, while even the lions and other beasts of prey often suffer hunger. What he says, then, is, that sooner shall the lions perish with hunger and want, than God will disappoint of their necessary food the righteous and sincere, who, content with his blessing alone, seek their food only from his hand. Whoever, therefore, shall in this way cast his cares upon God, and confide implicitly in his paternal goodness and bounty, shall live quietly and peaceably among men, and suffer no injury. If it is objected, that the good and the virtuous are not always exempted from penury, I answer, that the hand of God is stretched out to succour them in due season, when they are reduced to the greatest straits, and know not to what side to turn,[1] so that the issue always shows that we seek not in vain from him whatever is necessary to the sustenance of life.

11. *Come, children, hearken unto me, I will teach you the fear of Jehovah.*
12. *Who is the man who desireth life, loving days in which he may see good?*
13. *Keep thy tongue from evil, and thy lips from speaking deceit.*
14. *Turn away from evil, and do good; seek peace, and pursue it.*

[1] " Et ne sçavent plus de quel costé se tourner."—*Fr.*

11. *Come, children,*[1] *hearken unto me.* The Psalmist continues, with increased earnestness, to exhort the faithful, that they may know that nothing can be more profitable for them than to conduct themselves justly and harmlessly towards all men. As the greater part of men imagine that the best and the shortest way to attain a life of happiness and ease consists in striving to surpass other men in violence, fraud, injustice, and other means of mischief, it is necessary frequently to repeat this doctrine. Moreover, as it is necessary that the minds of men should be brought to a chastened and humble state, by calling them *his children,* he endeavours, by this gentle and courteous appellation, to allay all froward affections. None will stand unmoved amidst so many assaults, but those who have been endued by the Spirit of meekness with the greatest modesty. The prophet, therefore, tells them at the outset, that the rule of life which he prescribes can be observed and obeyed by those only who are meek and submissive. To the same purpose is the word *come,* and the command *to hearken;* and they imply, that men laying aside all wilfulness of spirit, and having subdued the ardour and impetuosity of their minds, should become docile and meek. He has put the *fear of the Lord* for the rule of a pious and holy life: as if he had said, Whilst virtue and righteousness are in every man's mouth, there are few who lead a holy life, and live as they ought; because they know not what it is to serve God.

12. *Who is the man who desireth life?* The prophet does not inquire if there be any man so disposed, as if all men voluntarily brought upon themselves the miseries which befall them; for we know that all men without exception desire to live in the enjoyment of happiness. But he censures severely the blindness and folly which men exhibit in the frowardness of their desires, and the vanity of their endeavours to obtain happiness; for while all men are seeking, and eagerly intent upon acquiring what is for their profit, there will be found scarcely one in a hundred who studies to purohase peace, and a quiet and desirable state of life, by just

---

[1] By this affectionate appellation, Hebrew teachers were wont to address their scholars.

and equitable means. The prophet therefore admonishes his disciples, that nearly the whole world are deceived and led astray by their own folly, while they promise themselves a happy life from any other source than the divine blessing, which God bestows only upon the sincere and upright in heart. But there is in this exclamation still greater vehemence, the more effectually to awaken dull and drowsy minds to the course of this world; as if he had said, Since all men earnestly desire happiness, how comes it to pass, that scarcely any one sets himself to obtain it, and that every man, by his own fault, rather brings upon himself various troubles?

13. *Keep thy tongue from evil.* The precept which David here delivers relates to a virtue which is very rare, namely, that we should be truthful and free from deceit in our discourse. Some, indeed, understand it in a much more extended sense, supposing that slander is condemned in this first clause. But it seems to me more simple, and more to the purpose, to understand this as of the same import with what he repeats in the second clause, that we should not speak *deceitfully* with our neighbours, so as that our words may prove the means of ensnaring them. And since nothing is more difficult than to regulate our discourse in such a manner as that our speech may be a true representation of our hearts, David calls upon us to exercise over it a strict and watchful control, not suffering it to run riot, lest it should prove the occasion of our deceiving others.

14. *Turn away from evil, and do good.* Here the Psalmist commands the children of God to abstain from all evil, and to devote themselves to the work of doing good to their neighbours. This verse is generally quoted as if David here treated of the two parts of repentance. The first step in the work of repentance is, that the sinner forsake the vices to which he is addicted, and renounce his former manner of life; and the second, that he frame his behaviour according to righteousness. But in this place we are more especially taught how we ought to deal with our neighbours. As it often

happens, that the man who is not only liberal, but also prodigal towards some, or, at least, helps many by acts of kindness, wrongs others by defrauding and injuring them, David, with much propriety, begins by saying, that those who desire to have their life approved before God, ought to abstain from doing evil. On the other hand, since many think, that provided they have neither defrauded, nor wronged, nor injured any man, they have discharged the duty which God requires from them, he has added, with equal propriety, the other precept concerning doing good to our neighbours. It is not the will of God that his servants should be idle, but rather that they should aid one another, desiring each other's welfare and prosperity, and promoting it as far as in them lies. David next inculcates the duty of maintaining peace: *Seek peace, and pursue it.* Now we know that this is maintained by gentleness and forbearance. But as we have often to do with men of a fretful, or factious, or stubborn spirit, or with such as are always ready to stir up strife upon the slightest occasion; and as also many wicked persons irritate us; and as others by their own wickedness alienate, as much as in them lies, the minds of good men from them, and others industriously strive to find grounds of contention; he teaches us not merely that we ought to seek peace, but if at any time it shall seem to flee from us, he bids us use our every effort without ceasing in pursuing it. This, however, must be understood with some limitation. It will often happen, that when good and humble men have done every thing in their power to secure peace, so far from softening the hearts of the wicked, or inclining them to uprightness, they rather excite their malice. Their impiety, also, often constrains us to separate from them, and to avoid them; nay, when they defy God, by proclaiming, as it were, open war against him, it would be disloyalty and treason on our part not to oppose and resist them. But here David means only that in our own personal affairs we should be meek and condescending, and endeavour, as far as in us lies, to maintain peace, though its maintenance should prove to us a source of much trouble and inconvenience.

15. *The eyes of Jehovah are upon the righteous, and his ears are open to their cry.*
16. *The face of Jehovah*[1] *is upon them that do evil, to cut off their remembrance from the earth.*
17. *They cried, and Jehovah heard them, and delivered them from all their troubles.*

15. *The eyes of Jehovah are upon the righteous.* The best support of our patience is a firm persuasion that God regards us, and that according as every man perseveres in a course of uprightness and equity, so shall he be preserved in peace and safety under his protection. In order, therefore, that the faithful may not think that they are exposed to the caprice of the world, while they are endeavouring to keep themselves innocent, and that they may not, under the influence of this fear, go astray from the right path, David exhorts them to reflect upon the providence of God, and to rest assured that they are safe under his wings. He says, then, that *the eyes of the Lord are upon the righteous*, to preserve them, in order that the good and simple may persevere the more cheerfully in their uprightness. At the same time, he encourages them to supplication and prayer, if at any time the world should unjustly persecute them. In saying that *the ears of the Lord are open to their cry*, he teaches that the man who is wantonly and unjustly persecuted, will find a ready and suitable remedy in all afflictions, by calling upon God as his avenger. On the other hand, he declares, that although God sometimes appears to wink at the misdeeds of men, and seems to overlook them, because he does not inflict immediate punishment upon them, yet nothing escapes his inspection. Whilst the wicked, says he, by reason of their impunity harden themselves in sin, God is watching, that he may *cut off their remembrance from the earth*, (1 Pet. v. 10.) He speaks particularly of this kind of punishment, because the ungodly not only expect that they shall be happy during their whole life, but also imagine that they shall enjoy

---

[1] That is, the anger of God. The *face* of God is often put for the *anger* of God, because this passion manifests itself particularly in the face. Thus in Lam. iv. 16, we read, "The anger [literally faces] of the Lord hath divided them." And in Lev. xx. 5, we read, " I will set my face [that is, my anger] against that man."

immortality in this world. Peter, in his First Epistle,[1] applies this passage very judiciously, for the purpose of assuaging our sorrows and appeasing our impatience, as often as the pride and arrogance of the wicked may carry us beyond due limits. Nothing is more useful for preserving our moderation than to depend upon God's help, and having the testimony of a good conscience, to rely upon his judgment. If it is objected, that good men experience the contrary, who, after having been long afflicted, at length find no help or comfort; I reply, that the aid which God affords to the righteous is not always made manifest, nor bestowed in the same measure; and yet he so alleviates their troubles as never to forsake them. Besides, even the best of men often deprive themselves of the help of God; for scarcely one in a hundred perseveres in such a course of integrity as not, by his own fault, to deserve the infliction of some evil upon himself. But as soon as they fall, lest sin should take root in them, God chastises them, and often punishes them more severely than the reprobate, whom he spares to utter destruction.[2] And yet, however much things may appear to be mingled and confused in the world, good men will find that God has not promised them help in vain against the violence and injuries of the wicked.

17. *They*[3] *cried, and Jehovah heard them.* The Psalmist's meaning is, that they are heard as often as they cry. This is a doctrine applicable to all times; and David does not merely relate what God has done once or twice, but what he is accustomed to do. It is also a confirmation of the preceding sentence, where he had said that the ears of the Lord

---

[1] In his First Epistle, (chap. iii. 10, 11, 12,) he quotes the 12, 13, 14, 15, and 16 verses of this psalm. He quotes from the Septuagint.

[2] "Lesquels il espargne pour un temps, afin de les ruiner eternellement." —"Whom he spares for a time, to destroy them eternally."—*Fr.*

[3] It is wicked men who are spoken of in the immediately preceding verse; but *they* here evidently refers not to them, but to the righteous, mentioned in the fifteenth verse; and, accordingly, in all the ancient versions, and in our English Bible, the words *the righteous* are supplied. It is supposed by those who make this supplement, that the word צדיקים, *tsaddikim*, has been lost out of the text. But if we read the 16th verse as a parenthesis, it will not be necessary to make any supplement, and the words may be read exactly as they are in the Hebrew, *They cried.*

are open to the cry of the righteous; for he now demonstrates by the effect, that God is not deaf when we lay our complaints and groanings before him. By the word *cry* we are taught, that although God defend the righteous, they are not exempt from adversity. He regulates the protection which he affords them in such a wonderful manner, as that he notwithstanding exercises them by various trials. In like manner, when we here see that deliverance is promised only to those who call upon God, this ought to prove no small encouragement to us to pray to him; for it is not his will that the godly should so regard his providence as to indulge in idleness, but rather that, being firmly persuaded that he is the guardian of their safety, they should direct their prayers and supplications to him.

18. *Jehovah is nigh to those who are broken of heart; he will save those who are bruised of spirit.*
19. *Many are the afflictions of the righteous: but Jehovah will deliver him from them all.*
20. *He keepeth all his bones: not one of them is broken.*[1]
21. *But malice shall slay the wicked; and those who hate the righteous shall be destroyed.*
22. *Jehovah redeemeth the soul of his servants, and those who trust in him shall not perish.*

18. *Jehovah is nigh to those who are broken of heart.* David here exemplifies and extends still more the preceding doctrine, that God is the deliverer of his people, even when they are brought very low, and when they are, as it were, half-dead. It is a very severe trial, when the grace of God is delayed, and all experience of it so far withdrawn, as that our spirits begin to fail; nay more, to say that God is nigh to the faithful, even when their hearts faint and fail them, and they are ready to die, is altogether incredible to human sense and reason. But by this means his power shines forth more clearly, when he raises us up again from the grave. Moreover, it is meet that the faithful should be thus utterly cast down and afflicted, that they may breathe again in God alone. From this we also learn, that nothing is more opposed to

[1] The last clause of this verse is applied in the Gospel of John (ch. xix. 36) to Christ, and represented as receiving its fulfilment in him.

true patience than the loftiness of heart of which the Stoics boast; for we are not accounted truly humbled until true affliction of heart has abased us before God, so that, having prostrated ourselves in the dust before him, he may raise us up. It is a doctrine full of the sweetest consolation, that God departs not from us, even when we are overwhelmed by a succession of miseries, and, as it were, almost deprived of life.

19. *Many are the afflictions of the righteous.* The Psalmist here anticipates the thought which often arises in the mind, "How can it be that God has a care about the righteous, who are continually harassed with so many calamities and trials? for what purpose does the protection of God serve, unless those who are peaceably inclined enjoy peace and repose? and what is more unreasonable, than that those who cause trouble to no one should themselves be tormented and afflicted in all variety of ways?" That, therefore, the temptations by which we are continually assailed may not shake our belief in the providence of God, we ought to remember this lesson of instruction, that although God governs the righteous, and provides for their safety, they are yet subject and exposed to many miseries, that, being tested by such trials, they may give evidence of their invincible constancy, and experience so much the more that God is their deliverer. If they were exempted from every kind of trial, their faith would languish, they would cease to call upon God, and their piety would remain hidden and unknown. It is, therefore, necessary that they should be exercised with various trials, and especially for this end, that they may acknowledge that they have been wonderfully preserved by God amidst numberless deaths. If this should seldom happen, it might appear to be fortuitous, or the result of chance; but when innumerable and interminable evils come upon them in succession, the grace of God cannot be unknown, when he always stretches forth his hand to them. David, therefore, admonishes the faithful never to lose their courage, whatever evils may threaten them; since God, who can as easily deliver them a thousand times as once from death, will never disappoint their expectation. What he adds concerning *their bones*, seems not a little to

illustrate the truth of this doctrine, and to teach us that those who are protected by God shall be free from all danger. He therefore declares, that God will take care that not one of their bones shall be broken; in which sense Christ also says, that "the very hairs of our head are all numbered," (Luke xii. 7.)

21. *But malice shall slay the wicked.* The Hebrew word רעה, *raäh,* which I have translated *malice,* some would rather render *misery,* so that the meaning would be, that the ungodly shall perish miserably, because in the end they shall be overwhelmed with calamities. The other translation, however, is more expressive, namely, that their wickedness, with which they think themselves fortified, shall fall upon their own heads. As David therefore taught before, that there was no defence better than a just and blameless life, so now he declares, that all the wicked enterprises of the wicked, even though no one should in any thing oppose them, shall turn to their own destruction. In the second clause of the verse he states, that it is for the sake of the righteous that it is ordered, that the ungodly are themselves the cause and instruments of their own destruction. *Those,* says he, *who hate the righteous shall be destroyed.* Let this, therefore, be to us as a wall of brass and sure defence; that however numerous the enemies which beset us may be, we should not be afraid, because they are already devoted to destruction. The same thing David confirms in the last verse, in which he says, that *Jehovah redeems the soul of his servants.* How could they be preserved in safety, even for a moment, among so many dangers, unless God interposed his power for their defence? But by the word *redeem* there is expressed a kind of preservation which is repugnant to the flesh. For it is necessary that we should first be adjudged or doomed to death, before God should appear as our redeemer. From this it follows, that those who hurry forward too precipitately, and are unable to realise God's power unless he appear speedily, working deliverance for them, intercept the communication of his grace. Moreover, that none might form their judgment of the servants of God by moral or philosophic

virtue only, as it is called, David specifies this as a principal mark by which they may be known, that they trust in God, on whom also their salvation depends.

PSALM XXXV.

So long as Saul was the enemy of David, the nobles, and such as at that time bore any authority, had (according to the subservient spirit which always prevails in the courts of kings) eagerly conspired to destroy an innocent man. They had also succeeded in inducing the common people to participate with them in their hatred and cruelty, so that all of them, from the highest to the lowest, burned with implacable hatred against him. But as he knew that the greatest part of them were thoughtlessly impelled to this by error and folly, and ignorance of the true state of affairs, he accounts those only his enemies who, from deliberate malice and wickedness, endeavoured in this way to please Saul, in order to obtain his favour. Against them he calls upon God for vengeance. And, first, as he was conscious of no crime, he alleges his innocence before God; and, secondly, as they sought to inflict unmerited punishment upon him, he implores God for deliverance. After he has complained of their impious cruelty, he calls down upon them the punishment which they deserved. Moreover, as in confident reliance upon the oracle of God, which had been spoken by Samuel, and the holy anointing, he hoped for a better issue, he intersperses throughout the psalm testimonies of his thankfulness. Finally, he concludes the psalm by saying, that after he has been delivered, he will celebrate the praises of God all his life.

¶ *A Psalm of David.*

1. *Plead my cause, O Jehovah! with them that plead against me; fight against them who fight against me.*
2. *Take the shield and the buckler, and rise up for my help.*
3. *Bring forth the spear, and oppose my persecutors: say unto my soul, "I am thy salvation."*

1. *Plead my cause, O Jehovah!* As the enemies of David not only avowedly sought to take away his life, but also troubled him by calumny and misrepresentation, he pleads for the redress of both these grievances. In the first place, by

appealing to God for his aid in defence of his cause, he intimates, that he has to do with wicked and maligning men. In the second place, by urging him to take up arms, he shows that he was grievously oppressed. It was a very dishonourable thing, that this holy man, alike eminent for his beneficence and inoffensiveness towards all men, and who by his courtesy and meekness had merited, both in public and private, the esteem and favour of all, was not permitted to escape the reproach and calumny of wicked men; but it is important for us to know this, and it sets before us a very profitable example. If even David did not escape the malice of wicked men, it ought not to seem wonderful or strange to us, if they blame and bite at us. The injuries they inflict upon us may be grievous and painful, but there is incomparable consolation presented to us in this consideration, that God himself interposes for our protection and defence against false accusations. Though calumniators, then, should arise, and tear us, as it were, to pieces, by falsely charging us with crimes, we need not be disturbed, so long as God undertakes to plead our cause against them. There can be no doubt, that in the second clause of the verse David implores God to resist the armed violence of his enemies. The amount of the whole is, that being falsely accused and cruelly persecuted, and finding no help at the hands of men, the Prophet commits the preservation of his life and his reputation to God.

2. *Take the shield.* These words certainly cannot be applied, in the strict and proper sense, to God, who has no need of the spear or buckler: for by the breath of his mouth alone, or merely with his nod, he is able to overthrow all his enemies. But although such figures at first sight appear rude, yet the Holy Ghost employs them in accommodation to the weakness of our understanding, for the purpose of impressing more effectually upon our minds the conviction that God is present to aid us. When troubles and dangers arise, when terrors assail us on every side, when even death presents itself to our view, it is difficult to realise the secret and invisible power of God, which is able to deliver us from all anxiety and fear; for our understandings, which are gross

and earthly, tend downward to the earth. That our faith, therefore, may ascend by degrees to the heavenly power of God, he is here introduced armed, after the manner of men, with sword and shield. In the same way, also, when he is in another place termed "a man of war," it is doubtless in adaptation to the imperfection of our present state, because our minds, from their limited capacity, could in no other way comprehend the extent of that infinite power, which contains in itself every form of help, and has no need of aid from any other quarter. This, therefore, is a prayer that God, by the exercise of his secret and intrinsic power, would show that he alone is able to encounter the whole strength and forces of the ungodly. Some suppose that the Hebrew word צנה, *tsinnah*, here used, means *a dart*, or some other kind of weapon; but as we have already seen, in the fifth psalm, that it properly signifies a *buckler*, I see no reason why it should be differently interpreted in this place. Nor is there any thing at all inconsistent in connecting here, as is often done in other places, the buckler and the shield.[1] If the expression here employed had been designed to signify a dart, or a similar weapon, it would have been more natural to connect it with the spear, of which mention is made in the following verse. David, then, first makes mention of defensive armour, praying that God would sustain and repel the assaults of the enemy. The Hebrew word רִיק, *rik*, which signifies *to unsheath*, or *make bare*, I take simply to mean, *to draw out*, or *bring forth*. The Hebrew word סְגוֹר, *segor*, which I have translated *to oppose*, literally signifies *to shut* or *to close*. But as David's meaning is, that God, by setting himself as a wall or rampart, would prevent his enemies from approaching him, it appears to me that I have faithfully translated it. At the same time, if any should prefer the translation to *shut*, or *close the way*, or to *impede it by some obstacle*, the meaning is

---

[1] The word rendered *shield* is in the Hebrew text מגן, *magen*, which was a short buckler intended merely for defence. The word rendered *buckler* is צנה, *tsinnah*, for an account of which see note, p. 64. The *tsinnah* was double the weight of the magen, and was carried by the infantry; the magen, being lighter and more manageable, was used by the cavalry. The *tsinnah* answered to the *scutum*, and the *magen* to the *clypeus*, among the Romans.—See *Paxton's Illustrations of Scripture*, vol. iii. pp. 366, 367.

substantially the same. The opinion of those who contend that it is a noun,[1] is not at all probable.

3. *Say to my soul.* Some expound these words thus: Declare to me by secret inspiration; and others, Make me to feel indeed that my salvation is in thy hand. In my opinion, David desires to have it thoroughly fixed in his mind, and to be fully persuaded that God is the author of his salvation. This he was unable, from the present aspect of things, to ascertain and determine; for such is the insensibility and dulness of our natures, that God often delivers us whilst we sleep and are ignorant of it. Accordingly, he makes use of a very forcible manner of expression, in praying that God would grant him a lively sense of his favour, so that being armed with this buckler, he might sustain every conflict, and surmount every opposing obstacle; as if he had said, Lord, whatever may arise to discourage me, confirm me in this persuasion, that my salvation is assuredly in thee; and although temptations drive me hither and thither, recall my thoughts to thee in such a manner, as that my hope of salvation may rise superior to all the dangers to which I shall be exposed;[2] nay, more, that I may become as infallibly certain as if thou hadst said it, that through thy favour I shall be saved.

4. *Let those who seek my soul be confounded and put to shame; and let those who devise my hurt be turned back, and brought to confusion.*
5. *Let them be as chaff before the wind, and let the angel of Jehovah thrust* [or *impel*] *them.*[3]
6. *Let their way be darkness and slipperiness, and let the angel of Jehovah pursue them.*
7. *For they have hid for me without cause their net in a pit, without cause they have digged a pit*[4] *for my soul.*

[1] Those who are of opinion that סגור, *segor*, is a noun, translate it "the scymitar," and read, "Draw out the spear, and the scymitar, to oppose my persecutors." According to Drusius, Vitringa, Michaelis, Dr Kennicott, and others, the word means σαγαρις, or scymitar, a sort of battle-axe, which was used by the Persians, Scythians, and other nations in ancient times.
[2] "Que l'esperance de mon salut surpasse tous les dangers qui me seront livrez."—*Fr.*
[3] "C'est, chasse et presse."—*Note, Fr. marg.* "That is, chase and pursue them."
[4] The allusion here is to the custom of digging pits and putting nets in them, covered with straw, &c., to catch wild beasts.

4. *Let those who seek my soul be confounded.* David now calls upon God to take vengeance upon his enemies; and he asks not only that he would disappoint and destroy their designs, but also that he would recompense them according to their deserts. In the first place, he desires that they may be confounded and put to shame in seeing their expectation and desire fail; and then he proceeds farther, desiring that while they imagine themselves to be firmly established, and deeply rooted, they may be like chaff or stubble. As the chaff is driven with the wind, so also he desires, that, being disquieted by the secret impulse of the angel of the Lord, they may never have rest. The imprecation which follows is even more dreadful, and it is this : that wherever they go they may meet with darkness and slippery places; and that in their doubt and perplexity the angel of the Lord would pursue them. In fine, whatever they devise, and to whatever side they turn, he prays that all their counsels and enterprises may come to a disastrous termination. When he desires that they may be driven by the angel of the Lord, we learn from this that the reason why the ungodly are troubled, though no man pursues them, is, that God smites them with a spirit of amazement, and distracts them with such fears that they tremble and are troubled.

The same thing he expresses more clearly in the following verse, praying that the angel of the Lord would drive them through dark and slippery places, so that reason and understanding might fail them, and that they might not know whither to go, nor what to become, nor have even time given them to draw their breath. We need not be surprised that this work should be assigned to the angels, by whose instrumentality God executes his judgments. At the same time, this passage may be expounded of the devils as well as of the holy angels, who are ever ready to execute the divine behests. We know that the devil is permitted to exercise his dominion over the reprobate; and hence it is often said that " an evil spirit from God came upon Saul," (1 Sam. xviii. 10.) But as the devils never execute the will of God, unless compelled to do it when God wishes to serve himself of them; the Sacred Scriptures declare that the holy and elect angels are in a much higher sense the servants of God. God, then, executes his judgments by the wicked and reprobate angels; but he gives the elect angels the pre-eminence over them. On this account, also, good angels only are called rightfully "principalities," as in Eph. iii. 10; Col. i. 16, and other similar passages. If it is objected that it is not meet that the angels, who are the ministers of grace and salvation, and the appointed guardians of the faithful, should be employed in executing judgment upon the reprobate, the explanation is simply this, that they cannot watch for the preservation of the godly without being prepared for fighting—that they cannot succour them by their aid without also opposing their enemies, and declaring themselves to be against them. The style of imprecation which the Psalmist here employs can be explained only by bearing in mind what I have elsewhere said, namely, that David pleads not simply his own cause, nor utters rashly the dicates of passion, nor with unadvised zeal desires the destruction of his enemies; but under the guidance of the Holy Spirit he entertains and expresses against the reprobate such desires as were characterised by great moderation, and which were far removed from the spirit of those who are impelled either by desire of revenge or hatred, or some other inordinate emotion of the flesh.

7. *For they have hid for me without a cause.* He here declares that he did not take the name of God in vain, nor call upon him for protection without just cause, for he openly asserts his innocence, and complains that he was thus severely afflicted without having committed any crime, or given any occasion to his enemies. It becomes us carefully to mark this, so that no one may rush unadvisedly into God's presence, nor call upon him for vengeance, without the assurance and testimony of a good conscience. When he says that he was assailed by stratagem, fraud, and wicked practices, there is implied in this a tacit commendation of his own integrity.

8. *Let confusion of which he is not aware come upon him; and let his own net which he hath hidden catch himself: let him fall into it with confusion.*
9. *And my soul is joyful in Jehovah, it shall be glad in his salvation.*
10. *All my bones shall say, O Jehovah! who is like thee, that*

deliverest the poor from him that is stronger than he, the poor and miserable from him that spoileth him?

8. *Let confusion of which he is not aware come upon him.* David again prays that God would cause to return upon the head of his enemies the mischief which they had directed against a just and an inoffensive man. The change from the plural to the singular number, even when the same subject is spoken of, is, we know, a thing very common among the Hebrews. Accordingly, what is here said of one man is applicable to all David's enemies in general, unless, perhaps, we are rather inclined to suppose that allusion is here made to Saul or some one of his nobles. But as it is certain that the prayer which he here offers against Saul as the head extends to the whole body, in other words, to all his followers,[1] it matters little in which way we understand it. The Hebrew word שׁוֹאָה, *shoah*, sometimes signifies *confusion*, and sometimes *destruction*; and, therefore, many translate it, *Let destruction*, or *desolation*, or *ruin*, *come upon him.* The other rendering, however, seems more suitable, for he immediately adds, *Let his own net which he hath hidden catch him, let him fall into it with confusion.* The way in which others render it, *Let him fall into destruction itself,* is certainly forced and unnatural. But the meaning of the clause will be brought out very suitable if it is viewed as a prayer of David, that as the wicked settle down like wine upon the lees, in present enjoyments, and fear nothing, as if they were placed beyond the reach of all danger, some calamity which they think not of may suddenly come upon them like a tempest, and overwhelm them. It never for a moment occurs to them as at all possible that their stratagems and craft, their wicked practices, and all the snares which they lay for the good and the simple, turn to the destruction of themselves who have devised them. David, therefore, very properly desires that they may fall with confusion into the nets which they have laid; in other words, that they may be filled with amazement and terror when they are suddenly and unexpectedly visited with calamity. The more unbounded and extravagant the

---

[1] " Qu'il fait yci contre Saul comme le chef, s'estend à tout le corps; c'est à dire, à tous ses adherens."—*Fr.*

exultation of men is, through their vainly and foolishly imagining that they shall escape unpunished, the more are they filled with amazement and fear when calamity suddenly overtakes them. I have, however, no doubt that David here refers to some strange and extraordinary calamity. Let *confusion*, then, of which he thinks not, come upon him; that is to say, when he shall have persuaded himself that all goes well with him, and promised himself peace in his deceitful fascinations, then let unwonted terror strike him to the heart, and let him feel by his tumultuous fear that he is caught in his own snares.

9. *And my soul is joyful in Jehovah.* Others read this in the optative mood, *May my soul rejoice in Jehovah, and may it be glad in his salvation.* But instead of continuing to express his desires, David, in my opinion, rather promises in this verse that he will be grateful to God. This is still more evident from the following verse, in which extolling very highly the goodness of God, he says that he will celebrate the remembrance of it with every member of his body. While, therefore, some ascribe to fortune, and others to their own skill, the praise of their deliverance from danger, and few, if any, yield the whole praise of it to God, David here declares that he will not forget the favour which God had bestowed upon him. My soul, says he, shall rejoice, not in a deliverance of the author of which it is ignorant, but in the salvation of God. To place the matter in a still stronger light, he assigns to his very bones the office of declaring the divine glory. As if not content that his tongue should be employed in this, he applies all the members of his body to the work of setting forth the praises of God. The style of speaking which he employs is hyperbolical, but in this way he shows unfeignedly that his love to God was so strong that he desired to spend his sinews and bones in declaring the reality and truth of his devotion.

10. *O Jehovah! who is like thee?* Here he explains more fully the nature of his joy in the salvation of God of which he had spoken, showing that it consisted in his ascribing en-

tirely to God the deliverance which he had obtained. Men, in general, praise God in such a manner that he scarcely obtains the tenth part of his due. But David, distinguishing him from all others, distinctly declares that the whole glory of his deliverance is due to him alone. And, certainly, we then only yield to God what belongs to him, when, investing him with his own power, we rest all our hopes on him. For what purpose does it serve, loudly to celebrate the name of God with our mouths, if we tear in pieces his power and goodness at our pleasure? David, therefore, in the true spirit of godliness, extols the greatness of God by this high encomium, that he is the guardian and defender of the poor, and rescues the needy and afflicted from the hand of those who oppress them; as if he had said, It is God's peculiar duty to succour the miserable. By these words we are taught to cling to the hope of better things in adversity; for the power and resources of our enemies, however great they may be, is no reason why we should lose our confidence, since God declares to us from heaven that he reigns expressly for the purpose of resisting the strong and powerful. If the children of this world, who employ their power in injuring and oppressing the weak, had the least degree of sound understanding, it would certainly serve to restrain their audacity, and prevent them proceeding farther in provoking the wrath of God.

11. *Violent witnesses rise up, they charge me with things which I know not.*
12. *They render me evil for good, to the bereaving*[1] *of my soul.*
13. *But as for me, when they were sick, my clothing was sackcloth: I afflicted my soul with fasting; and have poured my prayer into my own bosom.*
14. *I behaved myself towards him as if he had been my friend and brother: I humbled myself as one that mourneth heavily for his mother.*
15. *But they rejoiced at my halting, they gathered themselves together; yea, even the abjects whom I knew not gathered themselves against me: they have torn me with their lips, and have not ceased.*

11. *Violent witnesses*[2] *rise up.* The Hebrew is, *they shall rise*

---

[1] " C'est, desconforter."—*Note, Fr. marg.* "That is, to the discomfort."
[2] " עֵדֵי חָמָס, *witnesses of wrong* or *violence; i.e.*, witnesses deponing to acts of violence, as committed by the person accused. See Ps. xxvii. 12."—*Horsley.*

up; but in using the future tense, the Psalmist intimates that he is speaking of what he had suffered for a long time. And he complains that he was so oppressed with calumny that he had no opportunity of defending himself: than which nothing more grievous and painful can ever happen to those of an ingenuous mind, and who are conscious of no blame. Besides, he not only says that he had been falsely accused, but he also condemns the audacity and insolence of those who violently rose up to bear witness against him. To this belongs what he adds, *They charge me with things which I know not.* David then was not only spoiled of his worldly goods, and basely driven into exile, but was also accused and loaded with infamy under colour of justice. Being involved in such distress, he resorted directly to God, hoping that he would maintain his innocence. So ought the children of God to walk through good report and bad report, and patiently suffer reproach, until he assert and declare their innocence from on high. In old times, it was a common proverb among the heathen, " There is no theatre more beautiful than a good conscience;" and in this they uttered a noble sentiment; but no man can be sustained and supported by the purity of his conscience unless he has recourse to God.

12. *They render me evil for good.* David again shows that the malice of his enemies was of a very aggravated character, because they not only oppressed him wrongfully, seeing he was innocent, and had given them no occasion of offence, but also because even those who had received much enjoyment and many favours from him, recompensed him in a very strange and ungrateful manner. Such disgraceful conduct wounds the feelings of good men very severely, and seems quite intolerable. But it is an inexpressibly great consolation when we can testify before God, that we have attempted by every means in our power to soothe the minds of our enemies, and to bow them to gentleness, although, notwithstanding, they are hurried on by insatiable cruelty in desiring our hurt; for God will not suffer this barbarous and brutal ingratitude to pass unpunished. Their cruelty is farther expressed

when it is said that they endeavoured to bereave (for so it is properly in the Hebrew[1]) the soul of a meek and peaceable man; that is to say, to deprive it of comfort, and render it so desolate as to overwhelm it with despair and destroy it. David afterwards recounts certain acts of kindness which he had done them, and which, if they had had any sense of equity and humanity, ought to have been as so many sacred bonds of mutual love. He does not say that he aided them with money or with goods, or that he had by some other means exercised liberality towards them, for it may sometimes happen that when the hand is open the heart may be shut; but he mentions certain tokens of true and genuine love—that he lamented their misfortunes before God, and was troubled for them, as if he had mourned for the death of his mother; and, finally, that he felt for and took an interest in them as if they had been his own brothers. Since then he had thus laid them under high obligations to him, of what baser ingratitude could they be guilty than to vomit against him in his adversity the poison of their hatred? With respect to the meaning of the words, I take the term *sickness*, in this place, to signify metaphorically any kind of trouble or sorrow. David's meaning is, that as often as any calamity had befallen them he was a partaker of their grief. A good evidence of this was the prayer which he says he *poured out into his own bosom*. The proper meaning of the expression is, that he did not ostentatiously utter his prayers aloud before men, like many who pretend much more affection than they really feel, but that by praying in secret, and without making the world privy to it, he showed that he was sincerely and from the heart distressed by reason of their affliction. As we say that a man rejoices in his own bosom, who is satisfied with the secret and inward feeling of his heart, without declaring it to others, so also one may be said to weep or pray in his own bosom, who pours not forth his tears and prayers before men to secure their favour, but, contented with having God alone for his witness, conceals his emotions in his own heart. I do not, however, deny that in this manner of speaking there is

[1] " Ont tasché de rendre orpheline car il y a ainsi proprement en Hebrieu."—*Fr.*

expressed the attitude of one who prays, as if the Psalmist had said, that he bowed down his body, and prayed with his head hanging down, and his arms folded, as men in heaviness are accustomed to do.[1] But this especially we ought to regard as his meaning, that there was no dissimulation in his prayer. Some think that there is an imprecation in his words, and they explain them in this sense: Lord, if it is true that I have not desired all prosperity to them, let all mischief fall upon me: but this is a forced explanation. There is still another exposition, which has as little plausibility in it; and it is this: Because I profited nothing by praying for them, the fruit of my prayer returned to myself. The sense, which is more in unison with the purpose and also the words of the prophet, is, I prayed for them just as I pray for myself. But what I have already advanced concerning the secret affection of the Psalmist will, I hope, prove satisfactory to the judicious reader. With respect to *sackcloth* and *fasting*, he used them as helps to prayer. The faithful pray even after their meals, and do not observe fasting every day as necessary for prayer, nor consider it needful to put on sackcloth whenever they come into the presence of God. But we know that those who lived in ancient times resorted to these exercises when any urgent necessity pressed upon them. In the time of public calamity or danger they all put on sackcloth, and gave themselves to fasting, that by humbling themselves before God, and acknowledging their guilt, they might appease his wrath. In like manner, when any one in particular was afflicted, in order to excite himself to greater earnestness in prayer, he put on sackcloth and engaged in fasting, as being the tokens of grief. When David then, as he here tells us, put on sackcloth, it was the same as if he had taken upon himself the sins of his enemies, in order to implore from God mercy for them, while they were exerting all their power to accomplish his destruction. Although we may reckon the wearing of sackcloth and sitting in ashes among the number of the legal ceremonies, yet the exercise of fasting remains in

---

[1] "When the Orientals," says Boothroyd, " pray seriously in grief, they hide their face in their bosom: and to this custom the Psalmist here alludes. Rabbi Levi, Dathe, and others, explain it in like manner."

force amongst us at this day as well as in the time of David. When God, therefore, calls us to repentance, by showing us signs of his displeasure, let us bear in mind that we ought not only to pray to him after the ordinary manner, but also to employ such means as are fitted to promote our humility. In conclusion, the Psalmist says that he behaved and acted towards them as if each of them had been his brother.

15. *But they rejoiced at my halting.* I see no reason why interpreters should trouble themselves as they do about the word *halting.* Some conjecture that David had his leg put out of joint, and others suppose that he halted from some disease. But when we consider carefully the whole passage, nothing is more evident than that he refers by this expression to the calamities which befell him; as if he had said, As soon as they saw me begin to stagger and ready to fall, they did as it were gather together against me, and endeavoured entirely to overthrow me. There is, therefore, in this expression almost the same metaphor as we have already seen in the word *sickness.* Now, as men often relent at seeing the misfortunes of their enemies, so that they cease to hate or persecute those who are already miserably wretched, it was an evidence of the very cruel and fierce spirit by which David's former friends were actuated against him, when, upon seeing him cast down and afflicted, they were rather by this incited furiously and insolently to assail him. At the commencement he speaks only of a few; but immediately after, in order to show still farther the indignity which had been done to him, he adds to them the base and ignoble of the common people; not that he blames all alike, but that he may the better show with what bitter hostility he was assailed on all sides. It is probable that those who were then in power were as it were firebrands, who endeavoured to kindle every where the flame of hatred against David, that the people every where might rise up to destroy him, and strive with each other in this enterprise. And he repeats twice *that they gathered themselves together*, in order to show how resolute and determined they were in their opposition to him; unless, perhaps, some would

prefer to explain the words thus : They gathered themselves together, not only those who had some pretext for doing so, but even the lowest of the people. The Hebrew word נכים, *nekim,* literally signifies *the whipped,* or *beaten,*[1] but it is here to be understood as denoting base and disreputable persons. Some interpreters, indeed, derive it from the word כאה, *kaäh,* which signifies *to make sad,* and expound it actively, Those who make me sad : but the previous interpretation agrees better with the design of the passage, namely, that David was shamefully treated by the lowest dregs of the people. The words, *I knew not,* may be referred to the cause as well as to the persons. I, however, explain it as referring to the persons in this sense : So far from having any cause to complain that I have offended them, or done them any harm, I did not even know them. At the same time, these words may be understood as implying a complaint on the part of David, that the people were enraged against him without any cause, since he is conscious of no crime, and can conceive of no ground for such fierce hatred towards him. As to the last clause of the verse, also, although interpreters entertain different opinions, it appears to me that I have given the true and natural meaning. Literally it is, *they did cut, and ceased not;* but there can be no doubt that the language is metaphorical, and that the word *cut*[2] signifies that they opened their mouth ;

---

[1] The word is derived from נכה, *nakah, to strike* or *to smite.* The LXX. render it μαστιγες, *scourges;* and Jerome reads *percutientes, smiters,* in which he is followed by Ainsworth, who understands the word as meaning smiters with the tongue, or calumniators, and who thinks that the LXX., in translating it *scourges,* alluded to the scourge of the tongue, as in Job v. 21 ; and if *smiters* is the proper rendering, we may certainly conclude, that as this smiting is represented as done upon the person who was its object in his absence, it was a smiting by the tongue. At the same time, this critic observes, that the word may be read *the smitten,* that is, *abjects, vile persons,* as in Job xxx. 8. Dr Kennicott translates it by *verberones, whipt slaves, vile scoundrels.* Another meaning of the word, according to Buxtorff, is, *the wry-legged, the lame.* In this sense it is used in 2 Sam. iv. 4, and ix. 3 ; and hence the epithet of *Necho* was given to one of the Pharaohs, who halted in his gait. Thus it easily came to be employed as a term of contempt. Calvin and the translators of our English Bible agree in the meaning which they attach to this word.

[2] The verb קרע, *kara,* for *cut,* " is significant of tearing or rending, and by an easy metaphor, is applicable to wounds inflicted by evil speaking and slander."—*Walford.*

as if David had said, They have insolently poured forth with open mouth their scoffing and reproachful words against me. The additional clause in the sentence, *and ceased not,* is a repetition common in the Hebrew language, and is employed to express the vehemence with which David's enemies proceeded against him. It implies that there was no end or measure to their evil-speaking, and that they continued to pour forth with distended throats whatever first occurred to them.

16. *Among perfidious jesters at feasts, they gnash upon me with their teeth.*
17. *O Lord!*[1] *how long wilt thou look on? deliver my soul from their tumults, and my only one*[2] *from the lions.*
18. *I will magnify thee in the great congregation: I will praise thee before a great people.*[3]

16. *Among perfidious jesters.* Others translate it, *With hypocrites,* but in my opinion David simply relates the combination of his enemies. And the meaning of the expression is to this effect, That among men of a crafty disposition, who had been addicted to deceit, and were consequently lost to all sense of shame, the only and the constant subject of their deliberations was, how they might destroy this afflicted man. David again reverts to the leaders of the people, and to those in power, as the source whence all the mischief took its rise; for this description could not apply to a great part of the common people, who acted rather by thoughtless impulse. He therefore speaks particularly of the rulers, and others of a similar character, and accuses them of cruelty, saying, that they gnash their teeth upon him like furious

---

[1] Domine.—Lat. אדני, *Adonai.*—Heb. "More than fifteen copies collected by Dr Kennicott have יהוה here instead of אדני. Among which is one of the best manuscripts that has been collated. The Jews, in later ages, had a superstitious fear of pronouncing the word יהוה, and therefore inserted אדני or אלהים, in the place of it very frequently."—*Street.*

[2] "Asçavoir, mon ame unique; c'est à dire, solitaire et delaissee."—*Note, Fr. marg.* "Namely, my soul alone; that is to say, solitary and forsaken." See note 3, p. 432. In our English Bible the phrase is, "my darling;" but David rather means to intimate his forsaken and unprotected condition, unless God interposed in his behalf. Green reads, "my helpless *person.*"

[3] "Devant un grand peuple."—*Fr.* "C'est, beaucoup de peuple."—*Note, Fr. marg.* "That is, much people."

wild beasts. He first calls them *perfidious* or *wicked*, that he may the more easily obtain help and aid of God, as if calling upon him in the extremity of distress; and, secondly, he calls them *jesters* or *mockers*, by which he means that they have such effrontery, and are so far lost to all sense of shame, that there is nothing which they will not dare to do. As to the meaning of the word מָעוֹג, *maog*, which follows, interpreters are not agreed. Properly, it signifies bread baked upon the hearth upon the embers. Some, however, because they could not elicit from it a meaning suitable to the passage, have thought that it should be taken for talkative jesting, or idle speech. Others, presuming to give a still wider range to their fancy, have supposed the meaning of the Psalmist to be, that the scoffing of such persons was as bread to them, because they take pleasure in scoffing and jesting. To me, it appears that we ought to retain the proper signification of the word, while, at the same time, it may be understood in a twofold sense. Some taking מָעוֹג, *maog*, for *a cake* or *tart*, are of opinion that David here censures people of a delicate taste, who seek after fine and dainty fare, many of whom are always to be found in the courts of princes. Others rather suppose that he rebukes persons of a servile and sordid spirit, who, for the most trifling consideration, would employ their tongues in reviling others, just as in all ages there have been found men who, for a bit of bread, as we say, set their tongues to sale. When I carefully consider other passages in which David describes the nature and character of his enemies, I am disposed to think that those who indulged in jesting and scoffing at feasts, and who, in sitting over their cups, consulted about putting David to death, are here referred to. He therefore complains, that even in the midst of their feasting and banqueting, the ungodly, who had shaken off all shame, communed how they might take away his life.

17. *O Lord! how long wilt thou look on?* The meaning of the word which I have translated *how long*, is ambiguous in the Hebrew. In Latin it signifies, How long wilt thou see it, and suffer it without uttering a word? But the other interpretation is equally appropriate, namely, After having

seemed to take no notice of the matter for a long time, when wilt thou at length begin to see it? The meaning, however, is substantially the same, for David complains of God's long forbearance, declaring that while the wicked are running to every excess, God connives at them, and delays too much to take vengeance. And although God inculcates upon the faithful the duty of quietly and patiently waiting till the time arrive when he shall judge it proper to help them, yet he allows them to bewail in prayer the grief which they experience on account of his delay. At the same time, David shows, that in so speaking he is not carried headlong merely by the importunity of his desire, but that he is constrained to it by the extremity of his distress. For he says that they tumultuously rush upon him to take away his life, and he compares them to *lions*, and calls *his soul solitary*, or *alone*. Some think that the expression, *only soul*, means *dear and precious*, or *well beloved;* but such do not sufficiently consider the design of David, as has been stated in the 22d Psalm at the twenty-first verse.

18. *I will magnify thee in the great congregation.* In this verse David again engages to give thanks to God for all his goodness, since the faithful can render him no other recompense than the sacrifice of praise, as we shall see in Psalm cxvi. 17. Thus even whilst he was surrounded by the impetuous billows of fear and danger, he sets himself to the exercise of giving thanks, as if he had already obtained his desire; and by this he intended to encourage and confirm himself in the assurance of obtaining his requests. In this we may discern a striking and decided evidence of invincible fortitude, for though an outcast and a fugitive, destitute of all help, and, in short, in a state of great extremity and despair as to all his affairs, yet still he thinks of praising God's grace, and makes vows of solemn sacrifice to him, as if, in the midst of the darkness of death, he saw deliverance clearly shining upon him. And he speaks not only of giving thanks in private, but of such thanksgiving as those who were delivered out of any great perils were wont to yield in the public assembly, by the appointment of the law. Some

translate the latter clause of the verse *a strong and powerful people*,[1] but I do not see the propriety of it. It is a mere subtilty to argue that the Church is endued with great strength, and therefore is called a *strong people*. But as David simply means the great crowd and multitude of people who were wont to go up to the sanctuary to hold their solemn assembly before God, I have no doubt that when he speaks of the *great congregation*, and afterwards of *much people*, he only repeats, according to his custom, the same thing twice, for the Hebrew word is used in both these senses.

19. *Let not those who are my enemies wrongfully rejoice over me ; neither let those who hate me without a cause wink with the eye.*
20. *For they speak not peace ;*[2] *but devise deceitful words upon the clefts of the earth.*
21. *They have opened their mouth against me : they have said, Aha! aha! our eye hath seen it.*[3]
22. *O Jehovah! thou hast also seen it: keep not silence: O Lord! be not far from me.*
23. *Stir up thyself, and awake for my judgment, O my God! even for my cause, O my Lord!*

19. *Let not those who are my enemies wrongfully rejoice over me.* Because David's enemies already exulted in the hope of seeing his overthrow and destruction, he prays that God would not suffer them to realise a desire so wicked. In order to render God favourable to his cause, he again protests that they hated him without any fault or occasion on his part, and that it was their own malice which urged them to such cruelty against him ; for in order to secure the help of God, it is necessary to come before him with the testimony of a good conscience.

---

[1] Horsley takes this view. He reads, "*Among a mighty people;*" and observes, that this is the rendering of the Chaldee, and that עצם seems more properly to express strength or power than number.
[2] "C'est, ne tienent propos d'amis."—*Note, Fr. marg.* "That is, their discourse is not that of friends."
[3] "C'est, ce que nous desirions."—*Note, Fr. marg.* "That is, that which we desire." French and Skinner read, "Aha! aha! our eye seeth!" "that is," they observe, "beholds our enemy in the fallen condition in which we desire to see him. See verse 25, compare Ps. xcii. 11."

The Hebrew word שֶׁקֶר, *sheker*, which we have rendered *wrongfully*, is by some translated *deceitfully*, as if David meant that his enemies lay in wait for him. But this is to reason with too much subtilty. Besides, the repetition which immediately follows shows that he complains of their wilful hatred, inasmuch as of their own accord, and from deliberate design, they persecuted a man who had given them no cause of offence, but was their friend and benefactor. The Hebrew word קָרַץ, *karats*, here signifies *to wink with the eyes askance in mockery*, as in Psalm xxii. 8, it denotes, *to wag the head*, and *to shoot out the lip*.

In the following verse, that he may cherish still greater confidence in God, David again declares, that he has to do with enemies of an irreconcileable character, and who are fully bent upon cruelty. Of this we ought to be firmly persuaded, that the more grievously we are oppressed, so much the more certainly ought we to expect deliverance. He therefore says, that they speak of nothing but of tumults and slaughter. The meaning of the latter clause is somewhat obscure, arising from the ambiguous signification of the word רִגְעֵי, *rige*. As the word from which it is derived sometimes signifies *to cut*, and sometimes *to rest*, or *to be quiet and peaceable*, there are some who translate it *the meek and peaceable of the earth:* others translate it, *with the tranquil and easy of the earth;* meaning by this, those who live in the midst of riches and abundance, in the enjoyment of undisturbed repose. Both these seem to me to be forced interpretations. Others, too, though not more correctly, expound the word *in caves* or *secret places*, in order that, as they say, the wicked and deceitful counsels of such persons may not come to light. But it may be very appropriately rendered, *the clefts of the earth*, and by this metaphor are meant the miserable and afflicted, who are, as it were, broken and maimed. David, therefore, declares that as soon as his enemies see any opening, that is to say, some calamity befall him, they instantly put forth all their efforts to accomplish his destruction. Those who, in the time of his prosperity and power, never dared even to utter a word against him, began now, when they saw that his influence was feeble, to plot his ruin, just as we know that the wicked are for the most part persons of a servile and cowardly disposition, and assume not the tone of insolence save when an advantageous opportunity presents itself, as when the good and simple are in adversity. To the same purpose he represents them in the next verse, as crying out with open mouth, Aha! aha! and clapping their hands for joy that they saw David overcome, and, as it were, laid prostrate in the dust, a spectacle in which they took great delight.

22. *O Jehovah! thou hast also seen it.* There is in these words an implied contrast between the view which God is here represented as taking, and the sight at which, as we are told in the preceding verse, the ungodly rejoiced. The import of David's language is, You have rejoiced exceedingly at the sight of my miseries; but God also sees and takes notice of the cruelty and malice of those who feel a pleasure and gratification in seeing others afflicted and in trouble. David, however, in thus speaking, stays not to reason with his enemies, but rather addresses himself directly to God, and sets his providence as a rampart of defence in opposition to all the assaults of those who sought to shake his confidence, and who caused him much trouble. And certainly, if we would fortify ourselves against the scoffing and derision of our enemies, the best means which we can employ for this end is to overlook them, and to elevate our thoughts to God, and in the confidence of his fatherly care over us, to entreat him to show, in very deed, that our troubles are not unknown to him; yea, that the more he sees the wicked eagerly watching every opportunity to accomplish our ruin, he would the more speedily come to our aid. This David expresses by these various forms of expression—*Keep not silence, be not far from me, stir up thyself, awake for my judgment.* He might justly make use of such expressions, seeing he was already fully persuaded that God regards the poor and afflicted, and marks all the wrongs which are done to them. If, therefore, we would frame our requests aright, a clear conviction and persuasion of the providence of God must first shine into our hearts; nor is it necessary only that this should precede, in

point of order, all our desires; it must also restrain and govern them.

24. *Judge me, O Jehovah my God! according to thy righteousness; and let them not rejoice over me.*
25. *Let them not say in their heart, Aha! our soul!*[1] *let them not say, We have swallowed him up.*
26. *Let those who rejoice at my hurt be ashamed and confounded together; let those who magnify themselves against me be clothed with shame and dishonour.*
27. *But let those who favour my righteous cause shout and be glad, and let them say continually, Jehovah be magnified, who loveth the peace of his servant.*
28. *And my tongue shall declare thy righteousness and thy praise all the day.*

24. *Judge me, O Jehovah my God!* David here confirms the prayer of the preceding verse that God would be his defender, and would maintain his righteous cause. Having been for a time subjected to suffering as one who had been forsaken and forgotten, he sets before himself *the righteousness of God*, which forbids that he should altogether abandon the upright and the just. It is, therefore, not simply a prayer, but a solemn appeal to God, that as he is righteous, he would manifest his righteousness in defending his servant in a good cause. And certainly, when we seem to be forsaken and deprived of all help, there is no remedy which we can employ, more effectual to overcome temptation than this consideration, that the righteousness of God, on which our deliverance depends, can never fail. Accordingly, the Apostle Paul, in exhorting the faithful to patience, says in 2 Thess. i. 6, "It is a righteous thing with God to recompense tribulation to them that trouble you." Now David again appeals to God in this place, and entreats him to manifest his righteousness in restraining the insolence of his

---

[1] "C'est, nostre desir: nous avons ce que desirions: ou, nostre ame, assavoir s'esjouisse: comme on dit en nostre langue, Grande chere."— *Note, Fr. marg.* "That is, our desire: we have what we desire: or, our soul, that is to say, is glad: as we say in our language, Great cheer." French and Skinner read, "Let them not say in their hearts, Aha! our desire!" and observe, "that *our desire!* means our desire is accomplished."

enemies: for the more proudly they assail us, God is so much the more ready to help us. Besides, by again introducing them as speaking, he portrays in a graphic style the cruelty of their desires; and by this he means to show, that if things should happen according to their wishes, they would set no limit to their frowardness. But as the more they vaunt themselves, the more they provoke the wrath of God against them, David with good reason uses this as an argument to encourage his hope, and employs it for his support and confirmation in prayer.

26. *Let those who rejoice at my hurt be ashamed and confounded together.* This imprecation has already been expounded; and it is only necessary to remark, that there is peculiar force in the expression, *together,* or *at once.* It shows that it was not only one or two, but a great multitude, who waged war against him, and that he yielded not to the influence of fear, but believed that as soon as God should lift up his hand, he could at one stroke easily overthrow them all. When it is said that they seek after and *rejoice in David's hurt,* this shows that they were filled with cruel hatred against him. And when it is said, that they *magnify themselves against him,* this is a token of pride. David, therefore, in order to render them more hateful in the sight of God, represents them as filled with pride and cruelty. And as this form of prayer was dictated by the Holy Spirit to David, there can be no doubt that the end of all the proud shall be such as is here predicted, that they shall turn back overwhelmed with shame and disgrace.

27. *Let those who favour my righteous cause rejoice and be glad.* These two expressions, which are rendered in the optative mood, might have been translated with equal propriety in the future tense; but as this is a matter of little consequence, I leave it undecided. David here extols the deliverance which he asks of God, and exults in the results which should flow from it; namely, that it would be an occasion of general rejoicing and good hope to all the godly, while at the same time it would stir them up to cele-

brate the praises of God. He attributes to all the faithful the credit of desiring, that as an innocent man his righteous cause should be maintained. David, it is true, was the object of almost universal hatred among the simple and unsuspecting, who were imposed upon by false and unjust reports made concerning him; but it is certain that there were among the people some who formed a just and impartial estimate of things, and who were sorely grieved that a holy man, and one too whose benevolence was well known, should have been so unjustly and so wrongfully oppressed. And surely the common feelings of humanity require, that when we see men unjustly oppressed and afflicted, if we are not able to help them, we should at least pity them. When David uses the language, *Jehovah be magnified,* his design seems to be tacitly to set this in opposition to the pride of the wicked, of which he made mention above. As they presume in the pride of their hearts, and by their insolent and overbearing conduct, to obscure, as far as in them lies, the divine glory, so may the faithful, on the other hand, with good reason present the prayer that God would shine forth in the majesty of his character, and demonstrate in very deed that he exercises a special care over all his servants, and takes a peculiar pleasure in their peace. Finally, the Psalmist again declares, in the conclusion of the psalm, his resolution to celebrate in appropriate praises the righteousness of God, by which he had been preserved and delivered.

www.ingramcontent.com/pod-product-compliance
Lightning Source LLC
Chambersburg PA
CBHW052040290426
44111CB00011B/1564